Children's
Writers'
& Artists'
YEARBOOK
2012

D1635162

Children's Writers' & Artists'

YEARBOOK
2012

EIGHTH EDITION

**A directory for children's writers and artists
containing children's media contacts and
practical advice and information**

BLOOMSBURY
LONDON · BERLIN · NEW YORK · SYDNEY

© 2011 Bloomsbury Publishing Plc
50 Bedford Square, London WC1B 3DP

The publishers make no representation, express or
implied, with regard to the accuracy of the
information contained in this book and cannot
accept any legal responsibility for any errors or
omissions that may take place.

This book is produced using paper that is made
from wood grown in managed, sustainable forests.
It is natural, renewable and recyclable. The logging
and manufacturing processes conform to the
environmental regulations of the country of origin.

A CIP catalogue record for this book is available
from the British Library.

ISBN 978-1-4081-40062

Typeset by QPM from David Lewis XML
Associates Ltd

Printed in the UK by CPI William Clowes Ltd,
Beccles NR34 7TL

This edition of the *Children's Writers' & Artists' Yearbook* is dedicated to Rosemary Canter who sadly passed away in March 2011. Rosemary was one of the most respected agents in children's books, building a very strong list of writers and illustrators at PFD (Peters Fraser & Dunlop) before moving on to co-found United Agents. Rosemary contributed to the *Yearbook* for several years and will be sadly missed.

Contents

Foreword – Andy Stanton   ix

Books

Getting started – Alison Stanley   1
Notes from a Children's Laureate
  – Anthony Browne   75
Notes from Jacqueline Wilson   78
A word from J.K. Rowling   81
How it all began – Eoin Colfer   82
Notes from a successful children's author and
  illustrator – Lauren Child   84
Who do children's authors write for?
  – Michael Rosen   87
Spotting talent – Barry Cunningham   90
What makes a children's classic? – David Fickling   93
Writing and the children's book market
  – Chris Kloet   97
A year in view of children's publishing
  – Caroline Horn   101
Books for babies – Wendy Cooling   105
Writing books to read aloud – Anne Fine   109
Writing for girls – Louise Rennison   112
Writing for different genres – Malorie Blackman   115
Writing for a variety of ages
  – Geraldine McCaughrean   120
Fiction for 6–9 year-olds – Alison Stanley   124
Writing humour for young children
  – Jeremy Strong   126
Writing fantasy for children
  – William Nicholson   129
Writing horror for children
  – Anthony Horowitz   132
Writing historical novels for children
  – Michelle Paver   135
Writing for teenagers – Meg Rosoff   139
Writing crime fiction for teenagers
  – Anne Cassidy   143
Writing thrillers for teenagers
  – Sophie McKenzie   146
Teenage fiction – Gillie Russell   149
Writing series fiction for girls
  – Karen McCombie   152
Notes from a series author – Francesca Simon   155
Writing for the school market – Jim Green   157

Ghostwriting children's books – Di Redmond   161
What does an editor do? – Yvonne Hooker   164
Marketing, publicising and selling children's
  books – Rosamund de la Hey   168
From self-publishing to contract
  – Janey Louise Jones   173
Children's books and the US market
  – Richard Scrivener   177
Categorising children's books – Caroline Horn   181

Listings

Children's book publishers UK and Ireland   5
Children's book publishers overseas   28
Children's audio publishers   61
Children's book packagers   63
Children's book clubs   69
Children's bookshops   71

Poetry

Riding on the poetry roundabout – John Foster   185
An interview with my shadow – Brian Patten   189

Listings

Poetry organisations – Paul McGrane   191

Literary agents

How to get an agent – Philippa Milnes-Smith   201
Meet the parents: agent, author and the birth
  of a book – Stephanie Thwaites   205
Do you *have* to have an agent to succeed?
  – Philip Ardagh   208

Listings

Children's literary agents UK and Ireland   212
Children's literary agents overseas   220

Illustrating for children

Creating graphic novels – Raymond Briggs   227
Notes from the first Children's Laureate
  – Quentin Blake   229
Notes from a successful illustrator
  – David Lucas   231
Finding your own style – Emily Gravett   234
Presenting your portfolio to a publisher
  – Val Brathwaite   237

Eight great tips to get your picture book
  published – Tony Ross   240
Writing and illustrating picture books
  – Debi Gliori   244
The amazing picture book story – Oliver Jeffers   248
House of Illustration   255

Listings
Illustrators' agents   252

Publishing practice
Publishing agreements – Caroline Walsh   257
FAQs about ISBNs   262
Public Lending Right   264

Copyright
Copyright questions – Michael Legat   271
The Copyright Licensing Agency Ltd   274
Authors' Licensing and Collecting Society   276
Design and Artists Copyright Society   278

Magazines and newspapers
Writing for teenage magazines
  – Michelle Garnett   281

Listings
Magazines and newspapers for children   284
Magazines about children's literature and
  education   293

Television, film and radio
Commissioning for children's television
  – Anna Home   297
Writing comedy for children's television
  – Adam Bromley   299
Children's literature on radio and audio
  – Neville Teller   303
Writing to a brief – Di Redmond   310

Listings
Children's television and radio – Emma Hurrell   314

Theatre
Writing for children's theatre – David Wood   317
Adapting books for the stage – Stephen Briggs   322

Listings
Theatre for children   326

Resources for children's writers
Setting up a website – Suna Cristall   333
Learning to write for children – Alison Sage   338
Indexing children's books – Valerie Elliston   342

Listings
Children's writing courses and conferences   346
Online resources about children's books   348
Books about children's books   351

Societies, prizes and festivals
The Society of Authors   353
Society of Children's Book Writers &
  Illustrators   356
Booktrust   358
Seven Stories, the Centre for Children's Books   359
The Children's Book Circle – Rachel Boden   361
Federation of Children's Book Groups
  – Sinead Kromer   362
National Literacy Trust – better literacy for all   397

Listings
Societies, associations and organisations   364
Children's book and illustration prizes and
  awards   382
Calendar of awards   391
Children's literature festivals and trade fairs   392

Finance for writers and artists
FAQs for writers – Peter Vaines   399
Income tax – Peter Vaines   401
Social security contributions
  – Peter Arrowsmith   412

Index   421

'The *Children's Writers' & Artists' Yearbook* has two great virtues: the wealth of information it contains and the other is the impressive raft of advice and notes on every aspect of the business'
Quentin Blake

'The *Children's Writers' & Artists' Yearbook* is a goldmine of invaluable information, so good luck and get writing'
Francesca Simon

'Whenever people ask me about how to get their work for children published, or how to find their way around the world of writing and publishing for children, the first words to come out of my mouth are always: *Children's Writers' & Artists' Yearbook*'
Michael Rosen

'I wish you all the luck in the world. Don't be a ninny like me, practically giving up at the first rejection. Consult the excellent *Children's Writers' & Artists' Yearbook* and get going!'
Jacqueline Wilson

Foreword

Andy Stanton has been a medical secretary, a film script reader and a cartoonist, amongst other things. His favourite expression is 'good evening' and his favourite word is 'captain'. *You're a Bad Man, Mr Gum!* was his first book, published in 2006, and is the first in the nine-part *Mr Gum* series (Egmont). His other books are *Here Comes the Poo Bus!* (Puffin), *The Story of Matthew Buzzington* (Barrington Stoke) and *Sterling and the Canary*.

Good evening. You are holding in your hands one of two things. You are either holding one of the most powerful little books on the planet, a book which has the potential to CHANGE YOUR LIFE FOR EVER; or you are holding a cool little lifestyle accessory, a book which you can keep on your shelf to announce to yourself and others: 'Oh, I'm a writer-sort of person, I'm sure I'll use this book one day. But in the meantime, doesn't it look *professional*.' If you're holding the second version of the book, I'm not knocking you. For years before I got published I would frequently buy the latest copy of the *Writers' & Artists' Yearbook*, with the vague and magical idea that simply owning it was enough to effect an alchemical reaction in my life and turn me into a *writer*, with all the bunting, parades and adoring women that I imagined would naturally accompany such a position. Well, the years wore on and I discovered something quite annoying: The *Writers' & Artists' Yearbook*, and indeed the *Children's Writers' & Artists' Yearbook*, won't actually turn you into a writer. Take another look at the book you are holding right now and know the dreadful truth. However much you stroke this book; however prominently you display it on your shelves; however much you pray to it at night – there is one component you have to bring along yourself. And (double-annoyingly, because I am very lazy and hate working) that extra component is this: You must write something. You must do some work. And only then will this book become something that could CHANGE YOUR LIFE FOR EVER. It certainly changed mine. In 2002, I sat down and finally did the one thing I'd never done in all those years of wishing and longing and imagining all those adoring women. I wrote a story from start to finish. It was called *The Story of Mr Gum* and I wrote it partly to make my little cousins laugh, but mostly to see if I could actually finish a piece of work. Having written it, I promptly forgot about it for two years. When I rediscovered it, it was 2004 and I finally had a real and practical reason to buy the *Writers' & Artists' Yearbook*. But I found that fate had other, better plans for me, in the shape of the brand spanking new, first ever edition of the *Children's Writers'& Artists' Yearbook*. Just like its big brother, but so much easier! Now I wouldn't have to trawl through endless agents' listings, figuring out which ones accepted children's writers – no, every page of this publication was just for me. All the work had already been done. (Well, nearly all the work. I've already mentioned that one pesky component you'll have to provide yourself.) Within a month, the book had found me an agent. She's great, by the way, and she's in this latest edition too. But no plugs, Eve White, no plugs. A month or so after I found [unnamed agent] I had a publishing deal. And in 2006, Egmont published my little story as *You're a Bad Man, Mr Gum!*. Well, folks, it's been a pretty amazing ride since then. There are now nine *Mr Gum* titles, which have sold over a million copies in this country alone. Additionally, I've written two books for Barrington Stoke and published a truly revolting picture book with Puffin. And it all started here, in these pages. It's a shame it took me all that time to figure out how amazingly powerful this type of book can be. I hope it doesn't take you quite so long. See, it's a hard equation but it's fair. You get out what you put in. And if you put in something good, there's no book better qualified to help you reap your rewards (though a word of warning – the adoring women thing never really materialised). Well, that's enough from me. It's your turn now. You have here all the tools you need to CHANGE YOUR LIFE FOR EVER. So go to it! And the very best of luck.

Andy Stanton

Books

Getting started

You just have! By buying or borrowing the *Children's Writers' & Artists' Yearbook* you have taken the first step towards a potential new career in the field of children's publishing. Alison Stanley gives the benefit of her experience for success in this expanding market.

Whether you want to write for magazines, television, write or illustrate books, adapt for radio, get published in the UK or overseas, find an agent, illustrate greetings' cards, attend a festival, course or conference, or surf the children's literature websites, you will find the information on how to do it in this *Yearbook*.

But to help you on your way, here are ten top tips:

1. Read, read, read

• Read as many children's books as you can – picture books, young fiction, novels, teen reads, non-fiction, the classics, the prize-winners – and find out just what is being published… and what children like to read.

• Look at children's magazines and newspaper supplements as they will give you ideas about current trends.

• Read reviews in national newspapers, read children's literary magazines such as *Books for Keeps* and *Carousel* (see *Magazines about children's literature and education* on page 293).

2. Get out and about

• Visit your local bookshop and browse in the children's section.

• Go to your library and talk to the children's librarian. Children's books are read by children but usually bought by adults – so find out what parents, teachers, librarians and other professionals are recommending for young people.

• Visit Seven Stories, the Centre for Children's Books (see page 359).

• If you have children, don't just go by what they are reading, ask their friends too – children have wide reading tastes, just like adults. Ask permission to sit in on their school 'storytime' (or a literacy hour or a guided reading session if educational publishing is what you are interested in).

• Go to a festival! There are many literature festivals held throughout the year and most have children's literary events (see page 392). All children's literature festivals will have a sprinkling of new and well-known authors and illustrators in attendance, and most authors and illustrators will be accompanied by a representative from their publishing company. So you can see and hear the author/illustrator and even do a bit of networking with the publisher! You will also be guaranteed some fun. Festivals are also a useful way of seeing children's reactions to their favourite authors and books in an informal situation.

3. Watch, listen and... learn

• Familiarise yourself with the children's media: watch children's television and listen to children's radio programmes (see the *Television, film and radio* section beginning on page 297), and check out the websites listed throughout the *Yearbook*. Look at children's character merchandising and greetings cards.

• Enrol on a creative writing course where you can meet others who also want to write for children (see *Learning to write for children*, page 338). Or apply to do a postgraduate course in writing for young people, where you will be guided by published authors and other publishing professionals (see *Children's writing courses and conferences*, page 346).

4. Network

• Being an author or illustrator can be a lonely business – don't work in a vacuum. Talk to others of your discipline at festivals, conferences and book groups. Join the Federation of Children's Book Groups (see page 371) where you can network to your heart's content. Find out if there are any writer/illustrator groups in your area. If you are already published, join the Scattered Authors Society (see page 378).

5. Never underestimate the job in hand

• Writing and illustrating for children is not an easy option. Many people think they can dash off a children's story and a few sketchy illustrations and that they will be good enough to publish. But if you have researched the marketplace you will realise that it is a hugely competitive area and you have to be talented, have something original to say, have an unique style… and know how to persevere in order to get your work published and out to a wider audience.

6. Use your experiences

• Having your own children, or working in a child-related profession is helpful but shouldn't be relied on to bring you a new career as a children's writer or illustrator. (Never use this line when submitting a manuscript: 'I wrote this story for my children and they enjoyed it so please will you publish it?' Any story you write for your own children, grand-children, nieces, nephews, etc is likely to be enjoyed by them because children love atten-tion.) Publishers will only want to take on something that has appeal for a wide range of children – both nationally and internationally – never forget that publishing is a business. However, do use your experiences in terms of ideas, especially the more unusual ones, like seeing your first alien fall from the sky!

7. Research catalogues and websites

• Look at publishers' catalogues and websites, not just to find out what they are publishing, but because many of them give guidance for new writers and illustrators. When submitting a manuscript or portfolio to a publisher, it is a good idea to let them know that you know (and admire!) what they already publish. You can then make your case about where your submission will fit in their list. Let them know that you mean business and have researched the marketplace.

8. Submit your material with care

• First decide whether to approach an agent or to go it alone and submit your material direct to a publisher (see *How to get an agent* on page 201, *Do you have to have an agent to succeed?* on page 208 and *Publishing agreements* on page 257 for the pros and cons of each approach.) Check that the agent or publisher you are thinking of approaching accepts (a) unsolicited material, and (b) is interested in the type of work you are doing. For example, don't send your potential prize-winning novel to an educational publisher, and don't send your ideas for a Guided Reading Series at Key Stage 1 to a 'trade' publisher without an educational list. And don't send your illustrations for a children's picture book to an agent who only deals with teenage fiction – there will be zero interest from them and you will be very disappointed.

• Submit your work to the right publisher/agent and the right person within the company. Ring first to find out who the best person for your work might be, whether it be in a publishing company, an agency, a television production company or a children's magazine. Also ask whether they want a synopsis and sample chapters or the complete manuscript or, for artwork, a selection of illustrations or your whole portfolio.

• Presentation is important. For example, no editor will read a handwritten manuscript. It should be typed/word processed, using double spacing with each page clearly numbered. (Should an editor be interested in your work, it will be photocopied for all involved in the acquisition process to read. Photocopiers have a habit of chewing up pages and there's nothing worse than pages being missing at a crucial part of a novel.) If your manuscript is accepted for publication, the editor will want the text electronically.

• For illustrations, select work on a paper that can be easily photocopied – a white/cream background with no unusual textures for your first pitch (such as sandpaper or glass – yes, it really has happened!) And remember, publishers' photocopiers are notoriously bad at reproducing colour accurately, so if you are relying on the vibrancy of your colour to wow an art director, bear in mind that by the time they have been photocopied a few times for interested parties to see, the colours will not be the same. If your artwork is computer generated, send hard copies with your disk – it saves time when being shown around.

9. Identify your USP

• Ask yourself what the unique selling point (USP) of the material you are submitting for publication is. You may have an original authorial 'voice', you may have a particularly innovative illustration style or technique, or you may have come up with an amazingly brilliant idea for a series. If, after checking out the marketplace, you think you have something truly original to offer, then believe in yourself and be convincing when you offer it for publication.

10. Don't give up!

• Editors receive hundreds of manuscripts, and art directors receive hundreds of illustration samples every day. For a publisher, there are many factors that have to be taken into consideration when evaluating these submissions, the most important of which is 'Can we publish it successfully?' – i.e. 'Will it sell?'. Publishing is a big business and it is ever more competitive. Even after an editor or art director has seen and liked your work, there are many other people involved before something is acquired for publication: the marketing manager, the publicist, the rights director, the book club manager, the sales director and, of course, the financial director. You will find this mantra repeated again and again in many of the articles in this book: *Have patience, keep at it.* If you believe in your 'product' eventually someone else will too. And meanwhile, keep perfecting your craft. After all, you are doing it because you enjoy it, aren't you?

Alison Stanley has been a senior commissioning editor of children's fiction at Puffin Books and at HarperCollins Children's Books.

See also...
• *Notes from Jacqueline Wilson*, page 78
• *Who do children's authors write for?*, page 87

4 Books

- *Notes from a successful children's author and illustrator,* page 84
- *Spotting talent,* page 90
- *Writing for girls,* page 112
- *Writing for different genres,* page 115
- *Writing for a variety of ages,* page 120
- *Fiction for 6–9 year-olds,* page 124
- *Writing humour for young children,* page 126
- *Writing horror for children,* page 132
- *Writing historical novels for children,* page 135
- *Writing for teenagers,* page 139
- *Teenage fiction,* page 149
- *What does an editor do?* page 164
- *Writing for the school market,* page 157
- *Writing and illustrating picture books,* page 244
- *The amazing picture book story,* page 248

Books

Children's book publishers UK and Ireland

*Member of the Publishers Association or Publishing Scotland
†Member of the Irish Book Publishers' Association

Abbey Home Media Group Ltd
435–7 Edgware Road, London W2 1TH
tel 020-7563 3910 *fax* 020-7563 3911
email info@abbeyhomemedia.com
website abbeyhomemedia.com
Chairman Ian Miles, *Directors* Anne Miles, Emma Evans, Caroline Hansell

Activity books, board books, novelty books, picture books, non-fiction, reference books, audiotapes and CDs. Advocates learning through interactive play. Age groups: preschool, 5–10.

Alanna Books
46 Chalvey Road East, Slough, Berks. SL1 2LR
tel (01753) 573245
email www.alannabooks.com
website info@alannabooks.com
Children's picture books.

Philip Allan – see Hodder Education Group

Alligator Books Ltd
(Pinwheel Division)
Gadd House, Arcadia Avenue, London N3 2JU
tel 020-8371 6622 *fax* 020-8371 6633
email sales@pinwheel.co.uk
website www.alligatorbooks.co.uk

Children's licensed character titles, fiction, non-fiction, colouring and activity books. For submissions, see Pinwheel. Subsidiary of International Greetings Plc.

Pinwheel Children's Books (imprint)
website www.alligatorbooks.co.uk
Children's fiction, non-fiction, novelty and interactive titles and picture books. Ages 0–10 years.
   Submission details Unsolicited novelty book concepts, picture book MSS and illustration samples welcome – in writing only. No telephone submissions. Does not reply or return unsuccessful submissions. Address submissions to 'C. Swift – Bath' at the above address.

Amgueddfa Cymru – National Museum Wales
Cathays Park, Cardiff CF10 3NP
tel 029-2057 3155 *fax* 029-2057 3321
email books@museumwales.ac.uk
website www.museumwales.ac.uk
Head of Publishing Mari Gordon

Books based on the collections and research of Amgueddfa Cymru for adults, schools and children, in both Welsh and English.

Andersen Press Ltd
20 Vauxhall Bridge Road, London SW1V 2SA
tel 020-7840 8703 (editorial), 020-7840 8701 (general) *fax* 020-7233 6263
email andersenpress@randomhouse.co.uk
website www.andersenpress.co.uk
Managing Director/Publisher Klaus Flugge, *Directors* Philip Durrance, Joëlle Flugge, Rona Selby (editorial picture books), Charlie Sheppard (editorial fiction), Sarah Pakenham (rights), Mark Hendle (finance)

Picture books, and junior and teenage fiction. Recent successes include the *Elmer* series by David McKee and *Doing It* by Melvin Burgess. Other authors include Berlie Doherty, Michael Foreman, Sandra Glover, Julia Jarman, Henning Mankell, David McKee, Tony Ross and Jeanne Willis. Illustrators include Ralph Steadman and Max Velthuijs, winner of the 2004 Hans Christian Andersen Award for Illustration for his *Frog* series.
   Submission details For novels, send 3 sample chapters, a synopsis and return postage. Juvenile fiction should be 3,000–5,000 words long, and older fiction about 15,000–30,000 words. The text for picture books should be under 1,000 words long. No poetry or short stories. Do not send MSS via email.

Anness Publishing
88–89 Blackfriars Road, London SE1 8HA
tel 020-7401 2077 *fax* 020-7775 4441
email info@anness.com
website www.annesspublishing.com
Managing Director Paul Anness, *Publisher* Joanna Lorenz

Practical illustrated books on lifestyle, cookery, crafts, gardening, reference, health and children's non-fiction. Imprints: Lorenz Books, Southwater, Practical Pictures. Founded 1989.

Lorenz Children's Books (imprint)
website www.lorenzbooks.com
Non-fiction for children including art, science, history, maths.

Anova Children's Books – see Pavilion Children's Books

Anvil Books/The Children's Press†
45 Palmerston Road, Dublin 6, Republic of Ireland
tel (01) 4973628 *fax* (01) 496 8263

Directors Rena Dardis (managing), Margaret Dardis (editorial)

Children's Press: adventure fiction for ages 9–14. Anvil: Irish history and biography. Founded 1964.

Submission details Only considers MSS by Irish-based authors and of Irish interest. Send synopsis with IRCs (no UK stamps); unsolicited MSS not returned.

Arcturus Publishing Ltd

26–27 Bickels Yard, 151–3 Bermondsey Street, London SE1 3HA
tel 020-7407 9400 *fax* 020-7407 9444
email roberta.bailey@arcturuspublishing.com
website www.arcturuspublishing.com
Managing Director, Arcturus Children's Publishing Roberta Bailey

Children's non-fiction and school library books, including activity books, reference, education, geography, history and science.

Atlantic Europe Publishing Co. Ltd

Greys Court Farm, Greys Court, Henley-on-Thames, Oxon RG9 4PG
tel (01491) 628188 *fax* (01491) 628189
email info@atlanticeurope.com
website www.atlanticeurope.com,
www.curriculumvisions.com
Director Dr B.J. Knapp

Educational: children's colour illustrated information books, co-editions and primary school class books covering science, geography, technology, mathematics, history, religious education. Recent successes include the *Curriculum Visions* series and *Science at School* series. Founded 1990.

Submission details Submit via email to contactus@atlanticeurope.com with no attachments. No MSS accepted by post. Established teacher authors only.

Atom – see Little, Brown Book Group

AudioGO Ltd

St James House, The Square, Lower Bristol Road, Bath BA2 3BH
tel (01225) 878000
website www.audiogo.co.uk
Directors Mike Bowen (managing), Jan Paterson (publishing)

Large print books and complete and unabridged audiobooks: general fiction, crime, romance, mystery/thrillers, westerns, non-fiction. Does not publish original books. Imprints include BBC Radio Collection, Cover to Cover Classics, BBC Cover to Cover, Chivers Audiobooks, Chivers Children's Audiobooks. Formed in 2010 following the sale of BBC Audiobooks.

Aurora Metro

67 Grove Avenue, Twickenham TW1 4HX
tel 020-3261 0000 *fax* 020-8898 0735

email info@aurorametro.com
website www.aurorametro.com
Director Cheryl Robson

Drama (including plays for young people), fiction, non-fiction and translation.

Autumn Publishing

Appledram Barns, Birdham Road, Chichester, West Sussex PO20 7EQ
tel (01243) 531660 *fax* (01243) 538160
email autumn@autumnpublishing.co.uk
website www.autumnchildrensbooks.co.uk

Children's activity and learning books to provide a positive and fun learning experience. The *Help with Homework* series helps to bridge the gap between school and home learning; also educational wall charts, colouring, sticker and activity books, board books and picture story books. Formed in the late 1970s and now part of the Bonnier Publishing Group.

Submission details No responsibility is accepted for the return of unsolicited MSS.

Award Publications Ltd

The Old Riding School, The Welbeck Estate, Worksop, Notts. S80 3LR
tel (01909) 478170 *fax* (01909) 484632
email info@awardpublications.co.uk

Children's books: full colour picture story books; early learning, information and activity books. No unsolicited material. Founded 1954.

b small publishing limited

The Book Shed, 36 Leyborne Park, Kew, Richmond, Surrey TW9 3HA
tel 020-8948 2884
website www.bsmall.co.uk
Publisher Catherine Bruzzone

Activity books and foreign language learning books for 2–12 year-olds. No unsolicited MSS. Founded 1990.

Badger Publishing

Suite G08, Business & Technology Centre, Bessemer Drive, Stevenage, Herts. SG1 2DX
tel (01438) 791037 *fax* (01438) 791036
email info@badger-publishing.co.uk
website www.badger-publishing.co.uk
Publisher David Jamieson

Educational publishing for pupils and teachers across the curriculum, from foundation stage to Year 9, including books for reluctant readers and dual language books. Founded 2004.

Bantam Press (children's) – see The Random House Group Ltd

Barefoot Books Ltd

124 Walcot Street, Bath BA1 5BG
tel (01225) 322400 *fax* (01225) 322499

email info@barefootbooks.co.uk
website www.barefootbooks.com/uk
Editor-in-Chief Tessa Strickland, *Publishing Manager* Emma Parkin

Children's picture books, apps and audiobooks: myth, legend, fairytale, cross-cultural stories. See website for submission guidelines. Founded 1993.

Barrington Stoke*

18 Walker Street, Edinburgh EH3 7LP
tel 0131-225 4113 *fax* 0131-225 4140
email info@barringtonstoke.co.uk
website www.barringtonstoke.co.uk
Managing Director Sonia Raphael, *Editorial Manager* Kate Paice

Fiction for reluctant, dyslexic or under-confident readers: fiction for 8–12 year-olds with a reading age of 8+, fiction for teenagers with a reading age of 8+, fiction for 8–12 year-olds with a reading age of below 8, fiction for teenagers with a reading age of below 8, non-fiction for 10–14 year olds with a reading age of 8+, fiction for adults with a reading age of 8+, graphic novels. Resources for readers and their teachers. Publishes approx. 70 titles a year and has over 350 books in print. Founded 1998.

Submission details No unsolicited MSS. All work is commissioned from well-known authors and adapted for reluctant readers.

BBC Audiobooks Ltd – see AudioGO Ltd

BBC Children's Books – see Penguin Group (UK)

Belair – see Folens Publishers

A&C Black – see Bloomsbury Children's & Educational Division, Bloomsbury Publishing

Blackwater Press – see Folens Publishers

Bloomsbury Publishing Plc*

50 Bedford Square, London WC1B 3DP
tel 020-7494 2111
website www.bloomsbury.com
Founder & Chief Executive Nigel Newton, *Executive Director* Richard Charkin, *Group Finance Director* Wendy Pallot, *Non-executive Chairman* Jeremy Wilson, *Non-executive Directors* Ian Cormack, Sarah Jane Thomson, *Company Secretary* Michael Daykin
Media enquiries Katie Bond, Publicity Director, *tel* 020-7494 6012, *email* publicity@bloomsbury.com

A leading independent publicly quoted publishing house with 4 worldwide publishing divisions: Bloomsbury Adult, Bloomsbury Children's & Educational, Bloomsbury Academic & Professional and Bloomsbury Information. It operates through offices in the UK, the USA (see page 41), Germany (see below) and Australia (see page 28). No unsolicited MSS unless specified below. Founded 1986.

Bloomsbury Adult Division

Managing Director Richard Charkin, *Group Editor-in-Chief* Alexandra Pringle

Worldwide publisher for the general market of fiction and non-fiction including titles such as *Eat, Pray, Love* by Elizabeth Gilbert; *Operation Mincemeat* by Ben Macintyre, *The Finkler Question* (Man Booker Prize winner 2010) by Howard Jacobson and *The Guernsey Literary and Potato Peel Pie Society* by Mary Ann Shaffer. Other subjects include biographies/memoirs such as *Just Kids* by Patti Smith, politics, history, science; other titles include the *River Cottage* series by Hugh Fearnley-Whittingstall and reference books such as *Who's Who, Wisden Cricketers' Almanack* and *Reeds Nautical Almanac*. German language titles include *Neue Leben* by Ingo Schulze, *Ein Produktionsroman* by Péter Esterházy and *Das Jahr der Flut* by Margaret Atwood. Fiction and non-fiction titles published out of the USA include *Bobby Gold Stories* by Tony Bourdain, *Pearl of China* by Annchee Min and *My Horizontal Life* by Chelsea Handler.

Bloomsbury Children's & Educational Division

Managing Director Emma Hopkin, *Group Editor-in-Chief* Sarah Odedina, *Non-fiction and Education Publishing Director* Jayne Parsons
Children's – *Deputy Editorial Director* Emma Mathewson, *Commissioning Editor* Ele Fountain
Educational – *Commissioning Editors* Kate Paice (fiction), Helen Diamond (educational resources), Saskia Gwinn (non-fiction), Sheena Hodge (music)
Imprints include Adlard Coles Nautical, Berlin Verlag, A&C Black, Bloomsbury Audio, Bloomsbury Kinderbücher und Jugendbücher, Andrew Brodie (see page 8), Featherstone Educational (see page 12), Christopher Helm, Pica Press, Reeds Nautical Almanac, T&AD Poyser, Thomas Reed, Walker Books for Young Readers, USA (see page 60) and John Wisden & Co.

Children's. Worldwide publisher for readers of all ages up to 18 years including titles such as the *Harry Potter* series by J.K. Rowling, *Holes* by Louis Sachar and *The Graveyard Book* by Neil Gaiman. Recent successes include: for 0–5 years/preschool picture books, *The Selfish Crocodile* by Faustin Charles and Mike Terry, and *No Matter What* by Debi Gliori; for 5–8 years, *Wombles* by Elisabeth Beresford; for 8–11 years, *Mortlock* by Jon Mayhew, *Spilled Water* by Sally Grindley and *Princess Academy* by Shannon Hale; and for 11+ years, *Witch Child* by Celia Rees and *Refugee Boy* by Benjamin Zephaniah. No unsolicited MSS; send a synopsis with 3 chapters.

Educational. Educational publications and teacher resources for 5–14 year-olds include approx. 180 titles per year covering non-fiction subjects such as poetry, music and other reference, and fiction. Recent fiction titles include *Put Out The Light* by Terry Deary, Tom and Tony Bradman's *Space School* series and *Galaxy Patrol* by Jean Ure. Recent non-fiction titles include *RSPB Wild Things To Do with Woodlice* by Michael Cox and *My First Book of London* by Charlotte Guillain. Recent specialist educational titles include *Parents' Survival Guide to Maths Homework* by Andrew Brodie and *50 Fantastic Things* series by Sally and Phill Featherstone.

Submission details No submissions by email. Look at recently published titles and catalogues to gauge current publishing interests. Much of the list is educationally focused and publishes in series. Allow 8–10 weeks for a response.

Bloomsbury Verlag GmbH

(Berlin office of Bloomsbury Publishing)
Greifswalder Straße 207, 10405 Berlin
tel (49) 30443 845 0
website www.bloomsbury-verlag.de
Publishing contacts Birgit Schmitz, Dorothee Grisebach, Natalie Tornai (children's), *Managing Director/Geschäftsführer* Philip Roeder

Supports the worldwide publishing activities of Bloomsbury Publishing. Publishes German language high-quality fiction and non-fiction for adults and children. See Bloomsbury Adult, Bloomsbury Children's & Educational (imprint: Bloomsbury Kinderbücher und Jugendbücher), Bloomsbury Professional & Academic, Bloomsbury Information divisions.

Bodley Head Children's Books – see The Random House Group Ltd

Boxer Books Ltd

101 Turnmill Street, London EC1M 5QP
tel 020-7017 8980 *fax* 020-7608 2314
email info@boxerbooks.com
website www.boxerbooks.com

Innovative books for babies, toddlers and children: board books, novelty books, picture books and young fiction. Age groups: 0–12.

Bright Red Publishing

6 Stafford Street, Edinburgh EH3 7AU
tel 0131-220 5804 *fax* 0131-220 6710
email info@brightredpublishing.co.uk
website www.brightredpublishing.co.uk
Directors Sarah Mitchell, John MacPherson, Alan Grierson, Richard Bass

Educational publishing for Scotland's students and teachers. Founded 2008.

Brilliant Publications

Unit 10, Sparrow Hall Farm, Edlesborough, Dunstable LU6 2ES
tel (01525) 222292 *fax* (01525) 222720
email info@brilliantpublications.co.uk
website www.brilliantpublications.co.uk
Managing Director Priscilla Hannaford

Practical resource books for teachers and others concerned with the education of 0–13 year-olds. All areas of the curriculum published, but specialises in modern foreign languages, art and design, developing thinking skills and PSHE. Some series of books for reluctant readers, aimed at 7–11 year-olds. No children's picture books, non-fiction books or one-off fiction books. See 'Manuscripts guidelines' on website before sending proposal. Founded 1993.

British Museum Company Ltd*

38 Russell Square, London WC1B 3QQ
tel 020-7323 1234 *fax* 020-7436 7315
email publicity@britishmuseum.co.uk
website www.britishmuseum.co.uk
Director of Publishing Rosemary Bradley

The world's leading museum publisher, with a growing children's list including illustrated reference titles as well as activity and colouring books. Founded 1973.

Andrew Brodie

50 Bedford Square, London WC1B 3DP
tel 020-7494 2111
website www.bloomsbury.com

Children's, educational. Imprint of Bloomsbury Children's & Education division of Bloomsbury Publishing (see page 7).

Buster Books

9 Lion Yard, Tremadoc Road, London SW4 7NQ
tel 020-7720 8643 *fax* 020-7627 8953
email enquiries@mombooks.com
website www.mombooks.com/busterbooks
Managing Director Lesley O'Mara, *Publishing Director* Philippa Wingate

Non-fiction and gift books for young children. Publishes approx. 40 titles a year. Successes include *The Boys' Book*, *The Girls' Book* and a wide selection of doodle books.

Submission details Submit non-fiction (no fiction) with sae. Allow 1–2 months for response.

Cambridge University Press*

The Edinburgh Building, Shaftesbury Road, Cambridge CB2 8RU
tel (01223) 312393 *fax* (01223) 315052
email information@cambridge.org
website www.cambridge.org
Chief Executive of the Press Stephen R.R. Bourne, *Chief Operating Officer* Peter Phillips, *Managing Director, Academic Publishing* Andrew Brown, *Managing Director, Cambridge Learning (English Language Teaching and Education)* Hanri Pieterse

For children: curriculum-based education books and software for schools and colleges (primary, secondary and international). English language teaching for adult and younger learners.

For adults: anthropology and archaeology, art history, astronomy, biological sciences, classical studies, computer science, dictionaries, earth sciences, economics, e-learning products, engineering, English language teaching, history, language and literature, law, mathematics, medical sciences, music, philosophy, physical sciences, politics, psychology, reference, technology, social sciences, theology, religion. Journals (humanities, social sciences; science, technical and medical). The Bible and Prayer Book. Founded 1534.

Campbell Books – see Macmillan Publishers Ltd

Jonathan Cape Children's Books – see The Random House Group Ltd

Carlton Publishing Group

20 Mortimer Street, London W1T 3JW
tel 020-7612 0400 *fax* 020-7612 0401
email enquiries@carltonbooks.co.uk
website www.carltonbooks.co.uk
Chairman Jonathan Goodman, *Children's Editorial Director* Jane Wilsher

No unsolicited MSS; synopses and ideas welcome, but no fiction or poetry. Founded 1992.

Carlton Books (division)

Mass-market illustrated interactive children's books.

Caterpillar Books – see Magi Publications

Catnip Publishing Ltd

14 Greville Street, London EC1N 8SB
tel 020-7138 3650 *fax* 020-7138 3658
website www.catnippublishing.co.uk
Managing Director Robert Snuggs, *Commissioning Editor* Non Pratt

Children's books. New and previously published titles for children of all ages, with the emphasis on 8–12 year-olds. Acquires from overseas publishers, reissues out of print titles by top authors and commissions original books for children aged 5+. Publishes 22 books a year. Recent new books by Annette and Nick Butterworth, Joan Lingard, L.P. Howarth and Berlie Doherty. Founded 2005.
Submission details Will consider unsolicited MSS. Allow 3 months for response. No picture books.

CGP

Coordination Group Publications,
Kirkby-in-Furness, Cumbria LA17 7WZ
tel (0870) 750 1262 *fax* (0870) 750 1292
email info@cgpbooks.co.uk,
jane.towle@cgpbooks.co.uk
website www.cgpbooks.co.uk

Educational books centred around the National Curriculum, including revision guides and study books for GCSE, KS3, KS2, KS1 and A level. Subjects include maths, English, science, history, geography, ICT, psychology, business studies, religious studies, child development, design and techology, PE, music, French, German, Spanish, sociology.
Submission details On the lookout for top teachers at all levels, in all subjects. Potential authors and proofreaders should email Jane Towle with their name, subject area, level and experience, plus contact address, ready for when a project comes up in their subject area.

Paul Chapman Publishing – see SAGE Publications Ltd

Cherrytree Books – see Zero to Ten Ltd

The Chicken House

2 Palmer Street, Frome, Somerset BA11 1DS
tel (01373) 454488 *fax* (01373) 454499
email chickenhouse@doublecluck.com
website www.doublecluck.com
Managing Director & Publisher Barry Cunningham, *Deputy Managing Director* Rachel Hickman

Picture books, fiction for ages 5–8 and 9–11 and teenage fiction. Publishes approx. 25 titles a year. No unsolicited MSS. Recent successes include *Tunnels* by Roderick Gordon and Brian Williams, *The Road of the Dead* by Kevin Brooks and *Threads* by Sophia Bennett. Part of Scholastic Inc.

Child's Play (International) Ltd

Ashworth Road, Bridgemead, Swindon,
Wilts. SN5 7YD
tel (01793) 616286 *fax* (01793) 512795
email office@childs-play.com
website www.childs-play.com
Chairman Adriana Twinn, *Publisher* Neil Burden

Children's educational books: board, picture, activity and play books; fiction and non-fiction. Founded 1972.

Christian Education*

(incorporating RE Today Services and International Bible Reading Association)
1020 Bristol Road, Selly Oak, Birmingham B29 6LB
tel 0121-472 4242 *fax* 0121-472 7575
email enquiries@christianeducation.org.uk
website www.christianeducation.org.uk

Publications and services for teachers of RE including *REtoday* magazine, curriculum booklets, training material for children and youth workers in the Church. Worship resources for use in primary schools. Activity Club material and Bible reading resources.

Chrysalis Children's Books – see Pavilion Children's Books

Claire Publications

Unit 8, Tey Brook Craft Centre, Great Tey,
Colchester, Essex CO6 1JE
tel (01206) 211020 *fax* (01206) 212755
email mail@clairepublications.com
website www.clairepublications.com

Publisher and manufacturer of educational books and equipment, specialising in mathematics and literacy for children aged 5–15.

Books

Classical Comics
PO Box 7280, Litchborough, Towcester NN12 9AR
tel (0845) 812 3000
email info@classicalcomics.co.uk
website www.classicalcomics.com
Managing Director Clive Bryant

Graphic novel adaptations of classical literature.

Collins Education – see HarperCollins Publishers

Colourpoint Books
Colourpoint House, Jubilee Business Park,
Jubilee Road, Newtownards, Co. Down,
Northern Ireland BT23 4YH
tel (028) 9182 6339 *fax* (028) 9182 1900
email info@colourpoint.co.uk
website www.colourpoint.co.uk
Commissioning Editor Malcolm Johnston, *Marketing* Jacky Hawkes

Textbooks for Northern Ireland CCEA board.
Educational textbooks for KS3 (11–14 year-olds) KS3
Special Needs (10–14 year-olds), GCSE (14–16 year-olds) and A-Level/undergraduates (age 17+). Subjects
include business studies, English, geography, history,
HE, ICT, Irish, LLW, MVRUS, PE, physics, politics
and RE. Founded 1993.
Submission details Short queries by email. Full
submission in writing including details of proposal,
sample chapter/section to show ability to connect
with target age group, your qualification/experience
in the subject, full contact details and return postage.
Textbooks, workbooks and electronic resources all
considered.

The Continuum International Publishing Group Ltd
The Tower Building, 11 York Road,
London SE1 7NX
tel 020-7922 0880 *fax* 020-7922 0881
email info@continuumbooks.com
website www.continuumbooks.com
Ceo Oliver Gadsby, *Directors* Robin Baird-Smith
(publishing), Bob Marsh (finance), Ken Rhodes (sales
& marketing), Louise Cameron (production),
Publishers Sarah Campbell, Anna Fleming

Serious non-fiction, academic and professional,
including scholarly monographs and educational
texts and reference works in education, film, history,
linguistics, literary studies, media studies, music,
philosophy, politics; and in biblical studies, religious
studies and theology. Imprints: Burns & Oates,
Continuum, Network Continuum, T&T Clark
International, Thoemmes Press, Mowbray.
Education books include *Getting the Buggers to
Write* and *Getting the Buggers to be Creative* by Sue
Cowley.

Corgi Children's Books – see The Random House Group Ltd

Corner to Learn
Willow Cottage, 26 Purton Stoke, Swindon SN5 4JF
tel (01793) 421168 *fax* (01793) 421168

email neil@cornertolearn.co.uk
website www.cornertolearn.co.uk
Publisher Neil Griffiths

Books and learning materials aimed at teachers and
parents with young children. Imprint: Red Robin
Books (picture books).

cp publishing
The Children's Project Ltd, PO Box 2, Richmond,
Surrey TW10 7FL
tel 0845-094 5494
email info@childrensproject.co.uk
website www.socialbaby.com
Directors/Co-founders Helen Dorman, Clive Dorman

High-quality visual books that help parents and
carers better understand and communicate with their
children from birth. The Children's Project is
dedicated exclusively to supporting the family and
improved outcomes for children. It draws upon the
experience and expertise of parents, health
professionals and academics to provide up-to-date
information in a form that is easily accessible to
everyone – parents, carers and practitioners. Founded
in 1995; first books published 2000.

Crown House Publishing Ltd
Crown Buildings, Bancyfelin, Carmarthen SA33 5ND
tel (01267) 211345 *fax* (01267) 211882
email books@crownhouse.co.uk
website www.crownhouse.co.uk
Chairman Martin Roberts, *Directors* David Bowman
(managing director), Glenys Roberts, David
Bowman, Karen Bowman, Caroline Lenton

Publishes a range of teacher resources detailing the
latest and best techniques for enhancing learning and
teaching ability. List includes accelerated learning,
thinking skills, multiple intelligence, emotional
intelligence, mindmapping and music. Also publishes
titles in the areas of psychotherapy, business training
and development, Mind, Body & Spirit. Founded
1998.

Dean – see Egmont UK Ltd

Dorling Kindersley – see Penguin Group (UK)

Doubleday Children's Books – see The Random House Group Ltd

Dref Wen
28 Church Road, Whitchurch, Cardiff CF14 2EA
tel 029-2061 7860 *fax* 029-2061 0507
website www.drefwen.com
Directors Roger Boore, Anne Boore, Gwilym Boore,
Alun Boore, Rhys Boore

Welsh language publisher. Original, adaptations and
translations of foreign and English language full-
colour picture story books for children. Also activity
books, novelty books, Welsh language fiction for
7–14 year-olds, teenage fiction, reference, religion,

audiobooks and poetry. Educational material for primary and secondary school children in Wales and England, including dictionaries, revision guides and Welsh as a Second Language. Publishes approx. 50 titles a year and has 450 in print. Founded 1970.

Submission details No unsolicited MSS. Phone first.

The Educational Company of Ireland†

Ballymount Road, Walkinstown, Dublin 12, Republic of Ireland
tel (01) 4500611 *fax* (01) 4500993
email info@edco.ie
website www.edco.ie
Executive Directors Martina Harford (Chief Executive), Robert McLoughlin, *Commissioning Editors* Robert Healy, Michele Staunton

Educational (primary and post-primary) books in the Irish language. Publishes approx. 60–70 titles each year and has 600–700 in print. Ancillary materials include CD-Roms, CDs and audiotapes. Recent successes include *Sunny Street/Streets Ahead* Primary English Langue Programme, *Fonn 1, 2, 3* (Irish language publications for post-primary) and *Geo* (geography publication for post-primary). Trading unit of Smurfit Kappa Group – Ireland. Founded 1910.

Submission details Send an A4 page outlining the selling points and proposal, a draft table of contents and a sample chapter. Allow 3 months for response.

Educational Explorers (Publishers)

Unit 5, Feidr Castell Business Park, Fishguard SA65 9BB
tel/fax (08456) 123912
email enquiries@cuisenaire.co.uk
website www.cuisenaire.co.uk
Directors M.J. Hollyfield, D.M. Gattegno

Educational. Recent successes include: mathematics – *Numbers in Colour with Cuisenaire Rods*; languages – *The Silent Way*; literacy, reading – *Words in Colour*; educational films. No unsolicited material. Founded 1962.

Egmont UK Ltd*

239 Kensington High Street, London W8 6SA
tel 020-7761 3500 *fax* 020-7761 3510
email info@egmont.co.uk
website www.egmont.co.uk

Specialist children's publisher, selling more than 25 million books and 12 million magazines each year for babies to teenagers. Part of the Egmont Group, Europe's largest children's publisher telling stories through books, magazines, film, TV, music, games and mobile phones in 30 countries throughout the world. Founded 1878.

Egmont Press
email childrensreader@euk.egmont.com
Picture book and gift (ages 0+), fiction (ages 5+). Authors include Michael Morpurgo, Jenny Nimmo, William Nicholson, Helen Oxenbury, Enid Blyton, Andy Stanton, Julia Golding, Jan Fearnley and Lydia Monks. Characters include Winnie the Pooh and Tintin.

Submission details Will consider submissions sent by email but highly recommend that submissions are made through a literary agency. No submissions by post. Send a short synopsis and the first 3 chapters. Will not respond to individuals unless successful. See website for more details.

Egmont Publishing Group
Egmont Publishing represents licensed character publishing, including Thomas the Tank Engine, Mr Men, Wallace & Gromit, Postman Pat, Barbie, Bob the Builder, Waybuloo and Ben 10. Wide range of formats for children of all ages: storybooks, annuals, colouring, activity and sticker books, novelty books.

Egmont Magazines is the UK's second largest magazine publisher. Portfolio includes *Disney Princess, Barbie, Ben 10, Tinkerbell, Dora the Explorer, Fireman Sam, Go Girl, Toxic, Power Rangers, The World of Cars* and *Thomas & Friends.*

Evans Publishing Group*

2A Portman Mansions, Chiltern Street, London W1U 6NR
tel 020-7487 0920 *fax* 020-7487 0921
email sales@evansbooks.co.uk
website www.evansbooks.co.uk
Directors Brian Jones (managing), A.O. Ojora (Nigeria), Danny Daly (Finance), *UK Publisher* Su Swallow

Educational books, particularly preschool, school library and teachers' books for the UK, primary and secondary for Africa and the Caribbean. Submissions welcome but does not respond if unsuccessful. Part of the Evans Publishing Group. Founded 1908.

Faber and Faber Ltd*

Bloomsbury House, 74–77 Great Russell Street, London WC1B 3DA
tel 020-7927 3800 *fax* 020-7927 3801
website www.faber.co.uk
Chief Executive Stephen Page, *Publicity Director* Rachel Alexander, *Marketing Director* Jo Ellis, *Production Director* Nigel Marsh, *Rights Director* Jason Cooper, *Publishing Director Children's Books* Julia Heydon-Wells

High-quality general fiction and non-fiction, drama, film, music, poetry. For children: fiction for 5–8 and 9–12 year-olds, teenage fiction, poetry and some non-fiction. Authors include Paul McCartney, Ricky Gervais, G.P. Taylor, Ted Hughes, Philip Ardagh, Margaret Mahy, Pauline Fisk, Steve Voake, Harry Hill, Kenneth Oppel, Justin Richards, Betty G. Birney.

Submission details Only accepts submissions through an agent; no unsolicited MSS.

CJ Fallon

Ground Floor, Block B, Liffey Valley Office Campus, Dublin 22, Republic of Ireland

tel (01) 6166400 *fax* (01) 6166499
email editorial@cjfallon.ie
website www.cjfallon.ie
Executive Directors Brian Gilsenan (managing), John Bodley (financial)

Educational textbooks. Founded 1927.

Featherstone Education
50 Bedford Square, London WC1B 3DP
tel 020-7494 2111
website www.bloomsbury.com

A range of books for practitioners at Early Years and Foundation stage. Publishes approx. 50 titles each year. Imprint of Bloomsbury Children's & Education division of Bloomsbury Publishing (page 7).

David Fickling Books – see The Random House Group Ltd

Fidra Books
219 Bruntsfield Place, Edinburgh EH10 4DH
tel 0131-447 1917
email info@fidrabooks.com
website www.fidrabooks.com
Contact Rebecca Hearne, Editorial Assistant

Specialises in reprinting children's books ranging from 1930s adventure stories to iconic 1960s fantasy novels and from pony books to school stories. Founded 2005.

First and Best in Education
Earlstrees Court, Earlstrees Road, Corby, Northants. NN17 4HH
tel (01536) 399011 *fax* (01536) 399012
email sales@firstandbest.co.uk
website www.shop.firstandbest.co.uk
Contact Anne Cockburn (editor)

Education-related books (no fiction). Currently actively recruiting new writers for schools; ideas welcome. Send sae with submissions. Founded 1992.

Flame Tree Publishing
Crabtree Hall, Crabtree Lane, London SW6 6TY
tel 020-7386 4700 *fax* 020-7386 4701
email info@flametreepublishing.com
website www.flametreepublishing.com
Managing Director Frances Bodiam, *Publisher/ Creative Director* Nick Wells

Children's novelty books. Also for adults: music, reference, art, cookery. Part of The Foundry Creative Media Company Ltd. Founded 1992.

Floris Books*
15 Harrison Gardens, Edinburgh EH11 1SH
tel 0131-337 2372 *fax* 0131-347 9919
email floris@florisbooks.co.uk
website www.florisbooks.co.uk
Commissioning Editor Sally Martin

Children's activity books, novels, board and picture books. Also for adults: religion, science, philosophy,

holistic health, organics, Mind, Body & Spirit, crafts. Approx. 50 titles each year. Founded 1978.

Kelpies (imprint)
Contemporary Scottish fiction from picture books (for 3–6 year-olds) to novels (for 8–12 year-olds). Recent successes include *First Aid for Fairies and Other Fabled Beasts* by Lari Don and *You Can't Play Here!* by Angus Corby. Annual Kelpies Prize, see website.
Submission details Will consider unsolicited MSS. For novels send synopsis and sample chapters. For picture books send text and illustrations, text only or illustrations only. Include author/illustrator biography and sae for return of work. Must be Scottish in theme.

Folens Publishers*
Waterslade House, Thame Road, Haddenham, Bucks. HP17 8NT
tel (01844) 576 8115 *fax* (01844) 296 666
email folens@folens.com
website www.folens.com
Managing Director Adrian Cockell, *Director of Publishing* Peter Burton, *Primary Publisher* Zoe Nichols, *Secondary Publisher* Abigail Woodman

Primary and secondary educational books. Imprints: Folens, Belair. Founded 1987.
Submission details Will consider unsolicited MSS. Send synopsis, rationale and sample section by post or email. Material will be acknowledged on receipt; reply with decision to publish within 1–3 months.

Folens Publishers
Hibernian Industrial Estate, off Greenhills Road, Tallaght, Dublin 24, Republic of Ireland
tel (01) 4137200 *fax* (01) 4137282
email info@folens.ie
website www.folens.ie
Chairman Dirk Folens, *Managing Director* John O'Connor, *Primary Managing & Commissioning Editor* Deirdre Whelan, *Secondary Managing Editor* Margaret Burns

Educational (primary, secondary, comprehensive, technical, in English and Irish). Founded 1956.

Blackwater Press (imprint)
Senior Editor Sarah Deegan
Picture books and *Brainstorm* series of activity books. Recent successes include *Bin Bling* by Aoileann Garavaglia (activity book). Founded 1993.
Submission details Will consider unsolicited MSS. Send synopsis and first chapter. Allow 6 weeks for response.

David Fulton – see Taylor and Francis Group

Galaxy Children's Large Print – see AudioGO Ltd

Galore Park Publishing Ltd*
19–21 Sayers Lane, Tenterden, Kent TN30 6BW
tel (01580) 767200 *fax* (01580) 764142

website www.galorepark.co.uk

Educational textbooks and revision guides for students studying at independent schools. *So You Really Want To Learn* range of textbooks for children aged 11+ and *Junior* range for 8–10 year-olds. Courses include Latin, French, English, Spanish, maths and science. Founded 1999.

Gardner Education Ltd

The Old Manse, Rothiemurchus by Aviemore, Inverness-shire PH22 1QP
tel (0845) 230 0775 *fax* (0845) 230 0899
email education@gardnereducation.com
website www.gardnereducation.com

Specialists in literacy books and resources.

Ginn – see Pearson UK

GL Assessment

9th Floor East, 389 Chiswick High Road, London W4 4AL
tel 020-8996 3333 *fax* 020-8742 8767
email information@gl-assessment.co.uk
website www.gl-assessment.co.uk
Group Education Director Andrew Thraves

Independent provider of tests, assessments and assessment services for education. Its aim is to help educational professionals to understand and maximise the potential of their pupils and students. Publishes assessments for the 0–19 age group, though the majority of its assessments are aimed at 5–14 year-olds. Testing and assessment services include literacy, numeracy, thinking skills, ability, learning support and online testing. Founded 1981.

Gomer Press

Llandysul, Ceredigion SA44 4JL
tel (01559) 363090 *fax* (01559) 363758
email gwasg@gomer.co.uk
website www.gomer.co.uk, www.pontbooks.co.uk
Managing Director Jonathan Lewis, *Head of Publishing* Dylan Williams, *Editors* Sioned Lleinau, Rhian Evans

Picture books, novels, stories, poetry and teaching resources in the Welsh language relevant to Welsh culture. No unsolicited MSS; preliminary enquiry essential. Founded 1892.

Pont Books (imprint)
email editor@pontbooks.co.uk
website www.pontbooks.co.uk
Editor Viv Sayer

Picture books, novels, stories, poetry for children and teaching resources with a Welsh dimension. No unsolicited MSS; preliminary enquiry essential.

W.F. Graham

2 Pondwood Close, Moulton Park, Northampton NN3 6RT
tel (01604) 645537 *fax* (01604) 648414

email books@wfgraham.co.uk
website www.wfgraham.co.uk

Activity books including colouring, dot-to-dot, magic painting, puzzle, word search and sticker books. Also picture books and story books.

Granada Learning*

9th Floor East, 389 Chiswick High Road, London W4 4AL
tel 020-8996-3333 *fax* 020-8742-8767
website www.granada-learning.com

Educational multimedia company publishing innovative, assessment and curriculum-based resources for the UK and abroad. It has a catalogue of over 200 products for preschool children, primary and secondary, through to A level. Products are developed by teachers and educationalists. The Granada Learning Group includes Granada Learning Professional Development, GL Assessment (see page 13) and schoolcentre.net.

Gullane Children's Books

185 Fleet Street, London EC4A 2HS
tel 020-7400 1084 *fax* 020-7400 1037
email stories@gullanebooks.com
website www.gullanebooks.com
Publisher Simon Rosenheim

Picture and novelty books for children aged 0–8 years.

Hachette Children's Books*

338 Euston Road, London NW1 3BH
tel 020-7873 6000 *fax* 020-7873 6024
website www.hachettechildrens.co.uk
Managing Director Marlene Johnson

Hodder Children's Books (imprint)
Publishing Director Anne McNeil
Fiction, picture books, novelty, general non-fiction and audiobooks.

Orchard Books (imprint)
Publishing Director Megan Larkin
Fiction, picture and novelty books.

Franklin Watts (imprint)
Publishing Director Rachel Cooke
Non-fiction and information books.

Wayland (imprint)
Publishing Director Joyce Bentley
Non-fiction and information books.

Hachette UK*

338 Euston Road, London NW1 3BH
tel 020-7873 6000 *fax* 020-7873 6024
website www.hachette.co.uk
Chief Executive Tim Hely Hutchinson, *Directors* Jamie Hodder Williams (Ceo, Hodder & Stoughton, Headline, John Murray), Chris Emerson (Coo), Jane Morpeth (managing, Headline), Marlene Johnson

(managing, Hachette Children's), Peter Roche (deputy Ceo/Ceo, Orion), Malcolm Edwards (managing, Orion), Alison Goff (Ceo, Octopus), Ursula Mackenzie (Ceo, Little, Brown Book Group), Pierre de Cacqueray (finance), Richard Kitson (commercial), Dominic Mahony (group HR), Malcolm Edwards (managing, Hachette Australia), David Young (Ceo, Hachette Book Group USA), Clare Harington (group communications)

Part of Hachette Livre SA since 2004. Hachette UK group companies: Hachette Children's Books (page 13), Headline Book Publishing, Hodder Education Group, Hodder & Stoughton, Hodder Faith, John Murray, Little, Brown Book Group (page 16), Orion Group (page 19), Octopus Group, Hachette Ireland, Hachette Australia (page 28), Hachette New Zealand.

Haldane Mason Ltd

PO Box 34196, London NW10 3YB
tel 020-8459 2131 *fax* 020-8728 1216
email info@haldanemason.com
website www.haldanemason.com
Directors Sydney Francis, Ron Samuel

Illustrated non-fiction books and box sets, mainly for children. No unsolicited material. Imprints: Haldane Mason (adult), Red Kite Books (children's). Founded 1995.

Submission details Interested in non-fiction only; phone or email first to check interest.

HarperCollins Publishers*

77–85 Fulham Palace Road, London W6 8JB
tel 020-8741 7070 *fax* 020-8307 4440
also at Westerhill Road, Bishopbriggs, Glasgow G64 2QT
tel 0141-772 3200 *fax* 0141-306 3119
website www.harpercollins.co.uk
Ceo/Publisher Victoria Barnsley, *Publisher* Belinda Budge

For adults: fiction (commercial and literary) and non-fiction. Subjects include history, celebrity memoirs, biographies, popular science, Mind, Body & Spirit, dictionaries, maps and reference. All fiction and trade non-fiction must be submitted through an agent, or unsolicited MSS may be submitted to www.authonomy.com. Owned by News Corporation. Founded 1819.

HarperCollins Audio (imprint)
Head of Audio Jo Forshaw
See page 61.

HarperCollins Children's Books
website www.harpercollinschildrensbooks.co.uk
Publisher Ann-Janine Murtagh

Annuals, activity books, novelty books, picture books, painting and colouring books, pop-up books and book and tape sets. Fiction for 5–8 and 9–12 year-olds, teenage fiction and series fiction; poetry; film/

TV tie-ins. Publishes approx. 265 titles each year. Recent successes include (picture books) *The Tiger Who Came to Tea* by Judith Kerr, *Percy the Park Keeper* by Nick Butterworth, and *Duck in a Truck* by Jez Alborough; and fiction by Louise Rennison, Nicky Singer, Darren Shan and Michael Morpurgo. Books published under licence include *Noddy, Spiderman, The Simpsons, The Magic Roundabout, Dr Seuss* and *Paddington Bear.*

Submission details No unsolicited MSS: only accepts submissions via agents.

Collins Education (division)
Managing Director Nigel Ward
Books, CD-Roms and online material for UK primary and secondary schools and colleges.

Hawthorn Press

1 Lansdown Lane, Stroud, Glos. GL5 1BJ
tel (01453) 757040 *fax* (01453) 751138
email info@hawthornpress.com
website www.hawthornpress.com
'Books for a creative, peaceful and sustainable world'. Founded 1981.

Heinemann – see Pearson UK

Hippo – see Scholastic Ltd

Hodder Children's Books – see Hachette Children's Books

Hodder Education Group*

338 Euston Road, London NW1 3BH
tel 020-7873 6000 *fax* 020-7873 6325
website www.hoddereducation.co.uk, www.hachettelivreukco.uk
Chief Executive Thomas Webster, *Finance Director* Alex Jones, *Managing Directors* David Swarbrick (consumer learning), C.P. Shaw (tertiary), Lis Tribe (schools), *Editorial Directors* Robert Sulley (science and international), Steve Connolly (digital publishing), Jim Belben (humanities and modern languages), *Business Operations Director* Alyssum Ross, *Sales & Marketing Directors* Janice Tolan (schools and FE), Tim Mahar (trade, HE and health sciences), *Directors* Paul Cherry (Philip Allan), John Mitchell (Hodder Gibson)

Medical (Hodder Arnold), consumer education and self-improvement (Hodder Education and Teach Yourself), school (Hodder Education, Hodder Gibson and Philip Allan), dictionaries, reference and language publishing (Chambers). Part of Hachette Ltd (see page 13).

Hodder Gibson*

2A Christie Street, Paisley PA1 1NB
tel 0141-848 1609 *fax* 0141-889 6315
email hoddergibson@hodder.co.uk
website www.hoddergibson.co.uk,

www.hoddereducation.co.uk,
www.hachettelivre.co.uk
Managing Director John Mitchell

Educational books specifically for Scotland. No unsolicited MSS. Part of Hachette UK (see page 13).

Hodder Headline Ltd – see Hachette UK

Hogs Back Books Ltd
The Stables, Down Place, Hogs Back,
Guildford GU3 1DE
tel (01483) 506030
email enquiries@hogsbackbooks.com
website www.hogsbackbooks.com
Director/Commissioning Editor Karen Stevens

Children's picture books and teenage fiction.
Founded 2009.
   Submission details Welcomes texts and submissions from illustrators but cannot return material without prior arrangement.

Hopscotch Educational Publishing Ltd
St Jude's Church, Dulwich Road, London SE24 0PB
tel 020-7501 6736 *fax* 020-7978 8316
email sales@hopscotchbooks.com
website www.hopscotchbooks.com
Publishing Manager Angela Morano-Shaw

National Curriculum teaching resources for primary school teachers. Founded 1997.

Step Forward Publishing Ltd
Early years teacher resources.

Hutchinson Children's Books – see The
Random House Group Ltd

Igloo Books Ltd
Cottage Farm, Mears Ashby Road, Sywell,
Northants NN6 0BJ
tel (01604) 741116 *fax* (01604) 670495
email publishing@igloo-books.com
website www.igloo-books.com

Adult and children's: cookery, lifestyle, gift, trivia/crosswords, fiction (UK only); novelty, board, picture, activity books, education. Founded 2005.

Imperial War Museum
Lambeth Road, London SE1 6HZ
tel 020-7091 3064 *fax* 020-7416 5374
email mail@iwm.org.uk
website www.iwm.org.uk

In-house art and gift titles; also works in association with larger publishing houses on subjects such as military and social history, photography, children's books, gift, art and cookery.

Impress Books Ltd
Innovation Centre, Rennes Drive,
University of Exeter, Devon EX4 4RN
tel (01392) 262301 *fax* (01392) 262303

email enquiries@impress-books.co.uk
website www.impress-books.co.uk
Contact Richard Willis, Colin Morgan

'Quality thought-provoking titles for the enquiring general reader.' Established 2004.

Indepenpress Publishing Ltd*
25 Eastern Place, Brighton BN2 1GJ
tel (01273) 272758 *fax* (01273) 261434
email info@penpress.co.uk
website www.indepenpress.co.uk
Directors Lynn Ashman (managing), Grace Rafael (production)

Literary fiction, general fiction, children's fiction, selected non-fiction. Founded 1996.

Jolly Learning Ltd
Tailours House, High Road, Chigwell, Essex IG7 6DL
tel 020-8501 0405 *fax* 020-8500 1696
email info@jollylearning.co.uk
website www.jollylearning.co.uk
Director Christopher Jolly

Educational: primary and English as a Foreign Language. The company is committed to enabling high standards in the teaching of reading and writing. Publishes approx. 25 titles each year and has 200 in print. Recent successes include *Jolly Dictionary*, *Jolly Readers* and *Jolly Phonics Starter Kit*. Imprint: Jolly Phonics. Founded 1987.
   Submission details Unsolicited MSS are only considered for add-ons to existing products.

Miles Kelly Publishing
The Bardfield Centre, Great Bardfield,
Essex CM7 4SL
tel (01371) 811309 *fax* (01371) 811393
email info@mileskelly.net
website www.mileskelly.net
Directors Gerard Kelly, Jim Miles, Richard Curry

High-quality illustrated non-fiction and fiction titles for children and family: activity books, board books, story books, poetry, reference, posters and wallcharts. Age groups: preschool, 5–10, 10–15, 15+. See also entry in *Book packagers*. Founded 1996.

Kelpies – see Floris Books

Kingfisher – see Macmillan Publishers Ltd

The King's England Press
Cambertown House, Commercial Road, Goldthorpe,
Rotherham, South Yorkshire S63 9BL
tel/fax (01484) 663790
email sales@kingsengland.com
website www.kingsengland.com

Poetry collections for both adults and children. Successes include *The Spot on My Bum: Horrible Poems for Horrible Children* by Gez Walsh, *Always Eat Your Bogies and Other Rotten Rhymes* by Andrew

Collett, *Wang Foo the Kung Fu Shrew and Other Freaky Poems Too* by Chris White and *Vikings Don't Wear Pants* by Roger Stevens and Celia Warren. Founded 1989.

Also publishes reprints of Arthur Mee's *King's England* series of 1930s guidebooks and books on folklore, and local and ecclesiastical history.

Submission details See website for guidelines. Currently not accepting new unsolicited proposals.

Kingscourt/McGraw-Hill*

McGraw-Hill House, Shoppenhangers Road, Maidenhead, Berks. SL6 2QL
tel (01628) 502720 *fax* (01628) 635895
website www.mcgraw-hill.co.uk/kingscourt
General Manager Rob Ince

Educational publisher of resources for KS1–3, including *Big Books for Shared Reading*, *Guided Reading*, *Story Chest*, *Literacy Links Plus* and *Digital Resources*. Resources support the National Curriculum in England and Wales and the Curriculum for Excellence in Scotland, Northern Ireland curriculum and Curriculum 2000 in Wales. Part of the McGraw-Hill Companies. Founded 1988.

Jessica Kingsley Publishers*

116 Pentonville Road, London N1 9JB
tel 020-7833 2307 *fax* 020-7837 2917
email post@jkp.com
website www.jkp.com
Managing Director Jessica Kingsley

Psychology, psychiatry, arts therapies, social work, special needs (especially autism and Asperger Syndrome), education, law, practical theology and a small children's list focusing on books for children with special needs. Founded 1987.

Kube Publishing Ltd

(formerly the Islamic Foundation)
Markfield Conference Centre, Ratby Lane, Markfield, Leics. LE67 9SY
tel (01530) 249230 *fax* (01530) 249656
email info@kubepublishing.com
website www.kubepublishing.com
Managing Director Haris Ahmad

Books on Islam for adults and children.

Ladybird – see Penguin Group (UK)

Leckie & Leckie*

103 Westerhill Road, Bishopbriggs, Glasgow G64 2QT
tel 0141-772 3200 *fax* 0844-576 8131
email enquiries@leckieandleckie.co.uk
website www.leckieandleckie.co.uk

Educational resources. Dedicated to the ongoing development of materials specifically for education in Scotland, from Standard Grade Foundation to Advanced Higher Level and including new resources for the Curriculum for Excellence. Over 220 titles are currently available in the study guide range. Subsidiary of HarperCollins Publishers.

Frances Lincoln Ltd

4 Torriano Mews, Torriano Avenue, London NW5 2RZ
tel 020-7284 4009 *fax* 020-7485 0490
email reception@frances-lincoln.com
website www.frances-lincoln.com
Directors John Nicoll (managing), Maurice Lyon (editorial, children's books), Jon Rippon (finance), Gail Lynch (sales), Andrew Dunn (editorial, adult books), Helen Fraser, David Kewley, Sarah Roberts (non-executive)

Illustrated, international co-editions: gardening, architecture, environment, interiors, art, walking and climbing, gift, children's books. Founded 1977.

Frances Lincoln Children's Books (imprint)

Novelty books, picture books, fiction for 5–12 year-olds, art, science, religion, poetry.

Submission details Submit material either through an agent or direct.

Lion Hudson plc*

Wilkinson House, Jordan Hill Road, Oxford OX2 8DR
tel (01865) 302750 *fax* (01865) 302757
email info@lionhudson.com
website www.lionhudson.com
Managing Director Paul Clifford

Books for children and adults. Children's books include picture stories, illustrated non-fiction and information books on the Christian faith. Also specialises in children's Bibles and prayer collections. Founded 1971 as Lion Publishing; merged with Angus Hudson Ltd in 2003.

Little, Brown Book Group*

100 Victoria Embankment, London EC4Y 0DY
tel 020-7911 8000 *fax* 020-7911 8100
email info@littlebrown.co.uk
website www.littlebrown.co.uk
Ceo & Publisher Ursula Mackenzie, *Deputy Publisher* David Shelley, *Coo* David Kent, *Directors* Emily-Jane Taylor (finance), Richard Beswick (editorial), Antonia Hodgson (editorial), Robert Manser (group sales, publicity and marketing), Ben Groves-Raines (commercial), Diane Spivey (rights)

Hardback and paperback fiction and general non-fiction. No unsolicited MSS. Part of Hachette UK (see page 13). Founded 1988.

Atom (division)

website www.atombooks.co.uk
Publishing Director Tim Holman, *Editorial Director* Samantha Smith

Teen fiction with a fantastical edge.

Little Tiger Press – see Magi Publications

Longman – see Pearson UK

Macmillan Publishers Ltd*

The Macmillan Building, 4 Crinan Street, London N1 9XW

tel 020-7833 4000 *fax* 020-7843 4640
website www.macmillan.com
Chief Executive Annette Thomas, *Directors* Julian
Drinkall, S.C. Inchcoombe, D.J.G. Knight,
Dr A. Thomas, J. Wheeldon, A. Forbes Watson,
W.H. Farries, R. Gibb (Australia)

Pan Macmillan (division)
20 New Wharf Road, London N1 9RR
tel 020-7014 6000 *fax* 020-7014 6001
website www.panmacmillan.com
Managing Director Anthony Forbes-Watson,
Publishers Jon Butler (Macmillan non-fiction,
Sidgwick & Jackson, Boxtree), Jeremy Trevathan
(Macmillan fiction & Macmillan New Writing), Paul
Baggaley (Picador)
For adults: novels, literary, crime, thrillers, romance,
science fiction, fantasy and horror. Autobiography,
biography, business, gift books, health and beauty,
history, humour, travel, philosophy, politics, world
affairs, theatre, film, gardening, cookery, popular
reference. Publishes under Macmillan, Tor, Pan,
Picador, Sidgwick & Jackson, Boxtree, Macmillan
Audio, Macmillan New Writing. No unsolicited MSS
except through Macmillan New Writing. Founded
1843.

Campbell Books (imprint)
Editorial Director Suzanne Carnell
Early learning, pop-up, novelty, board books for the
preschool market.

Kingfisher (imprint)
tel 020-7014 6000 *fax* 020-7014 6001
Publishing Director Martina Challis
Non-fiction: activity books, encyclopedias, general
history, religion, art, music, philosophy, folklore,
language, mathematics, nature, science and
technology, novelty books, graded readers. Publishes
approx. 50 new non-fiction titles and has about 500
in print. Imprint of Macmillan Children's Books.

Young Picador (imprint)
Editorial Director Sarah Dudman
Literary fiction in paperback and hardback for the
young adult market.

Macmillan Education Ltd (division)
Macmillan Oxford, 4 Between Towns Road,
Oxford OX4 3PP
tel (01865) 405700 *fax* (01865) 405701
email info@macmillan.com
website www.macmillaneducation.com
Chief Executive Julian Drinkall, *Publishing Directors*
Alison Hubert (Africa, Caribbean, Middle East, Asia),
Kate Melliss (Spain), Sharon Jervis (Latin America),
Sue Bale (Dictionaries), Angela Lilley (International
ELT)
ELT titles and school and college textbooks and
materials in all subjects for the international
education market in both book and electronic
formats.

Magi Publications
1 The Coda Centre, 189 Munster Road,
London SW6 6AW
tel 020-7385 6333 *fax* 020-7385 7333
website www.littletigerpress.com,
www.caterpillarbooks.com,
www.stripespublishing.co.uk
Publishers Monty Bhatia, Jude Evans, Jane Harris,
Jamie Asher

Little Tiger Press (imprint)
email info@littletiger.co.uk
website www.littletigerpress.com
Publisher Jude Evans, *Editorial Director* Stephanie
Stansbie
Children's picture books, board books and activity
books for preschool age to 7 years. See website for
submissions guidelines. Founded 1987.

Caterpillar Books (imprint)
email jasher@caterpillarbooks.co.uk
website www.caterpillarbooks.com
Publisher Jamie Asher, *Managing Editor* Pat Hegarty
Books for preschool children, including pop-ups,
board books, cloth books and activity books.
Founded 2003.

Stripes (imprint)
email info@stripespublishing.co.uk
website www.stripespublishing.co.uk
Publisher Jane Harris, *Senior Editor* Katie Jennings
Fiction for children aged 6–12 years. Mainly series
publishing. Will consider new material from authors
and illustrators; see website for guidelines. Founded
2005.

Mantra Lingua TalkingPEN Ltd
Global House, 303 Ballards Lane, London N12 8NP
tel 020-8445 5123 *fax* 020-8446 7745
email info@mantralingua.com
website www.mantralingua.com,
www.talkingpen.co.uk, www.birdmike.co.uk
Managing Directors R. Dutta, M. Chatterji
Innovative TalkingPEN technology to support
language learning, literacy, and other areas of the
curriculum. Dual language books narrated in
multiple languages by the TalkingPEN. Considers
picture book MSS under 1,000 words, artwork
submission, and non-fiction proposals. Founded
1984.

Marshall Cavendish
5th Floor, 32–38 Saffron Hill, London EC1N 8FH
tel 020-7421 8120 *fax* 020-7421 8121
email info@marshallcavendish.co.uk
website www.marshallcavendish.co.uk
Managing Editor Susan McGing
English language teaching. Founded 1969.

Kevin Mayhew Ltd
Buxhall, Stowmarket, Suffolk IP14 3BW
tel (01449) 737978 *fax* (01449) 737834

Books

email info@kevinmayhew.com
website www.kevinmayhew.com
Directors Kevin Mayhew (chairman), Tim Messinger (sales and marketing), Barbara Mayhew

Christianity: prayer and spirituality, pastoral care, preaching, liturgy worship, children's, youth work, drama, instant art. Music: hymns, organ and choral, contemporary worship, piano and instrumental. Contact Manuscript Submissions Dept before sending MSS/synopses. Founded 1976.

Meadowside Children's Books

185 Fleet Street, London EC4A 2HS
tel 020-7400 1084 *fax* 020-7400 1037
email info@meadowsidebooks.com
website www.meadowsidebooks.com
Publisher Simon Rosenheim

Picture books, junior fiction and young adult fiction. Founded 2003.

The Mercier Press†

Unit 3, Oak House, Riverview Business Park, Blackrock, Cork, Republic of Ireland
tel 021-461 4700 *fax* 021-461 4802
email info@mercierpress.ie
website www.mercierpress.ie
Directors J.F. Spillane (chairman), C. Feehan (managing), M.P. Feehan

Books for adults and children. Subjects include Irish literature, folklore, history, politics, humour, current affairs, health, mind and spirit and general non-fiction. Founded 1944.

National Association for the Teaching of English (NATE)

50 Broadfield Road, Sheffield S8 0XJ
tel 0114-255 5419 *fax* 0114-255 5296
email info@nate.org.uk
website www.nate.org.uk
Chair Prof. Andrew Goodwyn, *Development & Communications Director* Ian McNeilly, *Publications Manager* Anne Fairhall

Educational (primary, secondary and tertiary): teaching English, drama and media. Publishes approx. 2 titles each year and has 70 in print. Recent publications include *Sharing not Staring* (lessons for the interactive whiteboard) and *The Complete Shakespearience*. Imprint: NATE. Founded 1963.
Submission details Submissions should be made via a 'Publication Proposal' form for consideration by the Publications Manager and 3 members of the Publications Board. Allow 3–6 weeks for response. Will consider unsolicited MSS.

Neate Publishing

33 Downside Road, Winchester, Hants SO22 5LT
tel (01962) 841479 *fax* (01962) 841743
email sales@neatepublishing.co.uk
website www.neatepublishing.co.uk

Directors Bobbie Neate (managing), Ann Langran, Maggie Threadingham

Non-fiction books, educational packs, CDs and posters for primary school children. Founded 1999.

Nelson Thornes Ltd*

Delta Place, 27 Bath Road, Cheltenham, Glos. GL53 7TH
tel (01242) 267287 *fax* (01242) 253695
email cservices@nelsonthornes.com
website www.nelsonthornes.com
Managing Director Mary O'Connor

Print and electronic publishers for the educational market: primary, secondary, further education, professional. Part of the Infinitas Learning group.

Jane Nissen Books

Swan House, Chiswick Mall, London W4 2PS
tel 020-8994 8203 *fax* 020-8742 8198
email jane@nissen.demon.co.uk
website www.janenissenbooks.co.uk

Reprinted fiction for 5–8 and 9–12 year-olds, teenage fiction and poetry. Publishes approx. 4 titles each year and has 36 in print. Recent successes include *Clever Polly and the Stupid Wolf* by Catherine Storr, and *Green Smoke* by Rosemary Manning. Seeking to publish more children's 'forgotten' classics. Founded 2000.
Submission details Personal recommendations welcome.

Nosy Crow

The Crow's Nest, 11 The Chandlery, 50 Westminster Bridge Road, London SE1 7QY
tel 020-7953 7677 *fax* 020-7953 7673
email hello@nosycrow.com
website www.nosycrow.com
Managing Director Kate Wilson, *Editorial Director* Camilla Reid

Children's books and apps. Founded 2010.

Oberon Books

521 Caledonian Road, London N7 9RH
tel 020-7607 3637 *fax* 020-7607 3629
email info@oberonbooks.com
website www.oberonbooks.com
Managing Director Charles Glanville, *Publisher* James Hogan, *Editor* Andrew Walby

New and classic play texts, programme texts and general theatre and performing arts books. Founded 1986.

The O'Brien Press Ltd†

12 Terenure Road East, Rathgar, Dublin 6, Republic of Ireland
tel (01) 492 3333 *fax* (01) 492 2777
email books@obrien.ie
website www.obrien.ie
Directors Michael O'Brien, Ide ní Laoghaire, Ivan O'Brien

For children: fiction for all ages; illustrated fiction series – *Panda Cubs* (age 3+), *Pandas* (age 5+), *Flyers* (age 6+) and *Red Flag* (8+); novels (10+) – contemporary, historical, fantasy; also non-fiction. Also for adults: biography, politics, history, true crime, sport, humour, reference. No adult fiction, poetry or academic. Founded 1974.

Submission details Unsolicited MSS (sample chapters only), synopses and ideas for books welcome – submissions will not be returned.

Orchard Books – see Hachette Children's Books

The Orion Publishing Group Ltd*
Orion House, 5 Upper St Martin's Lane, London WC2H 9EA
tel 020-7240 3444 *fax* 020-7240 4822
website www.orionbooks.co.uk
Directors Arnaud Nourry (chairman), Peter Roche (chief executive), Malcolm Edwards (deputy chief executive)

For adults: fiction and non-fiction and audio. Imprints include Everyman, Gollancz, Orion, Phoenix and Weidenfeld & Nicolson. Part of Hachette UK (see page 13). Founded 1992.

Orion Children's Books (division)
Publisher Fiona Kennedy, *Editorial Manager* Jane Hughes
Picture books, fiction for 5–8 and 9–12 year-olds, teenage fiction, series fiction and audio. Publishes approx. 50 titles each year and has about 350 in print. Recent successes include books by Francesca Simon, Michelle Paver and Sally Gardner. Imprint: Orion Children's Books.
Submission details Will consider unsolicited MSS. Allow 2 months for response. Submissions via agents take priority.

Oxford University Press*
Great Clarendon Street, Oxford OX2 6DP
tel (01865) 556767 *fax* (01865) 556646
email enquiry@oup.com
website www.oup.com
Ceo Nigel Portwood, *Group Finance Director* David Gillard, *Academic Journals & OUP USA Managing Director* Tim Barton, *UK Children's & Educational Division Managing Director* Kate Harris, *ELT Division Managing Director* Peter Marshall, *UK Human Resources Director* Caroline James-Nock, *Academic Sales Director* Alastair Lewis

Archaeology, architecture, art, belles-lettres, bibles, bibliography, children's books (fiction, non-fiction, picture), commerce, current affairs, dictionaries, drama, economics, educational (infants, primary, secondary, technical, university), encyclopedias, English language teaching, electronic publishing, essays, foreign language learning, general history, hymn and service books, journals, law, medical, music, oriental, philosophy, political economy, prayer

books, reference, science, sociology, theology and religion; educational software; *Grove Dictionaries of Music & Art*. Trade paperbacks published under the imprint of Oxford Paperbacks. Founded 1478.

Children's and Educational Division
Managing Director, Children's & Education Kate Harris, *Business Director Trade & Children's* Richard Hodson, *Children's Publisher* Liz Cross, *Dictionaries Publisher* Vineeta Gupta, *Schoolbooks: Business Director, Primary & Electronic* Rod Theodorou, *Business Director, Secondary & International* Phil Garratt, *Head of Publishing, Secondary English, Humanities, Languages & Cartography* Simon Tanner-Tremaine, *Publisher, Modern Foreign Languages & Classics* Frederique Jouhandin, *Publisher, Science Maths & Technology* Elspeth Boardley, *Head of Primary Literacy Publishing* Jane Harley.
Picture books, fiction, poetry and dictionaries. Authors include Tim Bowler, Gillian Cross, Julie Hearne and Geraldine McCaughrean.

Parragon Books Ltd
4 Queen Street, Bath BA1 1HE
tel (01225) 478888 *fax* (01225) 443681
email uk_info@parragon.com
website www.parragon.com
Managing Directors Paul Taylor, Stewart Bailey
Children's Publisher Venetia Davie, *Children's Licensed* Ayshea Scharf

Activity books, novelty books, picture books, fiction for 5–8 year-olds, reference and home learning, book and CD sets. Licensed character list. No unsolicited material.

Pavilion Children's Books
10 Southcombe Street, London W14 0RA
tel 020-7605 1400 *fax* 020-7605 1401
website www.anovabooks.com
Publisher Ben Cameron

Children's books: from baby and picture books to illustrated classics and interactive books. Part of the Anova Books Group. Submissions via an agent only.
Recent successes include *The Story of the Little Mole* by Werner Holzwarth, *War Boy* and *Classic Fairy Tales* by Michael Foreman, Quentin Blake's *Magical Tales* and Ralph Steadman's *Fly Away Peter*.

Payne-Gallway – see Pearson UK

PCET Publishing
(Pictorial Charts Educational Trust)
27 Kirchen Road, London W13 0UD
tel 020-8567 9206 *fax* 020-8566 5120
email info@pcet.co.uk
website www.pcet.co.uk

Visual resources for primary and secondary education: wallcharts, photopacks, activity books and other classroom accessories to support the National

Curriculum. Also has a charitable arm which provides funding and teaching resources for the developing world.

Pearson UK*

Edinburgh Gate, Harlow, Essex CM20 2JE
tel (0845) 313 6666 *fax* (0845) 313 7777
email schools@longman.co.uk
website www.pearsoned.co.uk
President Rod Bristow

Harcourt (imprint)

Educational resources for teachers and learners at Primary, Secondary and Vocational level. Provides a range of published resources, teachers' support, and pupil and student material in all core subjects for all ages. Imprints: Ginn, Heinemann, Payne-Gallway, Raintree, Rigby.

Longman (imprint)

Edinburgh Gate, Harlow, Essex CM20 2JE
tel (0800) 579579 *fax* (01279) 414130
email schools@longman.co.uk
website www.longman.co.uk

Educational: primary and secondary. Primary: literacy and numeracy. Secondary: English, maths, science, history, geography, modern languages, design and technology, business and economics, psychology and sociology.

Penguin Longman (imprint)

ELT.

York Notes (imprint)

Literature guides for students.

Penguin Group (UK)*

80 Strand, London WC2R 0RL
tel 020-7010 3000 *fax* 020-7010 6060
website www.penguin.co.uk
Chairman & Gobal Ceo John Makinson, *DK Ceo* Peter Field, *Penguin UK Ceo* Tom Weldon

Books for adults and children (see below). Adult subjects include biography, fiction, current affairs, general leisure, health, history, humour, literature, politics, spirituality and relationships, sports, travel and TV/film tie-ins. Adult imprints include Allen Lane, Dorling Kindersley, Fig Tree, Hamish Hamilton, Michael Joseph, Penguin, Penguin Classics, Rough Guides, Viking. Owned by Pearson plc.

Children's Division

Managing Director, Penguin Children's Francesca Dow, *Puffin Publishing Director (fiction)* Sarah Hughes, *Puffin Editorial Director (picture books)* Louise Bolongaro, *Puffin Editorial Director (Characters)* Kate Hayler, *Editorial Director, Classic Puffin* Elv Moody, *Publisher, Razorbill* Amanda Punter

Children's paperback and hardback books: picture books, board books, novelty books, fiction, poetry,

non-fiction, popular culture; and audio. Series: *Puffin Classics* and *Puffin Modern Classics.*
Submission details No unsolicited MSS or synopses.

Razorbill (imprint)

Publisher Amanda Punter
Commercial teen fiction. Launched 2010.

BBC, Ladybird, Warne

Category Publisher, Warne Nicole Pearson, *Editorial Director, Ladybird* Heather Crossley, *Publisher, Media and Entertainment* Juliet Matthews, *Publishing Director, Media and Entertainment* Eric Huang, *Art Director, Media and Entertainment* Kirstie Billingham, *Creative Director* Ronnie Fairweather

Specialises in preschool illustrated developmental books for ages 0–6, non-fiction 0–8; licensed brands; children's classic publishing and merchandising properties. No unsolicited MSS.

Dorling Kindersley (division)

website www.dk.com
Deputy Ceo John Duhigg

Illustrated non-fiction for adults and children: gardening, health, medical, travel, food and drink, history, natural history, photography, reference, pregnancy and childcare, film and TV.
Age groups: preschool, 5–8, 8+, family.

Penguin Longman – see Pearson UK

Phaidon Press Ltd

Regent's Wharf, All Saints Street, London N1 9PA
tel 020-7843 1000 *fax* 020-7843 1010
email enquiries@phaidon.com
website www.phaidon.com
Publisher Richard Schlagman, *Chairman* Andrew Price, *Directors* Amanda Renshaw (deputy publisher), James Booth-Clibborn

Visual arts, lifestyle and culture.

Phoenix Yard Books

Phoenix Yard, 65 Kings Cross Road, London WC1X 9LW
tel 020-7239 4968
email info@phoenixyardbooks.com, submissions@phoenixyardbooks.com (submissions)
website www.phoenixyardbooks.com
Commissioning Editor Emma Langley

Picture books, poetry and fiction for ages 3–13. Specialism in character publishing. Particularly seeking character-based young fiction (ages 6–9) and comics/graphic novel material. Founded 2009.
Submission details Will consider MSS either by post with sae or by email. Send covering letter, synopsis and up to 3 sample chapters. Allow 12 weeks for response. Illustration submissions: send artwork (not originals) by post or PDFs via email. Illustration samples are kept on file.

Piccadilly Press

5 Castle Road, London NW1 8PR
tel 020-7267 4492 *fax* 020-7267 4493

email books@piccadillypress.co.uk
website www.piccadillypress.co.uk
Managing Director & Publisher Brenda Gardner

Picture books, tween/teenage fiction, series fiction, parental advice trade paperbacks. Publishes approx. 25–30 titles each year and has over 200 in print. Recent successes include *Letters from an Alien Schoolboy* by Roo Asquith, *Desperate Measures* by Laura Summers and *Ruby and Grub* by Abi Burlingham and Sarah Warburton. Founded 1983. *Submission details* Will consider unsolicited MSS. Send synopsis and 3 sample chapters plus sae. Allow 6 weeks for response. Interested in publishing teenage books that deal with contemporary issues.

Picthall & Gunzi Ltd

21A Widmore Road, Bromley, Kent BR1 1RW
tel 020-8460 4032 *fax* 020-8460 4021
email chez@picthallandgunzi.demon.co.uk,
chris@picthallandgunzi.demon.co.uk
website www.picthallandgunzi.com
Managing Director Chez Picthall, *Publisher &
Editorial Director* Christiane Gunzi

High-quality, photographically illustrated non-fiction for children: activity books, board books, novelty books, early learning. Age groups: preschool and Key Stage 1. See also page 66.

Pinwheel Children's Books – see Alligator Books Ltd

Pipers' Ash Ltd

Pipers' Ash, Church Road, Christian Malford, Chippenham, Wilts. SN15 4BW
tel (01249) 720563 *fax* (0870) 0568916
email pipersash@supamasu.com
website www.supamasu.com
Editorial Director Alfred Tyson

Poetry, short stories; historical novels, biographies, plays, translations, general non-fiction. New authors with talent and potential encouraged. Founded 1976.

Point – see Scholastic Ltd

Pont Books – see Gomer Press

Poolbeg Press Ltd

123 Grange Hill, Baldoyle Industrial Estate, Dublin 13, Republic of Ireland
tel (01) 8321477 *fax* (01) 8321430
email info@poolbeg.com
website www.poolbeg.com
Directors Kieran Devlin (managing), Paula Campbell (publisher)

Children's and teenage fiction. Also adult popular fiction, non-fiction, current affairs. Imprint: Poolbeg. Founded 1976.

Portland Press Ltd

Charles Darwin House, 12 Roger Street, London WC1N 2JL

tel 020-7685 2410 *fax* 020-7685 2469
email editorial@portlandpress.com
website www.portlandpress.com
Directors Rhonda C. Oliver (managing), John Misselbrook (finance), John Day (IT), Adam Marshall (marketing)

Biochemistry and molecular life science books for graduate, postgraduate and research students. Illustrated science books for children: *Making Sense of Science* series. Founded 1990.

Priddy Books

4 Crinan Street, London N1 9XW
tel 020-7418 5515 *fax* 020-7418 85507
website www.priddybooks.com
Publisher Roger Priddy, *Publishing Manager* Claire Amos, *Art Director* Robert Tainsh, *Rights Manager* Emma Davies

Specialises in baby/toddler and preschool books: activity books, board books, novelty books, picture books.

Prim-Ed Publishing

Bosheen, New Ross, Co. Wexford, Ireland
tel (0870) 876 0151 *fax* (0870) 876 0152
email sales@prim-ed.com
website www.prim-ed.com
Managing Director Seamus McGuinness

Educational publisher specialising in copymasters (photocopiable teaching resources) for primary school and special needs lower secondary pupils. Books written by practising classroom teachers.

Puffin – see Penguin Group (UK)

QED Publishing

226 City Road, London EC1V 2TT
tel 020-7812 8600 *fax* 020-7253 4370
email qedpublishing@quarto.com
website www.qed-publishing.co.uk, www.quarto.com
Associate Publisher Zeta Davies, *Editorial Director* Jane Walker

Children's trade and education books. High-quality curriculum-friendly books designed to stimulate early learning in the classroom and home; also preschool. Series include *Storytime, Mighty Machines, Life Cycles, Warriors, People Who Help Us, Magic Handbooks, Awesome Animals, Great Big Book of…* series. Division of Quarto Publishing plc. Founded in 2003.

The Quarto Group, Inc.

226 City Road, London, EC1V 2TT
tel 020-7700 9000 *fax* 020-7253 4437
email info@quarto.com
website www.quarto.com
Chairman & Ceo Laurence Orbach, *Chief Financial Officer* Mick Mousley, *Creative Director* Bob Morley, *Director of Publishing* David Breuer

Independent publishing group encompassing traditional and co-edition publishing. Co-edition

Books

books are licensed to third parties all over the world, with best-selling titles often available in 20+ languages. UK-based operations include the following autonomously run business units/imprints: Quarto Publishing plc, Quintet Publishing Ltd, Marshall Editions, Quintessence, Quarto Children's Books/Design Eye (see below), QED Publishing Ltd, Quantum Publishing Ltd, qu:id, Aurum Press Ltd, Jacqui Small and RotoVision.

Quarto Children's Books Ltd
226 City Road, London EC1V 2TT
tel 020-7812 8626 *fax* 020-7253 4370
email quartokids@quarto.com, sueg@quarto.com
Publisher Sue Grabham, *Art Director* Jonathan Gilbert
Co-edition publisher of innovative Books-Plus for children. Highly illustrated paper-engineered, novelty and component-based titles for all ages, but primarily preschool (3+), 5–8 and 8+ years. Mainly non-fiction, early concepts and curriculum-based topics for the trade in all international markets. Opportunities for freelance paper engineers, artists, authors, editors and designers. Unsolicited MSS not accepted.

Quest – see Top That! Publishing plc

Ragged Bears Publishing Ltd
Unit 14A, Bennett's Field Trading Estate, Southgate Road, Wincanton, Somerset BA9 9DT
tel (01963) 34300
email info@raggedbears.co.uk
website www.raggedbears.co.uk
Managing Director Henrietta Stickland
Preschool picture and novelty books, first chapter books to young teen fiction. Emailed submissions preferred but if posted send sae. Do not send original artwork. Imprint: Ragged Bears. Founded 1994.

Raintree – see Pearson UK

The Random House Group Ltd*
20 Vauxhall Bridge Road, London SW1V 2SA
tel 020-7840 8400
website www.randomhouse.co.uk
Chairman/Ceo Gail Rebuck, *Deputy Ceo* Ian Hudson, *Directors* Larry Finlay (RHCB and Managing Director, Transworld), Mark Gardiner (finance), Brian Davies (Ebury Publishing and Managing Director, overseas operations), Richard Cable (Managing Director, Vintage Publishing), Garry Prior (sales), Mark Williams (Managing Director Distribution)

Subsidiary of Bertelsmann AG.
Group consists of 6 publishing companies comprising 40 imprints.

Random House Audio Books
tel 020-7840 8519 *fax* 020-7233 6127
Commissioning Editor Zoe Howes
See page 62.

Random House Digital
tel 020-7840 8400
Director of Digital Fionnuala Duggan

Random House Children's Books (company)
61–63 Uxbridge Road, London W5 5SA
tel 020-8579 2652 *fax* 020-8231 6737
website www.kidsatrandomhouse.co.uk
Publisher, Fiction Annie Eaton, *Publisher, Colour & Licensing & RHCSE* Fiona MacMillan, *Editorial Director, Fiction* Becky Stradwick, *Editorial Director, Fiction* Kelly Hurst, *Deputy Publisher, Picture Books* Sue Buswell, *Licensing* Jacqui Butler, *Art Director* Margaret Hope
Picture books, novelty and gift books, preschool and pop-ups, fiction, non-fiction and audio CDs.
Imprints: Bantam Press, Bodley Head Children's Books, Jonathan Cape Children's Books, Corgi Children's Books, Doubleday Children's Books, David Fickling Books, Hutchinson Children's Books, Red Fox Children's Books, Tamarind. No unsolicited MSS or original artwork or text.

Tamarind Books (imprint)
61–63 Uxbridge Road, London W5 5SA
tel 020-8231 6800 *fax* 020-8231 6737
email info@tamarindbooks.co.uk
website www.tamarindbooks.co.uk
Deputy Publisher Sue Buswell
Multicultural children's books. Fiction: picture books (ages 4–8), board books for babies (ages 0–3), board books for toddlers (ages 2–5). Non-fiction: biography (ages 8–12). Books feature on National Curriculum. Founded 1987.
Submission details Will consider unsolicited MSS with sae. Allow one month for response. Looking for books which give black children a high positive profile.

David Fickling Books (imprint)
31 Beaumont Street, Oxford OX1 2NP
tel (01865) 339000 *fax* (01865) 339009
email dfickling@randomhouse.co.uk
website www.davidficklingbooks.co.uk
Publisher David Fickling, *Editor* Bella Pearson
Picture books, fiction for 5–8 and 9–12 year-olds, teenage fiction and poetry. Will consider unsolicited MSS (first 3 chapters only); include covering letter and sae and allow 3 months for response. If possible, find an agent first. Founded 2000.

Ransom Publishing Ltd
Radley House, 8 St Cross Road, Winchester SO23 9HX
tel (01962) 862307 *fax* (05601) 148881
email ransom@ransom.co.uk
website www.ransom.co.uk
Directors Jenny Ertle (managing), Steve Rickard (creative)

Books for reluctant and struggling readers covering high interest age/low reading age titles, quick reads, reading schemes. Range of accompanying workbooks and teacher's guides. Series include *Goal!*, *Boffin Boy*, *Dark Man*, *Trailblazers*, *Siti's Sisters*, *321 Go!* and *Cutting Edge*. Will consider unsolicited MSS. Email in first instance. Founded 1995.

Reader's Digest Children's Publishing Ltd

The Ice House, 124–126 Walcot Street, Bath BA1 5BG
tel (01225) 473200 *fax* (01225) 460942
email lyndsey_crossing@readersdigest.co.uk
website www.rd.com, www.readersdigest.co.uk
Commercial Director Paul Stuart, *Contact* Lyndsey Crossing

Innovative, high-quality books designed to encourage children to use their creativity and imagination. Board, novelty, cinema and TV tie-ins. Licensed characters and brands. Also a wide range of children's religious titles. Fully owned subsidiary of Reader's Digest Association Inc. Founded 1981.

Red Bird Publishing

Kiln Farm, East End Green, Brightlingsea, Colchester, Essex CO7 0SX
tel (01206) 303525 *fax* (01206) 304545
email info@red-bird.co.uk
website www.red-bird.co.uk
Publisher Martin Rhodes-Schofield

Innovative children's activity packs and books produced with a mix of techniques and materials such as Glow in the Dark, Mirrors, Stereoscopic 3D, Moiré and other optical illusions. Authors are specialists in their fields. Activity books, novelty books, picture books, painting and colouring books, teaching books, posters: hobbies, nature and the environment, science. Age groups: preschool, 5–10, 10–15. No unsolicited MSS.

Red Fox Children's Books – see The Random House Group Ltd

Red Kite Books – see Haldane Mason Ltd

Rigby – see Pearson UK

Rising Stars*

PO Box 105, Rochester, Kent ME2 4BE
(0800) 091 1602 *fax* (0800) 091 1603
email info@risingstars-uk.com
website www.risingstars-uk.com

Educational publisher of books and software for primary school age children. Titles are linked to the National Curriculum Key Stages, QCA Schemes of Work, National Numeracy Framework or National Literacy Strategy. Approach by email with ideas for publishing.

Roar Publishing – see Magi Publications

Rockpool Children's Books Ltd

15 North Street, Marton, Warks. CV23 9RJ
tel/fax (01926) 633114

email info@rockpoolchildrensbooks.com
website www.rockpoolchildrensbooks.com
Creative Director Stuart Trotter

Picture books and board books. Founded 2006.

SAGE Publications Ltd*

1 Oliver's Yard, 55 City Road, London EC1Y 1SP
tel 020-7324 8500 *fax* 020-7324 8600
email info@sagepub.co.uk
website www.uk.sagepub.com
Directors Stephen Barr (managing), Katharine Jackson, Ziyad Marar, Richard Fidczuk, Phil Denvir, Clive Parry, Carol Irwin, Blaise Simqu (USA), Sara Miller McCune (USA), Paul R. Chapman

Primary/elementary education, children's development. Founded 1971.

Paul Chapman Publishing (imprint)

website www.paulchapmanpublishing.co.uk
Publisher Marianne Lagrange

Education: academic and professional books for students, practitioners and school leaders.

Salariya Book Company Ltd

Book House, 25 Marlborough Place, Brighton BN1 1UB
tel (01273) 603306 *fax* (01273) 693857
email salariya@salariya.com
website www.salariya.com
Director David Salariya

Children's non-fiction. Imprints: Book House, Scribblers, Scribo. Founded 1989.

Schofield & Sims Ltd

Dogley Mill, Fenay Bridge, Huddersfield HD8 0NQ
tel (01484) 607080 *fax* (01484) 606815
email post@schofieldandsims.co.uk
website www.schofieldandsims.co.uk
Chairman C.N. Platts

Educational: nursery, infants, primary; posters. Founded 1901.

Scholastic Ltd*

Euston House, 24 Eversholt Street, London NW1 1DB
tel 020-7756 7761 *fax* 020-7756 7795
website www.scholastic.co.uk
Chairman M.R. Robinson

Children's fiction and non-fiction and education resources for primary schools. Owned by Scholastic Inc. Founded 1964.

Scholastic Children's Books (division)

Euston House, 24 Eversholt Street, London NW1 1DB
tel 020-7756 7756 *fax* 020-7756 7795
email publicity@scholastic.co.uk
Managing Director Hilary Murray Hill, *Editorial Director, Non-Fiction* Jill Sawyer, *Editorial Director, Fiction* Clare Argar, *Editorial Director, Picture,*

Novelty, Gift Books Katherine Halligan, *Trade & Rights Director* Antonia Pelari

Activity books, novelty books, picture books, fiction for 5–12 year-olds, teenage fiction, series fiction and film/TV tie-ins. Recent successes include *Horrible Histories* by Terry Deary and Martin Brown, *His Dark Materials* trilogy by Philip Pullman and *Mortal Engines* by Philip Reeve. Imprints: Hippo, Point, Scholastic Fiction, Scholastic Non-fiction, Scholastic Press.

Submission details Will consider unsolicited submissions: send synopsis and sample chapter only.

The Chicken House
See page 9.

Scholastic Educational Resources (division)
Book End, Range Road, Witney, Oxon OX29 0YD
tel (01993) 893456
Managing Director Denise Cripps

Professional books and classroom materials for primary teachers and magazines (*Nursery Education Plus*, *Child Education Plus*).

Scholastic Book Clubs (division)
See page 69.

Scholastic Book Fairs (division)
See page 70.

SCP Publishers Ltd
(trading as Scottish Cultural Press)
Unit 6, Newbattle Abbey Business Park,
Newbattle Road, Dalkeith EH22 3LJ
tel 0131-660 6366 *fax* (0870) 285 4846
email info@scottishbooks.com
website www.scottishbooks.com
Directors Brian Pugh, Avril Gray

'Scottish books for children.' Picture books, history, reference and cookery. Publishes approx. 3 titles each year and has 32 in print. Recent successes include *Teach the Bairns to Cook/Bake* and *Classic Children's Games*. Also, for adults: Scottish non-fiction and Scots language. Founded 1992.

Submission details No unsolicited MSS. Send letter, phone or email before sending material. See website for submission guidelines.

Scripture Union
207–209 Queensway, Bletchley, Milton Keynes,
Bucks. MK2 2EB
tel (01908) 856000 *fax* (01908) 856111
email info@scriptureunion.org.uk
website www.scriptureunion.org.uk
Director of Ministry Delivery Terry Clutterham

Christian books and Bible reading materials for people of all ages; educational and worship resources for churches; adult fiction and non-fiction; children's fiction and non-fiction (age groups: under 5, 5–8, 8–10 and youth). Publishes approx. 40 titles each year for children/young people and has 200–250 in print.

Recent successes include The *Bible Storybook* range and *Essential 100* by Whitney Kuniholm. Scripture Union works as a charity in over 120 countries and publishes in approx. 20. Founded 1867.

Submission details Will not consider unsolicited MSS.

SEMERC – see Granada Learning

SEN Press Ltd
7 Cliffe Street, Hebden Bridge,
West Yorkshire HX7 8BY
tel (01422) 844822
email info@senpress.co.uk
website www.senpress.co.uk
Publisher Christine Clarke

Specialises in books that are accessible to young people (14–19 years) with severe learning difficulties. Founded 2003.

Short Books Ltd
3ᴀ Exmouth House, Pine Street, London EC1R 0JH
tel 020-7833 9429 *fax* 020-7833 9500
email clemmie@shortbooks.co.uk
website www.shortbooks.co.uk
Editorial Directors Rebecca Nicolson, Aurea Carpenter

Children's books: fiction and non-fiction. No unsolicited MSS. Founded 2000.

Simon & Schuster UK Ltd*
222 Gray's Inn Road, London WC1X 8HB
tel 020-7316 1900 *fax* 020-7316 0331/2
website www.simonandschuster.co.uk
Directors Ian Chapman (managing), Ingrid Selberg (children's publishing)

No unsolicited MSS. Founded 1986.

Simon & Schuster Children's Publishing
Children's Publishing Director Ingrid Selberg, *Fiction Editorial Director* Venetia Gosling, *Editorial Director, Picture Books & Novelties* Emma Blackburn, *Art Director* Nia Roberts

Activity books, novelty books, picture books, fiction for 5–8 and 9–12 year-olds, teenage fiction, series fiction, film/TV tie-ins. Publishes approx. 180–200 titles each year. Recent successes include *Aliens Love Underpants* by Claire Freedman, *Vampirates* by Justin Somper and the *Spiderwick* series by Holly Black and Tony Di Terlizzi.

Submission details No unsolicited MSS. Will only consider MSS via agents.

Smart Learning
PO Box 321, Cambridge CB1 2XU
tel (01223) 477550 *fax* (01223) 477551
email admin@smart-learning.co.uk
website www.smart-learning.co.uk

High-quality teaching and learning resources for both teachers and children – from the Foundation stage through to Key Stage 3. Publishes software and books to enhance the teaching and learning of ICT, Phonics, Literacy, PSHE and Citizenship and English.

Stacey International

128 Kensington Church Street, London W8 4BH
tel 020-7221 7166 *fax* 020-7792 9288
email info@stacey-international.co.uk
website www.stacey-international.co.uk
Chairman Tom Stacey, *Managing Director* Max Scott, *Finance Director* Patrick Kelly

Illustrated books for children aged 3–12. Publishers of the *Musgrove* series.

Storysack Ltd

Resource House, Kay Street, Bury BL9 6BU
tel 0161-763 6232 *fax* 0161-763 5366
email hello@resourcehouse.co.uk
website www.storysack.com

Storysacks for children aged 3+. Storysacks are cloth bags of resources to encourage children and parents to enjoy reading together. Each sack is based around a picture story book with a supporting fact book on a similar theme, a parent guide, characters and a game. Founded 1999.

Strident Publishing Ltd

22 Strathwhillan Drive, Hairmyres, Glasgow G75 8GT
tel (01355) 220588
email info@stridentpublishing.co.uk
website www.stridentpublishing.co.uk
Executive Director Keith Charters, *Commissioning Editors* Graham Watson, Alison Stroak

Fiction for ages 8–18, including fiction that will appeal to reluctant readers. Publishes 12–15 books a year. Authors include D.A. Nelson (winner of 2008 Royal Mail Awards for Scottish Children's Books), Catherine MacPhail, Linda Strachan, Gillian Philip, Paul Biegel, Emma Barnes, John Ward and Hazel Allan.
Submission details Email a proposed back cover book blurb together with the first 3 chapters. Founded 2005.

Stripes – see Magi Publications

Tamarind Books – see The Random House Group Ltd

Tango Books Ltd

PO Box 32595, London W4 5YD
tel 020-8996 9970 *fax* 020-8996 9977
email sales@tangobooks.co.uk
website www.tangobooks.co.uk
Directors Sheri Safran, David Fielder

Children's fiction and non-fiction novelty books, including pop-up, touch-and-feel and cloth books. Maximum 500 words. No poetry. Submissions with sae or by email.

Tarquin Publications

Suite 74, 17 Holywell Hill, St Albans AL1 1DT
tel (01727) 833866 *fax* (0845) 4566385

email info@tarquinbooks.com
website www.tarquinbooks.com
Director Andrew Griffin

Mathematical models, puzzles, codes and logic and paper engineering books for intelligent children. Publishes 7–8 titles each year and has 103 in print. Recent successes include *Mathematical Merry-go-round* and *A Handbook of Paper Automata Mechanisms*. Founded 1970.
Submission details Do not send unsolicited MSS. Send a one-page proposal of idea.

Taylor and Francis Group*

2 and 4 Park Square, Milton Park, Abingdon, Oxon OX14 4RN
tel 020-7017 6000 *fax* 020-7017 6699
email info@tandf.co.uk
website www.tandf.co.uk, www.informa.com
Managing Director, Taylor & Francis Books Jeremy North

Academic and reference books, including education. Imprints include CRC Press, Europa, Garland Science, Psychology Press, Routledge, Spon and Taylor & Francis.

The Templar Company Ltd

The Granary, North Street, Dorking, Surrey RH4 1DN
tel (01306) 876361 *fax* (01306) 889097
email info@templarco.co.uk, submissions@templarco.co.uk (submissions)
website www.templarco.co.uk
Managing & Creative Director Amanda Wood, *Sales & Marketing Director* Ruth Huddleston

Publisher and packager of high-quality illustrated children's books, including novelty books, picture books, pop-up books, board books, fiction, non-fiction and gift titles. Send submissions via email.

D.C. Thomson & Co. Ltd – Publications

2 Albert Square, Dundee DD1 9QJ
tel (0138) 222 3131
website www.dcthomson.co.uk
London office 185 Fleet Street, London EC4A 2HS

Publishers of newspapers and periodicals. Children's books (annuals), based on weekly magazine characters; fiction. For fiction guidelines, send a large sae to Central Fiction Dept.

TickTock Books Ltd

The Pantiles Chambers, 85 High Street, Tunbridge Wells, Kent TN1 1XP
tel 0870 381 2223
email info@ticktock.co.uk
website www.ticktock.co.uk

Children's non-fiction, fiction and preschool.

Tide Mill Press – see Top That! Publishing plc

Titan Books

144 Southwark Street, London SE1 0UP
tel 020-7620 0200 *fax* 020-7620 0032

Books

email editorial@titanemail.com
website www.titanbooks.com
Publisher & Managing Director Nick Landau, *Editorial Director* Katy Wild

Graphic novels, including *Simpsons* and *Batman*, featuring comic-strip material; film and TV tie-ins and cinema reference books. No fiction or children's proposals, no email submissions and no unsolicited material without preliminary letter. Email or send large sae for current author guidelines. Division of Titan Publishing Group Ltd. Founded 1981.

Top That! Publishing plc
Marine House, Tide Mill Way, Woodbridge,
Suffolk IP12 1AP
tel (01394) 386651 *fax* (01394) 386011
email info@topthatpublishing.com
website www.topthatpublishing.com
Chairman Barrie Henderson, *Directors* David Henderson (managing/digital publishing), Simon Couchman (creative), Stuart Buck (production), Douglas Eadie (financial), Daniel Graham (editorial), Dave Greggor (sales)

Top That! Kids (imprint)
Children's activity, picture, reference and gift books. Founded 1998.

Tide Mill Press (imprint)
Preschool novelty, picture and early learning books. Founded 2007.

Quest (imprint)
Children's internet-linked fiction and activity books. Founded 2008.

Trentham Books Ltd
Westview House, 734 London Road, Oakhill,
Stoke-on-Trent, Staffs. ST4 5NP
tel (01782) 745567 *fax* (01782) 745553
email tb@trentham.books.co.uk
Editorial office 28 Hillside Gardens, London N6 5ST
tel 020-8348 2174
website www.trentham-books.co.uk
Directors Dr Gillian Klein (editorial), Barbara Wiggins (executive)

Education (including specialist fields – multi-ethnic issues, equal opportunities, bullying, design and technology, early years), social policy, sociology of education, European education, women's studies. Does not publish books for use by parents or children, or fiction, biography, reminiscences and poetry. Founded 1978.

Trotman – see Crimson Publishing

Usborne Publishing Ltd
Usborne House, 83–85 Saffron Hill,
London EC1N 8RT
tel 020-7430 2800 *fax* 020-7430 1562
email mail@usborne.co.uk
website www.usborne.com

Publishing Director Jenny Tyler, *Editorial Director, Fiction* Rebecca Hill, *General Manager* Robert Jones

Activity books, novelty books, picture books, fiction for 5–8 and 9–12 year-olds, series fiction, reference, poetry and audio, YA fiction, ebooks. Reference subjects include practical, craft, natural history, science, languages, history, art, activities, geography. Publishes 300 titles each year and has about 1,500 in print. Imprint: Usborne. Founded 1973.
    Submission details Looking for high-quality imaginative children's fiction. Send correspondence to Rebecca Hill.

Walker Books Ltd
87 Vauxhall Walk, London SE11 5HJ
tel 020-7793 0909 *fax* 020-7587 1123
website www.walker.co.uk
Directors Roger Alexander (chairman, non-executive), David Heatherwick (group managing), Helen McAleer (managing), Jane Winterbotham (publishing), Jane Harris (sales), Alan Lee (production), *Publishers* Deirdre McDermott, Caroline Royds, Denise Johnstone-Burt, Gill Evans

Activity books, novelty books, picture books, fiction for 5–8 and 9–12 year-olds, teenage fiction, series fiction, film/TV tie-ins, plays, poetry and audio. Publishes approx. 300 titles each year and has 1,500 in print. Recent successes include the *Alex Rider* series by Anthony Horowitz, *Tamar* by Mal Peet, *The Runaway Dinner* by Allan Ahlberg and Bruce Ingman, and *Butterfly, Butterfly* by Petr Horáček. Imprint: Walker Books. Founded 1980.
    Submission details Write to the Editor. Allow 3 months for response.

Ward Lock Educational Co. Ltd
BIC Ling Kee House, 1 Christopher Road,
East Grinstead, West Sussex RH19 3BT
tel (01342) 318980 *fax* (01342) 410980
email wle@lingkee.com
website www.wardlockeducational.com
Directors Au Bak Ling (chairman, Hong Kong), Au King Kwok (Hong Kong), Au Wai Kwok (Hong Kong), Albert Kw Au (Hong Kong), *Company Secretary* Eileen Parsons

Primary and secondary pupil materials, Kent Mathematics Project: *KMP BASIC* and *KMP Main* series covering Reception to GCSE, *Reading Workshops*, *Take Part* series and *Take Part* starters, teachers' books, music books, *Target* series for the National Curriculum: *Target Science* and *Target Geography*, religious education. Founded 1952.

Warne – see Penguin Group (UK)

Franklin Watts – see Hachette Children's Books

The Watts Publishing Group Ltd – see Hachette Children's Books

Waverley Books Ltd
144 Port Dundas Road, Glasgow G4 0HZ
tel 0141-567 2841 *fax* 0141-567 2831

email info@waverley-books.co.uk
website www.waverley-books.co.uk
Publishers Ron Grosset, Liz Small
Children's fiction and non-fiction.

Wayland – see Hachette Children's Books

WingedChariot Press
7 Court Royal, Eridge Road, Tunbridge Wells,
Kent TN4 8HT
email info@wingedchariot.com
website www.wingedchariot.com
Directors Neal Hoskins, Ann Arscott
Children's books in translation. Founded 2005.

Wizard Books Ltd
Omnibus Business Centre, 39–41 North Road,
London N7 9DP
tel 020-7697 9695 *fax* 020-7697 9501
email wizard@iconbooks.co.uk
website www.iconbooks.co.uk/wizard
Directors Peter Pugh (chairman), Simon Flynn
(managing)
Gamebooks for 5–8 and 9–12 year-olds, reference
and narrative non-fiction. Recent successes include
Fighting Fantasy Gamebooks by Steve Jackson and Ian
Livingstone, *Big Numbers* by Mary and John Gribbin
and *Darkness Visible: Inside the World of Philip
Pullman* by Nicholas Tucker. Imprint of Icon Books
Ltd.

WizzBook Ltd
1 Stairbridge Court, Bolney Grange Business Park,
Haywards Heath, West Sussex RH16 2EH
tel (01444) 232889 *fax* (01444) 232142
email info@wizzbook.com
website www.wizzbook.com
Creative Director/Publisher Tony Potter
Fiction for children aged 4–12. Opportunities for
freelance writers and illustrators both for
commissioned and speculative work. Send
submissions to the Managing Editor with sae for
return. Founded 2008.

Wordsworth Editions Ltd
8B East Street, Ware, Herts. SG12 9HJ
tel (01920) 465167 *fax* (01920) 462267
email enquiries@wordsworth-editions.com
website www.wordsworth-editions.com
Managing Director Helen Trayler
Reprints of classic books: literary, children's; poetry;
reference; Special Editions; mystery and supernatural.
Founded 1987.

Y Lolfa Cyf.
Talybont, Ceredigion SY24 5HE
tel (01970) 832304 *fax* (01970) 832782

email ylolfa@ylolfa.com
website www.ylolfa.com
Director Garmon Gruffudd, *Editor* Lefi Gruffudd
Welsh-language popular fiction and non-fiction,
music, children's books; Welsh-language tutors;
Welsh- and Celtic-interest books in English. Founded
1967.

York Notes – see Pearson UK

Young Picador – see Macmillan Publishers Ltd

Zero to Ten Ltd
327 High Street, Slough, Berks. SL1 1TX
tel (0175) 357 8499 *fax* (0175) 357 8488
email sales@evansbrothers.co.uk
Publishing Director Su Swallow
Non-fiction for children aged 0–10: board books,
toddler books, first story books, etc. Submissions
welcome but does not respond to unsuccessful
submissions. Part of the Evans Publishing Group.
Founded 1997.

Cherrytree Books (imprint)
UK Publisher Su Swallow
Children's non-fiction illustrated books mainly for
schools and libraries.

ZigZag Education
Unit 3, Greenway Business Centre, Doncaster Road,
Bristol BS10 5PY
tel 0117-950 3199 *fax* 0117-959 1695
email submissions@publishmenow.co.uk
website www.zigzageducation.co.uk,
www.publishmenow.co.uk
Development Director John-Lloyd Hagger, *Strategy
Director* Mike Stephens
Teaching resources for UK secondary schools:
English, maths, ICT, geography, history, science,
business studies, politics. Founded 1998.

ZooBooKoo International Ltd
4 Gurdon Road, Grundisburgh, Woodbridge,
Suffolk IP13 6XA
tel (01473) 735346 *fax* (01473) 735346
email karen@zoobookoo.com
website www.zoobookoo.com
Sales Director Karen Wattleworth
Designer/manufacturer of ZooBooKoo Original Cube
Books, multi-level educational folding cube books.
Recent successes include *World Football, Human
Body, Kings and Queens, French Phrases* and *United
Kingdom.*

Books

Children's book publishers overseas

Listings are given for children's book publishers in Australia (below), Canada (page 30), France (page 33), Germany (page 34), Italy (page 34), the Netherlands (page 35), New Zealand (page 35), South Africa (page 37), Spain (page 38) and the USA (page 39).

AUSTRALIA

*Member of the Australian Publishers Association

ACER Press

19 Prospect Hill Road, Private Bag 55, Camberwell, Victoria 3124
tel (03) 9277 5555 *fax* (03) 9277 5500
email info@acer.edu.au
website www.acer.edu.au
General Manager/Publisher Annemarie Rolls

Publisher of the Australian Council for Educational Research. Produces a range of books and assessments including professional resources for teachers, psychologists and special needs professionals.

Allen & Unwin Pty Ltd*

83 Alexander Street, Crows Nest, NSW 2065
postal address PO Box 8500, St Leonards, NSW 1590
tel (02) 8425 0100 *fax* (02) 9906 2218
email info@allenandunwin.com
website www.allenandunwin.com
Directors Patrick Gallagher (Chairman), Paul Donovan (Executive Director), Robert Gorman (Ceo), David Martin (finance), Liz Bray (children's & young adult publishing)

Picture books, fiction for 5–8 and 9–12 year-olds, teenage fiction, series fiction, narrative non-fiction and poetry. Also adult/general trade books, including fiction, academic, especially social science and history. Imprint: Allen & Unwin. Founded 1990.

Submission details Will consider unsolicited MSS (but not picture book texts). Prefers to receive full MSS by post, with a brief synopsis and biography. Allow 3 months for response. Seeking junior fiction, quirky non-fiction by wise, funny, inventive authors with a distinctive voice.

Bloomsbury Publishing PTY Limited

(Sydney office of Bloomsbury Publishing)
Level 14, 309 Kent St, Sydney, NSW 2000
tel (612) 9994 8969
email csmanz@bloomsbury.com
website www.bloomsburyanz.com
Managing Director Kathleen Farrar

Supports the worldwide publishing activities of Bloomsbury Publishing: caters for the Australia and New Zealand territories. See Bloomsbury Adult, Bloomsbury Children's & Educational, Bloomsbury Professional & Academic and Bloomsbury Information on page 7.

Cengage Learning Australia*

Level 7, 80 Dorcas Street, South Melbourne, Victoria 3205
tel (03) 9685 4111 *fax* (03) 9685 4199
website www.cengage.com.au

Educational books.

Hachette Australia Pty Ltd*

Level 17, 207 Kent Street, Sydney, NSW 2000
tel (02) 8248 0800 *fax* (02) 2848 0810
email auspub@hachette.com.au
website www.hachette.com.au
Directors Malcolm Edwards (managing), Chris Raine, David Cocking, Louise Sherwin-Stark, Matt Richell, Fiona Hazard, Jodie Mann, Matt Hoy

General, children's. No unsolicited MSS.

Hachette Children's Books (division)

website www.hachettechildrens.com.au
Picture books, fiction for 5–8 and 9–12 year-olds, teenage fiction and series fiction. Publishes approx. 65 titles each year and has 750 in print. Recent releases include *The Arrival* by Shaun Tan.

Submission details Will not accept unsolicited MSS. Submit MSS via an agent.

HarperCollins Publishers (Australia) Pty Ltd Group*

postal address PO Box 321, 25 Ryde Road, Pymble, NSW 2073
tel (02) 9952 5000 *fax* (02) 9952 5555
website www.harpercollins.com.au
Publishing Director Shona Martyn, *Head of Children's* Cristina Cappelutto

Literary fiction and non-fiction, popular fiction, children's, reference, biography, autobiography, current affairs, sport, lifestyle, health/self-help, humour, true crime, travel, Australiana, history, business, gift, religion.

Little Hare Books*

Level 4, 50 Yeo Street, Neutral Bay, NSW 2089
tel (02) 9908 8222 *fax* (02) 9908 8666
email enquiries@littleharebooks.com
website www.littleharebooks.com

Publishes high-quality children's books in Australia, New Zealand and the UK: early childhood, picture books, fiction and puzzle/activity books.

Submission details Check website for details of when submissions are accepted.

McGraw-Hill Education*

Level 2, The Everglade Building, 82 Waterloo Road, North Ryde NSW 2113
postal address Private Bag 2233, Business Centre, North Ryde, NSW 1670
tel (02) 9900 1800 *fax* (02) 9900 1980
website www.macgraw-hill.com.au
Publishing Director Nicole Meehan, *Managing Director* Murray St Leger

Educational publisher: higher education, primary and secondary education (grades K–12) and professional (including medical, general and reference). Division of the McGraw-Hill Companies. Founded 1964.
 Submission details Always looking for potential authors. Has a rapidly expanding publishing programme. See website for author's guide.

Macmillan Education Australia Pty Ltd*

Melbourne office Level 1, 15–19 Claremont Street, South Yarra, Victoria 3141
tel (03) 9825 1000 *fax* (03) 9825 1010
email mea@macmillan.com.au
Sydney office Level 25, BT Tower, 1 Market Street, Sydney, NSW 2000
tel (02) 9285 9200 *fax* (02) 9285 9290
website www.macmillan.com.au
Managing Director Stewart Gill, *Primary Literacy Publisher* Col Gillespie, *Primary Teacher Resource and Text Publisher* Sharon Dalgleish, *Primary Library Publisher* Carmel Heron, *General Manager Secondary* Peter Saffin

Educational books.

New Frontier Publishing*

Suite 3 Level 2, 18 Aquatic Drive, Frenchs Forest, NSW 2086
tel (02) 9453 1525 *fax* (02) 9975 2531
email info@newfronteir.com.au
website www.newfrontier.com.au
Director Peter Whitfield

Aims to uplift, educate and inspire through its range of children's books. Activity books, picture books, fiction, dictionaries, textbooks. Caters for 5–10 year-olds.
 Submission details Unsolicited MSS accepted. Understanding of existing list crucial. Downloadable submissions pack available via website.

Pan Macmillan Australia Pty Ltd*

Level 25, 1 Market Street, Sydney, NSW 2000
tel (02) 9285 9100 *fax* (02) 9285 9190
email pansyd@macmillan.com.au
website www.macmillan.com.au
Directors James Fraser (publishing), Peter Phillips (sales), Andrew Farrell (publicity & marketing)

Commercial and literary fiction; children's fiction, non-fiction and character products; non-fiction; sport.

Pearson Education Australia*

Schools Division, 20 Thackray Road, Port Melbourne, Victoria 3207

tel (3) 9245 7111 *fax* (3) 9245 7333
email schools@pearsoned.com.au
website www.pearsoned.com.au/schools
Primary Publisher Corinne Atoune, *Secondary Publisher* Emma Roberts

Early fiction, non-fiction, geography, history, mathematics, textbooks, CD-Roms, interactive websites.

Penguin Group (Australia)*

250 Camberwell Road, Camberwell, Victoria 3124
tel (03) 9811 2400 *fax* (03) 9811 2620
postal address PO Box 701, Hawthorn, Victoria 3122
website www.penguin.com.au
Managing Director Gabrielle Coyne, *Publishing Director* Robert Sessions, *Publishing Director – Books for Children & Young Adults* Laura Harris, *Associate – Books for Children & Young Adults* Jane Godwin, *Executive Editor* Lisa Riley

Picture books, fiction for 5–8 and 9–12 year-olds, teenage fiction, series fiction and film/TV tie-ins. Also for adults: fiction and general non-fiction. Publishes approx. 85 titles each year and has about 500 in print. Recent successes include *Cuthbert's Babies* by Pamela Allen (picture book), *Rascal* books by Paul Jennings (younger readers) and *Saving Francesca* by Melina Marchetta (young adult). Children's imprints: Puffin (paperback). Founded 1935.
 Submission details Will consider unsolicited MSS but submit only one MS at a time. Send proposals to The Editor, Books for Children and Young Adults at the postal address (above). Enclose an sae for return of material. Does not accept proposals by email or fax.

Prim-Ed Publishing Pty Ltd

4 Bendsten Place, Balcatta, WA 6021
tel 618-9240-9888 *fax* 618-9240-1513
email mail@ricgrop.com.au
website www.prim-ed.com

Educational publisher specialising in blackline master or copymasters and student workbooks for schools and homeschoolers.

Puffin – see Penguin Group (Australia)

University of Queensland Press*

PO Box 6042, St Lucia, Queensland 4067
tel (07) 3365 7244 *fax* (07) 3365 7579
email uqp@uqp.uq.edu.au
website www.uqp.com.au
General Manager Greg Bain

Australian children's and young adult fiction. Submissions via agents only. Founded 1948.

The Quentaris Chronicles – see Hachette Children's Books (division)

Random House Australia Pty Ltd*

Level 3, Pacific Highway, North Sydney, NSW 2060
tel (02) 9954 9966 *fax* (02) 9954 4562

email random@randomhouse.com.au
website www.randomhouse.com.au
Managing Director Margaret Seale, *Publishing Director*
Jill Baker, *Children's Publisher* Linsay Knight,
Illustrated Publisher Jude McGee, *Sales & Marketing
Director* Carol Davidson, *Publicity Director* Karen
Reid

General fiction and non-fiction; children's,
illustrated. Imprints: Arrow, Avon, Ballantine,
Bantam, Black Swan, Broadway, Century, Chatto &
Windus, Corgi, Crown, Dell, Doubleday, Ebury,
Fodor, Heinemann, Hutchinson, Jonathan Cape,
Knopf, Mammoth UK, Minerva, Pantheon, Pavilion,
Pimlico, Random House, Red Fox, Rider, Vermilion,
Vintage, Virgin.Subsidiary of Bertelsmann AG.

Submission details For Random House and
Transworld Publishing, unsolicited non-fiction
accepted, unbound in hard copy addressed to
Submissions Editor. Fiction submissions are only
accepted from previously published authors, or
authors represented by an agent or accompanied by a
report from an accredited assessment service.

Scholastic Australia Pty Ltd*
76–80 Railway Crescent, Lisarow, Gostord,
NSW 2250
tel (02) 4328 3555 *fax* (02) 4323 3827
website www.scholastic.com.au
Publisher Andrew Berkhut

Children's fiction and non-fiction. Founded 1968.

Start-Ups – see Hachette Children's Books (division)

CANADA

*Member of the Canadian Publishers' Council
†Member of the Association of Canadian Publishers

Annick Press Ltd†
15 Patricia Avenue, Toronto, Ontario M2M 1H9
tel 416-221-4802 *fax* 416-221-8400
email annickpress@annickpress.com
website www.annickpress.com
Co-editors Rick Wilks, Colleen MacMillan, *Creative
Director* Sheryl Shapiro

Preschool to young adult fiction and non-fiction.
Publishes 8 picture books, 3 young readers, 3 middle
readers and 8 young adult titles each year. Recent
successes include – Fiction: *The Apprentice's
Masterpiece: A Story of Medieval Spain*, by Melanie
Little (ages 12+); Non-Fiction: *Pharoahs and Foot
Soldiers: One Hundred Ancient Egyptian Jobs You
Might Have Desired or Dreaded*, by Kristin Butcher,
illustrations by Martha Newbigging (ages 9–12); *The
Bite of the Mango*, by Mariatu Kamara with Susan
McClelland (ages 14+) Founded 1975.

Submission details Approx. 25% of books are by
first-time authors. No unsolicited MSS. For

illustrations, query with samples and sase to Creative
Director. Responds in 6 months.

Boardwalk Books – see Dundurn Press

Dundurn Press†
3 Church Street, Suite 500, Toronto,
Ontario M5E 1M2
tel 416-214-5544
email info@dundurn.com
website www.dundurn.com
President J. Kirk Howard

Popular non-fiction, fiction, scholarship, history,
biography, young adult, art. Part of the Dundurn
Group. Founded 1973.

Boardwalk Books; Sandcastle Books (imprints)
Young adult fiction.

Fitzhenry & Whiteside Ltd
195 Allstate Parkway, Markham, Ontario L3R 4T8
tel 800-387-9776 *fax* 800-260-9777
email godwit@fitzhenry.ca
website www.fitzhenry.ca
Publisher Sharon Fitzhenry

Fiction and non-fiction (social studies, visual arts,
biography, environment). Publishes 10 picture books,
5 early readers/chapter books, 6 middle novels and
7 young adult books each year. Founded 1966.

Submission details Approx. 10% of books are by
first-time authors. Emphasis is on Canadian authors
and illustrators, subject or perspective. Will review
MS/illustration packages from artists. Submit outline
and copy of sample illustration. For illustrations only,
send samples and promotional scheet. Responds in
3 months. Samples returned with sase.

HarperCollins Publishers Ltd*
2 Bloor Street East, 20th Floor, Toronto,
Ontario M4W 1A8
tel 416-975-9334
email hccanada@harpercollins.com
website www.harpercollins.ca
President David Kent

Literary fiction and non-fiction, history, politics,
biography, spiritual and children's books. Founded
1989.

Key Porter Books Ltd
6 Adelaide Street East, 10th Floor, Toronto,
Ontario M5C 1H6
tel 416-862-7777 *fax* 416-862-2304
email info@keyporter.com
Publisher Jordan Fenn

Fiction and non-fiction for all ages. Recent successes
include *Germania* by John Wilson (young adult);
American Raj by Eric Margolis (current events);
Contact Charlie by Chris Wattie (military history);
Stampede: The Rise of the West and Canada's New

Power Elite by Gordon Pitts (business); *Hockey Night in Canada: By The Numbers* by Scott Morrison (sports/hockey); *Ted Reader's Napoleon's Everyday Gourmet Grilling* by Ted Reader (cooking). For adults: fiction and non-fiction (nature, history, Canadian politics, conservation, humour, biography, autobiography, health). Founded 1981.

Submission details Approx. 30% of books are by first-time authors. No unsolicited MSS: only interested in submissions via literary agents. Responds to queries/proposals in 6 months. Length: picture books – 1,500 words; young readers, fiction – 5,000 words; middle readers, non-fiction – 15,000 words.

Kids Can Press Ltd[†]
25 Dockside Drive, Toronto, Ontario M54 0B5
tel 416-479 7000 *fax* 416-479 5437
email customerservice@kidscan.com
website www.kidscanpress.com/canada
Publisher Karen Boersma

Juvenile/young adult fiction and non-fiction. Publishes 6–10 pciture books, 10–15 young readers, 20–30 middle readers and 2–3 young adult titles each year. Recent successes include *Alphabeasts* by Wallace Edwards, Melanie Watt's award-winning *Scaredy Squirrel*, *If the World Were a Village* by David J. Smith and *Ryan and Jimmy and the Well in Africa Which Brought them Together* by Herb Shoveller. Publishers of *Franklin the Turtle* and *Elliot Moose* characters. Founded 1973.

Submission details Approx. 10–15% of books are by first-time authors. Submit outline/synopsis and 2–3 sample chapters. For picture books, submit complete MS. Responds in 6 months. Only accepts MSS from Canadian authors. Fiction length: picture books – 1,000–2,000 words; young readers – 750–1,500 words; middle readers – 10,000–15,000 words; young adult – over 15,000 words. Non-fiction length: picture books – 500–1,250 words; young readers – 750–2,000 words; middle readers – 5,000–15,000 words.

McGraw-Hill Ryerson Ltd*
300 Water Street, Whitby, Ontario L1N 9B6
tel 905-430-5000 *fax* 905-430-5020
website www.mcgrawhill.ca
President & Ceo David Swail

Educational and trade books.

Madison Press Books
1000 Yonge Street, Suite 303, Toronto, Ontario M4W 2K2
tel 416-923-5027 *fax* 416-923-9708
website www.madisonpressbooks.com
Publisher Oliver Salzmann

Illustrated non-fiction for 8–12 year-olds.

Napoleon & Company[†]
Church Street, Ste. 500, Toronto, Ontario M5E 1M2
tel 416-214 5544 *fax* 416-465-3241
email kmcmullin@dundurn.com
website www.napoleonandcompany.com
Publisher Sylvia McConnell, *Editor* Allister Thompson

Children's books and adult fiction. Founded 1990.

Nelson Education*
1120 Birchmount Road, Scarborough, Ontario M1K 5G4
tel 416-752-9448 *fax* 416-752-8101
website www.nelson.com
President Greg Nordal, *Vice President, Market Development* Chris Besse, *Senior Vice President, Media Services* Susan Cline, *Vice President, Higher Education* James Reeve

Educational publishing: school (K–12), college and university, career education, measurement and guidance, professional and reference, ESL titles. Division of Thomson Canada Ltd. Founded 1914.

Oberon Press
205–145 Spruce Street, Ottawa, Ontario K1R 6P1
tel 613-238-3275 *fax* 613-238-3275
email oberon@sympatico.ca
website www.oberonpress.ca

General fiction, short stories, poetry, some biographies, art and children's. Only publishes Canadian writers.

Orca Book Publishers[†]
Box 5626, Station B, Victoria, BC, V8R 6S4
tel 800-210-5277 *fax* 877-408-1551
email orca@orcabook.com
website www.orcabook.com

Books for children and young adults. No poetry. *Orca Echoes* (7–8 year-olds), *Young Readers* (8–11 year-olds), juvenile novels (9–13 year-olds), *Orca Currents* (intermediate novels aimed at reluctant readers with simple language and short, high-interest chapters), young adult fiction, *Orca Soundings* (high-interest teen novels aimed at reluctant readers). Recent successes include *Hero an Orca Young Reader* by Martha Attema and *The Puppet Wrangler* by Vicki Grant. Founded 1984.

Submission details Currently seeking picture book MSS of up to 1,500 words. Submit complete MS FAO Children's Book Editor. No queries.

Orca Echoes, Orca Young Readers (also called chapter books) and juvenile fiction: Contemporary stories or fantasy with a universal theme, a compelling, unified plot and a strong, sympathetic child protagonist who grows through the course of the story and solves the central problem him/herself. Well-researched stories dealing with, or taking their inspiration from, historical subjects, but not thinly disguised history lessons. Length: *Orca Echoes* 5,500–6,000 words; *Young Readers* 14,000–18,000 words; juvenile fiction 25,000–35,000 words. Send query with sample chapter FAO Children's Book Editor.

Stories for *Orca Currents* should have appropriate storylines for middle school (family issues, humour, sports, adventure, mystery/suspense, fantasy, etc) with strong plots, credible characters/situations. Awkward moralising should be avoided. Protagonists are between 12–14 years old and should be appealing and believable. Length: 14,000–16,000 words; 12–16 short chapters. Send a chapter-by-chapter outline and one sample chapter FAO Melanie Jeffs, Editor.

Teen or young adult fiction: Issue-oriented contemporary stories exploring a universal theme, with a compelling, unified plot and strong, sympathetic protagonist(s). Well-researched stories dealing with, or taking their inspiration from, historical subjects, but not thinly disguised history lessons. Length: up to 50,000 words. Send queries to Teen Fiction Editor.

Orca Soundings: Stories should reflect the universal struggles that young people face. They need not be limited to 'gritty' urban tales but can include adventures, mystery/suspense, fantasy, etc. Interested in humorous stories that will appeal to teens of both sexes. 'Disease-of-the-week' potboilers or awkward moralising should be avoided. Protagonists are between 14–17 years old and should be appealing and believable. Length: 14,000–16,000 words, 12–16 short chapters. Send a chapter-by-chapter outline and one sample chapter FAO Andrew Wooldridge, Editor.

Will consider MMS from Canadian writers only. No submissions by fax or email. See website for submission guidelines.

Pearson Canada*

(formerly Prentice Hall Canada and Addison-Wesley Canada)
26 Prince Andrew Place, Toronto, Ontario M3C 2T8
tel 416-447-5101 *fax* 416-443-0948
website www.pearsoned.ca
President Allan Reynolds

Academic, technical, educational, children's and adult, trade.

Penguin Group (Canada)*

90 Eglinton Avenue East, Suite 700, Toronto, Ontario M4P 2Y3
tel 416-925-2249 *fax* 416-925-0068
email online@ca.penguingroup.com
website www.penguin.ca

Literary fiction, memoir, non-fiction (history, business, current events). No unsolicited MSS; submissions via an agent only. Imprints: Penguin Canada, Viking Canada, Puffin Canada. Founded 1974.

Pippin Publishing Corporation

PO Box 242, Don Mills, Ontario M3C 2S2
tel 416-510-2918 *fax* 416-510-3359
email cynthia@pippinpub.com
website www.pippinpub.com
President/Editorial Director Jonathan Lovat Dickson

ESL/EFL, teacher reference, adult basic education, school texts (all subjects), general trade (non-fiction).

Raincoast Books†

2440 Viking Way, Richmond, BC V6V 1N2
tel 604-448-7100 *fax* 604-270-7161
email info@raincoast.com
website www.raincoast.com
Publisher Jesse Finkelstein

Non-fiction for adults. Fiction and non-fiction for children. Recent successes include *Waiting for Wings* by Lois Ehlert (picture book), *Genius Squad* by Catherine Jinks (juvenile fiction) and *Strange New Species* by Elin Kelsey. Imprints: Polestar, Press Gang.

Submission details Will not accept unsolicited MSS. Send a query letter via regular mail for the attention of the Editorial Department. For young adult fiction, submit query letter with a list of publication credits plus one-page outline of the plot. No queries via email. Allow up to 9 months for reply. Only accepts material from Canadian residents.

Random House of Canada Ltd*

1 Toronto Street, Suite 300, Toronto, Ontario M5C 2V6
tel 416-364-4449 *fax* 416-364-6863
website www.randomhouse.ca
Chairman John Neale

Adult and children's. Imprints: Canada, Doubleday Canada, Knopf Canada, Random House Canada, Seal Books, Vintage Canada. Subsidiary of Bertelsmann AG. Founded 1944.

Red Deer Press

195 Allstate Pky, Markham, Ontario L3R 4T8
tel 905-477-9700
email rdp@reddeerpress.com
website www.reddeerpress.com
Publisher Richard Dionne, *Children's Editor* Peter Carver

Literary fiction, sci-fi, non-fiction, drama, poetry, children's illustrated books, young adult fiction, teen fiction. Publishes books that are written or illustrated by Canadians and that are about or of interest to Canadians. Imprints: RJS (Robert J. Sawyer) Books (sci-fi). Publishes 14–18 new books per year. Founded 1975.

Submission details Children's picture books MSS from established authors with a demonstrable record of publishing success are preferred. Not currently accepting new MSS.

Ronsdale Press†

3350 West 21st Avenue, Vancouver, BC V6S 1G7
tel 604-738-4688 *fax* 604-731-4548
email ronsdale@shaw.ca
website www.ronsdalepress.com
Director Ronald B. Hatch

Canadian children's young adult novels. Founded 1988.

Sandcastle Books – see Dundurn Press

Scholastic Canada Ltd*

175 Hillmount Road, Markham, Ontario L6C 1Z7
tel 905-887-7323
email custserv@scholastic.ca
website www.scholastic.ca
Publishing Director Diane Kerner, *Art Director* Ms
Yüksel Hassan

Serves children, parents and teachers through a
variety of businesses including Scholastic Book Clubs
and Book Fairs, Scholastic Education, Classroom
Magazines, Trade, and Les Éditions Scholastic.
Publishes recreational reading for children and young
people from kindergarten to Grade 8 and educational
materials in both official languages. Its publishing
focus is on books by Canadians. Wholly owned
subsidiary of Scholastic Inc.
  Submission details No unsolicited MSS. Phone for
information on current submissions policy. Artists
may submit several photocopied samples of their
work and a brief résumé plus sase to the art director.
Never send originals.

Tundra Books Inc.†

75 Sherbourne Street, 5th Floor, Toronto,
Ontario M5A 2P9
tel 416-598-4786
email tundra@mccelland.com
website www.tundrabooks.com
Publisher Kathy Lowinger

High-quality children's picture books.

Whitecap Books Ltd†

351 Lynn Avenue, North Vancouver, BC V7J 2C4
tel 604-980-9852 *fax* 604-980-8197
website www.whitecap.ca
President Michael E. Burch, *Vice-President* Nicholas
S.M. Rundall, *Publisher* Robert McCullough

General: cooking, wine and spirit, gardening, travel,
health and wellbeing, history, biography, nature and
the environment. Also publishes juvenile fiction,
young adult fiction, non-fiction, picture books for
young children (nature, wildlife and animals). Recent
titles include *Saddle Island* series No 3: *Race to the
Rescue* by Sharon Siamon, *Take it to the Extreme* No
10: *Mountain Board Maniacs* by Pam Withers, and
Dogabet written and illustrated by Dianna Bonder.
  Submission details For children's illustrated fiction,
send complete MS. For all other submissions, send a
synopsis, a table of contents listing the chapters or
stories and their length, information about the
proposed illustrations or photographs (number
planned, b&w or colour), 1–3 sample chapters and
information about the author, including professional
background and previous publishing credits. Include
a sase with sufficient return postage, and if
submitting from outside of Canada, include an
international postal voucher.

Women's Press

180 Bloor Street West, Suite 801, Toronto,
Ontario M5S 2V6
tel 416-929-2774 *fax* 416-929-1926
email info@cspi.org
website www.womenspress.ca
Editor James MacNevin

The ideas and experiences of women: fiction, creative
non-fiction, children's books, plays, biography,
autobiography, memoirs, poetry. Owned by
Canadian Scholars' Press. Founded 1987.

FRANCE

L'Ecole des Loisirs

11 Rue de Sevres, 75006, Paris
tel (1) 42 22 94 10 *fax* (1) 45 48 04 99
email edl@ecoledesloisirs.com
website www.ecoledesloisirs.com
Managing Director Jean Fabre

Specialises in children's literature from picture books
to young adult fiction.

Flammarion

87 quai Panhard et Levassor, 75647 Paris Cedex 13
tel (1) 40 51 31 00 *fax* (1) 43 29 43 43
website www.flammarion.com
Managing Director Louis Delas

Leading French publisher. Children's imprints
include: Albums du Père Castor, Castor Poche,
Tribal, Etonnants Classiques, GF – Flammarion,
Chan – OK. Founded 1875.

Père Castor (imprint)
Children's Publisher Hélène Wadowski
Children's picture books, junior fiction, activity
books, board books, how-to books, comics, gift
books, fairy tales, dictionaries and records and tapes.
Covers ages 0–16.

Gallimard Jeunesse

5 rue Sebastien Bottin, 75328 Paris
tel (1) 49 54 42 00 *fax* (1) 45 44 39 46
website www.gallimard-jeunesse.fr
Children's Publisher Hedwige Pasquet

Publisher of high-quality children's fiction and non-
fiction including board books, novelty books, picture
books, pop-up books. Founded 1911.

Hachette Livre/Gautier-Languereau

43 quai de Grenelle, 75905 Paris Cedex 15
tel (43) 92 30 00 *fax* (43) 92 33 38
website www.hachette.com
Director Arnaud Nourry, *Editorial Director* Brigitte le
Blanc, *Artistic Manager* Maryvonne Denizet

Picture books and poetry. Publishes approx. 55 titles
each year. Recent successes include *Cyrano* by Tai
Marc Le Thanh and Rébecca Dautremer and

Books

Books

Princesses by Philippe Lechermeier and Rébecca Dautremer. Founded 1992.

Submission details Will consider unsolicited MSS. Allow 2 months for response.

Kaléidoscope

11 Rue de Sèvres, F–75006 Paris
tel (1) 45 44 07 08 *fax* (1) 45 44 53 71
email infos@editions-kaleidoscope.com
website www.editions-kaleidoscope.com
Children's Publisher Isabel Finkenstaedt

Specialises in up-market picture books for 0–6 year-olds. Founded 1988.

Editions Sarbacane

35 Rue d'Hauteville, 75010 Paris
tel (1) 42 46 24 00 *fax* (1) 42 46 28 15
email e.beulque@sarbacane.net
website www.editions-sarbacane.com
Publisher Emmanuelle Beulque

High-quality activity books, board books, picture books and general fiction for children from preschool age to 15 years.

Le Sorbier

7 rue de Savoie, 75006 Paris
tel (1) 40 46 43 20 *fax* (1) 40 46 43 31
website www.editionsdelamartiniere.fr
Publisher Françoise Mateu

High-quality picture books for children up to 10 years old and illustrated reference books for ages 9–12. Imprint of Editions de la Martiniere.

GERMANY

Carl Hanser Verlag

Vilshofener Strasse 10, 81679 München
tel (89) 998 30 191 *fax* (89) 944 03 6710
email info@hanser.de
website www.hanser-literaturverlage.de
Children's Publisher Ulrich Störiko Blume

High-quality hardcover books for all ages from preschool to young adults. Board books, picture books, fiction and non-fiction. Age groups: 3–10, 10–15, 15+. Founded 1993.

Carlsen Verlag

Völckersstrasse 14–20, D 22765 Hamburg
tel (40) 398040 *fax* (40) 39804390
email info@carlsen.de
website www.carlsen.de
Publisher Klaus Humann

Children's picture books, board books and novelty books. Illustrated fiction and non-fiction. Teenage fiction and non-fiction. Publishes both German and international authors including Stephenie Meyer, J.K. Rowling and Philip Pullman. Publisher of the *Harry Potter* series. Imprint: Chicken House

Deutschland. Age groups: preschool, 5–10, 10–15, 15+. Founded 1953.

Submission details Unsolicited MSS welcome but must include an sae for its return. Do not follow up by phone or post. For illustrations, submit no more than 3 colour photocopies and unlimited b&w copies.

Deutscher Taschenbuch Verlag (dtv junior)

Friedrichstrasse 1/A, D–80801 Munich
tel (89) 381 67281 *fax* (89) 346428
email verlag@dtv.de
website www.dtvjunior.de
Children's Publishing Director Anne Schieckel

Fiction and non-fiction for children and teenagers. Authors include Kate Di Camillo, Kevin Brooks and Ally Kennen. Founded 1971.

Ravensburger Buchverlag

Robert-Bosch-Straße 1, 88214 Ravensburg
tel (49) 751860 *fax* (49) 751 861289
email buchverlag@ravensburger.de
website www.ravensburger.de
Managing Directors Ulrike Metzger, Johannes Hauenstein, *Commissioning Editors* Sandra Schwarz, Sabine Zürn

Activity books, novelty books, picture books, fiction for 5–8 and 9–12 year-olds, teenage fiction, series fiction and educational games and puzzles. Publishes approx. 450 titles each year and has 1,500 in print. Founded 1883.

Submission details Will consider unsolicited MSS for fiction only. Allow 2 months for response.

ITALY

Edizoni Arka srl

Via Raffaello Sanzio, 7–20149, Milan
tel (39) 02 4818230 *fax* (39) 02 4816752
email arka@arkaedizioni.it
website www.arkaedizioni.it
Publisher Ginevra Viscardi

Picture books and some general fiction for preschool children and up to 10 years.

De Agostini Editore

Via Giovanni da Verrazano, 15-28100, Novara
tel (39) 0321 4241 *fax* (39) 0321 47128/6
website www.deagostini.it
Publisher Matteo Faglia

Illustrated books, books for schools.

Edizioni El/Einaudi Ragazzi/Emme Edizioni

Via J. Ressel 5, 34018 San Dorligo della Valle TS
tel (040) 3880311 *fax* (040) 3880330
email edizioniel@edizioniel.it
website www.edizioniel.com
Children's Publisher Orietta Fatucci

Activity books, board books, picture books, pop-up books, non-fiction, novels, poetry, fairy tales, fiction. Age groups: preschool, 5–10, 10–15, 15+. Publishes over 270 new titles per year.

Giunti Editore SpA
Via Bolognese, 165–50139, Florence
tel (39) 055 50621 *fax* (39) 055 5062298
email info@giunti.it
website www.giunti.it
Publishers Sergio Giunti, Camilla Giunti

Activity books, board books, novelty books, picture books, colouring books, pop-up books and some educational textbooks.

Arnoldo Mondadori Editore S.p.A (Mondadori)
Via Durazzo 4, 20134 Milan
tel (02) 2121-3214 *fax* (02) 2121-3220
email info.ragazzi@mondadori.it
website www.mondadori.it
Editor-in-Chief Fiammetta Giorgi

Activity books, board books, novelty books, picture books, painting and colouring books, pop-up books, how-to books, hobbies, leisure, pets, sport, comics, poetry, fairy tales, education, fiction and non-fiction. Age groups: preschool, 5–10, 10–15, 15+. Founded 1907.

Adriano Salani Editore S.p.A.
Via Gherardini 10, 20145 Milano
tel (02) 34597624 *fax* (02) 34597206
email info@salani.it
website www.salani.it
Publisher Luigi Spagnol

Picture books, how-to books, comics, gift books, fiction, novels, poetry, fairy tales. Age groups: preschool, 5–10, 10–15, 15.

THE NETHERLANDS

Lemniscaat BV
Posbus 4066, 3006 AB, Rotterdam
tel (31) 10 2062929 *fax* (31) 10 4141560
email info@lemniscaat.nl
website www.lemniscaat.nl
Publisher Boele van Hensbroek

Picture books, general fiction, fairy tales.

Rubinstein Publishing
Prinseneiland, 43-1013 LL, Amsterdam
tel (31) 20 4200772 *fax* (31) 20 4200882
email info@rubinstein.nl
website www.rubinstein.nl
Publisher Dik Broekman

Independent publisher specialising in audiobooks for children. Also produces novelty books.

Sjaloom & Wildeboer, Uitgevers
Postbus 1895, NL–1000BW, Amsterdam
tel (20) 6206263 *fax* (20) 4288540
email post@sjaloom.nl
website www.sjaloom.com
Children's Publisher Willem Wildeboer

Board books, novelty books, picture books, pop-up books, non-fiction, fiction for ages preschool, 5–10 and 10–15.

Submission details Welcomes new submissions (no disks) and illustrations. Include sae for return of material.

Van Goor
Papiermolen 14–24, 3994 DK Houten
tel (31) 30 7998300 *fax* (31) 30 7998398
website www.van-goor.nl
Publisher Marieke Woortman

High-quality picture books and activity books and literary fiction for age groups 6+ to young adults.

Zirkoon Uitgevers / Baekens Books
Schilpdel II, 2202 VA Noordwijk
tel (06) 516 06774 *fax* (07) 1364 7133
email info@baekensbooks.nl
website www.zirkoon.nl
Children's Publisher Iris Zuydewijn van de Roy

High-quality picture books, activity books, board books, novelty books, pop-up books, poetry, fiction and some non-fiction.

NEW ZEALAND

Member of the New Zealand Book Publishers' Association

David Bateman Ltd*
30 Tarndale Grove, Albany Business Park, Bush Road, Auckland
tel (09) 415 7664 *fax* (09) 415 8892
email bateman@bateman.co.nz
website www.bateman.co.nz
Chairman/Publisher David L. Bateman, *Directors* Janet Bateman, Paul Bateman (joint managing), Paul Parkinson (joint managing)

Natural history, gardening, encyclopedias, sport, art, cookery, historical, juvenile, travel, motoring, maritime history, business, art, lifestyle. Founded 1979.

Blue Balloon – see Scholastic New Zealand Ltd

Cengage Learning New Zealand*
Unit 4B, Rosedale Office Park, 331 Rosedale Road, Albany, North Shore 0632
postal address PO Box 33376, Takapuna, North Shore 0740
tel (09) 415 6850 *fax* (09) 415 6853

Educational books.

Books

Gecko Press*

PO Box 9335, Marion Square, Wellington 6141
tel (04) 801 9333 fax (04) 801 9335
email info@geckopress.com
website www.geckopress.com
Publisher Julia Marshall

Children's books: picture books, junior fiction and non-fiction. 'Translates and publishes award-winning, curiously good children's books from around the world'. Selects books strong in story, illustration and design, with a strong 'heart factor'. Established 2005.
Submission details See website for guidelines.

HarperCollins Publishers (New Zealand) Ltd*

31 View Road, Glenfield, Auckland 0627
tel (09) 443 9400 fax (09) 443 9403
email editors@harpercollins.co.nz
postal address PO Box 1, Shortland Street, Auckland
website www.harpercollins.co.nz
Managing Director Tony Fisk, Commissioning Editor Kate Stone

General literature, non-fiction, reference, children's.

McGraw-Hill Book Company New Zealand Ltd*

Level 8, 56–60 Cawley Street, Ellerslie, Auckland
postal address Private Bag 11904, Ellerslie, Auckland 1005
tel (09) 526 6200
website www.mcgraw-hill.com

Educational publisher: higher education, primary and secondary education (grades K–12) and professional (including medical, general and reference). Division of the McGraw-Hill Companies. Founded 1974.
Submission details Always looking for potential authors. Has a rapidly expanding publishing programme. See website for author's guide.

Mallinson Rendel Publishers Ltd – see Penguin Group (NZ)

MM House Publishing

752 Gladstone Road, Gisborne 3815, PO Box 539
tel (06) 868 7769 fax (06) 868 7767
email info@millymolly.com
website www.millymolly.com
Managing Director John Pittar

Picture books, gift books, fiction, education, interactive CD-Roms for preschool children and 4–8 year-olds. Promotes acceptance of diversity and sound values worldwide.

New Zealand Council for Educational Research

Box 3237, Education House, 178–182 Willis Street, Wellington 6011
tel (04) 384 7939 fax (04) 384 7933
email info@nzcer.org.nz
website www.nzcer.org.nz
Director Robyn Baker, Publisher David Ellis

Education, including educational policy and institutions, early childhood education, educational achievement tests, Maori education, curriculum and assessment, etc. Founded 1934.

Pearson Education New Zealand Ltd*

Private Bag 102902, Rosedale, North Shore 0745, Auckland
tel (09) 442 7400 fax (09) 442 7401
email customer.service@pearsonnz.co.nz
website www.pearsoned.co.nz
General Manager Adrian Keane

New Zealand educational books.

Penguin Group (NZ)*

Private Bag 102902, Rosedale, North Shore 0745, Auckland
tel (09) 442 7400 fax (09) 442 7401
website www.penguin.co.nz
Managing Director Margaret Thompson, Publishing Director Geoff Walker

Adult and children's fiction and non-fiction. Imprints: Penguin, Viking, Puffin Books. Founded 1973.

Random House New Zealand Ltd*

Private Bag 102950, North Shore Mail Centre, Auckland 0725
tel (09) 444 7197 fax (09) 444 7524
email admin@randomhouse.co.nz
website www.randomhouse.co.nz
Managing Director Karen Ferns

Fiction, general non-fiction, gardening, cooking, art, business, health, children's. Subsidiary of Bertelsmann AG. Founded 1977.

RSVP Publishing Company*

PO Box 47166, Ponsonby, Auckland 1144
tel/fax (09) 372 8480
email rsvppub@iconz.co.nz
website www.rsvp-publishing.co.nz
Managing Director/Publisher Stephen Ron Picard,
Sales & Marketing Director Chris Palmer

Fiction, metaphysical, children's. Founded 1990.

Scholastic New Zealand Ltd*

21 Lady Ruby Drive, East Tamaki, Auckland
tel (09) 274 8112 fax (09) 274 8114
email publishing@scholastic.co.nz
postal address Private Bag 94407, Botany, Auckland 2163
website www.scholastic.co.nz
Senior Editor Penny Scown

Picture books, fiction for 5–8 and 9–12 year-olds, teenage fiction and series fiction. Publishes approx.

40 titles each year and has over 200 in print. Imprint: Scholastic NZ. Founded 1962.

Submission details Not currently accepting unsolicited MSS from writers not already published by Scholastic New Zealand. See website download for further details. For picture books send copies of illustrations, *not* original artwork.

Weldon Owen Education*
Level 1, 39 Market Place, Auckland
tel (09) 358 0190 *fax* (09) 358 0793
email info@weldonowen.co.nz
postal address PO Box 91645, Auckland
website www.weldonowen.co.nz

Supplementary educational titles for school systems internationally. Produces literacy-teaching programmes for kindergarten through to Grade 6. Also resources for home schooling. Series include *Shockwave* (8–10 year-olds), *Brainbank* (4–9 year-olds) and *Worldscapes* (8–10 year-olds). Founded 2001.

SOUTH AFRICA

*Member of the Publishers' Association of South Africa

Cambridge University Press*
(African Branch)
Lower Ground Floor, Nautica Building,
The Water Club, Beach Road, Granger Bay,
Cape Town 8005
tel (021) 412 7800 *fax* (021) 419 8418
email capetown@cambridge.org
website www.cambridge.org/africa
Director Colleen McCallum

Distance learning materials and textbooks for sub-Sahara African countries, as well as primary reading materials in 28 local African languages.

Clever Books Pty Ltd*
2nd Floor, Melrose Arch Piazza, 34 Whiteley Road, Melrose North 2116
tel (011) 731 3300 *fax* (011) 731 3500
postal Private Bag X19, Northlands 214
email info@cleverbooks.co.za
website www.cleverbooks.co.za

Managing Director J. Steenhuisen

Educational titles for the RSA market. Owned by Macmillan South Africa. Founded 1981.

Educat Publishers Pty Ltd
40 Long Street, Maitland 7405, Cape Town
tel (21) 510 7680 *fax* (21) 511 8797
email educat@educat.co.za
website www.educat.co.za

Educational products including science and maths, product designs for schools and retail, as well as mass markets. Age groups: preschool, 5–10, 10–15, 15+.

Heinemann Publishers (South Africa)
Heinemann House, Building No 3,
Grayston Office-Park, 128 Peter Road, Sandton
postal address PO Box 781940, Sandton 2146
tel (0 11) 322 8600 *fax* (086) 687 7822
email customerliaison@heinemann.co.za
website www.heinemann.co.za
Managing Director Naëtt Atkinson

Educational publisher: school textbooks, library books, e-learning and professional development materials for all schools in South Africa.

Human & Rousseau
PO Box 5050, Cape Town 8000
tel (021) 406 3033 *fax* (021) 406 3812
email nb@nb.co.za
website www.humanrousseau.co.za

General Afrikaans and English titles. Quality Afrikaans literature, popular literature, general children's and youth literature, cookery, self-help. Founded 1959.

Best Books (imprint)
Education.

Jacklin Enterprises (Pty) Ltd
PO Box 521, Parklands 2121
tel (011) 265 4200 *fax* (011) 314 2984
email service@jacklin.co.za
Managing Director M.A.C. Jacklin

Children's fiction and non-fiction; Afrikaans large print books. Subjects include aviation, natural history, romance, general science, technology and transportation. Imprints: Mike Jacklin, Kennis Onbeperk, Daan Retief.

Maskew Miller Longman (Pty) Ltd*
PO Box 396, cnr Logan Way and Forest Drive,
Pinelands 7405, Cape Town 8000
tel (021) 532 6000 *fax* (021) 531 8103
email customerservices@mml.co.za
website www.mml.co.za
Publishing Director Jacques Zakarian

Educational and general publishers.

Nasou Via Afrika
PO Box 5197, Cape Town 8000
11th floor, 40 Heerengracht, Naspers Building,
Cape Town 8001
tel (021) 406 3528 *fax* (021) 406 3086
email customerservices@nasou.com
website www.nasou-viaafrika.com
Ceo Christina Watson

Educational materials for South African schools and FET colleges, for all learning areas and subjects at all grades/levels: languages materials, literature and other materials in all official languages of South Africa. Imprints: Acacia, Action, Afritech, Afro, Atlas, Bateleur Books, Collegium, Idem, Juta/Gariep, KZN

Books

Books

Books, Nasou; Stimela, Van Schaik (literature), Via Afrika, Y-Press, Lux Verbi/Protea.

NB Publishers (Pty) Ltd*

PO Box 879, Cape Town 8000
tel (021) 406 3033 *fax* (021) 406 3812
email nb@nb.co.za
website www.nb.co.za
Managing Director Eloise Wessels

General: Afrikaans fiction, politics, children's and youth literature in all the country's languages, non-fiction. Imprints: Tafelberg, Human & Rousseau, Pharos and Kwela. Founded 1950.

New Africa Books (Pty) Ltd*

99 Garfield Road, Claremont, Cape Town 7700
tel (21) 674 4136 *fax* (21) 674 3358
email info@newafricabooks.co.za
postal address PO Box 46962, Glosderry 7702
website www.newafricabooks.co.za
Publisher Jeanne Homnid

General books, textbooks, literary works, contemporary issues, children and young adult. Formed as a result of the merger of David Philip Publishers (founded 1971), Spearhead Press (founded 2000) and New Africa Educational Publishing.

Oxford University Press Southern Africa*

Vasco Boulevard, N1 City, Goodwood, Cape Town 7460
tel (021) 596 2300 *fax* (021) 596 1234
email oxford.za@oup.com
postal address PO Box 12119, N1 City, Cape Town 7463
website www.oxford.co.za
Managing Director E. Kotze

Reference books for children and school books: preschool and foundation, intermediate and senior phases; dictionaries, thesauruses, atlases and teaching English as a main and as a second language.

Shuter and Shooter Publishers (Pty) Ltd*

110 CB Downes Road, Pietermaritzburg 3201, KwaZulu-Natal
tel (033) 846 8700 *fax* (033) 846 8701
email sales@shuters.com
postal address PO Box 61, Mkondeni 3212, KwaZulu-Natal
website www.shuters.com
Managing Director Mrs P.B. Chetty

Core curriculum-based textbooks for use at foundation, intermediate, senior and further education phases. Supplementary readers in various languages; dictionaries; reading development kits, charts. Literature titles in English, isiXhosa, Sesotho, Sepedi, Setswana, Tshivenda, Xitsonga, Ndebele, isiZulu and Siswati. Founded 1925.

SPAIN

Grupo Anaya

C/ Juan Ignacio Luca de Tena, 15–28027 Madrid
tel (34) 91 3938800 *fax* (34) 91 7426631
website www.anaya.es
Managing Director Carlos Lamadrid

Non-fiction: education textbooks for preschool through to 15+.

Editorial Cruilla

Av. de la Marina, 54 Poligon Can Calderon, 08830 Sant Boi de Llobregat
tel (902) 123 336 *fax* (93) 630 8750
email editorial@cruilla.com
website www.cruilla.com
Publishing Director Josep Herrero

Activity books, novelty books, fiction for 5–8 and 9–12 year-olds, teenage fiction and poetry. Publishes approx. 120–130 titles each year. Recent successes include *El Vaixell de Vapor* (series), *Vull Llegir!* and *Molly Moon Stops the World/Molly Moon's Incredible Book of Hypnotism*. Subsidiary of Ediciones SM. Founded 1984.

Destino Infantil & Juvenil

Edificio Planeta, Diagonal 662–664, 08034 Barcelona
tel (93) 496 7001 *fax* (93) 496 7002
email destinojoven@edestino.es
website www.edestino.es
Children's Director Bueno Marta

Fiction for ages 6–16 years old. Picture books, pop-up books, fiction and some unusual illustrated books. Age groups: preschool, 5–10, 10–15, 15+.

Libros del Zorro Rojo

Sant Joan de Malta, 39, 202A, 08018 Barcelona
tel/fax (34) 93 3076850
email editorial@librosdelzorrorojo.com
website www.librosdelzorrorojo.com

Small independent publisher specialising in children's and young adult books. Main focus is picture books for young children and classics with high-quality illustrations for young readers.

Editorial Libsa

San Rafael 4, Poligono Industrail, 28108 Alcobendas/Madrid
tel (34) 91 6572580 *fax* (34) 91 6572583
email libsa@libsa.es
website www.libsa.es
President Amado Sanchez, *Children's Books Editor* Maria Dolores Maeso

Publisher and packager of highly illustrated mass market books: activity books, board books, picture books, colouring books, how-to books, fairy tales.

Random House Mondadori

Travessera de Gracia 47–49, 08021 Barcelona
tel (34) 93 3660300 *fax* (34) 93 200 2219

website www.randomhousemondadori.es

Preschool activity, novelty and picture books through to young adult fiction. Also a packager and printer.

Beasco (division)
Character publishing, including Disney and Fisher-Price.

Lumen (division)
Classics and illustrated books.

Montena (division)
Contemporary literary fiction including fantasy.

Vicens Vives SA
Avenida Sarriá 130–132, 08017 Barcelona
tel (93) 252 3700 *fax* (93) 252 3711
email e@vicensvives.es
website www.vicensvives.es
Managing Director Roser Espona de Rahola

Activity and novelty books, fiction, art, encyclopedias, dictionaries, education, geography, history, music, science, textbooks, posters. Age groups: preschool, 5–10, 10–15, 15+.

USA

*Member of the Association of American Publishers Inc.

Abingdon Press
201 Eighth Avenue, PO Box 801, Nashville, TN 37202–0801
tel 800-251-3320 *fax* 1800-836-7802
website www.abingdonpress.com
President Neil Alexander, *Vice President* Tammy Gaines

General interest, professional, academic and reference – primarily directed to the religious market; children's non-fiction. Imprint of United Methodist Publishing House.

Harry N. Abrams Inc.
115 West 18th Street, New York, NY 10011
tel 212-206-7715 *fax* 212-519 1210
email abrams@abramsbooks.com
website www.abramsbooks.com
Ceo/President Michael Jacobs

Art and architecture, photography, natural sciences, performing arts, children's books. No fiction. Founded 1949.

Harry N. Abrams Books for Young Readers
tel 212-519-1200
website www.abramsyoungreaders.com
Director, Children's Books Howard W. Reeves

Fiction and non-fiction: picture books, young readers, middle readers, young adult.
Submission details For picture books submit covering letter and complete MS, for longer works

and non-fiction send query and sample chapter with sase.

Absey and Co. Inc.*
23011 Northcrest Drive, Spring, TX 77389
tel 888-412-2739 *fax* 281-251-4676
email info@absey.biz
website www.absey.biz
Publisher Edward Wilson

Mainstream fiction and non-fiction, poetry, educational books, especially those dealing in language arts. Recent successes for young adult readers include *Where I'm From* by George Ella Lyon, *Poetry After Lunch* by Joyce Armstrong Carroll and *Just People and Paper, Pen, Poem* by Kathi Appelt; and picture books *Regular Lu* by Robin Nelson and *Stealing a Million Kisses* by Jennifer Skaggs.
Submission details For fiction query with sase. For non-fiction query with outline and 1–2 sample chapters.

Action Publishing, LLC
PO Box 391, Glendale, CA 91209
tel 323-478-1667 *fax* 323-478-1767
email info@actionpublishing.com
website www.actionpublishing.com

Children's picture books, young adult fiction, adult non-fiction.
Submission details See website for guidelines. Founded 1996.

Aladdin Paperbacks – see Simon & Schuster Children's Publishing Division

All About Kids Publishing
PO Box 159, Gilroy, CA 95021
tel 408-337-1866
email mail@aakp.com
website www.aakp.com
Publisher Mike G. Guevara, *Editor* Linda L. Guevara

Fiction and non-fiction picture books and chapter books. Recent successes include *A, My Name is Andrew* by Mary McManus-Burke (picture book) and *The Titanic Game* by Mike Warner (chapter book). Founded 1999.
Submission details See website for guidelines.

Alyson Publications, Inc.
245 West 17th Street, 12th Floor, New York, NY 10011
email publisher@alyson.com
website www.alyson.com
Editor Angela Brown

Picture books and young adult titles that deal with gay or lesbian issues. Recent successes include *Daddy's Wedding* by Michael Willhoite.
Submission details Picture books are only considered if text and illustrations are submitted together. For young adult books submit synopsis and

sample chapters with sase. See website for submission guidelines.

American Girl Publishing, Inc.
PO Box 620991, Middleton, WI 53562–0991
email middleton.bpsst@americangirl.com
website www.americangirl.com

Age-appropriate books and playthings to 'foster girls' individuality, intellectual curiosity and imagination'.

American Girl (imprint)
Advice and activity books for 8–12 year-old girls.
Submission details Publishes material to encourage girls' dreams and to reinforce their self-confidence and curiosity as they prepare to navigate adolescence in the years ahead. Invites proposals for well-focused concepts for activity books, craft books, or advice books. Also non-fiction specifically targeted to girls – if the approach would appeal to boys as well as to girls, submission is not appropriate. Proposals should include a detailed description of the concept, sample chapters or spreads, and lists or samples of previous publications, plus sase. Complete MSS are also acceptable. Founded 1985.

Amistad – see HarperCollins Publishers

Amistad Press – see HarperCollins Publishers

The Julie Andrews Collection – see HarperCollins Publishers

Atheneum Books for Young Readers – see Simon & Schuster Children's Publishing Division

Avisson Press, Inc.
3007 Taliaferro Road, Greensboro, NC 27408
tel 336-288-6989 *fax* 336-288-6989
email avisson4@aol.com
Publisher Martin Hester

Biography for young adults. Recent successes include *I Can Do Anything* by William Schoell and *The Girl He Left Behind* by Suzanne Middendorf. Founded 1995.
Submission details Submit synopsis and 2 sample chapters.

Avon Books – see HarperCollins Publishers

Bantam Books – see Random House Inc.

Barefoot Books
2067 Massachusetts Avenue, Cambridge, MA 02140
tel 617-576-0660 *fax* 617-576-0049
email publicity@barefootbooks.com
website www.barefootbooks.com

Barefoot Books 'celebrates art and story with books that open the hearts and minds of children from all walks of life'. Recent successes include *The Boy Who Grew Flowers* by Jen Wojtowicz, illustrated by Steve Adams (age 4–9, picture book). Founded 1993 (UK); 1998 (USA).
Submission details Length: 500–1,000 words (picture books), 2,000–3,000 young readers. Accepts unsolicited MSS. Send full MS and sase. Allow up to 6 months for response.

Barron's Educational Series Inc.
250 Wireless Boulevard, Hauppauge, NY 11788
tel 800-645-3476 *fax* 631-434-3723
email fbrown@barronseduc.com
website www.barronseduc.com
Chairman/Ceo Manuel H. Barron, *President/Publisher* Ellen Sibley

Series books for children aged 7–11, 12–16. Publishes 20 picture books, 20 young reader titles, 20 middle reader titles and 10 young adult titles each year. Recent successes include *Everyday Witch* by Sandra Forrester and *Word Wizardry* by Margaret and William Kenda. Also for adults: cookbooks, Mind, Body & Spirit, crafts, business, pets, gardening, family and health, art. Founded 1941.
Submission details Approx. 25% of books are by first-time authors. For fiction, query by email. For non-fiction, submit outline/synopsis and sample chapters with sase for response. Responds to MSS in 8 months. Send to Acquisitions Manager. See website for full details.
Reviews MS/illustration packages from artists: send query letter with 3 chapters of MS with one piece of final art, remainder roughs. For illustrations only send tearsheets or slides plus résumé. Responds in 2 months. Send to Bill Kuchler, Art Director.

Bick Publishing House
307 Neck Road, Madison, CT 06443
tel 203-245-0073 *fax* 203-245-5990
email bickpubhse@aol.com
website www.bickpubhouse.com

Adults: health and recovery, living with disabilities, wildlife rehabilitation. Non-fiction for young adults: philosophy, psychology, self help, social issues, science. Recent successes include *What Are You Doing with Your Life? Books on Living for Teenagers* by J. Krishnamurti; *The Teen Brain Book: Who and What Are You?, Talk: Teen Art of Communication,* and *Cosmic Calendar: The Big Bang to Your Consciousness* by Dale Carlson. Founded 1993.

Big Idea Entertainment
Building 2A, 230 Franklin Road, Franklin, TN 37064
tel 615-224-2200
email customerservice@bigidea.com
website www.veggietales.com
Senior Managing Editor Cindy Kenney

'To enhance the spiritual and moral fabric of society through creative media.' Children's/juvenile fiction and non-fiction, picture books for age 3+. Also books on child guidance/parenting, reference and gift books. Recent successes include *Lord of the Beans* by Phil Vischer (picture book) and *Mess Detectives* by Doug Peterson (storybook).

Submission details Material must be highly innovative and creative, and must conform to the Big Idea style. Send query with sase.

Blooming Tree Press
PO Box 140934, Austin, TX 78714
tel 512-921-8846 *fax* 512-873-7710
email email@bloomingtreepress.com
website www.bloomingtreepress.com
Publisher Miriam Hees

Fiction and non-fiction: picture books, young readers, middle readers, young adult.

Submission details For fiction send query letter; for non-fiction submit outline/synopsis and 3 sample chapters. For illustration send query letter to Regan Johnson. Founded 2000.

Bloomsbury Publishing USA
(New York office of Bloomsbury Publishing)
Suite 315, 175 Fifth Avenue, New York, NY 10010
tel 212-674-5151
email bloomsbury.kids@bloomsburyusa.com
website www.bloomsburyusa.com
Publishing Director George Gibson, *Other publishing contacts* Peter Ginna (non-fiction), Melanie Cecka (children's); *Chief Financial Officer* Peter DeGiglio

Supports the worldwide publishing activities of Bloomsbury Publishing Plc: caters for the US market. See Bloomsbury Adult, Bloomsbury Children's & Educational, Bloomsbury Professional & Academic, Bloomsbury Information on page 7.

Blue Sky Press – see Scholastic Inc.

Boyds Mills Press
815 Church Street, Honesdale, PA 18431
website www.boydsmillspress.com

Activity books, picture books, fiction, non-fiction, and poetry for ages 18 and under. Recent successes include *Drive* by Nathan Clement, *One Whole and Perfect Day* by Judith Clarke and *I'm Being Stalked by a Moonshadow* by Doug MacLeod. Publishes approx. 80 titles each year. Founded 1991.

Submission details Will consider both unsolicited MSS and queries. Send to above address and label package 'Manuscript Submission'. Looking for middle-grade fiction with fresh ideas and subject matter, and young adult novels of real literary merit. Non-fiction should be fun and entertaining as well as informative, and non-fiction MSS should be accompanied by a detailed bibliography. Interested in imaginative picture books and welcomes submissions from both writers and illustrators. Submit samples as b&w and/or colour copies or transparencies;

submissions will not be returned. Include sase with all submissions. Send art samples to above address and label package 'Art Sample Submission'.

Calkins Creek Books (imprint)
US history and historical fiction.

Front Street (imprint)
See page 45.

Wordsong (imprint)
Poetry.

Calkins Creek Books – see Boyds Mills Press

Candlewick Press
99 Dover Street, Somerville, MA 02144
tel 617-661-3330 *fax* 617-661-0565
email bigbear@candlewick.com
website www.candlewick.com
President/Publisher Karen Lotz, *Editorial Director/ Associate Publisher* Liz Bicknell

Books for babies through teens: board books, picture books, novels, non-fiction, novelty books. Publishes 160 picture books, 15 middle readers and 15 young adult titles each year. Recent successes include *The Astonishing Life of Octavian Nothing, Traitor to the Nation, Volumes I and II* by M.T. Anderson (young adult fiction), *Good Masters! Sweet Ladies! Voices from a Medieval Village* by Laura Amy Schlitz, illustrated by Robert Byrd (illustrated middle-grade fiction), and *A Visitor for Bear* by Bonny Becker, Illustrated by Kady MacDonald Denton (picture book). Subsidiary of Walker Books Ltd, UK.

Submission details Approx. 5% of books are by first-time authors. Submit MSS via a literary agent. No unsolicited MSS accepted. For illustrations, send résumé and portfolio for the attention of Art Resource Coordinator. Responds in 6 weeks. Samples returned with sase. Founded 1991.

Carolrhoda Books – see Lerner Publishing Group

Cartwheel Books – see Scholastic Inc.

Charlesbridge Publishing
85 Main Street, Watertown, MA 02472
tel 617-926-0329 *fax* 617-926-5775
email tradeeditorial@charlesbridge.com
website www.charlesbridge.com
President & Publisher Brent Farmer, *Vice President & Associate Publisher* Mary Ann Sabia

Board books, fiction and non-fiction picture books and transitional books for preschool–14 year-olds. Lively, plot-driven story books plus nursery rhymes, fairy tales and humorous stories for the very young. Non-fiction list specialises in nature, concept and multicultural books. Publishes 60% non-fiction, 40% fiction picture books and transitional books. Recent successes include *Sea Queens* by Jane Yolen, *The Searcher and Old Tree* by David McPhail, *Hello, Bumblebee Bat* by Darrin Lunde, *Life on Earth – and Beyond: An Astrobiologist's Quest* by Pamela S. Turner, *The Day-Glo Brothers* by Chris Barton and *The Importance of Wings* by Robin Friedman. Founded 1980.

Submission details Send full MSS; no queries. Responds to MSS of interest. Length: 1,000–10,000 words. For illustrations, send query with samples, tearsheets and résumé.

Chicago Review Press
814 North Franklin Street, Chicago, IL 60610
tel 312-337-0747 *fax* 312-337-5110
email frontdesk@chicagoreviewpress.com
website www.chicagoreviewpress.com
Publisher Cynthia Sherry

General publisher. Non-fiction activity books for children. Recent successes include *Exploring the Solar System: A History with 22 Activities* by Mary Kay Carson. Founded 1973.

Submission details Interested in hands-on educational books. See website for submission guidelines.

Chronicle Books
680 Second Street, San Francisco, CA 94107
tel 415-537-4200 *fax* 415-537-4460
email frontdesk@chroniclebooks.com
website www.chroniclebooks.com,
www.chroniclekids.com
Chairman & Ceo Nion McEvoy, *Publisher* Christine Carswell

Traditional and innovative children's books. Looking for projects that have a unique bent – in subject matter, writing style or illustrative technique – that will add a distinctive flair. Interested in fiction and non-fiction for children of all ages as well as board books, decks, activity kits, and other unusual or 'novelty' formats. Publishes 60–100 books each year. Also for adults: cooking, how-to books, nature, art, biographies, fiction, gift. Founded 1967.

Submission details For picture books submit MS. For older readers, submit outline/synopsis and 3 sample chapters. No submitted materials will be returned. Response approx. 3 months.

Clarion Books – see Houghton Mifflin Harcourt

Clear Light Books
823 Don Diego, Santa Fe, NM 87505
tel 505-989-9590 *fax* 505-989-9519
website www.clearlightbooks.com
Publisher Harmon Houghton

For adults: art and photography, cookbooks, ecology/environment, health, gift books, history, Native America, Tibet, Western Americana. Non-fiction for children and young adults: multicultural, American Indian, Hispanic.

Submission details Looking for authentic American Indian art and folklore. Send complete MS with sase.

CMX – see DC Comics

David C. Cook
4050 Lee Vance View, Colorado Springs, CO 80918
tel 719-536-0100
website www.davidccook.com

Christian education resources for preschool to teenagers.

Cooper Square Publishing
4501 Forbes Boulevard, Suite 200, Lanham, Maryland 20706
tel 301-459-3366
website www.northlandpub.com

Part of the Rowman & Littlefield Publishing Group. Founded 1949.

NorthWord Books for Young Readers (imprint)
11571 K–Tel Drive, Minnetonka, MN 55343
tel 952-933-7537 *fax* 952-933-3630
email mbohr@nbnbooks.com
website www.nbnbooks.com
Picture books and non-fiction nature and wildlife books in interactive and fun-to-read formats. Not accepting MSS at present. Founded 1989.

Rising Moon (imprint)
email editorial@northlandbooks.com
website www.northlandbooks.com
Illustrated, entertaining, and thought-provoking picture books for children, including Spanish–English bilingual titles. Founded 1998.

Submission details Seeking fresh picture book MSS about contemporary everyday life of children: edgy, innovative, spirited (e.g. *Do Princesses Wear Hiking Boots?* and *It's a Bad Day*). Also seeking exceptional Latino-themed picture books about multicultural living, contemporary issues, Latino role models (e.g. *My Name is Celia* and *Lupe Vargas and Her Super Best Friend*). Additionally seeking picture books that relate to western and southwestern USA, original stories with a Southwest flavour, fractured fairy tales (e.g. *The Treasure of Ghostwood Gully* and *The Three Little Javelinas*).

Two-Can Publishing (imprint)
website www.northlandbooks.com
Non-fiction books and multimedia products to entertain and educate 2–12 year-olds. Not accepting MSS at present.

Joanna Cotler Books – see HarperCollins Publishers

Cricket Books
Carus Publishing Company,
Cricket Magazine Group, 30 Grove Street, Suite C, Peterborough, NH 03458

email customerservice@caruspub.com
website www.cricketmag.com

Picture books, chapter books, poetry, non-fiction and novels for children and young adults. Recent successes include *Breakout* by Paul Fleischman and *Robert and the Weird & Wacky Facts* by Barbara Seuling, illustrated by Paul Brewer. Also publishes *Cricket*, the award-winning magazine of outstanding stories and art for 9–14 year-olds, and other magazines for young readers. Founded 1973. Division of Carus Publishing.

Submission details Not accepting MSS submissions at this time.

Crown Books – see Random House Inc.

Darby Creek Publishing – see Lerner Publishing Group

Dawn Publications

12402 Bitney Springs Road, Nevada City, CA 95959
tel 530-274-7775 *fax* 530-274-7778
website www.dawnpub.com
Editor & Co-Publisher Glenn Hovemann, *Art Director & Co-Publisher* Muffy Weaver

Picture books and biographies 'to assist parents and educators to open the minds and hearts of children to the transforming influence of Nature'. Recent successes include *How We Know What We Know About Our Changing Climate* by Lynne Cherry, photographed by Gary Braasch. Another new title is *Over in Australia: Amazing Animals Down Under* by Marianne Berkes, illustrated by Jill Dubin.

Submission details See website for guidelines.

DC Comics

1700 Broadway, New York, NY 10019
tel 212-636-5400 *fax* 212-636-5975
email dccomics@cambeywest.com
website www.dccomics.com

Activity books, board books, novelty books, picture books, painting and colouring books, pop-up books, fiction, fairy tales, art, hobbies, how-to books, leisure, entertainment, film/TV tie-ins, calendars, comics, gift books, periodicals, picture cards, posters, CD-Roms, CD-I, internet for preschool age to 15+.

DC Comics has published and licensed comic books for over 60 years in all genres for all ages, including super heroes, fantasy, horror, mystery and high-quality graphic stories for mature readers. Imprints: WildStorm, Vertigo. A Warner Bros. Company.

CMX (imprint)

Translated manga from Japan in its original format.

MINX (imprint)

Original graphic novels for teenage girls.

Delacorte Press Books for Young Readers – see Random House Inc.

Dial Books for Young Readers – see Penguin Group (USA), Inc.

Disney Books for Young Readers – see Random House Inc.

DNA Press

PO Box 9311, Glendale, CA 91226-0311
email editors@dnapress.com
website www.dnapress.com

Non-fiction books for adults and children on real estate, investing, business.

Submission details Children's books teach scientific concepts as part of the general context; all books should be oriented towards explaining science.

Dog-Eared Publications

PO Box 620863, Middleton, WI 53562–0863
tel/fax 608-831-1410
email field@dog-eared.com
website www.dog-eared.com

Children's nature books. No unsolicited MSS.

Tom Doherty Associates, LLC

175 5th Avenue, New York, NY 10010
tel 212-388-0100 *fax* 212-677-7456
email enquiries@tor.com
website www.us.macmillan.com/torforge.aspx

Fiction and non-fiction for middle readers and young adults. Publishes 5–10 middle readers and 5–10 young adult books each year. Recent successes include *Hidden Talents, Flip* by David Lubar (fantasy, ages 10+), *Briar Rose* by Jane Yolen (fiction, age 12+), *Strange Unsolved Mysteries* by Phyllis Rabin Amert (non-fiction). For adults: fiction – general, historical, western, suspense, mystery, horror, science fiction, fantasy, humour, juvenile, classics (English language); non-fiction. Imprints: Tor Books, Forge Books, Orb Books, Starscope, Tor Teen. Founded 1980.

Submission details For both fiction and non-fiction, submit outline/synopsis and complete MS. Responds to queries in one month; MSS in 6 months for unsolicited work. Fiction length: middle readers – 30,000 words; young adult – 60,000–100,000 words. Non-fiction length: middle readers – 25,000–35,000 words; young adult – 70,000 words. For illustrations, query with samples to Irene Gallo, Art Director. Responds only if interested.

Tor (imprint)

Science fiction and fantasy.

StarScape (imprint)

Science fiction and fantasy for ages 10–12.

Tor Teen (imprint)

Science fiction and fantasy for ages 12+.

Doubleday Books for Young
Readers – see Random House Inc.

Dover Publications Inc.
31 East 2nd Street, Mineola, NY 11501
tel 516-294-7000 *fax* 516-742-6953
website www.doverpublications.com

Activity books, novelty books, picture books, fiction for 5–8 and 9–12 year-olds, teenage fiction, series fiction, reference, plays, religion, poetry, audio and CD-Roms. Also adult non-fiction. Publishes approx. 150 children's titles and has over 2,500 in print. Recent successes include *Easy Noah's Ark Sticker Picture, How to Draw a Funny Monster* and *Pretty Ballerina Sticker Paper Doll*. Founded 1941.
   Submission details Will consider unsolicited MSS but write for guidelines.

Dragon Books – see Pacific View Press

Dragonfly Books – see Random House Inc.

Dutton Children's Books – see Penguin
Group (USA), Inc.

EDCON Publishing Group
30 Montauk Boulevard, Oakdale, NY 11769–1399
tel 631-567-7227 *fax* 631-567-8745
email info@edconpublishing.com
website www.edconpublishing.com

Supplemental instructional materials for use by education professionals to improve reading and maths skills. Includes early reading, *Classics* series, *Easy Shakespeare*, fiction and non-fiction, reading diagnosis and vocabulary books. Recent successes include adaptations of *A Midsummer Night's Dream* and *The Merchant of Venice*. Founded 1970.

Edupress
401 S. Wright Road, Janesville, WI 53547
tel 800-694-5827 *fax* 800-835-2329
email edupress@highsmith.com
website www.highsmith.com/edupress

Educational materials. Founded 1979.
   Submission details See website for guidelines.

Eerdmans Publishing Company
2140 Oak Industrial Drive NE, Grand Rapids, MI 49505
tel 616-459-4591 *fax* 616-459-6540
website www.eerdmans.com
President William B. Eerdmans, Jr

Independent publisher of a wide range of religious books, from academic works in theology, biblical studies, religious history, and reference to popular titles in spirituality, social and cultural criticism and literature. Founded 1911.

Eerdmans Books for Young Readers (imprint)
website www.eerdmans.com/youngreaders
Acquisitions Editor Jeanne Elders DeWaard, *Art Director* Gayle Brown

Picture books, biographies, middle reader and young adult fiction and non-ficiton. Publishes 12–18 books a year. Seeks MSS that are honest, wise and hopeful but also publishes stories that delight with their storyline, characters or good humour. Stories that celebrate diversity, stories of historical significance, and stories that relate to current issues are of special interest.
   Submission details Accepts unsolicited submissions. Send to Acquisitions Editor; responds in 4 months only to submissions of interest. For illustrations, send photocopies or printed media and include a list of books you have illustrated. Send to Gayle Brown. Samples will be kept on file; they will not be returned.

Egmont USA
443 Park Avenue South, Suite 806, New York, NY 10016
tel 212-685-0102
email egmontusa@egmont.com
website www.egmontusa.com

Picture books, children's and young adult fiction. Founded 2009.
   Submission details No unsolicited MSS; submissions accepted via literary agents only.

Encyclopaedia Britannica Inc.
331 North La Salle Street, Chicago, IL 60610
tel 312-347-7159 *fax* 312-294-2104
email international@eb.com
website www.britannica.com

Encyclopedias, reference books, almanacs, videos and CD-Roms for adults and children aged 5–15+.

Enslow Publishers, Inc.
Box 398, 40 Industrial Road, Berkeley Heights, NJ 07922–0398
tel 908-771-9400 *fax* 908-771-0925
email customerservice@enslow.com
website www.enslow.com
President Mark Enslow, *Vice President/Publisher* Brian Enslow

Non-fiction library books for children and young adults. Founded 1976.

Eos – see HarperCollins Publishers

Evan-Moor Educational Publishers
18 Lower Ragsdale Drive, Monterey, CA 93940
tel 1800-714-0971 *fax* 1800-777-4332
email marketing@evan-moor.com
website www.evan-moor.com
President Linda Hanger, *Publisher* Joy Evans

Educational materials for parents and teachers of children (ages 3–12): activity books, textbooks, how-to books, CD-Roms. Subjects include maths, geography, history, science, reading, writing, social studies, art and craft. Publishes approx. 50 titles each year and has over 450 in print. Recent successes include *Daily Paragraph Editing* (5-book series, grades 2–5) and *Nonfiction Reading Practice* (6-book series, grades 1–6). Founded 1979.

Submission details Less than 10% of books are by first-time authors. Query or submit outline, table of contents and sample pages. Responds to queries in 2 months; MSS in 4 months. See website for submission guidelines. For illustrations, send résumé, samples and tearsheets to the Art Director. Primarily uses b&w material.

Farrar, Straus and Giroux, LLC

website www.fsgbooks.com, www.fsgkidsbooks.com, mackids.com, macteenbooks.com
Publisher Simon Boughton

Farrar Straus Giroux Books for Young Readers

Margaret Ferguson Books Margaret Ferguson, *Frances Foster Books* Frances Foster, *Executive Editor* Wesley Adams, *Senior Editor* Janine O'Malley, *Associate Editor* Beth Potter, *Creative Director* Anne Diebel

Books for toddlers through to young adults: picture books, fiction for 5–8 and 9–12-year-olds, teenage fiction and poetry (occasionally). Publishes 70 hardcover originals plus 10 paperback reprints each year and has approx. 500 titles in print. Recent successes include *The Wall* by Peter Sís, *Way Down Deep* by Ruth White and *Someday This Pain Will be Useful to You* by Peter Cameron. Imprints: Frances Foster Books, Margaret Ferguson Books.

Submission details Approx. 10% of books are by first-time authors. Send query letter first but will consider unsolicited MSS. Include a covering letter containing any pertinent information about yourself, your writing, your MSS, etc and a sase for return of MSS. Address submissions to FSG Children's Editorial Department. Allow 3 months for response. Looking to publish books of high literary merit. For illustrations, send only 2–3 samples; do *not* send original artwork.

David Fickling Books – see Random House Inc.

Firebird – see Penguin Group (USA), Inc.

Flux Books/Llewellyn Worldwide

2143 Wooddale Drive, Woodbury, MN 55125–2989
tel 800-843-666 *fax* 651-291-1908
email brian@fluxnow.com,
submissions@fluxnow.com
website www.fluxnow.com
Publisher Bill Krause

Young adult: fiction for ages 12+ in all genres. Seeks to publish authors who see young adult as a point of view rather than a reading level. Looks for edgy, challenging books that try to capture a slice of teenage experience. Particularly interested in books that tell the stories of young adults in unexpected or surprising situations around the globe. Recent successes include *Leaving Paradise* by Simone Elkeles, debut novels *Lament* and *Ballad* by Maggie Stiefvater, and Laurie Faria Stolarz's debut *Blue is for Nightmares*.

Walter Foster Publishing Inc.

3 Wrigley, Suite A, Irvine, CA 92618
tel 800-426-0099 *fax* 949-380-7575
email info@walterfoster.com
website www.walterfoster.com
Chief Executive Ross Sarracino

Instructional art books for children and adults. Also art and activity kits for children. Subsidiary of Quayside Publishing Group.

Free Spirit Publishing

217 Fifth Avenue North, Suite 200, Minneapolis, MN 55401–1299
tel 612-338-2068 *fax* 612-337-5050
email help4kids@freespirit.com
website www.freespirit.com
President Judy Galbraith

Award-winning publisher of non-fiction materials for children and teens, parents, educators, and counsellors. Specialises in SELF-HELP FOR KIDS® and SELF-HELP FOR TEENS® materials which empower young people and promote positive self-esteem through improved social and emotional health. Topics include self-esteem and self-awareness, stress management, school success, creativity, friends and family, peacemaking, social action, and special needs (i.e. gifted and talented, children with learning differences). Publishes approx. 18–22 new products each year, adding to a backlist of over 100 books, audio tapes, and posters. Free Spirit authors are expert educators and mental health professionals who have been honoured nationally for their contributions on behalf of children. Founded 1983.

Front Street

815 Church Street, Honesdale, PA 18431
tel 570-253-1164
email contact@boydsmillspress.com
website www.frontstreetbooks.com
Editorial Director Larry Rosler, *Art Director* Tim Gillner

Books for children and young adults: picture books, fiction (5–8, 9–12, teenage). Recent successes include *The Adventurous Deeds of Deadwood Jones* by Helen Hemphill, *Child of Dandelions* by Shenaaz Nanji, and *Piggy* by Mireille Geus. Imprint of Boyds Mills Press. Founded 1994.

Submission details For fiction, submit the first 3 chapters and a plot summary. For picture books, submit the entire MSS. Include an sase if return required. Allow 3–4 months for response.

Fulcrum Resources*

4690 Table Mountain Drive, Suite 100, Golden, CO 80403

tel 303-277-1623 *fax* 303-279-7111
email fulcrum@fulcrumbooks.com
website www.fulcrum-books.com

Books and support materials for teachers, librarians, parents and elementary through middle school children in the subjects of science and nature, literature and storytelling, history, multicultural studies, and Native American and Hispanic cultures. Imprint of Fulcrum Publishing.

Gale Cengage Learning*
27500 Drake Road, Farmington Hills, MI 48331–3535
tel 248-699-4253
website www.gale.cengage.com

Education publishing for libraries, schools and businesses. Serves the K–12 market with the following imprints: Blackbirch Press, Greenhaven Press, KidHaven Press, Lucent Books, Sleeping Bear Press, UXL.

Greenhaven Press (imprint)
High-quality non-fiction resources for the education community. Publishes 220 young adult academic reference titles each year. Recent successes include the *Opposing Viewpoints* series. Founded 1970.
Submission details Approx. 35% of books are by first-time authors. No unsolicited MSS. All writing is done on a work-to-hire basis. Send query, résumé and list of published works.

KidHaven Press (imprint)
Non-fiction references for younger researchers.

Lucent Books (imprint)
Non-fiction resources for upper-elementary to high school students. Recent successes include *Women in the American Revolution* and *Civil Liberties and the War on Terrorism*.
Submission details No unsolicited MSS. Query with résumé.

Sleeping Bear Press (imprint)
email sleepingbearpress@cengage.com
website www.sleepingbearpress.com
High-quality picture books.

Laura Geringer Books – see HarperCollins Publishers

Golden Books for Young Readers – see Random House Inc.

Graphia – see Houghton Mifflin Harcourt

Greenhaven Press – see Gale Cengage Learning

Greenwillow Books – see HarperCollins Publishers

Grosset & Dunlap – see Penguin Group (USA), Inc.

Gryphon House, Inc.
10770 Columbia Pike, Suite 201, Silver Spring, MD 20901

tel 1800-636-0928 *fax* 1877-638-7576
website www.gryphonhouse.com

Early childhood (age 0–8) books for teachers and parents.
Submission details 'We look for books that are developmentally appropriate for the intended age group, are well researched and based on current trends in the field, and include creative, participatory learning experiences with a common conceptual theme to tie them together.' Send query and/or a proposal.

Hachai Publishing
527 Empire Boulevard, Brooklyn, NY 11225
tel 718-633-0100 *fax* 718-633-0103
email info@hachai.com
website www.hachai.com

Jewish books for children aged 0–8+.
Submission details Welcomes unsolicited MSS. Specialises in books for 2–4 year-olds and 3–6 year-olds. Looking for stories that convey the traditional Jewish experience in modern times or long ago, traditional Jewish observance, and positive character traits.

Hachette Book Group USA
237 Park Avenue, 16th Floor, New York, NY10017
website www.hachettebookgroup.com

Divisions: Center Street, Grand Central Publishing, Hachette Audio, Little, Brown and Company, Little, Brown and Company Books for Young Readers (page 51), Yen Press (see page 60). Imprints: Faith Words, Orbit, Windblown Media.

Handprint Books
413 Sixth Avenue, Brooklyn, New York 11215–3310
tel 718-768-3696 *fax* 718-369-0844
email info@handprintbooks.com
website www.handprintbooks.com
Publisher Christopher Franceschelli, *Executive Editor* Ann Tobias

A range of children's books: picture and story books through to young adult fiction. Imprints: Handprint Books, Ragged Bears, Blue Apple.
Submission details Welcomes submissions of MSS of quality for works ranging from board books to young adult novels. For novels, first query interest on the subject and submit a 7,500-word max. sample. Accepts MSS on an e-submission basis only, sent as attachments in a word processing format readily readable on a PC. Artwork should be sent as small jpegs; artists' website addresses may also be submitted. No series fiction, licensed character (or characters whose primary avatar is meant to be as licences), 'I-Can-Read'- type books, or titles intended primarily for mass merchandise outlets.

Harcourt School Publishers*
6277 Sea Harbor Drive, Orlando, FL 32887
tel 407-345-2000

website www.harcourtschool.com

Textbooks and related instructional materials for school and home use by students (grades PreK–6): reading, language arts, ESL, maths, science, social studies, art, health, professional development and electronic and online material. Division of Harcourt Inc. Founded 1919.

Harcourt Trade Publishers*

215 Park Avenue South, New York, NY 10003
tel 212-592-1034 *fax* 212-420-5850
website www.hmhbooks.com
President/Publisher Dan Farley, *Editorial Director* Liz Van Doren

Fiction and non-fiction (history, biography, etc) for readers of all ages. Part of the Harcourt Houghton Mifflin Book Group.

Harcourt Children's Books

Publisher Lori Benton, *Editorial Director, Harcourt Children's Books* Allyn Johnston

Quality picture books, contemporary and historical fiction for teen readers, board and novelty books, gift items, and non-fiction for children of all ages. Also reading and teacher guides for teachers of children aged 8–14+. The original publisher of such classics as *The Little Prince, Mary Poppins, The Borrowers, Half Magic, Ginger Pye*, and *The Moffats*. Recent successes include *Where Did That Baby Come From?* by Debi Gliori and Juliet Dove, *Queen of Love* by Bruce Coville (fiction, age 8–12). Imprints: Gulliver Books, Silver Whistle, Red Wagon Books, Harcourt Young Classics, Green Light Readers, Voyager Books/Libros Viajeros, Harcourt Paperbacks, Odyssey Classics, Magic Carpet Books.
Submission details Does not accept unsolicited query letters or emails, MSS and illustrations. Only accepts material via literary agents.

HarperCollins Publishers*

10 East 53rd Street, New York, NY 10022
tel 212-207-7000
website www.harpercollins.com
President/Ceo Brian Murray

Adult fiction (commercial and literary) and non-fiction. Subjects include biography, business, cookbooks, educational, history, juvenile, poetry, religious, science, technical and travel. Imprints: Amistad, Avon, Avon A, Avon Inspire, Avon Red, Caedmon, Collins, Collins Design, Ecco, Eos, HarperAudio, Harper Mass Market, Harper Paperbacks, Harper Perennial, Harper Perennial Modern Classics, HarperCollins, HarperEntertainment, HarperLuxe, HarperOne, William Morrow, Morrow Cookbooks, Rayo. No unsolicited material; all submissions must come through a literary agent. Founded 1817.

HarperCollins Children's Books (division)

1350 Avenue of the Americas, New York, NY 10019
tel 212-261-6500

website www.harperchildrens.com
President/Publisher Susan Katz

Children's classic literature. Imprints: Amistad Press, Julie Andrews Collection, Joanna Cotler Books, Eos, Laura Geringer Books, Greenwillow Books, HarperChildren's Audio, HarperCollins Children's Books, HarperEntertainment, HarperTeen, HarperTrophy, Rayo, Katherine Tegen Books.
Recent successes include *Goodnight Moon, Where the Wild Things Are, The Giving Tree*, and *Charlotte's Web*.
Submission details Does not accept unsolicited or unagented MSS.

Amistad Press (imprint)

Books by and about people of African descent on subjects and themes that have significant influence on the intellectual, cultural, and historical perspectives of a world audience.

The Julie Andrews Collection (imprint)

website www.julieandrewscollection.com

Books for young readers that nurture the imagination and celebrate a sense of wonder. Includes new works by established and emerging authors, out-of-print books, and books by Ms Andrews herself.

Avon Books (imprint)

Series and popular fiction for young readers: romance, mystery, adventure, fantasy. Series include *Making Out, Animal Emergency, Get Real*, and *Enchanted Hearts*, and authors include Bruce Coville, Beatrice Sparks and Dave Duncan.

Collins (imprint)

Non-fiction for toddlers to teens, including books published in conjunction with the Smithsonian Institution, the Emily Post Institute, and TIME for Kids, as well as Seymour Simon's award-winning titles and the classic *Let's-Read-and-Find-Out Science* series.

Joanna Cotler Books (imprint)

Literary and commercial picture books and fiction for all ages. Authors and illustrators include Clive Barker, Francesca Lia Block, Sharon Creech, Jamie Lee Curtis, Laura Cornell, Patricia MacLachlan, Barbara Robinson, Art Spiegelman, Jerry Spinelli and William Steig.

Eos (imprint)

Science fiction and fantasy.

Laura Geringer Books (imprint)

Publisher Laura Geringer

Fiction. Publishes 6 picture books, 2 young readers, 4 middle readers and one young adult title each year. Recent successes include *If You Take a Mouse to School* by Laura Numeroff, illustrated by Felicia Band (ages 3–7) and *The Dulcimer Boy* by Tor Seidler, illustrated by Brian Selznick (ages 8+). Authors and artists include William Joyce, Laura Numeroff, Felicia Bond, Bruce Brooks, Richard Egielski and Sarah Weeks.

Submission details Submissions via a literary agent only. Length: picture books – 500 words; young readers – 1,000 words; middle readers – 25,000 words; young adult – 40,000 words.

Greenwillow Books (imprint)

Books for children of all ages. Publishes 40 picture books, 5 middle readers and 5 young adult books each year. Recent successes indlue *Olive's Ocean* by Kevin Henkes.

Submission details No unsolicited MSS or queries. Unsolicited mail will not be opened or returned.

HarperChildren's Audio (imprint)

Offers best-selling children's books and young adult favourites in CD and audio cassette formats.

HarperCollins e-Books (imprint)

Middle-grade and young adult fiction. Many titles contain ebook features not found in print editions.

HarperEntertainment (imprint)

Film and TV tie-ins, from preschool through to teens. Recent titles include *The Chronicles of Narnia*, *Ice Age 2*, *X-Men*, *Charlotte's Web*, *Spider-Man* and *Shrek*.

HarperFestival (imprint)

Books, novelties and merchandise for children aged 0–6. Classic board books include *Goodnight Moon* and *Runaway Bunny*.

HarperTeen (imprint)

Books that reflect teen readers' own lives: their everyday realities and aspirations, struggles and triumphs. From topical contemporary novels to lighthearted series books, to literary tales. Authors include Meg Cabot, Walter Dean Myers, Louise Rennison, Chris Crutcher and Joyce Carol Oates.

HarperTrophy (imprint)

Children's books. Authors and illustrators include picture books by Maurice Sendak, *I Can Read* books by Arnold Lobel, novels by Laura Ingalls Wilder, E.B. White, Katherine Paterson and Beverly Cleary.

Rayo (imprint)

Culturally inspired Spanish, English and bilingual books, as well as translations of award-winning and highly popular English titles. The list celebrates the rich Latino heritage.

Katherine Tegen Books (imprint)

Story books that entertain, inform, and capture the excitement, the joys, and the longings of life.

TOKYOPOP (imprint)

Manga titles based on existing HarperCollins works, as well as original manga titles conceived by HarperCollins authors.

Health Press NA Inc.

2920 Carlisle Boulevard NE, Albuquerque, NM 87110
tel 505-888-1394 *fax* 505-888-1521
email goodbooks@healthpress.com
website www.healthpress.com

Books for children and adults on a wide variety of medical conditions to meet the need for easy access to responsible, accurate patient education materials.

Submission details Not currently accepting new MSS submissions.

History Compass LLC

25 Leslie Road, Auburndale, MA 02466
tel 617-332-2202 *fax* 617-332-2210
email info@historycompass.com
website www.historycompass.com

The history of the USA presented through the study of primary source documents. Recent successes include *Get a Clue!* (grades 2–8) and *Adventures in History* series (grades 4–8). Other series include *Perspectives on History* (grades 5–12+) and *Researching American History* (8–15 year-olds and ESL students). Also historical fiction for younger readers. Founded 1990.

Holiday House Inc.

425 Madison Avenue, New York, NY 10017
tel 212-688-0085 *fax* 212-421-6134
email info@holidayhouse.com
website www.holidayhouse.com
Vice President/Editor-in-Chief Mary Cash

General. Publishes 35 picture books, 10 young reader, 15 middle reader and 8 young adult titles each year. Recent successes include *Lafayette and the American Revolution* by Russell Freedman. Approx. 20% of books are by first-time authors.

Submission details Send entire MS. Only responds to projects of interest. Will review MS/illustration packages from artists: send MS with dummy and colour photocopies.

Henry Holt and Company LLC*

175 Fifth Avenue, New York, NY 10010
tel 646-307-5095 *fax* 212-633-0748
website www.henryholt.com, www.henryholtkids.com
Vice President and Publisher Laura Godwin

Books for young readers. Publishes 20–40 picture books, 4–6 chapter books, 10–15 middle-grade titles and 8–10 young adult titles each year. Founded 1866.

Submission details Approx. 15% of books are by first-time authors. Children's submissions: send full MS to submissions. No sase, publisher will respond only if interested. For illustrations: send samples to Patrick Collins, Creative Director.

Houghton Mifflin Harcourt*

222 Berkeley Street, Boston, MA 02116
tel 617-351-5000
website www.hmhco.com

Textbooks, instructional technology assessments, and other educational materials for teachers and students of all ages; also reference, and fiction and non-fiction for adults and young readers. Founded 1832.

Houghton Mifflin Books for Children (imprint)
222 Berkeley Street, Boston, MA 02116-3764
tel 617-351-5000 *fax* 617-351-1111
website www.hmhbooks.com
Associate Editor Erica Zappy, *Managing Editor* Ann-Marie Pucillo, *Creative Director* Sheila Smallwood
Fiction and non-fiction for all ages. Recent successes include *Actual Size* written and illustrated by Steve Jenkins and *Just Grace* by Charise Mericle Harper. Imprints: Clarion Books and Graphia.
Submission details For fiction, submit complete MS. For non-fiction, submit outline/synopsis and sample chapters. Responds within 4 months only if interested. For illustrations, query with samples (colour photocopies and tearsheets). Responds in 4 months.

Clarion Books (imprint)
215 Park Avenue South, New York, NY 10003
tel 212-420-5800 *fax* 212-420-5850
Vice-President & Associate Publisher, Clarion Books Dinah Stevenson
Board books, picture books, biographies, non-fiction, fiction, poetry and fairy tales for ages 5–15. Recent successes include *Flotsam* by David Wiesner. Founded 1965.
Submission details For fiction and picture books, send complete MSS. For non-fiction, send query with up to 3 sample chapters.

Graphia (imprint)
222 Berkeley Street, Boston, MA 02116-3764
tel 617-351-5000 *fax* 617-351-1111
Fiction and non-fiction for young adults, including poetry and graphic novels. Recent successes include *I Can't Tell You* by Hillary Frank and *Kid B* by Linden Dalecki.

Hunter House Publishers
PO Box 2914, Alameda, CA 94501–0914
tel 510-865-5282 *fax* 510-865-4295
email acquisitions@hunterhouse.com
website www.hunterhouse.com

Non-fiction books on physical, mental, and emotional health, including sexuality and relationships for adults, books for teens, and life skills and activity books for teachers. Recent successes include *The Highly Intuitive Child* and *101 More Drama Games for Children*. Founded 1978.

Hyperion Books for Children
114 Fifth Avenue, New York, NY 10010–5690
tel 212-633-4400 *fax* 212-633-4833
website www.hyperionbooks.com

Board and novelty books, picture books, young readers, middle grade, young adult, non-fiction (all subjects at all levels). Recent successes include *Don't Let the Pigeon Drive the Bus*, written and ilustrated by Mo Willems, *Dumpy The Dump Truck* series by Julie Andrews Edwards and Emma Walton Hamilton (ages 3–7) and *Artemis Fowl* by Eoin Colfer (young adult novel, *New York Times* bestseller). Imprints include Michael di Capua Books, Jump at the Sun, Volo. Founded 1991.
Submission details Approx. 10% of books are by first-time authors. Only interested in submissions via literary agents. For illustrations, send résumé, business card, promotional literature or tearsheets to be kept on file to Anne Diebel, Art Director.

Ideals Publications LLC
2630 Elm Hill Pike, Suite 100, Nashville, TN 37214
website www.idealsbooks.com

Picture books and board books for young children. Imprints: Candy Cane Press, GP Kids, Guideposts Books, Ideals Children's Books, Ideals Press, Ideals Interactive, Williamson Books. See website for submission guidelines. A Guideposts company.

Illumination Arts Publishing
PO Box 1865, Bellevue, WA 98009
tel 425-968-5097
email liteinfo@illumin.com
website www.illumin.com
Editorial Director Ruth Thompson

Picture books. 'Books to inspire the mind, touch the heart and uplift the spirit.' Successes include *All I See is Part of Me*. Founded 1987.
Submission details Length: 300–1,500 words.

Impact Publishers Inc.*
PO Box 6016, Atascadero, CA 93423–6016
tel 805-466-5917 *fax* 805-466-5919
email info@impactpublishers.com
website www.impactpublishers.com

Psychology and self-improvement books and audio tapes for adults, children, families, organisations, and communities. Recent successes include *The Divorce Helpbook for Kids*, *The Divorce Helpbook for Teens* and *Jigsaw Puzzle Family* by Cynthia MacGregor and *Teen Esteem: A Self-Direction Manual for Young Adults* by Pat Palmer and Melissa Alberti Froehner. Founded 1970.
Submission details Only publishes books which serve human development. Written by highly respected psychologists and other human service professionals. See website for guidelines.

Incentive Publications Inc.
2400 Crestmoor Road, Suite 211, Nashville, TN 37215
tel 615-385-2967
website www.incentivepublications.com
President Blake Parker

Supplemental resources for educators and students. Founded 1969.

Submission details Send a letter of introduction, table of contents, a sample chapter, and sase for return of material.

innovativeKids
18 Ann Street, Norwalk, CT 06854
tel 203-838-6400 *fax* 203-855-5582
email info@innovativekids.com
website www.innovativekids.com

Beginning reader books, activity books, infant/toddler books, preschool books and games, and science learning tools in a wide range of themes and subjects. Recent successes include *A Kid's Guide to Giving*, *Phonics Comics* series, *Groovy Tube* series and *iBaby* series. Founded 1999.

Just Us Books, Inc.
356 Glenwood Avenue East Orange, NJ 07017
tel 973-672-7701 *fax* 973-677-7570
email info@justusbooks.com
website www.justusbooks.com
Publisher Cheryl Willis Hudson

'Publishers of Black-interest books for young people,' including preschool materials, picture books, biographies, chapter books, young adult fiction. Focuses on Black history, Black culture and Black experiences. Founded 1988.
Submission details Currently accepting queries for young adult titles, targeted to 13–16 year-old readers. Work should contain realistic, contemporary characters, compelling plot lines that introduce conflict and resolution, and cultural authenticity. Also considers MSS for picture books and middle reader chapter books. Send a query letter, 1–2pp synopsis, a brief author biog that includes any previously published work, plus a sase.

Kaeden Books
PO Box 16190, Rocky River, OH 44116
tel 1800-890-7323 *fax* 440-617-1403
email info@kaeden.com
website www.kaeden.com

Educational publisher specialising in early literacy books and beginning chapter books. Founded 1986.
Submission details Seeking beginning chapter books and unique non-fiction MSS (25–2,000 words). Vocabulary and sentence structure must be appropriate for young readers. No sentence fragments. See website for complete guidelines.

Accepts samples of all styles of illustration but is primarily looking for samples that match the often humorous style appropriate for juvenile literature. Send samples, no larger than 8.5 x 11ins to keep on file.

Kar-Ben Publishing – see Lerner Publishing Group

KidHave Press – see Gale Cengage Learning

Kingfisher – see Houghton Mifflin Harcourt

Klutz – see Scholastic Inc.

Alfred A. Knopf Books for Young Readers – see Random House Inc.

Knopf Trade – see Random House Inc.

Wendy Lamb Books – see Random House Inc.

Laurel-Leaf Books – see Random House Inc.

LB Kids – see Little, Brown & Company

Lee & Low Books, Inc.
95 Madison Avenue, Suite 606, New York, NY 10016
tel 212-779-4400 *fax* 212-683-1894
email general@leeandlow.com
website www.leeandlow.com
Vice President/Editorial Director Louise May, *Associate Editor* Emily Hazel

Children's book publisher specialising multicultural literature that is relevant to young readers. The company's goal is 'to meet the need for stories that children of colour can identify with and that all children can enjoy and which promote a greater understanding of one another'.
Focuses on fiction and non-fiction for children aged 5–12 which feature children/people of colour. Of special interest are realistic fiction, historical fiction, and non-fiction with a distinct voice or unique approach. Does not consider folktales or animal stories.
Submission details MSS should be no longer 1,500 words for fiction and 3,000 words for non-fiction. Send MSS with a covering letter that includes a brief biography of the author, including publishing history, and stating if the MS is a simultaneous or an exclusive submission. No submissions via email. Writer will be contacted within 6 months if interested. Makes a special effort to work with artists of colour. Founded 1991.

Lerner Publishing Group
241 First Avenue North, Minneapolis, MN 55401–1607
tel 612-332-3344 *fax* 612-332-7615
email info@lernerbooks.com
website www.lernerbooks.com
Publisher Adam Lerner

Independent publisher of high-quality children's books for K–12 schools and libraries: picture books, fiction for 5–8 and 9–12 year-olds, teenage fiction, series fiction and non-fiction. Subjects include biography, social studies, science, sports and curriculum. Publishes approx. 200 titles each year and has about 1,500 in print. Founded 1959.
Submission details No unsolicited submissions for any imprint.

Carolrhoda Books (imprint)
website www.carolrhodabooks.com
Picture books aimed at 5–8 year-olds; longer fiction for age 7+, including chapter books and middle-grade and young adult novels; biographies. Authors and illustrators include Nancy Carlson and Jan Wahl. Recent successes include *Almost to Freedom* by Vaunda Micheaux Nelson, illustrated by Colin Bootman. Founded 1969.

Darby Creek Publishing (imprint)
High-interest, creative non-fiction and fiction titles for grades K–8.

Kar-Ben Publishing (imprint)
website www.karben.com
Books on Jewish themes for children and families. Subjects include the High Holidays, Passover, Sukkot and Simchat Torah, Hanukkah, Purim, Selichot, Tu B'Shevat, crafts, cooking, folk tales, and contemporary stories, Jewish calendars, music, and activity books. Founded 1974.

LernerClassroom (imprint)
website www.lernerclassroom.com
Non-fiction books and teaching guides for grades K–8 in social studies, science, reading/literacy and mathematics. Books are paired with teaching guides that are correlated to national and state standards.

Millbrook Press (imprint)
Maths, science, American history, social studies and biography for a younger age bracket.

Twenty-First Century Books (imprint)
Maths, science, American history, social studies and biography for Secondary school age bracket.

Arthur A. Levine Books – see Scholastic Inc.

Little, Brown & Company
1271 Avenue of the Americas, New York, NY 10020
tel 212-522-8700 *fax* 212-522-2067
email publicity@littlebrown.com
website www.hachettebookgroup.com

General literature, fiction, non-fiction, biography, history, trade paperbacks, children's. Founded 1837.

Little, Brown Books for Young Readers
website www.lb-kids.com, www.lb-teens.com
Publisher Megan Tingley, *Creative Director* Gail Doobinin
Picture books, board books, chapter books, novelty books and general non-fiction and novels for middle-grade and young adult readers.
   Recent successes include *The Gulps* by Rosemary Wells, illustrated by Marc Brown, *The Gift of Nothing* by Patrick McDonnell; *Chowder* by Peter Brown, *How to Train Your Dragon* by Cressida Cowell, *Atherton* by Patrick Carman, *Nothing But the Truth (and a Few White Lies)* by Justina Chen Headley,

Story of a Girl by Sara Zarr, *Eclipse* by Stephenie Meyer, *America Dreaming* by Laban Carrick Hill, and *Exploratopia* by The Exploratorium. Publishes approx. 1,135 books a year.
   Submission details Only interested in solicited agented material. Does not accept unsolicited MSS or unagented material. For illustrations, query Art Director with b&w and colour samples; provide résumé, promotional sheet or tearsheets to be kept on file. Does not respond to art samples. Do not send originals; copies only.

LB Kids (imprint)
Novelty and brand/licensed books focusing on interactive formats, licensed properties, media tie-ins, and baby and toddler-focused projects. Authors/artists include Sandra Magsamen, Rachel Hale and Ed Emberley.

Poppy (imprint)
Series for teenage girls, including *Gossip Girl* and *The It Girl*, *The Clique* and *The A-List*.

Llewellyn Worldwide – see Flux Books/ Llewellyn Worldwide

Lucent Books – see Gale Cengage Learning

Luna Rising – see Cooper Square Publishing

Margaret K. McElderry Books – see Simon & Schuster Children's Publishing Division

McGraw-Hill Professional*
2 Penn Plaza, 12th Floor, New York, NY 10121
tel 212-904-2000
website www.mhprofessional.com, www.mgeducation.com

Marshall Cavendish Benchmark
Marshall Cavendish Corporation,
99 White Plains Road, Tarrytown, NY 10591
tel 914-332-8888 *fax* 914-332-1082
email customerservice@marshallcavendish.com
website www.marshallcavendish.us

Non-fiction books for young, middle and young adult readers. Subjects include readers, American studies, the arts, biographies, health, mathematics, science, social studies, history, world cultures. Imprint of Marshall Cavendish Corporation.
   Submission details Non-fiction subjects should be curriculum-related and are published in series form. Length: 1,500–25,000 words. Send synopsis with one or more sample chapters and sample table of contents.

Marshall Cavendish Children's Books
Marshall Cavendish Corporation,
99 White Plains Road, Tarrytown, NY 10591
tel 914-332-8888 *fax* 914-332-1082

email customerservice@marshallcavendish.com
website www.marshallcavendish.us/kids

Picture books and novels for middle grade and teens. Send manuscripts to Margery Cuyler. Does not accept submissions via email. Imprint of Marshall Cavendish Corporation.

Milet Publishing, LLC

814 North Franklin Street, Chicago, IL 60610
email info@milet.com
website www.milet.com

Picture books in English; bilingual picture books; adventurous and international young fiction; language learning books.
Submission details Not currently accepting new submissions.

Milkweed Editions

1011 Washington Avenue South, Suite 300, Minneapolis, MN 55415
tel 612-332-3192 *fax* 612-215-2550
email editor@milkweed.org
website www.milkweed.org
Publisher Daniel Slager

Children's novels (ages 8–13). Recent successes include *Perfect* (contemporary) and *Trudy* (contemporary). For adults: literary fiction, non-fiction, books about the natural world, poetry. Founded 1979.
Submission details Full length novels of 90–200pp. No picture books or poetry collections for young readers. Submit complete MS. Responds in 6 months. Will consider simultaneous submissions.

Millbrook Press – see Lerner Publishing Group

MINX – see DC Comics

Mitchell Lane Publishers, Inc.

PO Box 196, Hockessin, DE 19707
tel 302-234-9426 *fax* 866-834-4164
email customerservice@mitchelllane.com
website www.mitchelllane.com
President Barbara Mitchell

Non-fiction for young readers, middle readers and young adults. Recent successes include *Art Profiles for Kids* series (middle-grade readers) and *Crisis in the Environment*.

Mondo Publishing*

980 Avenue of the Americas, New York, NY 10018
tel 888-886-6636 *fax* 888-532-4492
email info@mondopub.com
website www.mondopub.com

Classroom materials and professional development for K–5 educators.

Morgan Reynolds Publishing

620 South Elm Street, Suite 223, Greensboro, NC 27406

tel 1800-535-1504 *fax* 1800-535-5725
email editorial@morganreynolds.com
website www.morganreynolds.com

Biographies for juveniles and young adults. Recent successes include *Elizabeth I of England in the European Queens* series and *Ulysses S. Grant: Defender of the Union in the Civil War Generals* series. Founded 1993.
Submission details MSS of 25,000–30,000 words, with 8–10 chapters of 2,500–3,000 words each. See website for submission guidelines.

Thomas Nelson Publisher

PO Box 141000, Nashville, TN 37214
tel 800-251-4000
email publicity@thomasnelson.com
website www.thomasnelson.com
President and Ceo Michael Hyatt

Bibles, religious, non-fiction and fiction general trade books for adults and children. Founded 1798.

North–South Books

Ingram Publisher Services, One Ingram Boulevard, PO Box 3006, La Vergne, TN 37086–1986
tel 866-400-5351
website www.northsouth.com

Recent successes include *The Rainbow Fish* by Marcus Pfister and *Little Polar* by Hans de Beer. Publishes 100 titles a year. Imprint: Night Sky.
Submission details Not accepting queries or unsolicited MSS at this time.

NorthWord Books for Young Readers – see Cooper Square Publishing

The Oliver Press, Inc.

Charlotte Square, 5707 West 36th Street, Minneapolis, MN 55416–2510
tel 952-926-8981 *fax* 952-926-8965
email orders@oliverpress.com
website www.oliverpress.com

Non-fiction for young adults: history, biography, science. Curriculum-based series include *Profiles, Great Decisions, Innovators, Shaping America, Business Builders, In the Cabinet* and *Looking at Europe*. Clara House (division): books for younger readers on how things work.
Submission details Interested in receiving proposals that fit into an established series. Submit proposal, a résumé of previously published works and any applicable education or experience together with a writing sample similar to the reading level, style and subject to the book that is being proposed. No unsolicited MSS.

Orchard Books – see Scholastic Inc.

The Overlook Press*

141 Wooster Street, New York, New York 10012
tel 212-673-2210 *fax* 212-673-2296

website www.overlookpress.com
President & Publisher Peter Mayer

Non-fiction, fiction, children's books (*Freddy the Pig* series). Imprints: Ardis Publishing, Duckworth, Rookery Press. Founded 1971.

Richard C. Owen Publishers, Inc.

PO Box 585, Katonah, NY 10536
tel 800-262-0787 *fax* 914-232-3977
website www.rcowen.com
Contact Children's Book Editor

Books for grades K–8. Subjects include science, history and folktales.

Submission details All work must be submitted as hard copy. Books for Young Learners: Seeks high-interest stories with charm and appeal that 5–7 year-olds can read by themselves. Interested in original, realistic, contemporary stories, as well as folktales, legends, and myths of all cultures. Non-fiction content must be supported with accurate facts. Length: 45–1,000 words. Also beginning chapter books up to 3,000 words.

Oxford University Press*

198 Madison Avenue, New York, NY 10016
tel 212-726-6000 *fax* 919-677-1303
website www.oup.com/us
President Tim Barton

Fiction and non-fiction for children of all ages, including young adult. Subjects include art, biography and memoirs, history, literature, music, myths and fairy tales, poetry, reference, science, reference. Adults: all subjects, from agriculture to sociology.

Pacific View Press

PO Box 2897, Berkeley, CA 94702
tel 415-285-8538 *fax* 510-843-5835
email nancy@pacificviewpress.com
website www.pacificviewpress.com

Multicultural children's books, Traditional Chinese Medicine, Asia and Asian–American affairs.

Dragon Books (imprint)

Multicultural non-fiction and literature for children focusing on the culture and history of China, Japan, the Philippines, Mexico, and other countries on the Pacific Rim. Books are intended to encourage pride in and respect for the shared history that makes a people unique, as well as an awareness of universal human experiences. Recent successes include *Cloud Weavers: Ancient Chinese Legends* by Rena Krasno and Yeng-Fong Chiang and *Exploring Chinatown: A Children's Guide to Chinese Culture* by Carol Stepanchuk, illustrated by Leland Wong. Founded 1992.

Parragon Publishing

440 Park Avenue South, 13th Floor, New York, NY 10016

tel 212-629-9773 *fax* 212-629-9756
email info_northamerica@parragon.com
website www.parragon.com

Children's non-fiction books of all kinds, from activity to reference. Adult titles include cookbooks, lifestyle, gardening, history.

Peachtree Publishers

1700 Chattahoochee Avenue, Atlanta, GA 30318–2112
tel 404-876-8761 *fax* 404-875-2578
email hello@peachtree-online.com
website www.peachtree-online.com
President & Publisher Margaret Quinlin, *Submissions Editor* Helen Harriss

Specialises in children's books, from picture books to young adult fiction and non-fiction. Publishes 30–35 titles each year. Recent successes include *Dad, Jackie and Me* by Myron Uhlberg and Colin Bootman. No adult fiction. Founded 1977.

Submission details For children's picture books, send complete MSS; for all others, send query letter with 3 sample chapters and table of contents to Helen Harriss with sase for response and/or return of material. For illustrations, query with samples, résumé, slides, colour photocopies to keep on file. Samples returned with sase.

Pearson Education*

One Lake Street, Upper Saddle River, NJ 07458
tel 201-236-7000 *fax* 201-236-6549
email communications@pearsoned.com
website www.phschool.com, www.pearsoned.com

Educational secondary publisher of scientifically researched and standards-based instruction materials for today's Grade 6–12 classrooms with a mission is to create exceptional educational tools that ensure student and teacher success in language arts, mathematics, modern and classical languages, science, social studies, career and technology, and advanced placement, electives, and honors. Part of the Curriculum Division of Pearson Education, Inc.

Pearson Scott Foresman

One Lake Street, Upper Saddle River, NJ 07458
tel 201-236-7000 *fax* 201-236-6549
website www.pearsonschool.com

Elementary educational publisher. Teacher and student materials: reading, science, mathematics, language arts, social studies, music, technology, religion. Its educational resources and services include textbook-based instructional programmes, curriculum websites, digital media, assessment materials and professional development. Part of the Curriculum Division of Pearson Education Inc. Founded 1896.

Pelican Publishing Company*

1000 Burmaster Street, Gretna, LA 70053
tel 504-368-1175 *fax* 504-368-1195

Books

email editorial@pelicanpub.com
website www.pelicanpub.com
Publisher/President Milburn Calhoun

Children's books. Also travel guides, art and architecture books, biographies, holiday books, local and international cookbooks, motivational and inspirational works, social commentary, history.

Submission details Send a query letter and sase. No queries or submissions by email. No unsolicited MSS. Most young children's books are 32 illustrated pages when published; their MSS cover about 4pp when typed continuously. Proposed books for middle readers (ages 8+) should be at least 90pp. Brief books for readers under 9 may be submitted in their entirety. Founded 1926.

Penguin Group (USA), Inc.*

375 Hudson Street, New York, NY10014
tel 212-366-2000
email online@penguingroup.com
website www.us.penguingroup.com
President Susan Petersen Kennedy, *Ceo* David Shanks

Consumer books in both hardcover and paperback for adults and children; also maps, calendars, audiobooks and mass merchandise products.

Adult imprints: Ace Books, Alpha Books, Avery, Berkley Books, Dutton, Amy Einhorn Books/Putnam, Gotham Books, HP Books, Hudson Street Press, Jove, New American Library, Penguin, Penguin Classics, The Penguin Press, Perigee Books, Plume, Portfolio, Prentice Hall Press, G.P. Putnam's Sons, Riverhead, Sentinel, Signet Classics, Jeremy P. Tarcher, Viking.

Penguin Books for Young Readers (division)

Children's picture books, board and novelty books, young adult novels, mass merchandise products. Imprints: Dial Books for Young Readers, Dutton Children's Books, Firebird, Grosset & Dunlap, Philomel, Price Stern Sloan, Puffin Books, G.P. Putnam's Sons Books for Young Readers, Razorbill, Speak, Viking Children's Books, Frederick Warne. Founded 1996.

Dial Books for Young Readers (imprint)

President & Publisher Lauri Hornik

Children's fiction and non-fiction, picture books, board books, interactive books, novels. Publishes 35 picture books, 3 young reader titles, 6 middle reader titles and 9 young adult titles each year. Recent successes include *A Year Down Yonder* by Richard Peck (fiction, age 10+), *The Sea Chest* by Toni Buzzeo, illustrated by Mary Grand (fiction picture book, all ages), *A Strong Right Arm* by Michelle Y. Green (non-fiction, age 10+) and *Dirt on Their Skirts* by Doreen Rappaport and Lyndall Callan (non-fiction picture book, ages 4–8).

Submission details For picture books, send MSS. For longer works, query with no more than 10pp of MSS. Responds in 4 months. Send sase. No email queries. For illustrations, send samples with sase to Design Dept.

Dutton Children's Books (imprint)

President & Publisher Stephanie Owens Lurie

Picture books, young adult novels, non-fiction photographic books. Publishes 50% fiction, mostly young adult and middle-grade. Recent successes include *Leonard: Beautiful Dreamer* by Robert Byrd (non-fiction), *The Boy Who Spoke Dog* by Clay Morgan (middle-grade fiction), *Skippyjon Jones* by Judy Schachner (picture book) and *PREP* by Jake Coburn (young adult fiction). Founded 1852.

Submission details Approx. 10% of books are by first-time authors. No unsolicited MSS. Send query letter only; responds in 3 months. For illustrations, query with samples. Samples returned with sase.

Firebird (imprint)

Editorial Director Sharyn November

Science fiction and fantasy for teenagers and adults. Founded 2002.

Grosset & Dunlap (imprint)

Children's picture books, activity books, fiction and non-fiction. Publishes 175 books each year. Recent successes include *Zenda* (series) and *Strawberry Shortcake* (licence). Imprints: Grosset & Dunlap, Platt & Munk, Somerville House USA, Planet Dexter. Founded 1898.

Submission details Only interested in material via literary agent.

Philomel (imprint)

President & Publisher Michael Green

Fiction and non-fiction for all ages. Publishes 18 picture books, 2 middle-grade books, 2 young readers and 4 young adult books each year. Founded 1980.

Submission details Approx. 5% of books are by first-time authors. No unsolicited MSS. Fiction length: picture books – 1,000 words; young readers – 1,500 words; middle readers – 14,000 words; young adult – 20,000 words. Non-fiction length: picture books – 2,000 words; young readers – 3,000 words; middle readers – 10,000 words. For illustrations, query with samples: send résumé and tearsheets. Responds in one month. Samples returned with sase.

Price Stern Sloan (imprint)

Children's novelty/lift-flap books, activity books, picture books, middle-grade fiction, middle-grade and young adult non-fiction, graphic readers, books plus. Recent successes include *Inside the Little Old Woman's Shoe* by Chuck Reasoner, *Fear Factor Mad Libs* and *Elf*. Founded 1963.

Submission details No unsolicited MSS. Send query; responds in 3 weeks.

Puffin Books (imprint)

Publisher Eileen Bishop Kreit

Picture books, fiction for 5–8 and 9–12 year-olds, teenage fiction, series fiction and film/TV tie-ins. Publishes approx. 175–200 titles each year. Recent successes include *Rules of the Road* by Joan Bauer,

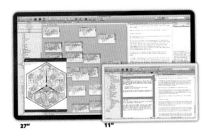

A Long Way from Chicago by Richard Peck and *26 Fairmount Avenue* by Tomie dePaola. Imprints: Firebird, Sleuth, Speak. Founded 1941.

Submission details Approx. 1% of books are by first-time authors. Will consider unsolicited MSS for novels only. Send with sase to Submissions Editor. Seeking to publish mysteries.

G.P. Putnam's Sons Books for Young Readers (imprint)
President & Publisher Nancy Paulsen

Children's hardcover and paperback books. Recent successes include *Fat Kid Rules the World* by K.L. Going (ages 12+), *Locomotion* by Jacqueline Woodson and *Atlantic* by G. Brian Karas (ages 4–8, non-fiction). Founded 1838.

Submission details For fiction, query with outline/synopsis and 1–3 sample chapters. Fiction length: picture books – 200–1,000 words; middle readers – 10,000–30,000 words; young adult – 40,000–50,000 words. For non-fiction, query with outline/synopsis, 1–2 sample chapters and table of contents. Non-fiction length: picture books – 200–1,500 words. Responds to queries in 3 weeks and to MS in 2 months. Write for illustrator guidelines.

Razorbill (imprint)
President & Publisher Ben Schrank

Young adult and middle-grade fiction and non-fiction.

Speak (imprint)
Publisher Eileen Bishop Kreit

Fiction for teenagers. Founded 2002.

Viking Children's Books (imprint)
Publisher Regina Hayes

Fiction, non-fiction and picture books for preschool–young adult. Publishes 70 books each year. Recent successes include *Strange Mr Satie* by M.T. Anderson (ages 5–8, picture book), *Restless* by Richard Wallace (ages 12) fiction, and *Open Your Eyes: Extraordinary Experiences in Far Away Places* (ages 12+, non-fiction). Founded 1925.

Submission details Approx. 25% of books are by first-time authors; receives 7,500 queries a year. No unsolicited MSS. Responds to artists' queries/submissions only if interested. Samples returned with sase.

Frederick Warne (imprint)
Managing Director Stephanie Barton

Original publisher of Beatrix Potter's *Tales of Peter Rabbit*. Founded 1865.

Philomel – see Penguin Group (USA), Inc.

Poppy – see Little, Brown & Company

Mathew Price Ltd
12300 Ford Street, Suite 455, Dallas, TX 75234
tel 972-484-0500

email info@mathewprice.com
UK Office Albury Court, Albury, Thame, Oxon OX9 2LP
tel (01844) 337000 *fax* (01844) 339938
email mathewp@mathewprice.com
website www.mathewprice.com
Chairman Mathew Price

Illustrated fiction and non-fiction children's books for all ages for the UK and international market. Specialist in flap, pop-up, paper-engineered titles as well as conventional books. Unsolicited MSS accepted only by email. Founded 1983.

Price Stern Sloan – see Penguin Group (USA), Inc.

Puffin Books – see Penguin Group (USA), Inc.

Simon Pulse Paperback Books – see Simon & Schuster Children's Publishing Division

Random House Inc.*
1745 Broadway, 10th Floor, New York, NY 10019
tel 212-782-9000 *fax* 212-302-7985
website www.randomhouse.com
Chairman/Ceo Markus Dohle

General fiction and non-fiction, children's books. Subsidiary of Bertelsmann AG.

Random House Children's Books (division)
website www.randomhouse.com/kids, www.randomhouse.com/teens

Board books, activity books, picture books, novels for preschool children through to young adult. Divisions: Kids@Random (RH Children's Books), Golden Books.

Knopf Delacorte Dell Young Readers Group
Editorial division of Random House Children's Books, incorporating Bantam Books, Beginner Books, Robin Corey, Crown Books, Delacorte Press Books for Young Readers, Doubleday Books for Young Readers, Dragonfly Books, David Fickling Books, First Time Books, Golden Books, Alfred A. Knopf Books for Young Readers, Landmark Books, Wendy Lamb Books, Laurel-Leaf Books, Picturebacks, Schwartz & Wade Books, Stepping Stone Books, Yearling Books.

Bantam Books (imprint)
website www.randomhouse.com/kids

Commercial paperbacks. Focus on TV and film. Not seeking new MSS at present.

Crown Books (imprint)
Juvenile fiction and non-fiction for ages 0–18.
Submission details Send query letter with sase to Acquisitions Editor.

Delacorte Press Books for Young Readers (imprint)
Literary and commercial novels for middle-grade and young adult readers, and educational/general interest

non-fiction. Authors include David Almond, Ann Brashares, Libba Bray, Caroline Cooney, Robert Cormier, Lurlene McDaniel, Phyllis Reynolds Naylor, Joan Lowery Nixon, Louis Sachar, Zilpha Keatley Snyder and R.L. Stine.

Submission details Approx. 90% of books are published via literary agents.

Doubleday Books for Young Readers (imprint)

Picture books for young readers and gift books for all ages.

Submission details Approx. 90% of books are published via literary agents.

Dragonfly Books (imprint)

Paperback picture books, ranging from concept picture books to read-together stories to books for newly independent readers.

David Fickling Books (imprint)

The first bicontinental children's book publisher. Publishes 12 books a year, all of which are chosen and edited in the UK.

Alfred A. Knopf Books for Young Readers (imprint)

Fiction and non-fiction for ages 0–18, from board books to novels to non-fiction. Authors and illustrators include Marc Brown, Robert Cormier, Leo and Diane Dillon, Carl Hiaasen, Leo Lionni, Christopher Paolini, Philip Pullman, Eric Rohmann, Judy Sierra and Jerry Spinelli.

Submission details Send query letter with sase to Acquisitions Editor.

Knopf Trade (imprint)

Paperback editions of middle-grade and young adult novels originally published in hardback by Alfred A. Knopf Books for Young Readers.

Wendy Lamb Books (imprint)

Acquisitions Wendy Lamb

Middle-grade and young adult fiction. Publishes 12 middle readers and young adult books each year. Authors include Christopher Paul Curtis, Peter Dickinson, Patricia Reilly Giff, Gary Paulsen, Meg Rosoff and Graham Salisbury. Founded 2002.

Submission details Approx. 15% of books are by first-time authors. Send query letter with sase and no more than 5pp (picture books) or 10pp (novels). Will review MS/illustrations packages from artists: query with sase for reply.

Laurel-Leaf Books (imprint)

Literature for teenagers, including reprints of contemporary and classic fiction, mystery, fantasy, romance, suspense, and non-fiction for ages 12+. Authors include Judy Blume, Caroline B. Cooney, Robert Cormier, Lois Duncan, S.E. Hinton, Lois Lowry, Scott O'Dell, Gary Paulsen, Philip Pullman and Jerry Spinelli. Laurel-Leaf also features the Readers Circle publishing programme.

Schwartz & Wade Books (imprint)

Directors Anne Schwartz, Lee Wade

Picture books. Authors include Tad Hills, Ronnie Shotter and Valorie Fisher. Founded 2005.

Yearling Books (imprint)

Affordable paperback books for 8–12 year-olds: contemporary and historical fiction, fantasy, mystery and adventure. Authors include Judy Blume, Christopher Paul Curtis, Patricia Reilly Giff, Norton Juster, Madeleine L'Engle, Lois Lowry, Gary Paulsen, Philip Pullman and Louis Sachar.

Random House/Golden Books Young Readers Group

1745 Broadway, New York, NY 10019
tel 212-782-9000
website www.randomhouse.com/kids, www.randomhouse.com/golden
Editor-in-Chief of Random House Books for Young Readers Mallory Loehr

Editorial division of Random House Children's Books. Classic titles such as *Tootle* and *Scruffy the Tugboat*. Established 1942.

Random House Books for Young Readers (imprint)

Variety and 'value' books for ages 6 months to young adult. Books range from *The Story of Babar* (1933) and *Dr Seuss*, to *Magic Tree House* and the *Junie B. Jones* books, and the *Step Into Reading* series.

Submission details Approx. 2% of books are by first-time authors. No unsolicited MSS: reserves the right to not return unsolicited material. All acquisitions are made via literary agents.

Golden Books for Young Readers (imprint)

Children's classic titles, including *Tootle*, *The Saggy Baggy Elephant*, *Scuffy the Tugboat*, and *The Poky Little Puppy*.

Submission details Approx. 2% of books are by first-time authors. No unsolicited MSS: reserves the right to not return unsolicited material. All acquisitions are made via literary agents.

Disney Books for Young Readers (imprint)

Colouring and activity books, storybooks, novelty books and early readers based on Disney properties. Films include *Toy Story 2*, *The Little Mermaid*, *The Lion King*, *Atlantis*, *Monsters, Inc.*, and *Finding Nemo*. Founded 2001.

Random House Large Print (division)

Fiction and non-fiction in large print.

Rayo – see HarperCollins Publishers

Razorbill – see Penguin Group (USA), Inc.

Rising Moon – see Cooper Square Publishing

Roaring Brook Press

175 Fifth Avenue, New York, NY10010
tel 646-307-5151

website http://us.macmillan.com/RoaringBrook.aspx
Publisher Simon Broughton, *Editorial Director* Neal
Porter *Books* Neal Porter, *Executive Editor* Nancy
Mercado

Picture books, fiction (including graphic novels) and
non-fiction for young readers, from toddler to teen.
Publishes about 40 titles a year. Recent successes
include *My Friend Rabbit* by Eric Rohmann (2003
Caldecott Medal winner), *The Man Who Walked
Between the Towers* by Mordicai Gerstein (2004
Caldecott Medal winner) and *A Sick Day for Amos*
illustrated by Erin Stead (2011 Caldecott Medal
winner). Imprint: First Second Books. Division of
Holtzbrink Publishers.

Submission details Does not accept unsolicited MSS
or submissions.

Running Press Book Publishers
2300 Chestnut Street, Suite 200, Philadelphia,
PA 19103
tel 215-567-5080
email perseus.promos@perseusbooks.com
website www.perseusbooksgroup.com/runningpress
Publisher Chris Navratil, *Directors* Bill Jones (design),
Greg Jones (editorial), Joanne Cassetti (production),
Craig Herman (marketing)

General non-fiction, science, history, children's
fiction and non-fiction, food and wine, pop culture,
lifestyle, photo-essay, illustrated gift books. Imprints:
Running Press, Running Press Miniature Editions,
Running Press Kids, Courage Books. Member of the
Perseus Books Group. Founded 1972.

Running Press Kids (imprint)
Picture books, activity books, young adult fiction.
Recent successes include *Cathy's Key* by Sean Stewart
and Jordan Weisman.

Scholastic Education*
557 Broadway, New York, NY 10012
tel 212-343-6100 *fax* 212-343-6189
website www2.scholastic.com

Educational publisher of research-based core and
supplementary instructional materials. A leading
provider in reading improvement and professional
development products, as well as learning services
that address the needs of the developing reader –
from grades pre-K to high school.

Publishes 32 curriculum-based classroom
magazines used by teachers in grades pre-K–12 as
supplementary educational materials to raise
awareness about current events in an age-appropriate
manner and to help children develop reading skills.
Magazines include *Scholastic News®*, *Junior
Scholastic®*, *The New York Times Upfront®*, *Science
World®*, *Scope®* and others, covering subjects such
as English, maths, science, social studies, current
events, and foreign languages. The magazine's online
companion, *Scholastic News Online* is the leading
news source for students and teachers on the internet.

Scholastic Education has also developed
technology-based reading assessment and
management products to help administrators and
educators quickly and accurately assess student
reading levels, match students to the appropriate
books, predict how well they will do on district and
state standardised tests, and inform instruction to
improve reading skills.

Its wholly owned operations in Australia, Canada,
New Zealand and the UK have original trade and
educational publishing programmes. Division of
Scholastic Inc.

Scholastic Library Publishing (division)
90 Sherman Turnpike, Danbury, CT 06816
tel 203-797-3500
website www.scholastic.com
Editor-in-Chief Kate Nunn

Online and print publisher of reference products.
Major reference sets include *Encyclopedia
Americana®*, *The New Book of Knowledge®*, *Nueva
Enciclopedia Cumbre®*, *Lands and Peoples* and *The
New Book of Popular Science*.

Scholastic Inc.*
557 Broadway, New York, NY 10012
tel 212-343-6100
website www.scholastic.com
Editorial Director Elizabeth Szabla

Innovative textbooks, magazines, technology and
teacher materials for use in both school and the
home. Scholastic is a global children's publishing and
media company with a corporate mission to instill
the love of reading and learning for lifelong pleasure
in all children. Founded 1920.

Scholastic Trade Books, Children's Book Publishing
Award-winning publisher of original children's
books. Publishes over 500 new titles per year
including the branding publishing properties *Harry
Potter®* and *Captain Underpants®*, the series *Clifford
The Big Red Dog®*, *I Spy™*, and Scholastic's *The
Magic School Bus®*, as well as licensed properties such
as *Star Wars®* and *Scooby Doo™*. Imprints: Blue Sky
Press®, Michael di Capua Books, Cartwheel Books®,
The Chicken House™, Graffix, Arthur A. Levine
Books, Little Shepherd, Orchard Books®, Point,
PUSH, Scholastic Paperbacks, Scholastic Press and
Scholastic Reference™.

Blue Sky Press (imprint)
Hardcover fiction and non-fiction, including novels
and picture books. Publishes 15–20 titles a year.
Recent successes include *To Every Thing There is a
Season* illustrated by Leo and Diane Dillon (all ages,
picture book) and *How Do Dinosaurs Say Good
Night?* by Jane Yolen, illustrated by Mark Teague.

Submission details Approx. 1% of which are by
first-time authors. Not currently accepting
unsolicited submissions due to a large backlog of
books. For illustrations, query with samples or

tearsheets. Responds only if interested; samples only returned with sase.

Cartwheel Books (imprint)

Fiction and non-fiction for very young readers. Non-fiction is mostly written on assignment or is within a series. Publishes 25–30 picture books, 30–35 easy readers and 15–20 novelty books each year.

Submission details Submissions via literary agents only: send complete MSS. Will respond in 6 months. All unsolicited material will be returned unread. Length: 100–3,000 words (picture books, easy readers). For illustrations, send samples and tearsheets to the Art Director with sase.

Klutz

How-to books packaged with the tools of their trade (from juggling cubes to face paints to yo-yos). Includes an educational product line for pre K–Grade 4 children in maths, reading and general knowledge. Products are designed for doing, not just reading: 'We think people learn best through their hands, nose, feet, mouth and ears. Then their eyes. So we design multi-sensory books'.

Arthur A. Levine Books (imprint)

Fiction and non-fiction, including picture books and young adult titles. Recent successes include *How Are You Peeling? Foods with Moods* by Saxton Freymann and Joost Elffers. US publisher of Harry Potter titles. Founded 1996.

Submission details Send query letter only in first instance.

Orchard Books (imprint)

Picture books, fiction and poetry for children and fiction for young adults. Publishes approx. 50 books each year. Recent successes include *Stuart's Cape* by Sara Pennypacker, illustrated by Martin Matje and *Where Are You Going? To See My Friend!* by Eric Carle and Kazuo Iwamura (picture book).

Submission details Approx. 10% of books are by first-time authors. Send query letter only (responds in 3 months): no unsolicited MSS. For illustrations, send tearsheets or photocopies (not disks or slides). Responds in one month. Samples returned with sase.

Scholastic Press (imprint)

Picture books, fiction for 5–8 and 9–12 year-olds, teenage fiction, poetry, religion and non-fiction for 3 year-olds–teenage. Publishes approx. 35–50 titles each year. Recent successes include *A Corner of the Universe* by Ann M. Martin, *Gregor the Overlander* by Suzanne Collins, *Zen Shorts* by Jon J. Muth, and *Old Turtle and the Broken Truth* by Douglas Wood and Jon J. Muth.

Submission details Will not consider unsolicited MSS. Send query letter or submit via an agent.

Schwartz & Wade Books – see Random House Inc.

Silver Moon Press

400 East 85th Street, New York, NY 10028
tel 800-874-3320 *fax* 212-988-8112
email customerservice@silvermoonpress.com
website www.silvermoonpress.com

Children's book publisher: test preparation, science, multiculture, biographies, historical fiction. Recent successes include *Stories of the States, Mysteries in Time* and *Adventures in America* series.

Simon & Schuster Children's Publishing Division*

1230 Avenue of the Americas, New York, NY 10020
tel 212-698-7200 *fax* 212-698-2793
website www.simonsayskids.com
Executive Publisher Jon Anderson, *Vice-President & Publisher* Valerie Garfield

Preschool to young adult, fiction and non-fiction, trade, library and mass market. Imprints: Aladdin Paperbacks, Atheneum Books for Young Readers, Libros para niños, Little Simon, Little Simon Inspirations, Margaret K. McElderry Books, Simon & Schuster Books for Young Readers, Simon Scribbles, Simon Pulse, Simon Spotlight. Division of Simon & Schuster, Inc. Founded 1924.

Aladdin Paperbacks (imprint)

Vice-President & Associate Publisher Ellen Krieger

Reprints successful hardcovers from other Simon & Schuster imprints (primarily). Recent successes include the *Pendragon* series and *Edgar & Ellen* series.

Submission details Accepts query letters with proposals for middle-grade series and single-title fiction, beginning readers, middle-grade and commercial non-fiction. Send MSS for the attention of the Submissions Editor. Send artwork submissions to Debra Sfetsios.

Atheneum Books for Young Readers (imprint)

Vice-President & Publisher Emma Dryden, *Editorial Director* Caitlyn Dlouhy

Picture books, chapter books, mysteries, biography, science fiction, fantasy, graphic novels, middle-grade and young adult fiction and non-fiction. Covers preschool–young adult. Publishes 20–30 picture books, 4–5 young readers, 20–25 middle readers and 10–15 young adult books each year. Successes include *Inexcusable* by Chris Lynch, *Once Upon a Time, the End (Asleep in 60 Seconds)* by Geoffrey Kloske and Barry Blitt, *Click Clack Quackity-Quack* by Doreen Cronin and Betsy Lewin, and *Kira-Kira* by Cynthia Kadohata. Includes Ginnee Seo Books and Richard Jackson Books.

Submission details Approx. 10% of books are by first-time authors. No unsolicited MSS. Send query letter only. Responds in one month. For illustrations, send résumé, samples and tearsheets to Ann Bobco, Design Dept.

Margaret K. McElderry Books (imprint)

Vice-President & Publisher Emma Dryden, *Executive Editor* Karen Wojtyla

Picture books, easy-to-read books, fiction (8–12 year-olds, young adult), poetry, fantasy. Covers preschool–young adult. Publishes 10–12 pciture books, 2–4 young reader titles, 8–10 middle reader titles, 5–7 young adult books each year. Recent successes include *Bear Stays Up for Christmas* by Karma Wilson and Jane Chapman, *The Water Mirror* by Kai Meyer, *Freaks* by Annette Curtis Klause, and *Where Did They Hide My Presents: Silly Dilly Christmas Songs* by Alan Katz and David Catrow.

Submission details Approx. 10% of books are by first-time authors. No unsolicited MSS. Fiction length: picture books – 500 words; young readers – 2,000; middle readers – 10,000–20,000; young adult – 45,000–50,000. Non-fiction length: picture books – 500–1,000 words; young readers – 1,500–3,000 words; middle readers – 10,000–20,000 words; young adult – 30,000–45,000 words. For illustrations, query with samples to Ann Bobco, Executive Art Director. Responds in 3 months. Samples returned with sase.

Simon Pulse Books (imprint)
Vice President & Publisher Bethany Buck, *Executive Editor* Jen Klonsky

Young adult series and fiction (primarily) and some reprints of successful hardcovers from other Simon & Schuster imprints. Recent successes include the *Uglies* trilogy by Scott Westerfield and the *Au Pair* books by Melissa de la Cruz.

Submission details Accepts query letters. Send MSS for the attention of the Submission Editor. Send artwork submissions to Russel Gordon.

Simon & Schuster Books for Young Readers (imprint)
Publisher Justin Chandu, *Editorial Director* David Gale, *Executive Editor* Kevin Lewis

Fiction and non-fiction, all ages. Recent successes include the *Pendragon* series including *The Rivers of Zadaa* by D.J. MacHale, *Arthur Spiderwick's Field Guide to the Fantastical World Around You* by Tony DiTerlizzi and Holly Black, and *And Tango Makes Three* by Pete Parnell, Justin Richardson and Henry Cole.

Submission details No unsolicited MSS. Send query letter only. Responds to queries in 2 months. Seeking young adult novels that are challenging and psychologically complex; also imaginative and humorous middle-grade fiction.

Paula Wiseman (imprint)
email paulawiseman@simonandschuster.com
Vice-President & Publisher Paula Wiseman

Picture books, fiction and non-fiction. Publishes 10 picture books, 2 middle readers and 2 young adult titles each year. Recent successes include *Double Pink* by Kate Feiffer and the *Amelia Notebook* series by Marissa Moss.

Submission details Approx. 10% of books are by first-time authors. Submit complete MSS. Length: picture books – 500 words; others standard length. Considers all categories of fiction. Will review MS/illustration packages from artists. Send MS with dummy.

Sleeping Bear Press – see page 46

Speak – see Penguin Group (USA), Inc.

StarScape – see Tom Doherty Associates, LLC

Sterling Publishing Co., Inc.
387 Park Avenue South, New York, NY 10016
tel 212-532-7160 *fax* 212-891-0508
email editorial@sterlingpublishing.com
website www.sterlingpublishing.com
President Marcus Leaver, *Vice-President/Editorial Director* Michael Fragnito

Adult non-fiction and children's board books, picture books and non-fiction. Subsidiary of Barnes & Noble. Founded in 1949.

Sterling Children's (imprint)
Non-fiction: crafts, hobbies, games, activities, origami, optical illusions, mazes, dot-to-dots, science experiments, puzzles (maths/word/picture/logic), chess, card games and tricks, sports, magic.

Submission details Non-fiction: Write explaining the idea and enclose an outline and a sample chapter. Include information and a résumé with regard to the subject area and your publishing history, and sase for return of your material. No email submissions. Send submissions FAO Children's Book Editor.

Sandy Creek (imprint)
Fiction and non-fiction for ages 0–14 including activity books, picture books, encyclopedias.

Flashkids (imprint)
Workbooks and flash cards for preschool, elementary, and middle school students.

Gareth Stevens Publishing
111 East 14th Street, Suite 349, New York, NY 10003
tel 800-542-2595 *fax* 877-542-2596
email customerservice@gspub.com
website www.garethstevens.com
Publisher Robert Famighetti

Educational books and high-quality fiction for 4–16 year-olds. Subjects include atlases and reference, arts and crafts, emergent readers, nature, science, maths, social studies, history and Spanish/bilingual. Publishes approx. 300 new titles each year and has over 1,000 in print. Part of Reader's Digest Association. Founded 1983.

Katherine Tegen Books – see HarperCollins Publishers

TOKYOPOP – see HarperCollins Publishers

Tor Books – see Tom Doherty Associates, LLC

Tricycle Press
PO Box 7123, Berkeley, CA 94707
tel 510-559-1600

website www.tricyclepress.com
President Philip Wood, *Publisher* Nicole Geiger

Children's picture books and board books, both fiction and non-fiction, and middle-grade novels. Subjects include life lessons and social skills, food and cooking, maths, science, nature, language arts, history, multiculturalism. Successes include *Hugging the Rock* by Susan Taylor Brown, *Mama's Milk* by Michel Elsohn Ross and illustrated by Ashley Wolff, *Where in the Wild* by David Schwartz and Yael Schy with photography by Dwight Kuhn. Founded 1993.

Twenty-first Century Books – see Millbrook Press

Two-Can – see Cooper Square Publishing

Viking Children's Books – see Penguin Group (USA), Inc.

VSP Books

PO Box 1723, Lorton, VA 22199
tel 800-441 1949 *fax* 703-684-7955
email mail@vspbooks.com
website www.vspbooks.com

Educational books for children about special and historic places. Recent successes include the *Mice Way to Learn* series and *Heartsongs* (poetry). Founded 1992.

Walker & Co.

175 Fifth Avenue, New York, NY 10010
tel 212-674-5151 *fax* 212-727-0984
website www.walkerbooks.com,
www.bloomsburykids.com
Publisher Emily Easton (children's), George Gibson (adult)

Picture books, non-fiction and fiction (middle grade and young adult). Publishes 20 picture books, 5–8 middle readers and 5–8 young adult books each year. Walker Books and Walker Books for Young Readers are imprints of Bloomsbury Publishing Plc (page 7).

Submission details Approx. 5% of books are by first-time authors. Approx. 65% of books are acquired via literary agents. Particularly interested in picture books, illustrated non-fiction, middle-grade and young adult fiction. No series ideas. Send 50–75pp and synopsis for longer works; send the entire MSS for picture books. Include sase for response only.

Weigl Publishers Inc.

350 5th Avenue, 59th Floor, New York, NY 10118
tel 866-649-3445 *fax* 866-449-3445
email linda@weigl.com
website www.weigl.com

Educational publisher: children's non-fiction titles. Recent successes include *The Backyard Animals* and *Learning to Write* series.

Albert Whitman & Company

250 South Northwest Highway, Suite 320,
Park Ridge, Illinois, IL 60068
tel 847-581-0033 *fax* 847-581-0039
email mail@awhitmanco.com
website www.albertwhitman.com

Books that respond to cultural diversity and the special needs and concerns of children and their families (e.g. divorce, bullying). Also novels for middle-grade readers, picture books and non-fiction for ages 2–12. Founded 1919.

Submission details Currently not seeking MSS for the *Boxcar Children® Mysteries* series. For picture books send complete MS; for longer works send a query letter with 3 sample chapters. Also interested in art samples showing pictures of children.

Paula Wiseman – see Simon & Schuster Children's Publishing Division

Wordsong – see Boyds Mills Press

Workman Publishing Company*

225 Varick Street, New York, NY 10014
tel 212-254-5900 *fax* 212-254-8098
email info@workman.com
website www.workman.com
Editor-in-chief Susan Bolotin

Popular non-fiction: business, cooking, gardening, gift books, health, how-to, humour, parenting, sport, travel. Founded 1968.

World Book, Inc.

233 North Michigan Avenue, Suite 2000, Chicago, IL 60601
tel 800-967-5325
website www.worldbook.com

Encyclopedias, reference sources, and multimedia products for the home and schools, including *World Book*. Recent publications include *World Book Student Discovery Encyclopedia*, a new *Childcraft – The How and Why Library* and *Animals of the World*. Founded 1917.

Yearling Books – see Random House Inc.

Yen Press

Hachette Book Group USA, 237 Park Avenue, New York, NY 10017
email yenpress@hbgusa.com
website www.yenpress.us

Graphic novels and manga in all formats for all ages. Division of Hachette Book Group USA. Founded 2006.

Children's audio publishers

Many of the audio publishers listed below are also publishers of books.

Abbey Home Media Group Ltd

435–437 Edgware Road, London W2 1TH
tel 020-7563 3910 *fax* 020-7563 3911
email emma.evans@abbeyhomemedia.com
Managing Director Anne Miles

Specialises in the acquisition, production and distribution of quality audio/visual entertainment for children. Best-selling children's spoken word and music titles are available on CD and cassette in the Tempo range including *Postman Pat*, *Watership Down*, *Michael Rosen*, *Baby Bright*, *Wide Eye*, *SuperTed* and *Golden Nursery Rhymes*.

Barefoot Books Ltd

124 Walcot Street, Bath BA1 5BG
tel (01225) 322400 *fax* (01225) 322499
email info@barefootbooks.co.uk
website www.barefootbooks.co.uk
Publisher Tessa Stickland, *Group Executive Editor* Emma Parkin

Narrative unabridged audiobooks, spoken and sung. Established 1993.

Barrington Stoke – see page 7

BBC Cover to Cover – see AudioGO Ltd

Bloomsbury Publishing Plc

50 Bedford Square, London WC1B 3DP
tel 020-7494 2111 *fax* 020-7734 8656
website www.bloomsbury.com
Contact Sarah Odedina

A broad selection of fiction and non-fiction. Baby books, picture books and fiction for children of all ages.

Chivers Children's Audiobooks – see AudioGO Ltd

Cló Iar-Chonnachta Teo.

Indreabhán, Conamara, Co. Galway, Republic of Ireland
tel (091) 593307 *fax* (091) 593362
email cic@iol.ie
website www.cic.ie
Ceo Micheál Ó Conghaile, *General Manager* Deirdre O'Toole

Predominantly Irish-language children's books with accompanying CD/cassette of stories/folklore/poetry. Established 1985.

CSA Word

6A Archway Mews, London SW15 2PE
tel 020-8871 0220 *fax* 020-8877 0712
email info@csaword.co.uk
website www.csaword.co.uk
Audio Director Victoria Williams

CDs of classic children's literature such as *Just William*, *Billy Bunter* and *Black Beauty*; also adult, classic and current literary authors. Founded 1991.

Dref Wen

28 Church Road, Whitchurch, Cardiff CF14 2EA
tel 029-2061 7860 *fax* 029-2061 0507
Directors Roger Boore, Anne Boore, Gwilym Boore, Alun Boore, Rhys Boore

Welsh language audiobooks. Founded 1970.

The Educational Company of Ireland

Ballymount Road, Walkinstown, Dublin 12, Republic of Ireland
tel (01) 4500611 *fax* (01) 4500993
email info@edco.ie
website www.edco.ie
Executive Directors Martina Harford (Chief Executive), Robert McLoughlin

Irish language CDs and audiotapes. Trading unit of Smurfit Kappa Group – Ireland. Founded 1910.

Hachette Children's

338 Euston Road, London NW1 3BH
tel 020-7873 6000 *fax* 020-7873 6024
website www.hodder.co.uk
Managing Director Marlene Johnson

Publishes outstanding authors from within the Hodder group as well as commissioning independent titles. The list includes fiction and non-fiction. Children's titles include *Winnie the Pooh*, *Wallace & Gromit* and the *Magic Roundabout Adventures*. Founded 1994.

HarperCollins Audio Books

77–85 Fulham Palace Road, London W6 8JB
tel 020-8741 7070 *fax* 020-8307 4440
website www.harpercollins.co.uk
Group Digital Director David Roth-Ey, *Director of Audio* Jo Forshaw

Publishers of a wide range of genres including fiction, non-fiction, poetry, Classics, Shakespeare, comedy, personal development and children's. All works are read by famous actors. Established 1990.

Ladybird Books

80 Strand, London WC2R 0RL
tel 020-7010 3000 *fax* 020-7010 6060
email ladybird@uk.penguingroup.com
website www.ladybird.co.uk
Marketing Director Rachel Partridge

Ladybird Books in book-and-CD format for children aged 0–8 years, including nursery rhymes, fairytales and classic stories as well as licensed character publishing.

Macmillan Digital Audio

20 New Wharf Road, London N1 9RR
tel 020-7014 6000 *fax* 020-7014 6001
email audiobooks@macmillan.co.uk
website www.panmacmillan.com
Digital Director Sara Lloyd

Children's titles include *The Gruffalo* by Julia Donaldson and Axel Scheffler. Also adult fiction, non-fiction and autobiography. Established 1995.

Naxos AudioBooks

40A High Street, Welwyn, Herts. AL6 9EQ
tel (01438) 717808 *fax* (01438) 717809
email info@naxosaudiobooks.com
website www.naxosaudiobooks.com
Managing Director Nicolas Soames

Classic literature, modern fiction, non-fiction, drama and poetry on CD. Also junior classics and classical music. Founded 1994.

The Orion Publishing Group Ltd

5 Upper St Martin's Lane, London WC2H 9EA
tel 020-7240 3444 *fax* 020-7240 4822
email salesinformation@orionbooks.co.uk
Audio Manager Pandora White

Adult and children's fiction and non-fiction. Established 1998.

Penguin Audiobooks

80 Strand, London WC2R 0RL
tel 020-7010 3000
email audiobooks@penguin.co.uk
website www.penguin.co.uk/audio
Audio Publisher Jeremy Ettinghausen

The audiobooks list reflects the diversity of the Penguin book range, including classic and contemporary fiction and non-fiction, autobiography, poetry, drama and, in Puffin Audiobooks, the best of contemporary and classic literature for younger listeners. Authors include Cathy Cassidy, Charlie Higson, Lauren Child, Roald Dahl and Eoin Colfer. Readings are by talented and recognisable actors. Over 300 titles are now available. Founded 1993.

Puffin Audiobooks – see Penguin Audiobooks

Random House Audio Books

20 Vauxhall Bridge Road, London SW1V 2SA
tel 020-7840 8400
email audioeditorial@randomhouse.co.uk
website www.randomhouse.co.uk/audio
Editorial Editor Zoe Willis

SmartPass Ltd

15 Park Road, Rottingdean, Brighton BN2 7HL
tel (01273) 300742
email info@smartpass.co.uk
website www.smartpass.co.uk,
www.spaudiobooks.com,
www.shakespeareappreciated.com
Managing Director Phil Viner, *Creative Director* Jools Viner

SmartPass audio education resources present unabridged plays, poetry and dramatisations of novels as guided full-cast dramas for individual study and classroom use. Student editions present the text with an explanatory commentary and teacher editions offer audio commentary options and CD-Rom classroom materials. Titles include *Macbeth, Romeo and Juliet, Twelfth Night, Henry V, Othello, King Lear, Hamlet, Julius Caesar, Shakespeare the Works, A Kestrel for a Knave, Animal Farm, An Inspector Calls, Great Expectations, The Mayor of Casterbridge, Pride and Prejudice, Classical Poetry* and *War Poetry*.

Usborne Publishing Ltd

Usborne House, 83–85 Saffron Hill, London EC1N 8RT
tel 020-7430 2800 *fax* 020-7636 3758
email mail@usborne.co.uk
website www.usborne.com
Publishing Director Jenny Tyler, *General Manager* Robert Jones

Founded 1973.

Walker Books Ltd

87 Vauxhall Walk, London SE11 5HJ
tel 020-7793 0909 *fax* 020-7587 1123
website www.walker.co.uk
Senior Editor Hannah Whitaker

Includes the best-selling fiction series *Alex Rider* and *The Power of Five* by Anthony Horowitz and titles by award-winning authors Michael Morpurgo, Mal Peet and Vivian French. Audio series for young children include *Listen and Join In!* – based on 12 classic picture books and featuring story readings, songs and activities; and the non-fiction picture book and CD series *Nature Storybooks*.

Children's book packagers

Many modern illustrated books are created by book packagers, whose particular skills are in the areas of book design and graphic content. In-house editors match up the expertise of specialist writers, artists and photographers who usually work on a freelance basis.

Aladdin Books Ltd

2–3 Fitzroy Mews, London W1T 6DF
tel 020-7383 2084 *fax* 020-7388 6391
email sales@aladdinbooks.co.uk
website www.aladdinbooks.co.uk
Directors Charles Nicholas, Bibby Whittaker

Full design and book packaging facility specialising in children's non-fiction and reference. Founded 1980.

The Albion Press Ltd

113 High Street, Avebury, Marlborough,
Wilts. SN8 1RF
tel (01993) 831094
Directors Emma Bradford (managing), Neil Philip (editorial)

Produces quality integrated illustrated titles from the initial idea to printed copies. Specialises in children's books: poetry, fairy tales, myths, Native Americans. Produces 4 titles each year. Founded 1984.

Submission details Will not consider unsolicited MSS. Interested in seeing fine samples of illustrations but no cartoons or technical drawings. Include sae.

Nicola Baxter Ltd

PO Box 215, Framingham Earl, Yelverton,
Norwich NR14 7UR
tel (01508) 491111
email nb@nicolabaxter.co.uk
website www.nicolabaxter.co.uk
Director Nicola Baxter

Full packaging service for children's books, from concept to disk or any part of the process in between. Produces both fiction and non-fiction titles in a wide range of formats, from board books to encyclopedias. Experienced in novelty books and licensed publishing. Opportunities for freelances. Founded 1990.

Bender Richardson White

PO Box 266, Uxbridge, Middlesex UB9 5NX
tel (01895) 832444 *fax* (01895) 835213
email brw@brw.co.uk
website www.brw.co.uk
Directors Lionel Bender (editorial), Kim Richardson (sales & production), Ben White (design)

Design, editorial and production of activity books, non-fiction and reference books. Specialises in non-fiction: natural history, science, history and educational. Packages approx. 60–70 titles each year. Founded 1990.

Submission details Writers should send a letter and synopsis of their proposal. Opportunities for freelances.

The Book Guild Ltd

Pavilion View, 19 New Road, Brighton BN1 1UF
tel (01273) 720900 *fax* (01273) 723122
email info@bookguild.co.uk
website www.bookguild.co.uk
Directors Carol Biss (managing), Janet Wrench (production)

Fiction for 5–8 and 9–12 year-olds. Produces approx. 10 children's titles each year. Offers a range of publishing options: a comprehensive package for authors incorporating editorial, design, production, marketing, publicity, distribution and sales; editorial and production only for authors requiring private editions; or a complete service for companies and organisations requiring books for internal or promotional purposes – from brief to finished book. Write for submission guidelines. Founded 1982.

Book Street Ltd

2 Vermont Road, London SE19 3SR
tel 020-8771 5115 *fax* 020-8771 9994
email graham@bwj-ltd.com

Designers and packagers of large format children's books for the international market.

Bookmart Ltd

Blaby Road, Wigston, Leicester LE18 4SE
tel 0116-275 9060 *fax* 0116-275 9090
email books@bookmart.co.uk
website www.bookmart.co.uk
Publishing Director Linda Williams

Colour illustrated titles: children's fiction and non-fiction, poetry, novelty books, pop-up books, activity books. Age groups: preschool, 5–10, 10–15.

Bookwork Ltd

Unit 17, Piccadilly Mill, Lower Street, Stroud,
Glos. GL5 2HT
tel (01453) 752521 *fax* (01453) 751544
email bookwork@compuserve.com
Directors Louise Pritchard (editorial), Alan Plank (production), Jill Plank (design)

Creates innovative books for children of all ages: activity books, board books, picture books, how-to books, reference books. Also supplies a full editorial and design service to other publishers. Imprint: Pangolin.

Books

Brainwaves Ltd
31 Chart Lane, Reigate, Surrey RH2 7DY
tel (01737) 224444 *fax* (01737) 225777
email keith@brainwavesbooks.co.uk
Editorial Director Keith Faulkner

Packager of activity books, board books, novelty books, picture books, pop-up books and gift books.

Brown Bear Books Ltd
1st Floor, 9–17 St Albans Place, London N1 0NX
tel 020-7424 5640 *fax* 020-7424 5641
Children's Publisher Anne O'Daly

Specialises in high-quality illustrated reference books and multi-volume sets for trade and educational markets. Opportunities for freelances.

John Brown Group – Children's Division
136–142 Bramley Road, London W10 6SR
tel 020-7565 3000 *fax* 020-7565 3060
email andrew.hirsch@johnbrownmedia.com
website www.johnbrownmedia.com
Ceo Andrew Hirsch (operations), Sara Lynn (creative)

Creative development and packaging of children's products including books, magazines, teachers' resource packs, partworks, CDs and websites.

Brown Wells & Jacobs Ltd
2 Vermont Road, London SE19 3SR
tel 020-8653 7670 *fax* 020-8653 7774
email graham@bwj-ltd.com
website www.bwj.org
Director Graham Brown

Design, editorial, illustration and production of high-quality non-fiction illustrated children's books. Specialities include pop-up and novelty books. Packages approx. 30–40 titles each year. Opportunities for freelances. Founded 1979.

Cambridge Publishing Management Ltd
Burr Elm Court, Main Street, Caldecote, Cambs. CB23 7NU
tel (01954) 214000 *fax* (01954) 214002
email initial.surname@cambridgepm.co.uk
website www.cambridgepm.co.uk
Managing Director Jackie Dobbyne, *Editorial Manager* Catherine Burch

Creative and highly skilled editorial and book production company specialising in complete project management of children's education, including special needs, ELT and illustrated non-fiction titles, from commissioning authors to delivery of final files to printer. Freelances should send their CVs to recruit@cambridgepm.co.uk. Founded 1999.

Cowley Robinson Publishing Ltd
(incorporating David Hawcock Books)
8 Belmont, Bath BA1 5DZ
tel (01225) 339999 *fax* (01225) 339995
email sales: anna.sainaghi@cowleyrobinson.com
Directors Stewart Cowley (publishing), David Hawcock, Phil Fleming (finance)

Specialises in children's novelty and paper-engineered formats for international co-editions. Licence and character publishing developments. Information and early learning. Founded 1998.

Creations for Children International
Steenweg op Deinze 150, 9810 Nazareth, Belgium
tel (9) 2446090 *fax* (9) 2446099
email info@c4ci.com, jan.meeuws@c4ci.com, marc.jongbloet@c4ci.com
website www.c4ci.com, www.inkypress.com
Directors Marc Barbier (business & sales), Marc Jongbloet (book publishing & sales), *Production Manager* Joost Demuynck, *Chief Editor* Mr Jan Meeuws

Packagers of high-quality mass market children's illustrated books, including fairy tale and classic adventure story books. Activity books, board books, colouring books, pop-up books, novelty books, picture books and non-fiction books.

Creative Plus Publishing Ltd
2nd Floor, 151 High Street, Billericay, Essex CM12 9AB
tel (01277) 633005 *fax* (01277) 633003
email enquiries@creative-plus.co.uk
website www.creative-plus.co.uk
Managing Director Beth Johnson

Provides all editorial and design from concept to finished pages for books, partworks and magazines. Specialises in licensed characters, make-and-do, illustrated non-fiction. Opportunities for freelances. Founded 1989.

Design Eye Ltd
226 City Road, London EC1V 2TT
tel 020-7812 8601 *fax* 020-7253 4370
email info@designeye.co.uk
website www.quarto.com/co_ed_designeye_uk.htm
Publisher Sue Grabham

Co-edition publisher of innovative Books-Plus for children. Highly illustrated, paper-engineered, novelty and component-based titles for all ages, but primarily children's preschool (3+), 5–8 and 8+ years. Mainly non-fiction, early concepts and curriculum-based topics for the trade in all international markets. Opportunities for freelance paper engineers, artists, authors, editors and designers. Unsolicited MSS not accepted. Founded 1988.

Elm Grove Books Ltd
Elm Grove, Marsh Lane, Templecombe, Somerset BA8 0TQ
tel (01963) 362498 *fax* (01963) 362982

email hugh@elmgrovebooks.com,
susie@elmgrovebooks.com
Directors Hugh Elwes, Susie Elwes
Packager of children's books. Founded 1993.

Graham-Cameron Publishing & Illustration

The Studio, 23 Holt Road, Sheringham,
Norfolk NR26 8NB
tel (01263) 821333 *fax* (01263) 821334
email enquiry@gciforillustration.com
and Duncan Graham-Cameron, 59 Hertford Road,
Brighton BN1 7GG
tel (01273) 385890
website www.gciforillustration.com
Partners Helen Graham-Cameron, Duncan
Graham-Cameron

Offers illustration and editorial services for picture
books, information books, educational materials,
activity books, picture books, non-fiction and
reference books. Illustration agency with 37 artists.
Do not send unsolicited MSS. Founded 1985.

Hart McLeod Ltd

14 Greenside, Waterbeach, Cambridge CB25 9HP
tel (01223) 861495 *fax* (01223) 862902
email inhouse@hartmcleod.co.uk
website www.hartmcleod.co.uk
Directors Graham Hart, Joanne Barker

Primarily educational and general non-fiction with
particular expertise in reading books, school texts,
ELT and electronic and audio content. Opportunities
for freelances and work experience. Founded 1985.

Hawcock Books

2 The Firs, Combe Down, Bath BA1 5ED
tel (07976) 708720
website http://hawcockbooks.co.uk

Designs and produces highly creative and original
pop-up art and 3D paper-engineered concepts. Most
experience is in developing, providing editorial for,
printing and manufacturing pop-up books and
novelty items for the publishing industry. Also
undertakes demanding commissions from the
advertising world for model-making, point-of-sale
and all printed 3D aspects of major campaigns.

HL Studios Ltd

Riverside House, Two Rivers, Station Lane,
Witney OX28 4BH
tel (01993) 881010 *fax* (01993) 882713
email info@hlstudios.eu.com
website www.hlstudios.eu.com

Primary, secondary academic education (geography,
science, modern languages) and co-editions (travel
guides, gardening, cookery). Multimedia (CD-Rom
programming and animations). Opportunities for
freelances. Founded 1985.

Hothouse Fiction Ltd

The Old Truman Brewery, 91 Brick Lane,
London E1 6QL
tel 020-3384 2609
email ben.horslen@hothousefiction.com
website www.hothousefiction.com
Directors Reg Wright, Richard Maskell, *Managing
Editor* Ben Horslen

Creative packager producing commercial series
fiction for children aged 5–teen. Genres include
fantasy, horror, romance, magical, historical, animals,
comedy and adventure. No unsolicited MSS. Supplies
a full brief for all its projects. Selects writers for
projects on the basis of unpaid writing samples, but
successful writers paid an advance and royalty for
published books. Welcomes new writers; visit website
to register.

Miles Kelly Packaging

The Bardfield Centre, Great Bardfield,
Essex CM7 4SL
tel (01371) 811309 *fax* (01371) 811393
email info@mileskelly.net
website www.mileskelly.net
Directors Gerard Kelly, Jim Miles, Richard Curry

Publishers of high-quality illustrated non-fiction titles
for children and family. See also page 15. Founded
1996.

Little People Books

The Home of BookBod, Knighton,
Radnorshire LD7 1UP
tel (01547) 520925
email littlepeoplebooks@thehobb.tv
website www.thehobb.tv/lpb
Directors Grant Jessé (production & managing),
Helen Wallis (rights & finance)

Packager of audio, children's educational and
textbooks, digital publications. Parent company:
Grant Jessé UK.

Marshall Editions Ltd

The Old Brewery, 6 Blundell Street, London N7 9BH
tel 020-7700 6764 *fax* 020-7700 4191
email JamesAshton-Tyler@marshalleditions.com
website www.marshalleditions.com
Publisher James Ashton-Tyler

Highly illustrated non-fiction for adults and children,
including history, health, gardening, home design,
pets, natural history, popular science.

Monkey Puzzle Media Ltd

Gissing's Farm, Fressingham, Eye, Suffolk IP21 5SH
tel (01379) 588044 *fax* (01379) 588055
email info@monkeypuzzlemedia.com
Director Roger Goddard-Coote

Offers a full packaging service from concept or
commission through to delivery of repro-ready disks

or film. Specialises in children's non-fiction and reference. Produces approx. 60 titles each year. Will consider unsolicited MSS and copies of illustrations with an sae. Founded 1998.

Orpheus Books Ltd
6 Church Green, Witney, Oxon OX28 4AW
tel (01993) 774949 fax (01993) 700330
email info@orpheusbooks.com
website www.orpheusbooks.com
Executive Directors Nicholas Harris (editorial, design & marketing), Sarah Hartley (production & design)

Produces children's books for the international co-editions market: activity books, novelty books, non-fiction and reference. Produces 8–20 titles each year. Welcomes samples from illustrators. Founded 1993.

Picthall & Gunzi Ltd
21A Widmore Road, Bromley BR1 1RW
tel 020-8460 4032 fax 020-8460 4021
email chez@picthallandgunzi.demon.co.uk, chris@picthallandgunzi.demon.co.uk
website www.picthallandgunzi.com
Managing Director Chez Picthall, Editorial Director & Publisher Christiane Gunzi

Offers a complete package, from initial concept to publication, producing high-quality, illustrated non-fiction for children of all ages: early learning, novelty, activity, board books, non-fiction.

Pinwheel – see Alligator Books Ltd

Playne Books Ltd
Park Court Barn, Trefin, Haverfordwest,
Pembrokeshire SA62 5AU
tel (01348) 837073
email info@playnebooks.co.uk
Design & Production Director David Playne, Editorial Director Gill Playne

Specialises in highly illustrated adult non-fiction and books for very young children. All stages of production undertaken from initial concept (editorial, design and manufacture) to delivery of completed books. Currently not considering new projects. Founded 1987.

Tony Potter Publishing Ltd
1 Stairbridge Court, Bolney Grange Business Park, Stairbridge Lane, Bolney, West Sussex RH17 5PA
tel (01444) 232889 fax (01444) 232142
email info@tonypotter.com
website www.tonypotter.com
Directors Tony Potter (managing), Christine Potter

Creates high-quality children's titles as a packager and occasionally publishes under its own imprints: Tony Potter Books and Over the Moon. Opportunities for freelance editors, designers and illustrators. Also creates custom-designed books and innovative paper-based products for children and adults, particularly for own-brand. Founded 1997.

The Puzzle House
Ivy Cottage, Battlesea Green, Stradbroke,
Suffolk IP21 5NE
tel (01379) 384656 fax (01379) 384656
email puzzlehouse@btinternet.com
website www.thepuzzlehouse.co.uk
Partners Roy Preston and Sue Preston

Editorial service creating crossword, quiz, puzzle and activity material for all ages. Founded 1988.

The Quarto Group, Inc.
226 City Road, London, EC1V 2TT
tel 020-7700 9000 fax 020-7253 4437
email info@quarto.com
website www.quarto.com
Chairman & Ceo Laurence Orbach, Chief Financial Officer Mick Mousley, Creative Director Bob Morley, Director of Publishing David Breuer

Independent publishing group encompassing traditional and co-edition publishing. Co-edition books are licensed to third parties all over the world, with best-selling titles often available in 20+ languages. UK-based operations include the following autonomously run business units/imprints: Quarto Publishing plc, Quintet Publishing Ltd, Marshall Editions, Quintessence, Quarto Children's Books/ Design Eye (see below), QED Publishing Ltd, Quantum Publishing Ltd, qu:id, Aurum Press Ltd, Jacqui Small and RotoVision.

Quarto Children's Books Ltd
226 City Road, London EC1V 2TT
tel 020-7812 8626 fax 020-7253 4370
email quartokids@quarto.com, sueg@quarto.com
Publisher Sue Grabham, Art Director Jonathan Gilbert
Co-edition publisher of innovative Books-Plus for children. Highly illustrated paper-engineered, novelty and component-based titles for all ages, but primarily preschool (3+), 5–8 and 8+ years. Mainly non-fiction, early concepts and curriculum-based topics for the trade in all international markets. Opportunities for freelance paper engineers, artists, authors, editors and designers. Unsolicited MSS not accepted.

Small World Design
72A Pope Lane, Penwortham, Preston,
Lancs. PR1 9DA
tel (01772) 750885 fax (01772) 750885
email sue.chadwick@smallworlddesign.co.uk
website www.smallworlddesign.co.uk
Partners Sue Chadwick, David Peet

Offers a writing, illustration, design and packaging service for preschool material, novelty, sticker and volume books, games, jigsaw puzzles and licensed products. Also publishes Small World Design ranges. Founded 1995.

Tangerine Designs Ltd*
5th Floor, The Old Malthouse, Clarence Street,
Bath BA1 5NS

website www.tangerinedesigns.co.uk

Packagers and international co-edition publishers of children's books. Brands include: *The Little Dreamers, Jolly Maties, Baby Eco, Little Eco.* Specialising in novelty books, book-plus and innovations. Submissions accepted from UK only; must enclose sae if return required. See website for submissions procedure. Founded 2000.

Tango Books Ltd
PO Box 32595, London W4 5YD
tel 020-8996 9970 *fax* 020-8996 9977
email sheri@tangobooks.co.uk,
edith@tangobooks.co.uk
website www.tangobooks.co.uk
Directors Sheri Safran, David Fielder, *Submissions* Edith Fricker (*tel* 020-8996 9973)

Creates and produces international co-productions of children's novelty books only (touch-and-feel, flaps, pop-ups, foils, etc). Publishes in UK under Tango Books imprint. No flat picture books. Produces mainly for the 0–6 age group but some for up to age 12. Books are highly visual with lots of illustrations and minimal text, except for non-fiction where there is scope for longer texts. Big multicultural novelty book list. Founded 1983.
  Submission details The max. word count for ages 0–6 is 500 words. Text should be for novelty format (repetition works well). No particularly British themes or characters. No poetry. Artwork: modern style, fresh and fun. Likes collage, bright and bold styles, pen and ink coloured in; less keen on watercolour unless very special. Send submissions with sae for their return or preferably by email. Allow one month for reply.

The Templar Company Ltd
The Granary, North Street, Dorking,
Surrey RH4 1DN
tel (01306) 876361 *fax* (01306) 889097
email info@templarco.co.uk,
submissions@templarco.co.uk (submissions)
website www.templarco.co.uk
Managing & Creative Director Amanda Wood, *Sales & Marketing Director* Ruth Huddleston

Publisher and packager of high-quality illustrated children's books, including novelty books, picture books, pop-up books, board books, fiction, non-fiction and gift titles. Send submissions via email.

Tiptoe Books
Bradley's Close, 74–77 White Lion Street,
London N1 9PF
tel 020-7520 7600 *fax* 020-7520 7606/7607
email enquiries@amberbooks.co.uk
website www.tiptoebooks.co.uk
Managing Director Stasz Gnych, *Deputy Managing Director* Sara Ballard, *Publishing Manager* Charles Catton, *Head of Production* Peter Thompson, *Design*

Manager Mark Batley, *Picture Manager* Terry Forshaw

Illustrated non-fiction, multi-volume sets, calendars and sticker books for children of all ages. Subjects include history, ancient civilizations, the natural world, fantasy and general reference. Opportunities for freelances. Children's books imprint of Amber Books Ltd.

Toucan Books Ltd
3rd Floor, 89 Charterhouse Street,
London EC1M 6HR
tel 020-7250 3388 *fax* 020-7250 3123
website www.toucanbooks.co.uk
Directors Robert Sackville West, Ellen Dupont

International co-editions; editorial, design and production services. Founded 1985.

Emma Treehouse Ltd
The Studio, Church Street, Nunney, Frome,
Somerset BA11 4LW
tel (01373) 836233 *fax* (01373) 836299
email sales@emmatreehouse.com
website www.emmatreehouse.com
Directors David Bailey, Richard Powell (creative & editorial)

Specialist creator of novelty books for children aged 0–7: bath books, books with a sound concept, cloth books, novelty books, flap books, touch-and-feel books. Packager and co-edition publisher with international recognition for its innovative and often unique concepts. The company has produced over 30 million books, translated into 33 different languages. Opportunities for freelance artists. Founded 1992

Tucker Slingsby Ltd
5th Floor, Regal House, 70 London Road,
Twickenham TW1 3QS
tel 020-8744 1007 *fax* 020-8744 0041
email firstname@tuckerslingsby.co.uk
website www.tuckerslingsby.co.uk
Directors Janet Slingsby, Del Tucker

Highly illustrated children's books from concept to delivery of disk or finished copies. Produces for preschool to teenage: activity books, novelty books, picture books, film/TV tie-ins, non-fiction, religion and reference. Produces approx. 50 titles each year. Founded 1992.
  Submission details Opportunities for freelances and picture book artists. Submit by post or email.

Umbrella Books
mobile (07971) 111256
email gary@allied-artists.net
website www.alliedartists-umbrellabooks.com
Contacts Gary Mills, Mary Burtenshaw

Packager of children's preschool novelty book formats.

David West Children's Books
7 Princeton Court, 55 Felsham Road,
London SW15 1AZ

Books

tel 020-8780 3836 fax 020-8780 9313
email dww@btinternet.com
website www.davidwestchildrensbooks.com
Proprietor David West, *Partner* Lynn Lockett

Packagers of children's illustrated reference books. Specialises in science, art, geography, history, sport and flight. Produces 40 titles each year. Opportunities for freelances. Founded 1986.

Windmill Books Ltd

1st Floor, 9–17 St Albans Place, London N1 0NX
tel 020-7424 5640 fax 020-7424 5641
Children's Publisher Anne O'Daly

Specialises in high-quality illustrated reference books and multi-volume sets for trade and educational markets. Opportunities for freelances.

Working Partners Ltd

Stanley House, St Chad's Place, London WC1X 9HH
tel 020-7841 3939 fax 020-7841 3940
email enquiries@workingpartnersltd.co.uk
website www.workingpartnersltd.co.uk
Chairman Ben Baglio, *Managing Director* Chris Snowdon, *Creative Director* Rod Ritchie, *Operations Director* Charles Nettleton

Children's and young adult fiction series: animal fiction, fantasy, horror, historical fiction, detective, magical, adventure. Recent successes include *Rainbow Magic, Beast Quest* and *Warriors*. Founded 1995.

Submission details Unable to accept any MS or illustration submissions. Pays advance and royalty; retains copyright on all work created. Selects writers from unpaid writing samples based on specific brief provided. Always looking to add writers to database; email writers@workingpartnersltd.co.uk to register details.

Zuza Books

7 St Christopher's Avenue, Cambridge CB3 0JD
tel/fax (01223) 368477
email zuza@zuzabooks.com
website www.zuzabooks.com
Managing Director Zuza Vrbova

Packager of interactive and educational cloth books for young children.

Children's book clubs

Not all the companies listed here are 'clubs' in the true sense: some are mail order operations and others sell their books via book fairs.

Baker Books

Manfield Park, Cranleigh, Surrey GU6 8NU
tel (01483) 267888 *fax* (01483) 267409
email enquiries@bakerbooks.co.uk
website www.bakerbooks.co.uk

School book club for children aged 3–16. Operates in the UK and in English medium schools overseas.

BFC Books for Children

BCA Groundwell, Hargreaves Road, Swindon, Wilts. SR25 5BG
tel (01793) 723 547
website www.booksforchildren.co.uk

Offers a wide range of books, DVDs and games for babies through to teenagers. Books include fiction, non-fiction and national curriculum-related material. Membership gives access to Books for Children website, and 12+ colour magazines per year offering books for sale. Conditions of membership: at least 4 books in first year must be ordered through the website or magazine. Part of the BCA Group.

Bibliophile

5 Datapoint, South Crescent, London E16 4TL
tel 020-7474 2474 *fax* 020-7474 8589
email orders@bibliophilebooks.com
website www.bibliophilebooks.com
Secretary Annie Quigley

To promote value-for-money reading. Upmarket literature and classical music on CD available from mail order catalogue (10 p.a.). Over 3,000 titles covering art and fiction to travel, history and children's books. Founded 1978.

The Book People Ltd

Park Menai, Bangor LL57 4FB
tel (0845) 6024040 *fax* (0845) 6064242
email sales@thebookpeople.co.uk
website www.thebookpeople.co.uk

Popular general fiction and non-fiction, including children's and travel. Monthly.

Children's Poetry Bookshelf

website www.childrenspoetrybookshelf.co.uk

This poetry book club offers poetry for 7–11-year-olds and its membership schemes are for parents and grandparents (with a gift membership), teachers and libraries. Its open access website has a lively and child-friendly area. Runs the Old Possum's Children's Poetry Competition over National Poetry Day each year. See also page 191.

International Schools Book Club (ISBC)

Scholastic Ltd, Windrush Park, Witney, Oxon OX29 0YD
tel (01993) 893474 *fax* (01993) 708159
email intschool@scholastic.co.uk
website www.scholastic.co.uk/isbc

International book club service for schools worldwide.

Letterbox Library

71–73 Allen Road, London N16 8RY
tel 020-7503 4801 *fax* 020-7503 4800
email info@letterboxlibrary.com
website www.letterboxlibrary.com

Specialises in children's books that celebrate equality and diversity. Also provides pre-selected packs for Sure Starts, children's centres and nurseries. Quarterly annotated catalogues. Operates as a non-profit-driven workers' co-operative. Orders taken online, by fax or by post.

Puffin Book Club

Catteshall Manor, Catteshall Lane, Godalming, Surrey GU7 1UU
Freephone tel (0500) 454 444 (UK), (1) 800 340 131 (ROI)
email customerservice@puffinbookclub.co.uk
website www.puffinbookclub.co.uk, www.puffinbookclub.ie

A schools-based book club that gives parents and children access to a fantastic range of discounted books from all the top publishers. It also helps schools to fill their classrooms and libraries with the best books as Puffin Book Club matches their school order value with the same value of free books.

Red House

PO Box 142, Bangor LL57 4ZP
tel 0845-606 4280 *fax* 0845-606 4242
email enquiries@redhouse.co.uk
website www.redhouse.co.uk

Helps parents to select the right books for their children at affordable prices. A free monthly magazine features the best of the latest titles on offer, young reader reviews and fascinating insight into the minds of popular children's writers. Sponsors the Red House Children's Book Award (page 388). Founded 1979.

Scholastic Book Clubs and Fairs

Euston House, 24 Eversholt Street, London NW1 1DB

tel 020-7756 7756 *fax* 020-7756 7799
email scbenquiries@scholastic.co.uk
website www.scholastic.co.uk,
http://clubs.scholastic.co.uk

Leading schools book clubs and fairs. Offers primary and secondary clubs and fairs.

Scholastic Book Fairs

Westfield Road, Southam, Warks. CV47 0RA
tel 0800 212281 (freephone)
website www.scholastic.co.uk/bookfairs
Managing Director Steven Thompson

Sells directly to children, parents and teachers in schools through 25,000 week-long events held in schools throughout the UK.

Travelling Book Company

(also known as Troubadour)
Express House, Crow Arch Lane, Ringwood, Hants BH24 1PD
tel (0800) 7315758 *fax* (01425) 471797
email enquiries@travellingbooks.co.uk
website www.travellingbooks.co.uk

Book fair operation selling books to children in schools in the UK (Celtic Travelling Book Company in Ireland) through easy-to-manage, well-stocked bookcases containing a wide range of books for all age groups. An editorial team works closely with teachers and parents to ensure a balanced collection and is headed up by Fiona Waters, the well-known writer, reviewer, publisher and bookseller.

Children's bookshops

The bookshops in the first part of this list specialise in selling new children's books and are good places for writers and illustrators to check out the marketplace. Most of them are members of the Booksellers Association and are well known to publishers. A list of second-hand and antiquarian children's bookshops follows.

Askews

218–222 North Road, Preston, Lancs. PR1 1SY
tel (01772) 555947 *fax* (01772) 254860
email enquiries@askews.co.uk
website www.askews.co.uk

Libraries and schools supplier.

Badger Books

email info@badger-publishing.co.uk
website www.badger-publishing.co.uk
Proprietors Nic and Janet Tall

Internet business specialising in selling modern reprints of sought after children's books.

Blast-Off Books

103 High Street, Linlithgow, Scotland EH49 7EQ
tel (01506) 844645 *fax* (01506) 844346
email info@blastoffbooks.co.uk
website www.blastoffbooks.co.uk

A dedicated children's bookshop for babies through to young adults, also stocking support materials for the Standard Grades and Highers. Wide range of materials for parents of, and teachers working with, children with specific learning needs such as dyslexia, autism, ADHD and Down Syndrome.

The Book House

93 High Street, Thame, Oxon OX9 3HJ
tel (01844) 213032 *fax* (01844) 213311
email anybook@the-book-house.demon.co.uk

Bookspread Ltd

6 Croxted Road, London SE21 8SW
tel 020-8670 1380 *fax* 020-8402 7886
email info@bookspread.co.uk
website www.bookspread.co.uk

A bookshop run by ex-teachers who offer advice and consultation as well as a mobile book service for schools. Also organises workshops and author visits to schools. Works in conjunction with the educational charity, the Children's Discovery Centre.

Bookworm Ltd

1177 Finchley Road, London NW11 0AA
tel 020-8201 9811 *fax* 020-8201 9311
email ruth.swindon@lineone.net
website www.thebookworm.uk.com

Brook Green Bookshop

72 Blythe Road, Brook Green, London W14 0HB
tel 020-7603 5999

email brookgreenbooks@btconnect.com
Children's bookshop.

Browns Books For Students

22–28 George Street, Hull HU1 3AP
tel (01482) 384660 *fax* (01482) 384677
email schools.services@brownsbfs.co.uk
website www.brownsbfs.co.uk

Supplies any book in print to schools, colleges and international schools. Full school servicing of books on request.

Chameleon Books

5 Milnyard Square, Peterborough PE2 6GX
tel (01733) 374717 *fax* (01733) 370607
email info@chameleongroup.co.uk
website www.chameleongroup.co.uk

Specialises in the supply of books and learning materials for schools and nurseries.

Chapter One Bookshop

136 Crockhamwell Road, Woodley, Reading RG5 3JH
tel/fax 0118-944 8883
email chapteronebookshop@yahoo.co.uk
website www.chapteronebookboxes.co.uk
Proprietors John and Mary Baker

General bookshop with specialisation in children's titles and teaching resource books. Also provides book boxes for reluctant readers to schools in the UK.

Childrens@Blackwells

Blackwells Bookshop, 50 Broad Street, Oxford OX1 3BQ
tel (01865) 333000
email mail.ox@blackwell.co.uk
website www.blackwell.co.uk

Children's Bookshop – Hay on Wye

Toll Cottage, Pontvaen, Hay on Wye, Herefordshire HR3 5EW
tel (01497) 821083 *fax* (08700) 517 746
email judith@childrensbookshop.com
website www.childrensbookshop.com
Proprietor Judith Gardner

New and secondhand children's books; collectibles.

The Children's Bookshop

1 Red Lion Parade, Bridge Street, Pinner, Middlesex HA5 3JD

tel 020-8866 9116 fax 020-8866 9116
email thechildrens.bookshop@virgin.net

Children's Bookshop (Huddersfield)
37–39 Lidget Street, Lindley, Huddersfield,
West Yorkshire HD3 3JF
tel (01484) 658013 fax (01484) 460020
email barry@hudbooks.demon.co.uk

Children's Bookshop (Muswell Hill)
29 Fortis Green Road, London N10 3HP
tel 020-8444 5500 fax 020-8883 8632
email admin@childrensbookshoplondon.co.uk
website www.childrensbookshoplondon.com

The Edinburgh Bookshop
219 Bruntsfield Place, Edinburgh EH10 4DH
tel 0131-447 1917
email shop@edinburghbookshop.com
website www.edinburghbookshop.com

Enchanted Wood
3–5 Kings Road, Shalford, Guildford GU4 8JU
tel (01483) 570088 fax (0870) 7052342
email sales@enchanted-wood.co.uk
website www.enchanted-wood.co.uk

Glowworm Books & Gifts Ltd
Unit 2, 5 Youngs Road, East Mains Industrial Estate,
Broxburn, West Lothian EH52 5LY
tel (01506) 857570 fax (01506) 858100
website www.glowwormbooks.co.uk

Specialises in supplying books for children, especially
those who find reading difficult due to physical or
special educational needs.

Golden Treasury (Southfields)
29 Replingham Road, London SW18 5LT
tel 020-8333 0167 fax 020-8265 1717
email southfields@thegoldentreasury.co.uk
website www.thegoldentreasury.co.uk

Heath Educational Books
Willow House, Willow Walk, Whittaker Road,
Sutton, Surrey SM3 9QQ
tel 020-8644 7788 fax 020-8641 3377
website www.heathbooks.co.uk

Supplies books only to schools and teachers in the
South of England. Large showroom.

Jubileebooks.co.uk
31A Vanburgh Park, Blackheath, London SE3 7AE
tel 020-8293 6060 fax 020-8465 5111
email enquiries@jubileebooks.co.uk
website www.jubileebooks.co.uk

Offers a wide range of children's books and resources
to schools. Organises literacy and book-related events
in the UK and worldwide. Service includes
consultancy, new library set-up, book fairs, author

visits, reading and writing projects, literacy inset and
training conferences. Established 1996.

Madeleine Lindley Ltd
Book Centre, Broadgate, Broadway Business Park,
Oldham OL9 9XA
tel 0161-683 4400 fax 0161-682 6801
email info@madeleinelindley.com
website www.madeleinelindley.com

Supplies books to schools, provides information
services and runs open days for teachers. Hosts
author/publisher events for teachers and children.

The Lion and Unicorn Bookshop
19 King Street, Richmond, Surrey TW9 1ND
tel 020-8940 0483 fax 020-8332 6133
email services@lionunicornbooks.co.uk
website www.lionunicornbooks.co.uk

A specialist independent children's bookshop
established in 1977. Holds regular author events,
offers services to schools, loyalty scheme and online
newsletter *The Roar*. Voted Independent Bookseller
of the Year, The British Book Industry Awards 2000.

Nickel Books
22A High Street, Sittingbourne ME10 4PD
tel (01795) 429546
email enquiries@nickelbooks.co.uk
website www.nickelbooks.co.uk

Specialises in children's books, from birth to teenage;
also books for parents.

Norfolk Children's Book Centre
Alby, Norwich NR11 7HB
tel (01263) 761402 fax (01263) 768167
email marilyn@ncbc.co.uk
website www.ncbc.co.uk

Specialist children's bookshop for readers of all ages.
Offers services to schools in East Anglia including
storytelling, talks to children and parents, approval
services and INSET for teachers.

Oundle School Bookshop
13 Market Place, Oundle, Peterborough PE8 4BA
tel (01832) 273523 fax (01832) 274611
email bookshop@oundle.co.uk
website www.oundleschool.org.uk

Peters Bookselling Services
120 Bromsgrove Street, Birmingham B5 6RJ
tel 0121-666 6646 fax 0121-666 7033
website www.peters-books.co.uk

Supplier of children's books to schools and libraries
with a comprehensive showroom and online ordering
facility. Provides book-related promotional material
and information including *tBkmag*, a reader
development magazine for 8–12 year-olds.

Rhyme & Reason
681 Ecclesall Road, Hunter's Bar, Sheffield S11 8TG
tel/fax 0114-266 1950

email richard@rhyme-reason.co.uk
website www.rhyme-reason.co.uk

New books for children of all ages. Special interest in social and emotional aspects of learning.

Roving Books Ltd (The Roving Bookshop)
Administration 3 Kirkby Road, Desford, Leicester LE9 9GL
tel (01455) 822192 *fax* (07005) 982306
email support@rovingbooks.com
Showroom inside the Leicester Wholefood Co-op, Unit 3, Freehold Street, Leicester LE1 2LX
tel 0116-251 9151
website www.rovingbooks.com, www.xybacard.com

Children's specialist bookseller, taking a comprehensive children's bookshop into schools for purchases by children, parents, teachers and schools. Promoting reading with the Jolly Roger Book Club and Xybacard. Specialist advice and supply of children's books for individuals and institutions.

Seven Stories – see page 359

Tales On Moon Lane
25 Half Moon Lane, London SE24 9JU
tel/fax 020-7274 5759
email info@talesonmoonlane.co.uk
website www.talesonmoonlane.co.uk
Proprietor Tamara Linke

Specialist children's bookshop which runs yearly children's literature festivals in May and October, as well as weekly storytelling sessions for preschool children.

Twist in the Tale
144 Station Road, Amersham, Bucks. HP6 5DW
tel (01494) 726234
email mail@twistinthetale.co.uk
website www.twistinthetale.co.uk

Specialist children's bookshop.

Victoria Park Books
174 Victoria Park Road, London E9 7HD
tel 020-8986 1124
email info@victoriaparkbooks.co.uk
website www.victoriaparkbooks.co.uk
Proprietors Jo and Cris De Guia

Specialist children's bookshop including dual language books. Reading groups for toddlers.

The Well Wisher Children's Bookshop
51 Long Street, Devizes, Wilts. SN10 1NP
tel/fax (01380) 722640
email wellwisher@btconnect.com
website www.wellwisher.biz
Contact Karen Hellewell

Specialist children's bookshop.

Willesden Bookshop
Willesden Green Library Centre, 95 High Road, London NW10 4QU
tel 020-8451 7000 *fax* 020-8830 1233
email books@willesdenbookshop.co.uk
website www.willesdenbookshop.co.uk

Specialist supplier of multicultural children's books (including many unusual and imported titles) to schools, nurseries, libraries and professional development agencies.

Young Browsers Bookshop
33 The Thoroughfare, Woodbridge, Suffolk IP12 1AH
tel (01394) 382832
email youngbrowsers@browsersbookshop.com
website www.browsersbookshop.com

Young Europeans Bookstore
5 Warwick Street, London W1B 5LU
email yeb@esb.co.uk
website www.younglinguists.com

A department of the European Bookshop offering a wide variety of material for young learners to learn foreign languages including picture books, reading material, songbooks, CDs, dictionaries, games and courses.

CHILDREN'S BOOKSELLERS FOR COLLECTORS

Blackwell Rare Books
48–51 Broad Street, Oxford OX1 3BQ
tel (01865) 333555 *fax* (01865) 794143
email rarebooks@blackwell.co.uk
website www.rarebooks.blackwell.co.uk

The Rare Books Department within Blackwell deals in early and modern first editions of children's books, among other subjects. Catalogues are issued periodically, which include modern and antiquarian children's books.

Bookmark Children's Books
Fortnight, Broad Hinton, Swindon, Wilts. SN4 9NR
tel (01793) 731693 *fax* (01793) 731782
email leonora-excell@btconnect.com
Contact Anne Excell, Leonora Excell

A mail-order bookseller, specialising in books for collectors, ranging from antiquarian to modern. A wide range of first editions, novelty and picture books, chap-books, ABCs, annuals, etc. Also a selection of vintage toys, games, dolls and nursery china. Catalogues of children's books and related juvenilia issued. Book search service available within this specialist area. Member of PBFA, exhibiting at PBFA book fairs in London, Oxford and Bath. Send sae. Established 1973.

Books

Mary Butts Books

219 Church Road, Earley, Reading RG6 1HW
tel 0118-926 1793
email mary.butts@tiscali.co.uk

Secondhand bookseller specialising in 19th- and
20th-century children's books for readers and
students rather than collectors. Mainly postal
business, but bookroom available on request. Free
book search.

Paul Embleton

12 Greenfields, Stansted, Essex CM24 8AH
tel (01279) 812627
email paulembleton@btconnect.com
website www.abebooks.com

Sells by post via the internet (some stock is on Abe)
and sends subject lists to regular customers. Receives
visitors by appointment. Specialises in books and
ephemera for the picture postcard collector and
maintains a good stock of children's books and
ephemera, mostly Victorian and Edwardian
chromolithographic by such publishers as Nister and
Raphael Tuck, and items of any age by collectable
illustrators.

Ian Hodgkins & Co Ltd

1 Clifton Villas, Springfield Road, Uplands, Stroud,
Glos. GL5 1TP
tel (01453) 755233 *fax* (01453) 755233
email enquiries@ianhodgkins.com
website www.ianhodgkins.com
Contact Simon Weager

Dealer in rare and out-of-print books and related
material. Specialist in Beatrix Potter and fairy tales
and 19th-century British art and literature. Free
catalogues in all specialist areas published regularly.

Robert J. Kirkpatrick

6 Osterley Park View Road,
London W7 2HH (private premises)
tel 020-8567 4521
email rkirkpatrick.molesworth@virgin.net

Secondhand bookseller specialising in stories about
boys' schools from 1800 to the present day. Also
public school studies, histories, etc.

Marchpane Children's Books

16 Cecil Court, Charing Cross Road,
London WC2N 4HE
tel 020-7836 8661 *fax* 020-7497 0567
email enquiries@marchpane.com
website www.marchpane.com

Antiquarian children's books only. Open Mon–Sat
11am–6.30pm.

Plurabelle Books

Michael Young Centre, Purbeck Road,
Cambridge CB2 8QL
tel (01223) 415671 *fax* (01223) 413241
email books@plurabelle.co.uk
website www.plurabellebooks.co.uk
Contact Michael Cahn

Secondhand bookseller specialising in academic
books on literature, reading, history of education and
children's literature. Free book search for out-of-
print books. Catalogue published 3 times a year.
Visitors welcome by appointment.

Ripping Yarns Bookshop

355 Archway Road, London N6 4EJ
tel 020-8341 6111
email yarns@rippingyarns.co.uk
website www.rippingyarns.co.uk

Vintage bookshop with a large general stock,
including poetry, politics, plays and ephemera. Has
an especially large collection of 19th and 20th century
children's books.

Rose's Books

14 Broad Street, Hay-on-Wye, Hereford HR3 5DB
tel (01497) 820013 *fax* (01497) 821554
email enquiry@rosesbooks.com
website www.rosesbooks.com
Contact Maria Goddard

Bookshop specialising solely in rare out-of-print
children's books and located in the international
book town of Hay-on-Wye. Stock available via
website. Catalogues and specialist lists issued
regularly. Open daily 9.30am–5pm. Children's books
purchased – single items or collections. Established
1986.

Henry Sotheran Ltd

2–5 Sackville Street, Piccadilly, London W1S 3DP
tel 020-7439 6151 *fax* 020-7434 2019
Contact Rosie Hodge

A large showroom with hundreds of important
children's books spanning 2 centuries, specialising in
first editions and attractive illustrated works by
pivotal artists. Issues 2 specialist children's book
catalogues free, on request.

Notes from a Children's Laureate

Anthony Browne was the Children's Laureate 2009–11. Here he shares his passion for picture books and explains the importance of the Shape Game to develop the act of looking.

It was a long road to become the Children's Laureate but I believe it all started with the Shape Game, a simple drawing game that my brother and I thought we'd invented when we were young. I have spoken of this game to children all over the world, and they've made me realise that its prevalence in my own childhood was by no means unique. Children everywhere have invented their own versions of the Shape Game. It has certainly been a very important part of my career, for I have played it in every book I've made.

The rules are very simple: the first person draws an abstract shape; the second person, ideally using a different coloured pen, transforms it into something. It seems that all children love this game and are very good at it – far better than adults are. It is an unfortunate part of growing up that we lose a great deal of contact with our visual imagination. The wonder with which we look at the world diminishes, and this inhibits both our inclination to draw (most adults give up entirely) and also our ability to draw with any real creative value.

Even though the Shape Game is great fun to play, I believe it also has a serious aspect. Essentially, the game is about creativity itself. Every time we draw a picture, or write a story, or compose a piece of music, we are playing the Shape Game. When children ask me (and they always do) where I get my inspiration from, I tell them it's from the same place that they get theirs – from things that happened to me when I was a boy, or things that happened to my own children, from other people's stories, from films, from paintings, or from dreams. There are so many sources of inspiration. Everything comes from somewhere else, and when we create something we're transforming our own experience into a picture, a book, or perhaps a piece of music. We are playing our own Shape Game.

In my early years my father was the landlord of a pub near Bradford and apparently I used to stand on a table in the bar and tell stories to customers about a character called Big Dumb Tackle (whoever he was). I spent much of my childhood playing sport, fighting and drawing with my older brother and then studied graphic design in Leeds. While I was at art college my father died suddenly and horrifically in front of me, and this affected me hugely. I went through a rather dark period which didn't sit very happily with the world of graphic design. After leaving college I dabbled rather unsuccessfully in the advertising world then heard about a job as a medical artist and thought that it sounded interesting – it was. I worked at Manchester Royal Infirmary for three years painting delicate watercolours of grotesque operations. It taught me a lot more about drawing than I ever learned at art college, and I believe it taught me how to tell stories in pictures. I thought that it was probably time to move on when strange little figures started appearing in these paintings – and so began a career designing greetings cards. I continued to do this for many years working for the Gordon Fraser Gallery.

Gordon Fraser became a close friend and taught me a lot about card design which was to prove very useful when I started doing children's books. I experimented with many styles and many subjects, from snowmen to dogs with big eyes to gorillas. I sent some of my designs to various children's book publishers and it was through one of these that I met Julia MacRae who was to become my editor for the next 20 years. She taught me much of what I know about writing and illustrating children's books.

In 1976 I produced *Through the Magic Mirror*, a strange kind of book in which I painted many of the pictures before I wrote the story. I followed this with *A Walk in the Park*, a story I was to revisit 20 years later with *Voices in the Park*. Probably my most successful book is *Gorilla*, and it was around the time it was published in 1983 that I was badly bitten by a gorilla whilst being filmed for television at my local zoo.

I have published 40 books and been very lucky to win awards for some of these – the Kate Greenaway Medal twice (page 384) and the Kurt Maschler 'Emil' three times. In 2000 I was awarded the Hans Christian Andersen Medal (page 382), which is an international award and the highest honour a children's writer or illustrator can win, and I was the first British illustrator to receive it. My books have been translated into 26 languages. My illustrations have been exhibited in many countries – USA, Mexico, Venezuela, Colombia, France, Korea, Italy, Germany, Holland, Japan and Taiwan – and I've had the pleasure of visiting these places and working with local children and meeting other illustrators.

In 2001–2 I worked at Tate Britain with children using art as a stimulus to inspire visual literacy and creative writing activities. It was during this time that I conceived and produced *The Shape Game*.

In 2009 I was appointed Children's Laureate. In this capacity, my aim was to encourage more children to discover and love reading, focusing particularly on the appreciation of picture books, and the reading of both pictures *and* words. I strongly believe that picture books are special – they're not like anything else.

Sometimes I hear parents encouraging their children to read what they call 'proper' books (that's books without pictures) at an earlier and earlier age. This makes me sad, as picture books are perfect for sharing, and not just with the youngest children. As a father, I understand the importance of the bond that develops through reading and talking about picture books with your child. I believe the best picture books leave a tantalising gap between the pictures and the words, a gap that's filled by the reader's imagination, adding so much to the excitement of the book. Picture books are for everybody at any age, not books to be left behind as we grow older.

I also try to encourage the act of looking. Research has shown that visitors to art galleries spend an average of 30 seconds looking at each painting, and considerably more time reading the captions. It's an unfortunate element of growing up that we can lose a great deal of contact with our visual imagination, and by encouraging children – and adults – to play the Shape Game I hope this will change.

In the best picture books the pictures contain clues; they tell you what characters are thinking or how they're feeling. By reading these clues we get a far deeper understanding of the story. In the UK we have some of the best picture book makers in the world, and I want to see their books appreciated for what they are – works of art.

In spite of my concerns about the state of the market for picture books, I am optimistic about the future. I realise now more than ever that I am incredibly lucky to love what I do. Straight after finishing art college I was disheartened because it seemed inevitable that in order to make a living from art I would have to make massive compromises. The experience of doing those advertising jobs made any dreams I once had seem futile. I was getting paid, but the fun of drawing had been taken away. I retrieved some of the fun when

I was a medical illustrator, and I enjoyed making many of the card designs, but it wasn't until I discovered picture books that I learned it was possible to have as much fun with a paintbrush as I had done as a child *and* get paid for it. This is what I love most about my job. What I do now is exactly what I did then: tell stories and draw pictures. Nothing much has changed, not even my approach. Drawing was always my favourite thing to do, and you could say that my career is comparable to other little boys growing up and being paid to play with Lego or dress up as cowboys!

I am also extremely lucky that I have been able to continue 'playing' for a living for so long. I could never stop drawing. Even if I was to give up doing it for a living I would carry on drawing for pleasure. But doing it for a living *is* doing it for pleasure, so there really is no reason to stop!

Anthony Browne was the Children's Laureate 2009–11. His most recent book is *Play the Shape Game* (Walker 2010).

See also...
• *Who do children's authors write for?*, page 87
• *Notes from Jacqueline Wilson*, page 78
• *Writing books to read aloud*, page 109
• *Notes from the first Children's Laureate*, page 229

Notes from Jacqueline Wilson

Jacqueline Wilson shares her first experience of becoming a writing success.

I knew I wanted to be a writer ever since I was six years old. I thought it would be the most magical job in the world. You could stay at home by yourself and write stories all day long.

I loved making up stories. I had a serial story permanently playing in my head. I used to mutter the words, acting each imaginary character in turn, but I soon learnt that this made people stare or giggle. I mastered the art of saying the words silently, experiencing all sorts of extraordinary adventures internally, while I sat staring seemingly blankly into space. No wonder I was nicknamed Jacky Daydream at school. My Mum thought I wasn't all there, and was forever giving me a shake and telling me not to look so gormless. She laughed at me when I confided that I wanted to be a writer. 'Don't be so daft Jac! Who on earth would want to read a book written by *you?*' she said.

She had a point. I was a totally unexceptional little girl, shy and anxious, barely able to say boo to a goose. My Mum wanted a daughter like Shirley Temple. She even permed my wispy hair to try to turn it into a cloud of golden ringlets. I ended up looking as if I'd been plugged into a light socket. I couldn't sing like Shirley, I couldn't tap dance like Shirley, and although I could recite long poems with dutiful expression I got so nervous performing I once wet myself on stage.

I didn't *want* to perform, well, certainly not in public. I would act out my stories enthusiastically whenever I was by myself, but I was a total shrinking violet in front of other people. I wasn't the life and soul of the party at school. I didn't clamour to have my friends round to play. I preferred playing elaborate imaginary games all by myself.

I saw a writing career as a wonderful grown-up version of these games. I suppose in a way it *is* – but I had no idea what it's *really* like to be a children's author. I don't think I've had a quiet day at home writing my book for weeks!

I suppose it used to be like that long ago. I've been writing children's books for the past 35 years. For the first 20 years very few people had ever heard of me. I wrote several books a year for a whole variety of publishers. They were published, and if I hunted high and low I occasionally saw one title in a bookshop down at the end of the Ws. I got a few pleasant reviews, and I was stocked in libraries, but that was about it. I've got copies of my first 40 books and they're all first editions – because they didn't go into any other editions. Publishing was so different in those days. You were kept on lists even if your books barely covered their advances – although eventually my first publisher told me they didn't see the point in buying any more of my books because they were never ever going to be popular.

I was upset, of course, but I felt their remarks were justified. I wrote about lonely imaginative children, all of them odd ones out. I thought that only odd children themselves would want to read them. I was worried that I'd never find another publisher but very luckily for me I was taken on by Transworld (now Random House Children's Books). I had the idea of writing a story about a fierce little kid in a children's home desperate to be fostered. I decided to tell it as if this child herself was writing her own life story. I wanted her to have a contemporary quirky kind of name. Something like... Tracy Beaker.

I knew I wanted the book to have lots of black and white illustrations as if Tracy herself had drawn them. I wanted several to a page, even in the margins. David Fickling was my editor then and he's always been very open to suggestions. 'Brilliant!' he said, rubbing his hands. 'I think I know just the chap too. He's done some wonderful illustrations for poetry books. His name's Nick Sharratt. Let's all meet.'

So Nick and I met in the publishing offices. We were both very shy at first. Nick seemed lovely and very talented but I wasn't quite sure he was wacky enough for Tracy-type illustrations. Then I needed to bend down to get a pen out of my handbag on the floor. I saw Nick's socks peeping out from his trouser hem – astonishingly bright canary yellow socks. I knew everything was going to be fine the moment I saw those amazing socks. In fact it became a running joke between us and I'd buy him ever more zany spotty stripy socks all colours of the rainbow.

We've worked on nearly 40 books together now and it's been just as magical as I'd hoped – but not at all as I'd imagined. I don't stay home all by myself and write my books. I have a beautiful book-lined study but I'm hardly ever in it. Most days I do my writing on trains or in the back of cars, scribbling frantically in my notebook on my way to endless meetings and events. I'm lucky enough to be able to write happily in these rather distracting conditions, though it's sometimes embarrassing if the train is crowded. I write in the first person, and my lovely Italian notebooks look like private journals. If a business man glances from his *Daily Telegraph* to my notebook, God knows what he thinks if he reads my fictional teenage girl musing; *I so fancy the boy I saw on the bus. How will I ever get to go out with him?*

People often ask me why I think my books have been so successful. I think there are several reasons, apart from sheer luck. They look great, with Nick's fantastic covers, and his lively black and white illustrations inside break up the text and make it less forbidding for inexperienced readers. I care passionately about language and play little word games with my readers, though I try to write in an immediate colloquial style through my child narrators. My publishers promote my books with energy and commitment. Nowadays they cosset me wonderfully when I embark on my three-week book tours, putting me up in luxurious hotels and giving me a delightfully cheery driver with a very comfortable car. But obviously you don't get this five-star treatment until your books sell in their millions. I believe the *real* secret of my success is the fact that I started doing many school and library visits early on, talking about my books. In fact I don't think there's a single county in the UK where I haven't given a talk.

I vividly remember my very first talk to a small docile group of Year 7s in a secondary school. I was so nervous I could barely eat breakfast beforehand. I hoped I acted like a reasonably competent sociable adult but inside I was still that shy little girl, terrified of performing. However, I could see the whole point of giving talks to children. It was a wonderful way of introducing them to the delights of reading in general, and to my own books in particular! That was why I was willing to put myself through this torture.

I didn't really know what to talk *about*. It seemed like terrible showing off simply talking about myself and my own work. I ended up reading an extract from Daisy Ashford's *The Young Visitors* to show that children could very occasionally have their work published, and then reading an extract from *Jane Eyre*, which had been my favourite book when I was 12. I realised soon enough that this was completely the wrong approach. The children thought the Daisy Ashford bizarre and *Jane Eyre* boring. They only livened up when I changed tack and talked about what I'd been like when I was young. I started to relate to them properly, and found I could tell them funny stories about myself as an earnest teenager, my experiences as a very junior journalist, and then chat to them about my latest book and how it came to be written.

I learnt how to give a talk – but it was a long time before I actually *enjoyed* doing it. I still got very fussed and anxious about it, and I hated it if I couldn't win every child over. After a while you learn that there will be an occasional kid who will give everyone a hard time. You just have to do your best and try to interest all the others. I slogged round several schools and libraries up and down the country every single week – and I learnt so much. This is where children's authors are so lucky. We can meet so many of our readers and find out what they like – and what they don't.

I only go to individual schools and libraries now as special favours to friends, but I still do many talks at festivals. Once you do something enough times you get so used to it you simply can't find it scary. I never get the slightest bit nervous now, even if I've got an audience of hundreds. I had to perform in the garden of Buckingham Palace in front of the Queen and 3,000 children and even that wasn't too worrying. It's just part of my job and I find it great fun.

But I got it right when I was six years old. The *most* magical part of being a writer is staying at home by myself and writing stories all day long.

Jacqueline Wilson has sold millions of books which have been translated into over 30 languages and have won many major awards. She was the Children's Laureate 2005–7. *Jacky Daydream* (Random House 2007) is an account of her own childhood. Her website is www.jacquelinewilson.co.uk.

See also...

- *Getting started*, page 1
- *A word from J.K. Rowling*, page 81
- *How it all began*, page 82
- *Who do children's authors write for?*, page 87
- *Writing for girls*, page 112
- *Writing for different genres*, page 115
- *Writing for teenagers*, page 139
- *Teenage fiction*, page 149

A word from J.K. Rowling

J.K. Rowling shares her first experience of becoming a writing success.

I can remember writing *Harry Potter and the Philosopher's Stone* in a café in Oporto. I was employed as a teacher at the language institute three doors along the road at the time, and this café was a kind of unofficial staffroom. My friend and colleague joined me at my table. When I realised I was no longer alone I hastily shuffled worksheets over my notebook, but not before Paul had seen exactly what I was doing. 'Writing a novel, eh?' he asked wearily, as though he had seen this sort of behaviour in foolish young teachers only too often before. '*Writers' & Artists' Yearbook*, that's what you need,' he said. 'Lists all the publishers and… stuff' he advised before ordering a lager and starting to talk about the previous night's episode of *The Simpsons*.

I had almost no knowledge of the practical aspects of getting published; I knew nobody in the publishing world, I didn't even know anybody who knew anybody. It had never occurred to me that assistance might be available in book form.

Nearly three years later and a long way from Oporto, I had almost finished *Harry Potter and the Philosopher's Stone*. I felt oddly as though I was setting out on a blind date as I took a copy of the *Writers' & Artists' Yearbook* from the shelf in Edinburgh's Central Library. Paul had been right and the *Yearbook* answered my every question, and after I had read and re-read the invaluable advice on preparing a manuscript, and noted the time-lapse between sending said manuscript and trying to get information back from the publisher, I made two lists: one of publishers, the other of agents.

The first agent on my list sent my sample three chapters and synopsis back by return of post. The first two publishers took slightly longer to return them, but the 'no' was just as firm. Oddly, these rejections didn't upset me much. I was braced to be turned down by the entire list, and in any case, these were real rejection letters – even real writers had got them. And then the second agent, who was high on the list purely because I like his name, wrote back with the most magical words I have ever read: 'We would be pleased to read the balance of your manuscript on an exclusive basis…'

J.K. Rowling is the best-selling author of the *Harry Potter* series (Bloomsbury). The first in the series, *Harry Potter and the Philosopher's Stone,* was the winner of the 1997 Nestlé Smarties Gold Prize and *Harry Potter and the Goblet of Fire* (2000) broke all records for the number of books sold on the first day of publication. The final book in the series, *Harry Potter and the Deathly Hallows*, was published in July 2007.

See also...
- *Notes from Jacqueline Wilson*, page 78
- *How it all began*, page 82
- *Who do children's authors write for?*, page 87
- *Spotting talent*, page 90
- *Fiction for 6–9 year-olds*, page 124
- *Writing for teenagers*, page 139
- *Teenage fiction*, page 149
- *The amazing picture book story*, page 248

How it all began

Eoin Colfer shares his first experience of becoming a writing success.

I have in my time purchased several copies of the *Writers' & Artists' Yearbook*, yet there is only one copy on my bookshelf. This, I suspect, is a condition common to most authors. When other writers visit my bat-cave – sorry, office – they don't bother asking for a signed first edition of my book, instead they make off with my *Yearbook* secreted up their jumpers. This inevitably happens shortly after I have completed the laborious task of attaching colour-coded paperclips to pages of interest. I know what you're thinking. Colour-coded paperclips. That explains a lot.

My obsession with the *Yearbook* began in the dark era of glitter eye shadow and ozone-puncturing hairdos known as the Eighties. I had recently finished college, and like all males in their twenties, knew all there was to know about the world. The population in general, I decided with humble altruism, deserved the benefit of my wisdom. And the best way to reach my prospective public was through literature.

So I wrote a book. Not content with that, I designed the cover. Multi-tasking even before the phrase was coined. This book qualified as a book because it had many words and quite a few pages. Secure in my sublime self delusion, I got hold of an industrial stapler, bound the whole lot together and crammed a copy into the nearest postbox. One copy would be sufficient, to the country's foremost publishers. I settled back on the family chaise longue and waited for the publisher's helicopter to land in the garden.

Seasons passed and the helicopter never materialised. Not so much as a postcard from the honoured house. Sighing mightily I widened my net, sending copies of my book to several other publishers. I got some replies this time. Would that I had not. Most were civil enough. We regret to inform you, etc… the opening phrase that haunts every writer's dreams. Still, at least they were polite. But a few less generic replies dropped onto my doormat. There was one note in which the handwriting deteriorated in spots, as the editor suffered from sporadic fits of laughter. A pattern was beginning to emerge. Could it be possible that my manuscript was flawed? Was there a chance that my presentation was not all that it could be? Did genius have to be packaged?

Help arrived in the form of an editor's response. 'We regret to inform you…' it began. Nothing new there. I was becoming inured. But there was an addendum pencilled below the type. Get the *Writers' & Artists' Yearbook*. It's worth the investment.

Reluctant as any Irish man in his twenties is to take advice from anyone besides his mother, I decided to act on this particular recommendation. The *Yearbook* paid for itself almost immediately. The mere act of purchasing the fat volume made me feel like a legitimate writer. I left the shop, making certain that my grip did not obscure the book title.

At home, I was amazed to discover that the *Yearbook* was not just a list of publishers. Every possible scrap of information needed by the upcoming or established writer was included (for more details buy the book. And if there are paperclips on this book, it is mine: please return it!) but what I needed to know was detailed under the heading 'Submitting material'. Next time, I vowed. Next time.

Next time turned out to be nearly a decade later. My self esteem had recovered sufficiently to brave the sae trail once more. So I wrote an introductory letter and an interesting summary of the book, and included the first 50 pages – double-spaced.

It worked. Two weeks later I had a publisher. Now I can't put the entire thing down to the *Yearbook*, but it certainly played its part. In public of course, I take all the credit myself. I am a writer after all. But packaging and presentation in my opinion made the difference between desktop and trash, to use a computer analogy.

A few years later my brothers advised me that I needed an agent, as they were running short on beer money. Once again the *Yearbook* was consulted. Not only were the agents listed but they were categorised. These *Yearbook* people were cut from the same cloth as myself. I could almost imagine their desks stacked with coloured paperclips.

My research paid off, and within weeks I was sitting in a top-class hotel treating my new agent to a flute of champagne. Although she insists it was a glass of Guinness in a Dublin pub and she paid.

Since then, I haven't looked back. Things are going well enough for me to be invited to write this article. If you are published and reading this book, hide it away and beware those with baggy jumpers. If you are as yet unpublished, then keep the faith and make sure that all around you can see the title.

Eoin Colfer has written several best-selling children's novels, including the *Artemis Fowl* books which have been translated into 44 languages and have won awards including British Children's Book of the Year, WHSmith Children's Book of the Year, Bisto Merit Awards and the South African Book Club Book of the Year. *Artemis Fowl* was recently voted the Puffin of Puffins celebrating the 70th anniversary of Puffin Books. His book *Half Moon Investigations* was turned into a hit TV series by the BBC and the first *Artemis Fowl* film is currently in production. Eoin's first crime novel, *Plugged*, was published in 2011 and he is currently working on the eighth and final *Artemis Fowl* book, which is due to be released in 2012.

See also...
- *Getting started*, page 1
- *Notes from Jacqueline Wilson*, page 78
- *A word from J.K. Rowling*, page 81
- *Who do children's authors write for?*, page 87
- *Spotting talent*, page 90
- *Fiction for 6–9 year-olds*, page 124
- *Writing for teenagers*, page 139
- *Teenage fiction*, page 149
- *The amazing picture book story*, page 248

Notes from a successful children's author and illustrator

Lauren Child describes how *Clarice Bean, That's Me* came to be published and shares her experiences of taking advice from publishers and editors.

My first attempt at writing a children's book was when I was 18 – my friend Bridget and I had an idea. Everything seemed simple – we were going to write a book, get it published and get on with something else. Almost immediately, and by sheer fluke, we had an interested publisher. We were invited along for a 'working lunch' to discuss the story development. The editor made some suggestions for improvement which we were quite happy about – we really had no objection to rewriting; we were happier still with the business lunch and were fuelled by the confidence of youth that life would always be this easy. We did nothing, of course, and the whole thing fell through which, with hindsight, was a relief – I think we would both be squirming now. It was a number of years later before I even thought to write anything else.

Please yourself

The next time I learnt the hard way, by trekking around uninterested publishers with my portfolio – something it would be almost impossible to do now, as no one wants to see unsolicited work. I used any contacts I had, however distant. I forced myself to phone complete strangers to try to get appointments and advice – something I hated doing. When I met with publishers they seemed to have very set views on what a children's book should be. I listened to their advice and always tried to write the book they wanted me to write. But, whenever I went back to them with my work, there was always something missing – I could never write the book they had in mind.

So, unable to interest publishers, no matter how hard I tried to give them what they said they wanted, I forgot about the whole project and got on with other things. One day, having reached a rather low point in my life, and having looked at every possible career path, a friend suggested that I leave my portfolio of designs, drawings and ideas with her so she could show it to her business manager who had created and managed various successful companies. On meeting this woman, I mentioned I had an interest in film and animation and also designing products for children and, although I had no relevant training, she suggested that I try to write a children's book because, hopefully, it would prove I could create characters and invent a world for them. I think that I was just at a point where I was ready to listen – perhaps because she was very successful, perhaps because it made sense, perhaps because she was a complete stranger.

I started to write the odd sentence, then draw a character, then write a bit more… there was no order to it, no plot structure. I wasn't even sure what I was writing, all I knew was that I was interested when I hadn't been before. I think it helped enormously that I wasn't fixated on creating the perfect children's book – it was merely a means to an end, a way to get into something else. I stopped being self-conscious about what I was doing and stopped trying to please everyone else. When I took this book – *Clarice Bean, That's Me* – to publishers, the difference was very obvious – they were all interested! However, no one was willing to take it on – they all thought it was unpublishable and they told me so. But I knew I had written something that had at least got their attention.

Listening to publishers

Nearly every publisher made suggestions of what I should change in order for this book to be published, some of them quite fundamental. I was told to drop the illustrations and simplify the text. I was told that varying fonts and integrating text and pictures was too complicated, that it would confuse young readers. I listened to them all; I considered what they had to say, but I knew they were all wrong – I knew they were wrong because I knew I wouldn't be happy with the end result. Because I had written something which felt right to me, it seemed better not to be published at all than to publish a book that wasn't really mine. After four or so long years, I eventually found a publisher who was willing to take the book on pretty much as it was.

And I think this is one of the most important things to know – how far will you go, how far *should* you go to be published? When it comes to this you have to follow your gut instinct. Despite my experience, I do think it is important to listen to what publishers have to say – it is always wise to listen, but it is not always right to take it on board. In the end, they can give you the benefit of their experience, but they cannot write the book for you, and you cannot write the book for them. As the writer, the book has to come from you. Of course, if more than one or two people pick up on the same thing then it may be worth following that advice, but for me it is never worth making a change when, after much consideration, it still feels wrong.

Know who you are writing for

When it comes to the question of writing for the 6–9 year-old market, I would say there is no formula. I don't write for 6–9 year-olds, I write for myself. My books are for anyone who wants to read them. For me, writing young fiction is less about writing for a particular audience or age group and more about telling a story that interests me. I have never thought 'Is this a book for 6–9 year-olds?' or 'Is this a book for 8–12 year-olds?'. I feel the same when writing picture books; they are there to be enjoyed by both adults *and* children because while the child looks at the pictures it is the adult who usually reads the story.

How does a writer come up with the interesting ideas in the first place? As an adult writing a children's book, is it helpful – even necessary – to have children of your own? My own view is that it is simply irrelevant. First, we have all been children and anyone who wants to write for children must have strong feelings from his or her own childhood to draw upon. But more importantly, good fiction writing is not about imitation – it is about imagination. Just as having children does not mean you have anything to say to them in book form, so not having children is no bar to writing in a manner to which they will respond. Writing for anyone is about having something to say – a point of view. Writing for children is no different. When it comes to writing fiction, I think that any good writer will see children as people first, and as children second. Of course the context of childhood experiences is different from those of adults, but there is no emotion experienced as a child which is not felt equally in adult life.

At the more practical level, I do not believe that there are any fixed rules. I know that many writers plot a book out before they start, and I had always been told that I needed to plot my books and understand where they were going if I was to write successfully. But

I never begin writing a book knowing how it is going to end. I never normally know how it is going to start either. I generally just begin with a sentence taken at random. For me, it is all about an idea taking hold, and the writing tends to be more about a feeling than anything. *Clarice Bean, Don't Look Now* began as a book about love and ended up being a book more about loss than anything else. I wrote a few sentences about Clarice's inability to sleep and from that the whole mood of the book was determined. I started to write about insomnia and then wondered why Clarice might experience this, which led to thinking about her worries, which in turn led to the idea that she might be feeling very insecure and start questioning things around her. So, in a way, a few sentences shaped the whole plot because they reflected something that I felt personally at the time. I didn't try to force a story that I wasn't interested in writing; instead it became a book about Clarice's anxieties, her inability to explain the world to herself, and some recognition on her part that not only is life something which cannot be controlled, but it's also something which can only be imperfectly understood.

I write a lot of material and read it over and over, until I see what themes are emerging and then I look for a way to hang it all together. Once it has a solid plot, I start to cut. Writing picture books is a very good discipline for writing novels because with just 800 or so words to play with, you have to decide what is important and what isn't: what exactly is this book *about*? Writing picture books makes you much less frightened of editing out the bits that you love. You really can't be indulgent, and have to pare your writing down to the essence of what that story is about. Although of course a novel gives you much more freedom – *Don't Look Now* was 42,000 words – I still consciously try to make sure that every chapter is pushing the story forward and has something to say.

A good editor

That brings me on to another important part – your editor. I really have to trust who I am working with. I rely so much on my editor because of the patchwork way I work. A good editor will let you debate back and forth until you've finally reached a point where you know that you can't make something any better. You do have to trust them because it is so easy to lose your perspective about your own work. You may think it's great and not listen to criticism, but more often than not you will get doubtful and think it's all rubbish, and that's where an editor can keep you believing in your work.

If there's a single piece of advice I could offer for writing fiction, it would be to write from the heart. When I wrote *Clarice Bean, That's Me*, I became passionate about what I was writing and found it exciting. If you're bored when you're writing, you will write a boring book. And no matter how hard you find the early stages, keep going. You just need to write and write until you've written the imitation stuff out of you. It is hard but it is very rewarding too. Writing is one of the best things in the world – a licence to discuss ideas – even if it's just with yourself.

Lauren Child's picture books have won many awards, including the Kate Greenaway Medal in 2000 for *I Will Not Ever Never Eat a Tomato* (2000); the Smarties Gold Award in 2002 for *That Pesky Rat* (2002); and the Smarties Bronze Award for *Clarice Bean, That's Me!* (1999); *Beware of the Storybook Wolves* (2000); and *What Planet Are You From, Clarice Bean?* (2001). In 2002 she published *Utterly Me, Clarice Bean*, the first of three Clarice Bean novels. In 2007 she illustrated a new edition of Astrid Lindgren's *Pippi Longstocking*. Her fourth Charlie and Lola book, *Slightly Invisible*, was published in 2010. Three animated TV series of *Charlie & Lola* have been shown on CBBC and on channels around the world. The first in a new series of children's novels featuring Ruby Redfort, *Look into My Eyes*, is due to be published in September 2011. Her website is www.milkmonitor.co.uk.

Who do children's authors write for?

When writing a children's book, who is an author really writing for? Michael Rosen shares his thoughts on this question and suggests what an author needs to take into account when writing.

People who can write for children don't come with a same format personality or a made-to-measure range of skills. We aren't people who can be easily categorised or lumped together. In part, this is because the world of children's books is constantly changing, starting out from a very diverse base in the first place. This derives from the fact that the world children inhabit is changing and indeed that there is a recognition within the children's books milieu that books are for everyone, not just one small section of the population.

In a way, this means that this is a great time to be writing or illustrating children's books. But that comes with a warning: diverse and changing – yes – but within a set of conventions (I won't say 'rules') and formats. Quite often, people who have written some stories or poems for children ask if I would take a look at them. Sometimes, the first problem that I can see with what they've written is that it doesn't 'fit in'. Or, another way of putting it, the writer hasn't taken a look at what's out there in the bookshops and schools and thought: how can I write something that could go alongside that book, or fit the same niche that that particular book occupies?

But what about artistic freedom? What about the rights of the writer to write about anything? Two things in response to that: nothing can stop you writing about anything you want to, however you want to. But there's no point in kidding ourselves that writing is really 'free'. We all write with our 'reading heads' on. That's to say, we write with the words, sentences, pages, chapters, plots, characters, scenes of the books we've read. If you say to yourself, 'I want to write a novel' or 'I want to write a picture book text', you're only doing so because your mind is full of novels or picture book texts. They are the 'already written' or the 'already read' material we write with. This affects everything we write, right down to the shape and structure of what we write, the tone we hit in the passages we write, the kinds of dialogue and thoughts we put into the writing. A crude analogy here is cooking. We cook with the ingredients that we are given. But more: if we say, we are going to make a cake, there is an understood outcome of what that will be (the cake), and an agreed set of ingredients that can arrive at that understood outcome. So, in a way, we not only cook with appropriate and given ingredients, we also cook with an understood outcome in mind. It has a shape, a smell and a taste that we expect the moment someone says, 'Here is a cake'. Our memory of past cakes prepares our mind and taste for what is to come. This set of memories of past writing and reading is what is in our mind as we write and indeed in the minds of the child readers as they sit down to something they can see is a book. These are what are known as the 'intertexts' we read and write with – memories of past texts.

Secondly, I would say that if you're interested in being published, then you have to look very, very closely at what publishers publish. This means looking at books not only from the point of view of what they say and how they say it. It means looking at what kind of book it is and inquiring whether there are other books like it. How would you categorise it? This asks you to put into your mind a sense of format, of shape, of outcome to guide you as you write. Another analogy: an architect who is asked to design a house knows that he or she has to create rooms that are high enough and large enough for people to live in, that there is a basic minimum of kitchen and bathroom, there is a door to get in and out of, and so on. If it fulfils these conditions, we will call it a house – and not a factory, or a warehouse, say. It's a great help sometimes to look at books from an architect's point of view: what is particular to a book that makes it work? Ask yourself, how did the writer reveal what was coming next? Or, how did the writer hold back and conceal what was coming next? (Writing is a matter of revealing and concealing!) How did the writer arouse your interest? Was it an invitation to care about the people or creatures in the story? Or was it more to do with events or happenings? Or both? Did the book announce itself as being of a particular genre: thriller, historical fiction, comedy, etc? How did it do that? What are the requirements of that genre? Or is it a hybrid?

If all this sounds too technical let me introduce you to someone: the child. If you say to yourself, I'm going to write for children, then even as you say this, you're putting an imagined child (or children) into your mind. This is what literary theorists call 'the implied reader'. We do this in several ways. There might be a real child we know. Robert Louis Stevenson wrote *Treasure Island* largely as part of his relationship with his stepson, Lloyd. But even though we might say, 'RLS wrote it for Lloyd', this doesn't really explain things. What Stevenson was doing, possibly without knowing it, was keeping a mental map of Lloyd's speech and personality in his mind, so as he wrote, he had his version of Lloyd in his head monitoring, guiding and censoring what he was writing.

There is no single way of importing the implied child reader into your head. Some writers do it from memory, connecting with the child they once were and using that version of themselves to guide them in what they write and how they write it. They use memories of what they liked to read, how they themselves spoke and thought and perhaps wrote, when they were a child. Others immerse themselves in the company of children – their own, their grandchildren, nephews and nieces or children in playgroups, nurseries or schools. And some do it by immersing themselves so thoroughly in children's books that they pick up the implied child reader from the actual books. And of course, it's possible to work a combination of all of these ways. What I don't think you can do is ignore them all.

In fact, what you write can't avoid an implied reader. That may seem odd, because you might say that you had no one in mind when you wrote this or that. The reason you can't avoid it is because the language we use comes already loaded up with its audience. So, if I write, 'Capitalism is in crisis', this is a phrase that implies an audience that first of all understands English, then understands the words 'capitalism', 'crisis' and the phrase 'in crisis'. But more than that, it's an audience that wants to read something like that and is, in a sense, hungry or prepared and sufficiently 'read' to want to read such a sentence – or, more importantly, to go on wanting to read what comes next. If I write, 'My Dad was attacked by a banana…' then I'm already positioning the reader to think about someone who is a child and that child is telling something a bit absurd or possibly funny, perhaps the beginning of a family anecdote or family saga. It's also a 'tease', in that a reader who 'gets it', will know that bananas don't attack anyone. It implies a reader who knows that. In other words, the 'implied reader' is 'inscribed' into what we write. In a way, these implied readers are stuck to the words, phrases, sentences, plots and characters we write.

This means that as we write – and when we go back over what we've written – we need to think about the implied reader we've put there. Who is the child who is going to 'get it'? Who is the child who won't? What kind of children are we talking to? What aspects of those implied children's minds and childhoods are we talking to? The fearful person in the child? The envious one? The yearning one? The lonely one? The greedy one? And so on.

A last thought: we talk of 'writing for children'. To tell the truth, I don't think we do just write for children. I think we write as a way for adults to join the conversations that adults have with adults, adults have with children, children have with children – on the subject of what it means to be a child and live your life as a child. Because it's literature, this conversation often comes in code, with ideas and feelings embodied in symbols (teddy bears, giants, etc), it arouses expectations and hopes (what's coming next?) and because it's literature that children can and will read, it often comes along according to predictable outcomes (getting home, getting redeemed, being saved) that remove the obstacles to unhappiness and imperfection that the story began with, and so on. Nevertheless, children's literature has a magnificent history of saying important things to many people, often in a context where adults are caring for children. I think that's a good thing to attempt.

Michael Rosen has been writing since he was 16 and published his first book in 1969. He was the Children's Laureate 2007–9 and has an MA and a PhD in Children's Literature. He is the co-director and Visiting Professor of the MA in Children's Literature at Birkbeck, University of London. His website is www.michaelrosen.co.uk.

Books

Spotting talent

Publishers and literary agents are not looking for what *they* like but for what children will like. Barry Cunningham famously accepted the manuscript of the first Harry Potter book which – as everyone knows – turned out to be the first of an international best-selling series. He explains here what he is looking for when he reads a new manuscript.

I'm a fan: I love reading and I love great stories. My background is in sales and marketing, and for many years I travelled with Penguin the length and breadth of the country – on tours with authors like Roald Dahl, to schools with the Puffin Book Club or to lonely writers' festivals.

It was during that time that I learnt the most important part of my trade – how children react to the books they love, the authors that they adore, and how they put up with the material that they are coerced into reading. Reluctant readers indeed!

So what I'm looking for is what *they* want, not what I like or what you think is good. More of this later.

First steps

All publishers get streams of brown envelopes – especially, like divorces, after Christmas or the summer holidays – when writers finally feel something must be done with that story they've been working on.

We read some part of everything we get. But, be warned, not every publisher does. So, ring up and find out what the publisher wants: sample, complete manuscript, or perhaps, like us, they only accept submissions at certain times of the year.

For most editors, first on the reading list are the submissions from agents, manuscripts recommended by other authors or by someone whose judgement they trust. So, if you know someone who knows someone – use the contact.

Next, know a little about the list you are submitting to: look at their catalogue or read some of their books. Let publishers know how much you like their publications (we all like those sorts of comments!) and how you think your novel might sit with the rest of their titles.

Then, write a short snappy synopsis – a page will do (I've had some that are as long as half the novel itself!). It should tell the publisher what the book is about, its characters and why they should read it.

Also include a little bit about you, the author. Don't forget that. It can be almost as important as anything else in these days of marketing and personality promotion (no, you don't *have* to be a vicar or an ex-glamour model, but it does give an impetus to read on…).

I worked with a very famous editor in my first job who was talking one day about her regular advice to first-time writers. Her advice began with a simple question – 'Have you thought of starting at Chapter 2?'

Strangely, I find myself repeating this regularly. Often I find the first chapter is tortured and difficult, before the writer relaxes into the flow of the story in Chapter 2. And often things improve if we start straight into the action, and come back and explain later. But more importantly, first novels often fail because the editor doesn't get past a poor opening section. Beginnings are crucial, because I know children won't persevere if the story has a poor start, either.

So what am I looking for?

Back to the heart of things...

There are writers who know a lot about children – they might be teachers or parents – so does this mean they can write more relevantly for young people? There are authors who know nothing about modern children, don't even really like children – does this mean they will never understand what a child wants? There are 'crossover' books that don't appear to be for real children at all. There are books with children in them that aren't children's books. Confused?

To me it's simple. Books that really work for children are written from a child's perspective through an age-appropriate memory of how the author felt and dreamed and wondered. The best children's writers carry that childhood wonder, its worry and concern, or even its fear and disappointment, around with them. They have kept the child within alive – so writing is not a professional task of storytelling for tiny tots but a simple glorious act of recreating the excitement of childhood.

That's part one of what you need. Part two, in my view, is a concentration on your audience. I've worked with adult writers too and there is a difference here. Children's authors are creating for a distinctly different readership – they need to think in a more *humble* way than if their work was for their contemporaries. What I mean is that they have to be mindful of how their work will impact on children. Characters must have convincing voices, descriptions must be good enough for children to visualise, and authors must be aware of things like children's attention span when it comes to detailed explanations.

But perhaps even more important is an awareness of the emotional effect of a story on a child. We must always remember their hunger for hope and a bright tomorrow, the closeness and importance of relationships – how easily a world can be upset by parents, or loss of an animal or a friend – and the way in which action really does speak to children, for fantasy and adventure is part of the process of literally growing an imagination.

(If all this means nothing to you, and writing for children is just another category, then I don't think you should bother. That's not to say all this should operate consciously in the mind of the new writer – but that's what a publisher seeks, and that's what I'm looking for.)

Categories and concepts

Everyone has read about the older children's market, and its lucrative crossover into the kind of children's book that adults buy for themselves. I think this will continue to be a growing phenomenon – but the best books in the field will still be clear in their intent: not looking 'over their shoulder' at adults, but true to themselves and their subjects.

I'm sure fantasy will continue to hold a firm following – but with the best books based around character and not simply wild lands and strange people. And historical fiction is poised for a come back for older children – showing the rich material and heritage we have in our shared everyday culture, as well as the 'big battles' of yore!

At last all kinds of young adult fiction has found a firm market and any number of clear voices: hard edged, romantic, comic, or a wild mixture of all three! Both here and in the USA the 13–17 age group has really started buying for themselves, and this is sure to demand more than just conventional 'problem issues' fare.

But my favourite category is the most neglected – real stories and novels for the 7–9 year-olds. This really was once the classic area of children's books, with the biggest names and the greatest longevity of appeal. Sadly, it has become the haunt of derivative series and boring chapter books. I predict a considerable revival, and it will be a great area for new talent.

Picture books seem to have had a much quieter time lately and are, perhaps, awaiting a revival with some newer attitudes. The success of cartoon novels and graphic story treatments for older readers must also hint at a new market here.

Language and setting

It's often said that, like exams, children's books are getting easier, that the language is getting 'younger' while the plots are getting more sophisticated. I don't think this is true. Certainly, for all markets, dialogue is more important than ever – and less time is taken in description.

Children are used to characters who say what they mean, and whose motivations and subtleties emerge in speech. But largely I think this makes for more interpretation and imagination. Descriptions now concentrate on setting and atmosphere, rather than telling us authoritatively what the hero or heroine feels. All to the good in my view, and something new writers for children should absorb.

Also welcome in contemporary children's books is the freeing up of the adult! These characters are no longer confined to small walk-on parts and 'parental' or 'villainous' roles. Nowadays, adults in children's novels are as well drawn as the children, sometimes as touchingly vulnerable people themselves. But as in life, the most potent and frightening image in any children's book remains the bad or exploitative parent.

International scope

Children's literature is truly one of our most glorious 'hidden exports'. British writers continue to be very successful around the world, particularly in the USA and Europe. It is worth remembering this – while setting is not so important as inspiration, obviously UK-centred plots, regional dialogue and purely domestic issues, if not absolutely necessary, are best avoided. But there is no need either – like a creaky old British film – to introduce 'an American boy' or mid-Atlantic slang to your work to appeal to another audience. This seldom works and is often excruciating!

The marketplace

The market still remains delightfully unpredictable. It is hopeless to look at last year's trends and try to speculate. The sound and timelessly good advice is to find your own voice and, above all, to write from the heart. If you can touch what moved you as a child or still moves the child within you, then there's your 'market appeal'. Whether it's aboard the frigate of your imagination or in the quieter, but equally dangerous seas of the lonely soul, skill and inspiration will win you your readership.

Oh, and finally, don't give up. As I once said to a certain young woman about a boy called Harry….

Barry Cunningham was the editor who originally signed J.K. Rowling to Bloomsbury Children's Books. He now runs his own publishing company, The Chicken House (see page 9), specialising in introducing new children's writers to the UK and USA. Notable recent successes include Cornelia Funke, Roderick Gordon, Brian Williams, Rachel Ward, Sophia Bennett, Janet Foxley and Lucy Christopher. The Chicken House and *The Times* jointly run an annual competition to find new writers; see page 389.

See also...
• *A word from J.K. Rowling,* page 81

What makes a children's classic?

David Fickling describes how he chooses a story for publication and hints at how it is crafted into the final book.

This is a variation of the age old exam question, the general one you attempted in a hyperventilating panic as a last resort and with a plunging heart because the question you had swotted up on had been unaccountably and unfairly omitted. This was the make-weight question that looked deceptively easy but you knew was a trap. But you couldn't resist it because it looked like you could write *something*. It was really only meant for the brainiest, to sort them out from us goats. So, if you want a considered, deeply reflective and wonderfully good-humoured and, more to the point, *beautifully written* answer, then may I respectfully refer you to Italo Calvino and his essay *Why Read the Classics?*. Answers to all the 'whys' and most of the 'whats' are in there. Calvino offers 14 increasingly mysterious and connected answers in all, and each one is a gem. There is little more to be added by way of definition. By implication Calvino leads the reader onto 'How do you write a classic?'. Of course the question asked of an editor is entirely different: 'How do you recognise a classic?', and that is the one I propose to attempt here in a deeply personal way with special reference to younger readers.

Recognising a good story

Recognition is everything. We publishers don't do much but recognise and act on the recognition. (The famous editor Maxwell Perkins just said we add enthusiasm.) 'No!' we say, 'We won't publish that'. Or 'Yes!' we say, 'I *love* this. Please please can we publish your story?' We are often wrong but at least we make a decision.

For good or ill, I am a potato print publisher. By which I mean that I do not analyse the decision (much) once it has been made. I am sent a story to consider for publication. I read the story (eventually). And if it moves me to laughter or tears or affects me in some other mysterious and powerful way and seems to be better than all the other things I am being asked to consider at that time, I say to myself 'Let's publish that'. In short, I *recognise* it. I *see* it, *make* it happen, *publish* it – 'there!' – like a potato print. I try to do all that as quickly as possible to the highest possible standard of manufacture. For the reader! Oh and I really like to meet the author, to see if we'll get on, and most of all to make sure they have tons of stories in them. There is really nothing in the world more exciting than meeting a writer with new stories to tell and a singing voice with which to tell them. And then to help bring those stories to readers. I am blessed.

A story is a whole thing in itself, like a melody, to which it is related. It must make sense in relation to itself. It is a wonderful pattern snatched out of the chaos. I try not to take it apart like a pocket watch fearing that I may not be able to reassemble it. It is not good if an author says back to you, 'Well if you know so much David, why don't you write it?'. As a young editor I once sent a five-page letter of quite brilliant, or so I thought, closely argued and typed editorial comments to an elderly experienced author who lived in Wales. My then boss received a sad note from his wife to the effect that Arthur (name changed) had been unfortunately taken to hospital after a heart attack. Nothing to do with David's letter of course, but . . . I have never since written such a letter even though I always write myself copious notes on a book. If I can, I boil those notes down to four or five practical points to say to the author in a relaxed way over lunch or a cup of coffee. Things 'said' can be more easily ignored, discarded, digested or given to the writer. Nowadays I never suggest that the author puts in any different ingredients. I never say, can we have some 'Tanks at the beginning' or could we have some 'Nude Women' or have you tried 'Vampires'? When I suggested to the late Jan Mark that she write about Japan, she reserved for me some choice language (not bad language, *choice*) that previously I had only heard her use about Tony Blair. Of course it was me that was interested in Japan, not Jan. I might venture something like, 'There seems to be something missing in chapter four, tho' I don't know what it is.' And the author might say, 'No there isn't, it's absolutely fine you fool'. To which I shall not demur. Or the author might say, 'Wow David, you are so right, you're a genius, we need some heavy artillery in there. I didn't tell you but I left out the pomegranates but now I am going to put them right back in. Thank you!! Thank you!!'. At this point my demeanour must be that of Beech the butler, or Jeeves. I may allow myself a raised eyebrow: 'Pomegranates' (*no inflection*). 'Very good sir. Will that be all?' P.G. Wodehouse contains in his butlers nearly all the editorial advice a good editor will ever need. The point here is that the story – however long – is the whole thing. I am interested in the whole thing and not just the parts.

When I was nine years old I can remember getting bored while reading the *Wind in the Willows* by Kenneth Graham, an acknowledged classic. The story seemed to be winging along quite merrily. I had been enjoying it. Mole, Rat, Badger and Toad were up and adventuring and then I came to Chapter Seven: *The Piper at the Gates of Dawn*. At that point the story gets interrupted by some long-winded poetical interlude (as it seemed to me at the time). Nowadays I am fond of poetical interludes. Not then. 'What was all that about?' my nine-year-old self asked himself. This is not to say my nine-year-old self was right. Recently I found myself editing the accumulated essays and articles of that amazing writer, Diana Wynne-Jones. Her young self was electrified by reading *Piper at the Gates of Dawn* at an even younger age and she believed reading and recognising the poetic brilliance of that chapter almost kick-started her career as a writer. My point is not about being correct but understanding all readers change over the course of their lives. My editorial point to Kenneth Graham would be this chapter may stop some readers and his answer could have been but it will inspire some too. I hope I would have said 'Okay, we'll leave it in.' Which brings me to the special circumstances in publishing for children. There really aren't any, apart from the fact that most of us are woefully bad at remembering what our minds were like when we were only seven years old. The single biggest error made by all of us publishers is to fail to empathise properly with the reader. Children suffer in particular.

I don't conduct research beforehand. I don't consult other people, unless they be members of the DFB editorial team. The DFB editorial team is like a gestalt mind, a hive mind. We are the editorial Borg. We always agree and no one can tell our opinions apart – in public. Behind the scenes we argue away like (polite) snarling dogs over a bone. Editors work well in teams. When I write 'I' I always mean 'We'. I certainly don't consult the accounts department, the marketing team, the sales department or the bookshop owner or anybody else in the book trade. I listen to them and respect them too, of course I do, but I don't consult them. I might pretend to consult them but I never really take any notice.

(Please don't worry on my account as none of them ever bother reading this kind of article because they are usually too busy grappling with the appalling reality of sales figures.) But most of all, I *never* consult children. How much better it is to be told a wonderful story rather than be asked to choose one. Sometimes I feel I'm sailing against the world's prevailing wind. Children don't want to be asked. They want to be given. Actually all human beings want to be given stories and to learn how to give them to others. If a child likes something, you learn that very quickly. If they don't like something, you learn that quicker. They are the most honest audience on this Earth. Anybody who has read to five year-olds and seen them peel off courteously to the sand pit will know this. Don't listen to all those comedians who talk about 'dying' in the clubs in Glasgow. They know nothing if they haven't 'died' in a nursery school. The test of a story for children is the intentness with which they listen and then how quickly they get their pencils out and start to write, draw or act their own stories. It is a guiding rule: Good stories promote creation, Classic stories promote a culture.

The editing secret

The point is, I have already made the decision to publish before the editorial stage, before any possibility of consultation, exulting inside myself as a reader. The recognition has already happened. I am in love. It's just a case of when not if.

It is in the editorial phase with the author where we check that the story is in as good a shape as it can be. This is really just another phase of the writer's work. It is the author who matters here, not the editor. This is the holy of holies, now, when classics are made. Editors may be useful in the early days, telling authors things they already know but haven't admitted to themselves or learned yet. Later on, good writers invariably know how to edit themselves. Then we editors are happy to be friends and supporters. This editorial phase is a secret, to be kept forever. The editing is important, not the editor. Any editing is like the scaffolding on a house: once the building is finished the scaffolding is taken away and forgotten. Once the story is published, that is how it is. Any new versions are new versions. The original story still stands and if we read it and loved it, we love it as we first read it. Were changes made? I am not saying. Was the first version different? None of your business! The author can talk about the building process if they want. The editor must never speak. It's not polite.

Another kind of group writing that is becoming more and more popular is where teams of writers get together to write stories. It happens a lot in films and television series, for example *The Simpsons*, etc. It has been done before: the great French storyteller Dumas had a lot of help. I admire this kind of writing but am not a practitioner. I like it because it raises the text and the reader's response above all other considerations. However, the set-up and the way of working needs to be established from the outset and all participants need to be given and to accept their due recognition as co-creators. This can be difficult, and besides, I suspect that there is always a presiding authorial mind that takes the decisions. For this reason I am happier with a clear editor/author demarcation. However it is written, the final version is the one to read.

Fairies and money

So you see it is not initially a matter of money, though the definition of Calvino's that most applies is No 6: 'A classic is a book that has never finished saying what it has to say'.

And clearly, if that is the case then it need never go out of print. And it will keep making money for the author and the publisher forever – publisher heaven! A publisher's definition of a classic is a book that never stops selling. But this does *not* mean that everything that sells is a classic, nor that all classics sell immediately.

I have no desire to rehearse the reasons why money is in charge as it will be obvious to all of you: the huge agglomeration into mighty international corporations, the demise of the Net Book Agreement, the adoption of new technology, the internet, the withering of story value, as stories become 'lost leaders' for other more profitable products and thus we crazily sell the most desired books at a loss and the newest and least reader-tested books are priced highest. All this is driven by the insane, bonkers drumbeat of the vast corporations searching for double-digit growth forever. . . . In my experience the people who work within corporations are nicer and cleverer than those outside. But they have been 'taken' and are dancing under the hill with the fairies and cannot stop. When the corporation throws them out eventually, they are bemused and cannot remember where they have been or why. I have seen the sales graphs soaring into the future, and still they climb on and on, faster and faster. Speed is killing the book. Everything has to happen faster these days. Mark my words, there will be a crash. The fairies are powerful but they are no good with money. Put the sales graphs away. Stop consulting. Put the story horse before the sales cart and pile the sales in the back. Of course the sales are important. We need to earn a living. I *love* sales. Like everyone else, I want more. But the way to more is to make things; stop fiddling and checking and get writing and making.

It is the story that matters. When I read a text that is new and original and hits the mark, I know. You know. Everyone knows. You would be deaf and blind not to feel the thrill of it. It is like seeing the northern lights or hearing the horns of elfland and the trumpets of the seventh cavalry sounding together. Or it could be just hearing Christopher's voice in *The Curious Incident of the Dog in the Night-Time*, it is not loud but is so clear and it sounds as if it has always been there and never been heard before.

Why you might ask do I get to choose? Who do I think I am? What gives me the right? You do, dear reader. You do. Thank you. Oh, and a favour, please stop asking our very best storytellers to do so many things. Personal appearances, opening shops, writing reviews, giving quotes. Hush children! They are working. There will be a new story all in good time.

What makes a children's classic? Wait and see.

David Fickling is a children's book editor and publisher. He started his career with Oxford University Press in 1977, moving on to Transworld and then to Scholastic UK. In 1999, David formed his own imprint, David Fickling Books, which is now based with Random House and publishes about a dozen titles per year in the USA, Australia and New Zealand as well as the UK. DFB's successful fiction titles include Philip Pullman's *Lyra's Oxford*, Mark Haddon's *The Curious Incident of the Dog in the Night-Time*, John Boyne's *The Boy in the Striped Pyjamas* and Linda Newbery's 2007 Costa Award-winning *Set in Stone*. In June 2008, the company started *The DFC*, which was published weekly and devoted to comic stories for children. *The DFC* featured mainly long-running serial stories with cliff-hangers and ran for 43 issues before, sadly, closing in March 2009. But *The DFC Library* – books comprising strips from *The DFC* – launched in March 2010, and David is thrilled to announce the launch of *The Phoenix* comic in 2012.

See also...
• *Who do children's authors write for?*, page 87

Writing and the children's book market

Thousands of new children's titles are published in the UK every year. Chris Kloet suggests how a potential author can best ensure that their work is published.

Despite the uncertain economy, the profile of children's books continues to be high, with the value of children's books sold in the UK in 2010 worth over £300 million. Yet it can be difficult for the first-time writer to get published. It is a diverse, overcrowded market, with many thousands of titles currently in print, available both in the UK and from elsewhere via the internet. Children's publishers tend to fill their lists with commissioned books by writers they publish regularly, so they may have little space for the untried writer, even though they seek exceptional new talent. This is a selective, highly competitive, market-led business. Your work will be vying for attention alongside that of tried and tested children's writers, as well as titles from celebrities such as sports and television personalities, and the offerings for children from established writers for adults, who seize the opportunity to widen their audience. Since every new book is expected to meet its projected sales target, your writing must demonstrate solid sales potential, as well as strength and originality, if it is to stand a chance of being published.

Is your work right for today's market? Literary tastes and fashions change. Publishers cater to children whose reading is now almost certainly different from that of your own childhood. In the present digital age, few want cosy tales about fairies and bunnies, jolly talking cars or magic teapots. Nor anything remotely imitative. Editors choose *original*, lively material – something witty, innovative and pacey. They look for polished writing with a fresh, contemporary voice that speaks directly and engages today's critical, tech-savvy young readers. These 'I want it and I want it now' children are used to multi-tasking via different platforms. Time poor, they are often easily bored.

Develop a sense of the market so that you can judge the potential for your work. Read widely and critically across the children's book spectrum for an overview, especially noting recent titles. Talk to children's librarians, who are expert in current tastes, and visit children's bookshops, both in the high street and online, and dedicated children's books websites, such as Lovereading4kids, Writeaway and Achuka. As you read, pay attention to the different categories, series, genres and publishers' imprints. This will help you to pinpoint likely publishers. Before submitting your typescript, ensure that your targeted publisher currently publishes in your particular form or genre. Request catalogues from their marketing department; check out their website. Consult the publisher's entry under *Children's book publishers UK and Ireland* (see page 5). Many publishing houses now stipulate 'No unsolicited MSS or synopses'. Don't spend your time and postage sending work to them; choose instead a publisher who accepts unsolicited work.

You might consider approaching a literary agent who knows market trends, publishers' lists and the faces behind them. Most editors regard agents as filters and may prefer submissions from them, knowing that a preliminary critical eye has been cast over them.

Picture books

Books for babies and toddlers are often board books and novelties. Unless you are also a professional illustrator they present few opportunities for a writer. Picture books are aimed at children aged between two and five or six, and are usually 32 pages long, giving 12–14 double-page spreads, and illustrated in colour.

Although a story written for this format should be simple, it must be structured, with a compelling beginning, middle and end. The theme should interest and be appropriate for the age and experience of its audience. As the text is likely to be reread, it should possess a satisfying rhythm (but beware of rhymes). Ideally, it should be fewer than 1,000 words (and could be much shorter), must offer scope for illustration and, finally, it needs strong international appeal. Reproducing full-colour artwork is costly and the originating publisher must be confident of achieving co-productions with publishers overseas, to keep unit costs down. It has to be said: it is a tough field.

Submit a picture book text typed either on single-sided A4 sheets, showing page breaks, or as a series of numbered pages, each with its own text. Do not go into details about illustrations, but simply note anything that is not obvious from the text that needs to be included in the pictures.

Younger fiction

This area of publishing may present opportunities for the new writer. It covers stories written for the post-picture book stage, when children are reading their first whole novels. Texts vary in length and complexity, depending on the age and fluency of the reader, but tend to be between 1,000 and 5,000 words long.

Some publishers continue to bring out titles under the umbrella of various series, each targeted at a particular level of reading experience and competency, although these are now often replaced by individual author series. Categories are: beginning or first readers, developing or newly confident, confident, and fluent readers. Note that these are not the same as reading schemes published for the schools market and do not require such a restricted vocabulary. Stories for the bottom end of the age range are usually short, straight-through narratives illustrated throughout in colour, whereas those for older children are broken down into chapters and may be illustrated in black and white. The table on page 99 lists publishers' requirements for some currently published series. Check that your material is correct in terms of length and interest level when approaching a publisher with a submission for a series.

General fiction

Many novels for children aged 9–12+ are published, not in series, but as 'standalone' titles, each judged on its own merits. The scope for different types of stories is wide – adventure stories, fantasies, historical novels, science fiction, ghost and horror stories, humour, and stories of everyday life. Generally, their length is 20,000–40,000 words. This is a rough guide and is by no means fixed. For example, J.K. Rowling's *Harry Potter* novels weigh in at between 600–750+ closely printed pages, and publishers now seem more willing to publish longer texts. Stories for this age group are enjoying more popularity, as publishers seek to adjust the balance of their lists following a recent emphasis on the teenage novel.

Perhaps more than in other areas of juvenile fiction, the individual editor's tastes will play a significant part in the publishing decision, i.e they want authors' work which *they* like. They, and their sales and marketing departments, also need to feel confident of a new writer's ability to go on to write further books for their lists – nobody is keen to invest in an author who is just a one-book wonder.

Publisher	Series name	Length	Age group	Comments
A&C Black	Chameleons	1,200 words; 48 pages	5–7	Colour illustrations throughout
	Black Cats	14,000–17,000 words; 96–128 pages	8–12	B&w illustrations throughout
Egmont Books	Green Bananas	500 words; 48 pages	4+	Colour illustrations
	Blue Bananas	1,000 words; 48 pages	5+	Colour illustrations
	Red Bananas	2,000 words; 48 pages	6+	Colour illustrations
Franklin Watts	Tiddlers	50 words; 24 pages	3–5	Colour illustrations throughout
	Tadpoles	70 words; 24 pages	4–6	Colour illustrations throughout
	Leapfrog	180 words; 32 pages	5–7	Colour illustrations throughout
	Hopscotch	350–400 words; 32 pages	5–8	Colour illustrations throughout
	Rhymes to Read	200 words; 24 pages	5–7	Colour illustrations throughout
Usborne Publishing	First Reading	400–1,000 words; 32–48 pages	5–6	Colour illustrations throughout
	Young Reading	1,000–5,000 words; 48–64 pages	6–9	Colour illustrations throughout
Walker Books	Walker Stories	1,800 words; 64 pages	5+	B&w illustrations throughout
	Racing Reads	8,000 words; 80–96 pages	7–9	B&w illustrations throughout

When submitting your work it is probably best to send the entire typescript. Although some people advise sending in a synopsis with the first three chapters, a prospective publisher will need to see whether you can sustain a reader's interest to the end of the book.

Teenage fiction

Some of the published output for teenaged readers is published in series but increasingly, publishers are targeting this area of the market with edgy, hard-hitting novels about contemporary teenagers, which they publish as standalone titles. The enormous success enjoyed in recent years by Stephenie Meyer's *Twilight* saga is dwindling, although other paranormal and gothic romance series still have a large 'young adult' readership. There is also a current vogue for post-apocalyptic dystopian fiction for the teenaged audience. Note also the rise in popularity of graphic novels for this age group, although the first-time writer is unlikely to find many opportunities here.

Non-fiction

There is a wide variety in the type of information books published for the young. Hitherto the province of specialist publishers catering for the educational market, the field now encompasses a range of presentations and formats, including electronic, which are attractive to the young reader. Increasingly, children who use the internet to furnish their information needs are wooed into learning about many topics via entertaining and accessible paperback series such as the *Horrible Histories* and *Murderous Maths* published by Scholastic, and highly illustrated titles by publishers such as Usborne and Dorling Kindersley. In writing for this market, it goes without saying that you must research your subject thoroughly and be able to put it across clearly, with an engaging style. Familiarise yourself with the relevant parts of the National Curriculum. Check out the various series and ask the publishers for any guidelines. You will be well advised to check that there is a market for your book before you actually write it, as researching a subject can be both time consuming and costly. Submit a proposal to your targeted publisher, outlining the subject matter and the level of treatment, and your ideas about the audience for your book.

Chris Kloet is Editor-at-Large at Walker Books. She has written and reviewed children's books and has lectured widely on the subject.

See also...
- *Who do children's authors write for?*, page 87
- *Year in view of children's publishing*, page 101
- *Writing for different genres*, page 115
- *Writing for a variety of ages*, page 120
- *Writing horror for children*, page 132
- *Children's literary agents UK and Ireland*, page 212

A year in view of children's publishing

Caroline Horn reviews the changes in the children's publishing industry.

Books

A sluggish high street, unhealthy levels of discounting and a downturn in the schools and library markets were just some of the challenges facing publishers as the recession continued to bite in 2010. By the end of 2010 all these had taken its toll and figures from Book Marketing Ltd (BML) showed that the number of children's books sold had fallen by 9% to 92 million. This was larger than the decline in the overall book market, which was down by 5% to 339 million. The fall was in part a result of the drop in sales of Stephenie Meyer's *Twilight* books, which made up a big chunk of children's sales in 2009.

Sales of children's books also fell in value, although the decline was not as steep. The value of children's books sold fell by 4% to £435 million, which was in line with the total book market fall of 4%, to £2,183 million.

Changes to chains

Another reason for the fall in children's sales was the closure of Borders at the end of 2009 during the busy pre-Christmas period. Borders had accounted for around 10% of publishers' business and its closure left Waterstone's and WHSmith dominating book sales on the high street. Further problems arose when HMV, the owner of Waterstone's, announced that it would be putting the chain up for sale in early 2011. As rumours circulated about a possible purchase by Tim Waterstone, the man who originally founded the chain, a relatively unknown name stepped in as the new owner, a wealthy Russian Alexander Mamut. Relief followed when he named James Daunt, owner of the successful independent chain, Daunt Books, as the new managing director in May 2011.

Independents, while struggling against the impact of online sales, the recession and high street rents, remain something of a star in the children's sector and publishers have been paying them more attention, especially since the disappearance of Borders and the uncertainty at Waterstone's.

What the independents are so good at is hand selling books, making individual recommendations for buyers so that independents' sales don't depend on bestsellers and the 'three for two' price-driven promotions in the chains. They offer a more distinctive range and give books that are often not backed by the chains a chance in the high street.

For all these reasons, publishers are delighted to see an independent bookseller at the helm of the new Waterstone's empire. What publishers anticipate from his appointment is more local selections by Waterstone's branches, so better reflecting their own consumers (and driving up sales), and less dependence by the chain on discounting. Time will tell if this will happen.

A shift to ebooks

The high street is now up against a number of pressures including rising rents, the economic downturn and competition from online sales and the supermarkets. However, the greatest potential threat to the future of booksellers remains ebooks and the industry's electronic future. While the children's sector will not be as immediately affected by this digital future since the devices are largely in the hands of adults, publishers and booksellers need to anticipate how the shift will transform the industry. By the end of 2012 it is thought that ebooks will account for about 10% of the market, not huge but a taste of things to come. In the USA, Amazon announced in summer 2011 that its Kindle editions were outstripping hardback and paperback sales combined.

In the children's sector, ebooks are expected to be embraced by the teen reader as quickly as they can lay their hands on cheaper (or free!) material; young people are generally expected to prefer reading books on their mobile phones rather than devices such as ebook readers – or traditional print on paper.

Until a child-friendly book device is developed for the child reader (the 'core' children's market is children aged 8–11), the printed book is probably safe. That said, J.K. Rowling's announcement in summer 2011 that she would launch her own Harry Potter website, Pottermore.com, and would also make Harry Potter ebooks available for the first time, shows the opportunities the digital arena offers to authors (at least the wealthy ones), taking complete control of their digital output. The focus of Pottermore.com is entirely on the Harry Potter books and additional written content from the author, not the games that many fans would have anticipated. It is a clear indication of how book-based brands could develop in the new digital era.

The preschool sector was expected to be the last market to switch over to digital reading devices; the cosy image of one-to-one sharing of a picture book is hard to dispel. However, the iPad and the development of other colour tablet devices could have a far-reaching affect on how picture books are shared with children. Already there is evidence that many mums are reaching for their iPhone to occupy a young child, rather than handing them the board books that would once have travelled with them. Publishers have responded by turning brands such as Elmer (Andersen Press) and Spot (Frederick Warne) into successful interactive apps.

Not all authors are happy to shift away from printed picture books, however. Indeed, Julia Donaldson (author of *The Gruffalo* and children's laureate) has refused to have her best-selling title turned into an app on the grounds that she wants children to be occupied with the story, its words and rhythm, not the gimmicks of an online device.

Despite the many perceived threats to its traditional publishing business, publishers are excited about the potential of the online environment for attracting new readers and for the ability it offers to reach consumers direct – even if the apps being sold today are typically 69 pence, or even free, compared to the £6.99 or £7.99 price of a traditional picture book. Most publishers are experimenting with new kinds of digital formats, or with revisiting their established brands such as Elmer.

Like J.K. Rowling's move on ebooks, authors are also getting excited about building direct routes to their own consumers and most now have some kind of online presence. This is certainly an area that is ripe for development in the future, particularly authors going direct and bypassing publishers, even if costs are currently too prohibitive for many authors to consider this option.

Threats to libraries

However, it is also true that away from the best-selling names, most children's authors are finding times tougher than ever before. It has never been easy to make a living as a children's author but the impact of discounting, the quick turnover of books on high street shelves, the threat to library lending rates (Public Lending Right) and cutbacks in schools spending on author visits is making life that much harder.

The fate of our public libraries has been causing huge concern within the industry for several years now, but particularly during this period as many libraries have been at the sharp end of local authority cuts, a result of the government's 'austerity package' to reign in national debt.

Libraries have seemed like a 'soft touch' in the first round of cuts and children's authors have been among a vanguard in fighting threatened closures, pointing out that public libraries often provide the only free access to books for children who do not have books at home. When presented with the 2011 CILIP Carnegie Medal for *Monsters of Men* (Walker Books), author Patrick Ness highlighted the irony of a government that espouses the fight for literacy, while at the same time removing children's access to books. Other reading initiatives, such as the Bookstart programme which gives free books to babies and young children, have also seen their funding drastically reduced.

By the end of 2010, at least 500 libraries were threatened with closure from an existing total of around 4,000 and that number could easily grow. Children's author Alan Gibbons, who founded Campaign for the Book to protest against public and school library closures, says it is still too early to predict the outcome for libraries. There have been legal challenges against threatened closures in regions such as Gloucester, since local authorities have a statutory duty to provide a 'comprehensive and efficient' library service. However, until such cases are resolved other closures and threatened closures will continue.

The government's 'big society' campaign – which aims to have more services run by volunteers – is also having an impact with some councils choosing to hand over libraries to 'local' control in the form of volunteers. What many are finding is that in the course of this handover, funding for librarians and book stock is being slashed – indeed some councils are even threatening to charge these local groups for keeping the library open.

School libraries have also been at the forefront of cost-cutting in schools with many seeing book budgets slashed, or the library closed entirely; while prisons are legally obliged to provide a library, schools are not. Thankfully there are very many examples of active and supported school libraries.

New trends

Given these combined pressures, libraries are inevitably expected to spend even less on books in the coming years. Combined with the uncertainties in the schools market and the growth of online information, the downturn in book spending is putting particular pressure on traditional non-fiction publishing. Some 90% of *Encyclopaedia Britannica's* sales, for example, are now electronic. According to BML, science and nature non-fiction publishing saw the biggest fall in sales in 2010.

Other areas that suffered a decline in sales in 2010 included activity books, licensed publishing, early learning books and horror and ghost stories. On the other hand, sales of adventure stories, classic fiction, picture books and poetry increased.

Science fiction and fantasy were also among the winners in 2010, reflecting a trend among teen readers to move away from the paranormal romance books that have dominated the shelves for a couple of years (thanks to Stephenie Meyer's *Twilight* series) and towards dystopian fiction instead with books like *The Hunger Games* (Suzanne Collins) leading the way. Specialists have pointed out that many teenagers are probably experiencing one of the most uncertain periods for households in living memory with many seeing their parents losing jobs, being threatened with losing their homes or at the very least, their holidays.

Teen/young adult publishing has continued to dominate publishers' interest and output, and booksellers' shelves. Waterstone's announced at the end of 2010 that it would, finally, take young adult fiction out of the children's department and house it in a distinct and separate area; US booksellers made this switch a few years ago. That will undoubtedly have a positive impact on sales of young adult fiction; most teenagers wouldn't be seen dead in a children's book department. It will also encourage adults to buy more teen fiction – many of Stephenie Meyer's fans, for example, were in their mid twenties.

The interest in teen publishing has, however, continued to impact negatively on the amount of publishing for the 'core' market, i.e. readers aged 8–11 years, and there continues to be an imbalance in publishing output. A number of publishers have said that they will adjust their publishing programmes this year to publish more for younger readers by summer 2011 but there was little evidence of this happening.

One of the problems publishers point to is the scarcity of strong fiction being generated by authors themselves, a chicken and egg situation where authors perceive publisher interest in the teen sector, and write accordingly. One of the biggest gaps, as in previous years, is in publishing and marketing of books for girl readers in this age group; when 'core' fiction is published, it generally has a strong boy protagonist with a girl side-kick; well-written books with a strong female lead are few and far between.

Optimism for children's books

Despite the current market difficulties, as we move through 2011 there are a number of areas for optimism. At the top of publishers' lists would be the Waterstone's move out of HMV's control; the bookseller has had a rocky few years and publishers hope to see that reverse under James Daunt's leadership. Finally, it has a managing director again who understands books and bookselling. The recession may also begin to ease and the high street to pick up. One of the strongest areas of growth over the last two years has been in supermarkets and publishers hope that this will continue; supermarkets can reach consumers who do not visit bookshops. Sainsbury's in particular has been driving book sales and in spring 2011 even launched its own brand titles.

Time will also bring a better understanding of the new digital era and what it means for the future not just of traditional print on paper, but of publishing houses and booksellers themselves. Publishers need to find new business models that can cope with much tighter margins, while booksellers need to find other ways to attract customers who could more easily download a book online. The future for children's books is open, and very much up for grabs.

Caroline Horn is Children's News Editor of the *Bookseller* and Editor of www.ReadingZone.com.

See also...
- *What makes a children's classic?*, page 93
- *Spotting talent*, page 90
- *Categorising children's books*, page 181

Books for babies

Books for babies can be wonderfully enjoyable for both infant and reader, and can give the child a head start in learning to learn. Wendy Cooling looks at what makes a successful book for a baby.

In recent years reading has become big news with the phenomenal success of the *Harry Potter* series, *His Dark Materials*, *Lord of the Rings* and such memorable events as World Book Day and the Big Read. Children's books are now being read by adults and people outside the book business have stopped asking in sympathetic voices: 'Do you ever do anything with adult books?'. Within this context the baby book market has been an area of real growth.

For babies

Publishers are not the kind of people who miss opportunities and they have responded with great creativity to this growing market. The Booktrust Early Years Awards (see page 383) celebrate the rich achievements of this publishing. One of the awards, the Best Book for Babies, looks at what makes a good book for the under ones. The first winner was Helen Oxenbury's *Tickle, Tickle* (Walker Books); it has been hugely successful and demonstrates many of the ingredients that add up to a really good book for a baby. The text is a joy to read aloud – very necessary as anyone with children will know that favourite books must be read again, and again, and again. Children don't understand all the words but they respond to the sound of the voice of someone who loves them and to the sound of the words. 'Splish, splash' and 'Tickle, tickle' resonate in the head because they sound good, they're great words to say and help the very youngest children to develop an ear for language that will later take them into reading. The invitation to adult and child to join in with the 'Tickle, tickle' is a winner too as the shared reading experience is always better if there's an element of fun and interaction. The illustrations are a delight as babies rule in this book; they fill every page as they squelch in the mud, splash in the bath and take readers through the pages to bedtime. Helen Oxenbury draws wonderful babies, both black and white, yet children just starting to talk will point to every one of them saying, 'Me, me, me, me.' So this is a book, a tough board book, for a baby to listen to, look at, play with and enjoy in the first two years of life. And, for those parents who worry excessively about learning, children who've enjoyed this book will find that they understand such things as alliteration and onomatopoeia when they come to them at school!

Even before *Tickle, Tickle* babies needed books made from cloth, books for the bath and books with no words at all. Helen Oxenbury's wordless books, first published in 1981, are still the best as her pictures are perfectly observed yet deceivingly simple. *Dressing* (Walker Books) is a good example as it really encourages the adult to talk as each page reveals a clear picture of a toddler progressing with the very complicated business of getting dressed. Many others have tried the wordless book but to do it well is no easy task. My favourite bath book is a small duck-shaped book *My First Duck* (published long ago by Blackie and now sadly out of print). It fits into a baby's hand and feels squidgy and wonderful when wet; it's a great first book as it tells a simple story in clear words and pictures. With a book like this babies learn to love books before they have any real idea about what books and stories – and ducks – are. They just know that the experience is fun and the voice of mum or dad is lovely and they want more of it!

Cloth books too are quite a creative challenge. A good one is *Farm* (Baby Campbell), a stuffed cloth book that crackles and crinkles as it's touched and uses black and white alongside just a little red – colours good for the very young child to pick out.

For innovation it's hard to beat another Baby Book Award winner, *Baby Faces* (Baby Campbell). This is a small board book with round pages joined by a string on which there is also a rattle. You can't move this book, or even turn a page without it making a noise – great, for shared reading with tiny children is often not quiet time! The title of this book describes it accurately as each round page reveals a baby's face and a minimal text as babies say 'hello', demonstrate moods and say 'goodbye'. This time the illustrations are black and white photographs, by Sandra Lousada, and they really do appeal to babies. The publisher has put lots of thought into this, picked up on the research that tells us that babies can focus on black and white long before they can pick out colours, and produced a superb first book for any baby. Baby Campbell also gave us another winning innovation – the buggy buddies – a series of tiny board books that can be attached to a buggy, cot or high chair and so always be accessible to the baby. These books look good and are very close to being toys but with them babies and toddlers learn how books work, learn to turn the pages and to look at the pictures even when no one has time to read to them.

Nursery rhymes

Nursery rhymes, traditional songs and action rhymes are great for all preschool children but there are never enough good, small collections for the very young. Some rhymes are quite violent but many are ideal to start with – hopefully they remind adults of the rhymes they listened to when they were young, because of course talking and singing to children is just as good as reading to them. Too often, nursery rhyme books are packed so full of words and pictures that they're too much for the early years, although children will of course love all the detail on the page as they get older. *Head, Shoulders, Knees and Toes*, illustrated by Annie Kubler (Child's Play), another prize-winner, is a good example for the youngest of children. It is quite a large board book and Annie Kubler's babies fill every page as they touch their head, shoulders, and laugh and giggle as they do it! This is a book that absolutely demands participation and is totally focused on the baby and on fun!

For a more sophisticated edition of a well-known rhyme there's *Twinkle, Twinkle!* (Templar). 'Twinkle, twinkle little star' is told on uncluttered backgrounds with star-shaped cut-outs that are perfect for little fingers to feel and explore. This is a tough and stylish board book that invites talk about shapes as it introduces a traditional poem – it's part of the excellent amazing baby series.

For a big nursery rhyme book it's hard to beat Sam Childs' *The Rainbow Book of Nursery Rhymes* (Hutchinson), for its generous page design, clear and warm pictures and wide range of rhymes – this is a book to last, a book for the bookshelf so it can be dipped into again and again well up to starting school. There is, however, no doubt that babies under one year old prefer the small book that they can hold themselves and keep in the toy box.

For toddlers

As babies grow into toddlers and develop better coordination there's nothing they like more than the lift-the-flap book – unless it's the touch-and-feel book! An example for really young children is Debi Gliori's *Where, Oh Where, Is Baby Bear?* (Orchard Books), offering a good introduction to her positive dad character, Mr Bear. Mr Bear is searching for Baby Bear and there's a flap to be lifted on every page until Baby Bear is discovered on the last page – and in the most obvious place. This is great for under one year-olds, with its delicious pictures and good rhyming text that children will try and gurgle along with before they start to talk. There are several bigger board books featuring Mr Bear for babies to move on to.

It's probably not necessary to mention two long-time winning lift-the-flap titles but I must. Eric Hill's *Where's Spot?* (Puffin) shows exactly what it takes to make a lasting baby book and so does *Dear Zoo* by Rod Campbell (Macmillan and Puffin) These books are worth examining by all would-be authors and illustrators of books for babies. What is it that makes children want to look and listen again and again once they know exactly where Spot is, and what will make the perfect pet?

Young children love to find characters they can read more and more about. As well as Spot and Mr Bear, current stars are Lucy Cousins' Maisy (Walker), Mick Inkpen's Kipper (Hodder), David McKee's Elmer (Andersen) and Tony Ross' Little Princess (Andersen). These characters all appear in board books as well as picture books and will still be enjoyed as children start school. *Weather*, a Little Princess board book, is one of the most delightful non-fiction books ever produced for babies; children who know her will happily learn with her many of the important things of life. All the characters mentioned are drawn with charm and love; all are very original and have the capacity to become friends. Many characters lack these qualities and never get beyond the third book.

What makes a classic picture book?

Babies who experience these exciting early books – and there are many more I could have mentioned – will soon be taking off into wonderful classic picture books such as *Each Peach Pear Plum* by Janet and Allan Ahlberg, *Where the Wild Things Are* by Maurice Sendak, *We're Going on a Bear Hunt* by Michael Rosen and Helen Oxenbury, and Eric Carle's *The Very Hungry Caterpillar*. If you're contemplating a career as an author and/or illustrator of picture books, look at these and at other great picture books carefully for there's a lot to learn – not least that every single word counts in a book for the very young.

What doesn't make a good picture book? The perfect picture book that has been reduced to board book format (why do publishers do it?) simply doesn't work – picture books are more sophisticated than that. Texts that lack rhythm and so really can't be read aloud should not be used. Crowded pages packed with the sort of detail that will intrigue a six year-old are obviously inappropriate for babies. Illustration that lacks quality and offers no interest to the child – and certainly none to the adult – should be abandoned.

So what *does* make a good picture book? Let's have great language packed with fine-sounding words that children will enjoy listening to. Let's have rhythm and rhyme that makes the reader want to turn the page and look/read on. Let's remember that the books are for the babies – it helps if adults enjoy them too but the baby must be at the heart of it. Let's value books for babies and celebrate them – they take children into a love of books and the start of a life as readers, and what could be more important? The right books can be nothing but good for babies, parents, carers, authors, illustrators and publishers – they make commercial and social sense.

About Bookstart

We've always known that an enormous amount of learning takes place in the preschool years and that reading books to babies is a positive thing to do. Yet it took the Bookstart research to really prove to us all that sharing books with children from a very early age can give them a positive advantage when they start school and can change family attitudes to books and book-buying. Bookstart was piloted by Booktrust in Birmingham in 1992 and aimed simply to give books to families when they attended the 7–9 month health check at their Health Centre, and to invite them to join the local public library.

Professor Barrie Wade and Doctor Maggie Moore of Birmingham University evaluated the project and continue to follow the progress of the first babies involved with Bookstart. When they started school this group of children were way ahead of the control group in all literacy-based tests and, rather unexpectedly, in all the numeracy tests. The children who had been read to at home were really ready for school and were able to start with confidence. They knew about stories, about rhyme and rhythm, and about shapes and numbers and most importantly, they knew that books could give great pleasure and that sharing could be fun – their learning from this early book experience was accidental, but very important learning.

Bookstart became established and with government support grew into a nationwide project now giving three packs of books and information about reading to preschool children. Not all Bookstart parents have enrolled their babies at the library but many more than ever before have, and many are buying books whether it be in bookshops, by mail order or at car boot sales, which has to be good for books and for babies.

Wendy Cooling MBE is a highly respected children's book consultant and reviewer, and winner of the 2006 Eleanor Farjeon Award. She taught English in Inner London comprehensives for many years before becoming head of the Children's Book Foundation (now Booktrust) where she initiated the Bookstart project. She is a regular guest on book-related radio and television programmes, and is the compiler of several children's fiction and poetry anthologies.

See also...
- *Writing and illustrating picture books,* page 244
- *Booktrust,* page 358

Writing books to read aloud

Best-selling author Anne Fine looks at why and how books are read aloud to children.

The first thing to say about writing books to read aloud is that they should be as much of a pleasure to read alone silently as any other story. Indeed, at first it's difficult to see where any differences might lie. Certainly when it comes to stories for the very young we tend to have a picture in our heads of the exhausted parent inviting the child to 'clean your teeth, hop into bed, and I'll read you a story'. And since all days are long for a parent, nobody wants their offspring to be worked into a frenzy all over again. So, in the classic bedtime stories for the younger child, there's very often a softer humour and a gentler tone, and a satisfactory and fulfilling ending.

And for the older child, there often isn't.

So, same old story really. No rules (or having to face the fact that rules appear to be there only for some other writer to irritate you intensely by making a fortune breaking them). But there are always the basic guidelines.

Keep things as simple as they can be for your particular story. With picture books you can of course assume that the child is propped up beside the reader, sharing each illustration as it comes along. But by the time the child is six, maybe they would prefer to snuggle down and shut their eyes to listen. So do you really have to take half a dozen sentences to describe the rigging, and the number and nature of the sails, and exactly how the ship was armed? Couldn't you just refer to it as 'the most magnificent galleon that ever sailed the seas' and leave it at that? After all, if those cannon ever come to be fired, we'll hear about it later.

Listeners are easily distracted. One minute they're all ears; the next, they're actually more interested in tracking the progress of a fly across the ceiling. Of course they're not going to admit they've lost the thread of the story, in case the parent snatches the opportunity to suggest they're too tired to listen and makes for the door, or the teacher decides it's time to move on to the workbooks. But their attention does stray. So it is best to try (as ever) to order your tale so you can start at the beginning and move on in sequence, steering clear of flashbacks.

On this matter of keeping things simple, does it sound mad to say that plots can be overrated? And never more so than in books designed to be read aloud to the young. In my own very short chapter book, *It Moved!*, Lily takes a stone in for Show and Tell and claims it sometimes moves, and we just get to see who in the class believes her and who doesn't, and how they all react over a day of watching it. In the *Stories of Jamie and Angus*, Jamie is an amiable child of about four in a perfectly normal household. His favourite soft toy is a little Aberdeen Angus bull. In the first story, Angus ends up in the washing machine when he's supposed to be 'dry clean only'. In another, the pair sort out the books in their bedroom according to their own rather strange shelving preferences. In yet another, they do little more than draw 'angry eggs'. The stories almost couldn't be more plain and domestic, and yet we still run through joy and misery, jealousy, anxiety, distress, fear, empathy, generosity, self-sacrifice, fury, resentment – the entire mercurial gamut of pre-school emotions. So do be confident that, especially for the very young, a tremendous amount can be forged from what seems, at first sight, not very much at all. With writing –

just as with practically everything else in life – it's not what you do but the way that you do it.

Children, like adults, have to *care* about what's being read. We adults tend to ask the 'Can I be *bothered* with these people?' question before returning a book, half-read, to the library. It's a test even harder to pass when you're writing for young ones. Remember Robert Browning:

> *If you want your songs to last*
> *Base them on the human heart*

because children love to identify with someone or something in the story – it doesn't really matter what. It could be another child, or a puppy, or even a lost pebble. But they do have to care. So perhaps it's best to make sure that, all the way through, your listener knows what your character (or puppy, or pebble) is feeling. And make sure that these are thoughts and emotions they will recognise. A child of six isn't 'disappointed that the weather is unpleasant'. It's all far more immediate. He feels the tears pricking because his socks are wet and his woolly hat is itching and his coat's too tight under his armpits. Ever heard them moan?

Joan Aiken once remarked that anyone who writes for the young 'should, ideally, be a dedicated semi-lunatic'. But you can go too far. The problem is one of differing – and shifting – levels of sophistication. What makes one child hoot with laughter will cause another to sneer, and there is in any case an entirely undefinable line between cashing in on a child's acceptance of the unlikely or the magical, and offering them something they think of as simply being 'stupid'. You might, for example, get away with the idea that the horse the child rescued from its cruel owner is being secretly kept in the garage, only to find your young readers baulking at the suggestion that Mum could walk in to fetch a screwdriver and not even notice it.

Avoid being arch. Of course there are differing levels at which many shared books can be read. The older reader often gets a sly chuckle out of things that sail right over the head of somebody smaller. But the joke does usually have to be at least potentially inclusive, so that, the tenth time around, out comes the thumb, down comes the chubby hand to stop you turning the page, and out comes the question: 'Daddy was just teasing them, really, wasn't he?' 'Mum *really* wanted to get back to reading the paper, didn't she?' In the benighted language of the National Curriculum, the child's already 'drawing inferences from text' (or, as we used to call it back in the good old days, 'reading').

Does it help to read your work aloud to children to see how it goes down? Not really, no. For one thing most children are notoriously polite and gentle with people they love, or strangers who come into class. And the sheer joy of having their opinions canvassed can send them haywire. One says, 'I liked this bit!' You beam, and all the other hands shoot up. 'I liked that bit!' 'And I liked that bit!' Everyone wants to have a go at the pleasure of shouting out to the visitor.

So trust your own judgement. You are the writer, after all. Try reading it aloud to an imaginary son or daughter or class. You'll soon notice which bits you're rushing through because they're tiresome, and which of the sentences you're tripping over because they're too clumsy or long. You'll realise that, yes, you *can* put that rather ambitious word into a story for four year-olds because the very context and the way in which it will be read out will make its meaning transparent.

Are there some subjects best avoided in books to be shared between adults and children? Again, it's hard to say. Some parents will read anything the child demands. Others, like teachers, will beach up on things like 'pottymouth' poetry ('Well, *you* just said bogey! And you just said poo *twice!*'). Or books that appear to encourage the child to relish – or, worse, be amused by – cruelty and the infliction of pain. I watched as at least 30 parents with small children trooped out of a book fair when one enthusiastic author read out a passage from one of his history books about red hot pokers being driven up people's bottoms. (I wondered, frankly, why the others stayed.) He may justifiably argue that he's sold hundreds of thousands of copies, but I would guess that few of them have been read aloud by squeamish parents to imaginative children before the lights go out. So use your sense.

What about *how* a book is read aloud? Should that make a difference to how you write it? I don't see how it can. After all, some readers treat the words in the old-fashioned way, and simply speak them with intelligence and inflections sympathetic to the meaning. They read, in short, as if it were a *book*. Others go half-mad, acting out every sentence, doing all the voices in different accents, shouting the yells and whispering the quiet bits. They treat the pages in front of them pretty well as a script for a stage performance. Like every other author whose work has been professionally recorded, I've shuddered through one actor's butchering of my work with his frantic showing off, and also been startled to find tears pricking as another has used her skills to mine a poignancy I had forgotten about or never even realised was there. It's their own voice that most writers hear in their head as they put down the words, so go along with that.

And that's the root of all writing, when it comes down to it. Your own voice. Children are strange. Ralph Waldo Emerson defined them as 'curly dimpled lunatics'. They assume that they're immortal. (Why else do adults have to step in so smartly and often, simply to keep them alive?) And children are at one with eternity. (When did you last see a nine year-old glance at a clock and say, 'My God! It's three already! And I've got nothing done!') Their lives may change immeasurably. See how the language of their stories has moved so seamlessly over the centuries from tumbledown cottages in dark forests, through secret gardens and kind governesses, to the babysitter and the stepbrother. But in their essential nature – however individual and various those natures may be – children have barely changed at all.

So the successful children's authors will always be those who can best make their work chime in with the child's capacity to understand and enjoy it. And since, like Walt Whitman, all children 'contain multitudes', that gives the writer enormous scope to get it very, very wrong or very, very right.

Anne Fine is one of the best known and most popular writers for children of all ages and was Children's Laureate 2001–3. She has twice won both the Carnegie Medal and the Whitbread Children's Book of the Year Award and at the Galaxy British Book Awards has twice been voted Children's Author of the Year. She has also won the *Guardian* Children's Fiction Prize and dozens of other awards in the UK and abroad. Her work is translated into over 40 languages. Anne also writes for adults. Her website is www.annefine.co.uk.

Writing for girls

Louise Rennison shares her thoughts about writing books for girls.

It still amuses me *a lot* when so called grown-ups have to read the titles of my books out loud. At one of my book launches, a middle-aged respectable-looking bloke in a suit was forced to say: 'And we are really looking forward to seeing *It's OK I'm Wearing Really BIG Knickers* at the top of the best-selling list'. Tee hee hee. I had to be practically carried to the loos because I was laughing so much when the same bloke announced the publication of my new book *Knocked Out By My Nunga-Nungas*. And this you see, in a nutshell, is the secret of my geniosity. I don't have to unleash my teenager within when I write Georgia's diaries because it is already unleashed and wandering around like a fool. (As I write this I am wearing my fluffy mules and a tiara, just in case I suddenly get asked to a party.) It is very restful being yourself(ish).

One of my first readings was in a bookshop in Brighton. It was a mixed adult and teenage audience and as usual I did *ad hoc* rambling. I told the audience that everything in the books was based on real life – my life – and that I had written *Angus, Thongs and Full Frontal Snogging* really quickly and used real people's names. I said I meant to change them before the book was published but forgot.

For instance, my loony school caretaker was nicknamed 'Elvis' because he once came to a school dance and did some exhibition twisting on stage until his back went and he had to be taken to casualty. Well, in the book he is called 'Elvis Attwood'. And guess what his name was in real life? Yes, Mr Attwood. Now you get the picture. Ditto 'Nauseating P. Green' and 'Wet Lindsay'.

Anyway, I was telling the audience that all the characters were real and the family in the book was my family in real life and so on and a woman said 'Well, how does your family feel about having all of their secrets revealed?' My mum was in the audience and I replied 'I don't know. Mum, how do you feel about having all of your secrets revealed?' Mum was slightly flustered by this because she wanted to be proud but also wanted to keep her distance, so she said 'Well, on the whole I think this is a very good book but of course the bits about me are grossly exaggerated.'

Another member of the audience said 'So did you really go to a fancy dress party dressed as a stuffed olive?' And, sadly, I had to admit it was true. I made the 'olive' bit out of green crêpe paper and chicken wire to make the round shape. Then I dyed my face, neck and head red for a pimento effect. It was quite funny at the time – well, it was when I was still in my room. The difficulty came when I tried to get out of my room. I had to go down the stairs sideways and I couldn't get in dad's Volvo. He told me I'd have to walk but offered to drive really slowly alongside me. I announced I would walk there by myself in that case and he got all dadish and said 'I don't want you wandering around the streets at night by yourself.' And I replied 'What would I be doing wandering the streets at night dressed as a stuffed olive? Gate crashing cocktail parties?'

But he didn't get it. Anyway, when I did get to the party (walking with dad driving his Volvo alongside me at five miles an hour) I had a horrible time. Initially, everyone laughed but later ignored me. I did have a dance by myself, but things kept crashing to the floor around me. In the end, the host asked me to sit down. I tried – but failed. Still, I did find out that I am not on my own *vis à vis* childishosity. At the end of the reading, a woman confided in me that she'd gone to a fancy dress party as a fried egg! We both shared a chuckle and I said 'Blimey what were we like?'And she replied 'No Louise, you don't understand, this was last week!'

What was I rambling on about? Oh yes – writing for girls. It's a hoot and I thoroughly recommend it. All you do is think about jokes, boys, snogging and lipstick. Perfect. I wish I had a useful tale to tell about how to write for girls, but the fact is that everything I have done has been sort of accidental. I wasn't intending to write books. In fact, years ago, I used to perform my own show entitled 'Stevie Wonder felt my face'. (He did actually feel my face… hang on a minute… 'Stevie Wonder' was also based on my real life. I am sensing a theme here…) Anyway, I was at the Edinburgh Festival doing my show and my first instinct was to reply 'Oooh no, I don't want to be stuck in a room writing by myself'.

I did eventually write my first book in 1999. I was a columnist on the London *Evening Standard* and I wrote a piece about having to have my shoes surgically removed. (Once again based on a real incident. I had forced my big fat feet into tiny strappy stilettoes out of sheer vanity, and then I fell out with my boyfriend and clip clopped off home in a high dudgeon (I lived on the other side of London). When I eventually got home, in the early hours, I fell asleep on the sofa fully clothed and still wearing my shoes. I woke up in the morning to find my feet had swollen up and my shoes were cutting into my feet. The shoes were embedded in my feet. I had shoefeet. My friends carried me to Charing Cross Hospital casualty to have them cut off.

The day after publication, Brenda Gardener from Piccadilly Press phoned me up and asked me to write a teenage girls diary and I asked why me? She said 'Because I have never read anything so childish and self obsessed as your article and I think you could do a really good job.' And the rest is historosity. But not very good advice for getting a book deal!

When I attempted to write the book, quite a few people pointed out that I am in fact not a teenager and haven't been one for quite some time. A very long time. A very very long time. Their advice was that I go and talk to some teenagers. I tried this straight away because I assumed it was possible to talk to teenagers – but it isn't – it is a hopeless task. You can't get any sense out of them at all and very often they do that helpless laughing thing. They know they should just stop it because if they don't someone will kill them, but they still can't stop. Anyway, I did attempt to speak to them for 'research' purposes. I asked one group of girls if they still did snogging. And they looked at me as if I had fallen out of someone's nose. They said 'SNOGGING? You say snogging. Snogging? How sad is that?' Then when I asked another group of girls, they looked at me in the same way and said 'Yeah, we say snogging, what else would you say you sad person?'

So, on the whole I more or less ignore what 'the youth' say. When I do readings and signings I am very often asked which are my favourite teenage books. My answer is – none. I don't read teenage books because I am not a teenager. In truth, I really am very ignorant about the whole 'teen' thing and that's how I want to stay. I deliberately don't read anyone else's books. I just plug into what I remember about my own teen times.

I recall parts of my teens very vividly. When I was 15 my family emigrated from Leeds to Whakatane, New Zealand. I'm sure I remember things around that time because of the high drama of what I went through. But I think that if I hadn't had any major drama to star in I would have made some up for myself. After all, every teenager is the star of their own melodrama. *Everything* matters and can potentially ruin your life – the way your fringe lies, a spot under your skin (*aka* a lurker) and I won't even go into the nose slimming measures.

Having an excellent memory definitely helps and I do credit myself with a head made for trivia. Did you know that your memory is like a muscle? The more I go back in time to remember, for example, my teenage friend's and my scoring system for snogging (graded one to ten – number five being a three-minute kiss with no breaks) the more I remember.

Of course, it helps if you are still on speaking terms with other people who were there at the same time. I am still in touch with my 'Ace Gang' from school and they can sometimes fill in the gaps in my memory. For instance, I was talking to my friend Rosie about one of our school teachers, Herr Kamyer. He had the double comedy value of being the only male teacher in an all-girls school and being German. I recalled a physics experiment he did using billiard balls on a tea towel to explain how molecules vibrate. At the time, I found this very funny and I put my hand up and said 'Herr Kamyer, what part does the tea towel play in the molecular structure?' And Herr Kamyer made his fateful mistake and replied 'Ach no, I merely use the tea towel to keep my balls still.' It was absolute pandemonium. I could not stop laughing even as I was taken to see the headmistress. Anyway, while Rosie and I were talking about this incident, she remembered something else about Herr Kamyer that I had completely forgotten. She recalled when he had taken our class by train to the Lake District. The train had slam doors on each side of the carriage and when the train pulled into the station Herr Kamyer leapt up said 'Ach here ve are' and stepped out of the door on the wrong side of the train and disappeared onto the track. Oh – happy days.

Writing for teenage girls is somehow timeless. The rites of passage that my mates and I went through in the Sixties are not so very different – emotionally – from girls now. Fashions have changed and the bands have different names but girls still strop around worrying about boys liking them and ignoring their long-suffering dads. Somewhere, even as I write this, a girl will be thinking 'For the teenage vampire party I could make one big eyebrow out of theatrical fur. That will be vair vair funny.'

Louise Rennison is the author of 11 books for teenage girls. Her most recent book is *Withering Tights* (HarperCollins 2010). Her other books are *Angus, Thongs and Full-Frontal Snogging, It's OK I'm Wearing Really Big Knickers, Knocked Out by My Nunga-Nungas, Dancing in My Nuddy-Pants, And That's When it Fell Off in My Hand, Then He Ate My Boy Entrancers, Startled by His Furry Shorts!, Love is a Many Trousered Thing* and *Stop in the Name of Pants!* A film based on the first two books, *Angus Thongs and Perfect Snogging*, was released in 2008.

See also...
- *Writing and the children's book market,* page 97
- *Writing for different genres,* page 115
- *Writing series fiction for girls,* page 152
- *Teenage fiction,* page 149
- *Writing for the school market,* page 157
- *Creating graphic novels,* page 227

Writing for different genres

Malorie Blackman looks at the different genres of children's books with a view to helping writers decide what kind of story they could write.

Take a trip to your local library or bookshop and peruse the children's section. (Also check out the books for young adults.) The books will probably be sorted into age ranges, for example books for babies and toddlers, books for the 5+ age range, books for 7+, 9+, 11+ and books for young adults or 14+. Take a closer look. There will probably be a separate poetry section (but not always) and a separate non-fiction or reference section. Take an even closer look. Are the books in the fiction section divided by genre? Probably not. There are so many different genres (and sub-genres) and so many books which span more than one genre that it would be a thankless task to sort books in this way. But we all have views on the types of stories we like to read – and write.

For the purposes of this article (and my sanity), I shall only be looking at the main fiction genres for children. My genre list is by no means definitive or exhaustive, but what I want to do is present some guidelines for some of the genres and some examples of books for further reading. Let me say straight away that a number of the books I've listed below quite happily overlap other genres as well. Take my own book for young adults, *Noughts and Crosses*, as an example. The story is about the friendship of two teenagers, Callum and Sephy, which eventually turns into a deep, undying love. Does that make it a romance/love story? The story takes place in an alternative version of contemporary Britain. So it's a fantasy story – right? Callum is a 'Nought' (white) and Sephy is a 'Cross' (black) and their society has strict demarcation lines where the two groups are not encouraged to integrate. Noughts are the minority and historically the ex-slaves of the Crosses. As the book takes an angled look at modern-day racism, does that make it a real life/contemporary story? Genre can be a hard one to pin down.

One of the first pieces of advice I received when I started writing was 'write about what you know'. Even though this advice is a useful starting point, I don't necessarily agree with it. After all, that's why we have imaginations, to take us outside of our own limited realm of experience. My advice would be to write what you *care* about rather than what you know. If you care about it, but don't know too much about it, then you'll take the trouble to find out, to do proper research. And if you care about it, then you'll write with a passion and a heart that will shine through.

Beware of choosing to write in a genre simply because it appears to be 'currently fashionable'. You may feel that you'll have more chance of being published or making money that way, but it's unlikely to be true. If you don't truly believe and feel every word you write, it will show. And what is 'currently fashionable' may not be so in one or two years' time. For a while in the mid to late 1990s, horror stories were the thing. Over the last few years, fantasy has been even bigger. But that also means there is more competition as every writer hoping to make some fast money jumps on that bandwagon. What makes your story more original, inventive and readable than the next one? If you can't answer that question, think long and hard about the type of story you are writing – and why.

Thrillers

Under this heading, I include the sub-genres of crime, ghost and horror stories. The key to thrillers is the battle between the protagonist or central character in your story and the antagonist or opponent. Your protagonist must have someone or something to battle against. Weak antagonists make for a weak story. Look at the *Harry Potter* stories for example (though they are not strictly speaking thrillers). Harry has to battle against the formidable Voldemort. Now if Voldemort was a weak enemy and easily vanquished, it would've made Harry's fight against him far less interesting. An antagonist doesn't have to be a person. It can be an organisation, the *status quo*, an object, but whatever it is, the reader should empathise with the protagonist's struggle against it.

Good examples: *I Am the Cheese* by Robert Cormier, *Cirque du Freak* series by Darren Shan.

Action

Always a favourite, action books are packed with incident. The most successful books in this genre certainly possess that page-turning quality which makes them incredibly hard to put down. Crime-busting spy thrillers are particularly popular. The protagonists are usually teenagers who invariably have to use their intelligence to get themselves out of myriad tricky situations.

Good examples: *Alex Rider* series by Anthony Horowitz, *Cherub* series by Robert Muchamore.

Mystery and adventure

These kinds of books catapult their readers into rip-roaring adventures. Most children love a puzzle element in a story and love the challenge of solving it. The puzzle element also provides that essential page-turning quality required for a successful book. The reader should not just want but *need* to know what is going to happen next. These types of stories, as well as thrillers, need endings which provide some resolution and a sense of closure. The puzzle presented in the story needs to be solved to be truly satisfying.

When I'm writing a mystery or an adventure story, I always make sure that the protagonist's troubles get worse in the middle of the story. Much worse. For example, in chapter one of my novel *Hacker*, one of the protagonists, Vicky, is accused of cheating in a Maths test by hacking into her teacher's computer to get the answers. But there's worse to come. When she gets home, she and her brother Gib find out that their dad has been arrested for siphoning off millions from the bank where he works. Worse is to come! Vicky and her brother have a huge bust up when Gib tells Vicky that her real parents drowned to get away from her and that she's not his sister and she never will be (Vicky is adopted). So not only does poor Vicky have her own school problems to deal with, she has to find a way to prove her dad innocent and find her own place within her family.

Good examples: *Wolf* by Gillian Cross, *Creepers* by Keith Gray.

Survival

Survival stories include stories where the protagonist finds himself or herself alone, with limited resources and having to rely on his/her wits to survive. These types of stories tend to involve a lot of interior monologue so that the reader can really get inside the head of the main character(s). The danger with this type of story is that the protagonist's plight can become a bit monotonous, so new, *believable* challenges have to be employed throughout the story and there has to be a real sense of jeopardy should the protagonist fail. These are great stories for having the protagonist learn a lot about themselves in the process. Characters in these books have to make a real emotional journey for the reader to care about them.

Good examples: *Wolf Brother* by Michelle Paver, *Kensuke's Kingdom* by Michael Morpurgo.

Animals and nature

There are two basic types of animal story – where real animals act in a 'realistic' way and anthropomorphosised animals, i.e. animals who are in fact humans. The latter allows children to identify with the main character(s) and to share in their adventures. Animals can be used to portray complex emotions in a way that is instantly identifiable to children but also one step removed. In this way, animals can be used to write stories about a number of difficult topics for younger children, such as bereavement or loneliness.

Good examples: *Watership Down* by Richard Adams, *The Sheep Pig* by Dick King Smith, *Fire, Bed and Bone* by Henrietta Branford.

Real life/contemporary

This is a vast genre which covers any kind of contemporary circumstance. These books – which are more than thrillers or mysteries – live or die by the central character(s). The protagonists don't necessarily need to be sympathetic, but we must empathise with them at least, otherwise readers won't bother to finish the book. This genre includes school and family stories, stories that deal with disfigurement or disability – the list is endless. When I write one of these stories, I always write a short five-page biography of each of my major characters: their favourite foods, their favourite types of music, their likes and dislikes, loves and hates, what their friends love about them, what their friends find annoying, etc. I will never start writing any novel until I know my main characters inside out. That way I'll know how they'll react in any given situation. And my characters become real people to me, and sometimes when I'm writing they'll behave in ways that surprise me. I take that as a good sign. It means my characters have really taken on a life of their own.

Good examples: *Holes* by Louis Sacher, *The Illustrated Mum* by Jacqueline Wilson, *Stone Cold* by Robert Swindells, *(Un)arranged Marriage* by Bali Rai, *Junk* by Melvin Burgess, *Speak* by Laurie Halse Anderson.

War

Unfortunately a genre which is always relevant. This genre allows the writer to examine the best and the worst of human nature.

Good examples: *Private Peaceful* by Michael Morpurgo, *I Am David* by Anne Holm, *Goodnight Mister Tom* by Michelle Magorian.

Romance and love stories

This is a popular genre for exploring relationships, and stories tend to be aimed at young adults.

Good examples: *Saskia's Journey* by Theresa Breslin, *Forever* by Judy Blume, *No Shame, No Fear* by Ann Turnbull.

Sports

This genre uses sport to illustrate and illuminate the major character(s) or society as a whole.

Good example: *Keeper* by Mal Peet, *McB* by Neil Arksey.

Fantasy

Hugely popular, this genre seems to have taken over from traditional myths and legends. It appeals to the sense that there is something inside or outside of us which we may or may not be able to control, and stories often contain a magical element.

Good examples: *Harry Potter* series by J.K. Rowling, *Artemis Fowl* by Eoin Colfer, *His Dark Materials* series by Philip Pullman.

Historical

Research, research, research. Do your research. For me, the best historical stories shine a light on the way we live now. This genre of course includes war, which is listed separately.

Good examples: *Hero* by Catherine Johnson, *Coram Boy* by Jamila Gavin.

Humour

Humour is always popular. It's easy and engaging to read but hard to do well. Anthony Horowitz's *Diamond Brother* series are fantastically funny crime novels and a particularly successful example of a fusion of genres. I've put them in this category though because for me, the antagonist in each of the *Diamond Brother* stories is almost incidental. I don't mean the books have weak antagonists; they don't. But it is the humour rather than the crimes in these stories that I more easily remember!

Good examples: *Angus, Thongs and Full Frontal Snogging* by Louise Rennison, *The Hundred Mile-an-Hour Dog* by Jeremy Strong, *I Know What You Did Last Wednesday* by Anthony Horowitz.

Science fiction

Science fiction is a vast genre. It can take you to other worlds, other times, other spaces and places, other minds. The writer who first turned me on to science fiction as a child was John Wyndham. I found his book *Chocky* totally mind-blowing. And it woke me up to the possibilities of science fiction. Science fiction isn't only spaceships and aliens from other planets – though there's nothing wrong with that! This genre allows for new technology and methodologies to be explored as in *Unique* by Alison Allen Grey, which explores the idea of cloning, or my own book, *Pig Heart Boy*, which uses as its starting point the whole notion of xenotransplantation (the transplantation of organs from one species into another). The title of my book gives away the species of the donor and the recipient!

Good examples: *Mortal Engines* by Philip Reeve, *Unique* by Alison Allen Grey, *Hex* by Rhiannon Lassiter.

Poetry/narrative verse

Over the last few years, there has been a welcome increase in the number of stories told in narrative verse. This genre is particularly useful for those children for whom unrelenting pages of prose can be quite daunting, but who still want to be told a story as opposed to reading a series of different poems on unrelated subject matter. Narrative verse stories contain all the drama and heart of prose stories but are an interesting form to use when telling the story. As a writer, you need to be very clear as to why you want to tell your story in this way. And bear in mind that narrative verse is very hard to translate, thus limiting foreign edition options – but don't let that stop you. If your story needs to be told in narrative verse – then go for it. Stories told this way should vary in rhyme, rhythm and cadence or they quickly become boring.

Good examples: *Love That Dog* by Sharon Creech, *Cloud Busting* by Malorie Blackman, *Locomotion* by Jacqueline Woodson.

Short stories

The sad fact is, short stories are a very hard sell. Random short stories across many different genres are an even harder sell. Short stories which focus on a particular genre may be easier to get published but not compared to writing a novel.

Good example: *A Thief in the Village and other stories* by James Berry.

Graphic novels

A number of well-known children's books have also had graphic novel editions published. These include *Stormbreaker* by Anthony Horowitz and *Artemis Fowl* by Eoin Colfer. Graphic novels are expensive to produce so it is rare for an unknown author to be published in this form by a children's publisher. Manga novels are becoming increasingly popular so this may change in the near future.

Fairy stories, myths and legends

These types of stories appear to have fallen out of fashion somewhat, which is a great shame. As a child I loved fairy stories and books of myths and legends from around the world. There was something very comforting in knowing that a true heart and a courageous spirit would eventually triumph over adversity. However as Rick Riordan shows, there's plenty of material in fairy stories and legends which can still be used and given a completely modern twist.

Good example: *Percy Jackson* series by Rick Riordan.

Malorie Blackman has written over 55 books for children, including picture books and novels for all ages and reading abilities. Her most recent books are *Boys Don't Cry* (2010) and *Double Cross*, the fourth in the *Noughts and Crosses* series. Malorie has received a number of awards including the FCBG Children's Book Award 2002 for *Noughts and Crosses*, a BAFTA for best children's drama with *Pig Heart Boy* in 2000 (also shortlisted for the Carnegie Medal), and the Smarties Silver Book Award 2004 for *Cloud Busting*. Her website is www.malorieblackman.co.uk and she is also on Facebook and Twitter.

See also...

- *Who do children's authors write for?*, page 87
- *Books for babies*, page 105
- *Writing for girls*, page 112
- *Writing for a variety of ages*, page 120
- *Fiction for 6–9 year-olds*, page 124
- *Writing humour for young children*, page 126
- *Writing fantasy for children*, page 129
- *Writing horror for children*, page 132
- *Writing historical novels for children*, page 135
- *Writing for teenagers*, page 139
- *Writing crime fiction for teenagers*, page 143
- *Writing thrillers for teenagers*, page 146
- *Writing for the school market*, page 157

Books

Writing for a variety of ages

Geraldine McCaughrean has written for both babies and adults – and all ages in between.
In this article she looks at the variety of writing forms she has been published in.

I spent my teenage years writing adult novels about things I knew nothing of, and (not surprisingly) having publishers turn them down. When I became an adult, I was published as an author of children's books, because at least I knew the world from a child's perspective: everyone has been a child. I was hugely prolific back then and, since each publication day felt like a fluke, constantly on the lookout for the chance to write more before my luck broke. It did not occur to me to specialise – in novels, in picture books, in educational or mainstream. Did you know that a baby's bath toy, if it has 25 words or more printed on it, becomes a book and exempt of VAT? I have reason to know this. I'm not proud, me.

Once my children's books started to win prizes, I was able to get adult novels published, too. Once, just once, I got paid the same for a 32-page picture book text that took a day to write as I got for a 600-page novel that had taken me two years. So which would I rather do? The answer is 'both', plus a few more titles for the ages in between, and a sprinkling of retellings for the fun of it. I have tried my hand at writing for almost every age, from toddler to adult. Three words are not enough to cover the many variants of Writing for Children. Each age range brings its own pleasures; each is as different from the others as crossword-puzzling is from writing a shopping list.

I confess that, when my daughter was small, I got very interested in writing picture books. As she grew older, my interest rose up in parallel with the pencil marks on the doorframe. Young children aren't much functional use, though, beyond their inspirational qualities. Horribly partisan, they love everything a parent or grandparent reads to them, regardless of merit. They only become really useful guinea-pigs later.

Picture books

At the core of a successful picture book is a good visual idea that hasn't already been done. Unfortunately, such ideas don't come along to order. And a nice little story won't cut it as a picture book text. Since the text is not there to describe the pictures, it has to do something else. You have, essentially, to lay 14 and a half visual opportunities in the lap of an artist, one for each spread plus the last verso.

The words mustn't vie with the pictures for room. The younger the age-pitch, the fewer the words – not just because the font size will be bigger, but because the child's concentration is shorter between page turns. A very young child's world does not extend far beyond home, parents, pets, toys and playschool, it's true. But within an astonishingly short time, nonsense, adventure, humour, delicious big words, sadness, bravery, magic, and wonder have all entered the child's ken. But whichever end of the scale you are writing for, there is always a third party to consider: the poor benighted soul who may be obliged to read this book over and over and over.

I once submitted a text, sure it would fail on grounds of conceptual sophistication. The young brain is slow to acquire the concept of Time, and this text was about a grandmother telling her granddaughter why she doesn't need a clock to tell her the time. It is my best-selling picture book, because grandparents love it. Children seem to, too, but then they haven't read Piaget's work on conceptual development so they don't know any better.

I embark on a picture book as I would poetry rather than prose, pouring on the word play and euphonious vocabulary, making the most of the aural splendour of words. It's almost sure to be read aloud, and small children love big language. After all, they have been acquiring new words every day without the aid of a dictionary, and are very good at it.

… Which is why writing for the next age bracket is more depressing.

School readers

Gone is the invitation to roll in glistening language like a lamb in dew. Grim school gates have clanged behind us and there is literacy fodder on the lunch menu. Over and above the big, famous reading schemes, *a lot* of books are published for use with learner-readers; it's nice work if you can get it. Well, it's work.

Here, it is all simple vocabulary, simply syntax and a list of prohibitions: no pigs, knives, alcohol, guns, occult… From the fairy-tale world of stepsisters hacking off their heels, and pigs boiling water in readiness for the salivating wolf on the roof, the child moves forward into a bald landscape where female tractor drivers commute between capital and full stop, avoiding unpleasantness and pork products on the way. I'm generalising, of course, but it feels 'cabin'd, cribb'd and confin'd'. The design is functional, the illustration generally cheap – and the editors rewrite your words, leaving you wondering why they didn't just write it themselves in the first place.

Younger fiction for independent readers

So the next, independent-reading phase – for, say, 7–9 year-olds – ought to offer a merciful relief. The sector is horribly dominated by collectible series, of course, and since you won't beat them, you may want to join them in Pink-Pong land: pink prettiness for girls and naughty nasties for boys. Heigh-ho. Surely there must be a Middle Way between the female tractor driver and the pink sequin fairy? There is, of course. There are some wonderful books out there that reward close reading – just not enough.

I began writing for this age group after sitting on a few judging panels, where oddly few attractive entries had been submitted for the 7–9 year-old category. I still think it is a neglected age group – and it's such fun to write for too, especially if your publisher can match you with a good sparky illustrator. Surely this is just the age when books should be covetable, tempting objects in themselves – miraculous little wedges of wonder with which to prop open new doors.

The best thing about writing for the primary age is that the school visits are more fun. Adult authors can be recluses if they want, so long as they are interesting recluses who can hint at a dark and sensational past during their 'rare and long-awaited' interviews. But if you're a children's author you do school visits. It's useful, informative, punctures any illusion of achievement, and, for many authors, is a way of making ends meet. In primary and middle schools the audience is largely on your side and ready to join in (even those who hate books). Some authors can win over Year 8s, 9s and 10s as well. It's just that I've been trying for 30 years, and coming away exhausted from willing them to like me, speak to me, forgive my crime of polluting the world with books they don't want to read. With forethought – think! – I *could* have confined myself to writing for Years 1–7 and saved myself a lot of tears.

Myth, legend and retellings

The National Curriculum – little as I care for it – has its advantages for a children's author. For instance, there are two 'Myth' slots (Years 5 and 7), which have brought the ancient

Books

gods out of their dingy library alcove and made them popular again. I keep going back to myth and legend, because they are an encounter with the Big Stuff: terror, love, creation, war, fate, heroism, atonement, death, Fate and God... It feels good to roam among the 'ageless' stories, where all narrative has its roots. And its juggernaut splendour crushes petty political correctness under its wheels without anyone even noticing.

I like to alternate original fiction with retellings of existing stories. After all, why incessantly create new beasts when there are magnificent old ones who have roamed the earth for centuries and should never be allowed to become extinct?

Teenage and young adult fiction

When history looks back on the last decade's fiction, will Black-and-Red look like the Plague sweeping Europe, killing the weaklings, leaving behind it empty fields and full graveyards? Some days it feels like it. I love writing for teenagers – just not the same teenagers who read Black-and-Red, since I have no insight into them whatsoever. I'm not going to attempt to 'get down wiv the undead' because I would be rubbish at it. I shall confine myself to writing for those who are experiencing adolescence much as I experienced mine. There may not be many of them (though surprising numbers creep out of the bushes when their peers aren't looking) but at least I'll get it right. There is nothing messier or more painful than a failed jump on to a bandwagon.

Even if the plague of vampires, angels and werewolves passes, it may leave one permanent scar. Bookshelves at Foyles bookshop in London are now divided into Teen Fiction and Young Adult (other shops have other labels). I admit I needed the distinction explained to me. Apparently, Teen Fiction covers gore, sex, horror, S&M soft porn, vampires, the Undead, occult, necro-fantasy and anything your mother would rather you didn't read. Young Adult covers... well, anything else (apart from Fantasy which has a bookcase of its own). Choose your destination now, you writers for teenagers, because your book will only be shelved in one of these places. It will be similarly categorised online, too.

Incidentally, Remedial Literacy books, for older readers with younger reading ages are *the* boom sector of the industry just now. (Sad but true.)

Older fiction

I have left my favourite category till last. And it's one marked for extinction. All research shows that the complex, linguistically challenging 12+ novel will be the first to go. So keep away. Those of us already aboard will go on baling with increasing frenzy, but why join a sinking ship? Why would you?

Perhaps because it is the most pleasurable, diverse, gratifying field of all. These readers have the skill and stamina to tackle a long book, can appreciate character, style and satire, tackle politics, philosophy, morality, and are open to new departures. They're still reading at age 12 because they like books! They have worked out that, inside a book, they are free from the oppression of either teacher or parent. No need yet to fan their libido or steer a path through their bleak angsty fantasies. The author is free to revel in language and character, to experiment, to cultivate fertile plots.

Consequently, the field is hugely overcrowded and is the area where contracts are being cancelled, projects abandoned, authors turned out of the circus to fend for themselves in the wild. Morale is understandably low.

Annoyingly, books decide for themselves what they want to be, and there is no point in cutting them off at the knees to pretend they are younger, or standing them on a chair to pretend they are older. However selfish it sounds, a book gains most from an author at ease with the story and writing for the joy of it. A book is only as old as it feels.

Children's books span such a variety of forms – far more than for adults. When you consider the distance between babyhood and teenage years, it is hard not to relish the number of possibilities strewn along the way.

Geraldine McCaughrean has been a full-time writer for 30 years and has produced over 160 books and plays. Six times shortlisted for the Carnegie Medal (which she won in 1989), her novels do not fit readily into any one category, but tend towards adventure. She won the chance to write a sequel to J.M. Barrie's *Peter Pan and Wendy* for Great Ormond Street Hospital; and *Peter Pan in Scarlet* was published in 2006 in 50 languages.

See also...
- *Books for babies*, page 105
- *Writing for different genres*, page 115
- *Fiction for 6–9 year-olds*, page 124
- *Writing for teenagers*, page 139

Books

Books

Fiction for 6–9 year-olds

Alison Stanley worked for many years as a commissioning editor of young fiction. She gives here what she regards as essential components of a good fiction book for younger readers.

When teaching six year-olds in the mid-1970s, 'reading' was something that involved a queue of children at my desk, waiting to be heard struggling through their less-than-stimulating reading scheme books. There had to be a better way of developing reading skills, especially as the delight of sharing real books with the children during 'storytime' at the end of the day, was such a marked contrast. I had no idea in those days about the business of publishing, and I certainly never imagined that many years later I would be commissioning books for that very same age group to read and enjoy. But without that classroom experience, I doubt that I would have begun to appreciate the needs of the young beginner reader. Nor would

Books for younger readers

Here are some of my favourite books for younger readers that have stood the test of time. Read them and you'll know what I mean!

Happy Families series by Janet and Allan Ahlberg (Puffin)

Horrid Henry series by Francesca Simon (Orion)

The Littlest Dragon by Margaret Ryan (Collins)

Mr Majeika series by Humphrey Carpenter (Puffin)

The Worst Witch by Jill Murphy (Puffin)

Spider McDrew by Alan Durant (Collins)

The Black Queen by Michael Morpurgo (Random House)

Morris the Mouse Hunter by Vivian French (Collins)

Clarice Bean by Lauren Child (Orchard Books)

Lizzie Zipmouth by Jacqueline Wilson (Random House)

There's a Viking in My Bed by Jeremy Strong (Puffin)

I have experienced that magical moment when a child just breaks through the reading skills barrier and begins to read unaided for the very first time. The anticipation in excitedly turning over the page to find out what happens next; the thrill of a guessed word being right; and the beginning of reading for pleasure are all magical moments to witness.

Beginner readers

What makes a good book for children just beginning to read on their own – one that will stimulate and motivate them, and let them know that reading is an enjoyable and rewarding activity?

Firstly and simply – beginner readers need good stories. Strong plots that are easy to follow, so that when faced with an unrecognisable word, the child can predict what is going to happen and be able to have a go at reading that 'difficult' word. Lively and appealing characters are essential too, especially if featured in more than one book.

Beginner readers like stories that reflect their experiences of the world but also ones that will stretch their imaginations. Stories with a fantasy element rooted in the real world where something ordinary becomes extraordinary in a familiar world, are always popular. The language of the stories should be rhythmic with plenty of repetition and alliteration. Sentences need to be short enough so they don't get split by a page turn, but long enough so that the story doesn't read in a stilted fashion.

Books for beginner readers require a generous typeface and good clear layout with plenty of illustrations giving clues to the text. This will help make the transition from shared picture books to reading alone a smooth one.

Last, but definitely not least, there is one vital thing to remember when writing stories for the beginner reader… beginner readers read *slowly*. Wacky, fast-paced humour within the text does not work when read word for word, very slowly. Humour in the text needs to be obvious, relate to the child's world and work when read at a snail's pace (see *Writing humour for young children* on page 126 for inspirational advice on writing funny fiction).

Ten questions

To summarise, the ten questions I ask when assessing manuscripts for younger readers are:

Plot
• Is it a good story?
• Will it make sense when read slowly?
• Will it keep the reader wanting to turn over the pages?
• Is the story strong enough to stand up to the competition?

Setting
• Is the story set in a world that children will be familiar with?
• Are there events in the story that children will relate to?

Characters
• Are the characters appealing and original?
• Are the characters rounded enough for the beginner reader to want further books about them?

Language
• Is the vocabulary suitable for the young beginner reader?
• Is there plenty of repetition, alliteration and rhythmic writing?

I would also want to know about the author. I'd want to know if the manuscript was written by a published author, and if so, do his or her books sell? (Never forget that publishing is a commercial venture!) If it is a new author, I'd like to know if he or she is seen to be a major new talent who will progress to write further books.

The editorial process can help with many of these points, but the originality and uniqueness of a story belong to the author. Because there are so many books written for this age group, it takes a special author to create something new and appealing, something that will stand the test of time.

Confident readers

Once children become fluent readers, there's usually no stopping them in their quest to read more, and soon move on to longer novels. It's at this stage that they are exploring the different genres – humour, horror, adventure, or themes such as school stories, animal stories and football stories, amongst others. They're also finding out which authors they like to read and will be actively seeking out new books by that author. Confident readers come in all shapes, sizes, ages and with different backgrounds and personalities and it is essential that this is reflected in a broad range of reading matter.

Alison Stanley was a commissioning editor at Puffin Books and at HarperCollins Children's Books, where she was responsible for developing the younger end of the fiction list. She also commissioned more than 40 titles for the Collins Education *Big Cat* series KS1 and 2.

See also...

• *Who do children's authors write for?*, page 87
• *Books to read aloud*, page 109
• *Categorising children's books*, page 181

Writing humour for young children

Like most adults, children love humour. But in both cases the joke will fall flat unless it is aimed at the right audience. Jeremy Strong has ten rules for writing humour for young children.

The snappy bit: some simple rules

1. Never allow your bum to become gratuitous.
2. Write wrong.
3. Self mutilation is highly recommended.
4. Words are essential.
5. Pulchritude? No way.
6. Inside every 20-plus there's an eight year-old trying to get out.
7. You calling me a wozzer? Mankynora!
8. Just who do you think you're talking to?
9. Surprise!
10. Ha! I laugh at death.

The expansive bit. We begin at the beginning, with Rule Nine. Surprise! Ha ha! That's pretty much self explanatory.

Rule Six: Inside every 20-plus there's an eight year-old trying to get out.

Years ago, when I first began writing for children, I was often asked (by adults) why it was that the stories I wrote seemed to appeal to children. You have to imagine an adult asking this question, in a tone of voice that mixes one part admiration to ten parts complete bewilderment. I used to answer, fairly truthfully, that only my exterior had aged along with my chronological age, and that I was still aged about eight inside. The adult would usually laugh and would go away as bewildered as they were before they'd asked the question. The point here is, I think, that it isn't possible to really understand except from a child's viewpoint. If you have forgotten what it was like to be a child then you're unlikely to understand.

Rule One: Never allow your bum to become gratuitous.

To make matters worse, adults often think the things that make children laugh are puerile. To some extent this is true and it is easy to make a child laugh by playing 'lowest common denominator' jokes – jokes that refer to farts, snot, bums, knickers, etc. But whilst employing these guaranteed tickle-sticks it is easy to forget that children also like quite sophisticated jokes.

As for the bums and farts, it's okay to pop them in here and there but, for the sake of at least some self respect, keep them to a minimum. Never let your bum be gratuitous.

Rule Four: Words are essential.

Children love word play, and they love 'knowing' jokes – for example, jokes that are aware of how bad they are, or referential jokes that make use of things familiar to them, the things that mark out their lives, such as school, parents, family.

Then there is the matter of what children can read and understand. Obviously, this is going to vary not only with age but with ability. Anyone who has taught junior age children knows that there are children of six who can read like 11 year-olds, and *vice versa*, with all shades in between and quite frequently further beyond. Nevertheless, as a writer, you need to aim towards the centre. In this article I am going to concentrate on 6–11 year-olds because those are the ages I taught for 17 years.

Let's look at language. Things need to be fairly simple. Shorter, rather than longer sentences work best. But like all rules this one can be deliberately misused. For example, at some appropriate point in a story you might wish to hurl yourself into some ever-increasing sentence that just seems to plunge on and on at a relentless pace and with reckless abandon like a runaway car because that happens to be one of the best ways your writing can capture the manic activity that is going on in your story at that particular point. Maybe it is a description of a runaway car. You get the point. Children respond to this positively because, anchored as it is in a normally short and simple style of writing, the over-long sentence becomes not only a writing device, but also a source of humour.

Rule Ten: Ha! I laugh at death.

As with comedy for other age groups, nothing is held sacred. You will, however, have to obey the obvious rules that generally apply to writing for children, and also steer clear of the PC police. You can be smutty, but not dirty. You can be unkind to animals, but they mustn't be in a circus, unless you're a signed up freedom fighter for 'Say no! to performing dumb creatures'.

You can laugh about death. (It's an emotional release. Honest.) You can even have stereotypes and clichés – but in this instance don't expect to get published.

Rule Two: Write wrong.

Children love to recognise things that are wrong, and this is where word play often has great effect. Characters that get their words or spellings wrong are a good source of humour, not only because it is funny in its own right, but because children love the empowerment of recognising what's wrong. (You will, incidentally, lose brownie points for using words like 'empowerment'.)

Rule Seven: You calling me a wozzer? Mankynora!

Invented words can also be a terrific source of enjoyment for both writer and reader, especially when they are used as expletives – sort of coded (and therefore safe) swear words. Mankynora! Wozzer yourself! Let's also take a look at sophistication. You have to ask yourself, am I writing a joke for an adult or a child? I know for a fact that I am guilty of putting jokes for adults in some stories – jokes I know only an adult will understand. (Or sometimes a joke that a child will get on one level, but where the adult will see a second 'hidden' joke or implication.) The reason I do this is because (a) I can't resist the temptation if it's a good one, (b) I like to remember that many of my books are read to children by adults, and so I am putting in something to make it more enjoyable for them, and (c) I don't do it often and I make sure that the vast majority of the humour is firmly in the child's grasp.

Rule Five: Pulchritude? No way.

Whilst on the subject of sophistication it is worth thinking about the words you use. With each word you need to ask yourself: can a child of 'x' years read and understand this word? Apply a bit of common sense. There are some words a child might not understand but it might be worthwhile introducing it to them, allowing the context to help reveal its meaning.

The word sophistication itself is a reasonable example. Many junior children would not understand it but, although it's long, it's not too difficult to work out what it says and you could argue that it's a good word for a child to know. On the other hand, the word 'pulchritudinous' is not only very hard for a child to work out but it is extremely unlikely you would need to use such a word when writing for junior children and if you do then you seriously need to reconsider what you are doing.

Rule Three: Self mutilation is highly recommended.

You have to be rigorously self disciplined about this. No matter how good a joke is you have to cut it out if it's not actually funny to your audience. The humour also needs to arrive and leave quickly. Anything that takes pages to set up is not worth it and the longer it takes the more likely it is that your writing will become increasingly false and unnatural as you struggle with all the scaffolding you require to hold up the joke.

Rule Eight: Just who do you think you're talking to?

It is a mistake to think that the things adults laugh at in children make good material for children's books. They don't, for the simple reason that it's funny to the adult watching the child, and not the other way round. All of this points to one of the cardinal rules for writing anything: be aware of your audience. Keep that firmly in mind and you can't go far wrong. I was going to finish by writing: May the fart be with you. Then I realised that it would be out of place and one fart too many. See what I mean?

Jeremy Strong writes humorous fiction for 8–11 year-olds. His books include *The Karate Princess* titles, and three Viking stories which were made into a popular television series. Jeremy won the Federation of Children's Book Groups Children's Book Award for *The Hundred-Mile-an-Hour Dog*. His first book for young teenagers, *Stuff*, won the 2006 Manchester Book Award. In 2008, *Beware! Killer Tomatoes* won four book awards, including the Sheffield Children's Book Award. New titles published by Puffin include *My Brother's Hot Cross Bottom*, *Krankenstein's Crazy House of Horror*, *Christmas Chaos for the Hundred Mile-an-Hour Dog* and *Batpants*.

See also...

- *Who do children's authors write for?*, page 87
- *Writing for different genres*, page 115
- *Writing comedy for children's television*, page 299

Writing fantasy for children

William Nicholson describes how he arrived at writing books for children and offers some advice to writers looking for success.

I entered the world of writing fantasy books late – I was just past 50 – and with a deliberate objective in mind. At the time my working days were mainly given to screenwriting. I wanted to break free from the various constraints that were limiting my writing and to write without a brief, and without the expectations or demands of others hovering over me. I told no one what I was up to. I wanted to set out on an adventure, without knowing where it would take me. I told myself that my new work would be 'for children', but more to free myself from the baggage that comes with the decision to write a grown-up novel. I made no attempt to calculate what children might want to read, or what vocabulary they could manage. My own children at the time were aged six, eight and 11, and I was fully aware of the explosion of new and exciting work in the field. As I began work I was just hearing tell of a popular new book featuring Harry Potter; but there were as yet no dreams of the millions to be made writing children's books.

I wrote as an escape, in precious hours stolen from proper paid work. My only rules were that I would keep my story vivid, moment by moment, and would follow my strongest emotions at each turn. The plot and the characters all grew out of simple but deeply felt emotions, rather than ideas: first, my rage at the over-testing of children in schools; then love for a gentle father; then terror of conformism among teenagers; and so on. In many cases, as I moved from scene to scene, I found myself developing a visual idea and only discovering later that it contained an emotional core, and was in fact driven by it. For example, the Mud People: these idle friendly folk who live in sewage began as a picture in my head, of the Underlake, a cavern beneath a city filled with a lake of sewage, lit by shafts of light where there are breaks in the ceiling rock. But as I developed the inhabitants I realised I was writing about a way of living I longed for myself, far removed from the antiseptic fear-based task-driven world we've created. In the same way the warring tribes of Barakas and Chakas began as an image of a great land-ship looming slowly over a dune horizon, and then developed into a satirical critique of the kind of military bravado that takes care to avoid any actual danger.

The point, I suppose, is that I was playing. I was allowing my imaginative self to go where it willed. This sounds like a recipe for sloppiness, but in fact as the book grew it became more and more clear to me what it was about, and what its natural style should be. I should also emphasise that as with everything I write, I planned the ending before I started work. This is my way of preventing a story from becoming aimless. I always know where I'm going, even though I don't know exactly how I'm going to get there. This open but directed way of working provides me with the two key aids to creativity: freedom and discipline.

By the time I finished I found to my great surprise that I had not after all written something outside my usual range: I had in fact been dealing all along in my usual adult obsessions, love, God and death. Most surprisingly, as was pointed out to me by others, the hero of my story was not an individual but a family. Far from following the usual template for children's books, in which the child hero has no parents, and is threatened by the world of adults, my main characters are all members of a close and loving family. This family is based on my parental family, and on my own family; both of which are of course central to my existence. The wonder of fantasy writing is that however far you roam from home, you end up telling the truth about yourself.

The result of all this was *The Wind Singer*. My agent read it, admired it, and explained the many ways in which it could be better. I rewrote extensively. She then placed it immediately with a fine publisher. It came out, it won prizes, and it's now in 25 languages. None of this could ever have been planned by me. However, once it was out, I realised I had an entire new career, which I have embraced with joy and energy. I developed the plot and characters of *The Wind Singer* in two more books, which became a trilogy called *The Wind on Fire*. Then I wrote an even more ambitious trilogy, *The Noble Warriors*, which is less widely read, but is perhaps the finest thing I've ever done. More recently I ventured into the world of realistic teen fiction, with *Rich and Mad*. That's seven teen novels in ten years, all written well past the age at which some are thinking of retirement. It's never too late.

Of course I've been helped in this career by the fact that I was already a successful writer in another field, and was already represented by an agency. However, I truly believe that anyone can get past the gatekeepers if they have the talent. A year ago I was one of the judges of the Costa Children's Book Award, and read some 45 novels, which had in turn been selected from a much longer list as the best of that year's crop. Some of the books I read were excellent, but most were poor. By this I don't mean that they were badly written, but that they were predictable, derivative, lacking in imaginative energy. Far too many seemed to believe that ceaseless manic invention is in itself exciting. But the poor reader, bewildered by yet another Tolkeinesque array of made-up names, and yet another set of intricate magic rules, loses patience and drifts away. The core of all great story telling is character. No amount of clever devising of alien worlds will make up for characters in whom the reader has no interest. Make us see and feel your hero, make us care passionately for him or her, and then you can do whatever you like.

How do you create characters the reader cares for? I think it's as simple as this: you have to care passionately about them yourself. And that means, however you disguise it, that you are your heroes. You're living through them. In the second book of my trilogy, *The Wind on Fire,* I found myself creating a character who was a beautiful 16-year-old princess called Sisi. I meant her to be a joke, a satire on girls who are so pretty they don't trouble to make friends. But as the story evolved I became more and more fascinated by Sisi, and she ended up playing a major role in the trilogy. What I had discovered, as I tell school audiences to their squirming delight, was that deep inside me there was a gorgeous 16-year-old princess trying to get out.

So here's my advice to aspiring writers of children's books, for what it's worth. Please read it in the knowledge that there are no rules, and your path may be very different to mine.

Explore your own fantasies. Harness the power of wish fulfilment. Get right in there with your characters and feel the ache in their hearts. Richard Adams wrote about bunny rabbits in *Watership Down*, but really he was writing about his own dreams of military glory. Don't try to write a bestseller in order to become as rich as J.K. Rowling.

Don't try to analyse the market. Write something no-one's ever seen before.

Test your work on others – it almost doesn't matter who, so long as they're not you. Then pay attention to what they say. If you can't take criticism and learn from it you have no future as a writer.

Don't give up. Most of the published books out there are poor, and most of the unpublished works you're in competition with are dire. Talented new work will find a publisher – agents and editors are looking for it all the time.

Don't give up the day job. Making a living as a writer is very hard. And anyway, you need the job to connect you to the world of other people. This is where you'll be finding your insights and your inspiration, though you may not realise it. Fantasy doesn't come from dreams, it comes from the real world. You may think your strange invented land ruled by robotic pigs comes straight from your subconscious, but actually those pigs are just people you know in disguise. They're probably you. How do you keep going in the face of rejection and disappointment? How do you know you're good enough to justify the time and effort and secret dreams? You don't. Either you can deal with this or you can't. But if you do keep going – if you listen to criticism and respond to it – if you keep going longer still – and listen to criticism again – and oh God, rewrite again – you'll make it. It took me 30 years of writing to get to *The Wind Singer*. I expect you'll make it sooner than I did.

William Nicholson is a screenwriter, playwright and novelist. He has written several books for older children including the award-winning *Wind on Fire* trilogy (Egmont). His most recent book for teenagers, *Rich and Mad*, was published in 2010 (Egmont). He also writes novels for adults but is perhaps best known as a highly acclaimed Hollywood screenwriter whose work includes *Elizabeth: The Golden Age*, *Shadowlands* and *Gladiator*.

See also...
• *Who do children's authors write for?*, page 87

Writing horror for children

'Nine stories you'll wish you'd never read' it warns on the cover of *Horowitz Horror*. Anthony Horowitz writes about writing horror for children and, aware of children's thirst for blood and intestines, airs the question of just how far an author can go.

As much as it's fun to be asked to write about writing, I hope anyone reading this will take it all with a medium-sized pinch of salt. The only incontrovertible law of writing I ever came upon was set down by my great hero, the American screenwriter William Goldman in *Adventures in the Screen Trade*. NOBODY KNOWS ANYTHING. It deserves the capital letters. If you're setting out to write a horror story for children, what follows may be useful. But your own instincts are probably better. Anyway, here is my experience for what it's worth.

I am currently writing a series of supernatural thrillers with the overall title of *The Power of Five*. The hero is a 14-year-old boy called Matt Freeman and in the first book, *Raven's Gate*, he finds himself arrested for attempted murder and sent on a fostering programme which lands him in the middle of a Yorkshire village, inhabited – as it turns out – by a coven of witches. Matt is chased by ferocious devil dogs and by the animated skeletons of dinosaurs. He is sucked into a bog, kidnapped and set up to be sacrificed. Anyone who tries to help him dies horribly. A policeman is killed in a car accident. A farmer is frightened to death. His own parents, of course, died long ago.

The second volume, *Evil Star,* begins with a madwoman immolating herself in a petrol tanker, shortly after murdering her live-in lover. The villain is a South American businessman who has been purposefully mutilated at birth. This time, Matt is beaten up by Peruvian police, robbed, starved, attacked by savage condors and… well, you probably get the idea.

Children love horror. You need look no further than the worldwide success of writers like Darren Shan to see it. Years ago, the *Goosebumps* series had covers that promised far more than the contents ever delivered but for a time they were littered across every school yard and made their author, R.L. Stine, a millionaire. Even the *Harry Potter* films have become progressively darker until the most recent instalment, which had one character cutting off his own hand, the death of a teenager and the truly hideous appearance of 'he who should not be named'.

And yet, the first – indeed the most crucial – question you have to ask yourself is: how far can you go? This is something of which I'm always painfully aware. Go into a classroom and talk to the children and you will discover that far enough is never enough. They want the blood, the intestines, the knife cutting through the flesh… the full monty. The problem, of course, is that if you give it to them you risk alienating the school librarians, bookshop buyers and the parents, and your book may never actually reach its intended audience.

When I visit schools, I always advise children to keep their own writing blood-free. Teachers don't like it, I tell them. I remind them that the scariest moment in any horror film is when the hand reaches for the door handle in the dark. That's when the music jangles and your imagination runs riot. What happens after the door is open is almost incidental. It seems to me that what you imagine will always be scarier than what you see – and this is a rule I apply to my own writing. For my money, the most effective passage in *Raven's Gate* comes when Matt gets lost, cycling through a wood in the dark. Every road brings him back to the same point. Slowly he begins to realise that he is never going to escape. There's no blood. No monsters. But it seems to work.

But at the same time – if you don't actually deliver, you're going to disappoint and so lose your audience. In my view, this is what went wrong with *Goosebumps* and it's the reason why they're no longer so popular. There has to be blood. How much of it and how far you go is up to you. Like I say, there are no rules. Take a look at the opening of Darren Shan's *Lord Loss*. The death of the parents leaves nothing to the imagination but teachers still love him. I don't know how he gets away with it.

Perhaps it's a question of context. A random act of violence or mutilation might seem very horrible in a book by, say, Jacqueline Wilson. But that's because her characters are so real, her world so recognisable. But when you write a horror story, you have a different departure point. Even before your readers buy the book, they know what to expect and they open it in exactly the same way as they might get on a ghost train at a fairground. They expect a certain number of skeletons and monsters and read the book in the knowledge that (a) it's only a ride, and (b) it will eventually deliver them back into the daylight.

The daylight, though, I think is important. I was genuinely shocked by the death of the teenager – Cedric Diggory – in *Harry Potter and the Goblet of Fire*. Not that J.K. Rowling needs to worry about the rules. But I've always thought that although it's reasonable to slap around your heroes, to frighten them and to hurt them, it's somehow irresponsible and wrong to kill them. No children have ever died in any of my books. Actually, none of them have ever felt real pain – again, because of the context. A child being chased by devil dogs through the swamps of Yorkshire may seem to be having a tough time. But that's nothing compared to a child in a London supermarket being slapped and screamed at by his mother. That, to me, is real horror.

Enough of these generalities. If you're thinking of writing something dark and scary for a young audience, here are just a few thoughts that might help.

• **You need an original story**. It may seem obvious but the realm of horror is stuffed with haunted castles, wicked stepmothers, evil magicians and all the rest of it. I know because I've used plenty of them myself. But a strong, simple idea will set you apart from the pack. Look at Justin Somper's success with *Vampirates*, a clever collision of swashbuckling and the supernatural. Or Garth Nix (*Mister Monday*) who time and time again comes up with hugely imaginative universes, completely new ideas.

• **Think about your central characters**. If they're likeable enough and idiosyncratic enough, you can – and will – get away with murder. There are some quite horrible things in Philip Pullman's *Northern Lights* with children kidnapped, stripped of their souls and turned into zombies. But we never doubt that Will and Lyra will win through.

• **Don't lose your sense of humour**. Mixing a few laughs in with the general mayhem doesn't lessen the horror. It helps the reader to deal with it. Paul Jennings, the Australian author, has produced some wonderfully twisted stories that would be far nastier if he didn't write with a smile.

• **Forget that you're writing for children**. This advice may seem incompatible with what I've already written but for me it's always been vital. If you sit at your desk with children in mind, it's all too easy for your work to become patronising and flabby. Of course it's important to consider levels of violence, what sort of language is applicable, how far you can go – but these should all be at the back of your mind. When I write horror, I try to scare myself. Darkness, solitude, the sense of being lost, the figure glimpsed out of the corner of your eye. I'm pretty sure that what scares children scares adults too. There's no need to cherry-pick, or to filter, the frissons!

• **Think visually.** The awful truth is that children are seeing more and more horror films with a 15 certificate, and they're also playing computer games with an incredible amount of electronic gore. Both films and games have a language which, I think, translates well to books. My generation was literary. Today's generation is visual. That's my theory, anyway, and I hope my audience will 'see' as much as read my work.

My intention has always been to entertain children – by which I mean neither educating them, improving them nor terrorising them. As to the last of these, I only ever got it wrong once. I wrote a short horror story (it's in *Horowitz Horror 2*) where the first letter of each sentence spelled out a message to the reader. That message went something along the lines of: 'As soon as you have read this, I'm coming to your house to kill you.'

About a year later, I received a note from a very angry and distressed mother who told me that she now had a traumatised daughter. My story, she said, was wilfully irresponsible and she suggested that I write a letter to her daughter, apologising.

I totally agreed. The next day I wrote a nice letter to the girl, explaining that I had intended to be mischievous rather than malevolent, that it was only a story, that she shouldn't have taken it so seriously.

Unfortunately, the first letter of every sentence in my letter spelled out: 'I am going to kill you too.'

Anthony Horowitz knew he wanted to be a writer when he was eight years old and was published for the first time when he was 22. He is perhaps best known for his *Alex Rider* novels, the first of which, *Stormbreaker*, was released as a major film in 2006. He has also written extensively for television, creating and writing the BAFTA-winning detective series *Foyle's War* and *Collision*. Among his other works, Anthony has written episodes for *Poirot*, *Midsomer Murders* and *Murder Most Horrid*. The ninth *Alex Rider* novel, *Scorpia Rising*, was published in 2011 and the tenth book in the series, *Yassen*, is due to be published in 2012. He has been appointed by the estate of Arthur Conan Doyle to be the official writer of a new Sherlock Holmes book, *The House of Silk*, due to be published in November 2011 by Orion. His website is www.anthonyhorowitz.com.

See also...
• *Who do children's authors write for?*, page 87
• *Writing for different genres*, page 115
• *Writing crime fiction for teenagers*, page 143
• *Writing for teenagers*, page 139

Writing historical novels for children

Michelle Paver shares her thoughts on how to approach writing historical novels for children and the importance of focusing on the story.

Books about how to get published sometimes advise new writers to research the market thoroughly. Read the competition, see what sells – that sort of thing. If that appeals to you, fine, but I've never liked the idea and have never done it. In my view it isn't necessary, or even a good thing. You might just find it confusing and intimidating, and it could put you off what you really want to write.

I think it's better to concentrate on the story *you* want to write. The characters. The premise. The historical setting. You may not even know *why* you want to write it. But you do, and that's the main thing.

The period

Before you make a start, though, it's worth asking yourself why you want to set the story in your chosen historical period. Are you especially attracted to it? Did you day-dream about it as a child; maybe you still do? Or does it simply have a vague appeal, perhaps based on having seen a few films or read some novels set in that time?

There's no harm in being drawn to a particular period for tenuous reasons. But if that is the case, I'd suggest that you become a little more familiar with it before deciding whether to use that time for your story. You'll need to know your chosen period pretty thoroughly; and if you decide halfway through writing your novel that it isn't quite as fascinating as you'd thought, then the chances are that the reader will think so too, and your story probably won't work. In short, you must be prepared to live and breathe it for months or even years.

The story is king

This would seem to be the logical point to talk about research, but I'm going to leave that for later because I don't think it's the most important thing. The most important thing is the story. Always. And particularly for children. In general, children don't read a book because it got a great review in *The Times*, or because they want to look impressive reading it on the train. They read it because they want to know what's going to happen next.

That might seem trite, but it's amazing how easy it is to forget, especially when you've done a ton of research on a particular period, and there are so many terrific things about it that you just can't wait to share with everybody else.

So it's worth reminding yourself that the basics of any good story need to be firmly in place: characters about whom you care passionately; a protagonist who wants or needs something desperately; perhaps a powerful villain or opposing force which poses a significant threat. Big emotions: anger, envy, pride, hate, loyalty, love, grief. And just because the book will be read by children, don't shy away from the bad stuff (although obviously, you'll need to handle it responsibly). Death, violence, neglect, loneliness. Children want to know. They're curious about everything.

The beginning

Everyone knows that the first page of a story is critical, but this is especially so for children. In fact, the first paragraph is even more critical. And the first sentence is the most critical of all.

This poses a special challenge if you're writing a historical novel. How do you root the story in the past without getting bogged down in clunky exposition?

There's no magic formula, but the idea of 'show, don't tell' is a good place to start. Perhaps you could begin with a situation that's specifically of that period, like a witch-burning. Or, as part of the story, weave in an object of the period, like a flint knife.

You might be tempted to write a 'prologue', like the ones they used to have at the beginning of old movies ('London, England. The Cavaliers and Roundheads are at War...'). By all means write one of these. I did, for the first draft of *Wolf Brother*. But you may well ditch it before you finish the final draft. You may find that by then it has done its work by helping to anchor you, the writer, in the period. If you leave it in, it might have a distancing effect for the reader, diminishing the immediacy of the story.

Telling the story

What I said about the beginning of the story goes for the rest of it, too. The challenge for the writer of historical novels is to make the reader 'live' the story along with the characters. Somehow you've got to make them see, feel, touch, taste that period – without resorting to wodges of boring description that might slow things down, or overdone 'period' dialogue which is tiring to read and may distance the reader.

Again, there's no formula, but a good guiding principle is to make the essential exposition an integral part of the story. Make this a story that couldn't really have happened at any other time in history – even though the emotions involved are universals with which the reader can readily identify.

If you do this, then it'll become fairly clear what needs to stay in and what should come out. And there will probably be a lot of cutting. Pare down the exposition to what's essential. For instance, you may not need to explain the background to the entire war; just the particular skirmish in which your heroine has been caught up.

And for the essential exposition, it can help to introduce it in a highly charged emotional way: perhaps an argument or a fight. 'Exposition as ammunition' was a favourite motto of the film-maker Ingmar Bergman and it's one that can serve you well. But don't get so hung up on explaining things that you lose sight of the emotional focus of the scene.

The same goes for 'period atmosphere'. I would think long and hard before including anything for this reason alone. Try to make your period details part of the story. Then cut them back, then cut them back some more. What you need is a swift, vivid, unforgettable image with *just* enough detail to bring it alive – but no more.

Research

Which brings me (finally) to research. Some novelists don't do any. If that works for them, that's great. But if you're setting your story in the past, I don't think you can get by without doing at least some. And probably rather a lot. You need to know, intimately, what it was like to live back then. It's the little everyday details which interest readers, particularly children. What did people eat, wear, live in? How did they fight, travel, work, entertain themselves? What did they *think*? How were they similar to us? How were they different? And the more you can actually experience some of this for yourself the better – for example, by location research, trying out the food of the period – because it will give you all sorts of intriguing ideas and insights that you couldn't have got in a library.

Bear in mind, too, that research isn't just a matter of getting the details right. It'll probably spark ideas for the story itself: incidents, twists, particular scenes. These are gold dust. Use them. (Provided, of course, that they work in the context of the story as a whole.)

Perhaps the hardest thing about research is that the vast bulk of what you've lovingly unearthed isn't going to make it into the final draft. Be ruthless about keeping *only* those details that you really need: either to move the story along, or to develop character, or to set the scene. And shun any whiff of teaching; this is a story, not a history lesson.

This means that you'll probably go through a rather painful process of cutting over the course of your first, second, and successive drafts. But don't grieve too deeply for your lost treasures. *You* know all that background, and your in-depth knowledge will give your writing an assurance that it wouldn't otherwise have.

Language and style

This can be especially tricky: a kind of balancing act between keeping the story and the characters accessible, while leaving the language with just enough special vocabulary or dialogue to remind us that we're in another time. All this without distancing us too much, or (just as bad) without obvious anachronisms.

I'm often asked if I write differently when I'm writing for children, as opposed to when I'm writing for adults. The answer is, no, not at all. For me, it's the nature of the story that dictates the language and the style. If you're writing a story set in a middle-class Victorian home, your vocabulary and style will be utterly different from that which you'd use if you were writing about a forest of the Stone Age.

Having said that, if children are going to be among your readers, one important thing to bear in mind is that lengthy flashbacks can weaken the force of a story by reducing its immediacy. Because children read to know what's going to happen next, it helps too, to have unexpected twists, surprises, action, high emotion, flashes of humour, and lots of dialogue, as well as the odd cliff-hanger chapter ending. You've got to give them a reason to turn the page; and to keep turning the pages, all the way to the end.

Who are you writing for?

'What age group are you "aiming" at?' is a frequently asked question. For myself, the answer is: none. Apart from a general idea that I'm not writing a picture book for six-year-olds, I prefer to leave age groups to editors and publishers, and concentrate on the story.

Besides, once you start thinking in terms of 'aiming' a story at a particular group of people, where does it end? For instance, say you're 'aiming' a story at 9–12 year-olds. Well, what kind of 9–12 year-olds? They're not a homogeneous mass. Boys or girls, or both? And what kind? Middle-class or underprivileged? Immigrant or home-grown? Gifted, average, or special needs? If you start thinking like that, you run the risk of killing your story.

The same thing goes for the publisher's Holy Grail of the 'crossover' novel that's read by both adults and children. If you have this at the forefront of your mind when you're writing, it's unlikely that you'll do justice to the story. It may well end up being a mess which *nobody* will want to read.

Although this may sound a bit uncompromising, I have the same view when it comes to trying out your story on your own children – if you have them – or on others. In my view, this is risky and I prefer not to do it. (Well, in my case, I couldn't, because I don't have children, and don't know any very well!) In fact, quite a few children's writers don't have children of their own, but what many do have is a strong memory of what it was like to be a child and an ability to write from a child's perspective. That's what you need. Not market research.

Being true to your story, knowing your chosen period inside out but only including the most telling of details…. Of course, none of this is going to guarantee success. But with luck, it'll improve your chances on the slush pile. *And* you'll have a lot more fun than if you'd been slavishly studying the market!

Michelle Paver is the author of the best-selling *Chronicles of Ancient Darkness* series, which has been published in 37 languages. The first book in the series, *Wolf Brother*, was published in 2004 and the others are *Spirit Walker*, *Soul Eater*, *Outcast*, *Oath Breaker* and *Ghost Hunter*, which won the 2010 Guardian Children's Fiction Prize. Her most recent book is an adult ghost story, *Dark Matter*, published in 2010 to critical acclaim, and she is now working on another series for children, *Gods and Warriors*, set in the Mediterranean Bronze Age. The books have also been recorded as audiobooks read by Ian McKellen.

See also...
* *Who do children's authors write for?*, page 87
* *Writing for different genres*, page 115

Writing for teenagers

Meg Rosoff describes how she came to write *How I Live Now* and offers some suggestions to bear in mind when writing for teenagers.

Despite the optimistic title of this piece, I know hardly anything about writing for teenagers.

Here's a metaphor. Let's say you have sex, get pregnant, and give birth to a baby who grows up to be a successful actor/scientist/politician. Everyone wants to know how you did it. You ponder the question. Was it the organic food? Piano lessons? Good genes? State school? Was it benign neglect? Fish oil? Dumb luck?

It may be possible to post-rationalise success, but it rarely rings true. How did I manage to write a book adolescents like? I read a lot. Procrastinated for years. Had five careers. Am a foreigner. Found a good agent. Was desperate.

The answer is probably all of the above, plus a few hundred things I haven't thought of yet. Writing does come easily to me, which (let's face it) helps a lot. I always *wanted* to be a writer. And much as I hate to give it any credit at all, my disastrous career in advertising turned out to be an excellent apprenticeship. I was also desperate to get out of advertising, which helped in a different way. But I never thought I could write a novel.

For one thing, I was never interested in plot and could never figure out where people got their ideas for stories. I am not the sort of mother with an endless supply of charming bedtime tales. I can't even tell a decent joke.

To make matters worse, I compared myself incessantly to the people I most admired – Jose Saramago, George Eliot, Shirley Hazzard – and knew I'd never be able to write a book *that good*. Which turned out to be true enough, but (in retrospect) blindingly irrelevant.

As for writing for teenagers, I am uniquely ill-equipped by virtue of my advanced age. I'm 53, which disqualifies me from talking like a teenager or knowing much about how teenagers act or dress or think, except insofar as I observe them walking past my North London home most mornings on the way to school, leaving a trail of incomprehensible slang and McDonald's wrappers behind them. (Of course my daughter – aged four when I wrote *How I Live Now* and now 12 – is beginning to provide concrete evidence of the workings of the teenage mind.)

So. The answer doesn't lie in storytelling ability, youth, or confidence. Nor will you find it in my powers of observation (mediocre, at best). I don't have an exceptional ear for dialogue or significant recall for past events. I'm terrible at history and hate research.

However… I have always had a morbid imagination (I can imagine a disaster in the most cheerful of scenarios) and a tendency to think like an adolescent. For me, teenage angst and midlife crisis got all caught up together at about the age of 20, and have been going along hand-in-hand ever since.

And I'm not the only hybrid freak around, the phenomenon of the middle-aged teenager is everywhere. Much of my generation was brought up on the idea that we never had to grow up, that we could wait forever to have children (whom we would raise as friends) that we could marry late or not at all, have powerful, well-paid jobs to which we would wear jeans and T-shirts, give ourselves grown-up toys for Christmas and birthdays (wide screen televisions, iPods, snowboarding kit, lava lamps) and never develop the gravitas our parents seemed to acquire magically and effortlessly at age 20.

When I was 25 (at which age my mother had married, bought a house and was pregnant with her second child) my friends and I were mooching around New York City, living in cockroach-riddled apartments, having affairs with inappropriate men, applying to art school, swapping illegal substances and going to all-night clubs. I married so late, my parents were convinced I was a lesbian. (How old was I? 33.)

My professional life followed a similar path. After seven jobs, three careers and a series of disastrous attempts to conform, I ended up in advertising, home to the hipsters at the end of the universe. Here was immaturity taken to its extreme: departments full of so-called creatives with goatee beards and stupid spectacles who played Xbox all day and called it work. The boys were joined by a tiny minority of females who changed their names from Susan and Mary to Cherokee and Zeus. And everyone pretended, day after day, that selling stuff nobody wanted was incredibly cool.

I got fired a lot from advertising, which seems fine today but at the time was discouraging. In retrospect, my relationship with advertising reminds me of a bad love affair – the sort that happens repeatedly when you lack the insight to realise that your taste in men (or in my case, careers) stinks. Being stuck in perpetual adolescence is all about lacking insight: lacking perspective, lacking wisdom, lacking everything in fact, except an enthusiasm that transcends failure. After failure. After failure.

As I moved from a 30-something adolescent to a 40-something adolescent, I ran up against the sobering consideration of having children. If your kids have parents who wear jeans, listen to Kings of Leon, and still don't understand the stock market, how are they supposed to act? My daughter started asking how to buy a house and the difference between credit and debit cards when she was six. She advises her father and me on how to dress, what car to drive, how to behave in public. She says she'd like to live in the American suburbs when she grows up, with a huge 4 x 4 and a spray-on tan. All her father and I can do is laugh (through our tears) and hope it passes.

But recently, something strange happened. Around my fortieth birthday, I began to notice I wasn't quite so lacking in perspective as before. I began to make certain observations, certain wise observations, like: *Life is short. I hate my job. Perhaps I should write a book.*

In July 2002, I gave myself a deadline: two years.

I took a two-month leave of absence from work, stole a plot from the horse books I loved as a kid and wrote a practice novel. It wasn't the finest work of literature, and I sincerely hope it will never see the light of day, but it worked. It had a story (an old story, but a story) and a bunch of characters. It moved smoothly from A to B, was moderately funny and faintly poignant. It looked like a book, it read like a book, and I thought, it may not be Henry James, but it ain't advertising either.

With that book I found myself an agent, who suggested I write another book (she didn't say, 'a better one' but I read between the lines). And when I asked for advice on how to write a 'proper book' for teenagers, she said 'Write the best book you can write'. If I had to condense this long rambling autobiography-disguised-as-advice into seven words, that would be it. Nothing wiser has come my way since.

Having stuck with me so far, you are no doubt panting for the good old-fashioned, opinionated, bullet-pointed advice on how to write for teenagers that this article promises and I'm more than happy to give it a shot. Remember, however, your grain of salt, and that for each suggestion that follows, I can already think of an exception.

• **There are no rules.** There are books for teenagers with sex and drugs and unhappy endings. There are 100-page books and 700-page books, moral and immoral world-views, books with no children in them, books that tackle the Spanish Inquisition, the holocaust, adultery, suicide, football. If you don't believe me about this lack of rules, take note of how many panel discussions at literary festivals are devoted to the subject 'What Makes a Young Adult Novel?' The reason they continue to ask the question is that nobody knows the answer.

• **Know how to write.** Really, it helps. If your true talent lies in baking bread, open a bakery.

• **If you're not lucky enough to be immature, regress.** Haul yourself back to the days when the world was opaque.

• **On the other hand, be wise.** The more you experience in life, the more wisdom you unconsciously stockpile. The broken relationships, the family rows, the children you raise, the friends you manage to hang on to (or not), the careers you try, the journeys you take – all these things separate you, the writer, from a genuine adolescent. I may not know much, but I do know that the thought of having to read a book written by an actual 15 year-old makes my blood run cold.

• **Cut to the chase.** Ten pages of exposition will lose all of your readers. Five pages will lose most of them. Even two paragraphs is dicey. So start fast. The average attention span of a 12 year-old these days is about half as long as whatever you're trying to tell them. (And having judged prizes for teenage books, I can tell you that judges with 50 books to read aren't much better.)

• **Don't try to write cool.** You will almost inevitably fail. Even if you have eight teenagers at home, your writing will somehow manage to expose you as the sad middle-aged person you are. At which point you will embarrass your friends and family and particularly your teenage children. They will gag and run out of the room and shout that you've ruined their lives, and they will be correct. I've often been asked how I managed to write like a teenager in *How I Live Now*. The answer is, I didn't. I wrote like an old jaded person thinking like a teenager.

• **Get a life.** OK, I'm prejudiced. But it helps to know something about a subject, any subject. And despite failed careers in journalism, PR, politics, publishing and advertising, I managed to pick up a great deal of useful training for writing novels, articles, screenplays, etc on the way.

• **Have a good story.** This is true of writing for anyone. It's amazing how many people forget. And as someone who's good at character but lousy at plot, I feel your pain. Steal a plot, if you have to. After all there are only two: (1) Stranger Comes to Town, and (2) The Journey.

• **Don't look for issues, they will find you.** I challenge anyone to write for teenagers without coming up against at least one of the following subjects: sex, drugs, the meaning of life, family conflict, friendship, the future of the world, self-image, self-loathing, difficult siblings, impossible parents, bullying, depression, overachievement, please someone stop me! *Animal Ark* is a wonderful series of books about fixing hurt animals and that's why 5–9 year-olds love it; but there's a reason that adults look back on Vonnegut and Dostoevsky and Kundera novels and say their lives were never quite the same afterwards.

• **Lie about everything except emotions.** England can be at war. Boys can read minds. Pigs can fly. But if you can't remember what it felt like to be depressed/vulnerable/in love, get a job writing *Animal Ark*.

• **Be passionate (see above).** Readers are.

• **Ignore the market.** By the time you figure out that vampire books are hot and write your vampire book, they will no longer be hot. Be the next big thing.

• **Listen to what other people have to say.** OK, OK. So 15 publishers turned down *Harry Potter*. But if 15 people say your story is dull, heavy handed and badly written, it's probably not the next *Harry Potter* in its current form.

• **Don't worry about your connections (or lack thereof).** Ask any agent, editor or bookseller and they'll all tell you the same thing: there is not an overabundance of terrific books around. So if you think you can write something amazing, don't worry about selling it. When you're ready to show it around, someone will sit up and take notice.

• **Write the best book you can write.**

It worked for me, anyway.

Meg Rosoff was born in Boston, USA, and lived in New York City for ten years before moving to London in 1989. She was fired from an impressive variety of jobs in publishing and advertising before writing *How I Live Now*, which won the Guardian Children's Fiction Prize in 2004 and is currently being made into a film. Her second novel, *Just in Case*, won the 2007 Carnegie Medal. She is also the author of *What I Was* and *The Bride's Farewell*. Her latest book is *There is No Dog* (Puffin 2011). Her website is www.megrosoff.co.uk.

See also...

• *Who do children's authors write for?*, page 87
• *Writing crime fiction for teenagers*, page 143
• *Writing thrillers for teenagers*, page 146
• *Teenage fiction*, page 149
• *Categorising children's books*, page 181

Writing crime fiction for teenagers

Anne Cassidy is the author of more than 25 novels for teenagers and she explains here why she thinks the crime genre is perfect for teenage fiction.

I love crime fiction and that's why I write it for teenagers. In my first book, *Big Girls' Shoes* (1990), two teenage girls overhear a murder during a phone call. In my most recent book, *Dead Time* (2012), a teenage girl sees a boy she hates get stabbed to death on a bridge over a railway line. The deaths are brutal and the books are dark. I make no apology for this. Crime fiction has to move the reader. The crimes have to be horrible so that the reader cares about the victim. I've locked up a victim in a container and left him to die. I've pushed a girl off a 16-story block of flats, I've drowned several hapless teens and I've even poisoned one with arsenic pasta. I have no mercy.

In 20 years I've written 25-plus novels for teenagers, all concerned with crime of one sort or another. I wrote a series in the 1990s called *The East End Murders* and in 2012 the first book of a new series called *The Murder Notebooks* will be published. In between I've written a line of standalone thrillers, most of which have a murder at their core.

Characters and narrative

Writing for teenagers is not different in kind to writing for adults. You have a particular audience and you have a story to tell. In my case the audience is teenagers and the stories I tell fall into the crime genre.

In general terms, books for teenagers have two main features. Firstly, the main character is usually a teenager and the story centres round them. This teenager has to be completely and utterly believable. This is a writer's first challenge. What you don't do is focus on the external features of today's teenagers; the music, the fashions, the mobile phones and the 'teen' speak patois are ephemeral. What you're really looking for is the emotional core of your teenage protagonist and for that you have to go back and find your own teenage self again. When I wrote my first teen novel I dredged up as many memories as I could. I listened to lots of the music I'd liked at the time (much of it still among my favourites). I looked at family photographs. I spoke to family members and thought back to my own schooldays, writing down a rough journal of anything and everything that I remembered; names, places, books, lessons, clothes, shops. I revisited my own past and what I found, when I got there, was a teenager who'd spent her teen years feeling hard done by, where the tantalising promises of near adulthood had become mired in the day-to-day life of being a schoolgirl/daughter/sister. There I found the emotional core of my teenager: the struggle to move forward into adulthood while everything seemed to pull her back. I realised that contemporary teenagers were no different. The fashions, the temperament and the reliance on electronic gadgets are all modern but at heart today's teens are the same as I was 40 years ago. They have within them that essential contradiction of adolescence; negotiating the passage to adulthood, shrugging off the child who they once were. So my teenage characters embody this struggle in one form or another.

The second feature of a teen book is that the story drives the novel. Novels for teenagers must have a strong narrative and this story has to move forward in every chapter. In general you cannot have pages and pages of musings about the meaning of life or overindulge in descriptive passages. But this doesn't mean that your story can't explore universal and important themes or that it cannot establish a sense of place. In my book *Looking for JJ*, a ten-year-old girl kills her friend and we meet her six years later when she is released from prison. The narrative follows her trying to live with a new identity. The theme of the book is forgiveness. Has she the right to expect a second chance in life after what she did?

The story of a crime teen novel should start when something dramatic is happening. *The Dead House* starts when the main character, Lauren, revisits the house in which her family were murdered ten years before. She alone survived. In *Forget Me Not* a child is abducted. In *Just Jealous* a girl is staring at the body of a boy who has been shot. The main character and others emerge through this early action and take shape quickly. By the end of the first chapter the reader should have a strong sense of story and character and an inkling of which direction the book is heading.

This is why I think the crime genre is so perfect for teenage fiction and why I have enjoyed writing it for so many years. A crime novel naturally starts with a dramatic event, often a murder. The main character is often involved in some aspect of the discovery of that murder. In a teen novel the main character will perhaps discover the body or be a friend of the victim, or perhaps he or she may be a murder suspect. The story will be told through his or her eyes whether it is in third or first person narrative. The rest of the novel will mirror an adult crime thriller in that there will be clues and red herrings, and secrets and lies will be exposed. There will be police involvement in some way and the tools of detection will be used – surveillance, research, interrogation. These things will happen whether the main character is a school student or a boy on the run. At the end of the book the killer will be exposed and the secrets revealed.

Language and savvy teenagers

Don't underestimate the teenage reader. Teenagers watch a lot of crime on television. When I visit schools I often ask them about it and they list anything from *CSI* to *Jonathan Creek* to *Morse* and *Poirot*. They are used to the complex narrative that a crime story necessarily needs. They like the twists and turns and the cliff-hangers and the secrets that emerge from the story. When teenagers are gripped by a story they will hold on to the various strands and read with gusto until they find out 'whodunnit'.

One of the main questions when writing for teenagers is *How explicit can the content be?* – which could be asked of any teenage novel. The writer is always writing with one eye on the reader and another on the 'gatekeeper': the librarian, teacher or parent. This is not just a matter of censorship. Teenagers as a group are not natural readers. They do not scour the review pages for new books and they do not haunt the shelves of Waterstone's. They often find their books through librarians, teachers and parents and then from word of mouth via friends. So these 'gatekeepers' are not to be feared but rather to be seen as your most demanding reader. They will not 'promote' your book unless they think it is really good. I think how explicit the content can be is a matter of taste and style rather than censorship. In crime fiction the question is particularly relevant. Modern crime fiction encompasses some truly stomach-turning gore but, again, the question for me is whether its plot delivers the shocks and surprises needed to make a good crime novel. If it does, then the gore is window dressing for a particular audience. I do not have serial killer/ torture violence in my books but this is an artistic decision rather than because of a fear of censorship. I think the taking of a small child or the murder of a mother and her baby or a teenage boy dying from a single punch is 'gore' enough. Who? Why? and How? are the questions that interest me.

My books are read by 12–14-year-olds onwards. The content is grown up and for this reason my characters are usually over 16. This is not a problem for the readers as teenagers like reading about older characters. It means, though, that my characters can do more grown-up stuff. A 17-year-old staying out all night or having a relationship is acceptable, whereas if the character was 14 it might cause added problems for the plot. My characters don't swear and I originally made this decision in part to avoid having my books kept out of school libraries just because of a couple of four-letter words. As time went on though and these four-letter words started to appear in other teen books it became a matter of choice. Conversation in novels is never realistic, it simply approximates to the way we think people speak; in sentences, cogently, without interruption. In reality speech is all over the place, fragmented and often incomprehensible. Likewise with swearing. If you stand near any group of teens you will be shocked at the range and frequency of swear words. If I were to try and replicate their speech the page would be peppered with four-letter words so I decided to leave them out altogether and let the reader supply them.

Series fiction and standalone novels

Crime fiction takes a number of forms but the most obvious two are series fiction and standalone novels. I have written both. The joy of a series is that it allows you to follow through on a group of characters and build a 'soap'-type plot from book to book. However, each book must stand up by itself and be a self-contained crime mystery. If a teenager picks book three of a series to read first they must have a satisfying plot and be informed of all the salient 'soap' developments without spoiling the enjoyment of reading books one or two. This is particularly relevant to me with my *Murder Notebook* series. These books are standalone murder mysteries but they all involve stepbrother Joshua and stepsister Rose who are both on a quest to find out about their parents' disappearance five years before. This disappearance is the continuing story of this series and each standalone murder mystery must in some way add to their knowledge of what happened to their parents. It's complicated but huge fun to do.

Standalone novels don't usually involve a 'detective' as such. They usually start with a teenager being drawn into some tricky situation and seeing how that teenager copes. In my book *Heart Burn*, Ashley owes a boy a favour. The favour he asks of her is illegal and dangerous. She agrees to help him and ends up fearing for her life. Standalone novels are often viewed as more 'literary' than series fiction. I think this is rubbish as series fiction has been written by many great writers. Patrick Ness has had his *Chaos Walking* series shortlisted for major awards and Kate Atkinson has given the adult crime novel a 'literary' feel with her *Case History* books.

What should you write – series or standalone novels? You should write the story that you want to write. If you have a good crime story to tell then decide which format it needs and write it. Don't underestimate your teenage audience. They are savvy and love a good murder mystery. Enough said!

Anne Cassidy is a full-time writer. She was a bank clerk and then a teacher. She is married and lives with her husband in Essex.

See also...
- *Writing for teenagers*, page 139
- *Teenage fiction*, page 149

Writing thrillers for teenagers

Sophie McKenzie considers the ingredients for writing a successful thriller for teenagers.

When people ask me what sort of books I write, I tend to reply that I write thrillers for teenagers. But actually, I do no such thing – at least not deliberately… I just write the kind of stories I like to read, involving characters I care passionately about. And I write to please myself – not for a specific audience. So here's the only rule I'm going to suggest you stick to – always write what matters to you… not what you think other people want, need or expect. Everything else (i.e. the rest of this article) is just my opinion – a few thoughts and suggestions that helped me and might be useful to you.

A strong story

This is definitely my number one requirement in a top thriller – whatever the age of the audience! Remember that a story is *not* simply an interesting situation, though it may start with one. In a story, stuff happens. A good way to check if you have a really interesting story is to look at whether the scenario you've created gives your main character something they really want or need – *and* a big fat problem that gets in the way of that ambition. In my book, *Girl, Missing,* for instance, Lauren *really* wants to find out who her birth mother is and whether she was stolen from her original home as a toddler. Her main problem, at the start of the story, is that her parents refuse to talk about her adoption. This also means that Lauren can't look to her parents to sort out her problem, thus ensuring the story follows one of the basic principles of children's fiction and gets the adults out of the way as fast as possible! It also deepens the problem, as Lauren starts to suspect that her adoptive parents may have been the ones who stole her from her birth mother.

High stakes

Your character's needs and problems must be important to them. If they care and you care, chances are you'll get your reader to care too.

There are millions of things your character might want or need to find fulfilment and/ or salvation. And a top story will certainly need an original twist. But there are a few fundamental ambitions that almost everyone relates to. Most thrillers and adventure stories revolve around one or more of the following, though there are others:

• Coming home. This is a common desire, especially in children's stories – I'm talking here about characters who are trying to find their way back home – like Dorothy in *The Wizard of Oz* – and about characters trying to find a new home – like Harry in Robert Westall's marvellous *The Kingdom by the Sea.*

• Working out who you really are and/or finding your place in the world. This is another huge need shared by characters in identity/rites of passage stories as varied as *Being* by Kevin Brooks and the *Pretties* series by Scott Westerfeld. This 'goal' is particularly common in teenage fiction – identity issues seem to resonate strongly with adolescents aware they are no longer children but not yet sure how to be adults.

• Then there's love. Will the boy get the girl; will the child be reunited with the parents?

• And, of course, there's survival. Whether your character's goal is to save his own life, the lives of those he loves or the entire planet, survival stories usually involve plenty of action and interesting villains. In fact, baddies often provide stories with the best problems: imagine the Harry Potter books without Voldemort or *101 Dalmatians* without Cruella de Vil.

Not worrying about taboo subjects

Personally I don't think there's any subject that can't be tackled. What counts is how you treat the material. Teenagers, like the rest of us, want to read about subjects that matter to them. Families, friendships, loss, guilt, identity, ambitions in work and in love – are all relevant. Sometimes I think teens get a raw deal. Just because young people are aware of difficult topics doesn't necessarily mean they want to read about them in a heavy duty way. Beware of turning your thriller into an 'issues' book in which the main character only 'angsts' and 'never acts'. If you want to write a thriller around a challenging topic, that's great. Just make sure there's a strong story holding the whole thing together. In *Blood Ties*, I wanted to write about how it might feel to discover, aged 15, you'd been cloned as a replacement for your dead sister. That could easily have been the starting point for a much less pacy book than the one I ended up writing, which attempts to weave its thought-provoking subject material in and out of a fast-moving action story.

A central character to care about and identify with

A good story *has* to involve individuals we care about. And a teenage novel will usually feature one or more teenage protagonists. If memory (I was a teen), personality (I act like a teen) and research (I talk to teens) don't help you imagine yourself into the head of an adolescent, then you may struggle to write teenage books!

The stories I like best often incorporate a relationship drama that bubbles under the main action. From a writing point of view, focusing on the development of a romantic relationship – as well as a high-octane thriller plot – helps make your characters more interesting and your story more meaningful. In *Blood Ties*, Theo and Rachel try to find out more about their respective fathers' involvement in human cloning work, which leads them into huge danger. And yet, the love story between them is always present as well.

Will boys read stories that contain an element of romance? Well, many won't, but I'm also certain that it's a complete myth to say that boys don't care about romantic relationships at all – they just don't want you to spend pages analysing them!

A clear sense of the point of view you're writing from

Whose story are you telling? Make sure you know, right from the start. Then try and keep that character at the centre of the action, moving the story along. In his commentary on the film adaptation of *The Lord of the Rings,* director Peter Jackson talks about the importance of turning the camera on the film's heroes at least every third shot. A useful tip – which translates in novel terms as follows: don't stray too far from what your main character can think, feel, see, touch, smell and hear. Writing from an omnipotent, narrator perspective is a perfectly valid choice but it does tend to distance the reader from the main character's mind. Almost all children love to identify with their heroes. And thrillers definitely benefit from the immediacy of a strong viewpoint.

Planning and plotting before you write

Some writers plan. Some don't. Personally, I like to plan the foundations – the outline of the story showing where the characters are going – before I start. But I save the fun stuff – showing how the characters are going to get there – for while I'm writing.

I came to the conclusion that planning was helpful after starting no fewer than 17 books in my first year of serious writing. Some of these had some merit – an interesting character here, an exciting scene there – but almost all of them fell apart by chapter five or so because the plots simply didn't pan out. Planning can feel like an overwhelming task. But unless you try and work through your story in advance, it's all too easy for the whole thing to crumble in your hands. This is, of course, particularly true for thrillers, which require suspenseful twists and turns in order to deliver their thrills!

Managing a plot is a bit like driving a chariot pulled by several huge, powerful horses. You have to concentrate on what you're doing – and be as fit and strong as possible – in order to hold together the reins and make sure that the various strands of the story you're weaving don't career down separate paths and send your chariot tumbling to the ground.

If you want to write thrillers, study thriller writers

I spent a lot of time studying other peoples' plots, working out how various authors whose plotting skills I admire handled that aspect of their writing. For instance, I read the first three books in Anthony Horowitz's *Alex Rider* series and wrote down everything that happened (literally, just the actions) that moved the story on.

That experience taught me many things – not least the value of breaking my plots into manageable amounts. When planning *The Set-Up*, the first book in my *Medusa Project* series, I knew halfway through the story that Nico, the main character, would discover the man he had trusted up to that point was actually plotting to betray him. This enabled me to break the story down into two halves, making it less daunting to plan each one.

Have a laugh along the way

Just because you're writing a thriller doesn't mean your story can't have its lighter moments. An ironic narrative voice, a character with a great sense of humour or a funny situation do more than make the reader laugh – they provide a release for tension, allowing the next plunge into suspense to be even more powerful.

Creating suspense – hooks and hangers

The most important chapter is the first – get that right, drawing your reader in with a dramatic 'inciting incident' (as Robert McKee puts it in *Story*) and you will, hopefully, have set up your story in an interesting way and hooked the reader in. Some sort of conflict is usually necessary here, as exemplified by one of the best kids' thriller first chapters I've ever read –*Thief* by Malorie Blackman. And never forget the power of D.R.A.T. – that's the Desperate Race Against Time, guaranteed to inject a shot of excitement into any story!

Cliffhangers are great too – whenever I'm coming to the end of a scene, I try and work out what I need to write to give the reader a pay off for sitting through that chapter – and what I can leave unexplained, as a hook to make them want to turn the next page.

And finally...

Here are my top three tips for producing a thrilling story: (1) Get into the story as fast as possible; (2) Make sure that every plot twist is unexpected but convincing; (3) Don't be indulgent... if what you've written doesn't move the story on, cut it.

In the end, if all else fails, remember that so long as you're trying to write the best book you're capable of writing, nothing else really matters. So don't give up.

Sophie McKenzie is the award-winning author of the thrillers, *Girl, Missing* and *Blood Ties*, which won the Red House Children's Book Award in 2009. She was born in London, where she still lives, and worked as a journalist and editor before concentrating full time on writing. Her most recent books include *Blood Ransom* (the sequel to *Blood Ties*) and *The Medusa Project* series, about a group of teenagers with psychic powers. Her website is www.sophiemckenziebooks.com.

Teenage fiction

Gillie Russell writes about teenage fiction from a publisher's pespective.

People often ask what the difference is between writing for teenagers and writing for adults. For me, the one significant difference is that teenagers come to books without a life experience. They are on the brink of self discovery, never having been plunged into the everyday grind of earning a living. They are open, honest and questioning as an audience and this, I believe, is why so many terrific writers want to write for this age group. Teenagers are challenging to write for and satisfyingly able to digest complex ideas. This often means that there are far too many 'issue'-based books on the market – not that these are badly written, often completely the reverse. But every major book fair will offer teenage books on incest, bullying, sibling rivalry, parental separation and drugs. Of course these kinds of books are important, but teenagers, like adults, need a varied diet. Teenagers like well-crafted stories in many genres – they love humour and history and fantasy, just as much as they like books which reflect their own worlds. They like inspirational and aspirational books where they can identify with the protagonists in a real way.

Getting teenagers to read

To lump teenage readers into one, all-encompassing bracket is not only dangerous but will ultimately reduce the choice of books available to them. We all know that teenagers who read don't necessarily want to continue reading 'children's books', that some seem to move seamlessly on to authors as varied as Agatha Christie and Isobel Allende, Ian Rankin and Margaret Atwood. This is partly because, though there are many wonderful writers for teenagers, no self-respecting young adult wants to venture into the 'children's' section of a bookshop – they would much rather hang out in Body Shop or HMV, or find books in the adult book displays or, sadly, stop reading books, entirely.

To attract teenagers to read at all is difficult; they don't like to feel manipulated, and life in secondary school nowadays makes it difficult to find time to read anything other than the books they are studying, The lead-up to major exams and the required reading tends to dominate their lives. This is why it is so important for children to develop the reading habit and reading stamina earlier in their lives – something which, hopefully, will never leave them, and the desire to lose themselves in a book.

As teenagers move away from the influence of their parents, it is important that, as well as having teachers to motivate and inspire them to read, there are bookshops which do the same. In the USA, for example, there are large areas devoted to 'young adult' books, sections of the bookshops which feel right for them, and are 'cool' places to be. Here in the UK it is sadly not the case. In most of the high street chains the children's areas are dominated by books for the much younger child. Hidden in amongst the books for the 8–12 year-olds there may be a few 'teenage' gems – but few teenagers venture into these areas and discover them. How about bookshops ranging teenage books like CDs, for example – in a rack, facing outwards – and organised by theme, with some short reviews?

Variety is the key

It is true that when we talk about books for teenagers, we tend to think automatically of gritty, contemporary fiction – rather like Melvyn Burgess's *Junk*, for example. But there are lots of books that young people like that are not specially written for teenagers. We need to remember that books for teenagers are any books, any genres, for the 12-plus age group. This band of children – from 12 up to young adult – can have any variety of tastes; they may like historical fiction, such as Celia Rees's *Witch Child*, humour, like Louise Rennison's *Angus, Thongs and Full Frontal Snogging* (to name just one of her deliciously funny and timeless teenage books), Philip Pullman's *His Dark Materials*, and David Almond's *Skellig*. A variety of genres, easy visibility in bookshops, the right covers and 'packaging' – all these things are hugely important to attract teenage readers. They are an intelligent and discerning audience, and when they discover an author they like, extremely loyal. Surely this is reason enough to make retailers think about being more imaginative in attracting teenage buyers?

The 'crossover' book

We talk a great deal these days of the 'crossover' book where an adult market has been identified for a children's book, a phenomenon which started with Harry Potter. Perhaps this is because publishers are desperately trying to attract a bigger section of the market for their authors, to make a double killing with one book. How true this *actually* is, I'm not sure, though occasionally a book which is stunningly original and exceptional, like *The Curious Incident of the Dog in the Night-Time*, can appeal to both markets, and even be successful in two editions. Another example of a 'crossover' book is *Across the Nightingale Floor* by Lian Hearn, which to some may feel more 'adult' than 'child', but which is hugely appealing to teenagers and doesn't feel at all patronisingly like a 'children's' book marketed at teens. How we market, package and position these 'crossover' books, such as Isobel Allende's *City of Beasts*, for example, occupies publishers constantly. Should they do one edition, sold into both adult and children's sections, or should there be two separate editions, one following the other? Or will teenagers who read discover Isobel Allende anyway, and thus make the publishing of a 'children's' edition completely redundant? Publishers certainly don't want to cannibalise their own book sales.

Is reading cool?

What we can say, post Harry Potter, is that reading is still 'cool' – that it is OK to be seen with a book on a bus or train. This can only be a good thing. It can only be fantastically exciting that there are queues outside bookshops for authors like Jacqueline Wilson, Philip Pullman, Darren Shan and, of course, J.K. Rowling.

Where do we go from here?

So where does this leave teenage fiction? How do we enable wonderful writers to reach their target audience? We try to keep publishing the talented authors who are offered to us, people like Mark Haddon who make a difference, who may write about 'issues' but don't set out to do so, but simply set out to write an engaging and compelling book. We keep trying to persuade retailers to recognise the importance of good teenage books – and I sincerely believe this is ultimately empowering, liberating and vital to their adult lives – and we have to be as innovative and imaginative as possible in the ways we think about presenting these books to our readers. Fewer books, better publishing, strong authors writing in different genres – this can be the only way forward. We have to keep on trying to publish the culturally important with the commercially successful in order to be able to produce books for our teenagers. We need to remember that, even in this relatively small area of our market, children need variety, complexity and vitality; they need adventure and fantasy and history and thrillers, humour and grit – everything, of course, that adult readers need, too.

We are privileged in our country to have truly wonderful authors writing for the teenage market – Michael Morpurgo's *Private Peaceful*, for example, which shows how world events impact on ordinary lives; Adele Geras, whose novel *Troy* is better than any history lesson; Peter Dickinson, Anthony Horowitz, Sherry Ashworth, Melvyn Burgess, Kevin Brooks, Nicky Singer… one can go on and on. There is new talent emerging all the time. Children's authors are now dominating the market in a way that was unheard of a few years ago, and this can only be a thrilling time for teenage fiction.

Gillie Russell was formerly Fiction Publishing Director at HarperCollins Children's Books and is now an agent at Aitken Alexander Associates.

See also...
- *Notes from Jacqueline Wilson*, page 78
- *A word from J.K. Rowling*, page 81
- *How it all began*, page 82
- *Writing for different genres*, page 115
- *Writing for teenagers*, page 139
- *Writing thrillers for teenagers*, page 146
- *Writing crime fiction for teenagers*, page 143

Books

Writing series fiction for girls

Karen McCombie outlines the challenges and offers tips on successfully writing series fiction.

'How many books have you written?' I'm typically asked at book talks.

'Umm…' I uselessly answer, always vowing to tot up my titles so I don't umm uselessly ever again. (At that question at least. I did umm a lot when a girl asked me recently which of my books was the worst. Ahem.)

Well, I've just counted, and there are 65 of them lining my office shelves, written over 13 years. It's a bit of a fearsome number, spread over a relatively short period, but that's due to the fact that (a) I come from a background of writing for teenage magazines where you have to crank out a feature by lunchtime or you're slacking, and (b) in the early days, I got paid £2.50 per book (near enough) and *had* to write speedily to make any money.

(I'm not so speedy these days, because I get paid more money, *and* because my optimum writing time used to be 3–7pm, which doesn't work now that I have a daughter. At 3pm, instead of knocking out an unstoppable word rate, I'm hovering outside the school gates with a Cheese String.)

Glancing along my slightly bowed shelves, it dawned on me that all but nine are one of a series, which I suppose does qualify me to write a feature-ette on the subject. And how did series suddenly become my thing? It wasn't deliberate. While I was still freelancing for magazines, I wrote a couple of standalone teen novels for Scholastic, which didn't exactly sprint up the Nielsen Bookscan charts. Luckily for me, my friend Marina Gask, then editor of the now-defunct *Sugar* magazine, came up with the idea of doing a younger 'Hollyoaks'-style series of books in conjunction with HarperCollins, with the *Sugar* branding. There were to be 20 books, written by three authors (Marina, myself and Sue Dando, former editor of the also defunct *Just Seventeen* magazine) all under one pseudonym (the jaunty 'Mel Sparke').

It wasn't an easy ride – the style and storylines were decided and endlessly amended by a disjointed committee of editors (fine) and magazine bigwigs (not so fine). The pay was terrible (both book and magazine publishers had to get a cut, leaving a whole lot of not much for the writers). It got slightly complicated when – with only a few titles under their belts – Marina was lured off to edit another magazine, and Sue announced she was pregnant, leaving me as the one and only Mel (Mc)Sparke.

But a frantic 12 out of the 20 books later, I'd come to like the pace of series, of getting to know and develop characters. In fact, my next teen standalone novel for Scholastic accidentally became a mini-series, when I developed two more books (*Bliss…* and *Wonderland*) using characters from a first (*My Funny Valentine*).

Scholastic then asked me to have a go at a slightly younger series. They wanted the ten to earlier teen mix; they wanted family and friends; they wanted funny. I wanted to be writing books full time, so I said yes, please, very fast. The series turned into *Ally's World*, which took me pleasantly by surprise when it became a bestseller. (Yay!)

Since then, there's been *Stella Etc*, *Sadie Rocks*, the slightly younger *Indie Kidd* series, plus this year's *You, Me and Thing* for Faber, interspersed with a bundle of novels.

So, what words of wisdom can I impart about series writing? Well, none, probably, so you'll have to accept these random noodlings instead.…

Have ideas that aren't going to bore you

Mull over strong/quirky/endearing characteristics for your, er, characters; you could be writing about them for a long time, if you're lucky, and you don't want to end up running out of empathy with them quickly. In fact, you want them to almost become embedded as virtual buddies in your brain. I was with a friend at London Zoo, melting at the sight of a Short-Eared Elephant Shrew (think mutant mouse/sparrow/mini-kangaroo crossover) and sighed, 'Tor would love that!'. 'Who's Tor?' asked my friend. 'The kid brother of Ally, from *Ally's World*...' I muttered back, wondering if I seemed deranged. (Not as deranged as a mutant mouse/sparrow/mini-kangaroo, to be fair.)

Also, choose a setting that has lots of possibilities. The town in the *Sugar*-branded series was made up and based on nowhere in particular, and I found it monstrously hard to get a handle on how big/small it was and geographically where things were/weren't.

When it came to *Ally's World*, I set it on my doorstep (Crouch End, North London), and happily referenced every park, pet shop, travelling fair and local caff with confidence.

Think of a story arc

I held my breath when Scholastic commissioned the first three *Ally's World*s, not sure how many it might run to. Six? Wonderful. I got my story arc in place, based on the mystery of just where Ally's missing mum might be. Oh, they want to stretch it to ten books? Wheee! Quick, take a look at the future titles and make that arc stretch without going wobbly. Oh, 14 you say? I think I did it – know I did it; I made that story arc extend without visible signs of bolted-on wiffle.

On the flip side, as a writer, your series might not run as long as you'd love it to, so be ready to reign in your arc and tie up all the loose ends without appearing to rush it. (Hey, it's a tricky one, but if writing's your job, it's just another technical problem you've got to solve without the reader noticing the slightest bump in the reading road.)

Make each book in the series a standalone novel

I'm lucky; not too many of my earlier efforts have been deleted from my back catalogue. (I've jinxed that now, of course. A whole pile of 'I'm sorry to say... and how many copies would you like to buy before your book(s) are pulped?' letters are in the post for sure.)

But just because something is in print, doesn't guarantee that it's going to be on every given bookshop shelf. So while the story arc arcs away, each book *must* be a standalone read. The girl who picks up *My Big (Strange) Happy Family* – No. 6 in the *Indie Kidd* series – has to love it for itself. She mustn't feel frustrated by the Great Unknown of what's gone before, even though she'll (hopefully) want to seek out the earlier instalments asap.

Which brings me on to the fact that you have to learn to recap on old storylines in a non-drab way. The first three chapters in a series book are torture. They take infinitely longer than the rest of the book, where the story can meander and unravel itself, unhindered by the problem of having to re-introduce characters and plots without (a) smacking your readers in the face with obviousness, and (b) boring them.

So what's the answer? A lot of thinking and rewriting, quite a bit of mucking around with the different techniques you can use to reiterate. In other words, the answer is that it's not easy, and you've just got to factor it in as something important to get right, and don't stress over the extra time it might take to fix.

Do what your readers love but don't repeat yourself

OK, so I know my readers like 'Funny, Family and Friends'. But coming off the back of *Ally's World*, it took a long time to figure out what I should do next. With *Stella Etc*, as well as the 3Fs, I added a touch of magic realism, a dollop of history and mystery, and sparked a heated debate amongst fans about the identity of a mental old lady in a meringue hat with a penchant for feeding fairycakes to overweight seagulls.

Sadie Rocks is a shorter, four-part series, in which I did the traditional 3Fs, but entertained myself with adding in splashes of black humour and a character who's a 17-year-old trainee funeral director with a sideline in stand-up comedy.

Scribble yourself a who's-who as you go

Stunningly important advice, all to do with continuity, which I regularly don't do, and regret it. But if you keep a notepad to hand with the sole purpose of jotting down names, eye colours, favourite foods, individual tics, family members, pets and predilections, you'll save yourself much angst and finger fatigue from flicking back through previous books while cursing yourself. (Yeah, says the author who gave the gran in the first *Ally's World* two different names, and has been alerted to the fact by endless eagle-eyed readers ever since, despite it being corrected in later print runs.)

Never bleed a good idea dry

I think Scholastic would have been happy bunnies if I'd extended the *Ally's World* series to 20, but I might have lost the will to live. I adored that family as if it was my own (well, the character of Ally was loosely based on my worrisome 13-year-old self, and Colin the three-legged cat was my neighbour's moggy and a regular visitor to my own cats' food bowls).

There was no way I wanted to drag out the series with potentially shoehorned-in plots; not when I was pleased with the books as they were and didn't feel any of the 14 were weaker than others (though the 11-year-old critic at my recent book talk might beg to differ).

But never say never to going back to something that's fun!

They kept emailing. They kept pleading for more. I resisted for a long, long time, till one *Ally's World* fan said, 'I'd *love* to read a whole book about Ally's ditzy older sister, Rowan!' And that one remark embedded itself in a dusty corner of my mind, eventually erupting as *The Raspberry Rules*, a linked-to-the-series novel about Ally's older, nuttier fairy lights-obsessed sister. It was a blast to write – like bumping into an old (slightly mad) friend.

Well, those are my noodlings; advice that I'm revisiting myself, now that I'm immersed in my latest series. Though my 'Who's who' continuity notes for *Thing* read rather strangely – 'Looks: like a squirrel crossed with a fairy crossed with a troll. Likes: doing rubbish magic.' You may have spotted that my main character isn't a teenage girl, just for once....

Karen McCombie lives in 'Ally's World' (i.e. Crouch End, North London) with her husband, young daughter and two furry purring machines. She has sold more than a million books, won zero awards, and is often to be found writing on her laptop at her local garden centre cafe, with the aid of cake. Her website is www.karenmccombie.com, where you can see a video of Karen, the garden centre cafe and the cake.

Notes from a series author

Francesca Simon shares her early experiences of success in writing for children.

I started writing stories when I was eight. Because I adored Andrew Lang's fairy tale collections, I wrote my own prince and princess stories. Unfortunately, like many would-be writers I was great at starting stories but terrible at finishing them. So I put my notebook away and thought maybe I'd be a lawyer. That is, until I was a Yale undergraduate and opened a law book. I read half a page, my eyes glazed, and I abandoned all thoughts of the legal profession.

After Oxford, where I read 'Old and Middle English' (very useful for all the alliteration in *Horrid Henry*), I fell into freelance journalism which I enjoyed. Then in 1989 my son Joshua was born and everything changed.

I love to read and we started looking at board books together from the time he was four months old. And I was suddenly overwhelmed with ideas for picture books. This surprised me, as I'd never had any interest in writing for children. When I fantasised about being a writer, I just assumed I would write for adults.

One publisher (who shall remain nameless) quickly returned my first story, 'Wriggling Fingers'. The editor not only hated the story, but obviously thought I was of unsound mind to think something so scary would appeal to babies. This rejection letter detailing my failings went on and on and on… Not a good start. I was clearly one of those deluded new mums who thought she could write for children.

But the ideas kept coming. And I kept writing stories and sending them off. An agent eventually took me on (thank you, *Writers' & Artists' Yearbook*). I got a lot of rejections but a few encouraging comments, for example 'This story isn't right for us, but please send us more of your work.' Then finally, about a year after I started writing, one absolutely amazing day, Julia MacRae Books accepted *Papa Forgot*, about a grandfather looking after his grandson, who forgets every single instruction the anxious parents have given him, but somehow they have a wonderful evening. I will always remember the moment when my agent rang to tell me that my first book was going to be published. For me, that's the day I became a writer. Soon after, Macmillan accepted *But What Does the Hippopotamus Say?*, an animal noise book featuring noisy kangaroos, camels, and yaks, as well as cows, horses and sheep. And then Hodder accepted *What's That Noise?*, which was based on one particular evening when my son, then a toddler, called me repeatedly up to his room because he kept hearing things that go bump. After that I started writing for children full time.

A year later, the brilliant Judith Elliott, who had just joined Orion to create a brand new children's list, turned down a story but asked to meet me. Would I consider writing a first-time reader?

Of course! So in 1993 I wrote a one-off comic story about two brothers, one horrid, one perfect, and their parents who favour the latter. As the eldest of four, I know something about sibling rivalry, and I have a very strong memory of those childhood battles. Plus, there is something irresistibly comic about families. Who hasn't been on the car journey from hell, or fought to the death for control of the TV remote?

Unfortunately, this was not what I'd been asked for. Judith pointed out that the language was much too difficult for a first reader (I foolishly never thought to read one) but she liked the story. Could I write three more, and then she'd publish Horrid Henry as a book for newly confident readers instead? (Hurrah for the creative editor!) I was terrified, as I'd never written to order before, but thought I could just about dream up three more stories about Horrid Henry and Perfect Peter. *Horrid Henry* wasn't an instant success: in fact it wasn't until the fourth book, *Horrid Henry's Nits*, that the series took off.

Looking back, much of my writing career seems accidental. If I hadn't had a child, I'd never have written for children. If Judith hadn't asked me to write a few more Horrid Henry stories, I would probably have filed *Horrid Henry's Perfect Day* with all my other rejects and my life now would be very different.

Francesca Simon has had over 50 books published, including the *Horrid Henry* series which has sold over 15 million copies, is published in 24 countries and is also an animated CITV series. She won the Children's Book of the Year in 2008 at the British Book Awards for *Horrid Henry and the Abominable Snowman* and *Horrid Henry and the Football Fiend* was the most borrowed children's library book in 2009. Her new book for older children, *The Sleeping Army*, is published by Faber and Profile (2011).

See also...

● *Writing to a brief*, page 310

Writing for the school market

Changes made to the National Curriculum provide educational writers with the opportunity to create up-to-date teaching aids. Jim Green outlines the relationship between the writer for schools and the publisher.

Picture the scene: a typical school classroom; a teacher, pupils, desks, chairs, a computer in the corner of the room, the atmosphere noisy and intense. The typical classroom is a boisterous environment with a learning focus. What makes this so clearly a place of learning? The presence of a teacher and pupils of course; but it's their interaction with the vast range of available learning resources that makes this such a special place. It's the textbooks, the revision aids, the educational software, the posters on the walls and the vast array of published materials to be found in every classroom that, when expertly used by teachers and eagerly consumed by pupils, make this a centre for learning. How did all these resources find their way into the classroom? Whose thought, creativity and effort went into their development? And how would someone approach the challenge of creating materials that will one day find their way into this exciting environment?

The short answer to all these questions is that most educational resources are the result of an involved collaboration between a writer and a publishing company. A motivated individual wanted to create new materials and a publishing company saw an opportunity to develop and produce them. Individual schools are free to select their own resources and to use a broad range of materials from a number of sources. However, schools in the state sector are obliged to follow the National Curriculum, and it is the context of a National Curriculum that is most significant in determining the nature of published materials for the educational sector.

The National Curriculum

The National Curriculum is an educational framework that covers the entire Primary and Secondary school age range, establishing specific subject-by-subject requirements, desired learning outcomes and thus a very clear route map through the educational system followed by teachers and learners. Published materials must be compliant with, and supportive of, the requirements of the National Curriculum in order for them to be viable for use in the classroom. The template provided by the National Curriculum can be seen as both a very useful guide to an individual school's resource requirements and, less positively, as a rather constricting straitjacket which allows little individuality either in the preparation of resources or the teaching of course subject matter. My favourite National Curriculum analogy is that it can be likened to a classical symphony or a haiku – both have a clear and somewhat rigid framework within which there is infinite space for the creation of uniquely individual content. Indeed, it is the creation of unique content within the framework of the National Curriculum that is the essential challenge facing all prospective educational writers and publishers.

Whilst teachers might find reassurance in the overall structure offered by the National Curriculum, its ongoing development gives teachers the problem of implementing curriculum changes into their classroom teaching on a regular basis. Many teachers complain that the evolving curriculum creates one of their largest challenges – no sooner have they updated teaching notes, assimilated new learning outcomes and developed their own strategies for teaching the curriculum requirements, than the process begins again. However, it is curriculum change that presents the greatest single opportunity for new writers to create new materials and to get them into use in the classroom. Indeed, it is in helping teachers deliver emerging areas of the curriculum that writers and publishers can be of most value to the teaching community. Curriculum change can generally be anticipated some time in advance of implementation, giving prospective writers time to prepare materials and publishers time to assess both the market and the proposed materials. Focusing time and effort on areas of the curriculum that are changing makes good sense for all interested parties – teachers, writers and publishers.

What do publishers look for when assessing educational materials?

The single, overarching requirement is an understanding of the requirements of teachers and learners, which can also be described as market knowledge. What do schools need? What will help teachers do an even better job of delivering the curriculum? What will enhance the educational experience of pupils? A writer with clear and compelling answers to these questions will be of great interest to publishing companies. Other criteria publishers apply when assessing educational materials include:

- **Writing ability.** Is the material coherent, clear and appropriate for the target age group?
- **Knowledge of subject.** Is the writer an expert in the subject matter?
- Does the writer have **experience teaching the material**?
- Is the writer **a known authority in the field**, whose published work will be recognised as coming from an authoritative source? (For example, materials created by a subject examiner are widely coveted by publishers.)
- **Is the material well organised?** Does it have a logical structure?
- How much thought has the writer given to the **visual presentation of the content**? Are there sample illustrations, diagrams or photographs?
- **Is theoretical content applied in a motivating way?** Are the examples relevant and interesting? Do examples clarify or confuse?
- **Will the end product have an advantage** over the products currently available to schools? Is this clear in the materials?
- **Will the writer be fun to work with?** The best resources grow from a genuine partnership between writer and publisher.
- **Does the material give the motivated learner opportunities to go further and learn more?** This could, for example, take the form of a suggested further reading list, a series of links to relevant websites or optional activities that extend the learners' understanding of subject matter.

What publishers do

Assuming the prospective writer has given thought to the above, that there is a curriculum need for the materials and that a publisher is keen to invest in development and production, what happens next? Or more succinctly, what is it that publishers actually do?! Publishers manage every stage of the development, production and promotion of a project. The publisher's role is to shape an original idea into an end product that articulates the original idea, whilst also supporting the curriculum and providing teachers with a resource that enhances the way they teach. The writer generally provides the creative impetus, the hard work of writing core content and, frequently, support to the sales and marketing of the end product. A more detailed list of the activities undertaken by a publisher includes:

• 18–24 months before publication: development of proposal; from an author's original idea the proposal is finalised, a contract agreed and the development timeline created.

• 6–24 months before publication: this phase includes the bulk of the writing and is when the writer's involvement is greatest. The publisher will provide input, feedback and guidance to the writer.

• 12 months before publication: initiation of marketing and promotional activities.

• 6–8 months before publication: coordination of reviews of the first draft of the manuscript. An editor will read the typescript and may also take advice from independent reviewers.

• 6–8 months before publication: copy-editing and preparing the typescript, commissioning of artwork, appointment of a picture researcher and clearance of copyright permission for sourced material.

• 6–8 months before publication: internal design and page layout.

• 6 months before publication: publisher will provide the author with a set of proofs for checking, these will also be sent to a professional proofreader and necessary corrections made to typescript.

• 4 months before publication: printing and binding.

• 2 weeks before publication: warehousing and release to market.

This is an overview of the process of creating educational materials that will hopefully be of use to anyone commissioned to write for the education market. However, we still need to look at the challenge of getting commissioned in the first place. This process will vary by publisher, indeed this process will vary between editors working at the same publishing house. What follows is a list of suggestions that will be of help to writers hoping to be commissioned to write for the school sector.

• **Make personal contact with the relevant editor**. The name of the editor responsible for a specific subject area will be available from the company switchboard. Call the editor to introduce yourself and your proposal prior to sending in sample materials. Materials sent to a generic 'Dear Sir/Madam' are rarely published.

• **When the time comes to send in sample materials, follow the publisher's requirements as closely as possible**. Most publishers will request a written overview of the project plus some comments on the needs of the prospective audience, as well as a draft table of contents and sample chapter. It's important to note that sending in too much material to an editor can be as unhelpful as sending in too little.

• **Ensure the material is 'fit for purpose'**. Does it solve a teaching problem? Does it meet an emerging curriculum requirement? Is it obvious to the reader that the material solves a problem/meets a curriculum requirement?

• **Ensure the end product has an advantage over currently available resources**. The existence of the National Curriculum means that there are ever smaller differences between the competing resources. A new product needs an 'edge', a point of distinction, that makes it more attractive to a teacher than the resource they currently use.

Summary

My intention is to provide helpful information that will assist in overcoming the challenges ahead. Should you feel daunted by any of the above it's important to remember that thousands of new products are published for the school market each year and many thousands of once-aspiring writers are now successfully published authors. The average classroom is packed with resources and this breadth of materials gives a lot of scope for new writers. Remember the classroom from the start of this article? A typical classroom will contain the work of around 100 different writers. Of course there will be long, lonely hours involved in the writing itself but once a publisher has committed to your project you'll be working as part of a team. The joy of making a direct contribution to education will make the effort worthwhile and when things get tough just imagine the excitement and interest created by well-written, well-published and genuinely motivating educational resources.

Jim Green has worked extensively in educational publishing in both the UK and North America and has been involved in creating a broad range of educational resources for schools.

Ghostwriting children's books

Di Redmond outlines the challenges and rewards for ghostwriters when working with celebrities.

Books

Publishers know that celebs sell. You've only got to run down the bestseller list to see that celebs' books are selling well – very well. But you can't help but wonder whether that footballer, pop star, fashion model or diva really wrote that children's book? It has to be said, sometimes not. Instead, publishers use professional ghostwriters, mainly because they can rely on them to deliver the manuscript on time and in the right publishable form and know it won't have wandered too far from the synopsis they approved at the beginning of the writing process. So, in our age of celeb writers, there are opportunities to be had for good ghostwriters.

How to become a ghostwriter

If you're interested in ghostwriting you'll need to put the word about by contacting agents and publishers. It's a genre that had never crossed my mind until I was approached by a publishing house. They were on a very tight schedule – they needed six books, 10,000 words each in three months and a synopsis by yesterday! I've written well over 100 books and have a good professional track record and I know from experience that there's nothing more reassuring to a publisher than a hard-selling synopsis. A good synopsis first and foremost tells a publisher that the ghostwriter can do the job in hand. This in turn increases their confidence when it comes to them pitching the sell to the chosen celeb. So, I make it my business to write a very clear synopsis. The whole process of laying down a foundation, outlining the chapters and describing the locations is as reassuring to me as it is to the publisher. As standard practice I usually write a synopsis for free: it helps to get the project moving and it also necessitates feedback from the editor and the celeb in question. I've always found this teamwork really useful as it means the ghostwriter, the editor and the celeb are in agreement at the start of the writing process.

The publishers like the 'ghost' to meet the celeb before the contract is signed. A working chemistry is important (if you can't stand the sight of each other there'll be no easy exchange and the book certainly won't get written). Another reason to meet the celeb is to get a feel for the 'tone' of the book you'll be writing. The celeb's major input is the book's subject matter which will have been chosen because of their interest or expertise in that subject. It might be about ballet dancing, show jumping, football or becoming a child pop idol. If the tone isn't forthcoming then it might be a part of your job to suggest one. For example, if the book is about show jumping, is it a posh show-jumping circuit or is it about kids at a local riding school? The subject matter stays the same but the tone will be different: one will be posh whilst the other will be gutsy. Whatever the choice of subject, the ghostwriter must be interested in it too otherwise the project will become unbearable. I was recently asked to ghostwrite a book but the subject matter was so alien to me I had to turn it down. It's best to be realistic about this right from the start otherwise you'll waste everybody's time, including your own, and you might eventually be fired for not coming up with the goods!

The celeb may furnish you with lots of material, or may not give you much more than his or her famous name. Each of my encounters has been different. I had a long meeting with one celeb then never saw her again; she was happy to jump start the project and leave it to me and the editorial team to get on with the job. Other celebs really want to get involved in the writing process. They might want to read every draft, make notes, and add comments, or even change the plot line. In terms of writing, especially if you're working to a tight deadline, waiting for feedback can be a time-consuming process if the celeb is, for example, filming abroad or playing in a World Cup match.

What does a ghostwriter do?

A large part of a ghost's job is to listen to and make sense of the story they're being told. Other people's stories (even famous celebs) can become rambling anecdotes that don't have much of a plot line, hold little tension and may not have a satisfactory conclusion. The ghost must be able to see the book's structure right from the beginning which is precisely why the initial synopsis is so vital. The ghost needs to keep the celeb on track, clear up inconsistencies in the story, establish what age group the book is being pitched at and clarify any publishing issues which may not be obvious to the celeb. For example, if it's a picture book you're writing and the celeb is going into great detail about the colour of the clothes the characters are wearing, the ghost can point out that the illustrations running through the book will make those details crystal clear. Similarly, the celeb may present you with material that is not suitable for the age range, for example if you're writing for 7–10 year-olds you won't want excessive kissing and cuddling. There are a lot of things to consider because even though the editor will probably already have discussed publishing issues with the celeb, it doesn't necessarily mean that he or she will have fully understood the differences between a 32-page picture book and a 10,000-word story with some black and white illustrations.

As a ghost you need to be able to write quickly because as a rule where celebs are involved there'll always be a tight deadline. They're busy people and when they decide to do a book they usually hit the ground running and want it instantly or certainly before they go off to meet the next demand on their time. Take as many notes as you can on that first meeting just in case you never see your celeb again and use a tape recorder if possible. Once your celeb is swept up into their next project you'll be lucky if you get an email or a phone call from them. Basically you're on your own with a deadline looming but any professional writer is used to that. Never be demanding: it doesn't work. As far as the celeb and, more importantly, their agent is concerned, you've been paid to do the job, so do it!

That said, it's another important part of a ghost's job to be diplomatic. Because it's the celeb's story you'll need to be subtle when pointing out any inconsistencies, especially with the celebs who need their ego massaging. If you're a good ghost, then you'll always have the backing of the editor as well as the celeb's agent, so most problems will be amicably sorted out.

What rights does a ghostwriter have?

The celeb might be generous and share the writing credit with the ghost or he or she might choose to ignore the ghost altogether. Make sure you know this kind of detail at the contract stage; there's no point in complaining later if you've signed your name away. Celebs don't see books – even their own – as big earners, and they're not when compared with the millions they net for, say, a lead part in a major film. Be aware from the outset that the celeb's agent and the publishing house which commissioned you will both take a cut. You'll undoubtedly be expected to sign a contract with a 'total buy-out clause' so don't auto-matically expect to get a royalty fee (some ghosts do but I never have). At best, there's a chance your name might appear on the inside back cover and if it does, this will guarantee you an annual Public Lending Right (see page 264) payment. You will also have to sign a confidentiality clause which means you can't go blabbing to the press or even chat to your mates about the contents of the book. People ask me over and over again, 'Isn't it frustrating not being able to say, I wrote that book?' The answer is no. In signing the contract you're giving the book away, you know from the word go that the celeb's glamorous picture will be on the back cover, her introduction will be on the first page, she'll be doing the book launch and the autograph signing and if the book's a huge success she'll be at the televised book award. I actually enjoy the reflected glory I get from being a ghostwriter and smile to myself when I see my celebs being interviewed about their books and how they personally enjoyed the new challenges that writing presented.

Whatever happens, don't be walked over. Fight for the best deal and stay focused on the fact that the book won't get written without you.

Lastly, don't expect a thank you crate of champagne or huge bouquet on publication because once that book is in print it really does belong to the celeb who never wrote it!

Di Redmond is a prolific writer for stage, radio and television. She has published over 100 books and is an established celebrity ghostwriter.

See also...
• *Writing to a brief*, page 310

What does an editor do?

Yvonne Hooker describes the varied and exciting aspects to an editor's job.

What does an editor do? Good question. Answers have ranged from reading all day to drawing the illustrations. However, baldly put, an editor's job is to acquire new titles and to oversee a book's progress from acquisition to publication, bringing the book in on time and on budget. Where the book goes, the editor follows – from finance and contracts, through design and production, to sales and publicity – making sure that their book, their baby, is getting the best possible treatment and the maximum attention. An editor is the book's champion throughout its life.

Acquiring

The demise of the publisher's slush pile in recent years means that most new books now come via agents. No editor wants to miss out on seeing the latest find from an agent. It's always possible that she will turn down a manuscript that will later become a runaway bestseller – publishing remains a gambling business – but the worst scenario of all is just not to have been offered the book in the first place. So, it is absolutely vital for the editor to be on close terms with all the relevant agents. She must make sure that the agent knows her tastes and is generally confident of her editorial skills and judgements, so that when a real plum of a book arrives, the agent will immediately think, 'Ah, x is just the editor for this,' and send it off.

No one can be an editor and not thrill to the sight of a new manuscript, so finding something you want to publish is a pulse-racing moment. What the editor has to do immediately is to get everyone else's pulse racing as well. She has to start the internal buzz. No book is going to succeed unless all the publishing departments are firmly behind it and it is the editor's job to get the enthusiasm going by talking the book up to key figures, and by presenting the book at the publisher's acquisitions meetings.

The editor will probably have to prepare some kind of financial spreadsheet showing that the book can be expected to make a profit. Figures are needed from sales, marketing, rights and so on and, in order to get the best possible forecasts, the editor has to convince all these other departments that here is a terrific new book which is an absolute must for the list.

In the meantime, the editor will have rung the agent to express her enthusiasm. Usually agents will say whether they are sending books to other publishers as well, but it's always prudent to check and to find out if interest has been expressed from any other quarter. If it has, and an auction situation is developing, then the editor has to make sure that everyone is aware of this, and that the offer is going to be ready on time. In these circumstances, the editor may prepare a particular pitch for the book: a presentation which will convince the author that this is the true home for the book with people who really understand it.

Although many other departments will be involved in the mechanics of the offer, it is the editor who will present it to the agent and who will negotiate all the terms of advance, royalties and rights. It would be rare for an offer for a book by a new author to be accepted as it stands. A certain amount of haggling will be expected and this is one instance where a cool head will serve an editor rather better than unbridled enthusiasm.

Sometimes, before the deal is concluded, the agent will want to have a beauty parade and take the author round to meet competing publishers. This is the editor's chance to woo the author face-to-face and, very often, though not always, the choice of editor will be the deciding factor. The author should be well aware that this is the person with whom he or she will be working most closely and that this will be a vital and all-important relationship. It is, of course, a professional one, and it is perfectly possible for author and editor to work together harmoniously even if they would never choose each other's company outside of publishing, but it does help to have a sense of rapport. No one else has as much contact with the author, and no one else fights as fiercely for the author's voice to be heard. Once the book is hers, the editor will be the author's champion. But she also has to remember that the book is required to make money for the publisher as well as the author.

Editing

The first stage the manuscript of the book goes through is editing: the process to arrive at a final text which is agreed upon by both the editor and the author. This is, rightly, a stage largely hidden from the rest of the world though, for both author and editor, it is the most rewarding part of the whole process. The editor is the first professional reader of the manuscript and her aim is to make the book the best it can possibly be. She will read it with a fine critical eye, checking for problems and seeing what can be done to put them right. These can range from the simple glitch (a week that lasts ten days or a dog that changes breed in the course of the story), to the emotional core (does a relationship have enough depth, would this character actually do or say this, is the emotional focus clear enough?) and the overall narrative structure (is the beginning punchy enough, does it take too long to get going, does it feel rushed at the end?).

This is the stage which cements the relationship between editor and author. It is a curiously intimate process, relying as it does on a basis of trust and a sharing of the creative process. There has to be absolute trust between author and editor. The author has to feel that he or she can rely upon the editor's critical skill and judgement; the editor has to feel that the author will receive editorial suggestions with serenity. It is taken for granted that editors will not make changes for the sake of it. Nor will they try to rewrite the book as they would have written it. It is, and will remain, the author's book. The whole process should be one of discussion and cooperation, with author and editor working together to make the book the very best it can be.

Every author has a different way of working with his or her editor. Some like to submit a finished manuscript, while others like to send in first ideas and chapters for editorial input as they go along. Any way the author wants to play it is fine with the editor. Sometimes, even the most experienced authors get stuck for some reason – finding the right voice, for instance – and it helps to meet with and talk to the editor. This is a vital and important part of the editorial role as writing is an incredibly lonely occupation and to be able to talk problems through with an interested and experienced reader can be a lifeline. The author–editor relationship can develop to the point where the editor will be one of the first people to be told about quite personal things – impending marriages and babies – and her advice can be sought about things which have nothing to do with work: the best way to cook roast potatoes, for instance (this has actually happened!). Editorial trust can extend beyond the book!

Copy-editing and proofing

When a final manuscript has been agreed between the author and editor, the text is ready to be copy-edited. Not many editors do this themselves nowadays, though most will have copy-editorial experience. This is not just because they do not have the time but it's good to have a fresh eye on the manuscript at this stage. The copy-editor marks up the manuscript for the typesetter, checks the grammar and spelling and acts as a safety net for any glitches which may have slipped through. Any word changes are checked with the author and, in any case, most authors are given the opportunity of seeing the copy-edited manuscript. This is the last opportunity to get everything right before the manuscript is typeset (and changes start costing money) so it is vitally important that everyone should be happy with it at this stage.

The copy-edited manuscript will then go off to be typeset. The editor, with the designer or text designer, will have chosen an appropriate text setting and any flourishes to chapter heads. If the book is to be illustrated, the editor will have marked appropriate places in the text for the illustrations. Both editor and author will be involved in choosing an illustrator, but this aspect is the responsibility of the design department.

When the proofs arrive from the typesetter a set will be sent to the author and another set will be proofread by a professional proofreader. The editor will see the proofs but will very rarely proofread the text, though every editor has the skill. This is a last opportunity for another fresh eye on the text to check for any errors.

While all this is going on, the editor will be busy with other aspects of the book. Having a final manuscript or bound proofs, if there are any, is an opportunity to remind everyone how good the book is, making sure it's not forgotten as other, newer titles are coming through. The editor may send the book out to well-known people in the hope of getting a useful quote for publicity purposes.

The cover

Getting the right cover for a book is of paramount importance. Although this is the design department's province, the editor has a vital role to play. She will need to discuss the book with the designer, and with the sales and marketing teams. Together they will decide on the approach to take, though the choice of artist will generally be in the hands of the designer. The editor may also have to write the cover copy if the publishing house does not have a separate blurb-writing department.

Because getting the right cover is so important, other departments such as sales and marketing will be involved and will have to approve. Of course, publishers want authors to be happy with the covers but authors very rarely have final approval of covers; it is generally accepted that this is an area where the publisher's judgement is final. It is the editor's job to send roughs and visuals of the cover to the author and, in rare cases of disagreement, to persuade them that the cover is absolutely the right one, or to suggest acceptable compromises.

Proof covers have to be ready at least six months before publication to allow for sell-in time. If that date slips, then the publication date has to move, so getting the cover through on time is a major editorial preoccupation.

Publication

Once the cover is done and the final text is going through, the editor's major work on the book is done. But she must keep it in the forefront of everyone's minds and keep the internal buzz growing. She will present the book at internal launch meetings and possibly also at sales conferences and presentations of lead and highlight titles. She will also be liaising with publicity and marketing on their plans to launch the book and will make sure that the author knows the publisher's publicity contact.

About a month before publication, early finished copies of the book will arrive on the editor's desk, hopefully looking wonderful. The editor will check through to make sure that everything is all right, and send an early copy to the author.

All the editor has to do then is to send the author a card on publication day, raise a glass at the launch party if there is one, read the reviews circulated by the publicity department, and make sure that the book is entered for every relevant prize going.

An editor has to have sound judgement, a fine critical eye and enormous funds of patience and sensitivity. It also helps to be a fast reader! Above all, she must be a consummate juggler, handling books at all their different stages – yet be able to drop everything in a crisis to concentrate on the one thing that matters: getting an author's book absolutely right, the book that he or she always hoped it would be.

Yvonne Hooker was Senior Editor at Puffin Books 1996–2008. She has now retired.

See also...
- *Getting started*, page 1
- *A word from J.K. Rowling*, page 81
- *How it all began*, page 82
- *Marketing, publicising and selling children's books*, page 168

Books

Marketing, publicising and selling children's books

The way in which books for children are marketed and publicised is different to the way the adult market is targeted. Rosamund de la Hey identifies the target audience for children's books and explains the various ways in which publishers can reach that audience.

What is marketing?

Marketing can be seen as an umbrella term that includes all the work a publisher does to promote or sell a book. Many people are not clear about the difference between marketing and publicity. Traditionally, marketing is categorised as anything paid for (posters, advertising, catalogues, etc) and publicity (such as review coverage and radio interviews) is free. There is a useful saying that every book must be sold three times – by the editor to the rest of the company, by the sales/marketing/publicity departments to the bookseller, and by the bookseller to the consumer.

How can authors help?

There are many ways authors can help to market their books from the start. Most publishers will send out an author questionnaire soon after acquiring the book. This will generally ask for information ranging from the name of his or her local bookshop, to background details which may offer a marketing or publicity hook. It can help to think of a biography as a series of tabloid headlines – for instance, a children's novelist whose previous career was that of a fighter pilot would be very interesting to teenage magazine editors with a young male readership. On the other hand, if there are areas an author would rather the press did not know about, he or she should tell the publicist, as otherwise innocent, but upsetting, mistakes may happen. Sometimes a mock interview with the publisher's publicist may help the author.

If a book covers a specialist area or issue – for example, Benjamin Zephaniah's *Face* deals with severe facial scarring – it's likely that the author will be able to give the publisher information about relevant organisations which would be interested in hearing about the book, and whose members may indeed buy it.

Events can form a crucial part of promoting a children's book. However, it's worth remembering that not all authors are comfortable in front of a room full of six year-olds.

Marketing children's books

One of the differences between marketing children's books and marketing adults' books is the timescale. Adult book launches are all tied round a very specific window of publication, whereas a children's publication, even if there is a splashy launch, tends to work more like a slow-burn candle.

Children's advertising is also dictated by both the target market – children and their parents – and by more limited budgets. While adult campaigns can assume that adults read a newspaper, take public transport and go shopping, children's sphere of influence tends to be more limited – school, the local sports centre, the library, the internet or television. Publishers must also decide whether they are targeting the child or the parent in advertising.

Publicity

In publicity terms, children's review space is more limited than for adult books, so the coverage happens when the space allows. Additionally, many of the important reviews for children's books happen in specialist magazines such as *Books for Keeps* and *Carousel* which are published only bi-monthly or quarterly.

Libraries

Libraries often receive the books some time after publication as each book needs to be adapted for library use. In school libraries, budgets can also be very tight so it may be months or years after publication that a school can afford to stock new titles.

Events

Unlike adult authors who will normally only do a book tour around publication, many children's authors and illustrators spend a great deal of their time doing events and workshops in schools and bookshops, and at the numerous literary festivals around the country throughout the year (see *Children's literature festivals and trade fairs* on page 392). For those who do get involved, the word-of-mouth benefits are well worth the effort. One of the best examples of this is Jacqueline Wilson, who was visiting schools up to three times a week long before her books became bestsellers. She still visits schools regularly year round, as well as touring bookshops and festivals with her new publications.

Direct marketing to schools

The children's market lends itself to direct marketing more than many other areas of trade publishing. This is largely because there is a captive market sitting in school for much of the year. However, marketing directly to schools does have its drawbacks. Teachers are very busy people who have to wade through enough paperwork without being sent endless publishers' catalogues. So, it is important for publishers to be clear and realistic about why they are sending material to schools. A children's educational publisher which also publishes a trade fiction list, may be more likely to be picked up by the Head of English because he or she is expecting to order course books from that catalogue.

Mailing a full trade publisher catalogue to every primary school headteacher in the country is also a very expensive exercise, for potentially little return. Some publishers do have a schools sales force who sell their list directly into schools; others use freelance reps to sell a limited selection from their list into schools. The appropriateness of either of these approaches will depend entirely on the type of list a publisher has.

World Book Day, however, provides many trade publishers with a positive platform to market to schools. For the past few years, a schools' pack has been sent out giving information to teachers and their pupils about World Book Day. Publishers that support World Book Day have the opportunity to insert marketing material (flyers, posters, etc) into the schools pack and know that the investment stands a better chance of paying dividends because it's more targeted.

Advertising in schools

Media agencies now sell poster sites within schools themselves. Books are arguably the perfect 'product' to advertise in this way – the teachers are keen to encourage reading and hopefully the advertisement will spark the interest of the children. This is an example of where jacket design is crucial. If the design is not sufficiently strong, it's unlikely catch the attention of the advertising-savvy children.

This type of advertising is not cheap and so is likely to be used rarely and be carefully timed. *Holes* by Louis Sachar, although winner of the prestigious Newbury Medal in the USA, was unknown in the UK until 1999. Bloomsbury marketed the hardback with a successful publicity-led campaign and when the paperback was published nine months later it targeted schools and ran a poster campaign within secondary schools. It is always hard to gauge the exact response to advertising of this type without commissioning expensive research (which is often more expensive than the original advertising costs). However, *Holes* has now sold half a million copies, helped in no small way by being extensively read for course work in schools.

Playground marketing

The phrase 'playground marketing' was widely used after the publication of *Harry Potter and the Philosopher's Stone* in 1997 and partly as a result of the book winning the Gold Smarties Book Prize that year. It is very hard to pin down exactly how playground marketing works except to say that it is a combination of many factors: school events, word of mouth, in-school advertising and the prizes network all play their part. The latter is especially important when the children themselves are involved in selecting the winner of a book prize. This now happens for many prizes, from the big national ones to strongly championed local prizes such as the Angus Book Award (see *Children's book and illustration prizes and awards* on page 382).

Playground marketing only works in tandem with mainstream publicity and child-focused campaigns. For example, when *Harry Potter and the Prisoner of Azkaban* was released in 1999, it was timed for 3.45pm, just after school finished for the day. This caused massive publicity as children streamed out of school and into bookshop queues to buy the book, giving the television cameras a visual hook.

Internet marketing

Many children's publishers are putting more emphasis on internet marketing. The reasons for this are fairly straightforward. In general, children are far more internet-aware than their parents, and tend to spend a lot more time on their computers than reading a book.

Most publishers have their own website and it's worth having a look at some examples to get an idea about what's out there. Some lead titles will be marketed on a specially created independent site as a key part of the overall marketing plan. For example, fantasy fiction often inspires addictive online games and quizzes, such as www.faeriewars.co.uk and www.artemisfowl.co.uk. However, these are expensive to set up and a great deal can be done to promote a book on the existing publisher website. Many publishers also use their sites to run readers' clubs and offer information to teachers.

Design

One of the key marketing tools for any book is the jacket image. If the book is fantastic but has a dull, or inappropriate jacket, not only will the bookseller be unwilling to stock it, but the reader will not be attracted to it, nor understand what kind of a reading experience it's 'selling'.

A good example of where a jacket can help to raise an already successful writer to the next level, is *Witch Child* by Celia Rees. Staring out of the jacket is the beautiful face of a young girl who commands the passer-by's attention with her piercing stare. The book jacket was cited by many booksellers as one of the key reasons why customers picked it up and it was subsequently shortlisted for the British Book Awards in their Book Cover image of the year.

Book jacket design is not only important in bookshops, it is also crucial in advertising. This is true for all advertising from standing out in a small trade advert in the *Bookseller* or *The School Librarian*, to staring down from the side of a London bus.

Trade sales and marketing

Sales and marketing have become more and more closely allied since the demise of the Net Book Agreement (NBA). This was abolished in 1995 and has meant the inexorable rise of the big discount as a way for booksellers to market to the consumer. The knock-on effect of this in the high street has been for publishers to compete with one another for their books to claim valued places in bookshop promotions, be they '3 for 2' offers or '£2 off' schemes. Although these do almost always generate higher sales for a title, they come at a price, and more and more publishers' marketing budgets are being devoted to funding bookshops to run these promotions.

As a result, the trend is for big books to get bigger and small titles to get lost and often disappear without trace. This in turn is polarising publishers' lists and making it a much harder business to break into.

Non-traditional book markets

Another knock-on effect of the NBA's demise is the rise of the supermarket as bookseller. Big supermarket chains such as Asda, Tesco and Sainsbury's are getting more and more involved in selling books, and it is now almost impossible to get onto the general bestseller lists without a supermarket presence for your title. They usually stock a very narrow range of titles but some, such as Asda, will occasionally try less well-known authors who publishers are pushing strongly. Bearing in mind that the likes of Tesco have in the region of 800 stores, this can transform the sales of a title on the basis of one retailer.

Book clubs/direct marketing sales

Book clubs have always marketed themselves using price and heavy advertising in the national press. Usually they offer deals whereby if you join you get several books very cheaply and you are then tied into a minimum level of book buying through the club for a specific period. Direct marketing companies such as The Book People have been incredibly successful in selling to customers in their workplace and through catalogues.

In the children's world, book clubs are especially important as there are more clubs devoted to children and their parents than there are for adults (see *Children's book clubs* on page 69). The children's market also has schools as a captive audience. Several clubs, including Scholastic and Troubadour, are set up to run 'book fairs' in schools in tandem with their mail order operations. They offer a hand-picked selection of what the club deems to be the most commercial and appropriate selection of titles. It is therefore crucial that any children's publisher has a very strong relationship with the clubs. They may stock a more narrow range than the high street, but they order in bulk and in many cases that one order can radically improve the viability of a book's print run.

The changing face of the children's marketplace

The past five or six years has seen a huge change in attitudes to children's publishing. One of the effects of this has been to generate far more high-profile – and expensive – marketing campaigns to launch new writers such as Eoin Colfer and Anthony Horowitz. In the past, these authors might have expected a publicity campaign and perhaps a poster for book-shops and libraries. However, for a small number of lead titles, now you will see major 'outdoor' advertising and read about them as front page news. Children's books are now winning the big prizes and taking up the kind of column inches that used to be reserved for the Salman Rushdies of this world.

However, this can distort the market and it should be emphasised that, generally speak-ing, children's books attract smaller marketing budgets than adults' books. This is down to simple economics: in general, children's books cost less than their adult equivalent. On the positive side, all this publicity has meant that the public awareness of good children's writing has been massively raised by the success of authors such as Rowling, Pullman and Wilson.

The 'crossover' book

The rise of the children's book prompted adults to find out what all the fuss is about and as a result the 'crossover' book was born. When Bloomsbury first published the Harry Potter books for the adult market with a specially designed discreet black and white jacket in 1998, it was for several reasons. Firstly, anecdotal evidence suggested that adults were reading the books already but that some felt embarrassed to be seen in public with a children's book. Secondly, even when *Harry Potter and the Chamber of Secrets* reached number one in the overall bestseller charts, booksellers refused to stock the books at the front of store. And finally, as a marketing concept, for fun, to see if it worked.

The results speak for themselves with the advent of adult editions of the Philip Pullman trilogy *His Dark Materials*, *Holes* by Louis Sachar and *Face* by Benjamin Zephaniah, the 'crossover' book has become a recognised marketing strategy that works when used for the right book. This theory has been taken a step further by the simultaneous publication of Mark Haddon's *The Curious Incident of the Dog in the Night-Time* in 2003 when Jonathan Cape and David Fickling Books brought out editions for both markets. This has proved a huge critical and commercial success.

Champion the book

One thing that will never change in marketing children's books is the very first sale that is made – by the editor to the publishing company. He or she must be able to inspire people to read and love the book they champion. In children's books, as with adult books, a very great deal comes down to the individual championing of one book above all others. This passion can make all the difference in marketing and selling, and it costs nothing.

Rosamund de la Hey was formerly Children's Marketing Director of Bloomsbury Publishing Plc and has been responsible for marketing J.K. Rowling's Harry Potter books, as well as other notable successes such as *Holes* by Louis Sachar and *Witch Child* by Celia Rees. With her husband, Bill, Rosamund opened a bookshop, café and giftshop in the Scottish Borders in 2008 called the Mainstreet Trading Company (www.mainstreetbooks.co.uk), which was voted Children's Bookseller of the Year and shortlisted for Independent Bookseller of the Year (Scotland and the North) in 2010.

See also...

- *What does an editor do?* page 164
- *Children's books and the US market*, page 177
- *Categorising children's books*, page 181
- *Magazines about children's literature and education*, page 293

From self-publishing to contract

Janey Louise Jones shares her tale of how she successfully self-published her first Princess Poppy book, which led to a contract with Random House and huge sales.

My journey to self-publishing

For some children, a bookshop has more delicious flavours than a sweetshop. I was one of those children. When I was a little girl, I wanted to be a writer *and* a princess. So, with my Princess Poppy books now selling in their millions around the world, I find myself reflecting on the life experiences which have led to me realising my childhood dreams.

People often say that the story of Princess Poppy, going from a childhood notion, to kitchen table, to self-published success, then on to a Random House contract, is a fairy tale in itself. Perhaps so, but even fairy tales are laced with problems and trials and self-publishing has been a very challenging experience. I highly recommend starting alone as a way of presenting a vision, proving strong sales and learning the full craft of producing a book – but it is not an easy process.

As a child, I saw witches at my window, and fairies in the moonlight. I loved ballet and the flower fairies, and made petal perfume. I was idealistic and romantic and although I was very loved, I never felt special enough. So I developed a perfectionist streak – always driven to do my very best. I began to express my feelings and identity through words. Like so many book lovers, I loved the physical look and texture of a book as much as what it said to me.

Growing up in the 1970s, it wasn't fashionable to be gender specific for children. Being ultra-feminine was frowned upon as frothy in a way that it isn't now. Did any other girls of the 1970s have a dark brown, checked, floor-length party dress, or was I especially unlucky? I felt a conflict between wanting to be educated, well read and serious on the one hand, and wanting to be a pretty fairy princess, on the other. Could I possibly be 'Fairy Blue Stocking'?

My favourite childhood books included *The Secret Garden*, *Little House on the Prairie*, *Little Women*, *The Children of the New Forest* and *The Diary of Anne Frank*. Later on, at Edinburgh University in the late 1980s, I became intrigued with the concept of 'the novel' and through my love of Victorian and early twentieth century authors, I was asked to contribute to *Chambers Dictionary of Literary Characters*. This was my first formal writing experience, which taught me the valuable lesson that when it comes to writing, effort and remuneration are not always commensurate.

Somehow, during my degree course, the wistful child within me resurfaced and I produced a storyboard for a magical, mythical character – Princess Poppy. People often ask me: 'Is she your child, your daughter?' (I have three boys). But no, she isn't my child, she is *me* as a child. I found it difficult to enter adulthood and Poppy beckoned me back to my childish dreams. So, the cliché that one's first and best work is autobiographical is certainly true for me.

Back at this early stage, I lacked confidence and direction, my ideas blowing in the wind – all too easily blown away. (It is so important to hold with your vision at this stage.) In fact, I was convinced by someone that there was no chance of such a character coming to life and so I actually put Poppy to one side for many years. I also heard the well-rehearsed adages that you can't write well until you're at an age when you've experienced life, and also that if you're a proper writer, it will just happen. There might be a bit of truth in these notions.

I became an English teacher, in an Edinburgh girls' school akin to that of Miss Jean Brodie. Then like any self-respecting princess in an ivory tower, I needed to be rescued by a dashing knight. Or, to put it another way, teaching wasn't much fun, and domesticity seemed more appealing. Conveniently, I fell in love with a Royal Marine Commando. This fitted neatly into my script. After a fairy tale wedding, I settled into the real 'grown-up' world of motherhood.

My main writing outlet in this period was a mother's answer to *Bridget Jones's Diary* – Jane Jones's Dairy – a kitchen sink drama of the daily intrigues of the 'stay-at-home-mum' with three infants under four years of age. My years of 'extreme mothering' definitely prepared me for the world of publishing and made my writing much more real and touching.

Curiously, Poppy re-emerged with great vibrancy when my grandmother died in 2000. I wrote about my wonderful granny, Emma Brown, in a eulogy entitled *Pale Pink, Lace and Pearls*. This piece of writing was so well received in my family, that I felt a burst of confidence, which is very elusive when little children take over your world. I finally left behind my own childishness and began to write as an adult, looking into childhood.

I found that Poppy was becoming an 'every girl' princess, instead of a traditional or mythical princess as she had been before. The theme of my Poppy stories is that through family love, every girl is a true princess. I don't like the idea of so-called 'alpha females' – lucky girls who are richer, prettier or smarter – every child has a right to feel equally special. Poppy is innocent, but not old-fashioned. Although I am nostalgic in some ways in my writing, I often think there is something rather brutal about girl stories of the 1950s, as if children were somehow less cherished then, so my books do not hark back. I prefer to reach the children who are growing up, right now, in the twenty-first century. Childhood is so precious and I want to prolong it, as most mothers do, so I attempt to evoke a world which is both contemporary and yet aspires towards a sweeter way of life.

Self-publishing Princess Poppy

As the Poppy book idea gathered energy, the story became quite focused. The decision to focus on one clear plot was a breakthrough after months of endless bright ideas. I plumped for a birthday party to introduce the heroine, her world and the cast of additional characters. The biggest challenge was with the visual, illustration side of my first book. I collected a roomful of reference materials: wild flowers, books, cards, magazines, fairies, photographs, butterflies, bridesmaids, princesses, tiaras and ballerinas. Slowly and almost imperceptibly, my own sketches became good enough for the trial book. Asking artists to sketch Poppy was potentially tricky. What if the publisher liked the pictures, but not the words, or *vice versa*? Arrangements between authors and illustrators at pitching stage have to be very clear cut.

I decided to self-publish when I became frustrated with the slow ways of the publishing world. I had sent off a few versions of Poppy, as well as some other ideas, and I'd had one helpful phone call from a publisher and some other words of encouragement – but no deal was in sight. I was in the Lake District when I realised that Beatrix Potter had self-published, along with many other stars such as Virginia Woolf, John Grisham and James Joyce. I decided there and then to speed up my career by producing the book as I imagined it. I had every confidence of it selling well. I dismissed the idea of using a firm specialising in self-publishing, even though some are perfectly respectable because I believed, and still do, that you can project manage it yourself and use your budget on strong production values instead of a middle-person.

There is something about making the financial investment which proves one's serious intentions: you can produce your book with plenty of trial copies for the cost of a holiday. I broke the self-publishing process down into the following ten-point battle plan:

1. Write a good, fast-paced story of the right length for your audience. (Ask for a few objective opinions. If there is not one common criticism, ignore all negative comments.) Remember: theme, character, plot and dialogue are the building blocks of any story.
2. Edit it objectively. (Ask a friend if necessary.) Know when to let go of words. Ask yourself if it is truly original. Innovate, don't imitate.
3. Illustrate it if it's a picture book. (Ask an artist to do this, either for a fee or as part of the pitch.)
4. Think of a wonderful jacket design, explore fonts, imagery and message.
5. Design and lay out the pages. (Use a professional designer who will also advise on a printer.)
6. Have it printed in sensible quantities. Use a printer who has produced 'perfect bound' books before, i.e. *not* those stapled down the spine, which would look amateurish. Test the market with a few hundred copies.
7. Hand-sell it to bookshops, both chains and independents.
8. Have it distributed. Ensure that the distributor has relationships with all the national chains.
9. Promote it to get it noticed (radio, television, articles).
10. Offer to do events and festivals to ensure ongoing sales.

After self-publishing: getting the deal and beyond

The first Princess Poppy book sold 40,000 copies in six months, which meant that the concept was noticed in the trade. All the main bookseller chains, as well as independents, were incredibly supportive. I was invited to visit headquarters of booksellers and soon the chains were distributing the book to their branches. All of this relied on good distribution, which is hard to find with only one title, but persistence is the key.

I paid for professional public relations which helped a lot, but is not essential. I began to be invited to book parties across Edinburgh and found that the publishing reps from large publishing houses were very willing to help. They took news of my book to London offices and soon I was being invited to these for meetings. At this point, I produced a second book, and a doll, which I feel showed the series potential of the Princess Poppy concept. But it was all getting too much for one person. I was running a business now, with printers to liaise with as well as the press, the distributors and events co-ordinators. When two offers for Poppy came in on my newly set up email, I didn't have to think twice about accepting.

I have been lucky enough to have a great relationship with my editor and publisher. Working with a major publisher requires the right amount of compromise, without losing personal direction and control. I believe in professional standards and feel that being part of an arts-based work cycle is no excuse for being chaotic. I always deliver texts on time and try not to be needlessly awkward or diva-ish. The author is simply a bit-part player in the successful production of a book. If you are incredibly hung up on ownership of rights, trademarks and the like, then self-publishing really might be best for you. Ironically, once you are published by a traditional publisher, you have to let all of that go.

I wouldn't change the way I did it, as I understand the whole world of publishing much more than I would have done otherwise. And I may never have got the deal at all, without self-publishing first. For those who say it is vain to self-publish, I would say, yes it is, as is the whole idea of wanting others to pay for your written words. But when one's main pleasure in life is reading, it makes perfect sense to create stories for others to enjoy. I can think of no better career, and when fan letters drop through the door, the whole process is complete.

Janey Louise Jones continues to write the *Princess Poppy* series for Random House. Her new ballet school series, *Cloudberry Castle*, is published by Floris Books and her new angel series, *St Celeste's*, is published by Usborne.

See also...
- *Writing for girls,* page 112
- *Writing series fiction for girls,* page 152

Children's books and the US market

Richard Scrivener outlines the possibilities for breaking into the US children's book market.

As L.P. Hartley once said of the past, America is a foreign country, they do things differently there. It is the biggest territory in the world for books, with immense opportunities, but with just as many pitfalls. Of course, the Brits have those US senators to thank, who some 200 years ago decided to make English the national language of their young nation. This does give British writers an edge over their Italian and French counterparts, although the competition for places is intense. So this article will briefly consider and note the general state of the US market, and then offer some general thoughts on what awaits a British writer who finds themselves about to be published in the United States of America.

Getting through the door

It's an old joke: the British and the Americans find their respective sandwiches very amusing. We think theirs are ridiculously big, they think ours are ridiculously small. The good news for authors is the 'big sandwich culture' has an enormous sales potential. The even better news is that, unlike their rock and pop counterparts, British authors have a brilliant track record in doing very well 'over there'. From A.A. Milne to J.K. Rowling, from Beatrix Potter to Philip Pullman, time and again the US market has shown itself more than receptive to the stories written on these wet islands. The knack is how to get in through the door.

I wouldn't recommend that a writer research the American market, then write a novel with that specifically in mind. One would most likely end up with a series of novels featuring a Christian wizard who loved *Star Trek* and looked after horses. No. As a writer, you simply have to write what you think is right. Practicalities say that you should begin with a UK publisher and editor in mind. However, you may choose to avoid subjects that might alienate the American market, though it's probably true to say the same issues apply in the UK.

The US market

Here are some basic facts and figures. (With apologies if this is a little like an economics lesson.) The US market is six times bigger than the UK's. The USA publish just about the same number of titles as in the UK – somewhere a little north of 130,000, of which around a quarter are children's books in various formats. The independent bookshop is still viable in the USA, and that's despite the massive growth of online sales via Amazon and the importance of retail chains such as Barnes & Noble and Borders. The library and institutional market whilst having suffered severe funding issues of late, still plays a stronger role in US publishing than its much ravaged British counterpart. The area of the greatest volume at retail, the mass market, is dominated by a couple of key players, with Walmart by far the largest company. The Asda-owning supermarket behemoth has a turnover larger than most countries. When it takes a book it will sell in great quantities.

Immediately one can see parallels with the UK, yet there is one noticeable difference and it's a crucial one for authors. In the delightful vicious pond that is the UK publishing market, publishers and retailers agree different discounts depending on the size of the account. In the USA you can't do that. It's basically the same discount if you're Mr Barnes Books of Biloxi or if you're Mr Barnes & Noble, though of course there are various legitimate ways around this. Nonetheless it sets the tone for the business.

As in the UK, the USA is dominated by the big 'conglomerate' publishers: Random House, Penguin, HarperCollins and Simon & Schuster. They all carry large lists, publishing sometimes as many as 800 books a year. Hardback publication is still the much preferred initial route for most novels and picture books with a paperback following sometime later. Review coverage in the USA for children's books is noticeably better than in the UK. *Publishers Weekly* (the US equivalent of the *Bookseller*; see *Magazines about children's literature and education* on page 293) always carries a children's section and features many thoughtful – and detailed – reviews. It would certainly be worth getting hold of a few copies of this excellent magazine to get a sense of the US market.

Alongside the usual names are other publishers which are less well known in the UK, but highly respected in the USA: Harcourt Brace, Farrar, Straus and Giroux and Houghton Mifflin. Some of these publishers have affiliates in the UK, others are part of major media companies. They have considerable clout in the marketplace and can certainly make things happen. For example: Farrar, Straus and Giroux is the US publisher of Louis Sachar's *Holes* and sold it to Bloomsbury in the UK which then published it to great acclaim. And then there was the film….

There are also a host of small hardback houses, independent general publishers who have children's lists, as well as mass market publishers who service the supermarkets. There is plethora of choice, each company with its own dynamic and ethos.

So how do I make it over there?
The principal question of interest to any author is how do I get published in the USA? As Bill Clinton used to say: that depends. If your book has been sold in the UK and the publisher has world rights and if that publisher has a US affiliate then most likely the affiliate will be the first port of call. This has the advantage of them knowing who to send it to and the fact that it's being published in the UK by the sister company will help. There should be a financial benefit to the author too – in that the royalty is paid 'straight through'. From a marketing perspective it could also mean that the publisher feels a global ownership of the author, and that would certainly help justify the necessary marketing investment.

But publishing isn't always that simple. The US affiliate may not like your book but this needn't be an issue *per se*. Nor indeed should it be a problem if the UK publisher doesn't have a US office because a good rights department will look to sell the title elsewhere. The cost of doing this for the publisher and the author is reflected in the cut of the deal retained by publisher.

If you have an agent, he or she may suggest selling US rights separately, in which case your manuscript or book will be submitted direct to US publishers. If you're really lucky, the agent may even be able to conduct an auction, but you have to be confident the book concerned will generate sufficient interest. There's nothing more embarrassing than a one-publisher auction.

In the case of picture books – there is no question of the publisher *not* getting world rights. Co-editions will need to be set up, so as broad a territory as possible is required to offset the high origination costs of publishing in full colour.

Changes, changes
Once your book has been sold, be prepared for further editorial comments! American editors nearly always make changes to the text to Americanise it. For example, rubbish

becomes garbage, nappy becomes diaper and sausage becomes hot dog. And it's not un-usual for a US editor to give more line by line comments and even request a different ending. Take these in your stride, sometimes it will help sell the book. On other occasions you may think it's a bridge too far. You'll have to take each battle as it comes.

Covers, too, require a sharp intake of breath. Invariably the US cover will be different. For reasons no one can understand, British and American cover sensibilities vary consid-erably. It's best really to let them get on with it. You have to trust that the publisher will know what sells in Des Moines. It may not look pretty to you, but if it sells, does it matter?

As in the UK, marketing is a critical factor in determining a book's success. Dumpbins, publicity, review coverage all add to the mix. The key thing is to have an editor who's supportive and a publishing organisation which supports the editor. The best marketing plans in the world can fall flat, whilst the unexpected bestseller can come from nowhere.

Being published in the USA means you'll get US fanmail! And, unless you happen to live there, you won't have that 'I'll just the check the stock in my local bookshop' oppor-tunity, that is unless you have American friends prepared to do it for you. (Though if you ring your US publisher to tell them about this, expect the same frosty response as you'd get from your UK publisher.)

Schools

Another point of difference with the USA is the schools market. School book clubs and book fairs are enormously important sales channels in the USA. A typical order quantity would be 50,000 units. Through club mailings and touring fairs, the principal player in this market is Scholastic, reaching virtually every American child at some stage or other. These titles are often discounted and acquired under licence from US publishers who grant schools 'reprint' rights. Royalties are generated via the net receipts from the sale of those rights and the ongoing sale of the book.

How did they do it?

It all sounds very exciting doesn't it? So how do I get invited to the party? Luck as much as anything plays an important part. Certainly you can't sit down and think I'm going to write a children's bestseller. Did J.K. Rowling ever think: 'I bet kids in Montana are going to love a story about an orphan trainee wizard attending a summer public school?' Who would have thought that Philip Pullman's version of *Paradise Lost* in which religion is castigated and God dies, would have been so popular in a country with such a wide Bible Belt?

So write what you want to write. Certainly it might be an idea to have more than one book in mind. America is after all the ultimate consumer country, if they like one, they'll want another – quickly. Series publishing is making a comeback in the USA and the UK. Good news if you can deliver the titles but this trend does make it harder for one-off pieces of fiction to reach an audience. And most likely a popular series will be made into a television show or even film – and then there's merchandising. But that's a whole other story.

Genres

As anywhere in the publishing world, genres come and go out of fashion. Supernatural fiction has been a hot category for some time now, with a particular emphasis on vampires. It may well be this bubble will burst as publishers' lists fill with titles featuring fanged

Books

creatures in various guises. Picture books have had a tough few years, but that said there are writers and artists who continue to sell very well in the USA. Again it will depend on the strength of the book – it will have to be outstanding. Probably the most difficult area is publishing for 5–8 year-olds. These books tend to feature school scenarios or make assumptions about reading levels. It is very difficult to sell these books in the USA, so I wouldn't have high hopes if that's your milieu. That's not saying, like a local wine, that there's anything wrong with it – it just doesn't travel long distances.

Teenage books have actually found a much greater audience in recent years. That's as much a British thing as an American factor. Though I personally would avoid writing what I call 'My Dad killed my Step Mum' fiction, there are plenty of American writers doing that. Non-fiction certainly can travel extremely well – although for some reason, humorous non-fiction is less successful.

In short, there are many reasons to be interested in the American market. And the obvious point is the sales potential. Imagine if all of Europe spoke English – okay they do, but at least no American cities have been trashed by English football fans. The infrastructure of US publishing is immensely impressive, it's full of talented and dedicated people who, like their British counterparts, love books. Find a home. Find an editor. Find a publisher. If you get all three in the USA, you'd be lucky, you may earn a few pennies. But whatever, if you're successful you'll have the satisfaction of knowing you're better than Oasis and Robbie Williams. *You* made it in America.

Richard Scrivener is the founder of the Creative Rights Agency.

Categorising children's books

When you walk into any high street bookstore the range of children's books can seem overwhelming. Once you look beyond the promotions and offers on the centre tables, however, the selections and layout start to make sense. Caroline Horn explains.

Retailers generally organise their children's book displays according to age ranges, making it easier for buyers to go straight to the section they want, be it baby board books or teen fiction. This approach also reflects how publishers 'segment' their lists.

Categorising children's books according to age groups is helpful as these categories generally reflect children's interests and reading abilities at key stages in their development. A book's format and subject matter, the presence of illustrations and the size of text and pagination, signal the intended age of its reader. So, for example, toddlers and preschool titles comprise short, illustrated picture books while young fiction books are mainly black and white text with short chapters, large text and some illustrations.

Large publishing houses will tend to cover the whole gamut of age ranges for children, from naught to young adult. They want their titles to win the loyalty of new parents from day one and to keep that loyalty all the way through to that child's teen years. Smaller, specialist publishers will often focus their lists on specific areas of children's publishing that reflect their in-house skills. Piccadilly Press, for example, is strong in teen fiction while Templar Publishing has developed a strong range of baby books.

Broadly speaking, children's books fit one of the following age groups: baby books (1–2 years), picture books (2–5 years), beginner readers (5–7 years), young fiction (6–8 years) and core fiction (8–12 years).

Teen titles and 'crossover books' (those that appeal to children or teenagers, as well as to adults) are in the top age range, i.e. 12 years plus. Non-fiction is also categorised according to age range and, often, National Curriculum subject areas.

There are, though, always exceptions and children's varied abilities and interests will mean that young readers will often cross these age bands. This is why including age guidance on books themselves – as they do with children's toys and clothing – has been such a contentious issue, one that publishers have actively avoided until now because of the wide variation in children's abilities and also their interests.

A nine year-old boy with reading difficulties could, for example, find himself reading a title that he sees is recommended for a child aged six, and there's nothing more guaranteed to put off a child from picking up another book – ever! New lists have been developed by publishers like A&C Black (*White Wolves* series) and Barrington Stoke to fill the gap for titles that can be enjoyed by older readers who are still struggling to read fluently, and reluctant readers.

In other cases, where perhaps an eight year-old child has the reading ability of an 11 or 12 year-old, that child would probably struggle with the subject matter intended for older readers.

Age ranging

However, while there are very good reasons for not giving specific age recommendations on book covers, this has not helped parents and other book buyers who are struggling to find the right title for children. Research by Book Marketing Ltd ('Expanding the Market') in 2004 indicated a high level of confusion by consumers when buying books for children. Until now, publishers have been heavily reliant on booksellers' ability to recommend the best book for individual children. However, in 2009 publishers bit the bullet and decided that they would introduce age guidance on fiction, and later picture books and non-fiction, with the aim of supporting consumers. Many new fiction titles now include an age guidance on the back cover, either 5+, 7+, 9+, 11+ or 13+.

Age ranging is the broadest tool publishers can use in categorising their lists but they will also build their lists' depth and range according to a variety of other factors, particularly genres that are popular such as fantasy, historical fiction, horror, thrillers, etc. Publishers will frequently revisit their lists to check where their 'gaps' are and how well each area is doing at any particular time. They pay special attention to how well their list serves the core market of 8–12 year-old readers.

Recent developments in fiction

In recent years, the British and American markets for children's fiction, particularly fantasy, have flourished thanks to authors such as J.K. Rowling (*Harry Potter*) and Philip Pullman (*His Dark Materials*) and the appetite among young readers for more 'big' fiction books seems insatiable. This has helped drive up author advances to unprecedented heights in the children's market, with the popularity of fantasy titles both here and in the US continuing to hold. This was not always the case. One of the reasons why *Harry Potter* was originally turned down was its length – publishers were wary of any books that were more than 40,000 words long, believing that children would not pick up hefty or challenging reads. Children's fantasy was also distinctly out of fashion, both among UK booksellers and foreign publishers, whereas today publishers are keen to find imaginative and challenging reads for children.

The market for 'crossover' fiction is another recent development – it was hard to envisage any demand by adults for children's books prior to *His Dark Materials* trilogy and *Harry Potter*. Today, though, publishers will look closely at a title's potential for crossover appeal. After all, selling to adults as well as to children instantly doubles a book's market. David Fickling Books and Random House exploited this by creating separate covers, for children and for adults, for *The Curious Incident of the Dog in the Night-Time* by Mark Haddon – the text was identical for both versions. Although very few novels can do so successfully, titles like Jonathan Stroud's *Bartimaeus Trilogy* (Random House Children's Books) and Jennifer Donnelly's *A Gathering Light* (Bloomsbury) can appeal to both adults and children or teen readers, and publishers are keen to find more books like these.

A more recent development in how books are categorised is by author 'brand'. Authors such as Jacqueline Wilson, Michael Morpurgo, Dick King-Smith and Eoin Colfer are all regarded as brands in their own right and, although these authors write for many different age ranges, their titles will often be displayed together on an author's 'shelf' in bookshops. Waterstone's, for example, has introduced new display cases in its children's sections to do just that, highlighting best-selling authors' work in individual sections. These key author 'brands' have a guaranteed – and large – audience. Jacqueline Wilson, who has sold more than 20 million copies across her titles, will regularly outsell adult bestseller titles with sales of her children's titles averaging about 50,000 copies a month. Readers are also loyal to series and Lemony Snicket's *A Series of Unfortunate Events* (Egmont) as well as Jeff Kinney's *Wimpy Kid* books have shown how successful these can be.

At the younger end of the market, sales of the *Horrid Henry* series by Francesca Simon (Orion) have encouraged publishers to develop more mass market series such as those based on the Felicity Wishes character (Hodder Children's Books) and *Rainbow Magic* (Orchard Books), as well as Random House Children's Books *Astrosaurs* series. Mass market series like these help to get 6–8 year-olds into the reading habit because they can recognise the books they have enjoyed and go back for more. Since young fiction books also tend to be relatively thin, a set of five or six books will help them to stand out on booksellers' shelves. More 'literary' series have also been developed for younger readers, with the production quality of the *Judy Moody* titles by Megan McDonald (Walker Books) and *The Spiderwick Chronicles* by Tony DiTerlizzi and Holly Black (Simon & Schuster) ensuring that they stand out from the crowd.

The next 'big thing'

But publishers know that they would be unwise to focus exclusively on areas that are ahead in today's climate – children's books is a cyclical business and what works today could be out of favour a few months down the line. Dorling Kindersley's approach to production was key to driving non-fiction sales in the Eighties while *Guess How Much I Love You* by Sam McBratney and illustrated by Anita Jeram (Walker Books) achieved a similar status for the picture book in the Nineties. In today's climate, however, non-fiction and picture books are struggling but it will only take a new taste, design or development to turn that around. People could easily be saying the same thing about fantasy fiction just a few years from now.

Publishers will regularly revisit and reshape their lists as a result of market changes like these. Walker Books, a notable picture book publisher, has in recent years strengthened its fiction list with lead authors including Anthony Horowitz and Kate DiCamillo, while Bloomsbury, which has traditionally focused on fiction, is now strengthening its picture book list. Traditional non-fiction publishers Kingfisher and Usborne have both recently moved into the fiction market, reflecting the greater focus on fiction.

Demographics are also responsible for changing tastes and shifting emphasis in publishers' lists. The number of children aged under 12 years is falling while the teen market is growing and this accounts for the increasing interest in young adult and crossover books. The demographic picture is similar in the USA, a key market for British publishers, so interest in teen fiction is likely to be maintained for some time. Teenage titles are, themselves, also categorised according to genres such as 'issue' books, crime, thrillers, etc. What is proving most successful among teen readers today are the romantic 'undead' novels inspired by Stephenie Meyer's *Twilight* series. Teen girls and young women can't get enough of them.

It goes without saying that writers need to know what areas a publisher specialises in before approaching them with manuscripts. A brilliant teenage title is likely to be rejected if the publisher's list does not include teenage books. Still worse, an inexperienced publisher could take on a teen novel but let it fall into oblivion by failing to market it to the correct audience.

That said, it is hard to second-guess what type of book publishers are looking for at any one time. A picture book publisher may still turn down a title, no matter how much they like it, if they have over-commissioned in that area or it is too similar to a title they are already publishing. Equally, even though booksellers' shelves are groaning under the weight

Books

of romantic gothic fiction, a book that stands out from the crowd will always find a home – publishers are continuously hunting for talented 'new voices'. In fact, 'debut author' has almost become a category in its own right as publishers strive to get unknown but promising authors into retail outlets.

It is also worth remembering that across the board, large publishing houses are reducing their children's output and that their lists are more structured and more focused than ever before. If a company has filled the gap for a dragon fantasy for a ten year-old reader, then they won't be looking for any more. Another publisher, however, might be looking for exactly that.

Caroline Horn is children's books editor at the *Bookseller* and editor of children's books website Reading Zone (www.readingzone.com).

See also...
• *Writing for a variety of ages*, page 120

Poetry
Riding on the poetry roundabout

Poet and anthologist John Foster writes about the difficulties involved in getting children's poetry published and offers some practical advice.

Today's children's poetry roundabout started spinning in the 1960s, when it was given a push-start by Spike Milligan, gathered momentum in the 1970s and 1980s with helping hands from the likes of Roger McGough, Allan Ahlberg and Michael Rosen, and increased in speed during the 1990s. You would think, therefore, that it might be easier for a newcomer to break in and to get their poems published these days than it was when I started anthologising and writing poetry some 30 years ago. However, the roundabout has slowed somewhat in the past decade and for the aspiring children's poet it can be as hard to get your poems published.

One reason, of course, is that there are now many more people specialising in writing children's poetry than there used to be and the competition is more fierce. Another is that there's an increasing number of established children's poets and that those people inevitably stand much more chance of getting a collection of their poems into print than someone who is unknown.

That said, anthologists like myself are always on the lookout for new voices, and if a good poem is submitted for an anthology, it doesn't matter who has written it – it will go in. When you're starting out, you have far more chance of getting one or two of your poems into some of the anthologies that are published annually than you have of getting a complete collection of your poems published. So if you are keen to find a ride on the poetry roundabout, it is better to discover what anthologies are in the pipeline and what specific poems are required than to try to place a single author collection. I had been anthologising and contributing poems to other anthologies for over ten years before my first book of original poems, *Four O'Clock Friday*, was accepted. And there are some very good children's poets – Julie Holder and John Kitching, for example – who have contributed to anthologies for many years, yet have never had collections of their own published.

Ask a publisher why there are many more anthologies than single poet collections and they will give you a simple answer: anthologies sell more copies. It is much easier to sell an anthology of school poems, such as 'Why do we have to go to school today?' than it is to sell 'The Very Best of A.N.Other Children's Poet'.

Get inspired by children

If you are undaunted by what I have said so far and still determined that you are going to write children's poetry and get it published, what tips can I offer?

Starting with the most obvious, get to know children's language. If you are writing poems about children's experiences from a child's point of view you must get the language right. It is, perhaps, not surprising that many of the most successful children's poets are from a teaching background – for example, Tony Mitton, Wes Magee, Judith Nicholls, Paul Cookson and Brian Moses. Teachers not only know what children's interests are, but they also know how children think and how they express themselves. So steep yourself in children's language, not just the language of your children or the children of friends, but of children from all sorts of backgrounds and cultures.

Try to arrange to visit schools in different areas. But always go through the correct channels with a letter to the literacy coordinator, copied to the head teacher, explaining the reasons you would like to visit. Schools these days are, quite rightly, very security-conscious. Visiting schools will give you the opportunity not only to talk with children, but to try out your poems too. There's nothing like a deafening wall of silence greeting that punchline you thought they would find so amusing to let you know that, in fact, the poem doesn't work!

Schools are also a good source of ideas. Many a poem comes from a child's tale or a teacher's comment. In one school I met a teacher called Mr Little, who was six foot six inches tall. He told me a story about a girl who had asked him: Were you big when you were little? This led to my poem 'Size-Wise' (below).

Our teacher Mr Little's really tall.
He's twice the size of our helper Mrs Small.
'Were you big when you were little?'
Sandra asked him.
'I was Little when I was little,
but I've always been big!'
he said with a grin.
'Have you always been small?'
Sandra asked Mrs Small.
'No,' said Mrs Small.
'I was Short before I got married,
then I became Small.
But,' she added, 'I've always been little.'
'That's the long and the short of it,'
said Mr Little.
'I've always been big and Little,
but she used to be little and Short,
and now she's little and Small.'

Visiting schools is worthwhile, too, because you can bring yourself up to date with how poetry is being used in the classroom. The literacy curriculum requires that children be introduced in the primary years to a wide range of poetic forms. There is an educational as well as a trade market for children's poems and it is worth knowing what the educational publishers might be looking out for.

Anthologies

Successful children's poets will tell you that many of their poems have been triggered by an anthologist's request for a poem on a particular theme. What then is the secret of getting a poem into an anthology?

It may seem to be stating the obvious but the first thing to do is to read the submissions letter closely. My filing cabinets are full of poems that have been given only a cursory glance, because it has become apparent from the first line that they are neither relevant to the theme of the anthology in question nor appropriate for the age group at which the anthology is aimed.

Having read the letter, one's first impulse is to consider whether any of the poems you have already written are suitable. There may well be one or two, particularly among those that are already published, but simply trawling through your file of unpublished poems to see if some of them can be made to fit in with the anthologist's demands is less likely to be successful than actually writing something new.

The key very often is to come up with something slightly different. Let's say you have been asked to contribute to a book of poems about pirates. You probably stand more chance of getting your poem selected if you write a poem about pirates who have become film stars, specialising in gangster parts, than if you write a poem about traditional pirates burying their treasure or making a captive walk the plank. Similarly, if you are writing about dragons, you are more likely to succeed in placing a poem about young dragons having a flying lesson (as I have done myself), or about a young dragon doing his party trick of lighting the candles on his birthday cake (as Ian McMillan has done) than a poem about a dragon fighting a knight. The wackier and more bizarre your idea is, the more chance you will have of your poem being chosen.

Another way of making your poem stand out from the crowd is to write it in a more unusual form. For example, instead of writing your poem about St George and the dragon in couplets, you could write it in the form of an encyclopedia entry, as a series of extracts from St George's diary or even as a text message. The more contemporary the form, the more likely it is to appeal, both to the anthologist and the reader.

Getting the idea is, of course, the hardest part. If you are stuck for a humorous idea, one way of trying to find one is to look in a book of jokes. I was racking my brains to come up with a new poem for a book of magic poems, when I came across this joke: Why are the ghosts of magicians no good at conjuring? Because you can see right through their tricks! This led to:

The ghost of the magician said:
'I'm really in a fix.
The trouble is the audience
Sees right through all my tricks!'

A word of caution: whereas it can pay to be risqué, both in terms of getting your poem selected and entertaining your readers, don't be rude just for the sake of it and, especially, don't be crude. Besides, you could easily get yourself labelled! During a performance in Glasgow, I included one or two poems which made references to 'bottoms' and 'knickers', getting the usual delighted response from the audience. However, I was taken aback when I asked them to suggest why the publishers won't allow me to illustrate my poetry books. Instead of giving me the expected – and correct – answer that my drawings are no good, the first boy I asked said: 'Because your poems are dirty!'

Before sending off your poems, make sure your name and contact details are given clearly beneath every poem. It is usually better, too, to put each poem on a separate page. Check with the anthologist before you submit your poems by email. Many anthologists prefer to receive hard copies, since they assemble the anthology by hand, rather than on the computer, and it saves them the chore of having to print out the poems themselves.

Also, don't send too many poems. As a rule of thumb it's usually best to send about five, and not more than ten. Of course, you will include what you think is your best and most suitable poem. But don't be surprised if it's not chosen and another one is. I'm constantly being asked why that happens. Usually it's because someone else has written a poem that's similar in content or form to your best one and it would not be appropriate to include two such similar poems. Whereas, with regard to your other poem, it either looks at the topic from a different angle or fills a gap that needs to be filled.

You won't make a fortune from getting your poem into an anthology, but once it is in print there's also the chance that it will be picked up and used by another anthologist. So my advice is: be prepared to accept any minor changes that the editor proposes, even if you prefer your original version of the poem. My own experience is that nine times out of ten any changes that have been suggested to my poems have actually improved them. One established poet actually calls me 'the poetry surgeon' because on several occasions I have suggested cutting whole verses from some of his poems. Professional that he is, he has agreed to accept the cuts, even if privately he knows, and I know, that he does not totally agree with them. And, of course, he has pocketed the fee!

Finally, the big question: how do you get yourself onto the anthologists' mailing lists? A simple request to have your name added won't necessarily do the trick. The anthologist needs to know that it is worth taking the time to send you a letter. So it's worth sending a sample of your poems (about five is enough) with a covering letter. But don't expect to be flooded with requests. There are only a very limited number of anthologies published annually. However, if the anthologist thinks your poems have potential, your name will be added to the list – the first step towards getting a ride on the children's poetry roundabout.

John Foster's latest collections of his own poems include *The Poetry Chest* (Oxford University Press) and *The Land of the Flibbertigibbets* (Salt). 'Size-Wise' is from *Making Waves* (Oxford University Press) ©John Foster; 'The Ghost of the Magician' ©John Foster. His latest anthology, *The Works 8*, is published by Macmillan Children's Books.

See also...
• *An interview with my shadow*, page 189

An interview with my shadow

Brian Patten talks about writing poetry.

Who are you?
I'm your shadow.

What's that you're eating?
It's the shadow of an apple.

Surely shadows can't detach themselves from walls and eat shadow-apples?
They can if they are writers' and poets' shadows.

Why do you write for children as well as for adults?
I don't know, it just happened that way. But I really do believe that writing for one is no easier than writing for the other. If somebody tries to write for adults and finds they aren't any good at it, then they will very likely be even worse at writing for children.

Can you really appreciate poetry at seven or even 11 years old?
Of course you can! Adults have no monopoly on feelings. I suspect that many adults never feel as intensely about things as they did when they were younger.

What are the best kinds of things to write about?
You can write about anything you want. Sometimes the weirder the better. At ten you will probably write very different poems than when you're 14 and when you are 40 you'll write different poems again.

How about telling stories through poems?
Very short stories, yes. But not long stories. For long stories children prefer prose, and quite rightly I think. Part of poetry is to do with condensing, not expanding. It is different if you are writing a series of poems about the same character or about a particular situation or unusual creatures, or seeing certain themes from different angles. Then snapshots can build up into a story. But there have been very few successful long story-poems written for children.

I thought poets were supposed to be daydreamers. Some people think poetry is a bit soft.
Modern poetry for children is usually anarchic – anything but soft. Having said this, there is an awful lot of bad so-called 'children's poetry' about. Almost as much as bad 'adult poetry'.

How so?
Well, there is more rhyme and word play in contemporary children's poetry than in contemporary adult poetry. People can make things rhyme, but they either don't or can't work on the scansion, and then the whole metrical structure falls apart. No matter how good an idea, it is the execution of the work that brings it to life.

Did you intend that last sentence to be ironic?
Yes. And it is true. Would-be writers forget it at their peril! Children won't be fobbed off with lazy work.

Poetry

Why did you begin writing poetry? Did anyone teach you?

No, one day I just started writing things down. You see, as a child I lived in this tiny house with three adults. They were all unhappy people. My mother was young and couldn't afford a place of her own, so we lived with my grandmother. My grandmother wore callipers and she dragged herself round the house by her hands. I remember thinking they were like talons.

What has this got to do with poetry and beginning to write it?

Everybody in that little house was miserable and they didn't talk to each other, and although they knew they were miserable and why they were miserable, they couldn't explain why.

You mean they could not express themselves?

Yes, and because they could not express themselves they kept everything walled up inside them, where it hurt and festered for want of light.

Were you like this as well?

To begin with. I don't know how it happened, or why, but I realised the only way I could express my feelings was by writing them down. I think that is how I started to become a poet. I began writing down what I felt. So really, I began writing poetry before I even began reading it. I needed to express my feelings and writing poetry was like writing a very intense diary.

Would you say you were a 'real' poet at that age? I mean, when you began writing did you think that you would ever become a professional poet?

No. That happened when I began changing words and moving lines around. When you begin to *make* something out of the words is when the professional element comes into play. A good poem is something that carries your feelings and ideas inside it. People remember a good poem because of the way it is written, just as much as because of what it says.

Would you like a bit of my apple?

I'm not sure. What does a shadow-apple taste like?

Brian Patten was born and bred in Liverpool. He writes poetry for adults and children and his most recently published books are *Collected Love Poems* (Harper Perennial 2007), *Selected Poems* (Penguin 2007) and *The Big Snuggle-Up*, illustrated by Nicola Bayley (Andersen Press 2011).

See also...
• *Riding on the poetry roundabout*, page 185

Poetry organisations

Poetry is one of the easiest writing art forms to begin with, though the hardest to excel at or earn any money from. Paul McGrane, Membership Manager at the Poetry Society, lists below the organisations which can help poets take their poetry further.

WHERE TO GET INVOLVED

The British Haiku Society

Longholm East Bank, Winglands, Sutton Bridge, Lincs. PE12 9YS
email enquiries@britishhaikusociety.org.uk
website www.britishhaikusociety.org.uk

The Society runs the prestigious annual James W. Hackett International Haiku Award, the Nobuyuki Yuasa Annual International Award for Haibun and the bienniel Sasakawa Prize worth £2,500 for original contributions in the field of haikai. It is active in promoting the teaching of haiku in schools and colleges, and is able to provide readers, course/ workshop leaders and speakers for poetry groups, etc. Write for membership details. Founded 1990.

Commonword

6 Mount Street, Manchester M2 5NS
tel 0161-832 3777
email admin@cultureword.org.uk
website www.cultureword.org.uk

Commonword is a valuable resource for poets and writers in the North West. It provides support, training and publishing opportunities for new writers. It has helped to launch the careers of many of the region's leading poets and strives to seek out new talent in unexpected places.

Creative Arts East

Griffin Court, Market Street, Wymondham, Norfolk NR18 0GU
tel (01953) 713390
email enquiries@creativeartseast.co.uk
website www.creativeartseast.co.uk

Creative Arts East is a fast-growing arts development agency which provides practical support to the arts community in Norfolk; directly promotes tours, exhibitions, and one-off performances and readings by professional artists and companies; and develops community-based arts projects which address social issues around isolation and disadvantage.

The agency was formally launched in 2002, and was set up to combine the collective expertise and energy of 4 smaller arts organisations: Rural Arts East, Norfolk Arts Marketing, Norfolk Literature Development and Create! Members receive the Norfolk Literature Network newsletter containing information, news, events listings and competitions.

Literature Wales

(formerly Academi)
3rd Floor, Mount Stuart House,
Mount Stuart Square, Cardiff Bay, Cardiff CF10 5FQ
tel 029-204 72266
email post@academi.org
website www.academi.org

The Welsh National Literature Promotion Agency which has a huge resource available for poets and poetry. It organises events and tours, promotes poets and poetry, offers poetry advice, locates poetry publishers, offers financial help to poets and to organisers wishing to book poets, and much more. To take advantage of their services you have to live or be in Wales, which has the largest number of poets per 1,000 population anywhere in the Western World.

The Poetry Book Society

The Dutch House, 307–308 High Holborn, London WC1V 7LL
tel 020-7831 7468 *fax* 020-7831 6967
email info@poetrybooks.co.uk
website www.poetrybooks.co.uk,
www.poetrybookshoponline.com,
www.childrenspoetrybookshelf.co.uk

This unique book club for readers of poetry was founded in 1953 by T.S. Eliot, and is funded by the Arts Council England. Every quarter, selectors choose one outstanding publication (the PBS Choice), and recommend 4 other titles, which are sent to members, who are also offered substantial discounts on other poetry books. The Poetry Book Society also administers the T.S. Eliot Prize, produces the quarterly membership magazine, the *Bulletin*, and has an education service providing teaching materials for primary and secondary schools. In addition, the PBS runs the Children's Poetry Bookshelf, offering children's poetry for 7–11 year-olds, with parent, school and library memberships and a new child-friendly website.

The Poetry Business

Bank Street Arts, 32–40 Bank Street, Sheffield S1 2DS
tel 0114-346 3037
email edit@poetrybusiness.co.uk
website www.poetrybusiness.co.uk

Dedicated to helping writers reach their full potential by running supportive workshops.

Poetry

The Poetry Can

12 Great George Street, Bristol BS1 5RH
tel 0117-933 0900
email admin@poetrycan.co.uk
website www.poetrycan.co.uk

The Poetry Can is one of the few literature organisations in the UK specialising in poetry. It organises events such as the Bristol Poetry Festival; runs a lifelong learning programme; offers information and advice in all aspects of poetry.

Poetry Ireland

2 Prouds Lane, Off St Stephen's Green, Dublin 2, Republic of Ireland
tel 353 (01) 478 9974 *fax* 353 (0) 478 0205
email info@poetryireland.ie
website www.poetryireland.ie

Poetry Ireland is the national organisation dedicated to developing, supporting and promoting poetry throughout Ireland. It is a resource and information point for any member of the public with an interest in poetry and works towards creating opportunities for poets working or living in Ireland. It is grant-aided by both the Northern and Southern Arts Councils of Ireland and is a resource centre with the Austin Clarke Library of over 10,000 titles. It publishes the quarterly magazine *Poetry Ireland Review* and the bi-monthly newsletter *Poetry Ireland News*. Poetry Ireland organises readings in Dublin and nationally, and runs a Writers-in-Schools Scheme.

Poetry on Loan

Unit 116, The Custard Factory, Gibb Street, Birmingham B9 4AA
tel 0121-246 2770
email jonathan@bookcommunications.co.uk
website www.poetryonloan.org.uk
Coordinator Jonathan Davidson

Poetry on Loan is a scheme to promote contemporary poetry through libraries in the West Midlands. There are 30 participating libraries and the scheme supports events, displays, stock collections and commissions. It also runs poetry projects for young people.

The Poetry Society

22 Betterton Street, London WC2H 9BX
tel 020-7420 9880 *fax* 020-7240 4818
email info@poetrysociety.org.uk
website www.poetrysociety.org.uk

The Poetry Society was set up to help poetry and poets thrive in Britain and is a registered charity funded by the Arts Council England. The Society offers advice and information to all, with a more comprehensive level of information available to members. Members receive copies of the UK's most prominent poetry magazine, *Poetry Review*, and the Society's newsletter, *Poetry News*, each quarter. The Society's website provides information, news, poetry links and a useful FAQ page, as well as an interactive regional guide to poetry organisations, venues, publishers, magazines and bookshops around the UK through its Poetry Landmarks of Britain section.

The Society also publishes education resources (see later); promotes National Poetry Day; runs Poetry Prescription, a critical appraisal service available to members and non-members (20% discount to members); provides an education advisory and training service, school membership, youth membership and a website. A diverse range of events and readings frequently take place at the Poetry Café and the Poetry Studio at the Society's headquarters in London. The Society also programmes events and readings in other regions of the UK.

Competitions run by the Society include the annual National Poetry Competition, which is one of the largest open poetry competitions in the UK with a first prize of £5000, the biannual Corneliu M. Popescu Prize for European Poetry in Translation and the Foyle Young Poets of the Year Award. Founded 1909.

The Seamus Heaney Centre for Poetry

c/o School of English, Queen's University Belfast, Belfast BT7 1NN
tel 028-9097 1070
email g.hellawell@qub.ac.uk
website www.qub.ac.uk/schools/SeamusHeaney CentreforPoetry Facebook: Seamus Heaney Centre for Poetry

The new Seamus Heaney Centre for Poetry (SHC) is designed to celebrate and promote poetry and artistic endeavour by poets from Northern Ireland. The Centre houses an extensive library of contemporary poetry volumes. It hosts regular creative writing workshops, a poetry reading group, and an ongoing series of readings and lectures by visiting poets and critics from all over the world. The SHC is chaired by the eminent poet, Ciaran Carson, and other resident poets include Medbh McGuckian.

Survivors Poetry

Studio 11, Bickerton House, 25–27 Bickerton Road, London N19 5JT
tel 020-7281 4654 *fax* 020-7281 7894
website www.survivorspoetry.com

A national charity which promotes the writing of survivors of mental distress. A Survivor may be a person with a current or past experience of psychiatric hospitals, ECT, tranquillisers or other medication, or a user of counselling services, a survivor of sexual abuse and any other person who has empathy with the experiences of survivors.

Tower Poetry Society

Christ Church, Oxford OX1 1DP
tel (01865) 286591
email info@towerpoetry.org.uk
website www.towerpoetry.org.uk

Tower Poetry exists to encourage and challenge everyone who reads or writes poetry. Funded by a generous bequest to Christ Church, Oxford, by the late Christopher Tower, the aims of Tower Poetry are to stimulate an enjoyment and critical appreciation of poetry, particularly among young people in education, and to challenge people to write their own poetry.

The Word Hoard

email hoard@phonecoop.coop
website www.wordhoard.co.uk

The Word Hoard is a not-for-profit cooperative of artists: writers, visual artists, makers, performers and musicians. Members have worked with text, music, performance, film and the visual arts in a variety of contexts with a huge range of people. They have also brought artists from abroad to the UK to play a part in projects and to work and teach around the country. Most of the projects have involved some kind of collaboration, between artists and between art forms.

WHERE TO GET INFORMATION

The first place to start is your local library. They usually have information about the local poetry scene. Many libraries are actively involved in promoting poetry as well as having modern poetry available for loan. Local librarians promote writing activities with, for example, projects like Poetry on Loan and Poetry Places information points in West Midlands Libraries.

Alliance of Literary Societies (ALS)

email l.j.curry@bham.ac.uk
website www.allianceofliterarysocieties.org.uk

The ALS is the umbrella organisation for literary societies and groups in the UK. Formed in 1973, it provides support and advice on a variety of literary subjects, as well as promoting cooperation between member societies. It produces an annual journal, *ALSo*....

Arts Council England

Head Office 14 Great Peter Street,
London SW1P 3NQ
tel 0845 300 6200 *fax* 0161-934 4426
website www.artscouncil.org.uk

Arts Council England has 9 regional offices and local literature officers can provide information on local poetry groups, workshops and societies (see page 364). Some give grant aid to local publishers and magazines and help fund festivals, literature projects and readings, and some run critical services.

Arts Council of Wales

Bute Place, Cardiff CF10 5AL
tel 0845 8734 900 *fax* 029-2044 1400
email info@artswales.org.uk
website www.artswales.org.uk

The Arts Council of Wales is an independent charity, established by Royal Charter in 1994. It has 3 regional offices and its principal sponsor is the Welsh Assembly Government. It is the country's funding and development agency for the arts supporting and developing high-quality arts activities. Its funding schemes offer opportunities for arts organisations and individuals in Wales to apply, through a competitive process, for funding towards a clearly defined arts-related project.

National Association of Writers' Groups (NAWG)

PO Box 9891, Market Harborough LE16 0FU
email secretary@nawg.co.uk
website www.nawg.co.uk

NAWG aims to bring cohesion and fellowship to isolated writers' groups and individuals, promoting the study and art of writing in all its aspects. There are over 150 affiliated groups and more than 100 associate (individual) members across the UK.

The Northern Poetry Library

County Hall, Morpeth, Northumberland NE61 2EF
tel 0845 600 6400 *fax* (01670) 511413
email ask@northumberland.gov.uk
website www.northumberland.gov.uk
Membership Free to anyone living in Northumberland, Tyne and Wear, Durham, Cleveland and Cumbria.

The Northern Poetry Library has over 15,000 titles and magazines covering poetry published since 1945. For information about epic through to classic poetry, a full text database is available of all poetry from 600–1900. The library has free public internet access. Founded 1968.

The Poetry Library

Level 5, Royal Festival Hall, London SE1 8XX
tel 020-7921 0943/0664 *fax* 020-7921 0939
email poetrylibrary@rfh.org.uk
website www.poetrylibrary.org.uk
Membership Free with proof of identity and current address

The principal roles of the Poetry Library are to collect and preserve all poetry published in the UK since

Poetry

about 1912 and to act as a public lending library. It also keeps a wide range of international poetry. It has 2 copies of each title available and a collection of about 40,000 titles in English and English translation. The Library also provides an education service (see under 'Help for young poets and teachers', below).

The Library runs an active information service, which includes a unique noticeboard for lost quotations, and tracing authors and publishers from extracts of poems. Current awareness lists are available for magazines, publishers, competitions, bookshops, groups and workshops, evening classes and festivals on receipt of a large sae. The Library also stocks a full range of British poetry magazines as well as a selection from abroad. When visiting the Library, look out for the Voice Box, a performance space for literature; a programme is available from 020-7921 0906. Open 11am–8pm Tuesday to Sunday. Founded in 1953 by the Arts Council.

The Poetry Trust

9 New Cut, Halesworth, Suffolk IP19 8BY
tel (01986) 835950
email info@thepoetrytrust.org
www.thepoetrytrust.org

The Poetry Trust is one of the UK's flagship poetry organisations, delivering a year-round live and digital programme, creative education opportunities, courses, prizes and publications. Over the last decade the Poetry Trust has been running creative workshops for teachers, and this extensive experience has been condensed into a free user-friendly handbook, *The Poetry Toolkit*. The Trust also produces *The Poetry Paper*, featuring exclusive interviews and poems.

The Scottish Poetry Library

5 Crichton's Close, Canongate, Edinburgh EH8 8DT
tel 0131-557 2876 *fax* 0131-557 8393
email reception@spl.org.uk
website www.spl.org.uk

The Scottish Poetry Library is the place for poetry in Scotland for the regular reader, the serious student or the casual browser. It has a remarkable collection of written works, as well as tapes and videos. The emphasis is on contemporary poetry written in Scotland, in Scots, Gaelic and English, but historic Scottish poetry – and contemporary works from almost every part of the world – feature too. They also have collections for the visually impaired. All resources, advice and information are readily accessible, free of charge. It holds regular poetry events, details of which are available on the library website. Founded 1984.

ONLINE RESOURCES

You can obtain a wealth of information at the click of a mouse these days. In addition to those listed above, good starting points are:

The Poetry Archive

website www.poetryarchive.org

The Poetry Kit

website www.poetrykit.org

The Poetry Society of America

website www.poetrysociety.org

WHERE TO GET POETRY BOOKS

See the Poetry Book Society, above. The Poetry Library provides a list of bookshops which stock poetry. For second-hand mail order poetry books try:

Baggins Book Bazaar

19 High Street, Rochester, Kent ME1 1PY
tel (01634) 811651 *fax* (01634) 840591
email godfreygeorge@btconnect.com
website www.bagginsbooks.co.uk

Secondhand bookshop with over half a million books in stock.

The Poetry Bookshop

The Ice House, Brook Street, Hay-on-Wye HR3 5BQ
tel (01497) 821812
website www.poetrybookshop.com

Peter Riley

27 Sturton Street, Cambridge CB1 2QG
tel (01223) 576422
email priley@dircon.co.uk
website www.aprileye.co.uk

Sweetens of Bolton

86 Deansgate, Bolton, Lancs. BL1 1BD
tel (01204) 528457 *fax* (01204) 522115

WHERE TO CELEBRATE POETRY

Festival information should be available from Arts Council England offices (see page 364). See also *Children's literature festivals and trade fairs* on page 392.

The British Council

10 Spring Gardens, London SW1A 2BN
tel 020-7389 3194 *fax* 020-7389 3199
website www.britishcouncil.org/arts-literature.htm

Send a large sae or visit the website for a list of forthcoming festivals.

Poems in the Waiting Room (PitWR)

Executive Chairman Michael Lee, PO Box 488, Richmond TW9 4SW
tel 020-8876 4379
email pitwr@blueyonder.co.uk
website www.pitwr.pwp.blueyonder.co.uk

PitWR is a registered arts in health charity which supplies short collections of poems for patients to read while waiting to see their doctor. First established in 1995, the poems cover both the cannon of English verse and contemporary works – poetry from Quill to Qwerty.

Poetry-next-the-Sea
24 Cleaves Drive, Walsingham, Norfolk NR22 6EQ
tel (01328) 820520, 738243
email whordleyclifford@homecall.co.uk
website www.poetry-next-the-sea.com

The genesis of Poetry-next-the-Sea occurred in 1997, when John Coleridge reasoned that an annual poetry festival on the North Norfolk coast could be a viable addition to the already established festivals at Aldeburgh and King's Lynn, and which would also be within reach of the literary and arts audiences in Norwich and East Anglia. The newsletter of the Friends of Poetry-next-the-Sea is *Wavelength* (2 p.a.), which is intended to present Friends' opinions on Poetry-next-the-Sea and on poetry in general. The editors are actively seeking letters, comments, articles and reviews for this lively and informative publication, with the aim of establishing a lasting dialogue between the festival and its supporters.

StAnza: Scotland's International Poetry Festival
email info@stanzapoetry.org
website www.stanzapoetry.org

StAnza is international in outlook. Founded in 1988, it is held each March in St Andrews, Scotland's oldest university town. The festival is an opportunity to engage with a wide variety of poetry, to hear world class poets reading in exciting and atmospheric venues, to experience a range of performances where music, film, dance and poetry work in harmony, to view exhibitions linking poetry with visual art and to discover the part poetry has played in the lives of a diverse range of writers, musicians and media personalities. The simple intention of StAnza is to celebrate poetry in all its forms.

WHERE TO PERFORM

In London, Express Excess and Aromapoetry are 2 of the liveliest venues for poetry performances and they regularly feature the best performers. Poetry Unplugged at the Poetry Café is famous for its open mic nights (Tuesdays 7.30pm). Poetry evenings are held all over the UK and those listed below are worth checking out. Others can be found by visiting your local library or your Arts Council office, or by visiting the Landmarks of Britain section of the Poetry Society website (www.poetrysociety.org.uk/content/landmarks).

Apples & Snakes Performance Poetry
The Albany, Douglas Way, London SE8 4AG
tel 0845 5213460
email info@applesandsnakes.org
website www.applesandsnakes.org

Carlton Poets
The Carlton Centre, Carlton Road, Weston-Super-Mare
email marilynedbrooke@hotmail.com

CB1 Poetry
32 Mill Road, Cambridge CB1 2AD
tel (01223) 363271 ext. 2725
email cb1poetry@fastmail.fm
website www.cb1poetry.org.uk

Clitheroe Books Open Floor Readings
29 Moor Lane, Clithence BB7 1BE
tel (01200) 444242
email joharbooks@aol.com

Coffee House Poetry
PO Box 16210, London W4 1ZP
tel 020-7370 1434
email coffpoetry@aol.com
website www.coffeehousepoetry.org

Dead Good Poets Society
96 Bould Street, Liverpool L1 4HY
tel 07903 563327
email sarah@deadgoodpoetssociety.co.uk
website www.deadgoodpoetssociety.co.uk

Express Excess
The Enterprise, 2 Haverstock Hill, London NW3
tel 020-7485 2659
website www.expressexcess.co.uk

Farrago Poetry
108 High Street, West Wickham, Kent BR4 0ND
tel 07905 078376
email farragopoetry@yahoo.co.uk
website http://london.e-poets.net

Farrago Poetry is a spoken word and performance poetry organisation based in London. It runs a range of events, from Spanish language poetry nights to events for elders, but is best known for pioneering slam poetry in the UK and for its links to the international performance poetry scene.

Hammer and Tongue
Hammer and Tongue HQ, The Old Music Hall, Oxford OX4 1JE
tel (01865) 403357
email events@hammerandtongue.co.uk
website www.hammerandtongue.co.uk

Morden Tower
Back Stowell Street, West Walls, Newcastle upon Tyne NE1 4XG

email mordentower@googlemail.com
website www.mordentower.org

Morden Tower is one of the UK's best known literary landmarks. Hundreds of poets have come from all over the world to give readings in this ancient turret room on Newcastle's city walls. Morden Tower readings started in 1964 and many poets have relished the experience of reading here with its fine acoustics, its warm, appreciative audiences and its gloriously battered architecture.

Poetry Café
22 Betterton Street, London WC2 9BX
tel 020-7420 9887
email poetrycafe@poetrysociety.org.uk

Tongues and Grooves
The Florence Arms, Florence Road, Southsea, Hants PO5 2NE
tel 07775 244573
email enquiries@tongues-and-grooves.org.uk
website www.tongues-and-grooves.org.uk

COMPETITIONS

There are now hundreds of competitions to enter and as the prizes increase, the highest being £5,000 (first prize in the National Poetry Competition and the Arvon Foundation International Poetry Competition), so does the prestige associated with winning such competitions.

To decide which competitions are worth entering, make sure you know who the judges are and think twice before paying large sums for an anthology of 'winning' poems which will only be read by entrants wanting to see their own work in print. The Poetry Library publishes a list of competitions each month (available free on receipt of a large sae).

Literary prizes are given annually to published poets and as such are non-competitive. An A–Z guide to literary prizes can be found on the Booktrust website (www.booktrust.org.uk). A current list of competitions can be found at www.poetrylibrary.org.uk/competitions

WHERE TO WRITE POETRY

Apples & Snakes
The Albany, Douglas Way, London SE8 4AG
tel 0845 5213460

A vital performance poetry agency dedicated to giving 'voice to challenging, diverse and dynamic poets…' Presents fortnightly shows at the Albany and holds occasional workshops. Founded 1982.

The Arvon Foundation
Lumb Bank – The Ted Hughes Arvon Centre, Heptonstall, Hebden Bridge, West Yorkshire HX7 6DF

tel (01422) 843714 *fax* (01422) 843714
email lumbbank@arvonfoundation.org
The Arvon Foundation at Totleigh Barton, Sheepwash, Beaworthy, Devon EX21 5NS
tel (01409) 231338 *fax* (01409) 231144
email totleighbarton@arvonfoundation.org
The Arvon Foundation at Moniack Mhor, Teavarren, Kiltarlity, Beauly, Inverness-shire IV4 7HT
tel (01463) 741675 *fax* (01463) 741733
email moniackmhor@arvonfoundation.org
The Hurst – The John Osborne Arvon Centre, Clunton, Craven Arms, Shrops. SY7 0JA
tel (01588) 640658 *fax* (01588) 640509
email thehurst@arvonfoundation.org
website www.arvonfoundation.org

The Arvon Foundation's 4 centres run 5-day residential courses throughout the year to anyone over the age of 16, providing the opportunity to live and work with professional writers. Writing genres explored include poetry, narrative, drama, writing for children, song writing and the performing arts. Bursaries are available to those receiving benefits. Founded in 1968.

Camden Poetry Group
Contact Hannah Kelly, 64 Lilyville Road, London SW6

Meets in Hampstead one Saturday per month from 6.30pm. Examples of work should be sent with a covering letter before coming to the first meeting.

Cannon Poets
22 Margaret Grove, Harborne, Birmingham B17 9JH
Meets at Moseley Community Development Trust, The Post Office Building, 149–153 Alcester Road, Moseley, Birmingham usually on the first Sunday of each month (except August) at 2pm
email info@cannonpoets.co.uk
website www.cannonpoets.co.uk

Cannon Poets have met monthly since 1983. The group encourages poetry writing through:

• workshops run by members or visitors
• break-out groups where poems are subjected to scrutiny by supportive peer groups
• 10-minute slots where members read a selection of their poems to the whole group
• publication of its journal, *The Cannon's Mouth* (quarterly).

Members are encouraged to participate in poetry events and competitions.

Centerprise Literature Development Project
136–138 Kingsland High Street, London E8 2NS
tel 020-7254 9632 ext. 211, 214 *fax* 020-7923 1951
website www.centerprisetrust.org.uk
Contact Eva Lewin, Catherine Johnson

Offers a range of creative writing courses, events, surgeries, advice and information resources plus links with other writers' organisations. Groups include the Women's Poetry Group and the Black Writers' Group. The project is committed to developing new writing from all community and ethnic groups.

City Lit
Keeley Street, London WC2B 4BA
tel 020-7492 2652, 020-7492 2600
email humanities@citylit.ac.uk
website www.citylit.ac.uk

City University Creative Writing and Poetry Courses
Northampton Square, London EC1V OHB
tel 020-7040 5060
website www.city.ac.uk

Epsom Writers' Workshop
Epsom Centre, 1 Church Street, Epsom
Contact Stella Stocker *tel* 020-8668 3816

Kent & Sussex Poetry Society
Camden Centre, Market Square, Tunbridge Wells, Kent TN1 2SW
email info@kentandsussexpoetrysociety.org
website www.kentandsussexpoetrysociety.org
Contact Joyce Mandel Water *tel* (01892) 530438

Lancaster University
Department of Continuing Education, Lancaster University, Ash House, Lancaster LA1 4YT
tel (01524) 592623/4
email conted@lancaster.ac.uk
website www.lancs.ac.uk

A range of part-time creative writing courses in various genres and at levels to suit both beginners and those with some experience.

The Poetry School
81–83 Lambeth Walk, London SE11 6DX
tel 020-7582 1679
website www.poetryschool.com

Offers courses and workshops in London, Manchester, York and the North East, Exeter and the South West, exploring key elements of poetic practice, complemented by lectures, discussions and seminars with some of the most renowned poets working today. Also international and online courses, and a postal tutorial service with Judy Gahagan and Myra Schneider.
    The website has extensive links to poetry information and resources on the internet. The Poetry School was founded in 1997 by 3 poets – Mimi Khalvati, Jane Duran and Pascale Petit.

Poets Anonymous
Contact Peter Evans, 70 Aveling Close, Purley, Surrey CR8 4DW

tel 020-8645 9956
email poets@poetsanon.org.uk
website www.poetsanon.org.uk

Meets at the Dog and Bull on the first Friday of each month at 8.15pm, £2/£1, and at the URC on the second Saturday of the month, 2.30–4pm, £1.50.

The Poet's House/Teach na hÉigse
Clonbarra, Falcarragh, County Donegal, Republic of Ireland
tel (074) 65470 *fax* (074) 65471
email phouse@iol.ie

The Poet's House runs 3 ten-day poetry courses in July and August. An MA degree in creative writing is validated by Lancaster University, and the Irish Language Faculty includes Cathal O'Searcaigh. The poetry faculty comprises 30 writers, including Paul Durcan and John Montagu.

Shortlands Poetry Circle
Ripley Arts Centre, 24 Sundridge Avenue, Bromley
email shortlands@poetrypf.co.uk
website www.poetrypf.co.uk/shortlands.html

South Norwood Writers' Workshop
South Norwood Centre, Sandown Road, London SE24 4XC
Contact Stella Stocker *tel* 020-8668 3816

Spread the Word
77 Lambeth Walk, London SE11 6DX
tel 020-7735 3111 *fax* 020-7735 2666
email info@spreadtheword.org.uk
website www.spreadtheword.org.uk

Surrey Poetry Circle
Friends Meeting House, 3 Ward Street, Guildford GU1 4LH
Contact Pat Earnshaw *tel* (01483) 274389

Meets on first and third Thursday of the month, 7.30–10pm.

Tŷ Newydd
Taliesin Trust, Tŷ Newydd, Llanystumdwy, Cricieth, Gwynedd LL52 0LW
tel (01766) 522811 *fax* (01766) 523095
email post@tynewydd.org
website www.tynewydd.org

Tŷ Newydd runs week-long writing courses encompassing a wide variety of genres, including poetry, and caters for all levels, from beginners to published poets. All the courses are tutored by published writers. Writing retreats are also available.

Wimbledon and Merton Poetry Group
Raynes Park Methodist Church, Worple Road, London SW20

Poetry

Contact Russell Thompson *tel* (07969) 597967, 020-8942 3685
email zznsh@yahoo.co.uk

Meets on first Tuesday evening of each month.

GROUPS ON THE INTERNET

It is worth searching for discussion groups and chat rooms on the internet.

British–Irish Poets
website www.jiscmail.ac.uk/archives/british-irish-poets.html
Discussion list (innovative poetry).

The Poem
website http://thepoem.co.uk/discussion.htm
Discussion forum.

Poetry Free-for-all
website www.everypoet.org/pffa
Post your poems and comment on others.

The Poetry Kit
website www.poetrykit.org/wkshops2.htm
List of online workshop/discussion sites.

Local groups
Local groups vary enormously so it is worth shopping around to find one that suits your poetry. Up-to-date information can be obtained from Arts Council England regional offices (see page 364).

The Poetry Library publishes a list of groups for the Greater London area which will be sent out on receipt of a large sae.

The Poetry Society organises local groups for its members – visit www.poetrysociety.org.uk/content/membership/stanzas/ for details.

HELP FOR YOUNG POETS AND TEACHERS

National Association of Writers in Education (NAWE)
PO Box 1, Sheriff Hutton, York YO60 7YU
tel/fax (01653) 618429
email paul@nawe.co.uk
website www.nawe.co.uk

NAWE is a national organisation, which aims to widen the scope of writing in education, and coordinate activities between writers, teachers and funding bodies. It publishes the magazine *Writing in Education* and is author of a writers' database which can identify writers who fit the given criteria (e.g. speaks several languages, works well with special

needs, etc) for schools, colleges and the community. Publishes *Reading the Applause: Reflections on Performance Poetry by Various Artists*. Write for membership details.

The Poetry Library
Children's Section, Royal Festival Hall, London SE1 8XX
tel 020-7921 0664
website www.poetrylibrary.org.uk

For young poets, the Poetry Library has about 4,000 books incorporating the SIGNAL Collection of Children's Poetry. It also has a multimedia children's section, from which cassettes and videos are available to engage children's interest in poetry.

The Poetry Library has an education service for teachers and writing groups. Its information file covers all aspects of poetry in education. There is a separate collection of books and materials for teachers and poets who work with children in schools, and teachers may join a special membership scheme to borrow books for the classroom.

Poetry Society Education
The Poetry Society, 22 Betterton Street, London WC2H 9BX
tel 020-7420 9894 *fax* 020-7240 4818
email education@poetrysociety.org.uk
website www.poetrysociety.org.uk

The Poetry Society has an outstanding reputation for its exciting and innovative education work. For over 30 years it has been introducing poets into classrooms, providing comprehensive teachers' resources and producing colourful, accessible publications for pupils. It develops projects and schemes to keep poetry flourishing in schools, libraries and workplaces. Schemes like Poets in Schools, Poet in the City and Poetry Places (a 2-year programme of residencies and placements, funded by the Arts Council's 'Arts for Everyone' lottery budget) have enabled the Poetry Society to give work to hundreds of poets and allowed thousands of children and adults to experience poetry for themselves.

Through projects such as the Respect Slam and The Foyle Young Poets of the Year Award the Poetry Society gives valuable encouragement and exposure to young writers and performers.

Schools membership offers publications, training opportunities for teachers and poets, a free subscription to *Poems on the Underground* and a consultancy service giving advice on working with poets in the classroom. *Poetryclass*, an INSET training project, employs poets to train teachers at primary and secondary level. Youth membership is available to 11–18 year-olds and provides advice on developing writing skills, access to publication on the Poetry Society website, quarterly issues of *Poetry News*, and poetry books and posters.

The Poetry Trust – see page 194

YOUNG POETRY COMPETITIONS

Children's competitions are included in the competition list provided by the Poetry Library (free on receipt of a large sae).

Foyle Young Poets of the Year Award

The Poetry Society, 22 Betterton Street,
London WC2H 9BX
tel 020-7420 9894 *fax* 020-7240 4818
email education@poetrysociety.org.uk
website www.poetrysociety.org.uk
Free entry for 11–17 year-olds with unique prizes.

Christopher Tower Poetry Prize

Christ Church, Oxford OX1 1DP
tel/fax (01865) 286591

email info@towerpoetry.org.uk
website www.towerpoetry.org.uk/prize/index.html

An annual poetry competition from Christ Church, Oxford, open to 16–18 year-olds in UK schools and colleges. The poems should be no longer than 48 lines, on a different chosen theme each year. Prizes: £3,000 (1st), £1,000 (2nd), £500 (3rd). Every winner also receives a prize for their school.

FURTHER READING

Baldwin, Michael, *The Way to Write Poetry*, Hamish Hamilton, 1982, o.p.
Chisholm, Alison, *The Craft of Writing Poetry*, Allison & Busby, 1997, repr. 2001
Chisholm, Alison, *A Practical Poetry Course*, Allison & Busby, 1997
Corti, Doris, *Writing Poetry*, Writers News Library of Writing/Thomas & Lochar, 1994
Fairfax, John, and John Moat, *The Way to Write*, Elm Tree Books, 2nd edn revised, 1998
Finch, Peter, *How to Publish Your Poetry*, Allison & Busby, 3rd edn, 2000
Forbes, Peter, *Scanning the Century*, Penguin Books, 2000
Hamilton, Ian, *The Oxford Companion to Twentieth Century Poetry in English*, OUP, 1996
Hyland, Paul, *Getting into Poetry*, Bloodaxe, 2nd edn, 1997
Livingstone, Dinah, *Poetry Handbook for Readers and Writers*, Macmillan, 1992
O'Brien, Sean, *The Firebox*, Picador, 1998, o.p.
Padel, Ruth, *52 Ways of Looking at a Poem*, Vintage, 2004
Padel, Ruth, *The Poem and the Journey*, Vintage, 2008
Reading the Applause: Reflections on Performance Poetry by Various Artists, NAWE, 1999
Riggs, Thomas (ed.), *Contemporary Poets*, St James Press, 7th edn, 2001
Roberts, Philip Davies, *How Poetry Works*, Penguin Books, 2nd edn, 2000
Sampson, Fiona, *Writing Poetry*, Robert Hale, 2009
Sansom, Peter, *Writing Poems*, Bloodaxe, 1994, reprinted 1997
Sweeney, Matthew and John Williams, *Teach Yourself Writing Poetry*, Hodder and Stoughton, 3rd edn, 2008
Whitworth, John, *Writing Poetry*, A&C Black, 2006

USA

Breen, Nancy, *Poet's Market 2009*, Writer's Digest Books, USA, 2008
Fulton, Len, *Directory of Poetry Publishers 2007–2008*, Dustbooks, USA, 2008
Fulton, Len, *The International Directory of Little Magazines and Small Presses 2007–2008*, Dustbooks, USA, 2008
Preminger, Alex, *New Princeton Encyclopedia of Poetry and Poetics*, Princeton University Press, 3rd edn, 1993

Literary agents
How to get an agent

Because children's publishing is highly competitive and the market is crowded, in this article
Philippa Milnes-Smith explains that finding an agent isn't child's play.

If you are currently just experiencing a vague interest in being a writer or illustrator, stop now. You are unlikely to survive the rigorous commercial assessment to which your work will be subjected. If you are a children's writer or illustrator, do not think that the process of getting published will be any easier than for the adult market. It's just as tough, if not tougher, partly because a lot of writers and would-be writers see writing for children as an easy option. It can't be that difficult to write a kid's book, can it? After all, it is just for kids....

Nowadays, too, there is extra competition in the children's field: the high profile of successes such as J.K. Rowling's *Harry Potter* series and Philip Pullman's *His Dark Materials* have drawn the attention of many professional writers who have previously only written for the adult market and who see it as a new and lucrative area for their talents. So, before embarking on a children's book/script/proposal for an exciting new children's character, remember that it is a highly competitive and crowded market you are entering.

So, what is a literary agent and why would I want one?

You will probably already have noticed that contacts for many publishers are provided in the *Children's Writers' & Artists' Yearbook*. This means that there is nothing to prevent you from pursuing publishers directly yourself. Indeed, if you can answer a confident 'yes' to all the questions below, and have the time and resources to devote to this objective, you probably don't need an agent.

• Do you have a thorough understanding of the publishing market and its dynamics?
• Do you know who are the best publishers for your book and why? Can you evaluate the pros and cons of each?
• Are you financially numerate and confident of being able to negotiate the best commercial deal available in current market conditions?
• Are you confident of being able to understand fully and negotiate a publishing or other media contract?
• Do you enjoy the process of selling yourself and your work?
• Do you want to spend your creative time on these activities?

An agent's job is to deal with all of the above on your behalf. A good agent will do all of these well.

Is that all an agent does?

Agents aren't all the same. Some will provide more editorial and creative support; some will help on longer-term career planning; some will be subject specialists; some will involve themselves more on marketing and promotion. Such extras may well be taken into consideration in the commission rates charged.

If I am writing and/or illustrating for children's books, do I need a specialist children's agent?

Most specialist children's agents would probably say you definitely need a specialist; many general agents will say you don't really need a specialist. In the end you will have to make up your own mind about whether an individual agent is right for your work and right for you as an individual. Knowledge, experience and excellent industry contacts (in the right companies and the right categories) are essential qualities in an agent who is going to represent you. If you are writing younger fiction, an agent whose expertise is in adult books with a few forays into young adult fiction probably won't have a full grasp of its potential. If your project is really something specifically for the schools and educational market it may well require different representation than a project for the consumer market: the audience (children) may be the same but projects for educational publishers tend to have to be tailored to the educational syllabus in a very particular way. You will need an agent who understands this (and there are very few).

If you are only interested in illustrating work by other people rather than developing your own projects and would like to try illustration work across a broad range of genres and formats, you may be best served by an artists' agent rather than a literary agent (see *Illustrators' agents* on page 252).

I am writing a text for an illustrated book – do I need to send illustrations with it for an agent to consider it?

No, not unless you are an accomplished illustrator or intend to do the illustrations yourself. The wrong illustrations will put off an agent as they will a publisher. A good text should be able to speak for itself. And never, in any case, send in original artwork, only send copies.

What if I have a brilliant novelty proposal, like a pop-up book? Do I need to show how it is going to look it its finished state?

If you can do it competently and it helps demonstrate how different and exciting your project is, you can certainly do this. But be prepared for the fact that you may need to make more than one, as the original runs the risk of getting damaged through handling or, when the worst comes to the worst, getting lost.

I have decided I definitely do want an agent. Where do I begin?

When I left publishing and talked generally to the authors and illustrators I knew, a number of them said it was now more difficult to find an agent than a publisher. Why is this? The answer is a commercial one. Running an agency is a costly thing and an agent will only take someone on if they can see how and why they are going to make money for the client and themselves (and, of course, a client who is making no money tends quickly to become an unhappy client). To survive just the basic costs, an agent needs to make commission and if an agent needs to fund sales trips on clients' behalf, often internationally, they need more commission. An agent also knows that if he or she cannot and does not sell a client's work, the relationship isn't going to last long.

So the agent just thinks about money?

Well, some agents may just think about money. And it is certainly what some authors and artists think about a lot. *But* good agents do also care about the quality of work and the clients they take on. They are professional people who commit themselves to doing the best job they can. They also know that good personal relationships count – and that they help everyone enjoy business more. This means that, if and when you get as far as talking to a prospective agent, you should ask yourself the questions: 'Do I have a good rapport with this person? Do I think we will get along? Do I understand and trust what they are saying?' Follow your instinct – more often than not it will be right.

So how do I convince them that I'm worth taking on?

Start with the basics. Make your approach professional. Make sure you only approach an appropriate agent who deals with the category of book you are writing/illustrating. Phone to check to whom you should send your work and whether there are any specific ways your submission should be made (if it's not clear from the listings in this *Yearbook* – see page 212). Only submit neat typed work on single-sided A4 paper and good quality copies of any artwork. Send a short covering letter with your project explaining what it is, what the intended audience is and providing any other *relevant* context. Always say if and why you are uniquely placed and qualified to write a particular book. Also, provide a CV (again, neat, typed, relevant). Think of the whole thing in the same way as you would a job application, for which you would expect to prepare thoroughly in advance. You might only get one go at making your big sales pitch to an agent. Don't mess it up by being anything less than thorough.

And if I get to meet them?

Treat it like a job interview (although hopefully it will be more relaxed than this). Be prepared to talk about your work and yourself. An agent knows that a prepossessing personality in an author is a great asset for a publisher in terms of publicity and marketing – they will be looking to see how good your interpersonal skills are. Do also take the chance to find out, if you are discussing children's projects in particular, how and where they submit their clients' work and how well they understand the children's market themselves. Also check that they have good relationships with the sort of publishers/media companies with whom you think your work belongs. Don't be afraid to question them on their credentials and track record. And if you have personal recommendations and referrals from other writers, publishers and other industry contacts, do follow these up. Ask, too, about representation overseas and at the key trade children's book fair(s) such as the one held annually in Bologna. If appropriate, ask about representation in other media. Is this agent going to get their clients' work noticed by the right people in the right places and sold for the best market rates?

Will they expect me to be an expert on children and the children's market?

Not as such, but they might reasonably expect you to have an interest in what children like and enjoy and show an understanding of a child's eye view of the world. Basically, an agent will be looking for a writer/illustrator who is in sympathy with the target audience. It also won't do any harm if you spend time at your local bookshop and/or library and befriend your local librarian or specialist children's bookseller to find out what books and authors are working well and if anyone is doing exactly what you plan to do. It's good, basic market research, as is browsing what else is available through internet retailers. For example, if you are planning a series of picture books about a ballet-dancing mouse you need to be aware that *Angelina Ballerina* is already out there.

And if they turn my work down? Should I ask them to look again? People say you should not accept rejection.

No means no. Don't pester. It won't make an agent change his or her mind. Instead, move on to the next agency who might feel more positive towards your work. The agents who reject you may be wrong. But the loss is theirs.

Even if they turn my work down, isn't it worth asking for help with my creative direction?

No. Agents will often provide editorial advice for clients but won't do so for non-clients. Submissions are usually sorted into two piles of 'yes, worth seeing more' and 'rejections'.

Literary agents

There is not another pile of 'promising writer but requires further tutoring'. To get teaching and advice, creative writing courses (see page 346) and writers' and artists' groups are better options to pursue. It is, however, important to practise and develop your creative skills. You wouldn't expect to be able to play football without working at your ball skills or practise as a lawyer without studying to acquire the relevant knowledge. If you are looking to get your work published, you are going to have to compete with professional writers and artists – and those who have spent years working at their craft.

There are also particular considerations that need to be given in the craft of writing children's books. In a picture book, the text needs to work specifically with the illustrations: the fewer words there are, the more they matter. In writing fiction for a young age group, where language and sentence construction have to be simple enough for a seven year-old child, the writer often has to work much harder to generate emotion and excitement and give the story personality. When illustrating children's poetry, the artist has to be able to develop and enhance the meaning of the words to just the right level. However you look at it, children's books are a demanding business.

Good luck!

Philippa Milnes-Smith is a literary agent and children' s specialist at the agency LAW (Lucas Alexander Whitley). She was previously Managing Director of Puffin Books and is a past president of the Association of Authors' Agents.

See also...
- *Meet the parents: Agent, author and the birth of a book*, page 205
- *Do you have to have an agent to succeed?*, page 208
- *Children's literary agents UK and Ireland*, page 212
- *Children's literary agents overseas*, page 220

Meet the parents: agent, author and the birth of a book

Stephanie Thwaites describes the agent's role in the route to a happy marriage between author and publisher.

Before I started work experience at Curtis Brown I had no idea what a literary agent did. Within my first year as an assistant I had tackled mountains of filing, collected dry cleaning, responded to fan mail (not addressed to me, however!), received a gift from Penhaligons, and drawn up my first audio rights contract. While my daily duties have certainly changed since then, the variety and excitement of the job still keeps my pulse racing and I never know what exactly will await me each morning.

As a children's agent, it amazes me that we haven't yet quashed the idea that writing for children is easy, or somehow easier than writing for adults. Shorter doesn't mean simpler. In fact, writing for children can be more difficult than writing for adults because of the very specific demands of the market. Quality writing alone won't work – a strong idea and engaging plot is vital. Then there's the challenge of finding the right voice, avoiding being patronising and keeping an energetic pace throughout. Thanks to a couple of high-profile success stories, new writers can start with inflated and unrealistic expectations. Part of our job as agents is to explain the business to new clients and to encourage them to have reasonable and achievable goals. While it is crucial to be positive and aim high, it is also worth remembering that there's really no such thing as an overnight success and children's authors often work incredibly hard for years before seeing the fruits of their labour. Young readers' taste evolves rapidly and it is not possible for writers and their representatives to rely on 'author loyalty' when it comes to building a career and body of work. This is a readership with an ever-changing face as new child readers discover new authors, and existing readers are continually moving on too. A lot of children's authors and illustrators have other jobs and don't rely solely on writing for their income. Many work tirelessly visiting schools, speaking to children, teachers and librarians, appearing at literary festivals and running workshops. More recently, writers have been encouraged to develop new skills – to create their own websites, use social networking , try blogging and even make Skype appearances. It's not enough for authors just to write and deliver their books – they are expected to promote them ever more energetically too.

The role of the agent

An agent is involved throughout the life of a book, and aims to support an author by acting as a sounding board for ideas, giving feedback on material before it reaches an editor, liaising with editors at different publishing houses, guiding the author, providing specialist industry knowledge and enabling them to find the right home for their book and to strike the best deal. An agent negotiates the terms, and often sells the translation, US, audio and film rights (collectively known as subsidiary rights), which can sometimes be as important as the original publishing deal. Agencies manage the accounting side – invoicing, chasing payments and checking royalty statements – together with handling miscellaneous requests.

Literary agents

Enormous changes are currently taking place in the publishing world and it is an agent's responsibility to keep abreast of new developments, for instance on issues surrounding ebooks, and to consider how their clients will be affected by these changes. A good agent will ensure their authors are in a position to seize new opportunities; and where a 'traditional' approach is not effective, the agent should be able to try other approaches and work with their authors to devise new strategies. Ideally, the relationship will be career-long for both agent and author. When the road is bumpy, the agent feels keenly the successes and disappointments of their authors. The unfortunate reality is that most authors will not become instant bestsellers and it can take years and a great deal of patience and determination for an author to build a strong foundation.

Manuscript submissions

It is natural to assume that agents spend all of their working day perusing manuscripts but in fact the majority of reading takes place outside of office hours. With limited time to focus on reading we have to be very selective about the submissions we read in full and unfortunately we often have to make decisions based on just three chapters. However, even before we reach the opening page, we will already have formed a first impression from the covering letter. A letter which is poorly executed, sloppy, riddled with spelling mistakes or addressed to 'Mr Curtis Brown' or 'Dear Editor' will not pique our interest. The letter should be arresting but not gimmicky; informative but brief. Writing the perfect letter is an art in itself. I prefer to receive just one page with an overview of the story, the age range of the target readership, an idea of where it could be positioned and a line or two about the author. It is important to remember that this may be your only opportunity to communicate with an agent and also bear in mind how many times a book will be pitched beyond this initial letter – to editors (in the UK, USA and translation markets), to their teams in-house, to buyers and to customers. Asserting that your own children have enjoyed it probably isn't the most persuasive argument to advance.

To give you the best chance at securing an agent it is worth starting your research well before submitting your manuscript. If you're reading this, no doubt you are already doing just that. Check that you are approaching the right agents – look at their interests and consider the writers and genres they represent. Make sure you follow submission guidelines and try to resist chasing up your manuscript too soon. It is not unheard of now for approaches to be made via Twitter. However, while Twitter can be a useful tool for following tweets by industry figures, my preference is to receive submissions in the usual way, through the post. Writing is, to an extent, a job like any other job. Just as you would research a company or industry before an interview, so should you do your homework before writing a covering letter. Reading other titles and reviewing what else is being published successfully will help give you a sense of the area you are writing into and of what might appeal to your target readership. If there's a gap in the market, sometimes there's a reason for that – it could be due to a lack of demand or just that it's the wrong moment for the subject. The books we might have enjoyed as children may not make it through an acquisitions meeting today where publishers have to assess costs and sales potential. However, while awareness of what is commercially viable is important, a great idea, story and characters are, as ever, essential. Writers should follow their instincts and inspiration and write what comes naturally.

The most satisfying success stories are the small, unlikely, unexpected ones. There's no substitute for a book that wins your heart. We've all heard reports of 22 publishers turning down a manuscript before one publisher takes a chance with it, offering a tiny advance and subsequently retiring on the profits as it becomes a blockbuster. The subjectivity and unpredictability of publishing can be simultaneously frustrating and thrilling and there's no feeling quite like reading a manuscript, by a new or existing author, and knowing that you're witnessing the early life of something remarkable.

As a new writer, sharing your work with others can be a terrifying experience, but inviting feedback is a good form of preparation. An editor I know came up with a brilliantly simple phrase: 'The end is not the end', which describes a key concept – you might think you've finished a manuscript but usually this is just the beginning. Publishing is a collaborative process and compromise is often necessary if you are to succeed. It is crucial to develop a thick skin or at least pretend to. Publishing a book involves many different parties and while you won't agree with all of them at all times it is important to be able to work as part of a team – albeit with the author as the star player.

Arranging a happy marriage

Just as an author might need to develop different skills and wear a number of hats, not just that of writer, so the agent will adopt a range of roles. Our strategies and activities might differ from client to client, project to project and day to day. To sum this up it might help to adopt a matrimonial analogy for the role of the agent in relation to author, and editor and publishing house. The agent can be seen as a bizarre hybrid of marriage broker, ceremony officiator, marriage counsellor and sometimes mother of the bride! How exactly? Well, we're responsible for helping the author to choose their publishing partner, introducing them to the right match – an editor who they will really connect with and a publishing house where they can thrive. Sometimes we might find there are several suitors and the agent will help the author weigh up the options and select the most suitable partner. So the agent acts as matchmaker for the 'author-bride', the principal player on the wedding day. Next we conduct the negotiations and handle the contractual side of the arrangement outlining each side's obligations. The agent, at this juncture, is a cross between cleric and the pre-nup lawyer. Combining two families is never easy, and the extended publishing family can include marketing and publicity departments, production, sales and accounting and rights teams, and ensuring good relations can sometimes be a challenge. The agent will keep a close eye on these areas and promote good communication and, hopefully, marital bliss. Ultimately, however, like the proud and loving Mother of the Bride we remain firmly on the side of the bride, representing her best interests and advising and guiding her, sharing her disappointments and rejoicing in her triumphs.

Stephanie Thwaites is a literary agent at Curtis Brown.

See also...
- *How to get an agent*, page 201
- *Do you have to have an agent to succeed?*, page 208
- *Children's literary agents UK and Ireland*, page 212
- *Children's literary agents overseas*, page 220

Literary agents

Do you *have* to have an agent to succeed?

Best-selling children's author Philip Ardagh has over 70 titles to his credit but chooses not to have a literary agent to represent him. In this article he tells us why.

There are a lot of people out there who think that they're children's writers ('I was a child myself once, you know') and who send unsolicited manuscripts directly to publishers in their hundreds – possibly thousands – every year. These manuscripts usually end up on what is called the 'slush pile'. Some publishers won't even read them. Some do but, usually, only after a very long time. Many manuscripts are very badly written or very badly presented. Some are perfectly good but a little too much like something already out there in the bookshops, or they lack that indefinable something that makes them stand out from the crowd. Others are perfectly good but are sent to completely the wrong publisher. The best children's fantasy novel ever isn't going to appeal to a publisher specialising in adult DIY manuals, is it? Getting an agent cuts through this process.

Having an agent

Firstly, if an agent submits a manuscript it's going to be to the publisher they think that it's best suited to, and probably to the most suitable editor within that company – more often than not someone they know or have had dealings with in the past. So your manuscript is being seen by the right people at the right place. It's also neatly bypassed the slush pile. It will actually get read. Hurrah! The agent has acted as a filter. The publisher knows that, if you've been taken on by a reputable agent, your words are probably *worth* reading. You're ahead of the game.

And if a publisher wants to publish your work, an agent knows the ins and outs of advances, royalties, escalators, foreign rights, and a million and one other things that makes the humble writer's head spin. Agents know the 'going rates' and will get you the very best deal they can. And, should there be problems further down the line, your agent can play the bad guy on your behalf – renegotiating contracts and doing the number crunching – whilst you only deal with the nice fluffy creative side with your editor.

That's the theory, of course, and much of it is true. They take their 10–15% but they're not a charity and, if they're on a percentage of your earnings, it's generally in their interest to make you as much money as possible, isn't it?

The question is: is it possible to be a successful children's author without an agent? Of course it is. Anything's possible. I'm an agentless author and I'm doing fine, but not without help, advice, common sense, good luck and, as time has passed, experience.

So what are the disadvantages of having an agent? If you've got the right agent, the answer is probably very few, if any. Sure, you're not earning the full advance or royalty because you're giving them a percentage but your manuscript may never have become a book (or the advance and royalty may have been much lower) if they didn't represent you in the first place. If you don't have an agent you don't get directly involved in every aspect of negotiation and discussion with your publisher because you've handed that role over. And if you like the on-hands approach (for that read 'are a control freak'), you may miss out on that but, over all, the pros seem to outweigh the cons.

If you're _not_ happy with your agent, though, it can be a very different story. You're not your agent's only client and you may feel – rightly or wrongly – that they're not giving you enough attention. Many is the writer and illustrator I know who has said, 'I find more work for myself than my agent does', or who isn't happy with the advance they've received and said, 'I'm not sure why my agent was so keen for me to agree to this deal.' Another familiar lament is, 'She seemed so enthusiastic when I first signed up, but now she's gone really quiet.' Your filter has become a barrier.

There may also be jobs which your agent is reluctant for you to take. In children's non-fiction, many authors are still paid flat fees, and small ones at that. Many agents will tell you not to touch them with a barge pole but – if you are at the beginning of your career – who knows what that little job might lead to? I once wrote the text to a book that owed its subsequent international success not to the beauty of my prose but to the illustrations and brilliant paper engineering. My fee was peanuts and, in immediate financial terms, it made no difference if the book sold three copies or 300,000. But it did my writing career the power of good. My name was associated with a successful title, I got known by various people within that particular publishing house, I went on to write many more books for them _with_ royalties, and added to my reputation, generating interest from other publishers.

Going it alone

I enjoy that getting-to-know aspect of developing a relationship with publishers and, when it comes to contracts, I have a very useful not-so-secret secret weapon. I may not have an agent but I can call on the contracts experts at the Society of Authors (see page 353). As a member of the Society, they'll go through a contract line by line for me, free and for nothing, offering comments, suggestions and advice. They also publish excellent easy-to-understand pamphlets on various aspects of publishing. If you're not already a member, rush out and join immediately! If you don't understand something, don't be afraid to ask.

Remember, whatever impression a publisher might give, there is very rarely such thing as a standard contract, written in stone, that can't be altered; sometimes significantly. Be prepared to concede some minor points, maybe, in return for sticking to your guns over a point which may really matter to you. (Different things matter to different writers.)

My big break came by luck, but luck borne out of developing contacts and making real friendships in the course of my agentless foray into the children's publishing world. The bulk of my 100 or so titles are non-fiction, but the bulk of my income and 95% of my recognition comes from my fiction, but one grew from the other. Because I was involved and enthusiastic, I was invited to promote one of my non-fiction titles at a sales conference. As a result of how I ad libbed at the conference, following a mighty cock-up, I was asked if I wrote fiction. _Awful End_ (my first Eddie Dickens book) was pulled out of the drawer and a deal was done. One thing had, indeed, led to another. Eddie's adventures are in over 30 languages and read around the world, and have picked up a few literary awards along the way.

Your rights

Publishers love to have world rights to your books. Agents love to sell the rights separately. You can see why. An agent will argue that they can get more for you (and therefore more for them) by selling foreign rights separately to foreign publishers – perhaps creating a US auction for your fabulous book, for example – rather than your signing everything over to your UK publisher in one fell swoop. If, however, you sell the world rights to your publisher, and you have a good relationship with them, they're in effect acting as your agent on foreign deals and can still negotiate some excellent ones *in consultation with you*. And, having your world rights, they can share in your international success when it comes, so may be more keen to nurture you (and your money-generating, recognition-building world rights) in the future than, possibly, another writer whom they only publish in the UK.

And remember, an advance is an advance of royalties. If the advance is small and the book is a success, it simply means that the advance is earned out sooner and the cheques start rolling in. My advance for *Awful End* was just a four figure sum, but the money I've earned from additional royalties has been very-nice-thank-you-very-much. And my advances for the later Eddie Dickens books and other fiction were significantly larger.

Making the right decision

I know from friends and colleagues that, when you're starting out, you can find it as hard to get an agent as a publisher, which is why some people choose to go straight for the publishing houses. My advice – and this may surprise some of you – is to stick at trying to get an agent. If I was starting out now, I'd do that. Having an agent from the beginning makes sense.

If you're dead against the idea, feeling convinced that you can do a great job (see Philippa Milnes-Smith's checklist on page 201) or are exhausted trying, there are a few obvious things you can do. Even now, I sometimes ask myself 'Am I getting the very best deal?' and 'Could an agent do better for me?' Financially, the answers to these are probably 'Maybe not' and 'Yes', but are these the right questions? Surely what I need to ask is: 'Am I happy with this deal?' 'Is it a reasonable sum reflecting what I think I'm worth and showing the commitment and understanding of the publisher?' And the answer to that is, more often than not, 'yes'. And remember, money ain't the be all and end all. A good working relationship with an editor and publisher who understand you, consult with you, nurture you and your writing, promote and market you in a way you're happy with is beyond price.

Approaching a publisher

But let's not get ahead of ourselves. One of the most important, important *important* – it's important, get it? – things you need to be sure of before sending a manuscript to an agent *or* a publisher is that it's ready to be seen. Some unpublished writers are so keen to show their work to others in the hope of getting it published as soon as possible that it's still in a very raw state. They're not doing themselves any favours. In fact, they could be ruining their chances. Sure, there is such a thing as overworking a piece, but you really need to be confident that it's about as good as it's going to get, especially if you're bypassing the agent route and going direct to the publisher. With no agent 'filter', you've got to be sure that you're representing yourself, through your work, in the very best possible light.

Look in bookshops to find out who publishes what. Once you've chosen a publisher, look them up in this *Yearbook*, find out their submissions procedure and ring them up. Ask the receptionist the name of the person you should send your manuscript or sample chapters to. This way you can address and write a letter to a particular person, rather than taking the 'Dear Sir/Madam' approach.

The covering letter you should write to the publisher is almost identical to the one for writing to a prospective agent in *How to get an agent* (page 201) except, of course, that you should also include the reason why you think they'd be the right people to publish your work.

Finally, do treat the business side of selling yourself as a business. It's not simply that 'the writing's the important bit' and that it'll 'sell itself'. Network, send in invoices on time, get in touch when you say you'll get in touch and be contactable (there's no excuse for dropping off the radar in this age of emails and mobile phones). If you're shy or don't like parties, still go to the ones you're invited to by your publisher. You never know what that chance meeting with that rather scruffy bloke by the chilli dips might lead to. He could end up turning your book into a 24-part television series.

Oh, and one last thing: never admit that, secretly, you enjoy writing so much that you'd happily be published for nothing. Ooops. Me and my big mouth!

Agented or agentless, good luck.

Philip Ardagh won the Roald Dahl Funny Prize for the first book in his new _Grubtown Tales_ series. Before that he was best known for his award-winning Eddie Dickens adventures, translated into over 30 languages. Philip is also author of Scholastic's non-fiction series, _Henry's House_, and his radio credits include having written and edited the BBC's first truly interactive radio drama series, _Arthur Storey and the Department of Historical Correction_. He has collaborated with Sir Paul McCartney and is an 'irregular regular reviewer' of children's fiction for the _Guardian_.

See also...
- _How to get an agent_, page 201
- _Meet the parents: Agent, author and the birth of a book_, page 205
- _Publishing agreements_, page 257
- _The amazing picture book story_, page 248

Literary agents

Children's literary agents
UK and Ireland

Cautionary note: The *Children's Writers' & Artists' Yearbook*, along with the Association of Authors Agents and the Society of Authors, takes a dim view of any literary agent who asks potential clients for a fee prior to a manuscript being placed with a publisher. We advise you to treat any such request with caution and to let us know if that agent appears in the listings below. However, agents may charge additional costs later in the process but these should only arise once a book has been accepted by a publisher and the author is earning an income. We urge authors to make the distinction between upfront and additional charges.

*Full member of the Association of Authors' Agents

The Agency (London) Ltd*
24 Pottery Lane, London W11 4LZ
tel 020-7727 1346 *fax* 020-7727 9037
email hd-office@theagency.co.uk
website www.theagency.co.uk
Children's Book Executive Hilary Delamere

Represents novelty books, picture books, fiction for all ages including teenage fiction and series fiction (home 15%, overseas 20%). Works in conjunction with overseas agents. No unsolicited material. No reading fee. Also represents screenwriters, directors, playwrights and composers; for more information email separately. Founded 1995.

Aitken Alexander Associates Ltd*
18–21 Cavaye Place, London SW10 9PT
tel 020-7373 8672 *fax* 020-7373 6002
email reception@aitkenalexander.co.uk
website www.aitkenalexander.co.uk
Agent Gillie Russell

Children's and young adult fiction. Submissions by post only: include first 3 chapters plus synopsis and short author biography. No reading fee. No picture books and no submissions by email.
    Children's authors include Mark Lowery, Louise Rennison and Moira Young. Founded 1977.

Darley Anderson Children's Book Agency Ltd*
Estelle House, 11 Eustace Road, London SW6 1JB
tel 020-7386 2674 *fax* 020-7386 5571
email assistant@darleyanderson.com
website www.darleyandersonchildrens.com,
www.darleyanderson.com
Directors Darley Anderson (managing), Madeleine Buston (deputy managing), Peter Colegrave (finance), *Financial Controller* Rosanna Bellingham

Children's fiction, non-fiction and picture books (home 15%, USA/translation 20%, film/TV/radio 20%). Send preliminary letter, synopsis and first 3 chapters. Return postage/sae essential for reply.

Clients include Cathy Cassidy, Phil Earle, Helen Grant, Michelle Harrison, S.B. Hayes, Lucy Jones, Michael Lawrence, Carmen Reid, Rob Stevens, Ahmet Zappa.

Author Literary Agents
53 Talbot Road, London N6 4QX
tel 020-8341 0442 *mobile* (07767) 022659
Contact John Havergal

Novels, thrillers, faction, non-fiction, graphic novels, and children's books, and graphic and illustrated media edutainment concepts (home 15%, overseas/ translations 20%, advertising/sales promotion one-third). Pitches to publishers and producers. Send first chapter, scene or section, and graphics samples (if any), plus a half/one-page plot or topic outline together with sae. No reading fee. Founded 1997.

The Bell Lomax Moreton Agency
James House, 1 Babmaes Street, London SW1Y 6HF
tel 020-7930 4447 *fax* 020-7925 0118
email info@bell-lomax.co.uk
website www.bell-lomax.co.uk
Executives Eddie Bell, Pat Lomax, Paul Moreton, June Bell

Quality fiction and non-fiction, biography, children's, business and sport. No unsolicited MSS without preliminary letter. No scripts. No reading fee. Founded 2000.

Jenny Brown Associates*
33 Argyle Place, Edinburgh EH9 1JT
tel 0131-229 5334
email lucy@jennybrownassociates.com
website www.jennybrownassociates.com
Contact Lucy Juckes

Represents children's writers and illustrators. Also adult fiction and general non-fiction. No reading fee. See website for submission guidelines.
    Clients include Keith Gray, Gaby Halberstam, Diana Hendry, James Jauncey, Johnny Meres, Kenneth Steven. Founded 2002.

Felicity Bryan Associates*

2A North Parade, Banbury Road, Oxford OX2 6LX
tel (01865) 513816 *fax* (01865) 310055
email agency@felicitybryan.com
website www.felicitybryan.com

Fiction for children aged 8–14, and adult fiction and general non-fiction (home 15%, overseas 20%). Translation rights handled by Andrew Nurnberg Associates; works in conjunction with US agents.

Children's authors include David Almond, Jenny Downham, Sally Gardner, Julie Hearn, Liz Kessler, Katherine Langrish, Graham Marks, Natasha Narayan, Linda Newbery, Annabel Pitcher, Meg Rosoff, Lauren St John, Matthew Skelton, Eleanor Updale, Jeanne Willis.

Celia Catchpole

56 Gilpin Avenue, London SW14 8QY
tel 0208-8255 4835
email celia@celiacatchpole.co.uk,
catchpolesubmissions@googlemail.com
(submissions)
website www.celiacatchpole.co.uk
Director Celia Catchpole, *Agent* James Catchpole

Agent for authors and illustrators of children's books for all ages. Send complete stories if under 5,000 words or first 3 chapters if longer. Founded 1996.

Conville & Walsh Ltd*

2 Ganton Street, London W1F 7QL
tel 020-7287 3030 *fax* 020-7287 4545
website www.convilleandwalsh.com
Contact Jo Unwin, *email* jo@convilleandwalsh.com

Picture books, fiction for 5–8 and 9–12 year-olds, teenage fiction, series fiction and film/TV tie-ins (home 15%, overseas 20%). Also handles adult literary and commercial fiction and non-fiction. Submit first 3 chapters, cover letter, synopsis and sae. No reading fee.

Children's authors include John Burningham, Kate Cann, Katie Davies, Rebecca James, Timothy Knapman, Astrid Lindgren Estate, P.J. Lynch, Joshua Mowll, Jacqui Murhall, Peadar O'Guilin, Niamh Sharkey, Nicky Singer, Steve Voake. Founded 2000.

Creative Authors Ltd

11A Woodlawn Street, Whitstable, Kent CT5 1HQ
tel (01227) 770947
email write@creativeauthors.co.uk
website www.creativeauthors.co.uk
Director Isabel Atherton

Fiction, women's fiction, literary fiction, non-fiction, humour, history, autobiography, memoir, Mind, Body & Spirit, health, cookery, arts and crafts, crime, children's fiction (home 15%, overseas 20%). Prefers email submissions.

Authors include Mark Beaumont, Lee Bullman, Janine Bullman, E.A. Hanks, Amanda Hallay, Sarah Herman, Adele Nozedar, Feargus O'Sullivan. Established 2008.

The Creative Rights Agency

17 Prior Street, London SE10 8SF
tel 020-8149 3955
email info@creativerightsagency.co.uk
website www.creativerightsagency.co.uk
Contact Richard Scrivener

Specialises in managing children's intellectual property: publishing, film and TV, interactive and licensing rights. Founded 2009.

Curtis Brown Group Ltd*

Haymarket House, 28–29 Haymarket,
London SW1Y 4SP
tel 020-7393 4400 *fax* 020-7393 4401/02
email cb@curtisbrown.co.uk
website www.curtisbrown.co.uk
Ceo Jonathan Lloyd, *Coo* Ben Hall, *Directors* Jacquie Drewe, Jonny Geller, Nick Marston, Sarah Spear
Books Jonny Geller (Managing Director, Books Division), Felicity Blunt, Anna Davis, Jonathan Lloyd, Vivienne Schuster, Elizabeth Sheinkman, Karolina Sutton, Stephanie Thwaites, Gordon Wise

Novels, general non-fiction, children's books and associated rights (including multimedia), as well as film, theatre, TV and radio scripts. See website for submission guidelines. Also represents playwrights, film and TV writers and directors, theatre directors and designers, TV and radio presenters and actors. Overseas associates in Australia and the USA. Founded 1899.

Eddison Pearson Ltd*

West Hill House, 6 Swains Lane, London N6 6QS
tel 020-7700 7763 *fax* 020-7700 7866
email info@eddisonpearson.com
website www.eddisonpearson.com
Contact Clare Pearson

Children's and young adult books, fiction and non-fiction, poetry (home 10%, overseas 15–20%). Small personally run agency. Enquiries and submissions by email only; email for up-to-date submission guidelines by return. No reading fee. May suggest revision where appropriate.

Authors include Valerie Bloom, Sue Heap, Caroline Lawrence, Robert Muchamore.

Fraser Ross Associates

6 Wellington Place, Edinburgh EH6 7EQ
tel 0131-553 2759, 0131-657 4412
email lindsey.fraser@tiscali.co.uk, kjross@tiscali.co.uk
website www.fraserross.co.uk
Partners Lindsey Fraser, Kathryn Ross

Annette Green Authors' Agency*

1 East Cliff Road, Tunbridge Wells, Kent TN4 9AD
tel (01892) 514275
email enquiries@annettegreenagency.co.uk
website www.annettegreenagency.co.uk
Partners Annette Green, David Smith

Literary agents

Full-length MSS (home 15%, overseas 20%). Literary and general fiction and non-fiction, popular culture, history, science, teenage fiction. No dramatic scripts, poetry, science fiction or fantasy. No reading fee. Preliminary letter, synopsis, sample chapter and sae essential.

Children's authors include Meg Cabot, Mary Hogan. Founded 1998.

Greene & Heaton Ltd*
37 Goldhawk Road, London W12 8QQ
tel 020-8749 0315 *fax* 020-8749 0318
email submissions@greeneheaton.co.uk
website www.greeneheaton.co.uk
Contact Nicola Barr

Children's fiction and non-fiction. Handles fiction for 5–8 and 9–12 year-olds, teenage fiction, series fiction, poetry and non-fiction. No picture books. Also handles adult fiction and non-fiction. Send a covering letter, synopsis and the first 50pp (or less) with an sae and return postage. Email submissions welcome but no reply guaranteed; type 'Children's' in subject line.

Children's authors include Helen Craig, Josh Lacey, Lucy Christopher. Founded 1963.

The Greenhouse Literary Agency
Stanley House, St Chad's Place, London WC1X 9HH
tel 020-7841 3959 *fax* 020-7841 3940
email submissions@greenhouseliterary.com
website www.greenhouseliterary.com
Director Sarah Davies, *Agent* Julia Churchill

Children's fiction from age 5 through to teen/young adult (USA/UK 15%, elsewhere 25%). Represents both US and UK authors. No picture books or non-fiction. No reading fee. Will suggest revision. Queries by email only, see website for details.

Authors include Sarwat Chadda, Lil Chase, Anne-Marie Conway, S.D. Crockett, Stephen Davies, Michael Ford, Harriet Goodwin, Jill Hathaway, Kathryn James, Lindsey Leavitt, Jon Mayhew, Megan Miranda, Leila Rasheed, Jeyn Roberts, Tricia Springstubb, Susanne Winnacker, Brenna Yovanoff. Founded 2008.

Marianne Gunn O'Connor Literary Agency
Morrison Chambers, Suite 17, 32 Nassau Street, Dublin 2, Republic of Ireland
email mgoclitagency@eircom.net
Contact Marianne Gunn O'Connor

Commercial and literary fiction, non-fiction, biography, children's fiction (home 15%, overseas 20%, film/TV 20%). No unsolicited MSS. Translation rights handled by Vicki Satlow Literary Agency, Milan.

Antony Harwood Ltd*
103 Walton Street, Oxford OX2 6EB
tel (01865) 559615 *fax* (01865) 310660

email mail@antonyharwood.com
website www.antonyharwood.com
Contacts Antony Harwood, James Macdonald Lockhart, Jo Williamson (children's)

General and genre fiction; general non-fiction (home 15%, overseas 20%). Will suggest revision. No reading fee.

Children's authors include Garth Nix. Founded 2000.

A.M. Heath & Co. Ltd
6 Warwick Court, London WC1R 5DJ
tel 020-7242 2811 *fax* 020-7242 2711
website www.amheath.com
Contact Sarah Molloy, Ben Illis

Fiction and non-fiction from age 5 to young adult (home 15%, USA/translation 20%). Handles fiction for 5–8 and 9–12 year-olds, teenage fiction, series fiction, film/TV tie-ins and non-fiction. Also handles adult literary and commercial fiction and non-fiction. Submit synopsis and sample chapters. No reading fee. Will suggest revision.

Children's authors include Nicholas Allan, John Dougherty, Nick Gifford, Caro King, Michelle Lovric, Joanna Nadin, Laura Powell, Susan Price, Leslie Wilson, the Estates of Noel Streatfeild, Helen Cresswell, Joan Aiken and Christianna Brand. Founded 1919.

David Higham Associates Ltd*
(incorporating Murray Pollinger)
5–8 Lower John Street, Golden Square, London W1F 9HA
tel 020-7434 5900 *fax* 020-7437 1072
email dha@davidhigham.co.uk
website www.davidhigham.co.uk
Managing Director Anthony Goff, *Books* Veronique Baxter, Anthony Goff, Caroline Walsh, *Foreign Rights* Ania Corless, Tine Nielsen, *Film/TV/Theatre* Nicky Lund, Georgina Ruffhead

Children's fiction, picture books and non-fiction (home 15%, USA/translation 20%, scripts 10%). Handles novelty books, picture books, fiction for 5–8 and 9–12 year-olds, teenage fiction, series fiction, poetry, plays, film/TV tie-ins, non-fiction, audio and CD-Roms. Also handles adult fiction, general non-fiction, plays, film and TV scripts; 35% of list is for the children's market. See website for submissions policy. No reading fee. Represented in all foreign markets.

Also represents illustrators for children's book publishing (home 15%). Submit colour copies of artwork by post or via email. Include samples that show children 'in action' and animals.

Clients (children's market) include Jenny Alexander, R.J. Anderson, Antonia Barber, Julia Bell, Joe Berger, Tim Bowler, Alan Brown, Mike Brownlow, Jos Carlyle, Charles Causley, Kathryn Cave, Jason Chapman, Lauren Child, Peter

Collington, Trish Cooke, Anne Cottringer, Cressida Cowell, Roald Dahl, Nicola Davies, Susie Day, Kady Macdonald Denton, Jane Devlin, Matt Dickinson, Berlie Doherty, Jonathan Emmett, Kat Falls, Anne Fine, Corina Fletcher, Susan Gates, Jamila Gavin, Maggie Gibson, Julia Golding, Kes Gray, Sally Grindley, Ann Halam, Carol Hedges, Leigh Hodgkinson, Belinda Hollyer, Meredith Hooper, William Hussey, Julia Jarman, Sherryl Jordan, Anna Kemp, Clive King, Bert Kitchen, Rebecca Lisle, Saci Lloyd, Jo Lodge, Tim Lott, Geraldine McCaughrean, Kirsty McKay, Tom McLaughlin, Hazel Marshall, Simon Mason, David Miller, Gwen Millward, Pratima Mitchell, Tony Mitton, Nicola Moon, Michael Morpurgo, Coleen Murtagh Paratore, Sarah Mlynowski, Jenny Nimmo, Martine Oborne, Clare O'Brien, Kate O'Hearn, Liz Pichon, Tamora Pierce, Chris Powling, Charlie Price, Lucy Daniel Raby, Gwyneth Rees, Adrian Reynolds, Jasmine Richards, Rachel Rooney, Nick Sharratt, Emily Smith, Alexander McCall Smith, Keris Stainton, Jeremy Strong, Frances Thomas, Theresa Tomlinson, Ann Turnbull, Jenny Valentine, A.M. Vrettos, Martin Waddell, Philip Webb, Alex Williams, Gina Wilson, Jacqueline Wilson and David Wojtowycz. Founded 1935.

Johnson & Alcock Ltd*
Clerkenwell House, 45–47 Clerkenwell Green, London EC1R 0HT
tel 020-7251 0125 *fax* 020-7251 2172
email info@johnsonandalcock.co.uk
website www.johnsonandalcock.co.uk
Contact Anna Power

All types of children's fiction and non-fiction (ages 8+), young adult and teenage fiction, (home 15%, USA/translation/film 20%). No short stories, poetry or board-/picture-books.

Send first 3 chapters (or 50pp), full synopsis, and brief covering letter with details or writing experience. No email submissions. No reading fee but return postage essential. Founded 1956.

LAW (Lucas Alexander Whitley Ltd)*
14 Vernon Street, London W14 0RJ
tel 020-7471 7900 *fax* 020-7471 7910
website www.lawagency.co.uk
Contacts Philippa Milnes-Smith, Holly Vitow

Children's books (home 15%, overseas 20%). Handles novelty books, picture books, fiction for 5–8 and 9–12 year-olds, teenage fiction, film/TV tie-ins, non-fiction, reference and audio. Send brief covering letter, short synopsis and 2–3 sample chapters. For picture books, send complete text and/or copies of sample artwork. Do *not* send original artwork. Sae essential. No email or disk submissions. Overseas associates worldwide. Founded 1996.

Lindsay Literary Agency
East Worldham House, Alton, Hants GU34 3AT
tel (01420) 83143

email info@lindsayliteraryagency.co.uk
website www.lindsayliteraryagency.co.uk
Directors Becky Bagnell, Kate Holroyd Smith

Literary fiction, serious non-fiction, children's (10–15%). No reading fee. Will suggest revision. Founded 2005.

Authors include Gina Blaxill, Sam Gayton, Mike Lancaster, Sue Lloyd-Roberts.

Christopher Little Literary Agency*
10 Eel Brook Studios, 125 Moore Park Road, London SW6 4PS
tel 020-7736 4455 *fax* 020-7736 4490
email info@christopherlittle.net
website www.christopherlittle.net
Contact Christopher Little

Fiction for 9–12 year-olds and teenage fiction (home 15%, overseas 20%); no illustrated children's or short stories. Also handles adult fiction and non-fiction. Send synopsis and first 3 chapters with an sae. No reading fee.

Children's authors include J.K. Rowling and Darren Shan. Founded 1979.

London Independent Books
26 Chalcot Crescent, London NW1 8YD
tel 020-7706 0486 *fax* 020-7724 3122
Proprietor Carolyn Whitaker

Specialises in teenage fiction (home 15%, overseas 20%). Handles fiction for 9–12 year-olds, teenage fiction and young adult fiction. Also handles adult fiction and travel; approx. one-third of list is for the children's market. Submit 2 chapters and a synopsis with return postage. No reading fee. Will suggest revision of promising MSS.

Authors include Simon Chapman, Joseph Delaney, Elizabeth Kay, Elizabeth Richardson, Craig Simpson, Chris Wooding. Founded 1971.

Jennifer Luithlen Agency
88 Holmfield Road, Leicester LE2 1SB
tel 0116-273 8863 and 0116-273 5697
website www.luithlenagency.com
Agents Jennifer Luithlen, Penny Luithlen

Children's fiction (home 15%, overseas 20%), performance rights (15%). Founded 1986.

Eunice McMullen Ltd
Low Ibbotsholme Cottage, Off Bridge Lane, Troutbeck Bridge, Windermere, Cumbria LA23 1HU
tel (01539) 448551
email eunicemcmullen@totalise.co.uk
website www.eunicemcmullen.co.uk
Director Eunice McMullen

Specialises exclusively in children's books, especially picture books and older fiction (home 10%, overseas 15%). Handles novelty books, picture books, fiction for all ages including teenage, series fiction and audio. No unsolicited scripts. Telephone or email enquiries only. No reading fee.

Authors include Wayne Anderson, Sam Childs, Caroline Jayne Church, Jason Cockcroft, Ross Collins, Emma Dodd, Charles Fuge, Maggie Kneen, David Melling, Angela McAllister, Angie Sage, Gillian Shields. Founded 1992.

Andrew Mann Ltd*

United House, North Road, London N7 9DP
email info@andrewmann.co.uk
website www.andrewmann.co.uk
Contacts Anne Dewe, Tina Betts, Louise Burns

Children's fiction and non-fiction (home 15%, overseas 20%). Handles picture books, fiction for 5–8 and 9–12 year-olds, teenage fiction, series fiction, film/TV tie-ins and non-fiction. Also handles adult fiction and scripts for TV, cinema, radio and theatre; 25% of list is for children's market. Submit synopsis and first 30pp. Email submissions only. No reading fee. Founded 1968.

Children's authors include Richard Byrne, Gina Douthwaite, Emily Gale, Joe Hackett, Judith Heneghan, Savita Kalhan, Kate Lennard, Katharine Quarmby, Anne Rooney, Andrew Weale, Jude Wisdom.

Sarah Manson Literary Agent

6 Totnes Walk, London N2 0AD
tel 020-8442 0396
email info@sarahmanson.com
website www.sarahmanson.com
Proprietor Sarah Manson

Specialises in fiction for children and young adults. See website for submission guidelines. Founded 2002.

Marjacq Scripts

34 Devonshire Place, London W1G 6JW
tel 020-7935 9499 fax 020-7935 9115
email enquiries@marjacq.com
website www.marjacq.com
Contact Philip Patterson (books), Isabella Floris (books), Luke Speed (film/TV)

All full-length MSS (home 10%, overseas 20%), including commercial and literary fiction and non-fiction, crime, thrillers, commercial, women's fiction, graphic novels, children's, science fiction, history, biography, sport, travel, health. No poetry. Send first 3 chapters with synopsis. May suggest revision. Film and TV rights, screenplays, documentaries: send full script with 1–2pp synopsis/outline. Interested in documentary concepts and will accept proposals from writer/directors: send show reel with script. Sae essential for return of submissions.

MBA Literary Agents Ltd*

(incorporating Merric Davidson Literary Agency)
62 Grafton Way, London W1T 5DW
tel 020-7387 2076 fax 020-7387 2042
email firstname@mbalit.co.uk
website www.mbalit.co.uk

Children's agents Diana Tyler, Meg Davis, Sophie Gorell Barnes, Laura Longrigg, Film & TV Jean Kitson

Fiction and non-fiction, children's books, and TV, film, radio and theatre scripts (home 15%, overseas 20%; theatre, TV, radio 10%; films 10–20%). See website for submission guidelines. Works in conjunction with agents in most countries. UK representative for the Donald Maass Agency, Martha Millard Agency and Frances Collin Agency. Founded 1971.

Authors include Catherine Webb, Brian Keaney, Mibi Thebo, Rebecca Promitzer, Sita Brahmachari, Christopher and Christine Russell.

Miles Stott Children's Literary Agency

East Hook Farm, Lower Quay Road, Hook, Haverfordwest, Pembrokeshire SA62 4LR
tel (01437) 890570
email nancy@milesstottagency.co.uk
website www.milesstottagency.co.uk
Director Nancy Miles, Associate Agent Victoria Birkett

Specialist in children's novelty books, picture books, fiction for 6–9 and 10–12 year-olds, young adult fiction and series fiction (from: home 15%, overseas 20%). Send covering letter, brief synopsis and 3 sample chapters. For picture books send complete text and/or copies of sample artwork (do not send original artwork). No reading fee. Sae essential.

Authors include Ronda Armitage, Dominic Barker, Frances Hardinge, Hiawyn Oram, Justin Richards. Founded 2003.

The No.1 Manchester Literary Agency

3rd Floor, Clayton House, 59 Piccadilly, Manchester M1 2AQ
tel 0161-904 0910
website www.theno1manchesterliteraryagency.co.uk
Contact Kathy Charvin, Karen James, Lorraine Birtwistle

Children's and adult fiction (home 15%, overseas 20%). Fiction for 5–8 and 9–12 year-olds and teenage fiction. Send covering letter, synopsis and the first 50pp (or less) with sae and return postage. No reading fee. Will suggest revision. Founded in 2009 to represent northern-based authors.

Pollinger Limited

(formerly Laurence Pollinger Ltd, successor of Pearn, Pollinger and Higham)
9 Staple Inn, Holborn, London WC1V 7QH
tel 020-7404 0342 fax 020-7242 5737
email info@pollingerltd.com
website www.pollingerltd.com
Managing Director Lesley Pollinger, Agents Joanna Devereux, Tim Bates, Leigh Pollinger, Hayley Yeeles

All types of general trade adult and children's fiction and non-fiction books; intellectual property developments, illustrators/photographers (home

15%, translation 20%). Overseas, media and theatrical associates. For submission guidelines see website.

Children's clients include Michael Coleman, Bridget Crowley, Catherine Fisher, Philip Gross, Frances Hendry, Hayley Long, Kelly McKain. Founded 1935.

Redhammer Management Ltd*
186 Bickenhall Mansions, Bickenhall Street, London W1U 6BX
tel 020-7486 3465 *fax* 020-7000 1249
website www.redhammer.info
Vice President Peter Cox

Specialises in works with international potential (home 17.5%, overseas 20%). Unpublished authors must be professional in their approach and have major international potential, ideally book, film and/or TV. Submissions must follow the guidelines given on the website. Do not send unsolicited MSS by post. No radio or theatre scripts. No reading fee.

Children's clients include Peggy Brusseau, Maria (M.G.) Harris, Michelle Paver, David Yelland. Founded 1993.

Rogers, Coleridge & White Ltd*
20 Powis Mews, London W11 1JN
tel 020-7221 3717 *fax* 020-7229 9084
email info@rcwlitagency.com
website www.rcwlitagency.com
Chairman Deborah Rogers, *Managing Director* Peter Straus, *Director* Patricia White, *Agent* Catherine Pellegrino

Children's fiction and non-fiction (home 15%, USA 20%). Handles novelty books, picture books, fiction for 5–8 and 9–12 year-olds, teenage fiction, series fiction, non-fiction and reference. No unsolicited MSS. No submissions by fax or email. No reading fee. Will suggest revision.

Children's authors include Mary Hoffman, Rhiannon Lassiter, Michelle Magorian, Richard Platt, Karen Wallace. Founded 1967.

Elizabeth Roy Literary Agency
White Cottage, Greatford, Nr Stamford, Lincs. PE9 4PR
tel (01778) 560672 *fax* (01778) 560672
website www.elizabethroyliteraryagency.co.uk

Children's fiction and non-fiction – writers and illustrators (home 15%, overseas 20%). Send preliminary letter, synopsis and sample chapters with names of publishers and agents previously contacted. Return postage essential. No reading fee. Founded 1990.

Uli Rushby-Smith Literary Agency
72 Plimsoll Road, London N4 2EE
tel 020-7354 2718 *fax* 020-7354 2718
Director Uli Rushby-Smith

Fiction and non-fiction, literary and commercial (home 15%, USA/foreign 20%). No poetry, picture books, plays or film scripts. Send outline, sample chapters (no disks) and return postage. No reading fee. Founded 1993.

Rosemary Sandberg Ltd
6 Bayley Street, London WC1B 3HE
tel 020-7304 4110 *fax* 020-7304 4109
email rosemary@sandberg.demon.co.uk
Directors Rosemary Sandberg, Ed Victor

Children's writers and illustrators, general fiction and non-fiction. Absolutely no unsolicited MSS: client list is full. Founded 1991.

Caroline Sheldon Literary Agency Ltd*
71 Hillgate Place, London W8 7SS
tel 0207-727 9102
email carolinesheldon@carolinesheldon.co.uk, pennyholroyde@carolinesheldon.co.uk
website www.carolinesheldon.co.uk
Contacts Caroline Sheldon, Penny Holroyde

All types of children's books plus adult fiction and non-fiction (home 15%, USA/translation 20%, film/TV 15%). All writing for children from picture books up through 7–9 year olds, 9–12 year olds to teenage fiction. All major genres including contemporary, comic, fantasy, historical series fiction and humour. Also non-fiction. Illustrators also represented. Also specialises in the sale of books to TV/film but not interested in non-book-originated merchandised characters.

Authors – send submissions by email only with Submissions/Title of work/Name of author in subject line. Include full introductory information about yourself and your writing and the first 3 chapters only or equivalent length of work.

Illustrators – send introductory information about yourself with samples. If submitting by email type Artist's Submission in subject line and attach samples of your work and/or link to your website. If submitting by post include printed samples and/or a disk with images saved as jpeg or tiff files together with a large sae. If available, include texts or book dummies. Founded 1985.

Dorie Simmonds Agency*
Riverbank House, One Putney Bridge Approach, London SW6 3JD
tel 020-7736 0002
Contact Dorie Simmonds

Children's fiction (UK/USA 15%; translation 20%). No reading fee but sae required. Send a short synopsis, 2–3 sample chapters and a CV with writing/publishing background.

Clients include award-winning children's authors.

The Standen Literary Agency
53 Hardwicke Road, London N13 4SL
tel/fax 020-8889 1167
website www.standenliteraryagency.com
Director Yasmin Standen

Children's fiction for all ages and picture books (home 15%, overseas 20%). Seeking new writers of fiction for all age groups. Send first 3 chapters and synopsis (one side of A4) with a covering letter by post only in first instance (no submissions via email) and sae. No reading fee. Also handles literary and commercial fiction for adults. 70% of list is children's writing. See website for further information.

Authors include Zara Kane, Zoe Marriott, Andrew Murray. Founded 2004.

Abner Stein*

10 Roland Gardens, London SW7 3PH
tel 020-7373 0456 *fax* 020-7370 6316
Contact Caspian Dennis, Arabella Stein, Sandy Violette

Fiction, general non-fiction and children's (home 10%, overseas 20%). Not taking on any new clients at present.

Sarah Such Literary Agency

81 Arabella Drive, London SW15 5LL
tel 020-8876 4228
email info@sarahsuch.com
website Twitter.com/sarahsuch
Proprietor Sarah Such

High-quality literary and commercial non-fiction and fiction for adults and children (home 15%, TV/film 20%, overseas 20%), including picture books. No reading fee. Will suggest revision. Submit synopsis and a sample chapter (as a Word attachment if sending by email) plus author biography. Sae essential for postal submissions. No unsolicited MSS or telephone enquiries. TV/film scripts for established clients only. No radio or theatre scripts, poetry, fantasy, self-help or short stories. Film/TV representation: Aitken Alexander Associates Ltd.

Authors include Matthew De Abaitua, Nick Barlay, Rob Chapman, John Harris Dunning, Rob Harris, John Hartley, Marisa Heath, Wayne Holloway-Smith, Antony Johnston, Louisa Leaman, Mathew Lyons, Sam Manning, Vesna Maric, David May, Jean Moorcroft-Wilson, Marian Pashley, Sarah Penny, John Rowley, Caroline Sanderson, Nikhil Singh, Sara Starbuck. Founded 2006.

United Agents*

12–26 Lexington Street, London W1F 0LE
tel 020-3214 0800
email info@unitedagents.co.uk
website www.unitedagents.co.uk
Agents Sarah Ballard, Jessica Craig (adult foreign rights), Caroline Dawnay, James Gill, Robert Kirby, Jodie Marsh (children's and young adult books), Rosemary Scoular, Simon Trewin, Charles Walker, Anna Webber, Jane Willis (children's foreign rights)

Fiction and non-fiction (home 15%, USA/translation 20%). No reading fee. See website for submission details. Founded 2008.

Ed Victor Ltd*

6 Bayley Street, Bedford Square, London WC1B 3HE
tel 020-7304 4100 *fax* 020-7304 4111
website www.edvictor.com
Contact Sophie Hicks

Fiction for all ages, film/TV tie-ins, non-fiction and audio (home 10%, overseas 20%). No short stories or poetry. Also handles adult fiction and non-fiction. No reading fee. No unsolicited MSS. No response to submission by email.

Children's authors include Herbie Brennan, Eoin Colfer, David Lee Stone, Oisín McGann, Siobhan Parkinson, Alexander Gordon Smith, Kate Thompson and Mark Walden. Founded 1976.

Watson, Little Ltd*

48–56 Bayham Place, London NW1 0EU
tel 020-7388 7529 *fax* 020-7388 8501
email office@watsonlittle.com
website www.watsonlittle.com
Contact Mandy Little, James Wills, Sallyanne Sweeney
Contact Mandy Little, James Wills, Sallyanne Sweeney

Fiction, commercial women's fiction, crime and literary fiction. Non-fiction special interests include history, science, popular psychology, self-help and general leisure books. Also children's fiction and non-fiction (home 15%, USA/translation 20%). No short stories, poetry, TV, play or film scripts. Not interested in purely academic writers. Send informative preliminary letter, synopsis and sample chapters.
Overseas associates The Marsh Agency Ltd; *Film and TV associates* The Sharland Organisation Ltd and MBA Literary Agents Ltd; *USA associates* Howard Morhaim Literary Agency (adult) and the Chudney Agency (children's).

Children's authors or illustrators include Jean Adamson, Stephen Biesty, Patricia MacCarthy, Margaret Mahy, Lynne Reid Banks, Stewart Ross.

AP Watt Ltd*

20 John Street, London WC1N 2DR
tel 020-7405 6774
fax 020-7831 2154 (books), 020-7430 1952 (drama)
email apw@apwatt.co.uk
website www.apwatt.co.uk
Directors Caradoc King, Linda Shaughnessy, Derek Johns, Georgia Garrett, Natasha Fairweather

Adults' and children's full-length MSS; dramatic works for all media (home 15%, overseas 20% including commission to foreign agent). No poetry. No reading fee. Does not accept unsolicited MSS or any other material. Send a query letter in first instance.

Authors include Quentin Blake, Melvin Burgess, Georgia Byng, Zizou Corder, Helen Dunmore, Dick King-Smith, Philip Pullman, Philip Ridley. Founded 1875.

Whispering Buffalo Literary Agency Ltd

97 Chesson Road, London W14 9QS
tel 020-7565 4737

email info@whisperingbuffalo.com
website www.whisperingbuffalo.com
Director Mariam Keen

Commercial/literary fiction and non-fiction, children's and young adult fiction (home 15%, overseas 20%). No reading fee. Will suggest revision. Founded 2008.

Eve White*

54 Gloucester Street, London SW1V 4EG
tel 020-7630 1155
email eve@evewhite.co.uk
website www.evewhite.co.uk
Contact Eve White

Picture books, fiction for 5–8 and 9–12 year-olds, teenage fiction and film/TV tie-ins (home 15%, overseas 20%). Also handles adult commercial and literary fiction and non-fiction; 50% of list is for the children's market. No reading fee. Will suggest

revision where appropriate. See website for up-to-date submission requirements.

Children's clients include Ivan Brett, Susanna Corbett, Tracey Corderoy, Jimmy Docherty, David Flavell, Miriam Halahmy, Abie Longstaff, Rachael Mortimer, Ciaran Murtagh, Kate Maryon, Gillian Rogerson, Andy Stanton. Founded 2003.

Susan Yearwood Literary Agency

2 Knebworth House, Londesborough Road, London N16 8RL
tel 020-7503 0954
email susan@susanyearwood.com
website www.susanyearwood.com
Contact Susan Yearwood

Literary and commercial fiction (home 15%, overseas 20%), including thrillers, general and young adult. Send first 30pp and a synopsis via email. No reading fee. Established 2007.

Children's literary agents overseas

Before submitting material, writers are advised to send a preliminary letter with a sase or IRC (International Reply Coupon) and to ascertain terms.

AUSTRALIA

Altair-Australia Literary Agency
PO Box 475, Blackwood SA 5051
tel/fax (8) 8278 5585
email altair-australia@altair-australia.com
website www.altair-australia.com
Agent Robert N. Stephenson

Specialises in science fiction and fantasy; also children's literature, mainstream literature, crime and mystery and action/adventure fiction (15–20%). Non-fiction material may be considered if queried first. Founded 1997.

Submission details Submit the first 3 chapters (up to 15,000 words) and 2pp synopsis for fiction/novel. Send whole MS plus reference details for non-fiction (do not include original graphics, films or photographs). Allow at least 12 weeks before querying.

Australian Literary Management
2–A Booth Street, Balmain, New South Wales 2041
tel (9) 818 8557
email alpha@austlit.com
website www.austlit.com

Fiction, non-fiction, fantasy, young readers and cartoons (home 15%). Telephone first, then submit a short synopsis and 2 chapters. No reading fee. Do not email. Does not suggest revision.
Children's authors include Pamela Freeman, Christine Harris, Glyn Parry, Laurie Stiller. Established 1980.

Bryson Agency Australia Pty Ltd
PO Box 13327, Law Courts PO, Melbourne 8010
tel (613) 9329 2517 *fax* (613) 9600 9131
email fran@bryson.com.au
website www.bryson.com.au
Contact Fran Bryson

Represents writers operating in all media: print, film, TV, radio, the stage and electronic derivatives; specialises in representation of book writers. Query first before sending unsolicited MSS. Not accepting until further notice.

Jenny Darling & Associates
PO Box 413, Toorak, Victoria 3142
tel (03) 9827 3883 *fax* (03) 9827 1270
email jda@jd-associates.com.au
website www.jd-associates.com.au
Contact Jenny Darling

Represents only a few children's authors. Open to all genres and ages. For picture books and up to end primary school, send the complete MS. For young adult, send the first 10pp in the first instance. Submit material by post, including return postage. See website for submission guidelines.

Golvan Arts Management
PO Box 766, Kew, Victoria 3101, Australia
tel (03) 9853 5341 *fax* (03) 9853 8555
email golvan@ozemail.com.au
website www.golvanarts.com.au
Manager & Director Debbie Golvan, *Director* Colin Golvan

Children's fiction and non-fiction (15%+GST). Handles picture books, fiction for 5–8 and 9–12 year-olds, teenage fiction, series fiction, film/TV tie-ins, non-fiction and plays. Also handles adult fiction and non-fiction, plays, feature film and TV scripts, visual artists and composers; 60% of list is for children's market. Read 'general information' section on website before sending a brief letter. Material sent to agency from outside of Australia will not be returned. No reading fee. Will suggest revision. Works with French, Chinese and Korean agents.
Children's authors include Nan Bodsworth, Terry Denton, Janine Fraser, Jayne Lyons, Paty Marshall-Stace, Sally Morgan, Wendy Orr, Greg Pyers, Alan Sunderland. Founded 1989.

CANADA

Melanie Colbert
17 West Street, Holland Landing, Ontario L9N 1L4
tel 905-853-2435
Contact Melanie Colbert

Children's authors and illustrators. Send initial query; no unsolicited MSS. Established 1985.

The Cooke Agency
278 Bloor Street East, Suite 305, Toronto, Ontario M4W 3M4
tel 416-406-3390 *fax* 416-406-3389
email agents@cookeagency.ca
website www.cookeagency.ca
Agents Dean Cooke, Sally Harding, Suzanne Brandreth, Mary Hu

Literary fiction, commercial fiction (science fiction, fantasy and romance), non-fiction (specifically narrative-driven works in the areas of popular culture, science, history, politics and natural history), and middle-grade and young adult books. No children's picture books, poetry or screenplays. Either submit query only by email (no attachments) or complete submission by post FAO Elizabeth Griffin. Represents more than 100 writers. Co-agents: Curtis Brown Canada, Greene & Heaton, The Turnbull Agency. Founded 1992.

Submission details See website at www.cookeagency.ca/submissions.htm to view submission guidelines.

Pamela Paul Agency

12 Westrose Avenue, Toronto, Ontario M8X 1Z9
tel 416-410-4395 *fax* 416-410-4949
email agency@interlog.com
Contact Pamela Paul

Children's fiction only. No unsolicited MSS. Established 1989.

Carolyn Swayze Literary Agency Ltd

W.R.P.O. Box 39588, White Rock,
British Columbia V4B 5L6
email reception@swayzeagency.com
website www.swayzeagency.com
Proprietor Carolyn Swayze

Fiction and non-fiction for teens and middle-grade readers. No romance, science fiction, poetry, screenplays or children's picture books. Eager to discover strong voices writing contemporary or supernatural stories if the metaphor reflects relevant themes.

Submission details No telephone calls: make contact by email or post. Send query including synopsis and short sample. Provide résumé, publication credits, writing awards, education and experience relevant to the book project. If querying by post include email or sase for return of materials. No original artwork or photographs. Allow 6 weeks for a reply. Founded 1994.

Transatlantic Literary Agency

2 Bloor Street East, Suite 3500, Toronto,
Ontario M4W 1A8
tel 416-488-9214 *fax* 416-929-3174
email info@tla1.com
website www.tla1.com
Contact Marie Campbell, Andrea Cascardi

Specialises in children's and young adult books: fiction, non-fiction. No unsolicited MSS. Founded 1993.

NEW ZEALAND

Glenys Bean Writer's Agent

PO Box 639, Warkworth
email info@glenysbean.com
website www.glenysbean.com
Directors Fay Weldon, Glenys Bean

Adult and children's fiction, educational, non-fiction, film, TV, radio (10–20%). Send preliminary letter, synopsis and sae. No reading fee. Represented by Sanford Greenburger Associates Ltd (USA). *Translation/foreign rights* the Marsh Agency Ltd. Founded 1989.

Richards Literary Agency

postal address PO Box 31–240, Milford,
Auckland 0620
tel/fax (649) 410-0209
email rla.richards@clear.net.nz
Staff Ray Richards, Elaine Blake, Judy Bartlam, Frances Plumpton

Children's fiction and non-fiction (home 15%, overseas 20%). Handles picture books, junior and teenage fiction, film/TV tie-ins, non-fiction and reference; educational (primary). Concentrates on New Zealand authors. Send book proposal with an outline and biography. No reading fee. Co-agents in London and New York.

Children's authors include Joy Cowley, Brian Falkner, Maurice Gee and Sally Sutton. Founded 1977.

Total Fiction Services

PO Box 46-031, Park Avenue, Lower Hutt 5044
tel (4) 565 4429
email tfs@elseware.co.nz
website www.elseware.co.nz

General fiction, non-fiction, children's books. No poetry, or individual short stories or articles. Enquiries from New Zealand authors only. Email queries but no attachments. Hard copy preferred. No reading fee. Also offers assessment reports, mentoring and courses.

SOUTH AFRICA

Cherokee Literary Agency

3 Blythwood Road, Rondebosch, Cape 7700
tel (021) 671 4508
email dklee@mweb.co.za
Director D.K. Lee

Children's picture books in translation (home 10%). Founded 1988.

SPAIN

RDC Agencia Literaria SL

C Fernando VI, No 13–15, Madrid 28004
tel 91-308-55-85 *fax* 91-308-56-00
email rdc@idecnet.com
Director Raquel de la Concha

Representing foreign fiction, non-fiction, children's books and Spanish authors. No reading fee.

Lennart Sane Agency AB

Infanta Mercedes 90, ES-28020 Madrid
tel 91-579-80-46 *fax* 91-579-89-84

email lennart.sane@lennartsaneagency.com
website www.lennartsaneagency.com
President Lennart Sane

Fiction, non-fiction, children's books, film and TV scripts. Founded 1965.

USA

*Member of the Association of Authors' Representatives

Adams Literary*

7845 Colony Road, C4 Suite 215, Charlotte, NC 28226
tel 704-542-1440 *fax* 704-542-1450
email info@adamsliterary.com
website www.adamsliterary.com
Agent Tracey Adams

Exclusively children's: from picture books to teenage novels (home 15%, overseas 20%). Strictly no unsolicited submissions. See website for guidelines. Founded 2004.

BookStop Literary Agency

67 Meadow View Road, Orinda, CA 94563
tel 925-254-2664 *fax* 925-254-2668
email info@bookstopliterary.com
website www.bookstopliterary.com
Contact Kendra Marcus

Exclusively children's fiction and non-fiction (home 15%). Represents both authors and illustrators. No reading fee.
   Submission details Send complete MS, sase for return of material and cover letter (include contact information, a short paragraph about your background, publishing credits and brief synopsis of MS). For non-fiction proposals send outline with 2 sample chapters. Illustrators should send colour and b&w samples. Do not send originals. Founded 1984.

Andrea Brown Literary Agency

1076 Eagle Drive, Salinas, CA 93905
tel 831-422-5925
website www.andreabrownlit.com
President Andrea Brown, *Senior Agent* Laura Rennert, *Associate Agents* Kelly Sonnack, Caryn Wiseman, Jennifer Rofe, Jennifer Laughran, Jamie Weiss Chilton, Jennifer Mattson, Mary Kole

Exclusively all kinds of children's books. Represents both authors and illustrators.
   Submission details Email submissions only. See website for guidelines. Founded 1981.

Pema Browne Ltd

11 Tena Place, Valley Cottage, NY 10989
email ppbltd@optonline.net
website www.pemabrowneltd.com
President Pema Browne, *Vice President* Perry J. Browne

Fiction, non-fiction and juvenile books (home/ overseas 20%). Only published children's book

authors will be accepted for review. Will only review MSS if never sent out to publishers; no simultaneous submissions to other agents. Send query with sase; no phone, fax or email queries with attachments. Founded 1966.

Browne & Miller Literary Associates

(formerly Multimedia Product Development Inc.)
410 South Michigan Avenue, Suite 460, Chicago, IL 60605
tel 312-922-3063 *fax* 312-922-1905
email mail@browneandmiller.com
website www.browneandmiller.com
Contact Danielle Egan-Miller

General fiction and non-fiction (home 15%, overseas 20%). Select young adult projects. Works in conjunction with foreign agents. Will suggest revision; no reading fee. Founded 1971.

Maria Carvainis Agency Inc.*

1270 Avenue of the Americas, Suite 2320, New York, NY 10020
tel 212-245-6365 *fax* 212-245-7196
email mca@mariacarvainis.com
President & Literary Agent Maria Carvainis

Young adult fiction (home 15%, overseas 20%). Also handles adult fiction and non-fiction. No reading fee. Query first; no unsolicited MSS. No queries by fax or email. Works in conjunction with foreign, TV and movie agents.

The Chudney Agency

72 North State Road, Suite 501, Briarcliff Manor, NY 10510
tel/fax 914-488-5008
email steven@thechudneyagency.com
website www.thechudneyagency.com
Contact Steven Chudney

Children's books. Focuses particularly on picture books, middle-grade novels and teenage fiction. No unsolicited submissions for non-fiction chapter books, middle-grade or teenage novels. Not interested in board books or lift-the-flap books; fables, folklore, or traditional fairytales; poetry or 'mood pieces'; stories for 'all ages'; or heavy-handed message-driven stories. Looking for author/ illustrator (one individual), who can both write and illustrate picture books. They must really know and understand the prime needs and wants of the child reader.
   Submission details Submit full text; include 3–5 art samples (not originals), a brief biography, and a sase for return of material. Founded 2002.

The Doe Coover Agency

PO Box 668, Winchester, MA 01890
tel 781-721-6000 *fax* 781-721-6727
email info@doecooveragency.com
website www.doecooveragency.com

Contact Doe Coover (non-fiction), Colleen Mohyde (fiction), Amanda Lewis (children's)

Specialises in non-fiction: history, popular science, biography, social issues, cooking, gardening; also literary and commercial fiction, children's (home 15%, overseas 10%). No romance, fantasy, science fiction, poetry or screenplays. Email queries accepted. Founded 1985.

Curtis Brown Ltd*
10 Astor Place, New York, NY 10003
tel 212-473-5400
Ceo Timothy Knowlton, *President* Peter Ginsberg, *Contacts* Elizabeth Harding, Ginger Knowlton, Anna J. Webman

Fiction and non-fiction, juvenile, film and TV rights. No unsolicited MSS; query first with sase. No reading fee; no handling fees.

Liza Dawson Associates*
350 Seventh Avenue, Suite 2003, New York, NY 10001
email queryliza@lizadawsonassociates.com
website www.lizadawsonassociates.com
Contact Liza Dawson

Fiction and non-fiction for adults and children (home 15%, overseas 20%). Promotes books of Jewish interest. Send query with email address, sase and first 5pp of MS.

Sandra Dijkstra Literary Agency*
PMB 515, 1155 Camino Del Mar, Del Mar, CA 92014
tel 858-755-3115
website www.dijkstraagency.com
President Sandra Dijkstra, *Sub-agents* Elise Capron, Taryn Fagerness, Kevan Lyon, Jill Marsal, Kelly Sonnack

Young adult, middle-grade, picture books and graphic novels. Fiction and non-fiction (home 15%, overseas 20%). Works in conjunction with foreign and film agents. All submissions must include synopsis and sase or IRC. No reading fee. Founded 1981.

Dunham Literary, Inc.*
156 Fifth Avenue, Suite 823, New York, NY 10010–7002
email dunhamlit@yahoo.com
website www.dunhamlit.com
Contact Jennie Dunham

Children's books (home 15%, overseas 20%). Handles picture books, fiction for 5–8 and 9–12 year-olds and teenage fiction. Also handles adult literary fiction and non-fiction; 50% of list is for the children's market. Send query letter in first instance by post, not by fax or email. Do not send full MS. No reading fee. Founded 2000.

Dwyer & O'Grady Inc.
PO Box 790, Cedar Key, FL 32625–0790
tel 352-543-9307 *fax* 603-375-5373

website www.dwyerogrady.com
Agents Elizabeth O'Grady, Jeff Dwyer

Exclusively children's books (home 15%, overseas 20%). Represents both authors and illustrators. Small agency; not looking for new clients.

Dystel & Goderich Literary Management*
1 Union Square West, New York, NY 10003
tel 212-627-9100 *fax* 212-627-9313
website www.dystel.com
Contact Michael Bourret, Jim McCarthy

Children's fiction (home 15%, overseas 19%). Handles picture books, fiction for 5–8 and 9–12 year-olds, teenage fiction and series fiction. Looking for quality young adult fiction. Also handles adult fiction and non-fiction. Send a query letter with a synopsis and up to 50pp of sample MS. Will accept email queries. No reading fee. Will suggest revision.
Children's authors include Antonio Pagliarulo, Kelly Easton, Sara Zarr, Anne Rockwell, Bernadette Rossetti, Richelle Mead, Carrie Ryan. Founded 1994.

Educational Design Services LLC
5750 Bou Avenue, Ste 1508, N. Bethesda, MD 20852
email blinder@educationaldesignservices.com
website www.educationaldesignservices.com
Contact B. Linder

Specialises in educational texts for K–12 market (home 15%, overseas 25%). No picture books or fiction. Send query with sase, or send outline and one sample chapter by email or with sase for return of material. Founded 1981.

The Ethan Ellenberg Literary Agency*
548 Broadway, Suite 5E, New York, NY 10012
tel 212-431-4554 *fax* 212-941-4652
email agent@ethanellenberg.com
website www.ethanellenberg.com
President & Agent Ethan Ellenberg

Fiction and non-fiction (home 15%, overseas 20%). Commercial fiction: thrillers, mysteries, children's, romance, women's, ethnic, science fiction, fantasy and general fiction; also literary fiction with a strong narrative. Non-fiction: current affairs, health, science, psychology, cookbooks, new age, spirituality, pop-culture, adventure, true crime, biography and memoir. No scholarly works, poetry, short stories or screenplays.
 Will accept unsolicited MSS and seriously consider all submissions, including first-time writers. For fiction submit synopsis and first 3 chapters. For non-fiction send a proposal (outline, sample material, author CV, etc). For children's works send complete MS. Illustrators should send a representative selection of colour copies (no orginal artwork). Unable to return any material from overseas. For response include a sase with correct US postage. Submissions without a sase will receive only an email response if interested. Founded 1983.

Flannery Literary
1140 Wickfield Court, Naperville, IL 60563
tel 630-428-2682
Contact Jennifer Flannery

Specialises in children's and young adult, juvenile fiction and non-fiction (home 15%, overseas 20%). Send query letter by post in first instance. Founded 1992.

Barry Goldblatt Literary LLC*
320 Seventh Avenue, PMB 266, Brooklyn, New York, NY 11215
tel 718-832-8787 *fax* 718-832-5558
email query@bgliterary.com
website www.bgliterary.com
Contact Barry Goldblatt

Specialises in young adult and middle-grade fiction, but also handles picture book writers and illustrators. No non-fiction. Has a preference for quirky, offbeat work. Query only.

Ashley Grayson Literary Agency*
1342 18th Street, San Pedro, CA 90732
tel 310-548-4672
email graysonagent@earthlink.net
Contact Ashley Grayson, Carolyn Grayson

Commercial fiction and literary fiction for adults and children. Handles foreign rights. No unsolicited MSS. Submit query letter and first 3pp of MSS. No calls or queries. No reading fee.
Clients include Bruce Coville, J.B. Cheany, David Lubar, Christopher Pike. Established 1976.

The Greenhouse Literary Agency
11308 Lapham Drive, Oakton, VA 22124
tel 703-865-4990
email submissions@greenhouseliterary.com
website www.greenhouseliterary.com
Director Sarah Davies

Children's fiction from age 5 through to teen/young adult (USA/UK 15%, elsewhere 25%). Represents both US and UK authors. No picture books or non-fiction. No reading fee. Will suggest revision.
Submission details Queries by email only, see website for details. Founded 2008.

John Hawkins & Associates Inc.*
(formerly Paul R. Reynolds Inc.)
71 West 23rd Street, Suite 1600, New York, NY 10010
tel 212-807-7040 *fax* 212-807-9555
website www.jhalit.com
President John Hawkins, *Vice-President* William Reiss, *Foreign Rights* Moses Cardona, *Other Agents* Warren Frazier, Anne Hawkins

Fiction, non-fiction, young adult. No reading fee. Founded 1893.

JCA Literary Agency Inc.*
174 Sullivan Street, New York, NY 10012
tel 212-807-0888

email tom@jcalit.com, tony@jcalit.com
Contacts Tom Cushman, Tony Outhwait

Adult fiction, non-fiction and young adult. No unsolicited MSS; query first.

Barbara S. Kouts, Literary Agent*
PO Box 560, Bellport, NY 11713
tel 516-286-1278 *fax* 516-286-1538
email bkouts@aol.com
Owner Barbara S. Kouts

Fiction and non-fiction, children's (home 15%, overseas 20%). Works with overseas agents. No reading fee. No phone calls. Send query letter first. Founded 1980.

kt literary
9249 S. Broadway 200–543, Highlands Ranch, CO 80129
tel 720-344-4728
email contact@ktliterary.com
website www.ktliterary.com
Contact Kate Schafer Testerman

Primarily middle-grade and young adult fiction but no picture books; also adult commercial fiction and narrative non-fiction. Seeking 'brilliant, funny, original middle-grade and young adult fiction, both literary and commercial; witty women's fiction; pop-culture narrative non-fiction'. Email a query letter and the first 3pp of MS in the body of the email (no attachments). No snail mail.
Clients include Maureen Johnson, Ellen Booraem, S. Terrell French, Stephanie Perkins, Josie Bloss, Matthew Cody. Founded 2008.

Gina Maccoby Literary Agency*
PO Box 60, Chappaqua, NY 10514
tel 914-238-5630
email Query@Maccobylit.com
Contact Gina Maccoby

Specialises in children's books: fiction, non-fiction, picture books, MS/illustration packages for middle grade and young adult (home 15%, overseas 20–25%). All queries by email. No unsolicited submissions. Founded 1986.

McIntosh & Otis Inc.*
353 Lexington Avenue, New York, NY 10016
tel 212-687-7400 *fax* 212-687-6894
email info@mcintoshandotis.com
website www.mcintoshandotis.com
Head of Children's Dept Edward Necarsulmer IV

Fiction for 5–8 and 9–12 year-olds, teenage fiction, series fiction, poetry and non-fiction for children (home 15%, overseas 20%). Also handles adult fiction and non-fiction. No unsolicited MSS for novels; query first with outline, sample chapters and sase. No submissions by email. No reading fee. Will suggest revision. Founded 1928.

Barbara Markowitz Literary Agency
PO Box 41709, Los Angeles, CA 90041
Agents Barbara Markowitz, Judith Rosenthal
Children's fiction: middle grade, young adult (11–15

year-olds) and historical (home 15%, overseas 15%). Seeking contemporary and historical fiction 35,000–50,000 words for 8–11 and 11–15 year-olds. No fables, fantasy or fairy tales; no illustrated books; no sci-fi.

Submission details Send query letter with sase or outline with 3 sample chapters. Send sase for return of material. Founded 1980.

Mews Books
20 Bluewater Hill, Westport, CT 06880
tel 203-227-1836 *fax* 203-227-1144
email mewsbooks@aol.com
Agents Sidney B. Kramer, Fran Pollak

Children's fiction, non-fiction, picture books, middle-grade and young adult books (home 15%, overseas 20%). Seeking well-written books of professional quality with continuity of character and story.

Submission details Send query letter with sase or outline and 2 sample chapters by regular mail (no email). Send sase for return of material. Founded 1974.

William Morris Agency Inc.*
(incorporating the Writers Shop, formerly Virginia Barber Literary Agency)
1325 Avenue of the Americas, New York, NY 10019
tel 212-903-1304 *fax* 212-903-1304
website www.wma.com
Senior VPs Jennifer Rudolph Walsh, Suzanne Gluck, Mel Berger, Jay Mandel, Tracy Fisher

General fiction and non-fiction (home 15%, overseas 20%, performance rights 15%). Will suggest revision. No reading fee.

Erin Murphy Literary Agency
2700 Woodlands Village, Suite 300–458, Flagstaff, AZ 86001–7127
tel 928-525-2056
website http://emliterary.com
President Erin Murphy, *Associate Agent* Ammi-Joan Paquette

Children's books: fiction, non-fiction, picture books, middle grade, young adult (home 15%, overseas 20%). No unsolicited queries or submissions; considers material only by referral or through personal contact such as at conferences. Founded 1999.

Muse Literary Management
189 Waverly Place, Suite 4, New York, NY 10014–3135
tel 212-925-3721
email MuseLiteraryMgmt@aol.com
website www.museliterary.com
Agent Deborah Carter

Children's and adult fiction and non-fiction (home 15%, overseas 20%). Looking for picture books, middle grade and young adult novels that bring something new to their bookselling category. Prefers writers who interact with the age group they are writing for. Originality and imagination are treasured. Actively persuing new writers with formal training and published authors who want to try something new. Prospective authors should be receptive to editorial feedback and willing to revise. Interested in intelligent books: no vulgar subject matter or books that copy others. Prefers queries by email with no attachments. If no response within 2 weeks, query again.

Alison Picard, Literary Agent
PO Box 2000, Cotuit, MA 02635
tel 508-477-7192
email ajpicard@aol.com

Adult fiction and non-fiction, children's and young adult (15%). No short stories, poetry, plays, screenplays or sci-fi/fantasy. No reading fee. Founded 1985.

Pippin Properties Inc.
155 East 38th Street, Suite 2H, New York, NY 10016
tel 212-338-9310 *fax* 212-338-9579
email info@pippinproperties.com
website www.pippinproperties.com
Contact Holly M. McGhee, Joan Slattery, Elena Mechlin

Exclusively children's book authors and artists (home 15%, overseas 25%), from picture books to middle-grade and young adult novels. Query with sase or by email. Founded 1998.

Susan Schulman, A Literary Agency*
454 West 44th Street, New York, NY 10036
tel 212-713-1633 *fax* 212-581-8830
email schulman@aol.com

Agents for negotiation in all markets (with co-agents) of fiction, general non-fiction, children's books, academic and professional works, and associated subsidiary rights including plays and film (home 15%, UK 7.5%, overseas 20%). No reading fee. Return postage required.

Stimola Literary Studio, Inc.*
308 Livingston Court, Edgewater, NJ 07020
tel/fax 201-945-9353
email info@stimolaliterarystudio.com
website www.stimolaliterarystudio.com
Contact Rosemary B. Stimola

Children's fiction and non-fiction, from preschool to young adult (home 15%, overseas 20%).
Submission details Most clients come via referral. Founded 1997.

S©ott Treimel NY*
434 Lafayette Street, New York, NY 10003
tel 212-505-0664

email jmc.st.ny@verizon.net
website www.scotttreimelny.com
President and founder Scott Treimel, *Contact* John M. Cusick

Exclusively children's books: middle-grade, young adult novels and MS/illustration packages by artist/illustrator only. No picture book MSS (home 15–20%, overseas 20–25%). Interested in seeing first chapter books, and middle-grade and teenage fiction. No religious books. Considers queries exclusively via an online submission form. Blog: ScottTreimelNY.blogspot.com. Founded 1995.

Ralph M. Vicinanza Ltd*

303 West 18th Street, New York, NY 10011-4440
tel 212-924-7090 *fax* 212-691-9644
Contacts Ralph Vicinanza, Christopher Lotts, Christopher Schelling, Adam Lefton

Fiction: literary, popular (especially science fiction, fantasy, thrillers), children's. Non-fiction: history, business, science, biography, popular culture. Foreign rights specialists. New clients by professional recommendation only. No unsolicited MSS.

Writers House LLC*

21 West 26th Street, New York, NY 10010
tel 212-685-2400 *fax* 212-685-1781
London agent: Ground Floor Flat, 24 Harvist Road, London NW6 6SH
020-8960 2966, 7534 494814
website www.writershouse.com
President Amy Berkower, *Juvenile & Young Agents* Stephen Malk, Susan Cohen, Ken Wright, Rebecca Sherman, Jodi Reamer

Fiction and non-fiction, including all rights; film and TV rights. No screenplays or software. Send a one-page letter in the first instance, saying what's wonderful about your book, what it is about and why you are the best person to write it. No reading fee. Founded 1974.

Illustrating for children
Creating graphic novels

Raymond Briggs has created many graphic novels and here he describes the process.

Book writers have such an easy time of it. They sit down, write their book and when they come to the end they send it off to the publisher. It might be long, it might be short, the publisher doesn't mind.

The writer needs no materials or equipment. He can do it all with a pencil and a Woolworth's pad. Even the typing may be done for him. Unlike the illustrator, he needs no paints, crayons, T-squares, set squares, brushes, dividers, spray cans, handmade paper and mounting boards, light boxes, cutting tables, guillotines, type scales, magnifier lamps, wall-to-wall display boards and masses of space. The writer can scribble it all in bed. (They often do.)

Drawing the book

For the picture book illustrator, when he has finished the writing, that is the easy bit done. His true task then begins.

First he has to design the book. Picture books have to be exactly 32 pages, not 33 or 31. This includes prelims. So the text has to be divided into fewer than 16 spreads. On rare occasions, the publisher may allow 40 pages, or on even rarer occasions 48, though this allowance may contain 'self-ends' which take up eight pages. (This is too technical to explain to book writers.)

Then, the illustrator becomes a typographer. He casts off the MSS, chooses a suitable font, decides on the type size, the measure and the leading, and has it set. Surprisingly, some writers I have met know nothing about typography. Some don't even know the name of the font their own book is set in! Some have never even set foot in a printer's.

If the book is strip cartoon with speech bubbles, the task is even greater as each speech bubble has to be individually designed. The size and shape of it is part of its expressive quality and once the bubble is finalised the illustrator becomes a hand-lettering expert and letters in, possibly many hundreds of words, trying to maintain a consistent style over many days' work. In America strip cartoon work is divided amongst several people: writer, pencilling-in artist, inker-in, and letterer. In England we are made of sterner stuff – 'blood, toil, tears and sweat' and we 'graphic novelists' do it all.

The illustrator then makes a dummy (a blank book) with the correct number of pages and of the exact size. If he is well established and commands respect from the publisher, the publisher may have a dummy made for him – but you need to be at least 60 years old to be granted this privilege. (You might have to show them your Bus Pass.) He then cuts up the type proofs (which used to be called 'galleys') and sticks them onto the dummy, imagining the pictures on the page as he does so. Again, for strip cartoons it is much more complicated – you have to consider not just what text goes on each spread but how many frames the text is to be divided amongst, and what size and shape the frames are to be.

This brings us to the next stage: designing the 'grid', i.e. how many rows of frames per page and the number of frames in each row there are to be. Places where small frames give way to a big picture, either vignetted or bled off, will be determined by the text itself, not only in terms of space but also by the feeling the text is trying to express.

Creating the action

When all this is done, it is time to stop book designing and start making the 'film'. You become the director. Who comes on from the left and who from the right? A slight nuisance is that the character on the left is the one who has to speak first. What are the characters doing and thinking and feeling? We have their words, but is there a subtext? Can this be expressed by body language? Is one of them angrily scrubbing the floor, whilst the other gazes moodily out of the window?

You then become the art director, designing the sets. Where does the scene take place? Indoors or outdoors? In the garden or in the street? What does a 1930s kitchen look like? How big is the room? What is the view from the window?

You also have to be the costume designer and the lighting designer. What would they be wearing at the time? Is it winter or summer? What were overcoats and hats like then? What did they wear on the beach? Should it be daylight or artificial light in this scene? What exactly was the look of gaslight? Does it need a dark ominous light or a happy morning light?

Then as the cameraman you have to decide where to shoot from. Close-up, long shot, or middle distance? Both characters in shot or one off-screen? Perhaps a speech bubble stays in the frame but the speaker is unseen, through a doorway or simply out of shot. Shall it be a high view looking down on the scene or a low angle looking up? It all depends on what the action is trying to convey.

Finally, you have to become the actor and feel yourself inside the character when you're drawing it. This is the essence of good narrative illustration. It is an odd bit of psychology. You have to be mentally in two places at once. One part of you is inside character, feeling what it is like to be huddled and running in the pouring rain, the other part of your brain is detachedly looking at this figure from a certain point of view, taking note of perspective. 'Ah yes, the lower leg will be foreshortened from this angle; we're looking down on the thigh and on the back; we can't see his face as his head is down and his arm is up. Will we see the sole of the shoe that is raised or is it edge on?'

The lucky writer need know nothing about human and animal anatomy, perspective, drawing, line tone or colour. All they have to do is write down some words! It's a doddle.

I wish I could do it.

Raymond Briggs is creator of *The Snowman*, *Fungus the Bogeyman*, *Father Christmas* and many other characters and stories for children, and *When the Wind Blows* and *Ethel and Ernest* for adults. Since leaving art school in 1957 he has been a writer and illustrator, mainly of children's books. He has written plays for the stage and radio and a few 'adult' books. In 2004 he designed the Christmas stamps for the Royal Mail, and was made a Fellow of the Royal Society of Literature, but his proudest achievement is going on the radio programme *Desert Island Discs*, twice. His fansite is www.toonhound.com/briggs.htm.

See also...
• *Notes from a successful children's author and illustrator*, page 84
• *Writing and illustrating picture books*, page 244

Notes from the first Children's Laureate

Quentin Blake was the first Children's Laureate (1999–2001).

I started life – my life as someone who does pictures to appear in print, that is – by doing illustrations and cartoons for magazines. It wasn't so long, however, before I got the idea that I would like to be on my own between two covers; or at least on my own with an author. There were various reasons. One was that I wanted to organise a sequence of images that would follow a narrative; another was to get into a wider range of subject matter, a wider range of mood and atmosphere than was supplied by humorous commentary on current everyday life. I had been trained as a teacher, and I thought it was possible that, as the humour I had to offer was mainly visual, children might appreciate it as much as adults. The prospect of children's books was an attractive one, but I had no idea at all about how to begin. In the event I asked a friend, John Yeoman, if he would write something for me to illustrate. He could read Russian and it was a sample Russian folk-tale that he offered to me, which I illustrated, and which we submitted to Faber and Faber. We fell on our feet. I think perhaps we had hoped for a picture book, but Faber said that if we could find another handful of stories they would publish them – and in due course they became a book called *A Drink of Water*.

So we were very lucky. We were spared the frustrating (and generally unavoidable) round of submissions, and we had something printed. And there is nothing, I suspect, so reassuring to a prospective commissioning editor as to see drawings actually in print.

Now (50 years later), holding the *Children's Writers' & Artists' Yearbook* in my hand, it's clear to me that, if we hadn't been as lucky as we were, how useful such a volume as this would have been. It has two great virtues. One, of course, is the wealth of information it contains. On the very first page of *Children's book publishers UK and Ireland* we discover that the Andersen Press, under the guidance of our friend Klaus Flugge, requires that the text for a picture book should be less than 1,000 words long – and doesn't want to receive it by email. Half a dozen pages later we discover that Faber and Faber won't look at unsolicited manuscripts – so we wouldn't have got far with them nowadays.

The other is an impressive raft of notes, comments and advice from practitioners in every aspect of the business. It's as good as a correspondence course in the creation of children's books. And as well as the sage advice of such examples as Raymond Briggs and Tony Ross, there are more recent personal reactions. I was fascinated to read accounts of self-discovery from Lauren Child, David Lucas and Oliver Jeffers. The great advantage of such a personal approach is that the advice you find there is not merely prescriptive. In fact, though there is useful advice to be had, nothing is certain. Conventional wisdom would no doubt say that a readership of eight and nine year-olds wouldn't want to be given a heroine years younger than themselves, nor would that age group want to read about a middle-aged bachelor trying to persuade a middle-aged woman to marry him. But Matilda is a huge success, and *Esio Trot* does pretty well too. The book that you now hold in your hand is a wonderful guidebook, but it's still nice to think that none of us know quite where we may be going.

Quentin Blake has always made his living as an illustrator, as well as teaching for over 20 years at the Royal College of Art, where he was Head of Illustration 1978–86. His first drawings were published in *Punch* when he was 16 and he continued to draw for *Punch*, the *Spectator* and other magazines over many years, and entered the world of children's books with *A Drink of Water* by John Yeoman in 1960. He has also collaborated with other writers such as Russell Hoban, Joan Aiken, Michael Rosen and, most famously, Roald Dahl. He has also illustrated classic children's books, and created much-loved characters of his own, including Mister Magnolia and Mrs Armitage. Since the 1990s Quentin Blake has curated shows in, among other places, the National Gallery, the British Library and the Musée du Petit Palais in Paris. His work can be seen in the wards and public spaces of several London hospitals and mental health units in England and Wales. His books have won numerous major prizes and awards. In 1999 he was appointed the first ever Children's Laureate and his book *Laureate's Progress* (Jonathan Cape 2002) records aspects of his two-year tenure.

See also...
- *Notes from a Children's Laureate*, page 75
- *Who do children's authors write for?*, page 87
- *Notes from Jacqueline Wilson*, page 78
- *Writing books to read aloud*, page 109

Notes from a successful illustrator

David Lucas shares his journey to being a successful illustrator and writer.

As a writer and illustrator I have been a slow starter. Ten years ago I was working in a shop and wondering if I'd ever achieve anything as an artist. I had been doing some illustration work for greeting cards and for a design company, but suddenly both companies went bust. There was, at the same time, huge turmoil in my personal life. It was one of those years when everything seems to go wrong at once. My life felt like a smoking ruin.

Since leaving college five years before, I'd been just going round in circles with no clear sense of direction – trying one thing after another, and the harder I tried the less I seemed to achieve. I had always dreamed of doing well as an artist, but I was actually so afraid of getting nowhere, so afraid of failure, that I couldn't stop chasing my tail. But until I stopped, until I came to a halt and calmly faced the fact of having failed in my efforts, I couldn't *begin* to succeed in anything. I had been in flight from my true self for years – working hard to maintain an elaborate disguise (I was the only one who was fooled), living in a whirl of activity, unable to be still and afraid to look into my heart.

But I had known exactly who I was as a teenager: I was a sentimental romantic, living in a world of my own. I spent most of my time drawing and writing, inventing characters and fantasy worlds and reading fairy tales and legends and books on magic and mysticism. My pictures were decorative and intricate, and I loved medieval art. I felt as if my life was full of meaning and purpose, that there was a magical force ordering the universe and I was convinced of the reality of the presence of God. I had encouragement and support from my family to be creative and I was allowed the freedom to be as peculiar as I liked. But I was isolated and withdrawn and, beyond my immediate family, I was more or less friendless.

Going to college broke the spell of my sealed world, and suddenly I had a lot of catching up to do. I badly wanted to fit in.

I made new friends, I did my best to be fashionable, and I forgot all about God and magic and fairy tales. I shuddered to think of the misfit I'd been. I rejected that teenage version of myself. I wanted to be cool. My pictures became deliberately trashy and fragmented, and I stopped writing stories.

How could I write stories? Stories only make sense if they are whole, with a beginning, middle and an end. I wanted novelty not wholeness. I cultivated an ironic take on everything – often not knowing if I was ever sincere about anything. I hid from *true* feeling – I didn't want to be seen to truly care.

Of course I was still just as emotional and sentimental, just as much a romantic, as I had always been. But I hid the truth of who I was as best I could because it only seemed to cause me trouble and embarrassment with people. Friends tried to tell me that I was fooling no one but myself, and I remember a college tutor saying to me, 'You shouldn't despise what comes naturally – it doesn't come naturally to everyone.' I half listened.

Over the next few years I drew constantly but more and more angrily and emptily, and I couldn't avoid the fact that my pictures were unappealing to people. When I was a teenager the few people who saw my pictures had responded so warmly, but now I knew that no one liked what I was doing at all. I did have plenty of friends – I certainly wasn't isolated

– but I had no idea who I was any more. It was harder and harder to pretend that all was well.

When at last everything fell apart I had to just stop. I had forgotten how to be alone and I'd never been any good at doing *nothing*. I needed to do both. I had to find a point of stillness, of calm stability, and just listen and look and not hide anymore. I spent months doing very little – just sitting staring out of the window or going for long walks. I had been keeping a journal for a few years, in a bid to make sense of things, but it was a mess of angry scrawls. Now I began writing clearly, neatly and slowly, in well-formed sentences. I began to try and define who I was. As I put into words what exactly I was best at, and what I uniquely had to offer, I realised that I was writing a *story* of who I was – the story of the conflict in my heart, the battle between having to be true to myself but not wanting to be alone.

And if I was writing a story, how did I want it to end? What did I really want to achieve? What were my true goals? Our lives are short, and our abilities are limited: fear of being defined, of admitting both our strengths and limitations, is the fear of death. Deep down I was still just a child, thinking I could do anything and be anything, and live forever. But by wanting everything I had ended up with nothing. I tried to imagine how I'd use my time if I knew I had only a couple of years to live. I knew that, above all, I wanted to tell *stories*. Writing a story that was satisfyingly complete, making a book that expressed the truth of who I was, *and* that connected with people – that would be the happy ending I was looking for. I set myself the simple goal of making the most beautiful books I could in whatever time I'd been given. It was an act of faith that if I spoke from my heart I would reach an audience.

My first book, *Halibut Jackson*, was about finding myself again, about being found out – by fate – being forced to drop the disguise, and be myself. And stepping out from behind that disguise was magically liberating. I felt like Scrooge on Christmas morning! I could *feel* again. I could forget about fashion and about trying to be cool, I could be openly sentimental and romantic. I could admit my love of nature and that I didn't much like the modern world. And I could once again draw fantastical pictures, and write fairy tales.

Of course the meandering path I had taken meant my work had broadened out and I was able to integrate some of those influences, but deep down I knew I was precisely the person I had been aged 14. And because I knew who I was again, and I knew all my ideas came from one source, I could be freely inventive, telling whimsical stories and making decorative pictures – drawing imaginary lands, fanciful architecture, unlikely costumes, fantastical flowers and blossoming trees full of bright-winged birds.

I found inspiration again in the medieval art I had loved as a teenager, and in folk art. And I realised that the art I loved was made by people who believed in magic, who believed in gods and spirits, whose work was decorative not just to be beautiful but because pattern-making is like weaving a magic spell of connectedness – the connectedness of all Creation.

As an artist and a storyteller, it is my job to connect: to reach out to an audience, to entertain people. It just took me a long time to see that there should be no conflict between being an entertainer and being true to myself.

For the last eight years I've made my living from children's books alone. I don't earn very much but I do OK, and my books are sold all around the world. Mostly I've written and illustrated picture books, but I have had one longer story published – an illustrated fable for both adults and children – and I'm working on a fantasy novel for teenagers which is a much more ambitious narrative.

This is an exciting time in children's books – a fertile time for new ideas and for new forms that haven't yet got a name. Publishers are open to any combination of words and pictures – from picture books to graphic novels and anything in between.

But of course the all-important thing is having a good story to tell.

Most stories are about emotional conflict – and the best stories are about the heart in conflict with itself, being torn in two directions. All my stories are autobiographical. I consciously use my own personal problems as a resource, as raw material to refine in order to make stories. (And luckily I do seem to have plenty of material.) For me, the germ of a story idea is a knot of dark energy, an inner conflict that I'm struggling to resolve, or at least understand. But I know that the deeper I look into my heart, the more I find that I share with everyone else. We all face more or less the same problems, we have to cope with the same sources of tension in our lives, the same kinds of inner conflict. Deep down we are all the same – our connectedness to one another is a hard fact not an airy, idealistic notion.

Stories work because people crave order and meaning and recognition, they want to recognise the same patterns of experience, the same inner struggles that they have felt themselves and they want to be offered the hope of a resolution, and if not always exactly a happy ending then some clear sense of completion and fulfilment. I felt torn between being true to myself and yet not wanting to feel alone. But this story at least ends happily.

David Lucas lives and works in Lewes, Sussex. His first book as author and illustrator, *Halibut Jackson* (Andersen Press 2003), was a 'Best Children's Book of 2004' in *Publishers' Weekly* in the USA. In 2008 he was chosen as one of the UK's Best New Illustrators by Booktrust. His website is www.davidlucas.org.uk.

See also...

- *Creating graphic novels*, page 227
- *Presenting your portfolio to a publisher*, page 237
- *Eight great tips to get your picture book published*, page 240
- *Writing and illustrating picture books*, page 244
- *The amazing picture book story*, page 248

Finding your own style

The 'style' of a good illustrator shines through no matter what the nature of the artwork is. Emily Gravett tells the tale of how she found her style.

When I saw that the theme of this article was 'finding your own style' it immediately brought back memories of my days at Brighton University where I studied illustration.

Not because university was the place that I found my own style, but because it was the place where I spent so much time, energy (and tears) searching for it. What I discovered was that, sadly, finding my own style wasn't like supermarket shopping. I couldn't just go to Aisle G and pay £10.99, or 50 sleepless nights, or my firstborn, etc and come away with a nice box of 'Gravett Style' (preferably tastefully packaged . . . I was an art student after all!).

So this is the story of how I *did* find my style.

I was the child of two talented and arty people. I had grown up with more than one set of coloured pencils and the expectation that I would do my (art-based) A levels and go straight on to art college. Unfortunately (for my parents) teenage rebellion hit me hard, and I didn't even get halfway through my first year of A-levels. I left sixth form, and home, on a sunny day with only a rucksack on my back, a lovely set of dreadlocks and a new and wonderful feeling of complete freedom. I liked the feeling of freedom so much that I spent the next eight years living in a bus as a new age traveller. During those years, thoughts of careers and job fulfilment were the last thing on my mind. The minutiae of living on the road absorbed much of each day. When we weren't being evicted, my partner and I spent our time cooking, cleaning, fetching water and wood, digging holes and a thousand other jobs that living in ancient vehicles with very little money and no plumbing or electricity involve.

I also drew. The big advantage of living in a bus is that the view from the window changes a lot, and so I could sit and draw the world outside from the comfort of my own home with a cup of tea and my slippers on. (So not that different from now!)

Life changed after I gave birth to my daughter. Although being dirty had been somewhat a badge of honour for my partner and me, I wasn't so keen for our daughter to grow up being spat at in public. So after nearly a year of searching we eventually found a small cottage to rent in rural Wales. We parked the bus in the garden and went about setting up the idyllic life. A vegetable plot, cosy fires, and time to play and watch our (lovely clean) daughter grow up. It should have been perfect, but somehow it wasn't.

Horses got in and trampled the vegetables, the fire smoked, and the time to play turned into hours of boredom in an isolated area without the community of travellers we were used to. Living in a house was more expensive than in the bus so my partner started working. I found that the days stretched emptily before me. Our daughter wasn't the content little baby we'd envisaged and cried and cried (and then cried some more). The only thing that seemed to pacify her (and me) was endless readings, and re-readings of her picture books. I spent on average about four hours a day on the sofa with her reading. We had to put up new shelves to house her expanding picture book collection!

She was turning the pages to Jez Alborough's *Where's My Teddy?* long before she could talk! I loved the books, and I loved our hours together on the sofa reading (well. . . until my voice went – which it did frequently!) It was often the only time when I felt like I was succeeding at being a parent. The more we read, the more I started to really look at the books. I began to notice the way individual authors and illustrators used shape/colour/text and the structure of the book to communicate their ideas, and started to wonder if I could do the same.

About this time my partner brought home a prospectus for the local community college. He'd had enough of working for minimum wage and wanted to train as a plumber. Looking through the prospectus I saw that they had an art foundation course. I applied, got a place, and loved it. Within the first week a fantasy began to shape in my mind, which developed into a 'Master Plan'. We would up-sticks and move somewhere that I could do an illustration degree. I won't bore you with the details of the following year, but it involved a lot of hard work, frustration, sleepless nights and worry sprinkled with large doses of excitement of the type I'd not experienced since the day I left home.

It wasn't easy, but eventually I got myself a place at Brighton University. We packed up our belongings, waved goodbye to the cottage and the bus, and set off to start our new life.

It wasn't what I expected. I had somehow imagined that at university there would be a lot of teaching and that drawing would be central, but I think in common with most universities the course was much more self directed and conceptual. I struggled. The first year was the worst. We were asked to tear down any notion of what we did – or where we were going work-wise. Often tutors would examine the back of artwork, or wax lyrical over a squiggle in a sketchbook rather than the project we'd just spent the previous six weeks slaving over. By the end of the first year I felt totally disillusioned and that my work had lost any merit and individuality it might have once had. I felt I was constantly trying to chase the approval of the tutors, and failing.

But by far the worst parts of my first year at university were the class crits. For anyone lucky enough never to have experienced one, a 'crit' (short for critique) is when the class gets together and looks at each other's work to give constructive criticism with the aim of helping their fellow students' progress. The crits on my foundation year had been frightening (mainly because I knew I'd have to stand up and explain my work in front of the class – public speaking wasn't my strong point!), but university crits were frightening in a whole different way! The most positive thing that could be hoped for in a class crit was disinterested disdain, but more often than not it felt like a competition in nastiness. They were HORRIBLE!

At the end of the first year we were set the project of illustrating a selection of letters from Edward Gorey's ABC *The Gashleycrumb Tinies*, an alphabet of children's deaths. I'd never seen Edward Gorey's work before (and avoided looking at it until after the project), but was excited by the narrative. I really enjoyed myself, and eventually finished a piece of work that I was pleased with. It felt like I was heading in the right direction at last! I went to the end-of-project crit scared but hopeful. The crit was an all-day, whole class affair (i.e. the worst kind). They started at ten o'clock in the morning, and didn't finish until after five. Needless to say my project went down like a lead balloon!

The comment that still (quite vividly) sticks in my mind was 'it looks the same as all your other work' to which I retorted that although it was recognisably my 'style' I disagreed that it was like anything else I'd produced that year. This opened the floodgates, and the tutor informed me that developing 'style' too early was dangerous for an illustrator.

After that I'm ashamed to say that I swore, and then cried. To which was added (fairly, I think in this case) the observation that I also don't take criticism well. I went home and stomped and ranted (and cried some more) and vowed never to go back to university again (me, not take criticism well?!) At this point my lovely patient partner who had just moved 300 miles and was struggling to support us by unblocking nasty things from strangers' u-bends produced a set of drain rods, and told me there was always another option.

So of course I went back, but it did make me think long and hard about style, and what it means to me. That crit was a turning point for me at university. It forced me to sit down and examine exactly what I was doing, and I discovered that what I was doing was everything that the tutors asked me to, without considering if it was something that interested me, or was right for me. I'd spent the whole year thinking that if I did exactly what they asked, that my work would improve, but without hearing that all I really was being asked to do was to think. From that day on I listened to all their advice, and I thought about all their advice, but I also thought about what was right for my work and me. I decided to follow the avenues that excited me. I started to spend a lot of time studying the structure of books and how the structure relates to the contents. For example I made a concertina book about an accordionist, and a cautionary tale of playing with fire inside a box of matches. I was lucky that my university had a well-equipped bookbinding department where we were taught to make books properly. It's something that I still love to do, and often make a few hand-bound copies of my books. I also relaxed my drawing, and let myself draw any way I wanted to. If drawing wasn't right for whatever I was working on I found something that was. I started to gauge the success of a project not by what the tutors thought but what *I* thought, and how much pleasure it had given me.

Looking back, I think I probably misunderstood the tutor on that day of the bad crit. I think that what he meant when he was so derisive about 'style' was purposefully setting out to create a particular 'look' in your work, to follow fashion or to try to be different. I agree that this is a bad thing. Pretending to be something you're not is never going to keep you satisfied for long. When I use the word 'style' I mean it more as a fingerprint that shines through and makes each piece of work recognisably belong to its creator, whether the work is written, painted, or doodled on the back of an envelope with a biro! To me style is a subconscious expression of who you are, rather than what you are trying to be, and is as individual as your own handwriting. I think that an individual's style is just an outward sign of their personality, and personality is shaped by the experiences you've already had in your life, and will continue to develop with every triumph, catastrophe, and evening spent watching *Big Brother* with a cup of tea . . .

So that's the story of how I found my style, not after all at university (although that's maybe where I recognised it) but somewhere in the 30 years before that.

I still haven't worked out if all that self doubt and gazing at squiggles was a necessary part of the whole process of becoming an illustrator. I don't think there's any magic formula that must be followed for success. Like style, and the process of discovering your own, I'm sure it's an individual journey. For me the three years spent studying provided the time I needed to think, draw, and develop, and most importantly to realise that I already had my own style. As do you!

Emily Gravett won the Macmillan Prize for Illustration for *Wolves*, which was published in 2005 and also won many other prizes. Her most recent books are *Monkey and Me* and *The Rabbit Problem* (Macmillan Children's Books 2010).

Presenting your portfolio to a publisher

Identifying an appropriate publisher for your work is the first step to gaining a commission for illustration. Val Brathwaite outlines how to present your samples and approach a publisher.

The best way to start when deciding how to show your work to publishers is to research the market. Think about the type of illustration you would like to do and the areas of publishing that appeal to you. Take some time to look at the different publishers and the kinds of books they publish and where your work would be suitable. Research the styles of illustration that are selling: visit specialist children's bookshops (see page 71) or bookshops with a good children's department to examine a wide variety of books.

Once you have identified the publishers you feel are most appropriate for your work, make a list of the ones to contact. This *Yearbook* contains pretty much all the contact details you'll need. If a particular listing doesn't include the name of the person to send your submission to, then call the publisher to find out. This could be the Art Director, Art Editor, Designers or a specific name. If your work crosses over into both children's and adult publishing, you should send your work to both departments. It is also very important to find out how each publisher prefers samples to be supplied, i.e. by email, CD or colour copies. Always check this because it will vary from publisher to publisher. It really helps if you're able to arrange an appointment to see someone in person, as good advice and feedback on your work will stand you in good stead for future submissions. Whatever you do, don't drop off your folder expecting it to be viewed unless you have made a prior arrangement – chances are it won't be and, even worse, it might get lost! And never spontaneously drop in to a publisher on the off chance there'll be someone willing to see you. It won't happen so always phone or email for an appointment first.

Presenting your work

It might sound obvious but always select the best work from your portfolio. Show the work you feel happy and confident with – not the stuff you don't feel strongly about! And don't include too much – usually10–15 pieces are sufficient. If you have a variety of styles, show a selection of work. For example, if you work in colour as well as in black and white line then show samples of both, and if your illustration style works for both children's and adult books or you have a different style for older age group books, show this too. It can take some time to break into the children's market so if your work lends itself to adult publishing, editorial and/or advertising, look to cross over into these markets. It all adds to gaining all round experience and further developing your style. Many well-known children's illustrators have started in other areas of illustration.

And it goes without saying, give due thought to how your work is presented – you are an artist after all. Clean and well-presented work shows that you are organised and proud of your work. A good quality portfolio with plastic compartments for each sample looks very neat and is easy to view.

Picture books

If you want to break into the picture book market and think you have a good idea, conduct a thorough research of which houses are publishing the type of book where it would fit. If it is a novelty book, make sure the publishers you approach have a novelty list. There is no point sending in an idea to a publisher which doesn't publish novelty books as they won't start a new list just to accommodate your idea! Don't waste your time making basic mistakes like this – ensure you are targeting the right publishers otherwise it's effort and expense down the drain. When presenting ideas for a picture book, a few sample illustrations are adequate along with the text, which can be printed onto A4 paper. Send jpegs or PDFs by email if that's what the publisher wants. If you have created a full 'book dummy' with illustrations and text in place as a college project or at some other point in your career, be prepared to make some changes to suit a particular publisher. Adapting each presentation to cater to each individual house may be more time consuming, but it will certainly increase your chances of getting a deal.

Each publisher will have a different format in mind as they have their own ways and ideas of making a book a financially viable investment. Also be aware that picture book publishers will be looking to sell co-edition rights and so will be keen to know that potential new books have an international appeal and that the art is as universal as possible.

If you are primarily an illustrator and don't write text to accompany your drawings, pay extra attention to the presentation of your work. And be encouraged as publishers are always on the lookout to find great illustrators for authors and need many different styles of illustration. But there is a downside – picture book publishing is one of the most difficult areas to break into, as there is fierce competition and chances are you'll be turned down several times before you get a break. So be prepared to keep trying and be patient. Having lots of experience in researching the market, submitting your work, and talking to publishers and getting feedback will help you to continually develop your work to suit the needs of your target audience.

Preschool books

The preschool market is very diverse, ranging from simple concept board books to pop-up novelty and interactive books. These ideas can come from an illustrator, author or the publisher. Submitting an idea for this category as a rough dummy, a more finished spread together with the text is adequate.

Young illustrated fiction

Black and white line art is a good way into the book illustration market. Many children's publishers have illustrated fiction lists for young readers which carry very varied styles of illustration, from a fun cartoon look to more delicate or decorative illustrations. If you are able to work in line as well as colour this will help to broaden your prospect of being commissioned by a publisher.

Older fiction and teen fiction

The fiction market for older readers usually requires cover illustrations only. Cover art tends to be one-off commissions, unless you are lucky enough to be asked to illustrate a series. Undertaking cover work is a very good way to build up your contacts and it can allow you to carry out single jobs with several different publishers simultaneously. Again it is important to research the market and be sure to target only those publishers which your work will suit, for example there is no point in presenting illustrations to a publisher which only uses photographs.

Promotional material

Promotional material can be a very good way of introducing yourself, and postcards are a great approach. If the person you send a sample to likes your work, you'll be put on file and hopefully contacted in the future. Or better than that, if your postcard arrives on their desk at the right time, you might get called straightaway! It's a convenient, compact and non-intrusive way of showing an example of your work and leaving a (hopefully) memorable sample along with your contact details when approaching several publishers at once. A website is also an excellent way of showcasing your illustrations and is easy for people to view your work. Including the address on any printed samples you send out or emailing a link is helpful.

Follow up

Fingers crossed, when you send your postcards, email your jpegs or conclude your face-to-face meeting with the publisher of your choice, you'll secure a commission/deal. However, it's quite likely that you might not get any response or be waiting for a reply for a long time. If your work was received positively the first time, then follow this up say, six months later with any relevant new work you've produced in the interim. A gentle reminder can help push things along if you're sure your work is right for that publisher. There's every chance that publisher may not have had any suitable work for you the first time you approached them but six months down the line a project may have arisen.

Never be afraid to contact a publisher after a reasonable amount of time (3–4 months) has passed. In-house teams are always busy and constantly working to deadlines and seeing new people all the time, so follow-up is important to increasing your chances of securing work with them. But be sensible and patient about it: don't call right away as the publisher will need time to consider your work, talk to others in the department and see what work they have which will match your talents. A pushy approach can be all it takes for the publisher to dismiss you as a potential freelance illustrator – regardless of the quality of your work. Never forget the degree of competition there is out there and the need for you to be professional, reliable and easy to work with.

And last but by no means least, the main thing is don't give up. If you really want to illustrate for the children's book market and believe your work matches the needs of particular publishers then you must keep trying. It can take a long time to establish yourself but if you're good enough, you'll get there.

Good luck!

Val Brathwaite is the Design Director at Bloomsbury Children's Books.

See also...

- *Creating graphic novels*, page 227
- *Notes from a successful illustrator*, page 231
- *Eight great tips to get your picture book published*, page 240
- *Writing and illustrating picture books*, page 244
- *The amazing picture book story*, page 248

Eight great tips to get your picture book published

Tony Ross gives some sound advice for illustrators and writers of children's picture books.

I have always had the uncomfortable feeling that if I can get published, anyone can. A belief that being published is something that only happens to other people, holds some very good writers and illustrators back.

Assuming you have drawings – or a story – to offer, there are several ways to go about it. Probably the best way is to have a publishing house in the family! Failing that, all is not lost.

Work can be sent directly to a publisher's office. Most editors receive a good amount of unsolicited work, so be patient with them for a reply. A stamped addressed envelope for its return is always appreciated, bearing in mind that the majority of work submitted is refused. At the beginning of a career, refusal is quite normal and a great deal about yourself and your talent can be gleaned from this experience. Sometimes, advice gained at this stage can change your future.

Starting on a drawing career is an exciting time and I think it's a good idea to get yourself in perspective. Visit the library and some bookshops to look at all the styles that are around. Get a sense for what's out there: you don't want to regurgitate it, but to get a feel for the parameters. You can learn a lot, maybe more than you learned at art school, from looking at great artists such as Edward Ardizzone, E.H. Shepard, Maurice Sendak and Chris Van Allsburg.

Great Tip No 1: Use black and white

There is great appeal in working in full colour but it's good to remember black and white. Sometimes a publisher may have a black and white project waiting for an illustrator, while all of the big interest is going into the coloured picture book list. Some of the greatest children's books are illustrated in black and white – A.A. Milne and E.H. Shepard made one of the greatest partnerships with those tiny black ink drawings contributing so much to a great classic. Not a bad place to start, eh?

Ink drawing is simple in the hands of a master but not easy. That unforgiving fluid! Wonder at the uncomplicated, straightforwardness of the Pooh drawings. Consider Toad in *The Wind in the Willows*. When he applied to do the illustrations, Kenneth Graham said to Shepard: 'I have seen many artists who can draw better than you, but you make the animals live.' Can you learn anything from that? Look at Ardizzone's ability to draw mood. He can show both a summer afternoon and a cold November morning simply by using black ink. There is so much to look at, so much to learn from.

Try to include black and white work in your folder. Also include a series of perhaps 30 drawings, such as a fully illustrated story, where you show your ability to be consistent with the characters and the style, without repetition or irrelevance (like the radio programme *Just a Minute*!).

It is a duty of an illustrator to be able to read – that is to try and understand the writer's aims – and to help them rather than to inflict a totally different angle onto the book (again, think of the Milne and Shepard partnership). Much of this comes down to being sensitive enough to recognise the tone of the writing, and skilful enough to draw in the same tone. So the importance of really taking an interest in the story cannot be overstressed. In the text, there will be either clues, or blatant instructions to help the drawings gel. Be very aware.

Great Tip No 2: Experiment

I have known illustrators who convinced themselves that they couldn't use black ink. Mostly this was because they were using the wrong ink, the wrong pen, and/or the wrong paper. Types of black ink vary: waterproof behaves differently from water soluble. Fine nibs and broad nibs each give a totally different result, as does an old fountain pen or a sharpened stick. Try ten different inks, 50 different nibs, odd sticks and all the papers you can find: tracing, layout, calendered, five different cartridges, smooth and rough water-colour, handmade, wrapping paper, anything at all. It's a case of finding the combination that suits your hand and your intention. Your own genius, unrecognised at art school, could surprise you.

Many of the points I've made about black and white work also apply to colour. The marriage of image to text will be in your hands, but it must work.

Great Tip No 3: Choose the right words

I am hesitant to give advice to writers. After all, there are few rules, and the next J.K. Rowling may read this. My own view is really quite simple, and rather obvious. I write mainly for under eight year-olds, so my stories are as short as I can make them. I feel that it is good to have a magnetic first sentence, and an ending that EXPLODES WITH SURPRISE. I think that the ending is the most important part of the story. The bit in the middle should waft the reader along, remembering that the *sound* of words and sentences can be a useful tool.

I like stories to be either funny or scary. *Very* funny, or *very* scary. To be dull is the worst thing in the world! That sounds so obvious, but it gets overlooked. If you are not excited with your work, maybe nobody else will be either.

A picture book has about 23 pages of text (but this can be flexible). I think those pages should have fewer than 2,000 words; 1,000–1,500 is good. One word per page would be great, if the one word was brilliant. As brilliant as the story. Don't be frightened of editing out surplus words. One brilliant one will work better than a dozen mundane ones.

Don't fall into the mindset that writing for children is easy. It has all the disciplines of writing for adults, with the added problem of understanding a child's mind and world. The great writers have a passport to a child's world – think of Roald Dahl. I have seen many brilliant ideas, with less than brilliant pictures, make wonderful books. I have seen a bad idea saved by wonderful illustrations. So, writing style apart, be your own concept's greatest critic. It is quite natural to be protective of your baby, of your story. But try to remember that there are a lot of good editors out there and it will be in your own interest to consider their advice. So don't be a young fogey: be flexible, listen, understand experi-enced points of view. This can be a good time to change for the better, and to start a relationship with one publishing house that may serve you for a lifetime.

Great Tip No 4: Choose what you draw

Don't plan huge drawing problems into your submitted roughs. They may be accepted, and the editor will expect the final art to be better than the roughs.

I illustrate my own writing. This appeals to me for all sorts of reasons, few of them noble. Firstly, I get all of the available fee or/and royalty because I don't have to let half or more go to a writer. Secondly, if there is something I don't like to draw, I don't write about it! For instance, most of my stories take place in the summer, because I prefer to handle trees with their leaves on.

Illustrations being worked on to be published is not the place to practise your drawing. *Practise, change, experiment* all the time, but not in a publishing project. Your finished illustrations must be as good as you can make them. I know an illustrator who won't draw feet, always hiding the ends of legs in grass, water, behind rocks, etc. This is okay if the text will allow; a well-drawn puddle is better than a badly drawn foot any day. It is better to think around a drawing problem, than just to go along with it.

Great Tip No 5: Experiment with your main character

Before you start, try drawing your main character (the most important visual element of the story) in all sorts of ways. A day spent doing this can be so valuable. Getting the main character right can indicate ways to proceed with the whole book.

Great Tip No 6: Think global

Remember that editors react well to stories with wide appeal, rather than minority groups. Foreign sales are in everyone's interest, so try to allow your work to travel. Rhyme is sometimes difficult to translate, as are unusual plays on words.

Great Tip No 7: Plan the whole book

Do little mock-up books for yourself to plan what text goes on which page. This helps to get the story right throughout the book. A 32-page children's book (the most common extent for a picture book) includes covers, end papers, title and half-title pages. This leaves you 23–25 pages to play with. These little mock-ups are for your own use, not to be presented as roughs, so they can be quite work-a-day.

By working out what text goes on which page you will get some sort of an idea of which illustrations go where. Just as the drawings are creative, so is their use on the page. If you use a full double-page spread, another can be expected on the next page. But imagine the effect if the next page explodes with huge typography, and tiny pictures? I am not suggesting you do this, only reminding you that pages of a book are there to be turned, and the turning can be unpredictable and adventurous. Book design is important, along with everything else.

Great Tip No 8: Persevere

So much to do, so much to remember. The main thing is, every children's illustrator and writer I know who has kept trying has got there in the end and been published. But I've also seen great talents give up far too early. Remember that rejection is normal: it's only someone's point of view. Some great books have had long hunts for a publisher. Be open to change and always bear in mind that editors have the experience that you may lack and an editor's advice is meant to help you, not choke you off. However, not all of their advice may apply in your case, so try to recognise what applies to you. When I worked in advertising, I had an art director who said: 'Half of what I say is rubbish. Trouble is, I don't know which half.'

And a reminder

Don't waste time by sending work to publishers who don't publish material like yours. Libraries and bookshops are worth exploring to familiarise yourself with which publishing houses favour what types of work. Research of this kind is time well spent.

Try to show your work in person so that you get a chance to talk, and learn. Do not, however, just drop in. Make an appointment first and hope that these busy people have some time available.

There are also agents prepared to represent new talent (see *Illustrators' agents* on page 252). Of course, an agent will charge a percentage of work sold, but my dad used to say, 'Seventy-five per cent of something is better than 100% of nothing.'

I am troubled by giving advice. I can't help thinking of the young composer who approached the slightly older Mozart and asked, 'Maestro, how should I compose a concerto?' to which Mozart replied, 'You are very young, perhaps you should start with a simple tune'. The young composer frowned and argued: 'But, Maestro, *you* composed a concerto when you were still a child!' 'Ah yes,' said Mozart, 'but I didn't have to ask how?'

Tony Ross is a renowned illustrator of international repute and the creator of such classics as *The Little Princess* and *I Want My Potty*. His first book was published in 1976 and since then he has illustrated more than 900 books including the *Dr Xargle* series, created with the author Jeanne Willis and the *Horrid Henry* series written by Francesca Simon.

See also...

- *Notes from a successful children's author and illustrator*, page 84
- *Creating graphic novels*, page 227
- *Writing and illustrating picture books*, page 244
- *The amazing picture book story*, page 248

Illustrating for children

Writing and illustrating picture books

Debi Gliori tells the story of how she started writing and illustrating children's books.

The prospect of spending your life making children's books has a great deal to recommend it, not least the fact that you will never have to buy those nasty big itchy rolls of rockwool to insulate the walls of your home ever again. Twelve thousand or so volumes will do the job far better. Following the children's books career path will ensure that books will pour into your home, year after year, yours and other people's; foreign editions and large-print versions; pop-ups and boards; collections and anthologies; so many that you might think about studying 'Elementary Bookshelf Building for Beginners and Fumblethumbs' before your piles of books reach to the ceiling. You will also be forced to develop a pronounced and sincerely apologetic grovel each time your postman staggers laden to your door – after all, his sciatica/lower back pain/slipped disc is *entirely your fault*.

Tottering heaps of hardbacks notwithstanding, I can say, with hand-on-heart, that being a children's author and illustrator is the best job in the world. I'm not alone in this opinion. Some years ago, a midwife visited me in the studio I work from in my garden and said, apropos of nothing: 'Eee lass, you've landed with your bum in the butter'.

Unsurprisingly, I looked suitably horrified. (What *was* this, pray? Surely not more indignities to be visited upon my person in the name of childbirth?) Seeing my expression, she hastily explained that what she had *meant* was that I was exceedingly fortunate to be paid to do what I love best. 'Bum in the butter' huh? Takes all sorts. But hey, Gentle Reader, it was not always thus. Back in the mists of that ghastly period of human history known as the Eighties when I set off on this Quest for Publication, I recall that I underwent a long period of major struggle during which many lentils were consumed. This was a lengthy phase which also involved dressing in the morning *in* bed, serious layering of woolly jumpers and, I kid you not, bathrooms so cold that one's toothbrush *froze*.

After graduation from Edinburgh College of Art, I trawled round London publishers with my too-big portfolio and quickly realised that good picture book texts were as rare as talking bears. While illustrators, such as I'd been studying to become, were everywhere in abundance. Encouraging, *not*.

Stubborn is my middle name. That's right, Debi Stubborn Gliori – I know it's weird, but parents... pffff, what can I say? Anyway, stubbornly I decided that there was no way that I was going to take on a badly paid job to 'support' my unpaid non-existent career in children's books. That would be *two* jobs. I mean, get real. Nor did I much fancy the kind of grinding-noble-poverty-consumption-in-a-garret artist's lifestyle afforded by a complete lack of cash. Mercenary little beast that I was, I picked up as many well-paid advertising jobs as possible (illustrating whisky labels and smoked salmon packaging, mainly) and in my spare time hauled myself off to libraries and bookshops and did my research. Who was publishing what? Why were these books published rather than, say, *mine*? What was fashionable and why? Did retellings work? Were books for babies no-brainers? Trust me, it wasn't all that hard for me to see what was required from a good picture book. I won't insult your intelligence by telling you. You know this stuff. Or if you don't, you'll pick it up quickly.

So, armed with a rough idea of what first publishers, then parents and finally, children might want (the order is, sadly, significant), I holed myself up in a 1.2 square metre cupboard and wrote a book which, joy of joys, was picked off the Walker Books slush pile and published. Read my lips: at that point, I had no 'in' in publishing – no contacts, no money and no influence. I was a single parent living in a freezing cold, damp cottage waaaaay out in the sticks in Scotland. And yet, and yet, and yet, I managed to get my book published. The message here is Take Heart. It *can* be done.

Making a picture book the Gliori way

How I go about starting to make a book from scratch is another matter. All of us approach the process of creating picture books from a multitude of different directions. For what it's worth, here's how I go about it. Although I always start with the text, nine times out of ten the initial idea for a book arrives in my head as a couple of images that I know I'd love to paint. Unsurprisingly, I never experience a burning desire to make a book that involves cars or horses, mainly because I cannot draw either. On the other hand, I love landscapes. So, for example, there's a scene in one of my early books called *Mr Bear Babysits* in which Mr Bear is walking home by moonlight through trees, and all around him are baby animals, birds and insects being tucked in for the night. Immediately that image sparks off a series of questions. What season would this be set in? Answer – summer, because then I can draw golden moonlit fields and haystacks. What time is it? Probably after midnight. Why is Mr Bear out so late? Maybe he's having a *liaison dangereux* with Mrs Grizzle-Bear… or then again, perhaps not. Let's imagine he's been babysitting for the Grizzle-Bear cubs. How many? Three. Heavens, poor Grizzle-Bears, they must *really* need a night off. What are the cubs like? Rumbustious. Has Mr Bear got kids of his own? Is he going home? Is this the end or is it the beginning? You can see the process, can't you? By trying to supply answers to my own questions, I am effortlessly beginning to build a framework round which I could start to construct a narrative.

I wouldn't like you to think that it's easy though. Frequently, the entire framework begins to assume the tensile properties of overcooked tagliatelle, at which point I will decide that this is an idea that's not ready to be written yet. I have several of these raw and palely loitering things tucked away in various notebooks, and once in a while I'll drag them out into the unforgiving daylight; poke, prod and play with them until they turn to mush at which point, with deep regret, I'll put them back and try a different tack. Sometimes, to my delight, the poking and prodding succeeds and a picture book text emerges, oozing and flubby in parts, but with a decent story at its heart. Over the course of the next month, I'll return to that text and read it out loud until my ears bleed, because reading out loud is the single best way for me to expose flaws, glitches and bumpy bits before I self-edit in what I blithely imagine to be a ruthlessly incisive fashion.

Afterwards, breathless and pink with the unaccustomed exertion, I type it out and email it to my editor. When I was a beginner, I would assemble a thick envelope in which I included the following items for editor-seduction purposes: one lovingly typed covering letter on headed stationery, one double-spaced (with Tippex blobs) manuscript (both typed and corrected on an ancient manual typewriter bought in a junk shop), a set of thumbnail sketches showing how I anticipated pacing the text and pictures over 32 pages, two hideously expensive colour photocopies of two spreads of artwork and one sae for the return of said hideously expensive samples. And then I would wait… and wait… and wait.

These days, if my editor likes my initial idea, she usually lets me know the same day I emailed it. This has little to do with talent, and everything to do with expediency. These days my editor knows my work and she trusts me. From past experience, she is fairly certain that come hell or high water, or even both, simultaneously, along with some obstetric complications thrown in for good measure, three months after she has read and approved my text, I will deliver detailed black and white pencil roughs showing how I intend each spread to look. For her part, she will comment on the roughs, sending them back to me with a tactful and light powdering of Post-it notes. Only *suggestions*, Debi. Put that axe down. Five months afterwards, I will deliver camera-ready artwork and ten minutes after that, my editor and I will be raising that first of many flutes of champagne to our lips in celebration. What, at ten o'clock in the morning? Damn straight.

Proofs and publication

Back when I was starting out, nothing much happened after I delivered a book. There was a lull and then the first proofs arrived – a stage I loved, and still love, because suddenly your whole book appears to fall into focus – it looks like a real book at last and it's one of many identical copies, thus saving me from my illustrator's artwork-related paranoia about someone accidentally dropping a slice of raw tomato onto it. Before you dismiss me as neurotic, Gentle Reader, let me say that this tomato-on-watercolour-artwork-falling-incident really happened. He'll never walk again without a limp, though. After the heady rush of seeing my work in proof form, came the not-so heady rush of publication day, which came… and went, unremarked. Sometimes there would be a wee card in the post, signed by everyone who'd had anything to do with the book; sometimes a bunch of flowers would arrive from my publisher, bestowing a kind of temporary London-glamour on my Scottish hovel. Sometimes I'd cook something special for my family, or bake a cake or just sit in my studio and gnaw my fingernails off one by one, wondering just how far we could make 10% of not a lot stretch.

These days, I'm so involved with my next project that I'll have achieved a measure of distance from the book just published; so much so that I have been known to stare at a beautiful bouquet of flowers and wonder if my publisher thinks I've had another baby. Surely not? Maybe I did – perhaps I'd better just go and check the pram, just in case….

The exact timing of Publication Day can become a bit blurred when your book is released early in order to maximise sales at, say, a book festival. Actually, given the levels of author hospitality on offer, *everything* can get a little blurred during book festivals. By the time you get to Publication Day it's quite hard not to feel a little anti-climatic. What happens to your book from now on is, by and large, out of your hands. It's the day that unpublished authors dream of: the day you see *your* book in print. Perhaps I'm just an old cynic, but seeing my book in mint condition in bookshops doesn't press any of my buttons whatsoever. No, what *I* want to see is *my* book being read till it *falls to bits*. I want to see the date-stamp page at the front of a library copy of one of my books full to the brim with the inky evidence of many withdrawals. *That's* the whole point. Being *read* – not being published.

But first you have to get published, and that's why we're here; you reading and me attempting to spout wisdom like an illustrator's version of the Delphic Oracle. Did anyone remember to bring me a goat, by the way? Problem is, I'm not an oracle, and nor am I a teacher. All that I know is based my own experience of the business. Your experience will be significantly different. Without sitting down beside you and looking over your text or your portfolio, the best advice I can give is *keep going*. Be stubborn – if you want to be published, you're going to have to be rhinoceros-like in your determination as well as acquiring a rhino-hide to shrug off those slings and arrows of unkind comment. Follow your own star, even if it's a redundant Russian satellite. Er, learn how to put up bookshelves and develop a series of nifty recipes for lentils. And good luck: like all the best things in life, the process of learning how to make picture books is well worth the effort.

Debi Gliori has written and illustrated many picture books and her best-loved titles include *No Matter What* and the *Mr Bear* series. She is also the author of the *Pure Dead...* series of novels for older children and the *Witch Baby and Me* series of books for in-between-picture-books-and-novels children. She lives in Scotland and works from her International Shedquarters at the bottom of her garden.

See also...
- *Creating graphic novels*, page 227
- *The amazing picture book story*, page 248
- *Notes from a successful children's author and illustrator*, page 84

Illustrating for children

The amazing picture book story

Oliver Jeffers tells the story of how his first picture book came to be published.

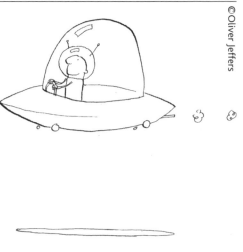

© Oliver Jeffers

In this, the 21st century, anything is possible. We drive flying cars, live in bubbles, go to the moon for our summer holidays and we can freeze and heat things instantly. People can do whatever they want, and in some cases get paid for it, even writing and illustrating children's books. And in this age of possibility, they can even be picked from the slush pile. That's what happened to me. Although I still believe I'm one of the luckiest people alive, and this article isn't much beyond bragging, hindsight and other people would suggest there is more to it than that. One thing that hasn't changed with all our technological advancements is the fundamental need for children's picture books on a number of levels. From educating enquiring young minds, and entertaining both children and adults alike at bedtime (and not just adults who have children, and not just at bedtime) to pushing the boundaries of style and content within the broader worlds of both art and literature. Children's books are art, and all true artists do what they love first and hope to make a living second. Creating a piece of work to the absolute best of an ability is an artist's priority. Getting paid is a bonus. The same goes for those who create children's books. (I bet if you were to ask someone like Quentin Blake, if he wasn't getting paid to make children's books, would he do it anyway and just be poor? He'd probably say 'yes' but also have a second job working at some moon resort or other.)

Anyway, so back to me bragging about how I'm one of the luckiest people in the world and get to do what I love for a living. Well, sort of living as the money isn't great, and I sell proper paintings as well, and between the two I can pay my mortgage. But I do have a publisher that publishes my books and I'm going to tell you how that happened. The story itself is actually quite business-like and boring so I'll throw in a few creative exaggerations for effect.

The story begins

It all started when I had just defeated the Admiral of the Swiss Navy in a sword fight, and sat at the edge of a fish market pier for a think. I had known all along that I liked to draw pictures and I liked to write, and I had been putting the two together for a while in my paintings. I even bought and collected children's picture books both for my own enjoyment and as research for my paintings. But it wasn't until a good friend suggested I attempt a children's book of my own that I seriously considered it as a direction to take my life. So, as I sat there dangling my legs off the pier, I had my first idea for a children's book, about a boy who tries to catch the reflection of a star in the water, not unlike the Brer Rabbit story of the *Moon and the Mill Pond*.

After a year out, I carried the idea into my final year studying Visual Communication (specialising in illustration) at the University of Ulster in Belfast in 2000, having to hold down a second job as a racecar driver to pay for my tuition. I developed self-portrait doodles to narrate my thesis that year, which eventually developed into the character used in the book. In the second half of my final year I used my picture book concept as a piece of coursework, deciding to see how far I could take it to a finished product. This involved getting the words right, and the pictures right, and more importantly, the balance between the two right.

Looking, thinking children's books

To get the words right, I read my manuscript to as many six year-olds as I could find (you'd be amazed how many there are: I reckon if they were all to jump at once something big would break, like London Bridge or at least a phone box or two), slowly tweaking the story based on the feedback I was getting. To get the pictures right I used the unending help of my older brother Rory who basically has a lot more sense than I do. And to get the balance right we both looked at hundreds of other picture books to see what everyone else had done. That was when the earthquake happened and Rory had to balance 58 books on his head to save them from falling down a crack to the molten core of the earth.

In the process of getting the balance right, I noticed a few things about how good picture books seem to work. The one that sticks out most is about how they seem to appeal across all ages without being forced. They aren't condescending, but at the same time they aren't inaccessible. There just seems to be a natural universal appeal to both children and adults – and let's face it, they need to appeal to adults, as however well a six year-old is doing, they're unlikely to stick their hand in their pocket and pull out a tenner in a bookshop!

OK, so in the second half of 2001, after I had finished developing my idea and finished my degree, and after the initial euphoria of never having to write another thesis in my life wore off, and during that slightly intimidating, 'I actually have to do something with my life now!' phase, I decided I would get my book published. I looked at what was

© Oliver Jeffers

around in the bookshops and thought that what I had created was as good as, if not better, than anything else that was out there, and confidence and self belief are important tools when you need to be self motivated. My first step was to buy the *Writers' & Artists' Yearbook* and I then began to look at which publisher would be lucky enough to receive my manuscript. Alright, I wasn't that confident, in fact, having worked in Waterstone's for a few years and armed with a very minimal knowledge of the publishing world, I knew I was in for a long and trying road of numerous attempts contacting publishers, repeatedly saying 'have you read it yet?'

Apart from using the *Yearbook* to research which publishers I should send my idea to, I also referred to my own collection of children's picture books, the collection that would make any six year-old jealous. I looked to see who had published what, paying particular attention to my favourites, and which publishers popped up more often.

My next step was to figure out what exactly to send them. There are hundreds and thousands of unsolicited ideas that reach publishers every year and my objective was to stand out among those. To be noticed. By asking, I found that what publishers like to see in a proposal for a new book was the manuscript and a few samples of the illustrations to give a broad idea of the feel for the book. I invested a bit of money into producing 100 copies of a small spiral bound 'sample', with the manuscript at the start and ten full-colour illustrations after, which I put into an envelope with a letter outlining who I was and what I was trying to do, and a self-addressed envelope for them to contact me. I also included a small portfolio (and I mean small, eight prints that were 14cm square each) of other examples of my paintings and illustrations in the hope that if a particular publisher didn't pick up on my book idea, at least I might be able to get a few commissions while I was waiting.

A few phone calls later and I had found out who looked after the children's division in each appropriate publishing house, and addressed my envelope to them. The point being that it would arrive at a real person's desk instead of an anonymous room that was only used for hostage situations or when they ran out of chairs. I spent a while drawing up a big chart showing which publishers I had sent an envelope to, their contact name and number, date last contacted, and room for comments. I sent an envelope to the ten biggest publishers in the UK, and the ten biggest in USA, figuring I'd start at the top and work my way down.

© Oliver Jeffers

© Oliver Jeffers

Illustrating for children

The envelopes were opened

Expecting a healthy dose of being ignored and avoided, you can perhaps imagine my surprise when, the next afternoon, as I was entertaining the Sultan of Brunei and his wonderful wife Delilah, I received a phone call from a publisher in London during the course of which they expressed their desire to publish my book. It had arrived on the desk of a young editorial assistant: she had opened it, liked what she saw, and had immediately decided to do something about it. That offer was followed a week later by one from a US publisher in New York City, where something similar happened. I forgave the US publisher for their delay, as they are geographically further away.

And it was as simple as that. I met with both publishers, and between the three of us we were able to devise a cunning plan that would enable both of them to publish the book.

Told you I was lucky, I may as well have won the lottery. But as someone wiser than me once said, 'It's all about healthy measures of luck and hard work!' or was that 'work and hard luck?' I can't remember, but the point is that I set myself an objective and was quite methodical and logical in my efforts to get there. Like most businesses, I had an idea, I developed it, then invested time, thought, and money in selling it. But if I hadn't already sold it, I'd still be trying to, and I'd still be having the same ideas for my next books, only wearing cheaper shoes, eating Weetabix for dinner, and maybe sending off an application to that moon resort too.

The end. Or rather, the beginning….

Oliver Jeffers makes art. From figurative painting and installation to illustration and picture book making, his work has been exhibited and published in New York, Dublin, London, Sydney, Washington DC, Belfast and elsewhere. His picture books are published by HarperCollins UK and Penguin USA and include *Lost and Found*, *The Incredible Book Eating Boy* and, most recently, *The Great Paper Caper*. Picture book awards include the Smarties Award, Irish Book of the Year, and the Blue Peter Book of the Year, as well as shortlists for the British Book of the Year, the Roald Dahl Funny Award and the Greenaway Medal. Oliver was brought up in Northern Ireland and now lives and works in New York.

See also...
- *Getting started*, page 1
- *Eight great tips to get your picture book published*, page 240
- *Writing and illustrating picture books*, page 244
- *Notes from a successful children's author and illustrator*, page 84

Illustrators' agents

Before submitting work, artists are advised to make preliminary enquiries and to ascertain terms of work. Commission varies but averages 25–30%. The Association of Illustrators (see page 366) provides a valuable service for illustrators, agents and clients.

*Member of the Society of Artists Agents †Member of the Association of Illustrators

Advocate

56 The Street, Ashtead, Surrey KT21 1AZ
tel 020-8879 1166 *fax* 020-8879 3303
email mail@advocate-art.com
website www.advocate-art.com
Director Edward Burns

Has 5 agents representing 110 artists and illustrators. Supplies work to book and magazine publishers, design and advertising agencies, greeting card and fine art publishers, and gift and ceramic manufacturers. Also has an original art gallery, stock library and website in German, Spanish and French. Founded as a co-operative in 1996.

Allied Artists/Artistic License

mobile (07971) 111256
email info@allied-artists.net
website www.allied-artists.net
Contacts Gary Mills, Mary Burtenshaw

Represents over 40 artists, all of whom illustrate children's books. Specialises in highly finished realistic figure illustrations and stylised juvenile illustrations for children's books. Extensive library of stock illustrations. Commission: 33%. Founded 1983.

Arena*†

Arena Illustration Ltd, 31 Eleanor Road,
London E15 4AB
tel (0845) 050 7600
email info@arenaillustration.com
website www.arenaillustration.com
Contact Tamlyn Francis

Represents 30 artists working mostly for book covers, children's books and design groups. Average commission 25%. Founded 1970.

The Art Agency

The Lodge, Cargate Lane, Saxlingham Thorpe,
Norwich NR15 1TU
tel (01508) 471500 *fax* (01508) 470391
email artagency@me.com
website www.the-art-agency.co.uk

Represents more than 40 artists producing top-quality, highly accurate and imaginative illustrations across a wide variety of subjects and for all age groups, both digitally and traditionally. Clients are children's fiction and non-fiction publishers. Include sae with submissions. Do not email portfolios. Commission: 30%. Founded 1992.

The Artworks†*

12–18 Hoxton Street, London N1 6NG
tel 020-7729 1973
email info@theartworksinc.com
website www.theartworksinc.com
Contact Lucy Scherer, Stephanie Alexander, Alex Gardner

Represents 20 artists for illustrated gift books and children's books. Commission: 25% advances, 15% royalties.

Beehive Illustration

42ᴀ Cricklade Street, Cirencester, Glos. GL7 1JH
tel (01285) 885149 *fax* (01285) 641291
email info@beehiveillustration.co.uk
website www.beehiveillustration.co.uk
Contact Paul Beebee

Represents over 70 artists specialising in ELT (English Language Teaching) books, education and general publishing illustration. Commission: 25%. Founded 1989.

The Bright Agency

Studio 102, 250 York Road, London SW11 3SJ
tel 020-7326 9140
email vicki@thebrightagency.com
website www.thebrightagency.com

Represents artists for children's publishing covering all ages.

Bright Art Licensing

Studio 102, 250 York Road, London SW11 3SJ
tel 020-7326 9140
email emma@brightartlicensing.com
website www.brightartlicensing.com

Focuses on the greeting card/gift and licensing/merchandising industries.

Jenny Brown Associates – see page 212

Celia Catchpole Ltd

56 Gilpin Avenue, London SW14 8QY
tel 020-8255 4835 *fax* 020-8255 4835
email celiacatchpole@yahoo.co.uk
website www.celiacatchpole.co.uk
Proprietor Celia Catchpole

Represents 9 artists specialising in artwork for picture books and storybooks for ages 0–12. Submit samples as A4 photocopies. Commission: 15%. Founded 1996. See also page 213.

The Copyrights Group Ltd

(A Chorion company)
4th Floor, Aldwych House, 81 Aldwych,
London WC2B 4HN
tel 020-7406 7406 *fax* 020-7406 7464
email reception@chorion.co.uk
website www.copyrights.co.uk
Chairman Nicholas Durbridge, *Creative Director*
Linda Pooley

Leading licensing organisation with an international team of staff working together to represent writers, artists and the owners of quality characters, fine art and brand names for licensing to manufacturers of consumer products and for consumer promotions. Properties include *Peter Rabbit, Paddington Bear, Spot, Flower Fairies, Jacqueline Wilson, Horrible Histories, Ivory Cats, The Snowman, Father Christmas* and *The Wombles.*

Graham-Cameron Illustration

The Studio, 23 Holt Road, Sheringham,
Norfolk NR26 8NB
tel (01263) 821333 *fax* (01263) 821334
email enquiry@gciforillustration.com
and Duncan Graham-Cameron, Graham-Cameron
Illustration, 59 Hertford Road, Brighton BN1 7GG
tel (01273) 385890
website www.gciforillustration.com
Partners Helen Graham-Cameron, Duncan
Graham-Cameron

Represents 37 artists and undertakes all forms of illustration for publishing and communications. Specialises in educational, children's and information books. Telephone before sending A4 sample illustrations with sae. Do not send MSS. Founded 1985.

David Higham Associates Ltd – see
page 214

John Hodgson Agency

38 Westminster Palace Gardens, Artillery Row,
London SW1P 1RR
tel 0171-580 3773 *fax* 0171-222-4468

Represents 6 artists producing children's material. Specialises in children's picture books for 0–8 year-olds. Phone before sending samples. Enclose an sae with samples. Commission: 25%. Founded 1965.

The Illustration Cupboard

22 Bury Street, London SW1Y 6AL
tel 020-7976 1727
email john@illustrationcupboard.com
website www.illustrationcupboard.com
Chief Executive John Huddy

A London art gallery which specialises in the exhibition and sale of original book illustration

artwork from around the world. It represents over 150 different leading illustrators and displays their work in group and single artist exhibitions with an annual catalogue produced every November. Founded 1996.

LAW (Lucas Alexander Whitley Ltd)

14 Vernon Street, London W14 0RJ
tel 020-7471 7900 *fax* 020-7471 7910
website www.lawagency.co.uk
Contacts Philippa Milnes-Smith, Holly Vitow

Illustrations for children's publishing for ages 0–16. Submit copies of samples (not originals) together with an sae for their return plus a covering letter and CV. No submissions by email or disk accepted. Commission: 15% (20% overseas). See also page 215. Founded 1996.

David Lewis Agency

Worlds End Studios, 134 Lots Road,
London SW10 0RJ
tel 020-7435 7762 *mobile* (07931) 824674
fax 020-7351 5044
email davidlewis34@hotmail.com
website www.davidlewisillustration.com
Director David Lewis, *Associate Director* Ramon Johns

All kinds of material for all areas of children's publishing, including educational, merchandising and toys. Represents approx. 25 artists, half of whom produce children's material. Also considers complete picture books with text. Send A4 colour or b&w copies of samples with return postage. Commission: 30%. Founded 1974.

Frances McKay Illustration

18 Lammas Green, Sydenham Hill, London SE26 6LT
tel 020-8693 7006 *mobile* (07703) 344334
email frances@francesmckay.com
website www.francesmckay.com
Proprietor Frances McKay

Represents 20+ artists producing children's material, largely for book publishers and packagers. Also considers MSS for young children. Submit illustrations for age 4+ with an original slant, either as jpegs on CD, as low-res scans by email or send copies by post with sae. Commission: 25–35%. Founded 1999.

The Monkey Feet Illustration Agency

Oakwood Cottage, 107 Grove Lane, Cheadle Hulme,
Cheshire SK8 7NE
tel 0808 1200 996
email enquiries@monkeyfeetillustration.co.uk
website www.monkeyfeetillustration.co.uk
Director Adam Rushton

Represents 48 artists creating work for children's book publishers, design agencies, greeting card companies and toy manufacturers. Commission: 15–30%. Founded 2002.

Illustrating for children

NB Illustration

40 Bowling Green Lane, London EC1R 0NE
tel 020-7278 9131 *fax* 020-7278 9121
email info@nbillustration.co.uk
website www.nbillustration.co.uk
Directors Joe Najman, Charlotte Berens, Paul Najman

Represents 50+ artists, of whom 10% produce
children's material for picture books and educational
publishing. Submit samples either as web address by
email or by post with an sae. Commission: 30%.
Founded 2000.

The Organisation*†

The Basement, 69 Caledonian Road, London N1 9BT
tel 0845-054 8033 *fax* 020-7833 8269
email lorraine@organisart.co.uk
website www.organisart.co.uk
Contact Lorraine Owen

Represents 60 artists, 75% of whom produce
children's material for all ages. Can supply both
traditional and digital illustration for all markets,
including the children's and educational book
markets. Also produces illustrations for other print
markets, advertising, packaging and editorial. Before
submitting samples research the website. New artists
must not have a similar style to one already
represented. Send samples either by email or on a CD
by post, or send printed images with sae. Average
commission: 30%. Founded 1987.

Plum Pudding Illustration

9 Lydden Road, London SW18 4LT
tel 020-3004 7135 *fax* 020-3004 7136
email info@plumpuddingillustration.com
website www.plumpuddingillustration.com
Contact Mark Mills

Represents 60+ artists, producing illustrations for
children's publishing (all genres), advertising,
editorial, greetings cards and packaging. See website
for submission procedure. Commission: 30%.
Founded 2006.

Sylvie Poggio Artists Agency

36 Haslemere Road, London N8 9RB
tel 020-8341 2722 *fax* 020-8374 1725
email sylviepoggio@blueyonder.co.uk
website www.sylviepoggio.com
Directors Slyvie Poggio, Bruno Caurat

Represents 40 artists producing illustrations for
publishing and advertising. Commission: 25%.
Founded 1992.

Elizabeth Roy Literary Agency

White Cottage, Greatford, Nr Stamford,
Lincs. PE9 4PR
tel/fax (01778) 560672
website www.elizabethroyliteraryagency.co.uk

Handles illustrations for children's books. Only
interested in exceptional material. Illustrators should
research the children's book market before sending
samples, which must include figure work. Send by
post with return postage; no CD, disk or email
submissions. See also page 217. Founded 1990.

Caroline Sheldon Literary Agency Ltd

71 Hillgate Place, London W8 7SS
tel 020-7727 9102
email carolinesheldon@carolinesheldon.co.uk,
pennyholroyde@carolinesheldon.co.uk
website www.carolinesheldon.co.uk,
www.carolinesheldonillustrators.co.uk
Contacts Caroline Sheldon, Penny Holroyde

Represents a select list of leading illustrators working
mainly in children's books. Also author/illustrators.
Send introductory information about yourself and
samples by email only (type Artist's Submission in
subject line and attach samples and/or link to your
website). Also specialises in the sale of books to TV/
film but is not interested in non-book-originated
merchandised characters. See also page 217. Founded
1985.

Specs Art

93 London Road, Cheltenham, Glos. GL52 6HL
tel (01242) 515951
email roland@specsart.com
website www.specsart.com
Partners Roland Berry, Stephanie Prosser

Represents 30 artists, all of whom produce children's
material for all ages. High-quality illustration and
animation work for advertisers, publishers and all
other forms of visual communication. Specialises in
licensed character illustration. Submit about 6 jpegs
by email. Commission: 25%. Founded 1982.

Vicki Thomas Associates

195 Tollgate Road, London E6 5JY
tel 020-7511 5767 *fax* 020-7473 5177
email vickithomasassociates@yahoo.co.uk
website www.vickithomasassociates.com
Consultant Vicki Thomas

Represents approx. 50 artists, three-quarters of whom
produce children's material for all ages. Specialises in
designing gift products and considers images for
publishing, toys, stationery, clothing, decorative
accessories, etc. Submit samples as photocopies with
a covering letter. Commission: 30%. Founded 1985.

United Agents

12–26 Lexington Street, London W1F 0LE
tel 020-3214 0800
email info@unitedagents.co.uk
website www.unitedagents.co.uk
Agent Jodie Marsh

Represents illustrators of children's books for all ages
(home 15%, USA/translation 20%). See website for
submission details. Founded 2008.

House of Illustration

Plans for a centre of excellence for illustration are under way.

Illustrating for children

When it opens, the House of Illustration will be the world's first centre dedicated to the art of illustration in all its forms. It will be a home for illustration past and present, international and British, where visitors will be able to see and experience this most accessible and popular art form in a wide variety of ways. Illustration will get the critical attention it deserves, revealing the creative processes behind it and the way in which it impacts on our daily lives.

Further information

House of Illustration
website www.houseofillustration.org.uk

In 2002, Quentin Blake, Britain's pre-eminent and internationally acclaimed illustrator, gathered together a group of people who all share the passionate wish that illustration should have a home of its own. Since then, two critically acclaimed and commercially successful temporary exhibitions have been mounted in connection with this project:
• *Fifty Years of Quentin Blake* at Somerset House in London broke box office records with 28,500 visitors, and
• *What Are You Like?* opened at Dulwich Picture Gallery in 2008 and toured the UK during 2009 and 2010.
In addition, a series of education workshops in London schools to explore the power of illustration in primary school teaching and learning began in 2009.

The proposed home for the House of Illustration is a refurbished Victorian building in the King's Cross regeneration area of London and a £6.5 million capital campaign has been launched. When it opens, it will attract visitors from the general public, including children and young people, and illustration students. It will be a creative hub for illustrators of all varieties, from the worlds of books, advertising, botany, medicine, science and fashion. In the meantime, the House of Illustration website is serving as its base.

Publishing practice
Publishing agreements

Before signing a publisher's agreement, it should be thoroughly checked. Caroline Walsh introduces the key points of this very important contract.

So, you've done the difficult bit and persuaded a publisher to make an offer to publish your book. But how do you know if you're getting a fair deal? And what should you be looking out for on the contract? I would always advise an author or illustrator to engage an agent. An agent will ensure that the contract gives you the best possible chance of maximising your income from a book. Alternatively, the Society of Authors (see page 353) and the Writers' Guild of Great Britain (see page 381) will both check publishing agreements for their members. In addition, there are lawyers who specialise in publishing contracts and for those who prefer to go it alone, there are some useful books on the subject listed at the end of this article.

What follows is a whistle-stop tour around the key points of a publishing contract, especially for those writing for children. To begin, the offer from the publisher should come in writing clearly setting out exactly what rights the publisher wants to license and what they are willing to pay for those rights. A contract is a business agreement for the supply of goods or performance of work at a specified price. Normally, that payment comes as an advance against royalties. Occasionally, a flat fee payment is appropriate, but a royalty allows the author to share in the income from a book throughout its life and is therefore generally preferable. Perhaps the most important point of all is that you make sure you fully understand which rights are being licensed under the contract and aren't seduced merely into worrying about the advance and royalty (tempting though they may be!)

Publishers' agreements often have useful headings for each clause and I've used some of those headings here for ease of reference.

Licence

The very first thing to be clear about is what is being licensed to the publisher. For a new book one expects to grant to the publisher, for the legal term of copyright, the exclusive right to publish and sell the work in certain forms. The standard grant is of 'volume form', which means all book forms (hardback, paperback, other formats). However, the offer or contract may also state other forms, for example serial (newspaper and magazine rights) or audio rights. Some publishers' contracts include all-encompassing wording such as 'all media forms currently in existence and hereinafter invented'. This in effect hands control to the publisher of a wide range of rights, including electronic, dramatic (film, television, radio), merchandising and so on. In such a case, it's likely that the author's share of income from such rights will be less than it would be were the author to reserve those rights and have them handled separately.

Territory

Territory states *where* the publisher has the right to sell or sub-license the book. For picture books of all kinds, fiction and non-fiction, UK publishers generally require world rights as the UK market alone is not large enough to sustain the costs of four-colour printing. US publishers are lucky enough to have a sufficiently large home market to mean they are not reliant on foreign sales and therefore will not always require world rights.

For fiction (i.e. novels) a judgement needs to be made about which territories should be granted to the publisher. English language rights are made up of two large mutually exclusive territories: the UK and Traditional British Commonwealth (including or excluding Canada) on the one hand and the USA, its dependencies and the Philippines on the other. The rest of the world is considered an open market. One could grant Traditional British Commonwealth rights in the English Language to a publisher, thereby reserving American and translation rights to be sold separately. Or one could grant World English Language rights, so the publisher can sell on US rights while translation rights are held in reserve to be sold separately. Or again, one could grant world rights to the originating publisher.

When thinking of granting a wide range of territories to a publisher, it is worth checking out how proactive and successful their foreign rights department is. It may be possible to speak to the foreign rights manager and find out for yourself if they have a good track record. An agent will have an informed view on a publisher's expertise in this area and furthermore, they will probably either be experienced themselves in selling foreign and US rights, or will work with associate agencies in all the different language territories. Publishers will take 15–30% share on US and foreign sales and, if you have an agent too, their commission will also be deducted before you receive your percentage. Agents will generally charge 15–20% on US and foreign sales.

Advances

We've all read the newspaper headlines about huge advances, but the fact is most children's book advances currently fall within the range of £1,000–£25,000. For books that will be published in the trade (i.e. by a mainstream publishing house and where the book will appear in bookshops) most offers are framed as an advance against royalties. Advances may be paid in one go, on signature, but don't be surprised if the publisher proposes paying half on signature and half on publication, or in thirds (signature, delivery and publication), or even in quarters (signature, delivery, hardback publication, paperback publication), though the latter is more common when the advance offered is substantial.

Royalties

As a very basic rule of thumb, hardbacks attract a 10% base royalty and paperbacks 7.5%. Bear in mind that on picture books these figures will be shared between author and illustrator. Sometimes, children's black and white illustrated fiction titles also bear a small royalty for the illustrator, which will come out of the total royalty. Most novelty books, including board books, work on a smaller royalty, for example 5% or even less because of the high production costs and relatively low retail price.

Ideally, the royalty will escalate to a higher level when a certain number of sales have been achieved and this can prove to be very important if a book becomes a long-running success.

For a trade book the royalties should ideally be based on the recommended retail price for home sales. Export sales and sales to book clubs or book fairs are usually calculated on the publisher's price received (or net receipts). The contract should set out each type of sale and list the appropriate royalty rate. Nowadays particular attention needs to be paid to 'high discount' clauses in contracts. However good the main home sales royalty is, a disadvantageous high discount clause can mean that disappointingly few of the sales attract the full royalty and consequently revenues will be much reduced. This is especially important now because retailers are pushing publishers hard on discounts. An agent will be used to negotiating carefully on precisely this kind of area to secure the best possible terms.

Co-edition royalties

As previously mentioned, picture books in the UK are very dependent upon publishers selling American and foreign language co-editions. Therefore, it is important to note on the contract what the author's share of any such co-edition deals will be. These generally fall under two categories in the contract:

• If the UK publisher prints for the foreign publisher, the books are usually sold for a fixed price per copy as 'royalty inclusive' and the author's and artist's share will be expressed as a percentage of the publisher's price received. These deals help to get the book published by bringing the unit cost down and they begin the process of earning out the advance.

• US and foreign language sales also fall under the heading of subsidiary rights. In this case, the UK publisher may or may not print the books, but the US or foreign publisher will have agreed to pay an advance and royalty for the right to sell the book in their territory (a 'royalty exclusive' deal). The author's and artist's share in this instance shouldn't be less than 50% and it could be much more. If a book is particularly sought after by foreign or US publishers, such a royalty exclusive deal could mean that the original UK advance is earned out immediately.

Subsidiary rights

Other subsidiary rights include reprint rights (large print, book club, paperback reprint, etc), serial rights (the right to publish in newspapers and magazines), anthology and quotation rights, educational rights, audio rights and so on. There will usually be a percentage listed against each right and that is the author's share of any deal. Generally the author receives at least 50% on these deals and more in the case of serial, US and translation rights. The rights listed in the sub-rights clause should be checked against the opening grant of rights clause to see that they conform.

Delivery and publication

There should be clauses in the contract that state the agreed delivery date of the book and give some indication of what is expected, for example 'a work for children to be written and illustrated by the said author to a length of not more than 25,000 words plus approximately 50 black and white line illustrations'. There should also be an undertaking by the publisher to publish the work within a stated time period, for example 'within 12 months from delivery of the complete typescript and artwork'. There might also be an indication of what the published price will be.

Copyright and moral rights

As you are licensing your work, you should retain copyright and there should be a clause that obliges the publisher to include a copyright line in every edition of the work published or sub-licensed by them. The author's moral rights are also often asserted within the contract.

Production

Though the publishers will generally insist on having the final decision regarding details of production, publication and advertising, they should agree to consult meaningfully with the author over the blurb, catalogue copy, jacket and cover design. There should also be an undertaking to supply the author with proofs for checking and enough time for the author to check those proofs.

Accounts

Publishers usually account to authors twice a year for royalties earned. Even if the advance has not earned out, the publishers should still send a royalty statement. Royalty statements are notoriously enigmatic and vary from publisher to publisher. Mistakes on royalty statements are more common than one might like to think and an agent will be used to checking royalty statements carefully and taking up any anomalies with the publisher.

In addition to the twice-yearly accounting, once the initial advance has been earned out, an agent will be able to ensure that any substantial income from sub-rights deals (e.g. in excess of £100) will be paid immediately.

Electronic or ebook rights

The electronic or ebook market is growing quickly, with a proliferation of devices and formats for accessing ebooks coming on to the market. Publishers are rushing books into ebook format and establishing protocols with online retailers. Ebook development currently encompasses several different forms: straightforward verbatim text; 'enhanced' ebook, i.e. with added material such as author interviews; 'apps' for smart phones; and some children's novels are even available in a 'game' format for reading on one of the popular handheld devices. Authors should take care to retain the right of approval over every aspect of these enhanced electronic editions.

At the time of writing, standard ebook royalties are hovering around 25% of the publisher's price received, but this is often subject to review after a fixed period to enable both sides to take account of changing practice. As this part of the market is fluid and expanding, it's wise to keep your options open if you can.

Reversion

It's important to ensure that the author can get back the rights to their book if the publisher either fails to stick to the terms of the contract or lets the book go out of print. Historically, if the publisher left a book out of print for 6–9 months after receiving a written request to reprint it, rights would revert. However, ebook and print-on-demand formats mean that standard 'stock level' reversion clauses no longer provide adequate protection and new triggers for reversion need to be agreed. This might be a rate of sale or revenue threshold. It is well worth reclaiming rights to out-of-print books as it may well be possible to re-license them later on.

Assignment

A small but important clause that may need to be added states that the publishers shall not assign the rights granted to them without the author's express written consent. This gives the author at least a degree of control over the book's destiny if the publishing company runs into trouble or is sold.

Educational publishers' contracts

Many children's authors begin as writers for educational publishers and quite a number continue to work in this field alongside producing books for the trade market. Educational publishers usually commission tightly briefed work. Advances are generally modest and the royalties are based on the publishers' price received. However, substantial sums can eventually be earned. Educational publishers usually expect to be granted a very wide range of rights and while it makes sense to grant audio or electronic rights where the publisher has the capacity to produce or license such formats for their market, it may be possible and desirable to reserve, for example, dramatic and merchandising rights. However, discretion is needed here. If, for example, the publisher is commissioning writers to create stories about a given set of characters created by the publisher, then the publisher will rightly expect to control such rights.

That really is a scratching of the surface of publishing agreements. Do take advice if you don't feel confident that the contract presented to you is fair. It seems a very obvious thing to say but always read a publishing agreement carefully before signing it and if anything in it isn't clear, ask for an explanation. Remember, too, that it's a negotiation and that despite publishers' talk of 'standard terms' and 'standard agreements', it is always possible to make amendments to contracts.

Caroline Walsh is a literary agent and a director of David Higham Associates Ltd (www.davidhigham.co.uk). She specialises in the children's book market.

Useful reading

Clark, Charles (ed.), *Publishing Agreements: A Book of Precedents*, Tottel Publishing, 7th edn, 2007

Flint, Michael F., *A User's Guide to Copyright*, Tottel Publishing, 6th edn, 2006

Jones, Hugh and Benson, Christopher, *Publishing Law*, Routledge, 3rd edn, 2006

Publishing practice

FAQs about ISBNs

The ISBN Agency receives a large number of enquiries about the ISBN system. The most frequently asked questions are answered here.

What is an ISBN?

An ISBN (International Standard Book Number) is a product identifier used by publishers, booksellers and libraries for ordering, listing and stock control purposes. It enables them to identify a specific edition of a specific title in a specific format from a particular publisher. The digits are always divided into six parts, separated by spaces or hyphens. The six parts can be of varying length and are as follows:

Contact details

ISBN Agency for UK and Ireland
3rd Floor, Midas House, 62 Goldsworth Road, Woking GU21 6LQ
tel (01483) 712215 *fax* (01483) 712214
email isbn.agency@nielsen.com
website www.isbn.nielsenbook.co.uk

• Prefix element – distinguishes the ISBN from other types of product identifier which are used for non-book trade products; three-digit number that is made available by GS1. Prefixes that have already been made available by GS1 are 978 and 979, but there may be a further prefix allocation made in the future as required to ensure the continued capacity of the ISBN system.
• Group Identifier – identifies a national, geographic or language grouping of publishers. It tells you which of these groupings the publisher belongs to (not the language of the book).
• Publisher Identifier – identifies a specific publisher or imprint.
• Title Number – identifies a specific edition of a specific title in a specific format.
• Check Digit – this is always and only the final digit which mathematically validates the rest of the number.

Since January 2007 all ISBNs are 13 digits long. The older ten-digit format can be converted to the 13-digit format by adding the 978 EAN prefix and recalculating the check digit.

Do all books need to have an ISBN?

There is no legal requirement for an ISBN in the UK and Ireland and it conveys no form of legal or copyright protection. It is a product identifier.

What can be gained from using an ISBN?

If you wish to sell your publication through major bookselling chains, or internet booksellers, they will require you to have an ISBN to assist their internal processing and ordering systems. The ISBN also provides access to bibliographic databases such as Nielsen Book's database and information services, which are organised using ISBNs as references. These databases are used by the book trade – publishers, booksellers and libraries – for internal purposes, to provide information for customers and to source and order titles. ISBNs are also used by Nielsen Book's order routing and sales analysis services to monitor book sales. The ISBN therefore provides access to additional marketing opportunities which assist the sales and measurement of books and other published media.

Where can we get an ISBN?

ISBN prefixes are assigned to publishers in the country in which the publisher is based by the national agency for that country. The UK and Republic of Ireland Agency is run by Nielsen Book. The Agency introduces new publishers to the system, assigns prefixes to new and existing publishers and deals with any queries or problems in using the system. The UK ISBN Agency was the first ISBN agency in the world and has been instrumental in the set up and maintenance of the ISBN. Publishers based elsewhere will not be able to get numbers from the UK Agency but may contact them for details of the relevant agency in their market.

Who is eligible for ISBNs?

Any organisation or individual who is publishing a qualifying product for general sale or distribution to the market is eligible (see 'Which products do not qualify for ISBNs?').

What is a publisher?

It is sometimes difficult to decide who the publisher is and who their agent may be, but the publisher is generally the person or body which takes the financial risk in making a product available. For example, if a product went on sale and sold no copies at all, the publisher is usually the person or body which loses money. If you get paid anyway, you are likely to be a designer, printer, author or consultant of some kind.

How long does it take to get an ISBN?

In the UK and Ireland the 'Standard' service time is ten working days. There is also a 'Fast Track' service, which is a three-working day processing period.

How much does it cost to get an ISBN?

In the UK and Ireland there is a registration fee which is payable by all new publishers. The fees during 2011 are £118.68 including VAT for the Standard service and £181.08 including VAT for the Fast Track service. A publisher prefix unique to you will be provided and allows for ten ISBNs. Larger allocations are available where appropriate.

ISBNs are only available in blocks. The smallest block is ten numbers. It is not possible to obtain a single ISBN.

Which products do not qualify for ISBNs?

Calendars and diaries (unless they contain additional text or images such that they are not purely for time-management purposes); greetings cards, videos for entertainment; documentaries on video/CD-Rom; computer games; computer application programs; items which are available to a restricted group of people, e.g. a history of a golf club which is only for sale to members or an educational course book only available to those registered as students on the course.

Can I turn my ISBN into a barcode?

Prior to 2007 ISBNs were only ten digits long, whereas the appropriate barcode was 13 digits long and was derived from the ISBN by adding a prefix and recalculating the check digit. From 1 January 2007 the appropriate barcode number will be the same as the 13-digit ISBN. Further information about barcoding for books is available on the Book Industry Communication website (www.bic.org.uk).

What is an ISSN?

An International Standard Serial Number is the numbering system for journals, magazines, periodicals, newspapers and newsletters. It is administered by the British Library, *tel* (01937) 546959.

Publishing practice

Public Lending Right

Under the PLR system, payment is made from public funds to authors (writers, translators, illustrators and some editors/compilers) whose books are lent out from public libraries. Payment is made once a year, and the amount authors receive is proportionate to the number of times that their books were borrowed during the previous year (July to June).

The legislation

Public Lending Right (PLR) was created, and its principles established, by the Public Lending Right Act 1979 (HMSO, 30p). The Act required the rules for the administration of PLR to be laid down by a scheme. That was done in the Public Lending Right Scheme 1982 (HMSO, £2.95), which includes details of transfer (assignment), posthumous registration, renunciation, trusteeship, bankruptcy, etc. Amending orders made in 1983, 1984, 1988, 1989 and 1990 were consolidated in December 1990 (SI 2360, £3.90). Some further amendments affecting author eligibility came into effect in December 1991 (SI 2618, £1), July 1997 (SI 1576, £1.10), December 1999 (SI 420, £1), July 2000 (SI 933, £1.50), June 2004 (SI 1258 £3) and July 2005 (SI 1519, £3).

Further information

Public Lending Right
PLR Office, Richard House, Sorbonne Close, Stockton-on-Tees TS17 6DA
tel (01642) 604699 *fax* (01642) 615641
website www.plr.uk.com,
www.plrinternational.com
Contact The Registrar

Application forms, information, publications and a copy of its *Annual Report* are all obtainable from the PLR Office. See website for further information on eligibility for PLR, loans statistics and forthcoming developments.

PLR Management Board
Advises the Registrar on the operation and future development of the PLR scheme.

How the system works

From the applications received, the Registrar of PLR compiles a register of authors and books which is held on computer. A representative sample of book issues is recorded, consisting of all loans from selected public libraries. This is then multiplied in proportion to total library lending to produce, for each book, an estimate of its total annual loans throughout the country. Each year the computer compares the register with the estimated loans to discover how many loans are credited to each registered book for the calculation of PLR payments. The computer does this using code numbers – in most cases the ISBN printed in the book.

Parliament allocates a sum each year (£7.45 million for 2010/11) for PLR. This Fund pays the administrative costs of PLR and reimburses local authorities for recording loans in the sample libraries. The remaining money is then divided by the total registered loan figure in order to work out how much can be paid for each estimated loan of a registered book.

Limits on payments

Bottom limit. If all the registered interests in an author's books score so few loans that they would earn less than £1 in a year, no payment is due.

Top limit. If the books of one registered author score so high that the author's PLR earnings for the year would exceed £6,600, then only £6,600 is paid. No author can earn more than £6,600 in PLR in any one year.

Money that is not paid out because of these limits belongs to the Fund and increases the amounts paid that year to other authors.

The sample

Because it would be expensive and impracticable to attempt to collect loans data from every library authority in the UK, a statistical sampling method was employed instead. The sample represents only public lending libraries – academic, school, private and commercial libraries are not included. Only books which are loaned from public libraries can earn PLR. Consultations of books on library premises are excluded from PLR.

The sample consists of the entire loans records for a year from libraries in more than 30 public library authorities spread through England, Scotland, Wales and Northern Ireland. Sample loans represent around 20% of the national total. All the computerised sampling points in an authority contribute loans data ('multi-site' sampling). The aim has been to increase the sample without any significant increase in costs. In order to counteract sampling error, libraries in the sample change every three to four years. Loans are totalled every 12 months for the period 1 July–30 June.

An author's entitlement to PLR depends, under the 1979 Act, on the loans accrued by his or her books in the sample. This figure is averaged up to produce first regional and then finally national estimated loans.

ISBNs

The PLR system uses ISBNs (International Standard Book Numbers) to identify books lent and correlate loans with entries on the PLR Register so that payments can be made. ISBNs are required for all registrations. Different editions (e.g. 1st, 2nd, hardback, paperback, large print) of the same book have different ISBNs.

Publishing practice

Summary of the 28th year's results

Registration: authors. When registration closed for the 28th year (30 June 2010) there were 34,836 authors and assignees.

Eligible loans. Of the 309 million estimated loans from UK libraries, 132 million belong to books on the PLR register. The loans credited to registered books – 42% of all library borrowings – qualify for payment. The remaining 58% of loans relate to books that are ineligible for various reasons, to books written by dead or foreign authors, and to books that have simply not been applied for.

Money and payments. PLR's administrative costs are deducted from the fund allocated to the Registrar annually by Parliament. Operating the Scheme this year cost £756,000, representing some 10% of the PLR fund. The Rate per Loan for 2010/11 was 6.25 pence and was calculated to distribute all the £6.7 million available. The total of PLR distribution and costs is therefore the full £7.45 million which the Government provided in 2010/11.

The numbers of authors in various payment categories are as follows:

*356	payments at	£5,000–6,600
366	payments between	£2,500–4,999.99
877	payments between	£1,000–2,499.99
938	payments between	£500–999.99
3,649	payments between	£100–499.99
17,180	payments between	£1–99.99
23,366	TOTAL	

* Includes 230 authors whose book loans reached the maximum threshold

Authorship

In the PLR system the author of a book is the writer, illustrator, translator, compiler, editor or reviser. Authors must be named on the book's title page, or be able to prove authorship by some other means (e.g. receipt of royalties). The ownership of copyright has no bearing on PLR eligibility.

Co-authorship/illustrators. In the PLR system the authors of a book are those writers, translators, editors, compilers and illustrators as defined above. Authors must apply for registration before their books can earn PLR. This can now be done online through the PLR website. There is no restriction on the number of authors who can register shares in any one book as long as they satisfy the eligibility criteria.

Writers and/or illustrators. At least one must be eligible and they must jointly agree what share of PLR each will take. This agreement is necessary even if one or two are ineligible or do not wish to register for PLR. Share sizes should be based on contribution. The eligible authors will receive the share(s) specified in the application. PLR can be any whole percentage. Detailed advice is available from the PLR office.

Translators. Translators may apply, without reference to other authors, for a 30% fixed share (to be divided equally between joint translators).

Editors and compilers. An editor or compiler may apply, either with others or without reference to them, to register a 20% share. An editor must have written at least 10% of the book's content or more than ten pages of text in addition to normal editorial work and be named on the title page. Alternatively, editors may register 20% if they have a royalty agreement with the publisher. The share of joint editors/compilers is 20% in total to be divided equally. An application from an editor or compiler to register a greater percentage share must be accompanied by supporting documentary evidence of actual contribution.

Dead or missing co-authors. Where it is impossible to agree shares with a co-author because that person is dead or untraceable, then the surviving co-author or co-authors may submit an application without the dead or missing co-author but must name the

Most borrowed children's authors

1	Daisy Meadows	11	Lucy Cousins
2	Jacqueline Wilson	12	Janet & Allan Ahlberg
3	Francesca Simon	13	Enid Blyton
4	Mick Inkpen	14	Fiona Watt
5	Julia Donaldson	15	Tony Ross
6	Lauren Child	16	Vivian French
7	Terry Deary	17	Eric Hill
8	Ian Whybrow	18	Jeanne Willis
9	Roderick Hunt	19	Jeremy Strong
10	Roald Dahl	20	Michael Morpurgo

This list is of the most borrowed authors in UK public libraries. It is based on PLR sample loans in the period July 2009–June 2010. It includes all writers, both registered and unregistered, but not illustrators where the book has a separate writer. Writing names are used; pseudonyms have not been combined.

co-author and provide supporting evidence as to why that co-author has not agreed shares. The living co-author(s) will then be able to register a share in the book which reflects individual contribution.

Providing permission is granted, the PLR Office can help to put co-authors (including illustrators) in touch with each other. Help is also available from publishers, the writers' organisations, and the Association of Illustrators.

Life and death. First applications may *not* be made by the estate of a deceased author. However, if an author registers during their lifetime the PLR in their books can be transferred to a new owner and continues for up to 70 years after the date of their death. The new owner can apply to register new titles if first published one year before, or up to ten years after the date of the author's death. New editions of existing registered titles can also be registered posthumously.

Residential qualifications. With effect from 1 July 2000, PLR is open to authors living in the European Economic Area (i.e. EU member states plus Norway, Liechtenstein and Iceland). A resident in these countries (for PLR purposes) must have their only or principal home there.

Eligible books

In the PLR system each separate edition of a book is registered and treated as a separate book. A book is eligible for PLR registration provided that:
- it has an eligible author (or co-author);
- it is printed and bound (paperbacks counting as bound);
- copies of it have been put on sale (i.e. it is not a free handout and it has already been published);
- it is not a newspaper, magazine, journal or periodical;
- the authorship is personal (i.e. not a company or association) and the book is not crown copyright;
- it is not wholly or mainly a musical score;
- it has an ISBN.

Statements and payment

Authors with an online account may view their statement online. Registered authors who do not have an online account receive a statement posted to their address if a payment is due.

Sampling arrangements

To help minimise the unfairnesses that arise inevitably from a sampling system, the Scheme specifies the eight regions within which authorities and sampling points have to be designated and includes libraries of varying size. Part of the sample drops out by rotation each year to allow fresh libraries to be included. The following library authorities have been designated for the year beginning 1 July 2011 (all are multi-site authorities). This list is based on the nine government regions for England plus Northern Ireland, Scotland and Wales.

• East – Essex, Suffolk
• East Midlands – Northamptonshire
• London – City of London, Islington, London Libraries Consortium (Barking & Dagenham, Brent, Ealing, Enfield, Hackney, Havering, Newham, Redbridge, Richmond Upon Thames, Tower Hamlets, Waltham Forest, Wandsworth)
• North East – Middlesbrough, Sunderland
• North West & Merseyside – Blackburn with Darwen, Salford, Sefton
• South East – East Sussex
• South West – LibrariesWest (Bath and North East Somerset, Bristol, North Somerset, Somerset, South Gloucestershire)

Most borrowed children's fiction titles

	Author	Title	Publisher	Year
1	Julia Donaldson (illus. Axel Scheffler)	*The Gruffalo*	Macmillan Children's	1999
2	Francesca Simon (illus. Tony Ross)	*Horrid Henry and the Football Fiend*	Orion Children's	2006
3	Claire Freedman and Ben Cort	*Aliens Love Underpants!*	Simon & Schuster	2007
4	Stephenie Meyer	*Eclipse*	Atom	2008
5	Stephenie Meyer	*Breaking Dawn*	Atom	2008
6	J.K. Rowling	*Harry Potter and the Deathly Hallows*	Bloomsbury	2007
7	Stephenie Meyer	*Twilight*	Atom	2007
8	Stephenie Meyer	*New Moon*	Atom	2007
9	Giles Andreae (illus. Nick Sharratt)	*Pants*	David Fickling	2003
10	Jacqueline Wilson (illus. Nick Sharratt)	*Cookie*	Doubleday	2008
11	Francesca Simon (illus. Tony Ross)	*Horrid Henry and the Abominable Snowman*	Orion Children's	2007
12	Francesca Simon (illus. Tony Ross)	*Horrid Henry Robs the Bank*	Orion Children's	2008
13	Francesca Simon (illus. Tony Ross)	*Horrid Henry Meets the Queen*	Orion Children's	2004
14	Michael Rosen (illus. Helen Oxenbury)	*We're Going on a Bear Hunt*	Walker	1989
15	Maurice Sendak	*Where the Wild Things Are*	Red Fox	2000
16	Eric Hill	*Where's Spot?*	Puffin	1983
17	Jacqueline Wilson (illus. Nick Sharratt)	*Hetty Feather*	Doubleday	2009
18	Julia Donaldson (illus. Axel Scheffler)	*Stick Man*	Alison Green	2008
19	Jacqueline Wilson (illus. Nick Sharratt)	*My Sister Jodie*	Doubleday	2008
20	Francesca Simon (illus. Tony Ross)	*Horrid Henry and the Mega-Mean Time Machine*	Dolphin	2005

- West Midlands – Telford and Wrekin, Warwickshire
- Yorkshire & The Humber – North Yorkshire, Rotherham
- Northern Ireland – The Northern Ireland Library Authority
- Scotland – East Ayrshire, Glasgow, Scottish Borders
- Wales – Cardiff, Denbighshire and Flintshire, Monmouthshire.

Participating local authorities are reimbursed on an actual cost basis for additional expenditure incurred in providing loans data to the PLR Office. The extra PLR work mostly consists of modifications to computer programs to accumulate loans data in the local authority computer and to transmit the data to the PLR Office at Stockton-on-Tees.

Most borrowed classic children's titles

	Author	Title	Publisher	Year
1	Roald Dahl (illus. Quentin Blake)	The BFG	Puffin	2007
2	Ian Beck	Chicken Licken	OUP	2003
3	Michael Bond (illus. R.W. Alley)	Paddington in the Garden	HarperCollins	2008
4	Dodie Smith (illus. David Roberts)	The Hundred and One Dalmations	Egmont	2006
5	Michael Bond (illus. R.W. Alley)	Paddington Here and Now	HarperCollins	2008
6	Enid Blyton	The Secret Seven	Hodder	2006
7	Enid Blyton	Secret Seven Adventure	Hodder	2006
8	Lewis Carrol (illus. Helen Oxenbury)	Alice Through the Looking-glass and What She Found There	Walker	2009
9	Roald Dahl	Fantastic Mr Fox	Puffin	2009
10	Roald Dahl (illus. Quentin Blake)	The Vicar of Nibbleswicke	Penguin	1992
11	Roald Dahl (illus. Quentin Blake)	George's Marvellous Medicine	Cape	2003
12	Enid Blyton	Secret Seven on the Trail	Hodder	2006
13	Sam Taplin	Night Night Stories	Usborne	2008
14	Roald Dahl (illus. Quentin Blake)	The Giraffe and the Pelly and Me	Puffin	2004
15	Michael Bond (illus. Peggy Fortnum)	A Bear Called Paddington	Collins	2003
16	L. Frank Baum (intro Cornelia Funke, illus. David McKee)	The Wizard of Oz	Puffin	2008
17	Charles Dickens (illus. Barry Ablett)	Oliver Twist	Usborne	2006
18	Enid Blyton	Well Done, Secret Seven	Hodder	2006
19	Michael Bond (illus. R.W. Alley)	Paddington and the Grand Tour	Collins	2003
20	C.S. Lewis (illus. Pauline Baynes)	The Lion, the Witch and the Wardrobe	Collins	1998

Reciprocal arrangements

Reciprocal PLR arrangements now exist with the German, Dutch, Austrian and other European PLR schemes. Authors can apply for overseas PLR through the Authors' Licensing and Collecting Society. Authors resident in the European Economic Area can also now register for Irish PLR through the Irish PLR Office (www.plr.ie). Further information on PLR schemes internationally and recent developments within the EC towards wider recognition of PLR is available from the PLR Office or on the international PLR website.

Most borrowed children's non-fiction titles

	Author	Title	Publisher	Year
1	David McKee	*Elmer's First Counting Book*	Anderson	2007
2	Characters created by Lauren Child	*I Completely Know About Guinea Pigs*	Puffin	2008
3	Mick Inkpen	*One Year with Kipper*	Hodder Children's	2006
4	Illus. Annie Kubler	*Peek-a-book: Nursery Games*	Child's Play	2005
5	Mick Inkpen	*One Year with Kipper*	Hodder Children's	2007
6	Lauren Child	*Charlie and Lola's Opposites*	Orchard	2007
7	Lauren Child	*Charlie and Lola's Numbers*	Orchard	2007
8	Stella Blackstone (illus. Christopher Corr)	*My Granny Went to Market*	Barefoot	2006
9	Lauren Child	*Charlie and Lola's Colours*	Watts	2007
10	Jacqueline Wilson (illus. Nick Sharratt)	*Totally Jacqueline Wilson*	Doubleday	2007
11	Jacqueline Wilson (illus. Nick Sharratt)	*Jacky Daydream*	Doubleday	2007
12	Lauren Child	*Charlie and Lola's Shapes*	Orchard	2007
13	Characters created by Lauren Child	*Look After Your Planet*	Puffin	2008
14	Lauren Child	*Charlie and Lola's Animals*	Watts	2007
15	Lauren Child	*Charlie and Lola's Things*	Orchard	2007
16	Fiona Watt (illus. Stephen Cartwright)	*Touchy-feely 123*	Usborne	2008
17	Dave King	*My First Numbers*	Penguin	2009
18	Mick Inkpen	*First Kipper: Colours*	Hodder Children's	2008
19	Terry Deary (illus. Martin Brown)	*Knights*	Scholstic	2006
20	Fiona Land	*Baby Touch Shapes*	Ladybird	2008

Copyright
Copyright questions

Copyright is a vital part of any writer's assets, and should never be assigned or sold without due consideration and the advice of a competent authority, such as the Society of Authors, the Writers' Guild of Great Britain, or the National Union of Journalists. Michael Legat answers some of the most commonly asked questions about copyright.

Is there a period of time after which the copyright expires?

Copyright in the European Union lasts for the lifetime of the author and for a further 70 years from the end of the year of death, or, if the work is first published posthumously, for 70 years from the end of the year of publication. In most other countries of the world copyright exists similarly for the lifetime and for either 50 years or 70 years after death or posthumous publication.

If I want to include an extract from a book, poem or article, do I have to seek copyright? How much may be used without permission? What happens if I apply for copyright permission but do not get a reply?

It is essential to seek permission to quote from another author's work, unless that author has been dead for 70 years or more, or 70 years or more has passed from the date of publication of a work published posthumously. Only if you are quoting for purposes of criticism or review are you allowed to do so without obtaining permission, and even then the Copyright, Designs and Patents Act of 1988 restricts you to 400 words of prose in a single extract from a copyright work, or a series of extracts of up to 300 words each, totalling no more than 800 words, or up to 40 lines of poetry, which must not be more than 25% of the poem. However, a quotation of no more than, say, half a dozen words may usually be used without permission since it will probably not extend beyond a brief and familiar reference, as, for example, Rider Haggard's well-known phrase, 'she who must be obeyed'. If in doubt, always check. If you do not get a reply when you ask for permission to quote, insert a notice in your work saying that you have tried without success to contact the copyright owner, and would be pleased to hear from him or her so that the matter could be cleared up – and keep a copy of all the relevant correspondence, in order to back up your claim of having tried to get in touch.

If a newspaper pays for an article and I then want to sell the story to a magazine, am I free under the copyright law to do so?

Yes, provided that you have not granted copyright or exclusive use to the newspaper. When selling your work to newspapers or magazines make it clear, in writing, that you are selling only First or Second Serial Rights, not your copyright.

If I agree to have an article published for no payment do I retain any rights over how it appears?

Whether or not you are paid for the work has no bearing on the legal situation. However, the Moral Rights which apply to books, plays, television and radio scripts, do not cover you against a failure to acknowledge you as the author of an article, nor against the mutilation of your text, when it is published in a newspaper or magazine.

I want to publish a photograph that was taken in 1950. I am not sure how to contact the photographer or even if he is still alive. Am I allowed to go ahead and publish it?

The Copyright, Designs and Patents Act of 1988 works retrospectively, so a photograph taken in 1950 is bound to be in copyright until at least 2020, and the copyright will be owned by the photographer, even though, when it was taken, the copyright would have belonged to the person who commissioned it, according to the laws then in place. You should therefore make every effort to contact the photographer, keeping copies of any relevant correspondence, and in case of failure take the same course of action as described above in relation to a textual extract the copyright owner of which you have been unable to trace.

I recently read an article on the same subject as one I have written. It contained many identical facts. Did this writer breach my copyright? What if I send ideas for an article to a magazine editor and those ideas are used despite the fact that I was not commissioned? May I sue the magazine?

Facts are normally in the public domain and may be used by anyone. However, if your article contains a fact which you have discovered and no one else has published, there could be an infringement of copyright if the author who uses it fails to attribute it to you. There is no copyright in ideas, so you cannot sue a writer or a journal for using ideas that you have put forward; in any case you would find it very difficult to prove that the idea belonged to you and to no one else. There is also no copyright in titles.

Does being paid a kill fee affect my copyright in a given piece?

No, provided that you have not sold the magazine or newspaper your copyright.

Do I need to copyright a piece of writing physically – whether an essay or a novel – or is it copyrighted automatically? Does it have to carry the © symbol?

Anything that you write is your copyright, assuming that it is not copied from the work of someone else, as soon as you have written it on paper or recorded it on the disk of a computer or on tape, or broadcast it, or posted it on the internet. It is not essential for the work to carry the © symbol, although its inclusion may act as a warning and help to stop another writer from plagiarising it.

Am I legally required to inform an interviewee that our conversation is being recorded?

The interviewee owns the copyright of any words that he or she speaks as soon as they are recorded on your tape. Unless you have received permission to use those words in direct quotation, you could be liable to an action for infringement of copyright. You should therefore certainly inform the interviewee that the conversation is being recorded and seek permission to quote what is said directly.

More and more newspapers and magazines have versions both in print and on the internet. How can I ensure that my work is not published on the internet without my permission?

Make sure that any clause granting electronic rights to anyone in any agreement that you sign in respect of your work specifies not only the proportion of any fees received which you will get, but that your agreement must be sought before the rights are sold. Copyright extends to electronic rights, and therefore to publication on the internet, in just the same way as to other uses of the material.

I commissioned a designer to design a business card for me, and I paid her well. Does the design belong to me or to her?

Copyright would belong to the designer, and not to the person who commissioned it (as is also true in the case of a photograph, copyright in which belongs to the photographer). However, copyright in the business card might be transferred to you if a court considered you to have gained beneficially from the card.

Michael Legat became a full-time writer after a long and successful publishing career. He is the author of a number of highly regarded books on publishing and writing.

See also...
- *The Society of Authors*, page 353
- *Authors' Licensing and Collecting Society*, page 276
- *Design and Artists Copyright Society*, page 278
- *The Copyright Licensing Agency Ltd*, page 274

Copyright

The Copyright Licensing Agency Ltd

The Copyright Licensing Agency (CLA) licenses organisations to copy extracts from copyright publications on behalf of the authors, publishers and visual creators it represents. CLA's licences permit photocopying, scanning and emailing of articles and extracts from books, journals and magazines, as well as digital and online publications. CLA issues licences to schools, further and higher education, businesses and government bodies. The money collected is distributed to rights owners to ensure that they are properly rewarded for the use of their intellectual property.

Why was CLA established?

CLA was set up by its owners, the Authors' Licensing and Collecting Society (ALCS) and the Publishers Licensing Society (PLS) and has an agency agreement with the Design and Artists Copyright Society (DACS), which represents visual artists, such as photographers, illustrators and painters.

Further information

The Copyright Licensing Agency Ltd
Saffron House, 6–10 Kirby Street,
London EC1N 8TS
tel 020-7400 3100 *fax* 020-7400 3101
email cla@cla.co.uk
website www.cla.co.uk

CLA exists to represent creators and publishers by licensing the copying of their work and promoting the value of copyright generally. This way CLA helps to protect the value of creativity.

How CLA helps artists and writers

CLA allows licensed users access to millions of titles worldwide. In return, CLA ensures that artists and writers, along with publishers, are fairly recompensed through the payment of royalties derived from the licence fees which CLA collects and distributes.

Through this collective licensing system CLA is able to provide users with the simplest and most cost-effective means of obtaining authorisation for photocopying and scanning of published works, albeit under strict copy limits.

CLA has licences which enable digitisation of existing print material, enabling users to scan and electronically send extracts from printed copyright works.

CLA has recently also launched a series of new licences for business and government which allow users to re-use and copy from born digital electronic and online publications. Writers and publishers can benefit further from the increased income generated from these licences which operate under the same copy limits as the established photocopying licences.

Who is licensed?

CLA's licences are available to three principal sectors:
• education (schools, further and higher education);
• government (central, local authorities, public bodies); and
• business (businesses, industry and the professions).

CLA offers licences to meet the specific needs of each sector and user groups within each sector. Depending on the requirement, there are both blanket and transactional licences available. Every licence allows the photocopying of most books, journals, magazines and periodicals published in the UK.

International dimension

Many countries have established equivalents to CLA and the number of such agencies is set to grow. Nearly all these agencies, including CLA, are members of the International Federation of Reproduction Rights Organisations (IFRRO).

Through reciprocal arrangements covering more than 30 overseas territories including the USA, Canada and most EU countries, CLA's licences allow copying from an expanding list of international publications. CLA receives monies from these territories for the copying of UK material abroad and passes it on to UK rightsholders.

Distribution of licence fees

The fees collected from licensees are forwarded to publishers, authors and visual artists via PLS, ALCS and DACS respectively, and the allocation of fees is based on subscriptions, library holdings and detailed surveys of copying activity. To date, CLA has collected and distributed over £460 million to rightsholders since its establishment. For the year 2008/9 over £52 million was paid to creators and publishers.

Enabling access, protecting creativity

CLA believes it is important to raise awareness of copyright and the need to protect the creativity of artists, authors and publishers. To this end, it organises a range of activities such as copyright workshops in schools, seminars for businesses and institutions and an extensive programme of exhibitions and other events.

CLA believes in working positively together with representative bodies in each sector, meaning legal action is rare. However, organisations – especially in the business sector – are made aware that copyright is a legally enforceable right and not a voluntary option. CLA's compliance arm, Copywatch, is active in these sectors to educate users and seek out illegal copying.

By supporting rightsholders in this way, CLA plays an important role in maintaining the value of their work, thereby sustaining creativity and its benefit to all. Through protection of this sort the creative industries in the UK have been able to grow to support millions of jobs and to produce over 8% of UK GDP.

Copyright

Authors' Licensing and Collecting Society

The Authors' Licensing and Collecting Society is the rights management society for UK writers.

The Authors' Licensing and Collecting Society (ALCS) is the UK collective rights management society for writers. Established in 1977, it represents the interests of all UK writers and aims to ensure that they are fairly compensated for any works that are copied, broadcast or recorded.

A non-profit company, ALCS was set up in the wake of the campaign to establish a Public Lending Right to help writers protect and exploit their collective rights. Today, it is the largest writers' organisation in the UK with a membership of approximately 80,000. In the financial year of 2010/11, £25.2 million in royalties were paid out to writers.

The Society is committed to ensuring that the rights of writers, both intellectual property and moral, are fully respected and fairly rewarded. It represents all types of writers and includes educational, research and academic authors drawn from the professions: scriptwriters, adaptors, playwrights, poets, editors and freelance journalists, across the print and broadcast media.

Internationally recognised as a leading authority on copyright matters and authors' interests, ALCS is committed to fostering an awareness of intellectual property issues among the writing community. It maintains a close watching brief on all matters affecting copyright both in the UK and internationally and makes regular representations to the UK government and the European Union.

The Society collects fees that are difficult, time-consuming or legally impossible for writers and their representatives to claim on an individual basis, money that is nonetheless due to them. To date, it has distributed over £250 million in secondary royalties to writers.

Over the years, ALCS has developed highly specialised knowledge and sophisticated systems that can track writers and their works against any secondary use for which they are due payment. A network of international contacts and reciprocal agreements with foreign collecting societies also ensures that British writers are compensated for any similar use overseas.

The primary sources of fees due to writers are secondary royalties from the following.

Membership

Authors' Licensing and Collecting Society Ltd
The Writers' House, 13 Haydon Street,
London EC3N 1DB
tel 020-7264 5700 *fax* 020-7264 5755
email alcs@alcs.co.uk
website www.alcs.co.uk
Chief Executive Owen Atkinson

Membership is open to all writers and successors to their estates at a one-off fee of £25 for Ordinary membership. Members of the Society of Authors and the Writers' Guild of Great Britain have free Ordinary membership of ALCS. Operations are primarily funded through a commission levied on distributions and membership fees. The commission on funds generated for Ordinary members is currently 9.75%. Most writers will find that this, together with a number of other membership benefits, provides good value.

Photocopying

The single largest source of income, this is administered by the Copyright Licensing Agency (CLA – see page 274). Created in 1982 by ALCS and the Publishers Licensing Society (PLS), the CLA grants licences to users for the copying of books and serials. This includes schools, colleges, universities, central and local government departments as well as the British Library, businesses and other institutions. Licence fees are based on the number of people who benefit and the number of copies made. The revenue from this is then split between the rightsholders: authors, publishers and artists. Money due to authors is transferred to ALCS for distribution. ALCS also receives photocopying payments from foreign sources.

Digitisation

In 1999, the CLA launched its licensing scheme for the digitisation of printed texts. It offers licences to organisations for storing and using digital versions of authors' printed works, which have been scanned into a computer. Again, the fees are split between authors and publishers.

Foreign Public Lending Right

The Public Lending Right (PLR) system pays authors whose books are borrowed from public libraries. Through reciprocal agreements ALCS members receive payment whenever their books are borrowed from German, Belgian, Dutch, French, Austrian, Spanish and Irish libraries. Please note that ALCS does not administer the UK Public Lending Right, this is managed directly by the UK PLR Office; see page 264.

ALCS also receives other payments from Germany. These cover the loan of academic, scientific and technical titles from academic libraries; extracts of authors' works in text-books and the press, together with other one-off fees.

Simultaneous cable retransmission

This involves the simultaneous showing of one country's television signals in another country, via a cable network. Cable companies pay a central collecting organisation a percentage of their subscription fees, which must be collectively administered. This sum is then divided by the rightsholders. ALCS receives the writers' share for British programmes containing literary and dramatic material and distributes it to them.

Educational recording

ALCS, together with the main broadcasters and rightsholders, set up the Educational Recording Agency (ERA) in 1989 to offer licences to educational establishments. ERA collects fees from the licensees and pays ALCS the amount due to writers for their literary works.

Other sources of income include a blank tape levy and small, miscellaneous literary rights.

Tracing authors

ALCS is dedicated to protecting and promoting authors' rights and enabling writers to maximise their income. It is committed to ensuring that royalties due to writers are efficiently collected and speedily distributed to them. One of its greatest challenges is finding some of the writers for whom it holds funds and ensuring that they claim their money.

Any published author or broadcast writer could have some funds held by ALCS for them. It may be a nominal sum or it could run into several thousand pounds. Either call or visit the ALCS website – see box for contact details.

Copyright

Design and Artists Copyright Society

Established by artists for artists, the Design and Artists Copyright Society (DACS) is the UK's leading visual arts rights management organisation.

About DACS

As a not-for-profit organisation, DACS translates rights into revenues and recognition for a wide spectrum of visual artists.

DACS offers three rights management services – Copyright Licensing, Artist's Resale Right and Payback – in addition to lobbying, advocacy and legal advice for visual artists.

DACS is part of an international network of rights management organisations. Today DACS represents nearly 60,000 artists and in 2010, it distributed over £7.2 million to artists and their beneficiaries. See website for more information about DACS and its services.

Payback

Each year DACS pays a share of royalties to visual artists whose work has been reproduced in UK magazines and books or broadcast on UK television channels. DACS operates this service for situations where it would be impractical or near impossible for you to license your rights on an individual basis, for example when a university wants to photocopy pages from a book which features your work. Every kind of visual artist can claim Payback. If you are an illustrator, sculptor, cartoonist, photographer or any other type of visual artist, you can make a claim.

Artist's Resale Right

The Artist's Resale Right entitles artists to a royalty each time their work is resold by an auction house, gallery or dealer subject to certain conditions. Visual artists who benefit from this service include fine artists, bookbinders, photographers, sculptors, furniture designers and ceramicists to name but a few. See website for details of eligibility criteria. DACS ensures artists receive their royalties from qualifying sales not just in the UK but also internationally through our network of rights management organisations. The Right is capped at €12,500 to protect the art market. From 1 January 2012, in the UK the Right will be fully implemented to enable artists' heirs and beneficiaries to benefit from these royalties.

Copyright licensing

For artists to manage their copyright it can be a complex and time-consuming process. However, DACS' Copyright Licensing service provides an effective way for artists to manage the licensing of their rights, by ensuring terms, fees and contractual arrangements are all in order and in their best interests. Copyright licensing benefits artists and their estates when their work is reproduced for commercial purposes – for example on t-shirts or greetings cards, in a book or on a website. DACS provides advice and support if an artist's work is used without their permission. Artists who use this service are also represented globally through our international network of rights management organisations.

Copyright facts

• Copyright is a right granted to visual artists under law.

• Copyright in all artistic works is established from the moment of creation – the only qualification is that the work must be original.

• There is no registration system in the UK; copyright comes into operation automatically and lasts the lifetime of the visual artist plus a period of 70 years after their death.

• After death, copyright is usually transferred to the visual artist's heirs or beneficiaries. When the 70-year period has expired, the work then enters the public domain and no longer benefits from copyright protection.

• The copyright owner has the exclusive right to authorise the reproduction (or copy) of a work in any medium by any other party.

• Any reproduction can only take place with the copyright owner's consent.

• Permission is usually granted in return for a fee, which enables the visual artist to derive some income from other people using his or her work.

• If a visual artist is commissioned to produce a work, he or she will usually retain the copyright unless an agreement is signed which specifically assigns the copyright. When visual creators are employees and create work during the course of their employment, the employer retains the copyright in those works.

See also...

• *Copyright questions,* page 271

Copyright

Magazines and newspapers
Writing for teenage magazines

Teenage magazines can be a lifeline to adolescent girls but writing for this market is very specialised. Michelle Garnett explains what writers for teenage magazines need to know.

Life for teen girls is tough. Raging hormones, changing body bits, annoying boys and constant peer pressure, all gang up to present one huge challenge for them. And that's where teen magazines come to the rescue, providing escapism and reassurance for their confused readers. But before even thinking about submitting your work to any teen mag, it's vital to get a firm grasp on what they're all about. Most mags tend to fall into two categories – 'Lifestyle' and 'Entertainment':

• The Lifestyle titles (think *Bliss*) provide info on anything relevant to teen girls' lives, from reports on way-out new style trends and self-help features to dish out advice on coping with bullies to tips on bagging a buff boyfriend and gritty real life stories.

• The Entertainment titles (think *Top of the Tops Magazine*) focus on celeb, music, TV and film gossip with lashings of star interviews, celeb quizzes, posters and song words.

Both categories tend to overlap slightly, with the Lifestyle titles including a juicy dollop of celebrity gossip and interviews and the Entertainment titles enjoying a sprinkling of fashion and self-help advice.

These days, with teens spending piles of their pocket money on mobile phone top-up cards and quick-fix junk food there's heaps of competition amongst the teen mags for high sales. So covers *have* to be attention grabbing. Cover lines must offer exclusivity (e.g. a gripping heart-to-heart with the latest *X Factor* winner), fresh ideas (new revelations about the murky depths of teen boys' minds) and aspirational promises (easy steps to looking fab *whatever* your body shape). Cover images must be non-threatening (girls looking friendly, not bitchy), eye-popping (topless, and most importantly, hairless boy totty is usually a firm favourite) and colourful (you can't beat a flash of fluoro to help you stand out). Most mags also rely on 'free gifts' to help boost their 'come buy me!' appeal.

Teen mag readership

But who are these teen girls that we're trying to persuade to part with their precious pocket money? If you're intending to aim your features at this discerning group of individuals you'd better get to know all you can about them.

On the whole, teen readers are demanding, streetwise, fickle consumers who want to be treated with respect but view adulthood with apprehension, often clinging to the comforts of childhood to help them feel secure and safe when the pressure gets too much.

Here's the scientific bit… Did you know that typical teen readers tend to fall into four *very* revealing categories? First off, there's the 'Obsessive Fan'. This girl has to be the first to know any gossip. She'll usually be infatuated with one boy in particular – often this will be a celeb whose cute face will be plastered all over her bedroom wall, school locker, books, etc. She'll spend every last penny on anything (including mags) that contains a fleeting mention of him. Sometimes her affections will be focused on a 'real' boy – it's been known for Obsessive Fan types to keep a secret stash of her 'crush souvenirs', containing such gems as a dirty fork that he once used in the school canteen!

Next there's the 'Fashionista'. This girl is crazy about fashion. She'll spend hours flicking through the style pages desperate for inspiration for her weekly shopping trips to New Look and Top Shop. The more creative Fashionista will copy the step-by-step customising guides to give her outfits that individualistic edge. She'll be an expert with her make up brush and unsurprisingly, will be very image conscious. She might pretend that she doesn't need to read features on 'detox diets to make your skin glow' but she'll devour them in secret and then pass on her newly acquired tips to her gang.

Then there's the 'Reality Lover'. This girl is addicted to Jeremy Kyle and TV soaps. She'll greedily devour tragic real life stories. It doesn't matter whether the tale relates to a famous celeb or an ordinary 15 year-old from Leeds – so long as it's majorly grim, with a positive ending, she'll be hooked. It's no surprise that she's a fan of reality TV shows and dramas and loves gossiping about the latest shocking antics on *I'm a Celebrity… Get Me Out of Here* or *Desperate Housewives*. In fact, it's reading about other people's lives that provides her with some comfort and reassurance about her own life.

Lastly, there's the 'Info Gatherer'. This girl is a true magazine junkie! She uses her mag fix to get high on knowledge that'll help her make sense of the world around her and will elevate her status in her gang. She's not fussy about what she reads, is less street-sussed than other girls in her class and becomes easily bored. She'll often have three different mags on the go at a time but will just as happily plough through her mum's mags too.

But in case you're thinking, 'Hey, I was a teen once – I *know* what they're like' just remember one thing… 21st century teen readers are very different from those even just ten years ago. These days' teens have much less to rebel about. The majority are actually best mates with their mothers and instead of shocking them with new pillar-box red highlights they'll be out shopping with their trendy mums and swapping clothes! They're also worldly wise and surprisingly ambitious about their future prospects.

Oh and don't think you can ever pull the wool over teen readers' eyes – they're sharp and quick to judge and if you get even the smallest fact wrong, they'll pick you up on it!

Considering writing for teen mags

So, now you've considered the kind of reader you'll be speaking to via your feature, it's time to get cracking, yes? No! It may sound mind-numbingly obvious but the first step when considering submitting material to a teen mag is to actually read a copy of that magazine! It's amazing how many times I've received suggestions for short fiction pieces when we don't actually feature those kind of stories in the magazine.

Familiarise yourself with the content, the look and the feel of the magazine. Many mags get revamped quite frequently to keep ahead of the competition, so it's wise to regularly browse through the latest issues to stay up to date.

A quick glance at the mag should tell you which kind of teen it's aimed at and therefore how you should tailor your copy or artwork to the targeted reader. As a writer it's vital to soak up the tone of the copy. Is it streetwise and fast-paced or cheesy and fun? Are there any phrases or words that pop up on a regular basis, giving an insight into the kind of language the average reader uses? Features for the older Lifestyle magazines tend to adopt a punchy, straight-talking approach with, where appropriate, more caring 'big sister' tone when tackling sensitive subjects. A magazine aimed at younger readers, such as *Top of the Pops Magazine*, veers towards a more excitable, upbeat tone, with the tendency to paint the pop world as bright, crazy and inoffensive.

Consider the tone of the actual subject matter too. Is it serious and gritty? Is it frivolous and tongue-in-cheek? Are there clear sections within the magazine which consist of a running theme? *Bliss* magazine features a strong 'real life stories' section which caters for their readers love for a dramatic, juicy read.

Another angle to reflect on is the topicality of the copy and pictures. When contributing ideas to a monthly mag think of a quirky spin you can give your idea to help give what could be a tried and tested subject a fresh makeover. If you're intending to submit ideas to a weekly mag then you need to prove that you've got your finger on the pulse. Think about how you can make your work up to date and relevant. Ask yourself, 'What's affecting teens' lives right *now*?' Are they crumbling under the pressure of exams? Is there a huge blockbuster film on the horizon that's set to capture their imaginations?

When *High School Musical* was first released it was noticeable how most titles were quick to spot the potential popularity of the film. By the time the third instalment hit the big screen, Hollywood star Zac Efron had firmly established himself as a teen heartthrob and his appearance in the film as the student Troy Bolton encouraged a stream of Zac-inspired features to whet readers' appetites. Paparazzi and studio shots of the actor were in high demand and real life titbits and Zac Efron quizzes were a staple diet for several months.

And of course, think seasonal. A few months prior to the summer holidays, monthly teen titles will be dreaming up cover-worthy concepts for the ultimate boredom buster feature. Conjure up a trend-based, original idea and you could find yourself commissioned to produce a hefty eight-page special.

Getting noticed

Finally… how to get yourself noticed amongst a sea of competition from other freelancers. Sometimes it's all about timing. It may be worthwhile to find out if the mag you're hoping to submit work to has a set date each week or month when feature ideas are discussed so that you can ensure your suggestions land in the Features Editor's email box just when he or she is tuned into an ideas brainstorm. Don't go the bother of sending in a fully completed article. If your idea is strong, a catchy headline and brief synopsis will grab their attention and the sheer mention of a juicy real life case study will be enough to get them salivating! And if you have a specialist subject area (style, real life stories, celebrity interviews) it could be worth suggesting a meeting with the relevant team member – if you impress them with your expertise you could bag yourself a regular commission.

But most importantly of all – don't give up. If you don't hear back immediately it doesn't necessarily mean your idea's been discarded. Many teen mag offices are hectic environments in which pressured deadlines often take on a life of their own. Your contact is probably furiously chasing a lead on a reality TV star's love life trauma, while trying to persuade a gang of shy 14 year-old lads to confess their first date hells and batting around that ever niggling question: 'how am I going to make our lovely readers feel entertained, shocked, reassured and hooked by my magazine this issue?' And hopefully that's when *your* life-saving email will come to light! Good luck!

Michelle Garnett was editor of *Sneak* magazine from April 2002 to May 2005. Previously, she worked for ten years in various roles in the entertainment industry including deputy editor of *Top of the Pops Magazine*, producer of *cd:uk news*, editor of *worldpop.com*, writer of pop band biographies and (her most bizarre job to date…) official news reporter for Reuters on the Backstreet Boys four-day round-the-world promotional trip (2000). She now freelances as a writer and editor for various publications.

Magazines and newspapers for children

Listings of magazines about children's literature and education start on page 293.

Adventure Box
Bayard, 1st Floor, 2 King Street,
Peterborough PE1 1LT
tel (01733) 565 858 *fax* (01733) 427 500
email contact@bayard-magazines.co.uk
website www.bayard-magazines.co.uk
Editor-in-chief Simona Sideri, *Art Director* Pat Carter
10 p.a. £39 p.a.

Aimed at 6–9 year-old children starting to read on their own. Each issue contains an illustrated chapter story plus games, an animal feature, nature activity and a cartoon. Length: 2,500–3,000 words (stories). Specially commissions most material. Founded 1996.

All About Animals
BBC Worldwide Ltd, Woodlands, 80 Wood Lane,
London W12 0TT
email allaboutanimals@bbc.co.uk
website www.bbcmagazines.com
Every 4 weeks £2.99

Animal facts, features about wildlife and pets, and puzzles, quizzes and posters for 7–11 year-old girls.

Animal Action
RSPCA, Wilberforce Way, Southwater, Horsham,
West Sussex RH13 9RS
tel (0300) 123 0100
website www.rspca.org.uk
Editor Sarah Evans
7 p.a. £1.99, £11 p.a.

RSPCA membership magazine for children under 13 years old with animal news, features, competitions and puzzles.

Animals and You
D.C. Thomson & Co Ltd, Albert Square,
Dundee DD1 9QJ
tel (01382) 223131 *fax* (01382) 322214
email animalsandyou@dcthomson.co.uk
185 Fleet Street, London EC4A 2HS
tel 020-7400 1030 *fax* 020-7400 1089
Every 3 weeks £2.99

Features, stories and posters for girls who love animals. Founded 1998.

Aquila
New Leaf Publishing Ltd, PO Box 2518, Eastbourne,
East Sussex BN21 2BB
tel (01323) 431313 *fax* (01323) 731136
email info@aquila.co.uk
website www.aquila.co.uk
Editor Jackie Berry
Monthly £40 p.a.

Dedicated to encouraging children aged 8–13 to reason and create, and to develop a caring nature. Short stories and serials of up to 3 parts. Occasional features commissioned from writers with specialist knowledge. Approach in writing with ideas and sample of writing style, with sae. Length: 700–800 words (features), 1,000–1,100 words (stories or per episode of a serial). Payment: £75 (features); £90 (stories), £80 (per episode). Founded 1993.

Art Attack
Panini UK, Brockbourne House, 77 Mount Ephraim,
Tunbridge Wells TN4 8AR
tel (01892) 500143 *fax* (01892) 545666
email paninicomics@panini.co.uk
website www.paninicomics.co.uk
Editor Simon Frith
Monthly £2.25

Magazine to complement the TV show *Art Attack*. Step-by-step instructions on creative things to make and do.

Astonishing Spider-Man
Panini UK, Brockbourne House, 77 Mount Ephraim,
Tunbridge Wells TN4 8AR
tel (01892) 500100 *fax* (01892) 545666
email astonspid@panini.co.uk
website www.paninicomics.co.uk
Editor Brady Webb
Every 2 weeks £2.95, £76.70 p.a.

Avengers Unconquered
Panini UK, Brockbourne House, 77 Mount Ephraim,
Tunbridge Wells TN4 8AR
tel (01892) 500100 *fax* (01892) 545666
email paninicomics@panini.co.uk
website www.paninicomics.co.uk
Editor Scott Gray
Every 4 weeks £2.95

Barbie
Egmont Magazines, 239 Kensington High Street,
London W3 6SA
tel 020-7761 3500 *fax* 020-7761 3510
website www.egmontmagazines.co.uk
Editor Rebecca Boxer

Every 3 weeks £2.50

Magazine for 3–8 year-old girls. Provides the reader with news from the ever-changing world of Barbie from pretty princess to cool chic, with a constant focus on aspects of fashion, friends and fun.

Batman: Legends
Titan Publishing Group Ltd, Titan House, 144 Southwark Street, London SE1 0UP
tel 020-7620 0200 *fax* 020-7620 0032
website www.titancomicsuk.com
Editor Ned Hartley
6 p.a. £2.60

The Beano
D.C. Thomson & Co. Ltd, 2 Albert Square, Dundee DD1 9QJ
email adigby@dcthompson.co.uk
185 Fleet Street, London EC4A 2HS
tel 020-7400 1030 *fax* 020-7400 1089
Editor Alan Digby
Weekly £1.35

Comic strips for children aged 6–12. Series, 11–22 pictures. Artwork only. Payment: on acceptance.

Ben 10 Magazine
Egmont UK Ltd, 239 High Street Kensington, London W8 6SA
email info@egmont.co.uk
website www.egmont.co.uk
Every 3 weeks £2.45

The official Ben 10 magazine aimed at 4–6-year-old children. Includes an 8pp comic strip, activities, fact files and posters. Founded 2009.

Blast Off!
RNIB, PO Box 173, Peterborough PE2 6WS
tel 0303-123 9999 *fax* (01733) 375001
email editorial@rnib.org.uk
website www.rnib.org.uk
Editor Racheal Jarvis
Monthly 29p (export £1.78)

Braille general interest magazine for blind and partially sighted children aged 7–11. Also available electronically.

Bliss
Brockbourne House, 77 Mount Ephraim, Tunbridge Wells, Kent TN4 8BS
tel (01892) 500100 *fax* (01892) 545666
email bliss@panini.co.uk
website www.blissmag.co.uk
Editor Leslie Sinoway
Monthly £2.50

Glamorous young women's glossy magazine. Bright, intimate, A5 format, with real life reports, celebrities, beauty, fashion, shopping, advice, quizzes. Payment: by arrangement. Founded 1995.

Bob the Builder
BBC Worldwide Ltd, BBC Woodlands, 80 Wood Lane, London W12 0TT
tel 020-8433 2000 *fax* 020-8433 2941
website www.bbcmagazines.com/bobbuilder
Editor Siobhan Keeler
Every 3 weeks £2.25

Stories, puzzles, stickers and activities built around Bob and his team for children aged 3–5 and their parents.

Braille at Bedtime
RNIB, PO Box 173, Peterborough PE2 6WS
tel 0303-123 9999 *fax* (01733) 375001
email editorial@rnib.org.uk
website www.rnib.org.uk
Editor Racheal Jarvis
Every 2 months 87p (export £4.15)

Braille short fiction magazine for blind and partially sighted children aged 7–11.

Cars Magazine
Egmont UK Ltd, 239 High Street Kensington, London W8 6SA
email info@egmont.co.uk
website www.egmont.co.uk
Monthly £2.30

Aimed at 4–7-year-old boys featuring characters from the Disney movie Cars with comic strips, games, puzzles and activities. Founded 2008.

CBeebies Animals
BBC Worldwide Ltd, Media Centre, 201 Wood Lane, London W12 7TQ
tel 020-8433 2000
Every 4 weeks £2.35

Aimed at preschool children who love both CBeebies and animals, with fun facts, stories, puzzles, etc.

CBeebies Art
BBC Worldwide Ltd, Media Centre, 201 Wood Lane, London W12 7TQ
tel 020-8433 1291
email cbeebiesart@bbc.com
Editor Steph Cooper
Every 4 weeks £2.99

Aimed at preschool children who like art; linked to popular CBeebies art brands. Including Mister Maker, Get Squiglet, Louie and Doodle Do.

CBeebies Weekly Magazine
BBC Worldwide Ltd, Media Centre, 201 Wood Lane, London W12 7TQ
tel 020-8433 2496
email cbeebiesweekly@bbc.co.uk
website www.cbeebiesmagazine.com
Editor Steph Cooper
Weekly £1.99

Weekly preschool magazine with educational content targeted at $3\frac{1}{2}$-year-olds. Actively promotes learning through play. Showcases new characters, presenters and programmes as they appear on the CBeebies channel. Founded 2006.

Charlie and Lola

BBC Worldwide Ltd, Woodlands, 80 Wood Lane, London W12 0TT
tel 020-8433 2356
email charlieandlolamagazine@bbc.co.uk
website www.bbcmagazines.com
4-weekly £2.75

Interactive arts and crafts magazine for preschool children.

Commando

D.C. Thomson & Co. Ltd, Albert Square, Dundee DD1 9QJ
tel (01382) 223131 *fax* (01382) 322214
8 per month £1.45

Fictional stories set in time of war told in pictures. Scripts: about 135 pictures. Synopsis required as an opener. New writers encouraged; send for details. Payment: on acceptance.

The Dandy Xtreme

D.C. Thomson & Co. Ltd, Albert Square, Dundee DD1 9QJ
tel (01382) 223131 *fax* (01382) 322214
PO Box 305, London NW1 1TX
tel 020-7400 1030 *fax* 020-7400 1089
email cgraham@dthompson.co.uk
Editor Craig Graham
Fortnightly £1.99

Comic strips and features for boys aged 7–10 years. Picture stories with 7–10 pictures per page, 1–4pp per story. Promising artists are encouraged. Payment: on acceptance.

Discovery Box

Bayard, 1st Floor, 2 King Street, Peterborough PE1 1LT
tel (01733) 565858 *fax* (01733) 427500
email contact@bayard-magazines.co.uk
website www.bayard-magazines.co.uk
Editor Simona Sideri
10 p.a. £37 p.a.

Photographs and short texts to introduce children aged 9–12 to animals and their habitats. Includes historical events retold as picture stories and a range of topics and experiments to develop children's scientific knowledge; also photographs showing the variety of lifestyles around the world. Plus games, fun facts, short story, recipe, quizz, cartoon. Specially commissions most material. Founded 1996.

Disney & Me

Egmont Magazines UK, 239 Kensington High Street, London W8 6SA
tel 020-7761 3500 *fax* 020-7761 3510
website www.egmontmagazines.co.uk
Every three weeks £2.30

Entertaining and fun reading source for 3–6 year-olds with authentic illustrations based on original Disney animation. Includes stories, games, puzzles, posters, colouring pages and reader's letters.

Disney Girl

Panini UK, Brockbourne House, Mount Ephraim, Tunbridge Wells TN4 8BS
tel (01892) 500100 *fax* (01892) 545666
email paninicomics@panini.co.uk
website www.paninicomics.co.uk
Every 4 weeks £1.99

Magazine for 7–12 year-old girls combining features with Disney properties such as *High School Musical*, *Camp Rock* and the latest Disney film releases. Includes fashion, crafts, hobbies, pets, posters, quizzes, etc.

Disney Tinker Bell

Egmont Magazines UK, 239 Kensington High Street, London W8 6SA
tel 020-7761 3500 *fax* 020-7761 3510
website www.egmontmagazines.co.uk
Monthly £2.50

Aimed at 5–7 year-old girls. Published under the Disney franchise spawned from the novels *Fairy Dust* and *The Quest for the Egg* by Gail Carson Levine. Founded 2006.

Disney's Princess

Egmont Magazines UK, 239 Kensington High Street, London W8 6SA
tel 020-7761 3500 *fax* 020-7761 3510
website www.egmontmagazines.co.uk
Every 2 weeks £2.10

Magazine for 4–7 year-old girls to enter the magical world of Disney heroines through stories, crafts and activities. Founded 1998.

Doctor Who Adventures

BBC Worldwide, Media Centre, 201 Wood Lane, London W12 7TQ
tel 020-8433 3386
email dwa@bbc.co.uk
Editor Natalie Barnes
Weekly £2.99

Magazine for 6–12 year-old fans of *Doctor Who*. Readers are immersed into the world of the Doctor, taking them on an adventure into time and space, with monsters and creatures, excitement, action, adventure and humour. Founded 2006.

Doctor Who Magazine

Panini UK, Brockbourne House, 77 Mount Ephraim, Tunbridge Wells TN4 8BS
tel (01892) 500100 *fax* (01892) 545666
email paninicomics@panini.co.uk
website www.paninicomics.co.uk
Editor Tom Spilsbury
Every 4 weeks £4.20

Dora the Explorer

Egmont Magazines UK, 239 Kensington High Street, London W8 6SA
tel 020-7761 3500 *fax* 020-7761 3510
Editor Rebecca Jamieson
Monthly £1.75

Magazine for preschool children based on the Dora the Explorer character. Content includes puzzles, stories, posters and basic educational elements. Payment: by arrangement.

Essential X-Men

Panini UK, Brockbourne House, 77 Mount Ephraim, Tunbridge Wells TN4 8AR
tel (01892) 500100 *fax* (01892) 545666
email paninicomics@panini.co.uk
website www.paninicomics.co.uk
Editor Scott Gray
Every 4 weeks £2.50

Fifi and the Flowertots

BBC Worldwide Ltd, Media Centre, 201 Wood Lane, London W12 7TQ
tel 020-8433 2000
website www.fifiandtheflowertots.com
Every 4 weeks £1.99

Magazine aimed at 3–5 year-old children and based on the *Fifi and the Flowertots* TV programme. It mirrors the values of fun, friendship and creativity with activities and stories. Parent's notes are included to encourage joint participation and added enjoyment to the magazine. Founded 2006.

Fireman Sam Magazine

Egmont UK Ltd, 239 High Street Kensington, London W8 6SA
email info@egmont.co.uk
website www.egmont.co.uk
Monthly £2.25

Magazine for preschool children with a range of activities based around the Fireman Sam characters.

FirstNews

4th Floor, Shand House, 14–20 Shand Street, London SE1 2ES
email newsdesk@firstnews.co.uk
website www.firstnews.co.uk
Editor Nicky Cox, *Editorial Director* Piers Morgan
Weekly Fri £1.10

An inspiring, educational and entertaining national newspaper and website for 7–14 year-olds with news, sport, showbiz, interviews and in-depth features. It aspires to raise the profile of children's views and opinions in society. Founded 2006.

Fun to Learn Bag-o-Fun

Redan Publishing Ltd, Suite 2, Prospect House, Belle Vue Road, Shrewsbury, Shrops. SY3 7NR
tel (01743) 364 433 *fax* (01743) 271 528

email info@redan.com
website www.redan.co.uk
8 p.a. £3.99

Magazine, magic painting and colouring books, with at least 3 gifts, for preschool children and their parents to encourage early educational activities. Compiled of popular characters, including Mr Men, Peppa Pig, Clifford's Puppy Days, Dora the Explorer, Guess with Jess and many more, to help bring to life stories and activities whilst developing basic educational skills.

Fun to Learn Discovery

Redan Publishing Ltd, Suite 2, Prospect House, Belle Vue Road, Shrewsbury, Shrops. SY3 7NR
tel (01743) 364 433 *fax* (01743) 271 528
email info@redan.com
website www.redan.co.uk
2 p.a. £3.99

A magazine covering the National Curriculum's Early Foundation Stage. It has a different theme every issue, providing preschool children with stories and activities based on Halloween and Christmas.

Fun to Learn Favourites

Redan Publishing Ltd, Suite 2, Prospect House, Belle Vue Road, Shrewsbury, Shrops. SY3 7NR
tel (01743) 364 433 *fax* (01743) 271 528
email info@redan.com
website www.redan.co.uk
Every 2 weeks £1.99

A magazine for preschool children compiled of stories and activities using popular children's TV characters including Dora the Explorer, Mr Men, Scooby-Doo, Peppa Pig and more. It includes a pull-out workbook with 75 reward stickers, based on one of these characters, for parent and child inter-activity, with activities including counting, matching, puzzles and colouring.

Fun to Learn Friends

Redan Publishing Ltd, Suite 2, Prospect House, Belle Vue Road, Shrewsbury, Shrops. SY3 7NR
tel (01743) 364 433 *fax* (01743) 271 528
email info@redan.com
website www.redan.co.uk
Every 2 weeks £1.99

Magazine for preschool children and their parents to encourage early educational activities. Compiled of stories and activities using popular children's TV characters including Clifford's Puppy Days, Ben & Holly's Little Kingdom, Humf, Dora the Explorer and Peppa Pig. Includes a 24pp pull-out workbook with 75 reward stickers based on one of these popular characters for parent and child inter-activity, with activities including counting, matching, puzzles and colouring. The content supports the National Curriculum's Early Years Foundation Stage.

Fun to Learn Peppa Pig

Redan Publishing Ltd, Suite 2, Prospect House, Belle Vue Road, Shrewsbury, Shrops. SY3 7NR

tel (01743) 364433 *fax* (01743) 271528
email info@redan.com
website www.redan.co.uk
Every 2 weeks £1.99

Interactive magazine for girls and boys aged 3–7 with stories, activities and puzzles based on the TV show, *Peppa Pig*. Supports the National Curriculum's Early Years Foundation Stage and includes a pull-out workbook with 75 reward stickers.

Futurama (UK)

Titan Publishing Group Ltd, Titan House, 144 Southwark Street, London SE1 0UP
01795 414815
email futurama@titanemail.co.uk
website www.titanmagazines.com
Editor Andrew James
Monthly £3.65

Girl Talk

BBC Worldwide, Media Centre, 201 Wood Lane, London W12 7TQ
tel 020-8433 1296
email girltalk.magazine@bbc.co.uk
website www.bbcmagazines.com/girltalk
Editor Samantha Robinson
Fortnightly £2.99

Magazine for children aged 7–12 years old. Contains pop, TV and film celebrity features, personality features, quizzes, fashion, competitions, stories. Length: 500 words (fiction). Payment: £75. All material is specially commissioned. Founded 1997.

Girl Talk Extra

BBC Worldwide Ltd, Woodlands, 80 Wood Lane, London W12 0TT
tel 020-8433 1010
email girltalk.magazine@bbc.co.uk
website www.bbcmagazines.com
Monthly £2.99

Small format sister title to *Girl Talk*.

Go Girl Magazine

Egmont Magazines, 239 Kensington High Street, London W8 6SA
tel 020-7761 3500
website www.gogirlmag.co.uk
Editor Emma Prosser
Every 3 weeks £2.50

Magazine for 7–11-year-old girls including fashion, beauty, celebrity news and gossip. Payment: by arrangement. Founded 2003.

Goodie Bag Mag

D.C. Thomson & Co Ltd, Albert Square, Dundee DD1 9QJ
tel (01382) 223131 *fax* (01382) 225511
185 Fleet Street, London EC4A 2HS
tel 020-7400 1030 *fax* 020-7400 1089

website www.goodiebagmag.co.uk
Monthly (Thurs) £2.99

Features, fashion, puzzles pin-ups, stories, quizzes, competitions. Founded 2003.

Guiding Magazine

17–19 Buckingham Palace Road, London SW1W 0PT
tel 020-7834 6242 *fax* 020-7828 8317
email guiding@girlguiding.org.uk
website www.girlguiding.org.uk
Editor Jane Yettram
Quarterly

Official magazine of Girlguiding UK. Articles of interest to women of all ages, with special emphasis on youth work and the Guide Movement. Length: up to 600 words. Illustrations: line, half-tone, colour. Payment: £300 per 1,000 words. Please contact editor with proposal first.

Headliners

Rich Mix, 35–47 Bethnal Green Road, London E1 6LA
tel 020-7749 9360 *fax* 020-7729 5948
email enquiries@headliners.org
website www.headliners.org
Director Fiona Wyton

An award-winning news agency charity (does not publish a magazine or newspaper) that offers young people aged 8–18 the opportunity to write on issues of importance to them, for newspapers, radio and TV. Founded 1995.

High School Musical

Panini UK, Brockbourne House, Mount Ephraim, Tunbridge Wells TN4 8BS
tel (01892) 500100 *fax* (01892) 545666
email paninicomics@panini.co.uk
website www.paninicomics.co.uk
Monthly £2.10

Interviews and behind-the-scenes gossip about *High School Musical*.

In the Night Garden

BBC Worldwide Ltd, Woodlands, 201 Wood Lane, London W12 7TQ
tel 020-8433 2356
website www.bbcmagazines.com
Fortnightly £1.99

Magazine for prechool children with activities and *In the Night Garden* stories.

Junior Puzzles

Puzzler Media Ltd, Stonecroft, 69 Station Road, Redhill, Surrey RH1 1EY
tel (01737) 378700 *fax* (01737) 781800
email enquiries@puzzlermedia.com
website www.puzzler.com
Editor Mike Murphy
6 p.a. £2.40

Entertainment for 7–12 year-old children with a variety of puzzles, e.g. spot the difference, wordsearch, kriss kross, dot to dot, crosswords, mazes.

Kids Alive! (The Young Soldier)

The Salvation Army, 101 Newington Causeway, London SE1 6BN
tel 020-7367 4911 *fax* 020-7367 4710
email kidsalive@salvationarmy.org.uk
website www.salvationarmy.org.uk/kidsalive
Editor Justin Reeves
Weekly 50p (£25 p.a. including free membership of the Kids Alive! Club)

Children's magazine: pictures, scripts and artwork for cartoon strips, puzzles, etc; Christian-based with emphasis on education re addictive substances. Payment: by arrangement. Illustrations: half-tone, line and 4-colour line, cartoons. Founded 1881.

KISS

3 Ely Place, Dublin 2, Republic of Ireland
tel (01) 480 4700 *fax* (01) 480 4799
website www.kiss.ie
Editor Nathalie Marquez-Courtney
Monthly €2.80

Articles on fashion and beauty, celebrities, entertainment, fashion and relationships for 13–18 year-old girls. Ireland's only teen magazine.

Marvel Heroes

Panini UK, Brockbourne House, Mount Ephraim, Tunbridge Wells TN4 8BS
tel (01892) 500100 *fax* (01892) 545666
email paninicomics@panini.co.uk
website www.paninicomics.co.uk
Every 4 weeks £2.50

Comic strips, games and news on the Marvel heroes.

Match of the Day

BBC Worldwide Ltd, Media Centre, 201 Wood Lane, London W12 7TQ
tel 020-8433 3438
email shout@motdmag.com
website www.motdmag.com
Weekly £1.99

Aimed at football-mad children with star interviews, match results, gossip and quizzes. Also includes an 8pp pull-out football skills guide.

The Max

RNIB, PO Box 173, Peterborough PE2 6W7
tel (0303) 123 9999 *fax* (01733) 375001
email editorial@rnib.org.uk
website www.rnib.org.uk
Editor Racheal Jarvis
Monthly 47p (export £3.05)

Braille magazine for blind and partially sighted men aged 16–19. Also available electronically. Includes

features on the music scene, sport, interviews with personalities and a problem page. Will consider unsolicited submissions but most material has previously appeared in mainstream print magazines.

Mighty World of Marvel

Panini UK, Brockbourne House, 77 Mount Ephraim, Tunbridge Wells TN4 8AR
tel (01892) 500100 *fax* (01892) 545666
email paninicomics@panini.co.uk
website www.paninicomics.co.uk
Editor Scott Gray
Every 4 weeks £2.50

Missy

RNIB, PO Box 173, Peterborough, Cambs. PE2 6WS
tel 0303-123 9999
email editorial@rnib.org.uk
website www.rnib.org.uk
Editor Chris James
Monthly 49p (export £3.39)

Braille general interest magazine for blind and partially sighted girls aged 12–15. Also available electronically.

Mizz

Panini UK, Brockbourne House, 77 Mount Ephraim, Tunbridge Wells TN4 8AR
tel (01892) 500100 *fax* (01892) 545666
email mizz@panini.co.uk
website www.mizz.com
Editor Karen O'Brien
Fortnightly £2.30

Articles on any subject of interest to girls aged 10–14. Approach in writing. Payment: by arrangement. Illustrated. Founded 1985.

The Newspaper

Young Media Holdings Ltd, PO Box 400, Bridgwater TA6 9DT
tel 0845-094 0646
email editor@thenewspaper.org.uk
website www.thenewspaper.org.uk
Managing Editor Phil Wood
6 p.a. Subscription only

Newspaper aimed at 8–14-year-old school children for use as part of the National Curriculum. Contains similar columns as in any national daily newspaper. Not currently looking for new writers/articles. Founded 2000.

Play & Learn Thomas & Friends

Egmont Magazines, 239 Kensington High Street, London W3 6SA
tel 020-7761 3500 *fax* 020-7761 3510
website www.egmontmagazines.co.uk
Fortnightly £2.10

Magazine for 3–6 year-old children with activities and stories involving Thomas characters. A companion to KS1 programmes of study.

PONY Magazine

Headley House, Headley Road, Grayshott,
Surrey GU26 6TU
tel (01428) 601020 *fax* (01428) 601030
Editor Janet Rising
13 p.a. £2.99

Lively articles and short stories with a horsy theme
aimed at readers aged 8–16. Technical accuracy and
young, fresh writing essential. Length: up to 800
words. Payment: by arrangement. Illustrations:
drawings (commissioned), photos, cartoons.
Founded 1949.

Postman Pat

Panini UK, Brockbourne House, Mount Ephraim,
Tunbridge Wells TN4 8BS
tel (01892) 500100 *fax* (01892) 545666
email paninicomics@panini.co.uk
website www.paninicomics.co.uk
Editor Patrick Bishop
Every 4 weeks £1.99

Pure

RNIB, PO Box 173, Peterborough PE2 6WS
tel 0303-123 9999 *fax* (01733) 375001
email editorial@rnib.org.uk
website www.rnib.org.uk
Editor Chris James
Monthly 47p (export £3.05)

Braille magazine for blind and partially sighted girls
aged 16–19. Also available electronically. Includes real
life stories, celebrity interviews and beauty features.
Will consider unsolicited submissions but most
material has previously appeared in mainstream print
magazines.

Puzzler Quiz Kids

Puzzler Media Ltd, Stonecroft, 69 Station Road,
Redhill, Surrey RH1 1EY
tel (01737) 378700 *fax* (01737) 781800
email reception@puzzlermedia.com
website www.puzzler.com
Editor Jackie Guthrie
6 p.a. £2.50

Puzzles and quizzes for 7–11 year-old children to
help build reading, writing and mathematical skills.

Scooby-Doo

Panini UK, Brockbourne House, 77 Mount Ephraim,
Tunbridge Wells TN4 8BS
tel (01892) 500100 *fax* (01892) 545666
email paninicomics@panini.co.uk
website www.paninicomics.co.uk
Editor Ed Caruana
Monthly £2.25

Shout

2 Albert Square, Dundee DD1 9QJ
tel (01382) 223131 *fax* (01382) 200880

email shout@dcthomson.co.uk
185 Fleet Street, London EC4A 2HS
tel 020-7400 1030 *fax* 020-7400 1089
website www.shoutmag.co.uk
Editor Maria Welch
Fortnightly £2.20

Magazine for 11–14 year-old girls. Pop, film and
'soap' features and pin-ups; general features of teen
interest; emotional features, fashion and beauty
advice. Payment: on acceptance. Founded 1993.

Showtime Magazine

Panini UK, Brockbourne House, Mount Ephraim,
Tunbridge Wells TN4 8BS
tel (01892) 500100 *fax* (01892) 545666
email paninicomics@panini.co.uk
website www.paninicomics.co.uk
Every 4 weeks £1.85

Magazine for preschool children featuring the most
popular preschool TV characters from all channels.

Simpsons Comics

Titan Publishing Group Ltd, Titan House,
144 Southwark Street, London SE1 0UP
tel 020-7620 0200 *fax* 020-7803 1803
website simpsonsmail@titanemail.com
website www.titanmagazines.com
Editor Rona Simpson
Monthly £3.20

Reprints the US *Simpsons Comics* material with
localised letters page and some other features.

Simpsons Comics Presents

Titan Publishing Group Ltd, Titan House,
144 Southwark Street, London SE1 0UP
tel 020-7620 0200 *fax* 020-7803 1803
email simpsonsmail@titanemail.com
website www.titanmagazines.com
Editor Rona Simpson
Monthly £3.20

Sparkle World

Redan Publishing Ltd, Suite 2, Prospect House,
Belle Vue Road, Shrewsbury SY3 7NR
tel (01743) 364 433 *fax* (01743) 271 528
email info@redan.com
website www.redan.com
Every 3 weeks £2.45

Magazine aimed at 4–9 year-old girls with stories and
activities based on a dazzling selection of the most
popular licensed characters, including Rainbow
Magic, Littlest Petshop, Polly Pocket, Strawberry
Shortcake, My Little Pony and Angelina Ballerina. A
fun and educational magazine for young girls who
love everything that glitters.

Spectacular Spider-Man

Panini UK, Brockbourne House, Mount Ephraim,
Tunbridge Wells TN4 8BS

tel (01892) 500100 *fax* (01892) 545666
email specspidey@panini.co.uk
website www.paninicomics.co.uk
Editor Patrick Bishop
Every 3 weeks £1.99

SpongeBob SquarePants

Titan Magazines, Titan House,
144 Southwark Street, London SE1 0UP
tel 020-7620 0200 *fax* 020-7803 1803
email spongebob@titanemail.com
website www.titancomicsuk.com
Editor Rona Simpson
Every 3 weeks £2.70

Star Trek Magazine

Titan Magazines, Titan House,
144 Southwark Street, London SE1 0UP
tel 020-7620 0200 *fax* 020-7803 1803
Editor Paul Simpson
13 p.a. £27.99

Up-to-date news about every aspect of *Star Trek*,
including all TV series and films, cast interviews,
behind-the-scenes features and product reviews.
Payment: by arrangement. Founded 1995.

Star Wars Clone Wars Comic

Titan Publishing Group Ltd, Titan House,
144 Southwark Street, London SE1 0UP
tel 020-7620 0200 *fax* 020-7803 1803
email swcomicmail@titanemail.com
website www.titanmagazines.com
Editor Andrew James
Every 4 weeks £2.50

Features 8–10pp originated UK *Clone Wars* comic
strips, features, puzzles, etc.

Storybox

Bayard, 1st Floor, 2 King Street,
Peterborough PE1 1LT
tel (01733) 565858 *fax* (01733) 4275000
email contact@bayard-magazines.co.uk
website www.bayard-magazines.co.uk
Editor-in-chief Simona Sideri
10 p.a. £37 p.a.

Aimed at 3–6 year-old children. A range of stories
with rhyme and evocative pictures to stimulate
children's imagination and introduce them to the
delights of reading. Each issue presents a new, full-
colour, 24pp story created by teams of internationally
acclaimed writers and illustrators for laptime reading.
A non-fiction section linked to a theme in the story
follows, together with pages of games and craft ideas.
Includes games, an animal feature, science and a
cartoon. Founded 1996.
    Submission details Length: 500–1,000 words
(stories). Requirements: rhyme, repetition, interesting
language. Specially commissions most material.
Payment: by arrangement.

tBkmag

4 Froxfield Close, Winchester SO22 6JW
tel (01962) 620320
email guy@newbooksmag.com
website www.newbooksmag.com
Editor Helen Boyle, *Send material to* Guy Pringle,
Publisher
Quarterly £1.99

Extracts and activities from the best new books for
8–12 year-olds. Specially commissions all material.
Email for a free introductory copy. Founded 2001.

Thomas & Friends

Egmont Magazines, 239 Kensington High Street,
London W8 6SA
tel 020-7761 3500 *fax* 020-7761 3510
website www.egmontmagazines.co.uk
Fortnightly £2.35

Magazine for 3–6 year-old children designed to
encourage early reading skills and all-round child
development using stories and activities involving
Thomas and all his friends. Each issue contains
posters, colouring pages, competitions and readers'
letters and pictures as regular features.

Tom and Jerry

Panini UK, Brockbourne House, 77 Mount Ephraim,
Tunbridge Wells TN4 8AR
tel (01892) 500100 *fax* (01892) 545666
email paninicomics@panini.co.uk
website www.paninicomics.co.uk
Editor Ed Caruana
Every 4 weeks £1.99

Top of the Pops

BBC Worldwide Ltd, Media Centre, 201 Wood Lane,
London W12 7TQ
tel 020-8433 3910
website www.bbcworldwide.com/magazines
Editor Peter Hart
Monthly £2.30

'The celebrity gossip bible for teenagers.' Primarily
aimed at teenage girls (ages 10–14), the magazine
strives to provide all the celebrity knowledge
teenagers could want. It aims to make the reader feel
part of an exclusive club, to transport them behind
the scenes so they get a real sense of what really goes
on in the world of the stars. Founded 1995.

Toxic Magazine

Egmont Publishing Group,
239 Kensington High Street, London W8 6SA
tel 020-7761 3500
website www.toxicmag.co.uk
Editor Frank Tennyson
Fortnightly £2.50

Topical lifestyle magazine for 8–12 year-old boys.
Includes competitions, pull-out posters, reviews and
jokes. Covers boys' entertainments, sports, video

games, films, TV, music, fashion and toys. Slapstick humour. Showcases latest products, events and trends. Payment: by arrangement. Founded 2002.

Toybox

BBC Worldwide Ltd, Media Centre, 201 Wood Lane, London W12 7TQ
tel 020-8433 1291
email toyboxmagazine@bbc.com
Editor Steph Cooper
Every 4 weeks £2.99

Magazine with workbook and stickers, plus free gifts, for 3–5 year-olds, with stories, puzzles, quizzes and colouring-in. Featuring characters from CBeebies.

2000 AD

Riverside House, Osney Mead, Oxford OX2 0ES
email publicrelations@2000adonline.com
website www.2000adonline.com
Weekly, Wed £2.25

Cult sci-fi comic. A cocktail of explosive sci-fi and fantasy, infused with a mean streak of irony and wry black humour, *2000 AD* has been a proving ground for young writers and artists, and many of the biggest names in comics today honed their skills within its pages. Founded 1977.

Vibe

RNIB, PO Box 173, Peterborough PE2 6WS
tel 0303-123 9999 *fax* (01733) 375001
email editorial@rnib.org.uk
website www.rnib.org.uk
Editor Racheal Jarvis
Monthly 45p (export £3.05)

Braille general interest magazine for blind and partially sighted boys aged 12–15. Also available electronically.

The Voice

6th Floor, Northern & Shell Tower, 4 Selsdon Way, London E14 9GL
tel 020-7510 0340 *fax* 020-7510 0341
email newsdesk@the-voice.co.uk
website www.voice-online.co.uk
Editor Steve Pope
Weekly 85p

Weekly newspaper for black Britons. Includes news, features, arts, sport and a comprehensive jobs and business section. Illustrations: colour and b&w photos. Open to ideas for news and features on sports, business, community events and the arts. Founded 1982.

Young Voices

website www.young-voices.co.uk
Editor Dionne Grant
Monthly, 2nd Tues of each month £2.40
News, features, reviews, showbiz highlights and current affairs for 11–19 year-olds. Founded 2003.

Waybuloo

BBC Magazines, BBC Worldwide Ltd, Media Centre, 201 Wood Lane, London W12 7TQ
tel 020-8433 1291
email waybuloo@bbc.com
website www.waybuloo.com
Editor Steph Cooper
Every 3 weeks £2.35

Magazine for prechool children based on CBeebies programme *Waybuloo*.

Wolverine and Deadpool

Panini UK, Brockbourne House, 77 Mount Ephraim, Tunbridge Wells TN4 8AR
tel (01892) 500100 *fax* (01892) 545666
email paninicomics@panini.co.uk
website www.paninicomics.co.uk
Editor Scott Gray
Every 4 weeks £2.50

Young Scot

Rosebery House, 9 Haymarket Terrace, Edinburgh EH12 5EZ
tel 0131-313 2488 *fax* 0131-313 6800
email info@youngscot.org
website www.youngscot.org
Editor Fiona McIntyre
Quarterly Free with *Scottish Daily Record* and at selected venues

The latest news, features, discounts, and competitions for young Scots aged 12–26. Offers incentives, information and opportunities to people in this age group to help them make informed choices, play a part in their community, and make the most of their free time and learning.

Young Writer Magazine

5th Floor, 31–32 Park Row, Leeds LS1 5JD
tel (0113) 200 2929 *fax* (0113) 200 2928
email youngwriter@writersnews.co.uk
website www.youngwriter.org
Editor Matthew Hill
3 p.a. £3.75, £10 p.a.

Specialist magazine for young writers under 18 years old: ideas for them and writing by them. Includes interviews by children with famous writers, fiction and non-fiction pieces, poetry; also explores words and grammar, issues related to writing (e.g. dyslexia), plus competitions with prizes. Length: 750 or 1,500 words (features), up to 400 words (news), 600 words (short stories – unless specified otherwise in a competition), poetry of any length. Illustrations: colour – drawings by children, snapshots to accompany features. Payment: most children's material is published without payment. Free inspection copy. Founded 1995.

Magazines about children's literature and education

Listings of magazines and newspapers for children start on page 284.

Armadillo

Louise Ellis-Barrett, c/o Downsend School,
1 Leatherhead Road, Leatherhead, Surrey KT22 8TJ
email armadilloeditor@googlemail.com
website http://sites.google.com/site/
armadillomagazine
Editor Louise Ellis-Barrett
4 p.a. Free

Online children's book review magazine including
reviews, interviews, features, competitions and
profiles. Linked to a blog for weekly children's book
news updates, issues posted March, June, September
and December. New reviewers and writers always
welcome. Founded 1999.

Books for Keeps

1 Effingham Road, London SE12 8NZ
tel 020-8852 4953 *fax* 020-8318 7580
email enquiries@booksforkeeps.co.uk
website www.booksforkeeps.co.uk
Editor Rosemary Stones
Bi-monthly, free online

Features, reviews and news on children's books.
Readership is both professionals and parents.
Founded 1980.

The Bookseller

VNU Entertainment Media Ltd, 5th Floor,
Endeavour House, 189 Shaftesbury Avenue,
London WC2H 8TJ
tel 020-7420 6006 *fax* 020-7420 6103
email felicity.wood@thebookseller.co.uk
website www.thebookseller.com
Editor-in-Chief Neill Denny, *Features Editor* Tom
Tivnan
Weekly £4.40, £170 p.a.

Journal of the UK publishing and bookselling trades.
The *Children's Bookseller* supplement is published
regularly and there is news on the children's book
business in the main magazine. Produces the
Children's Buyer's Guide, which previews children's
books to be published in the following 6 months. The
website holds news on children's books, comment on
the children's sector, author interviews and children's
bestseller charts. Founded 1858.

Carousel – The Guide to Children's Books

Ephraim Phillips House, 54–76 Bissell Street,
Birmingham B5 7HP

tel 0121-622 7458
email carousel.guide@virgin.net
website www.carouselguide.co.uk
Editor Jenny Blanch
3 p.a. £11.25 p.a. (£16 p.a. Europe; £19 p.a. rest of
world)

Reviews of fiction, non-fiction and poetry books for
children, plus in-depth articles; profiles of authors
and illustrators. Length: 1,200 words (articles); 150
words (reviews). Illustrations: colour and b&w.
Payment: by arrangement. Founded 1995.

Child Education PLUS

Book End, Range Road, Witney OX29 0YD
tel (01926) 887799 *fax* (01926) 883331
email childed@scholastic.co.uk
website www.scholastic.co.uk/childedplus
Publishing Director Paula Hubbard
Bi-monthly £19.98 p.a.

For teachers concerned with the education of
children aged 4–11. Articles by specialists on practical
teaching ideas and methods. Length: 600–1,200
words. Payment: by arrangement. Profusely
illustrated with photos and artwork; also two A2
colour posters. Founded 1924.

Mary Glasgow Magazines

Scholastic UK Ltd, Westfield Road, Southam,
Warks. CV47 0RA
tel (01926) 815560
email orders@maryglasgowmags.co.uk
website www.maryglasgowmagazines.com

Publisher of 16 magazines for learners of English,
French, German, and Spanish. Also publishes a series
of resource books for teachers of English as a foreign
language. Wholly owned subsidiary of Scholastic Inc.

Inis – The Children's Books Ireland Magazine

Children's Books Ireland,
17 North Great George Street, Dublin 1,
Republic of Ireland
tel (1) 872 7475 *fax* (1) 872 7476
email info@childrensbooksireland.ie
website www.childrensbooksireland.ie
Editors Dr Patricia Kennon, Mr David Maybury
Quarterly €4

Reviews and articles on Irish and international
children's books. Readership of parents, teachers,

librarians and children's books specialists. Founded 1989.

Junior

Magicalia Publishing Ltd, 15–18 White Lion Street, London N1 9PG
tel 020-7843 8800
email editorial@juniormagazine.co.uk
website www.juniormagazine.co.uk
Editor Catherine O'Dolan
Monthly £3.50

Glossy up-market parenting magazine aimed at mothers of children aged 0–8 and reflects the shift in today's society towards older mothers and fathers who have established their careers and homes. Intelligent and insightful features and the best in fashion. Specially commissions most material. Welcomes ideas for articles and features. Payment: £150 per 1,000 words (articles/features/short fiction), £300 per feature (colour and b&w photos/artwork). Founded 1998.

The Lion and the Unicorn

Project MUSE, 2715 North Charles Street, Baltimore, MD 21218-4319
tel 410-516-6989 *fax* 410-516-6968
email muse@muse.jhu.edu
website www.press.jhu.edu/journals/lion_and_the_unicorn/
$114 p.a., 3 p.a.

A theme- and genre-centred journal of international scope committed to a serious, ongoing discussion of literature for children. The journal's coverage includes the state of the publishing industry, regional authors, comparative studies of significant books and genres, new developments in theory, the art of illustration, the mass media, and popular culture. It has become noted for its interviews with authors, editors, and other important contributors to the field, such as Mildred Wirt Benson, Robert Cormier, Chris Crutcher, Lensey Namioka, Philip Pullman, and Aranka Siegal. Special issues have included 'Violence and Children's Literature' and 'Folklore In/And Children's Literature.' Includes a book review section and each year publishes a general issue and 2 theme issues. Project MUSE is part of the Johns Hopkins University Press.

Literacy

UK Literacy Association, University of Leicester, Leicester LE1 7RH
tel 0116-223 1664 *fax* 0116-223 1665
email admin@ukla.org
website www.ukla.org, www.blackwellpublishing.com
Editor Kathy Hall, Department of Education, University College Cork, Lee Holme, Donovan's Road, Cork, Ireland (*email* k.hall@ucc.ie)
3 p.a. (subscription only)

The official journal of the UK Literacy Association

(see page 380) and is for those interested in the study and development of literacy. Readership comprises practitioners, teachers, educators, researchers, undergraduate and graduate students. It offers educators a forum for debate through scrutinising research evidence, reflecting on analysed accounts of innovative practice and examining recent policy developments. Length: 2,000–6,000 words (articles). Illustrations: b&w prints and artwork. Formerly known as *Reading – Literacy and Language*. Published by Blackwell Publishing. Founded 1966.

NATE Classroom (National Association for the Teaching of English)

NATE, 50 Broadfield Road, Sheffield S8 0XJ
tel 0114-255 5419 *fax* 0114-255 5296
email info@nate.org.uk
website www.nate.org.uk
Editor Anne Fairhall
3 p.a.

The official magazine of the National Association for the Teaching of English (NATE), available as part of its membership. A mix of entertaining and practical articles for both primary and secondary teachers of English, with a review section addressing children's fiction and texts for teachers. Also publishes a professional journal, *English Drama Media* (3 p.a.), a research journal, *English in Education* (3 p.a.) and a newsletter, *NATE News* (3 p.a.).

Nursery Education Plus

Scholastic Ltd, Book End, Range Road, Witney, Oxon IX29 0YD
tel (01993) 893456 *fax* (01993) 893222
email earlyyears@scholastic.co.uk
website www.scholastic.co.uk/nurseryedplus
Editor Tracey Brand
Monthly £38.25 p.a.

News, features, professional development and practical theme-based activities for professionals working with 0–5 year-olds. Activity ideas based on the Early Learning Goals. Material mostly commissioned. Length: 500–1,000 words. Illustrations: colour and b&w; colour posters. Payment: by arrangement. Founded 1997.

Nursery World

Haymarket Business Media, 174 Hammersmith Road, London W6 7JP
tel 020-8267 8409
email news.nw@haymarket.com
website www.nurseryworld.co.uk
Editor Liz Roberts
Weekly £1.50, £65 p.a.

For all grades of primary school, nursery and child care staff, nannies, foster parents and all concerned with the care of expectant mothers, babies and young children. Authoritative and informative articles, 800 or 1,300 words, and photos, on all aspects of child welfare and early education, from 0–8 years, in the UK. Practical ideas, policy news and career advice. No short stories. Payment: by arrangement. Illustrations: line, half-tone, colour.

Practical Parenting

Magicalia Limited, 15–18 White Lion Street, Islington, London N1 9PD
tel 020-7843 8800
website www.practicalparenting.co.uk
Editor Daniella Delaney
Monthly £2.80

Articles on parenting, baby and childcare, health, psychology, education, children's activities, personal birth/parenting experiences. Send article by email to jenny.stallard@magicalia.com. Illustrations: colour photos, line; commissioned only. Payment: by agreement. Founded 1987.

Publishers Weekly

71 West 23 Street, 1608 New York, NY 10010, USA
tel 212-377-5500 *fax* 646-746-6631 *fax* 646-746-6738
website www.publishersweekly.com
Editor Diane Roback

The international news magazine of the $23 billion book industry. Covers all segments involved in the creation, production, marketing and sale of the written word in book, audio, video and electronic formats. In addition to reaching publishers worldwide, it influences all media dealing with the acquisition, sale, distribution and rights of intellectual and cultural properties.
   Children's books for review, from preschool to young adult, should be sent to Diane Roback, Children's Books Editor – all reviews are prepublication. Also send to her story suggestions on children's publishing, new trends, author or illustrator interviews, etc for the weekly *Children's Books*. Diane also edits the listings for new children's books twice a year for the Spring and Fall Children's Announcements issues. Fax (do not email) any story pitches or queries concerning review submissions of children's books, review enquiries and editorial guidelines for submission of children's books for review. Founded 1873.

Report

ATL, 7 Northumberland Street, London WC2N 5RD
tel 020-7930 6441
email report@atl.org.uk
website www.atl.org.uk
Editors Alex Tomlin, Charlotte Tamvakis
9 p.a. £2.50, £15.50 p.a., £27 p.a. overseas, Free to members

The magazine from the Association of Teachers and Lecturers (ATL). Features, articles, comment, news about nursery, primary, secondary and further education. Payment: minimum £120 per 1,000 words.

Right Start

Ten Alps Publishing, 9 Savoy Street, London WC2E 7HR
tel 020-7878 2338 *fax* 020-7379 6261
email lynette@rightstartmagazine.co.uk
website www.rightstartmagazine.co.uk
Editor Lynette Lowthian
Bi-monthly £2.50, £10.90 p.a.

Features on all aspects of preschool and infant education, child health and behaviour. No unsolicited MSS. Length: 800–1,500 words. Illustrations: colour photos, line. Payment: varies. Founded 1989.

The School Librarian

The School Library Association, Unit 2, Lotmead Business Village, Lotmead Farm, Wanborough, Swindon SN4 0UY
tel (01793) 791787 *fax* (01793) 791786
email info@sla.org.uk
website www.sla.org.uk
Editor Steve Hird
Quarterly £81 p.a.

Official journal of the School Library Association. Articles on school library management, use and skills, and on authors and illustrators, literacy, publishing. Reviews of books, CD-Roms, websites and other library resources from preschool to adult. Length: 1,800–3,000 words (articles). Payment: by arrangement. Founded 1937.

The TES

26 Red Lion Square, Holborn WC1R 4HQ
tel 020-3194 3000
fax 020-3194 3202 (news), 020-3194 3200 (features)
email newsdesk@tes.co.uk, features@tes.co.uk
website www.tes.co.uk
Editor Gerard Kelly
Weekly £1.40

Education newspaper. Articles on education written with special knowledge or experience; news items; books, arts and equipment reviews. Check with the news or picture editor before submitting material. Outlines of feature ideas should be emailed. Illustrations: suitable photos and drawings of educational interest, cartoons. Payment: standard rates, or by arrangement.

TES Magazine

Weekly Free with TES
Magazine for teachers focusing on their lives, inside and outside the classroom, investigating the key issues of the day and highlighting good practice. Length: 800 words max.

The TES Cymru

Sophia House, 28 Cathedral Road, Cardiff CF11 9LJ
tel 029-2066 0201 *fax* 029-2066 0207
email cymru@tes.co.uk
website www.tes.co.uk/cymru
Editor Gerard Kelly
Weekly £1.40

Education newspaper. Articles on education, teachers,

teaching and learning, and education policy in Wales. Length: up to 800 words (articles). Illustrations: line, half-tone. Payment: by arrangement. Founded 2004.

The TESS

Thistle House, 21–23 Thistle Street,
Edinburgh EH2 1DF
tel 0131-624 8333 *fax* 0131-467 8019
website www.tes.co.uk/scotland
Editor Neil Munro
Weekly £1.50

Education newspaper. Articles on education, preferably 800–1,000 words, written with special knowledge or experience. News items about Scottish educational affairs. Illustrations: line, half-tone. Payment: by arrangement. Founded 1965.

The Times Educational Supplement – see The TES

The Times Educational Supplement Scotland – see The TESS

Under 5

Pre-school Learning Alliance,
The Fitzpatrick Building, 188 York Way,
London N7 9AD
tel 020-7697 2500 *fax* 020-7697 8607
website www.pre-school.org.uk
Editor Mandy Murphy
10 p.a. £30 p.a.

Articles on the role of adults, especially parents/preschool workers, in young children's learning and development, including children from all cultures and those with special needs. Length: 600–1,200 words. Founded 1962.

Television, film and radio
Commissioning for children's television

Anna Home offers guidelines for writing for children's television programmes.

What are the classic children's television titles? *Blue Peter*, of course, *Magpie*, *Bagpuss*, *Grange Hill*, *My Family Are Aliens*, *Bob the Builder*, *Teletubbies*, etc. Children's television embraces a multitude of different kinds of programming, all of which requires writers. *Blue Peter* is not the kind of programme which gets commissioned cold – it evolved over the years through various production teams – but what is fundamental to its success is its makers' knowledge of its audience and how that audience has changed over the years. *Teletubbies*, and more recently *In the Night Garden*, are exactly the same: their creator Anne Wood spent months researching the target audience and testing ideas before committing to them. So....

• **Rule One.** Know your audience and the age range that you are aiming for.

• **Rule Two.** Know the schedules. Be aware of the available slots and the kind of programmes which go into them, and study the output and the varying requirements of the different channels. CITV has commissioned almost no new programmes since 2007 and seems unlikely to do much more in the immediate future. CBBC and CBeebies are the main commissioners catering for their specific age ranges; Five only caters for preschool. Nick, Cartoon Network and Disney do commission in the UK but only on a small scale. CBBC now has a 360 degree policy, i.e. all programmes need to be created with a variety of platforms and outlets in mind. They only have one commissioning round a year, although they are happy to discuss ideas at other times. Also go to 'Meet the Commissioner' meetings, network, and study the broadcasters' websites.

• **Rule Three.** Learn how to write proposals and how to pitch them (remember that commissioners receive hundreds of proposals in a year). Presentation, clarity and passion are all important. This is a very competitive world and if you get an opportunity to pitch in person know how to do it as it may be your only chance to impress. Rehearse well, have your props prepared (if appropriate) and don't waffle. You have to convince the commissioner that your project has a real USP (unique selling point) and that you can deliver it.

• **Rule Four.** Have some idea of what your project is going to cost and be prepared to defend that costing. Few broadcasters fully fund commissions any more and you need to be aware of how to find matching deficit funding. Sometimes a writer may team up with an independent producer who will cover this part of it. As a writer you will probably already have an agent, but that agent may not be an expert in terms of accessing television or film work. Check this out as many writers have two agents – one for their publishing activities and another for television and film.

Children's television drama

The BBC is now virtually the only commissioner of children's drama although Sky produced a film version of *Skellig* in 2009. The current policy is to concentrate on investing in big event dramas which will differentiate the channel – for example *The Roman Mysteries*. There are a very limited number of Sunday teatime slots.

Smaller scale adaptations are still commissioned especially if they have a long running potential, for example *Tracy Beaker*. If you find a book which you think would work for television, you'll have to buy an option before you take it to the producer or commissioner. As a result of the huge success of *Harry Potter*, *Lemony Snickett,* etc the cost of optioning children's books has risen steeply and the potential 'biggies' are snapped up before publication. However, there are a number of excellent children's books published every year which could make good television and you might pick up the next 'big thing', so keep an eye on what is happening in the children's publishing world, read the trade magazines and try to get to know children's publishers. When you are looking at books consider whether they have potential beyond one book or a limited series. Commissioners are always looking for something which has the possibility to go to more than one series and to become a franchise or brand. Once you have secured your option write a brief treatment of how you see the television version working and submit it together with the book either to an independent producer, or to a commissioner – remembering the rules outlined above.

Animation

Animation is the most prolific and potentially the most financially rewarding children's genre, but it is rather specialised. There are certain things that work in cell or model animation and there are things that don't, so it is well worth studying successful animated series. Remember that this really is a visual medium and often words are minimal – think *Pingu*! In fact, the *Yoko Toto Yakamoto* series (which has no words) has won two BAFTA Children's Writer Awards. The alternative is to start with a book or a series of characters and then approach an animation production house. You don't have to provide the visuals, but you do need to remember that animation needs to be a minimum of 26 episodes in the first series with the potential to go to 104 episodes or more. Animation also needs to have international appeal as most animated series are international co-productions. Lastly, if you can, it's worthwhile trying to learn a little bit about how animation works technically – it will help you identify the right kind of books or ideas.

Comedy and comedy-drama

Comedy and comedy-drama has become an increasingly popular part of children's television output. It's mainly studio based, relatively cheap to make and it works well in the schedule. The same comments about potential longevity apply in terms of the series and you should always have this in mind. Having said all this however, the main thing is to write something that you really want to write and you think will work for the audience on television, something that you care about and are passionate about and are really able to visualise and able to sell to those cynical commissioners.

Good luck.

Anna Home is Chief Executive of the Children's Film and Television Foundation. Previously she worked in children's programmes at both the BBC and ITV. Latterly she was Head of CBBC for 11 years, responsible for commissioning all the children's output. Her career began on *Playschool*, she started *Grange Hill* and her last commission was *Teletubbies*.

Writing comedy for children's television

Adam Bromley looks at types of comedy, the parameters of writing comedy for children's television and describes the commissioning process.

Writing comedy for children's television presents numerous challenges: it is both liberating and restrictive. Today, this target audience is more discerning than ever and they have a wide choice of television channels and entertainment options. If a comedy show doesn't deliver in a few minutes viewers will look elsewhere and perhaps channel surf or switch on a games console. Budgets for making programmes are ratcheted downwards than upwards. Also, editorial restrictions for children's television are extensive and need to be considered at every stage in the writing process.

But don't be disheartened by these challenges because children are more imaginative than adults and as an audience they will be more receptive to more outlandish ideas than conservative adult audiences.

The first question

Before you start on the time-consuming, frustrating and drawn-out process of 'making it' as a comedy writer, there's one question you should ask yourself: 'Can I write funny material?' It's surprising how many aspiring comedy writers never take a moment to be objective about their own work. You have to be tough on yourself because the chances of getting a show commissioned are low. The majority of scripts never get past the initial filtering process by producers and script readers. At every stage the numbers are whittled down. So the odds of any given script actually becoming a television programme are stacked against a writer from day one. Hard work and dedication will take you a long way, but if you can't deliver the comedy then think again. Try out what you've written on children and observe their reaction. You can rely on children to display their honest opinions. Don't rely on adults to give you mere confidence-boosting words of encouragement about your work. You don't need to wow your audience with the first thing you write. But you do need to raise a laugh somewhere along the way. If, after looking at yourself objectively, you do reckon that you may have that potential, the next step is to find out more about your chosen medium.

Budgets and briefs

Children's television has two special features that a writer should be aware of at every stage of writing: low budgets and a restrictive editorial brief. Budgets for programmes are around a fifth of comparable adult television shows so it's worth considering programme budgets when devising an idea. Commissioners are more likely to be attracted to proposals that can be realised on these lower sums than shows with a cast of hundreds and requiring numerous special effects. But don't make the mistake of thinking that a lower budget means lower quality. For example, Monty Python's *Life of Brian* was shot on a very low budget. The use of coconuts clapped together in place of horses for the knights was an ingenious way of overcoming the lack of funds for the horses. Whilst it's not a writer's job to get mired in the detail of how a scene could be shot, you should try to get a sense of what to avoid. Complex ideas which require large casts, major set builds and extensive use of special effects or large amounts of expensive post production are the obvious pitfalls.

The other unique aspect to children's television is its editorial concerns, which are wide ranging and can be tricky to master. In terms of content, swearing, sexual references, blasphemy or realistic violence are absolutely taboo. Your point of reference should be the content of a U or PG-rated film at the cinema. Watch a good variety of children's television and films to get an innate sense of what the boundaries are. As with the budgets, it's more productive to see these editorial rules as something that will force you to be a better writer than just a burden. Often new comedy writers rely on dark, violent scenarios because mastering a scene that relies on word play and a clever premise is beyond them. This tighter control of content means that the writer cannot fall back on shock tactics or explicit language to achieve a reaction which is, in the long run, a better way to progress.

There is an additional concern known as 'imitative behaviour'. Children are more suggestible and have a lower sense of risk and personal safety. In anything you write avoid any action that, if copied by children, might harm them, for example swallowing lots of tablets, forcing things into their mouths, throwing household objects at people. This may pose problems if you've got slapstick gags, which are a reliable mainstay of children's comedy. Be wary of any highly realistic scenarios as opposed to cartoonish ones. If the above sounds limiting, the flipside is that children will readily make greater leaps of imagination than adults. Don't forget that you're writing for an audience that remains fresh and open-minded in a way few adults are. Working within these ground rules is a small price to pay for an appreciative audience.

Comedy writing itself naturally divides into three main areas: sketches, scripted comedy and gag writing.

Scripted comedy

Scripted comedy covers a number of forms, including comedy narrative that has an unfolding story which links week by week and sitcom in which each episode is largely self contained. The three keys to writing good scripted comedy are number one: character; number two: character; and number three: character.

Everything starts and ends with your principal characters. Witty one-liners and elaborate plot structures are worthless unless they flow from strong central characters. For creating comedy characters, it's useful to think of them as embodying certain key personality traits and to make that inform everything they do. As we're dealing with comedy, don't make your characters too pleasant. There's nothing very amusing, for example, about a family sitcom where everyone gets on wonderfully well, is understanding, supportive and helpful. That may be a good environment to raise children, but it makes for tedious television. Characters don't work in isolation so put together a mix of characters that will spark against one another. Comedy, like drama, needs tension. So if you have a dysfunctional family that lives in a house so huge they never need to interact with one another, there's no friction for comedy to happen. But if you put them in a pokey flat where they're always getting in one another's way, then you've got fertile comic territory.

If you want to devise characters that will appeal to a children's audience, a mix of adults and children will be the most likely to work, preferably of different generations. Children won't be interested in mid-life crises, office politics or single women in their twenties looking for love. Generational conflict with families is an ideal starting point. But as with everything, there are no rules.

So long as your audience can find some point of connection, there's no reason why your lead couldn't be an alien or from another century. It all depends on how that character is presented so consider how your characters will connect with the wider audience. A child's frame of reference is different to that of an adult and children want comedy that reflects that. Remembering that you're writing not just for yourself but for hundreds of thousands of strangers will help guide you towards broader, more accessible characters. Make sure that the comedy flows from the characters themselves and doesn't just happen around them. Your comic leads need to initiate much of the action. In comedy things should go wrong most of the time so the leads should be the authors of their own misfortunes rather than having random events simply happen.

Sketch writing

Sketch writing presents other challenges, not least that many ideas have been done before. Common mistakes new writers make with a sketch is to start with a confused or muddled premise. Alternatively, they have a good premise and do nothing with it. The premise of a sketch is the one-line summary of a funny idea. If you can't summarise the sketch into one line and if that summary doesn't make you laugh, then there's probably something at fault with the original idea. Once you've got a promising sketch idea, it should develop as the piece unfolds. Even though the sketch may be only two minutes of airtime, you'll have to give some kind of twist or progression to sustain the audience's interest over that period. Even ten seconds of dead air in a television programme can feel like an eternity. Write your sketches longer and then trim them back. Another good rule is to not let a sketch run for longer than two minutes.

Gag writing

Gag writing is a discipline all of its own. When writing standalone jokes, practise does make perfect and it's critical that you test your material on audiences. It can be intimidating but there's no better way to find out if what you've written makes audiences laugh. Your main avenue for gag writing is the scripted links in entertainment shows.

The commissioning process

Once you have material ready to submit, understanding the commissioning process can save a lot of wasted effort. The first hurdle for a writer is to get anyone, whether it's a producer or an agent, to take an interest in their work. Getting a programme commissioned is a long, frustrating process and it's integral to that process to have someone promoting your cause – typically a producer.

From a new writer's perspective, agents can help from an early stage to get your script past the initial filtering stage. Producers and development executives are generally more receptive to scripts sent to them by agents, as they act as a form of quality control. Don't despair, if you send an unsolicited script or proposal to a producer or editor, it will be read... eventually.

One mistake writers often make is to send out copies of their script to every producer working in children's television with a general covering letter. This is never a good idea. It sends out a signal that the writer in question couldn't be bothered to do some research on who might be interested in their script. Finding out who makes which shows is relatively easy as all the major channels have information lines if you miss the end credits of shows. A bit of research goes a long way. You should follow up that script with a phone call or email. Although your script may represent months of hard toil to you, remember that producers work on other shows and that reading scripts is a low priority for them.

If you are able to get a producer to take an interest in your work, often the next natural step is not to immediately pitch your own programme ideas but to work on existing shows, perhaps writing episodes of a long-running sitcom, devising sketch ideas or writing additional material for entertainment shows. This is a good bridging stage as you'll get a better feel of the production and commissioning process. It's also a great opportunity to improve your writing craft without the exposure of a solo project. Nearly all comedy writers started out writing on other people's shows. The longer you spend writing in a professional environment, the better you'll get. Meeting deadlines and turning work around in a short time frame are not disciplines new writers acquire by writing on their own but they are an important part of being a successful television writer. Being funny on demand is a tough task and it's part of the craft.

In the long run most writers are more interested in getting their own solo ideas commissioned. Be prepared for a lot of frustration and disappointment if you follow this route. There are relatively few programme slots available in any given year. Commissioners tend to favour tried and tested writers over new names. There's no conspiracy to exclude new talent, however. When money is in short supply, opting for a safe pair of hands is a form of insurance policy. All of which means that, as a new writer, you'll have to be that much more impressive than an established one to get noticed. In spite of all this, if you deliver funny, original and accessible scripts, sooner or later you'll be noticed and they will make it on screen.

Adam Bromley is a freelance producer and director for TV and radio. He produced *Tiny and Mr Duk's Huge Show* and *Stupid* for CBBC, *Bash* for BBC3, *Jesusboy and the Goatherd* for E4, as well as numerous hit comedies for BBC Radio 4, including *Think the Unthinkable*, *The Now Show*, *Hut 33* and *Recorded for Training Purposes*.

See also...
- *Commissioning for children's television*, page 297
- *Writing humour for young children*, page 126

Children's literature on radio and audio

The technologies for transmitting the spoken word to children are developing rapidly. Neville Teller describes the fast-changing world of radio and audio, and explores what a writer for the microphone needs to know, and how to break into this market.

'Read me a story' – one of childhood's perennial cries. Until radio arrived, parents found little relief from it (palming it off on grandma or auntie was perhaps the best bet). But from its very beginning, radio included in its schedules stories read aloud for children. So, for part of the time at least, the loudspeaker was able to provide a fair substitute for mummy or daddy by providing literature, specially prepared for performance at the microphone, read by professional actors.

Very early on, actors learned that performing at the microphone was a new skill – the techniques were specialised and quite different from those required on the stage. Writers, too, had to acquire a whole range of new skills in preparing material for radio. Two things quickly became apparent. First, the time taken to read a complete book on the air would be far too long to be acceptable, and in consequence most books would need to be abridged. Secondly, literature simply read aloud from the printed page often failed to 'come across' to a listening audience, because material produced to be scanned by the eye is often basically unsuited to the requirements of the microphone.

Today there are two main outlets in this country for aspiring writers and abridgers for children in the radio/audio sphere: BBC radio and audiobook publishers.

How has this market reached its present position?

Radio

Children's radio in the UK has certainly had its ups and downs. It came into existence in December 1922, just a few weeks after the BBC itself was born, and for some 40 years the daily 'Children's Hour' became an established and much-cherished feature of life in the UK.

However, in the 1960s the imminent death of radio was a generally accepted prognostication. So, starting in 1961, children's radio was slowly but surely strangled on the dubious, if not specious, grounds that children no longer had the time or inclination to listen to radio. Television, it was argued, was their medium of choice. So first the much-loved title Children's Hour was dropped, then the time allotted to programmes 'For the Young' (as it was subsequently called) was cut back. Finally, in March 1964, the programme was put out of its agony.

The demise of children's radio naturally evoked a massive groundswell of protest. In response – although the BBC of the day had clearly lost faith in it – they did grant some sort of reprieve. Stories had always featured strongly in its schedules, so Story Time – a programme of abridged radio readings – started life in the old Children's Hour slot with a strong bias towards children's literature. It was not long, however, before more general literature began to be selected. Finally, in 1982, the programme was dropped. For the next 20 years the only regular children's programme left on BBC radio was Listen with Mother, the 15-minute programme for the under-fives.

The comeback started slowly, and then suddenly gathered momentum. Early in the new millennium the BBC – moved, doubtless, by mounting evidence of the undiminished popularity of radio – decided to reintroduce a regular programme for children. All they could offer at the time was a 30-minute programme each Sunday evening on Radio 4 called *Go4It*, a magazine-type show which would include a ten-minute reading. Children's literature had – to mix metaphors and create a glorious vision – re-established a toehold on the airwaves, and I found myself abridging books for the programme like *The Lion, The Witch and the Wardrobe* by C.S. Lewis and *The Wolves of Willoughby Chase* by Joan Aiken. Unfortunately this renaissance was typically short lived. *Go4It* was axed on 24 May 2009.

But the door had been pushed ajar and much more was to follow, for in the autumn of 2002 the BBC launched its new digital radio channel, BBC7, and its schedules included, as a basic ingredient, daily programmes for children using live performers and incorporating readings from children's literature, both current and classic. These abridgements were specially prepared and read for the two daily shows: *The Big Toe Radio Show* for older children and – it goes without saying – *The Little Toe Radio Show* for the youngsters. I prepared a considerable number of books for these programmes, including not only classical children's literature like *Robinson Crusoe* and *The Prince and the Pauper*, but also more general classics specially prepared for younger listeners like *20,000 Leagues Under the Sea* and *Oliver Twist*. The Big Toe programme also featured up-to-the-moment favourites such as Anthony Horowitz's series about his boy secret agent, Alex Rider, the *Artemis Fowl* novels by Eoin Coffer, Terry Pratchett's *A Haul of Sky* and *The Amazing Maurice*, and Jackie French's *Callisto* series. For younger listeners, I abridged books like the *Whizziwig* series by Malorie Blackman, the *Lily Quench* books by Natalie Jane Prior, and Kaye Umansky's *The Silver Spoon of Solomon Snow*.

Children's radio had been re-established, and all seemed set fair. Then, towards the end of 2006, came news of major changes. The BBC's digital television channel for the youngest children, CBeebies, had been proving an enormous success. The BBC decided that the time was ripe to exploit this advantage. Lateral, not to say radical, thinking was applied. *The Little Toe Radio Show* was to be converted into a radio extension of CBeebies and would be renamed *CBeebies on BBC7* (and later as *CBeebies on BBC Radio 7*). The radio programme would be promoted on the television show, and child viewers would be urged to tune in for more CBeebies on the air.

Big Toe Books consisted of readings drawn from the programme's extensive archive of children's literature, including my own abridgements of, among many others, *Bootleg* by Alex Shearer, *Stop the Train* by Geraldine McCaughrean, *Huckleberry Finn* by Mark Twain, *Slaves of the Mastery* and *Firesong* by William Nicholson, *Stig of the Dump* by Clive King, *The BGF* by Roald Dahl, *The Little House on the Prairie* by Laura Ingalls Wilder, *Dream Master* by Theresa Breslin, and *Point Blanc* by Anthony Horowitz.

Nothing lasts for ever, and 2011 saw big changes in BBC digital radio generally, and in its children's radio programming in particular. As from 2 April, BBC Radio 7 was transmogrified into BBC Radio 4 Extra. With the transformation came a new shape to children's radio – almost a return to the Children's Hour concept of yesteryear. CBeebies and *Big Toe Books* were both abandoned. Now each day Radio 4 Extra transmits *The Four O'Clock Show* – a one-hour programme devised specifically for children, and always including abridged readings of children's literature. On Sundays at 4pm a *Young Classics* radio drama is scheduled, with dramatisations of books like *The Wizard of Oz*, *Chitty-Chitty Bang-Bang*, *Treasure Island* and *Black Beauty*. This continuous stream of radio programming for children is produced by an enhanced Children's Unit situated in Glasgow.

Audiobooks

Audiobooks are literary works of all types, some abridged, some unabridged, read by actors and now generally available in CD format. From what was virtually a standing start in the late 1980s, annual sales of audiobooks are now pushing £75 million. In excess of five million audiobooks are purchased in the UK annually, and children's literature forms a significant proportion of that total.

Nowadays, it is common for major publishers to launch a fair number of their new books, including books for older children, in printed and audiobook form simultaneously. Publishers of books for younger children often adopt the 'twin pack' concept – packaging book and audiobook together – so that children can read and listen at the same time. This development has mushroomed since 2003, when HM Revenue & Customs decided that such products could be zero-rated for VAT.

In March 2009 ECOFIN (the EU's Economic and Financial Affairs Council) agreed to reduce VAT on audiobooks from 15% to 5%. As a result, within the next few years audiobook publishers may be able to charge significantly less for both their digital and physical audiobooks.

How children listen

The ways in which children can – and increasingly do – listen to the readings intended especially for them are multiplying at what seems an ever-increasing rate.

The digital radio channel, BBC Radio 4 Extra is also transmitted online (where it can be heard simul-streamed and also through 'Listen Again'), and via satellite and cable television sets.

Audiobooks, too, have now burst through the confines of the CD to become available as downloads, via a range of online outlets including Audible, Apple iTunes, AudioGo (the new name for BBC products) and a growing list of other suppliers, including the US book chain Barnes & Noble and the UK's Random House. Taken together, they have an enormous and expanding list of children's books available for downloading, and stories are proving a popular second-best to music for many children for their personal iPods and mobiles. Subscribers either pay for downloads book by book, or pay a monthly fee for the right to download a specific number of titles. In-car MP3 playback, via the car radio, is now becoming widely available at very modest cost, and this method of listening is likely to rival the in-car audio or CD player for keeping children happy on long journeys.

Amazon has over 30,000 children's audiobooks available to be purchased and downloaded. Users can then start listening within seconds, transfer the audiobook to a computer, iPod or other device, or burn it to a CD. There are other specialist providers of audiobooks for children, such as Audio Stories 4 Kids (www.kidsaudiobooks.co.uk/mp3_downloads.htm).

According to recent research in the USA, nearly a third of children aged 6–10 are regular users of digital audio players. As a result, Audible launched AudibleKids.com, where children can download books directly onto their digital audio players. But the site also offers children a social networking community, where they can talk about books with each other, and with parents, teachers and even authors.

The mobile phone is now regarded by many people, and especially the younger generations, as an essential part of one's personal equipment. Children are increasingly accessing not only digital radio and the internet via their mobile phones, but also audiobooks. Launched internationally in 2008, the Vodafone 'Books on Mobile' operation is a partnership between Vodafone and GoSpoken.com, a website dedicated to putting audiobooks and ebooks on mobiles. Most leading audiobook publishers in the UK, including the BBC, have signed up to the new service. The technology used is known as HSDPA (High-Speed Downlink Packet Access), and originally this permitted a three-hour audiobook to be downloaded to a mobile phone – and paid for – in three minutes. Since then, even faster times have been introduced by Vodafone. Other providers, such as Mobcast, are also now crowding into the marketplace, and evidence is mounting that children are taking advantage of this flexible access to read-aloud literature.

For the past two years the coffee chain, Starbucks, has been offering their regular customers free internet access to visit the online iTunes store, where they can instantly purchase music and other products on offer. iTunes has a large stock of audiobooks, including many for children and young people.

Kindle 2 – the newest version of Amazon's ebook reader – hit the UK early in 2009. Roughly the dimensions of a paperback but paper-thin, it can download a novel in about 30 seconds either for you to read on its 6-inch wide screen or – and this was the innovation – for it to be read aloud to you (albeit in a somewhat robot-like voice).

Apple's iPad, a tablet computer, took the UK by storm in May 2009. Its many functions include their eBook application (or 'app' as it's now commonly called), akin to Amazon's Kindle and preferred by many.

Another new phenomenon is 'podiobooks', or podcast audiobook novels, released on the internet in instalments, and free. They are often made available at the same time in the form of a PDF ebook (i.e. to be downloaded and read on the computer screen, on an ebook reader, or on a new generation mobile phone). They are often offered together with a range of stickers, ringtones and wallpapers – all designed to appeal to the young market. The pioneer was Scott Sigler, whose website offers free audio fiction on a regular basis. Most podiobooks so far have been in the fields of science fiction and fantasy. Other 'podio-authors' may branch out into different types of writing. But the whole concept is aimed particularly at young people, and is likely to encourage audio listening in the younger age groups.

The message of all this for writers is that the radio/audio market is mushrooming, and that the technological developments and innovations seem designed to appeal particularly to the internet-savvy younger generations. If you are keen to break into the rapidly changing world of children's literature on radio and audio, it seems worthwhile to persevere.

Writing for the microphone

Putting unabridged audiobook readings to one side, what does the aspiring radio/audio children's writer need to know, and how can he or she break into the rather specialised world of abridging children's literature for the microphone?

As in all professional fields, the tyro is faced with the classic Catch-22 situation: radio producers and audio publishers are reluctant to offer commissions to people without a track record, while it is of course impossible to gain a track record without having won a commission or two. The only advice is to keep plugging away, hoping for that elusive lucky break – and the only consolation on offer is that even the most experienced of today's professionals was once a complete novice.

But what of the techniques that need to be applied in converting material produced for the printed page into a series of scripts that can be performed by an actor with ease at the microphone, and bring real listening pleasure to the child at the other end?

Getting to grips with abridging books for the microphone requires, in the first instance, the application of some simple arithmetic. Take a book of around 70,000 words. Children's radio usually devotes about ten minutes' airtime to its reading slot, and producers allow up to 14 episodes for each book. In ten minutes, an actor can read about 1,450 words. It is clear, therefore, that normally the abridger will be required to reduce the wordage from 70,000 to no more than 20,300 words. In other words, one can be required to remove up to 70% of the original.

The audio field has different requirements. Books abridged for audio are today usually produced in CD format. CDs can accommodate some 70 minutes of airtime, which translates to about 11,000 words. So a 140-minute abridgement is presented in the form of two CDs, and will allow the abridger about 22,000 words.

An abridgement – is that the same as a précis? I think not. A précis writer's objective is to reproduce the sense of an original in fewer words. The skill of the abridger lies in doing that while, in addition and quite as important, retaining the character of the original writing. That demands the capacity to respond sympathetically to the feel of an author's style and to be able to preserve it, even when large chunks of the original are being cut away. Abridging for radio goes beyond even this, for the writer must fulfil his or her commission through the medium of that highly technical artefact, the radio script.

How much liberty is the abridger allowed in translating the printed to the spoken word, while reducing the wordage? Some audiobook producers ask for the minimum of interference with the published text; some radio producers are content for the abridger to adapt the original freely, so as to enhance the actor's performance at the microphone. The different approaches reflect the fact that, in acquiring radio reading rights, the BBC retains editorial independence over the final product, while the granting of abridged audio rights is often conditional on the original writer's approval of the abridged text. So audio producers, reluctant to run the risk of rejection, sometimes allow the abridger very little freedom.

Nevertheless it is an undoubted fact that the requirements of eye and of ear do not always coincide, and that a message easily absorbed from the printed page can become surprisingly garbled if transmitted unamended at the microphone.

In crafting a radio/audio script the needs of the listener must be one of the prime considerations. The needs of the actor who will read it at the microphone are another. The writer must keep in the forefront of the mind the fact that the script has to be performed. The words must 'flow trippingly on the tongue'. With audio the listener is in control, and can switch on or off whenever convenient. However, a radio script needs shape. On the air, ten minutes on an emotional plateau can be pretty boring. *Crescendi* and *diminuendi* are called for. A good plan is to provide a modest peak of interest about halfway through the script, and work up to a climax at the end, leaving the listener anxious for more of the story.

Principles, principles – what about practice? Let me offer a modest illustration, assuming I'm abridging for radio.

'How are you going?' Harriet said, stifling a yawn.
'The Oxford bus,' returned Pam.

Nothing wrong with that – on the printed page. If faced with it, though, the experienced radio abridger would feel it necessary to present it somewhat along the following lines:

Harriet stifled a yawn.
'How are you going?'
'The Oxford bus,' said Pam.

Why? Let's take the points in order.

Harriet said.

If the speaker's name instantly follows a piece of reported speech, and especially a question, a moment of confusion can arise in the listener's mind. In this instance, it could be unclear for a second whether 'Harriet' is included in, or excluded from, the question. It might be: *'How are you going, Harriet...?'*

The meaning is soon resolved, of course, but impediments to understanding are best eliminated.

'Stifling a yawn' is an indication of the way in which the words were said. If the actor is to provide that indication, he or she needs to know ahead of the speech how it is to be delivered. Moreover, taking the original version, if the actor stifles a yawn while saying Harriet's speech, and then reads 'said Harriet, stifling a yawn,' the passage becomes tautologous.

For this reason it is best to cut back to a bare minimum all indications in the text of how speeches are delivered – 'grimly', 'lugubriously', 'chuckling merrily', and so on. It is better to leave it to the actor and the producer to interpret most of them.

There are no apostrophes on the air. By and large, 'said' is the best radio indicator of speech. An alternative is to precede speech by some description of the speaker, and to insert the words spoken with no further indication of who is speaking. Thus:

Harriet stifled a yawn.
'How are you going?'

It is clearly Harriet speaking.

'The Oxford bus,' returned Pamela.

Two points here. Almost all the literary variants of 'said' ring false through the loudspeaker or headphones – 'cried', 'riposted', 'remarked', 'answered', and so on. For reading purposes, most are best replaced with 'said' (or better, wherever possible, omitted altogether) and the speech in question left to the actor to interpret. In this instance, 'returned' is particularly difficult for the listener – again, for no more than a moment – but is 'returned' part of the speech? *'The Oxford bus returned...?'* It is surely best to eliminate obstacles to understanding.

This peek into the radio/audio abridger's toolbox might leave one thinking that the business is all gimmick and no heart – noses pressed up so hard against tree trunks that there is no time for the wood. It is certainly necessary in this field, as in any other, for basic techniques to be acquired and then absorbed to the point where they become second nature. Only then can they be applied to ensure that the radio and audio media are used to interpret a writer's intentions as fully and as honestly as possible.

It is, though, equally essential that the abridger of children's books reproduces, as far as possible, the plot, atmosphere and character of the original. The aim must be to leave the listener with as complete a feeling of the original book as possible, given the technical limitations of time and wordage. It is, in short, an essential aspect of the radio/audio writer's craft to keep faith with the author.

Neville Teller MBE has been contributing to BBC radio for over 50 years. He has well over 250 abridgements for radio readings to his credit, some 50 radio dramatisations and over 200 audiobook abridgements. His most recent children's abridgements include *Bootleg* by Alex Shearer, *Kidnapped* by Robert Louis Stevenson, *Sunning* by Kenneth Oppel, *The Fall of Fergal* and the *Awful End* series by Philip Adagh, *A Hatful of Sky* by Terry Pratchett, and *Muddle Earth* by Paul Stewart and Chris Riddell. Neville Teller is a past chairman of the Society of Authors' Broadcasting Committee and of the Audiobook Publishing Association's Contributors' Committee. He was made an MBE in 2006 'for services to broadcasting and to drama'.

See also...
- *Children's audio publishers*, page 61
- *Writing to a brief*, page 310
- *Children's television and radio*, page 314

Television, film and radio

Writing to a brief

Writing to a brief is an exacting process in which the writer has to produce work to satisfy others as opposed to exploring their own project ideas. The writer may work with others as part of a team when script writing or collaborate with an artistic director when adapting a play. Di Redmond looks at three aspects of writing to a brief for children.

Writing to a brief is enormously varied. I never know what's going to land on my desk – it could be anything: a children's animation series, a set of books, a live action drama script or a stage play. When you're writing to a brief you have to be able to absorb material very quickly and you must be disciplined enough to put your own ideas on the back burner. If you twist the commissioner's brief in order to accommodate what you want to write you'll very soon be out of a job!

Animation
The writing team

An animation series is usually commissioned in blocks of 26 or 52 ten-minute episodes. US companies like to have big commissioning meetings with 10–12 writers sat around the table brainstorming for 2–3 days. UK companies prefer smaller more intimate groups of 6–8 writers brainstorming for a day at most, often just a morning! You might be invited to these meetings through your agent or through your own personal contact with the animation house or broadcaster. After the meeting you pitch ideas and if they are approved you become one of the writing team, which can be an uplifting experience – after all we writers work on our own so interacting with other writers is the equivalent of a party! Most writers are open and generous with their ideas, although there can be an initial shyness as nobody wants to make a fool of themself. My advice is to not hold back as the more you share together the more you can generate together.

On a financial note, every stage of the writing process should be covered in your writer's contract, from the writers' meeting where you should receive a full day's fee plus travelling expenses, to separate payments for the Treatment, Draft 1, Draft 2, and the Final Polish Draft. If a contract along these lines isn't offered in advance I'd be extremely wary of attending any meeting.

The writing process

Working from the 'Bible', a document which contains everything the writer needs to know from character descriptions to locations and props, the writing process begins in earnest. It's a real bonus if the 'Bible' contains a fully executed script as it is the best template to work from: an added bonus would be a promo tape to give you the chance to see the characters and hopefully hear their 'speak'. Hearing Neil Morrisey as Bob the Builder on a promo CD crystalised Bob's character for me and made the writing process so much fun and a lot easier too. Your writing will be hugely affected by the animators' criteria. CGI (computer-generated image) animations like *Magic Roundabout* and *Noddy in Toyland* are vastly different from stop frame puppetry animation like the original *Noddy*, *Postman Pat* and *Fifi and the Flowertots*. A puppet like Bob the Builder costs upwards of £8,000 and will be limited in what it can and cannot do. It's best to sort out all practical problems with the animators at an early stage so you don't waste time writing scripts that are impossible to execute. Even when your storyline is nothing more than a basic idea on half a page of A4 check with the animators that it's workable: for example, if it's about bubbles make sure the studio can do bubbles, if it's about autumn check with the animators that they can do falling leaves. There's nothing more frustrating than getting to Draft 1 stage only to discover that one of the main elements in the story can't be animated. You'll be left seething that you've spent a week writing a draft that has to be ripped apart and started all over again. Be bold and ask the practical questions right at the start.

When you finally get the red light to go to Draft 1, i.e. the Treatment has been approved, the real *fun* begins! I have sat at my desk and laughed till I cried at my characters and the daft situations they've got themselves into. Remember that behind the lively dialogue other things are happening simultaneously: movement within the set, facial expressions, sound effects and music too. Sometimes a single word of dialogue like 'Okay!' will have instructions to camera that cover half a page. Matching dialogue to camera shots is a precise skill which I find hugely challenging and very satisfying.

Storylines

Sometimes a few storylines are developed when the writing team is together – just enough to get the team kick-started. The writers may be invited to choose a storyline that grabs them and develop it into a three- or four-page treatment which is a detailed scene-by-scene breakdown of a ten-minute episode. After this writers usually develop further storylines in their own time, in my case when I'm walking the dogs or listening in on children's conversations in the supermarket! A series of images (generally comical) will suddenly pop into my head which make me laugh out loud. If I'm lucky these will form the basis of my plotline. The first script is without doubt the hardest because no matter how good the 'Bible' is you've still got to breathe life into the characters, get the 'beats' of the show and come in on time. If the script is too long it will be edited down before it's recorded so try to make sure that it's the right length before you send it off to the broadcaster. A ten-minute script with opening and closing credits is around 13–15 pages depending on the font size you use. After completing a couple of scripts you're usually on a roll. However, there have been some shows which I couldn't engage with as the subject matter left me cold and I had to bow out gracefully. The commissioners will be looking for scripts that contain humour, warmth, clarity and an understanding of the age group the programme is pitched at. If it's about garden gnomes then keep it in the garden; if it's about a builder then the building job will be essential to every story; if it's about a postman then he has to do his post round. Most scripts, even if they're only ten minutes long, have a main plot and a sub-plot which have to be reconciled at the end of the episode. Make sure your sub-plot doesn't swamp your main plot and make doubly sure your main plot echoes the criteria of the series. Some commissionaires insist on a three-act writing structure, with three questions underpinning the story line – What's the goal? What's the risk? What does the character learn? This might seem like a big ask but once you've got used to it as a writing process it can be useful as it highlights the dramatic peaks in the story and you always know what you're building up to.

The script editor

A good script editor coordinates the scripts and makes sure the series has one voice, whether it's a ballerina, a little pig, a runaway train or a naughty boy. Writers have different styles, which is why they've been chosen to do the job. The script editor with her overall view of the show will make changes to scripts and she'll also keep an eye on the timing. She has the sensitive task of liaising with the commissioner and the producer on the writers' behalf. Sometimes you *don't* want to see the notes the producer has made: they may be too abrupt or confusing. A good script editor will work on the notes before handing them on to the writers to make the necessary changes.

Stage plays

As well as writing my own stage plays I've also adapted stage plays from the classics such as *Hard Times* by Charles Dickens and Homer's *The Odyssey*. The Dickens play was commissioned by the Cambridge Youth Theatre for the Edinburgh Festival with a cast of 30, and *The Odyssey* was staged at the Polka Theatre for Children in London with a cast of six!

When briefed by an artistic director writers should listen hard to his or her requirements and it is imperative that they take on board the limitations of the budget. Theatres usually have to work on a shoestring budget. If too much is spent on props and costumes it may be at the cost of the funding for an actor, so be prepared to adapt and compromise.

Adapting from the classics

Adapting from a text such as a classic is an exacting exercise. The two books I adapted couldn't have been more different but the process was exactly the same. I read both books until I knew them backwards: with that knowledge under my belt I felt at liberty to explore the plotlines within the stories and look for modern day angles on how to dramatise them.

The brief for *The Odyssey* was to write a 90-minute play with a ten-minute interval for 8–12 year-olds. *The Odyssey* is full of sex! For instance, Odysseus loiters too long with Circe and nearly dies in his desire to reach the Sirens! In order not to shock my young audience I found a way around this sensitive area by bringing in the crew who made humorous references to Odysseus' behaviour. In one of my scenes Eurylochus says, 'It's time we set sail.' Castor nods towards Odysseus locked in the arms of Circe the Witch and says, 'I don't think the captain's ready for that yet, mate!' The language of Homer is hauntingly beautiful but certainly not pitched at children. The hardest part of writing the play was adapting the language and the plot so that the audience could understand what was going on without destroying the nobility of the original piece. Working closely with the artistic director, I wrote three drafts of the play before I felt I'd got it right, by which time I was so familiar with the gods and heroes of Ancient Greece that they felt like my extended family! It's a knowledge I've never lost and have since written four books based on classical Greek heroes. That's another great thing about writing: you can transpose a story from one art form to another!

Book series

A book series may be commissioned as a result of a writer pitching an idea to a publisher, or a publisher may have spotted a gap in the market which a writer has been invited to fill. The books vary in length – 2,000–40,000 words – depending on the age range.

I've written three series of books based on football which I knew nothing about but finished up the world's expert on the offside trap! I went on to write several more series based on show jumping, a stage school, a veterinary practice, a drama queen, and an eight-book series based on bridesmaids! A lot of research goes into my books. With my show-jumping series I virtually lived at the livery yard, trailing the head groom and asking questions like, 'Where do show jumpers go when they're not show jumping? How do you treat a lame horse? What's the best fitness diet? Do show jumpers need special shoes and saddles?' I've always been very lucky in finding professionals who allowed me into their lives and let me watch them at work, though I have had a few nasty shocks in the process. Once I found myself masked and gloved in an operating theatre at a vet's surgery watching a Newmarket racehorse under the scalpel; but I fled the premises (and my note taking) when a couple brought in a large snake that needed treatment! You *really* do have to know your subject when you're writing this kind of specialist book. The readers certainly know their stuff and are highly critical of any inaccuracies, so be careful what you write otherwise you'll get letters of complaint!

Di Redmond is a prolific writer for children's television. She has worked for Aardman Animation, CBBC, CITV, HIT Entertainment, Cosgrove Hall, Milkshake, Nikelodeon, Nick Jn, CBC (Canada), Cyber Group (France) and Ki-Ka (Germany). Her credits include *Magic Roundabout, Bob the Builder, Postman Pat, Roary the Racing Car, Tweenies, Fifi Forget-me-Not* and *Angelina Ballerina*. She also writes for stage and radio and has published over 100 books, and is a ghostwriter.

See also...
- *Children's literature on radio and audio,* page 303
- *What does an editor do?,* page 164

Television, film and radio

Children's television and radio

Emma Hurrell provides listings to help writers make contact with the world of television.

Children's television
Submitting scripts to BBC Television

BBC writersroom
Brock House, 3rd Floor, 19 Langham Street, London W1A 1AA
email writersroom@bbc.co.uk
website www.bbc.co.uk/writersroom
Creative Director, New Writing Kate Rowland,
Development Producer Paul Ashton

BBC writersroom is the first point of call at the BBC for unsolicited scripts and new writers. It identifies and champions new writing talent and diversity across BBC children's, drama and narrative comedy programmes. New writers are strongly advised to visit the website for more detailed information on what type of work can be submitted and how to submit it. As well as submission guidelines, the comprehensive website provides advice on scriptwriting, contacts, interviews with prominent writers and BBC executives, formatting templates, free downloadable scripts from BBC productions, details of current opportunities and events, blogs and useful links. Writers can sign up for the monthly newsletter on the homepage. From time to time national and regional open competitions for writers are held. All writers submitting scripts are considered for targeted professional writing schemes and workshops.

Children's Department
MediaCityUK, Salford Quays M50 2EQ
tel 020-8743 8000
website www.bbc.co.uk/commissioning/briefs/tv/browse-by-genre
Director, Children's Joe Godwin

Children's is a self-commissioning, self-scheduling department managing its own production unit. For detailed information on CBBC and Cbeebies, go to the website and select either CBBC or CBeebies.

CBBC
email cbbcdrama.submissions@bbc.co.uk (Drama Submissions Dept)
website www.bbc.co.uk/writersroom/writing/guidelines_cbeebies
Controller Damian Kavanagh

CBBC is for children aged 6–12. It offers a distinctive schedule of original drama, animation, comedy, news, factual programming and events on a variety of platforms as well as interactive applications (online, WAP, SMS, enhanced TV) that allow children to get involved, to connect with CBBC and to explore topics

further. The CBBC channel runs 7am–7pm and CBBC output runs on BBC ONE and BBC TWO. Independent suppliers should send proposals to Damian Kavanagh, and drama, acquisitions and animations enquiries should be made to Steven Andrew via the e-Commissioning system. If you are an experienced writer with TV, radio, or theatre credits or have an agent and are interested in writing for new or existing children's drama series, email a 30-minute writing sample for TV and your CV to the CBBC Drama Submissions Department.

CBeebies
Controller Kay Benbow

CBeebies is the BBC's first truly tri-media brand, offering TV, radio and web services on all digital platforms. CBeebies offers a rich portfolio of content on its website, including the Radio Player, and through its TV outlets. It is therefore a multi-platform commissioner not just a TV commissioner. Independent suppliers should send all proposals to Kay Benbow (via e-Commissioning). Enquiries concerning acquisitions and animations should also be made to Kay Benbow (but proposals must be submitted via e-Commissioning).

The CBeebies digital TV channel (on satellite, cable and Freeview) is on air 6am–7pm daily. CBeebies TV may also be found on BBC TWO, which runs complementary schedules – sometimes simulcasting the CBeebies channel across weekday mornings. CBeebies radio is now only available via the website.

Other television networks

Pact is the UK trade association representing and promoting the commercial interests of independent feature film, TV, digital, children's and animation media companies. For a full list of children's independent TV and film production companies visit its website (www.pact.co.uk).

BabyTV
Baby Networks Ltd, PO Box 63107, London W14 4AA
email info@babytvchannels.com
website www.babytv.com

Dedicated content for infants and toddlers broadcast 24 hours a day. Many original series aimed at early learning and skills development. BabyTV has also recently launched an Online Player, through which its programmes can be viewed via a computer. Part of Fox International Channels.

Boomerang
Turner House, 16 Great Marlborough Street, London W1F 7HS

tel 020-7693 1000
website www.boomerangtv.co.uk

Cartoon entertainment broadcast 24 hours a day. Operated by Turner Broadcasting.

Cartoon Network

Turner House, 16 Great Marlborough Street, London W1F 7HS
tel 020-7693 1000
website www.cartoonnetwork.co.uk

Cartoon entertainment broadcast 24 hours a day. Operated by Turner Broadcasting. Cartoon Network has 2 sister channels:
• **Cartoon Network Too (CN Too)** Original and modern classic cartoons broadcast 24 hours a day.
• **Cartoonito** *website* www.cartoonito.co.uk Preschool cartoon entertainment.

Channel 4

124 Horseferry Road, London SW1P 2TX
tel 020-7396 4444
website www.channel4.com
Ceo David Abraham, *Chief Creative Officer* Jay Hunt, *Commissioning Editor, Education* Jo Twist

Channel 4 is a publicly owned, commercially funded public service broadcaster and transmits across the whole of the UK, except some parts of Wales, which are covered by the Welsh language S4C. Channel 4 also operates a number of other services, including the free-to-air digital TV channels E4, More4, Film4 and 4Music, and an ever-growing range of online activities, Channel 4's bespoke video-on-demand service 4oD and standalone digital projects. As a publisher–broadcaster, Channel 4 does not produce its own programmes but commissions them from more than 300 independent production companies.

Channel 4 does not currently commission and broadcast children's programmes but a key component of their diverse educational content and services is interactive digital media projects aimed at 10–19 year-olds in the UK. These can be games or web-based projects which help young people to understand the world they live in and learn life skills to achieve their personal potential and make the decisions that affect their futures.

Channel 5

10 Lower Thames Street, London EC3R 6EN
tel 020-8612 7000
website www.channel5.com
Director of Programmes Jeff Ford, *Commissioning Editor, Children's* Jessica Symons

Channel 5 is a publisher–broadcaster and works with independent production companies to provide its programmes. It usually only accepts programme proposals from independent production companies. Channel 5 brands include the original channel, 5; digital channels 5* and 5 USA; and video-on-demand service Demand 5.

Children's strand Milkshake offers age-appropriate programmes, games, songs, dances, stories, and competitions for preschool children (2–7 year-olds). Milkshake is on Channel 5 Saturday and Sunday 6–10am and weekdays 6–9.15am. Channel 5 commissions, co-produces and acquires preschool programming with a wide range of different deals and arrangements. Increasingly, co-productions are dominant. Budget contributions have ranged from 10–100%. Channel 5 also commissions short form live-action series for preschool children.

CITV

The London Television Centre, Upper Ground, London SE1 9LT
tel 020-7157 3000
website www.citv.co.uk
Programme Manager Jamila Metran

The ITV Network is responsible for the commissioning, scheduling and marketing of network programmes on ITV1 and its digital channel portfolio, ITV2, ITV3, ITV4 and CITV. Programmes from ITV are provided by ITV's in-house production unit and by the independent sector. CITV is on air 6am–6pm and targeted at 2 distinct age groups: preschool and 4–10 year-olds.

Disney Channel UK

Chiswick Park, Building 12, 566 Chiswick High Road, London W4 5AN
tel 020-8636 2000
website www.disneychannel.co.uk
Programming Director Jonathan Boseley

A cable and satellite network run by the Walt Disney Company. It specialises in programming for children aged 6–14, with the exception of weekend primetime when it is aimed at ages 9–14, and shows original series and movies, as well as third party programming. It has 3 sister channels:
• **Disney Cinemagic** Shows Disney classics.
• **Disney XD** Primarily aimed at boys aged 6–14, it features live action films, animated shows, as well as sports coverage.
• **Disney Junior** Specialises in educational programming for children aged 2–6.

Nickelodeon UK

15–18 Rathbone Place, London W1H 1HU
tel 020-7462 1000
website www.nick.co.uk
Programming Director Debbie MacDonald

Nickelodeon UK currently comprises 3 channels which target children aged 2–12:
• **Nickelodeon** *website* www.nick.co.uk Key shows with a specific focus on live action comedy.
• **NickToons** *website* www.nicktoons.co.uk Animation plus top toons aimed primarily at boys aged 6–9, although the channel has broad appeal. Looking to acquire comedy-driven animation but will consider action series with a comedy skew.

• **Nick Jr** *website* www.nickjr.co.uk Dedicated preschool channel targeting 2–5 year-olds. The programming encourages active participation as opposed to passive viewing. Nick Jr 2 broadcasts Nick Jr shows but on a different schedule.

POP

CSC Media Group Ltd, 37 Harwood Road, London SW6 4QP
tel 020-7371 5999
website www.popfun.co.uk
Director of Programmes Francesca Newington

Cartoons and pop music videos with 3 sister channels:
• **Pop Girl** *website* www.popgirlworld.com Cartoons, live action and pop music videos for a more female audience.
• **Tiny Pop** *website* www.tinypop.com Cartoons and pop music videos for preschool children.
• **Kix!** Cartoons, extreme sports and music videos aimed at a more male and teen audience.

Radio Telefís Éireann (RTÉ)

Donnybrook, Dublin 4, Republic of Ireland
tel (01) 208 3111
website www.rte.ie
Commissioning Editor, Young People's Programmes Sheila DeCourcy

RTÉ is a Public Service Broadcaster, a non-profit-making organisation owned by the Irish people. RTÉ operates 2 complementary TV channels, RTÉ One and RTÉ Two; 4 radio stations; and 7 digital services. RTÉ also publishes the *RTÉ Guide*, operates teletext service, RTÉ Aertel, and provides information via its website. RTÉ is also a major contributor to the arts and supports 5 performing groups.

RTÉ Television broadcasts for its younger audiences on its second channel, RTÉ Two. For 0–6 year-olds RTÉjr delivers a mix of both original and acquired live action and animation programming 8.30am–3.30pm on weekdays and early mornings at the weekend. TRTÉ is for 7–15 year-olds and delivers a mixed schedule 3.30–5.30pm weekdays and on weekend mornings. Two Tube is for older teens and young adults and runs 5.30–7pm. All of the original programming is complemented by fresh online content on the websites and on digital radio.

S4C

Parc Ty Glas, Llanishen, Cardiff CF14 5DU
tel 029-20747444
website www.s4c.co.uk
Interim Chief Executive Arwel Ellis Owen, *Head of Children's Services* Sian Eirian

Welsh language digital channel S4C is one of the UK's 5 public service broadcasters providing a mixed-genre channel of drama, sport, factual, news, entertainment and culture and also offers a comprehensive service for children: Cyw for younger viewers, Stwnsh for older children and programmes for teenagers. Programmes are commissioned from independent production companies with content also produced by BBC Wales and ITV Wales. The channel is available on all digital TV platforms in Wales, plus broadband, and has a video-on-demand service. There are subtitles for non-Welsh speakers and learners, with signing and audio description for the deaf and the hard of hearing.

Children's radio

BBC Children's Radio

website www.bbc.co.uk/radio4extra/features/family-friendly

'Family friendly' programming is available on Radio 4 Extra aimed at children and their parents/carers.
• *The 4 O'Clock Show* is a mix of quizzes, stories, comedy clips and interviews. Contact Elizabeth Clark, Series Producer.
• *Young Classics* – new dramas for all ages broadcast on Sundays. Contact Mary Kalemkerian, Head of Programmes.

CBeebies radio is now only available to download from the CBeebies website at www.bbc.co.uk/cbeebies/radioplayer. See the CBeebies TV section for contact details.

BBC School Radio

Room MC3 D5, Media Centre, BBC White City, 201 Wood Lane, London W12 7QT
email schoolradio@bbc.co.uk
website www.bbc.co.uk/schoolradio

Provides audio resources to support teaching across a wide range of primary curriculum areas. The programmes offer a varied, flexible and convenient resource with learning outcomes which carefully target curriculum objectives. A range of programmes include existing copyright material while others require original scriptwriting. Send an email to the Editor for further details.

Fun Kids

Folder Media, 96ᴀ Curtain Road, London EC2A 3AA
tel 020-7739 7879
website www.funkidslive.com

A British children's digital radio station (not national) providing programming to entertain children age 10 and under with a mixture of songs, stories, competitions and news of events. Available to listen via the website or on DAB Digital Radio across London and South East England.

Emma Hurrell previously worked at the BBC for 14 years as a Business Manager in TV and as a Project Manager, providing key senior management support for the launch of the BBC's digital services. She is currently freelancing.

Theatre
Writing for children's theatre

Writing plays for children is not a soft option. David Wood considers children to be the most difficult audience to write for and shares his thoughts here about this challenge.

'Would you write the Christmas play?' These six words, uttered by John Hole, Director of the Swan Theatre, Worcester, unwittingly changed my life, setting me off on a trail I'm still treading over 40 years later. It wasn't a totally mad question, even though I was then cutting my teeth as an 'adult' actor/director – and indeed I have managed to continue these so-called mainstream activities to a limited degree ever since. No, it had already struck me that children's audiences were important and, by doing magic at birthday parties since my teens, I had already developed an aptitude for and delight in entertaining children.

At Worcester I had organised Saturday morning children's theatre, inveigling my fellow repertory actors into helping me tell stories, lead participation songs and perform crazy sketches. And I was still

Further information

TYA (Theatre for Young Audiences)
website www.tya-uk.org
TYA is the UK Centre of ASSITEJ (International Association of Theatre for Children and Young People). The website lists most of the companies currently in production. In association with Aurora Metro Press publishes *Theatre for Children and Young People* (see 'Further reading'), a comprehensive collection of articles about the development of children's theatre and theatre-in-education in the UK over the last 50 years.

National Theatre Bookshop
National Theatre, South Bank, London SE1 9PX
tel 020-7452 3456 *fax* 020-7452 3457
email bookshop@nationaltheatre.org.uk
website www.nationaltheatre.org.uk

French's Theatre Bookshop
52 Fitzroy Street London W1T 5JR
tel 020-7255 4300 *fax* 020-7387 2161
website www.samuelfrench-london.co.uk

haunted by the memory of seeing, a couple of years earlier, a big commercial panto in which the star comedian cracked an off-colour joke to a matinee house virtually full of children, got an appreciative cackle from a small party of ladies in the stalls, then advanced to the footlights and said, 'Let's get the kids out of here, then we can get started!'. In the dark I blushed and my hackles rose. How dare this man show such disdain for the young audience whose parents' hard-earned cash had contributed towards his doubtless considerable salary? It set me thinking about how few proper plays were then written and performed for children. There were traditional favourites like *Peter Pan* in London, the occasional *Wizard of Oz*, *Toad of Toad Hall* and *Alice in Wonderland* in the regions but that was about it. Nothing new. Later I discovered my assessment had been too sweeping. There were several pioneers out there presenting proper plays for children, including Brian Way (Theatre Centre), Caryl Jenner (Unicorn), John Allen (Glyndebourne Children's Theatre) and John English (Midlands Arts Centre), but their work was not then widely recognised. Their contribution to the development of children's theatre in the UK cannot be overestimated. Also, in 1965, the Belgrade Theatre, Coventry had created the first theatre-in-education company, touring innovative work into schools; and early in 1967 I had acted in the first production of the TIE Company at the Palace Theatre, Watford.

Theatre

So writing *The Tinder Box* for Christmas 1967 seemed a natural opportunity and, although I don't think it was very good, it paved the way for me to write around 70 (so far) plays that try to trigger the imagination, make children laugh, cry and think, and hopefully lead them towards a love of theatre. The journey hasn't always been easy. It is frustrating that children's theatre is still often perceived as third division theatre; funding for it is less than for its adult counterpart, even though it often costs as much, sometimes more, to put on, and always commands a lower seat price; critics generally ignore it; and most theatre folk seem to think it is only for beginners or failures, a ridiculous belief, since children are the most difficult and honest audience of all – and yet the most rewarding when we get it right.

Let's pause briefly to talk terminology. The phrase 'children's theatre' means different things to different people. Whereas 'youth theatre' clearly implies that young people are taking part in the play, 'children's theatre' can mean not only children performing but also (more correctly, in my view) theatre produced by adults for children to watch. And, although I have occasionally, and enjoyably, written plays for children to perform (*Lady Lollipop*, from Dick King-Smith's book) or for children to take part in alongside adults (*The Lighthouse Keeper's Lunch*, from Ronda and David Armitage's book and *Dinosaurs and All That Rubbish*, from Michael Foreman's book), the vast majority of my plays have been written for professional actors to perform for children. Don't get me wrong. Participation by children is hugely beneficial and worthwhile, but I like to feel my plays might provide the inspiration to encourage them to want to do it themselves. I believe that children respond to exciting examples that inspire them. I also believe that children are more likely to, say, want to learn to play a musical instrument if they see and hear the best professional musicians playing in a concert. They are more likely to want to excel at football if they see – live or on television – the best professional teams displaying dazzling skills.

So any advice I can offer about children's theatre is mainly aimed towards writers who would like to create plays for grown-ups to perform for children. Having said that, it has always surprised me that several of my professionally performed plays have been subsequently put on by schools and youth groups who cope, showing tremendous flair and imagination, with tricky technical demands. I sometimes wish I could write more plays specifically for schools and youth groups, but I think I might be tempted to oversimplify (which would be patronising) or to try to write enough roles for a very large cast, which might dilute the content and fail to provide a satisfying structure.

Encouragingly, the professional children's theatre scene today is much healthier than when I started. There are many more touring companies (see page 328) large and small, producing high-quality work for all ages. There has been an exciting explosion in the amount of work for under-fives. And at last we have two full-time children's theatre buildings – Unicorn and Polka – who put on their own plays as well as receive other companies' work. They are both in London, and the big hope is that there will in the future be many more such beacons in other cities and towns. Children are entitled to their own theatre, and creating theatre buildings especially for them, run by committed professionals, is the best way to improve the quantity, quality and status of the work. Alongside that, our major theatres, including the National and the Royal Shakespeare Company, should be setting an example by making children's theatre an integral part of their programming, rather than occasionally mounting a children's play as an optional extra. And this means more than coming up with an annual Christmas show.

Study the market

Go and see shows. Which companies are doing what? How many cast members can they afford? Are they looking for original plays as well as adaptations of successful books with big titles and box office appeal? Try to meet the artistic directors, to discuss what they might be looking for. What size spaces are the companies playing in? Studios? Large theatres? Do they have facilities for scene-changes? Is there flying? Incidentally, restrictions on cast size and staging possibilities are not necessarily a bad thing. Well-defined parameters within which to work can be a help not a hindrance. I was asked to write a play for the Towngate, Basildon, a theatre that had no flying, not much stage depth and virtually no wing space. And I was allowed a cast of only six. At first I despaired but then managed to think positively and wrote *The Gingerbread Man*, which ended up paying the rent for 30 years! The play is set on a giant Welsh dresser. No props or scenery come on or off stage during the show – the basic set is self-contained. And the six characters are joined by the off-stage voices (recorded) of the 'Big Ones', the human owners of the dresser.

It may be putting the cart before the horse to worry about where and how your play might be performed – before you've written it! But it really is foolish to start before finding out what might be practical and realistic. Quite frankly, a cast of 20, or even a dozen, is going to be out of the question for most professional companies, so if your idea demands such numbers, maybe you should approach a school, a youth drama group or an amateur dramatic society instead.

Rather than rely on others, might you be in a position to create your own openings? Many children's theatre practitioners, including myself, have had to start by 'doing it themselves'. I, like Richard Gill, Vicky Ireland and Annie Wood (former artistic directors of the Polka Theatre) not only write but also direct. And Richard Gill, Tim Webb (Oily Cart), Guy Holland (Quicksilver) and I (Whirligig), went as far as to create companies to produce our own work, because we knew we were unlikely to get other companies to put it on. The TYA (Theatre for Young Audiences) website (see box) lists most of the companies currently in production, and is a useful first port of call to see the scope of the work.

What 'works' for children?

A good, satisfying story makes a helpful start, told with theatrical flair. By that I mean that we should use theatrical techniques to spark the imagination of the audience – scenery, costume, sound, lighting, puppetry, magic, circus skills, masks, mime, dancing and music. The physical as well as the verbal can help to retain the attention and interest of children. Page after page of two characters sitting talking are likely to prove a turn-off. It's better to see them do something rather than just talk about it. I try to introduce lots of 'suddenlies' to help keep the audience riveted to their seats, wanting to know what happens next. I've often said that my life's work has been dedicated to stopping children going to the lavatory. Suddenlies – a new character appearing, a sound effect, a lighting change, a surprise twist, a musical sting – can be a huge help. Compare it to the page-turning appeal of a successful children's book.

Play ideas can be found in fairy tales, myths and legends, traditional rhymes and popular stories. Be careful, however, not to waste time adapting books in copyright, unless you have got the necessary permission – no public performances, paid or unpaid, can be given without this. Approach the publisher or the author's agent to discover if the stage, rights are available and, if they are, how much it might cost to acquire them for a year or two.

Theatre

Or you might use an incident from history, a pertinent modern social issue, such as conservation, or the real life of an inspirational or controversial person. Or you could explore a social problem especially relevant to children, like single-parent families or bullying.

In my book *Theatre for Children: A Guide to Writing, Adapting, Directing and Acting* I identify useful ingredients for children's plays. They are really fairly obvious – things that we know children respond to. They include animals, toys, fantasy, a quest, goodies and baddies, humour, scale (small characters in large environments and *vice versa*), a child at the centre of the story. And justice – think *Cinderella*. Children, like adults, have a strong sense of fairness and will root for the underdog. Roald Dahl's stories, seven of which I have been lucky enough to adapt, all use this. Sophie (in *The BFG*), James (in *James and the Giant Peach*) and Boy (in *The Witches*) are all disadvantaged orphans whose strength of character leads them through immense difficulties to eventual triumph. They are empowered to succeed in an adult-dominated world, and children identify with them.

The use of audience participation is an option much argued about by children's theatre practitioners. Many hate it. For some plays, it would, indeed, be totally inappropriate. But for others it can be exciting and fun. I'm not talking about basic panto participation – 'he's behind you!' – though even this can be used on occasion with integrity. I'm talking about what I call 'positive participation', in which the audience contribute to the action by helping or hindering, by having ideas or by taking part in a 'set piece'. In *The Selfish Shellfish* they create a storm to fool an oil slick. In *Meg and Mog Show* (for very small children), they make springtime noises and movements to encourage Meg's garden to grow. In *The See-Saw Tree* they vote on whether to save an ancient oak or allow it to be cut down to make way for a children's playground. In *The Gingerbread Man* they help catch the scavenging Sleek the Mouse under an upturned mug. Their contribution is crucial to the development and resolution of the plot. In *The Twits* the audience fools Mr and Mrs Twit by making them think that they, the audience, are upside down. They all remove their shoes, put them on their hands and stretch their arms up while lowering their heads! The sight of a thousand children all doing this, with joy and not a shred of cynicism, is pure magic to me.

I don't believe that a children's play has to have a moral, a self-improving message for the audience. But I do believe a children's play should *be* moral, presenting a positive attitude and an uplifting, hopeful conclusion. And I resent the notion that children's plays should always be written to tie in with the national curriculum. Many do, but the educationalists shouldn't dictate our agenda – the tail shouldn't wag the dog.

Before you start

I strongly recommend that you create a synopsis, outlining the events in story order. This leads to clarity of storytelling, to the disciplined pursuit of a through-line, with not too many subplots that could end up as time-wasting, irrelevant cul-de-sacs. For myself it would be foolish to think I had the brilliance to start a play with only an initial idea and just let my imagination lead me through uncharted waters. I find it far better to let the juices flow during the synopsis stage and, when it comes to writing the play, to conscientiously follow through my original instincts with not too many diversions.

Good luck with getting your first play produced. Getting it published may need determination. It was a very special day for me when Samuel French accepted (after initial rejections) *The Owl and the Pussycat Went to See...*, my second play, co-written with Sheila Ruskin. After its first production at Worcester, I beavered away to get it on stage in London and, thanks to several friends helping financially, managed to produce it at the Jeannetta Cochrane Theatre. To save money I directed it myself. We were lucky enough to get two rave reviews. I approached Samuel French again. They came to see it and, hallelujah, offered to publish it. Since then their loyalty has been more than gratifying – they still publish most of my efforts. There are now several specialist children's play publishers, many of whom also act as licensees of amateur performances. The National Theatre Bookshop and French's Theatre Bookshop stock a fair number of plays and, when searching for a publisher, it is worth checking out their shelves. The internet can help too. Tap in the names of successful children's playwrights, like Mike Kenny, Charles Way or the late Adrian Mitchell and see what comes up.

I find that the challenge of writing a play for children never gets easier, however many times I go through the process. It certainly isn't a soft option, i.e. easier than writing a play for adults. And it carries, I believe, a big responsibility. I always worry that I haven't the right to fail! The last thing I want to do is write something that might put children off theatre for life. I'm aware that many in the audience will be first-time theatre-goers, some of whom never asked to come! It's so important to get it right, to enthuse them so much they can't wait to return. And this is where the passion comes in. Most children's theatre practitioners are passionate about what they do, with an almost missionary zeal to stimulate and delight their audience. Also, we all know that, unlike adult audiences who tend to sit quietly and clap at the end, even if they've hated the play, our children's audiences won't be – and shouldn't be – so polite. It is palpably obvious when we 'lose' them. We are dedicated to using our experience and instinct to 'hold' them, to help them enjoy the communal experience of a theatre visit and willingly enter the spirit of the performance. The buzz I get from being in an auditorium of children overtly having a great time – listening hard, watching intently, reacting, feeling, letting the play take them on a special, magical, unique journey – is a buzz I constantly strive for. I suppose that's really why I do it.

David Wood OBE has been dubbed 'the national children's dramatist' by *The Times*. His plays are performed regularly on tour, in the West End and all over the world. In 2006, for the Queen's 80th birthday party celebrations, he wrote *The Queen's Handbag*, which was broadcast live from Buckingham Palace Gardens and watched by 8 million viewers on BBC1. In 2011, four of his adaptations were seen on tour in the UK: *Goodnight Mister Tom, Shaun the Sheep, George's Marvellous Medicine* and *The Tiger Who Came to Tea*. His website is www.davidwood.org.uk.

Further reading
Stuart Bennett (ed.), *Theatre for Children and Young People*, Aurora Metro Press, 2005
Wood, David, with Janet Grant, *Theatre for Children: A Guide to Writing, Adapting, Directing and Acting*, Faber and Faber, 1997

See also...
- *Adapting books for the stage*, page 322
- *Writing to a brief*, page 310

Theatre

Adapting books for the stage

Stephen Briggs ponders the challenges and rewards of dramatising other people's novels.

Why me?

Stephen Briggs? Stephen Briggs? Who on earth is Stephen Briggs to write about adapting novels for the stage?

Well, many years ago I wrote a stage version of *A Christmas Carol* for my amdram group... no, stick with me on this.... *Then*, a few years later I adapted two Tom Sharpe novels (these were for one-off productions and the scripts are now long gone). *However*, my overwhelming – and more recent – experience has been with dramatising the novels of Sir Terry Pratchett. I've now adapted 18 of Terry's books and 15 have so far been published – four for Transworld/Doubleday, three for Samuel French, two for Oxford University Press and six for Methuen Drama (now at A&C Black). These have been staged by amateur groups in over 20 countries from Zimbabwe to Antarctica (yes, really, Antarctica) and by professional groups in France and the Czech Republic. I also co-scripted the mini-dramatisations used by Sky One to promote their big budget television movies of Terry's *Hogfather* and *Colour of Magic*.

I have been involved in amateur theatre since I left school. Not just acting, but also directing, choreography, set design/construction, costume design/construction – even including brewing mulled wine for the audiences in our chilly medieval theatre. None of this makes me an expert, not by any interpretation of the word, but I was the one who had to make my scripts work on stage since I also directed them. I was also able to get useful and honest feedback from the original author. Hopefully I've learned a few lessons along the way, which I'm happy to pass on.

Dialogue

When you watch a film, a lot of screen time is taken up by fancy stuff – Imperial star cruisers roaring through space, ill-fated liners ploughing the waves, swooping pan shots over raddled pirate ships. In a play, you don't get any of that stuff. The dialogue has to drive the action.

The methods used to adapt a novel for the stage are as varied as the authors you try to adapt. Terry Pratchett, like Charles Dickens, writes very good dialogue and the scenes already leap from the page. Other authors make greater use of narrative which the adapter has to weave into the play as well, if they are to keep to the spirit of the original work. Terry is well known for his use of footnotes and, for some of the plays, I even included the Footnote as a 'character' – a Brechtian alienation device, for those who want a more literary justification.

Keep it simple

Terry Pratchett writes 'filmically' – his scenes cross-cut and swoop like a screenplay. On the silver screen, you can set a scene visually in a second. On the stage it can take longer, and you have to give the audience a chance to realise where they are if they are to have any chance of keeping up with the – often quite complex – plot.

It's important to remember that a theatre audience doesn't have the luxury of being able to re-read a page, or skip back to check a plot point – they (usually) get to see the play only once. It's vital, therefore, to ensure that important plot points are not lost along the way while one is tempted to keep in other favoured scenes from the much longer novel.

Keep it moving

Novelists are not constrained by budget – they can destroy cities, have characters who are 60-foot long dragons, write vital scenes involving time travel and other difficult concepts. These can initially appear to be a challenge for anyone without the budget of Industrial Light and Magic.

When I write, I have the good fortune to be writing for a theatre which has very limited space – on and off stage – and virtually no capacity for scenic effects. This makes staging the plays a nightma…, ahem… a challenge, but the benefit is that my adaptations can be staged virtually anywhere. I don't write them with essential big effects or big set changes. Of course, drama groups with huge budgets can go wild with all that – but the plays can work without it.

Plays which demand massive set changes or pose huge scenic problems are likely to put off many directors working to a tight budget. It's different if you're Alan Ayckbourn, of course… onstage swimming pool, floating river cruiser… no problem.

People say that radio has the best scenery. Allowing the audience to fill in the gaps can not only save on costly wood and canvas but, on occasions, can even be more effective than an expensive but stagey scenic effect. After all, Shakespeare's *Antony and Cleopatra* includes a sea battle between two great navies – all seen by two blokes standing on a hill.

The plays – like the books – have to keep moving. Scenes need to flow fairly seamlessly into one another. Set changes slow things down. I get to see large numbers of productions of my plays and the general rule is that the ones with frequent set-changes are the ones which plod.

Writing for schools

Two of my plays were written specifically for classroom use. I had to bear in mind that the plays were as likely to be used for reading in a classroom as well as for production on a stage. So I tried to keep the amount of stage directions to a minimum because I know all too well from reading plays with my own amateur drama group that the need to read through huge chunks of explanatory stuff in italics, interspersed with snippets of uninformative dialogue, is very tedious. Here is an example (not, I hasten to add, an extract from a real play):

(As Smithers looks out of the window, Bert rushes downstairs, carrying an aspidistra in a brass bowl. He passes, but fails to notice, the gorilla. He trips and falls, dropping the plant and pot on Smithers' head)
SMITHERS: Oof!
(Smithers picks up a broom from the floor and chases after Bert. They run into the kitchen and out again, up the stairs and across the landing. Bert takes a wad of banknotes out of his pocket and throws them at Smithers)
BERT: Take that!

It was also important to try to avoid characters with just 'one line and a cough'. Nothing is worse in a read-through than to be given the role of 'King of France' only to find that the character speaks one line on page one and then is silent for the rest of the play. Except,

Theatre

perhaps, being allocated a role meant for someone of the opposite sex and then finding it contains dialogue that will invite ridicule from the rest of the class…' I fink I've got a beard coming through' or 'Oh la, I feel so pretty; I do love wearing frilly pink underwear'.

I also try to ensure that whatever special effects are mentioned should be either easily achievable or not essential and again, that the plays can be performed with the minimum amount of scenery.

The two plays I wrote for OUP were the only ones I had written which I would not be staging myself. It was really fascinating (and quite gratifying) to see the plays staged by schools and to find that they *worked*.

How do I start?
• **I read the book.** Then I read the book again. I then put it down, leave it for a week and write down all the main plot points I can recall, and a rough list of scenes. That should give me a rough shape for the play. Anything I've forgotten to include can probably go high up on the list of potential material to cut.

• **I write it.** I sit down and write the script. At this stage I don't try to keep to a specific length; I just adapt the book, making mental notes of any scenes that show potential for trimming, cutting or pasting into another as I go along. My overall plan is to keep the play to around two hours. If, when I get to the end, the play is too long, I then go back and look again at each scene and character to ensure they can justify their place in the script.

• **I dump it.** Reducing a 95,000-word novel into a 20,000-word play means that there will have to be an element of trimming. The trick, I suppose, is to ensure that the cuts will not be too glaring to the paying audience ('I reckon if we cut out the Prince of Denmark, we can get *Hamlet* down to an hour and a half, no problem'). Hopefully, there will be subplots, not vital to the main story, which can be excised to keep it all flowing. But even so, occasionally tough decisions have to be made once all the fat's been removed and one is forced to cut into muscle and bone (as it were). It's important to let stuff go – even if it's a favourite scene in the book, or a favourite character.

• **I share it.** It's good then to let someone else read it. It's all too easy to get so far into the wood that you can no longer see the trees. Being challenged on the decisions you made in adapting the book is a very good thing. I'd certainly recommend anyone adapting a book to have the script read by someone who knows the book well, and who can point out any important plot omissions. It is also good to have your script read by someone who does *not* know the book and who can ask the 'what on earth does that mean?' questions.

It's useful for me that many of my drama club are not *Discworld* 'fans'. Their outsider's view of the script is extremely useful. I also then have the luxury of amending the script in rehearsal to tidy up scenes, add in bits and take bits out. This means that the script which is submitted to the publishers is then fully tried and tested.

Some golden rules
It's difficult to be hard and fast about 'rules' for adapting books, but here are a few useful guidelines that I do try to stick to:

• **Don't change the principle plot** – there's no point in calling a play *Bram Stoker's Dracula* if you're then going to have Dracula surviving at the end and starting up a flourishing law firm in Whitby.

• **Never sacrifice 'real' scenes in order to add in some of your own** – after all, you've chosen to adapt the author's work because, presumably, you admire their writing. If you think you can improve on their humour/drama/characterisation you should really be writing your own plots and not torturing theirs!

• **Use the author's dialogue whenever possible** – same as the above, really. Also try to attribute it to the right character whenever practicable.

• **Don't add characters** – stick to the ones the author has given you.

• **Don't be afraid to cut material** – after all, you're trying to squeeze a 300-page novel into a two-hour play; you just can't fit everything in, so don't try. Anything which does not advance the main plot should be on your list for potential dumping if your play overruns.

• **If it doesn't *need* changing – don't change it!**

As well as the 18 plays he mentions in his article, **Stephen Briggs** is the co-author, with Terry Pratchett, and illustrator, of *The Discworld Companion, The Streets of Ankh-Morpork, The Wit & Wisdom of Discworld* and a small raft of other publications emanating from Terry Pratchett's *Discworld* books. He reads the unabridged audio versions of Terry's books for Isis (in the UK) and for HarperCollins (in the USA). In 2005 he was awarded an Audie (a US industry award) for his reading of Terry's *Monstrous Regiment* and in 2009 he received an Odyssey Award for his recording of Terry's *Nation* for Harper Audio. In 2010 he won two awards from *AudioFile* magazine for his recording of *Unseen Academicals*. He can be contacted at sbriggs@cix.co.uk.

See also...

• *Writing to a brief,* page 310

Theatre

Theatre for children

London and provincial theatres are listed below; listings of touring companies start on page 328.

LONDON

Polka Theatre

240 The Broadway, London SW19 1SB
tel 020-8543 8320 *fax* 020-8545 8365
email admin@polkatheatre.com
website www.polkatheatre.com
Artistic Director Jonathan Lloyd

Exclusively for children aged 0–13, the Main Theatre seats 300 and the Adventure Theatre seats 80. It is programmed 18 months–2 years in advance. Theatre of new work, with targeted commissions. Founded 1967.

Soho Theatre

21 Dean Street, London W1D 3NE
tel 020-7478 0117 *fax* 020-7287 5061
email jules@sohotheatre.com
website www.sohotheatre.com

Aims to discover and develop new playwrights, produce a year-round programme of new plays and attract new audiences. Producing venue (144-seat theatre) of new plays and comedy. The Writers' Centre offers an extensive unsolicited script-reading service and provides a range of development, the Westminster Prize, a thriving Young Writers' Programme, commissions and seed bursaries and more. There is also a large self-contained studio space with 85-seat capacity plus theatre bar, restaurant, offices, rehearsal, writing and meeting rooms. Primarily for adults but has staged *The Gruffalo* and *Private Peaceful*. Founded 1972.

Theatre-Rites

Unit 612 Erlang House, 128 Blackfriars Road, London SE1 8EQ
tel 020-7928 4875 *fax* 020-7928 4347
email info@theatre-rites.co.uk
website www.theatre-rites.co.uk
Artistic Director Sue Buckmaster

Creates devised theatre for family audiences and young people using a mix of performance, installation, puppetry, video and sound. Working internationally and within the UK, the company creates site-specific and touring productions. Founded 1995.

Unicorn Theatre

147 Tooley Street, London SE1 2HZ
tel 020-7645 0500 *fax* 020-7645 0550
email stage.door@unicorntheatre.com
website www.unicorntheatre.com

Artistic Director Tony Graham, *Associate Artistic Director* Rosamunde Hutt, *Associate Director & Literary Manager* Carl Miller, *Associate Artist (Literary)* Charles Way

At the end of 2005 Unicorn moved into its new theatre near Tower Bridge, where it produces a year-round programme of theatre for children and young people (0–19 years). In-house productions of full-length plays with professional casts are staged across 2 auditoriums, alongside visiting companies and education work. Unicorn rarely commissions plays from writers who are new to it, but it is keen to hear from writers who are interested to work with the Unicorn in the future. Its aim is for its work to be artistically led, truthful, and insistent on the primacy of imagination. It asks: does the play matter to children; does it have a sense of poetry; does it contain a child's perspective; is it drama; can it transcend and transform?

Do not send unsolicited MSS as Unicorn does not have the resources to read and respond to them in appropriate detail. Send a short statement describing why you would like to write for Unicorn and a CV or a summary of your relevant experience.

Whirligig Theatre

14 Belvedere Drive, London SW19 7BY
tel 020-8947 1732 *fax* 020-8879 7648
email david.woodplays@virgin.net
Artistic Director David Wood

Formerly a touring company, it is open to suggestions from theatres for one-off productions.

Young Vic Theatre Company

66 The Cut, London SE1 8LZ
tel 020-7922 2922
email info@youngvic.org
website www.youngvic.org
Artistic Director David Lan

Metropolitan producing theatre producing great plays of the world repertoire. Founded 1969.

PROVINCIAL

The Byre Theatre of St Andrews

Abbey Street, St Andrews KY16 9LA
tel (01334) 475000 *fax* (01334) 475370
email enquiries@byretheatre.com
website www.byretheatre.com

Offers an exciting year-round programme of contemporary and classic drama, dance, concerts, comedy and innovative education and community events. Operates a blend of in-house and touring productions. Education programme caters for all ages with Youth workshops and Haydays (for 50+). Offers support for new writing through the Byre Writers, a well-established and successful playwrights group.

Chichester Festival Theatre

Oaklands Park, Chichester, West Sussex PO19 6AP
tel (01243) 784437 *fax* (01243) 787288
email admin@cft.org.uk
website www.cft.org.uk
Artistic Director Jonathan Church

Summer Festival Season April–Oct in Festival and Minerva Theatres together with a year-round education programme, autumn touring programme and youth theatre Christmas show. Unsolicited scripts are not accepted.

Clwyd Theatr Cymru Theatre for Young People

Mold, Flintshire CH7 1YA
tel (01352) 701565 *fax* (01352) 701558
email education@clwyd-theatr-cymru.co.uk
website www.ctctyp.co.uk,
www.clwyd-theatr-cymru.co.uk
Director Tim Baker, *Education Producer* Anne Plenderleith, *Education Co-ordinator* Jane Meakin, *Education Administrator* Nerys Edwards

An organisation dedicated to both enlightening young people through theatre and creating an audience for the future through theatre production and related activities. Also the home of Clwyd Theatr Cymru.

Contact Theatre Company

Oxford Road, Manchester M15 6JA
tel 0161-274 0600/0601
website www.contact-theatre.org
Artistic Director Baba Israel

Multidisciplinary arts organisation focused on working with and for young people aged 13–35.

The Egg

Sawclose, Bath BA1 1ET
tel (01225) 823409 (reception and administration)
email egg.reception@theatreroyal.org.uk
website www.theatreroyal.org.uk/the-egg

Part of the Theatre Royal Bath, the Egg is a purpose-built theatre for young people and their families. It hosts and produces shows for children and young people alongside a year-round participation and outreach programme for people aged 2–25. Opened in 2005.

Everyman Theatre

7 Regent Street, Cheltenham, Glos. GL50 1HQ
tel (01242) 512515 *fax* (01242) 224305
email admin@everymantheatre.org.uk
website www.everymantheatre.org.uk

Chief Executive Geoffrey Rowe, *Director of ReachOut* Paul Milton

Regional presenting and producing theatre promoting a wide range of plays. Small-scale experimental, youth and educational work encouraged in The Other Space studio theatre. Contact the Director of ReachOut before submitting material.

Leeds Children's Theatre

c/o The Carriageworks Theatre, The Electric Press, 3 Millennium Square, Leeds LS2 3AD
email info@leeds-childrens-theatre.co.uk
website www.leeds-childrens-theatre.co.uk

One of the many amateur dramatic societies based at The Carriageworks Theatre. A member of the Leeds Civic Arts Guild, Leeds Children's Theatre stages 2 shows each year. It is dedicated to the principle of quality, affordable children's entertainment in order to encourage the introduction of the theatrical experience to young children. It covers most aspects of theatrical production. Membership is open to all young people. Workshops for children of all ages. Adult membership is also available. Founded 1935.

Leighton Buzzard Children's Theatre

12 Linslade Road, Heath and Reach, Leighton Buzzard, Beds. LU7 0AU
tel (01525) 237469
email sally@lbct.org
website www.lbct.org

A community-based group which exists to introduce young people to the joy of theatre, to develop theatre craft and to enhance enjoyment of performance through community involvement. It offers a unique opportunity to young people aged 5–18 to act, sing, dance, improvise, communicate, have fun and learn.

Library Theatre Company

St Peter's Square, Manchester M2 5PD
tel 0161-234 1913 *fax* 0161-274 7055
email ltcadmin@manchester.gov.uk
website www.librarytheatre.com
Contact Artistic Director

Produces mostly contemporary drama with a major play for children and families at Christmas. A recent family production was Neil Bartlett's version of *Great Expectations*. Will consider scripts from new writers. Allow 4 months for response.

Norwich Puppet Theatre

St James, Whitefriars, Norwich NR3 1TN
tel (01603) 629921 (box office), 615564 (admin.)
fax (01603) 617578
email info@puppettheatre.co.uk
website www.puppettheatre.co.uk
General Manager Ian Woods

Norwich Puppet Theatre is the base for a professional company which creates and presents its own

Theatre

productions at the theatre, as well as touring to schools and venues throughout the UK and to international venues and festivals. Founded 1979.

Nottingham Playhouse

Nottingham Playhouse Trust Ltd, Wellington Circus, Nottingham NG1 5AF
tel 0115-947 4361 *fax* 0115-947 5759
website www.nottinghamplayhouse.co.uk/playhouse
Chief Executive Stephanie Sirr, *Artistic Director* Giles Croft, *Director of Roundabout and Education* Andrew Breakwell

Works closely with communities of Nottingham and Nottinghamshire.
   Roundabout is the Theatre in Education company of Nottingham Playhouse. Produces plays and workshops for children and young people, and training and support for teachers. Since 1973 Roundabout has commissioned and produced nearly 300 new plays for schools, young people and the families. Submissions are accepted for reading as part of an assessment procedure but almost all productions are commissioned.

Queen's Theatre, Hornchurch

(Havering Theatre Trust Ltd)
52 Billet Lane, Hornchurch, Essex RM11 1QT
tel (01708) 462362 *fax* (01708) 462363
email info@queens-theatre.co.uk
website www.queens-theatre.co.uk
Artistic Director Bob Carlton

500-seat producing theatre serving outer East London with permanent company of actors/musicians presenting 8 mainhouse and 4 TIE productions each year. Treatments welcome; unsolicited scripts may be returned unread. Also offers writer's groups at various levels.
   The Queen's Youth Theatre Programme provides the opportunity for young people aged 7–18 to become involved in drama. There is no selection process on the basis of experience or ability.

Royal Shakespeare Company

The Courtyard Theatre, Southern Lane, Stratford-upon-Avon, Warks. CV37 6BB
tel (01789) 272227
email education@rsc.org.uk
website www.rsc.org.uk
Artistic Director Michael Boyd, *Company Dramaturg* Jeanie O'Hare

Based in Stratford-upon-Avon, produces a core repertoire of Shakespeare alongside modern classics and new plays as well as the work of Shakespeare's contemporaries. Commissions adaptations of well-known novels and stories for Christmas shows. Works with contemporary writers, encouraging them to write epic plays. The Literary department seeks out writers it wishes to work with or commission. Does not read unsolicited work, but does monitor the

work of emerging writers in production nationally and internationally.
   The Company is currently undergoing a 4-year rebuilding programme transforming the Royal Shakespeare Theatre and the entire Waterside complex of studios, rehearsal rooms, actors' cottages and workshops. The theatre is being remodelled to create state-of-the-art facilities for artists.

Sherman Cymru

Senghennydd Road, Cardiff CF24 4YE
tel 029-2064 6901 *fax* 029-2064 6902
email admin@shermancymru.co.uk
website www.shermancymru.co.uk
Director Chris Ricketts, *General Manager* Margaret Jones, *Literary Manager* Siân Summers, *Associate Directors* Arwel Gruffydd, Amy Hodge

Produces two Christmas productions (Under and Over 7s) and actively seeks high quality work for children and young people as part of programming. Commissions writers for projects with young people. Participatory work with youth theatres for 5–25 age range. Founded 2007.

TOURING COMPANIES

Arad Goch

Stryd Y Baddon, Aberystwyth, Ceredigion SY23 2NN
tel (01970) 617998 *fax* (01970) 611223
email post@aradgoch.org
website www.aradgoch.org
Artistic Director Jeremy Turner

The company performs in Welsh and English and tours nationally throughout Wales, and occasionally abroad. It uses a visual and imagistic style often drawing both on contemporary physical theatre and on traditional performance techniques. The company is particularly interested in enabling children and young people to recognise and appreciate their own unique cultural identity though theatre. Some of the company's work is based on traditional material and children's literature but it also commissions new work from experienced dramatists and new writers. As well as creating productions which are performed in theatres, Arad Goch also creates many theatre-in-education projects for junior and secondary schools and offers seminars/workshops about this specialist work to teachers and to college and university students. Founded 1989.

Booster Cushion Theatre

75 How Wood, Park Street, St Albans, Herts. AL2 2RW
tel (01727) 873874 *fax* (01727) 872597
email admin@booster-cushion.co.uk
website www.booster-cushion.co.uk

Theatre company formed specifically to work with children to encourage them to take a greater interest in books. It has performed to over 300,000 people in schools and theatres in the UK using pop-up books up to 3m tall and concertina books over 5m wide.

All shows are solo performing shows using mime, voice and some sign language. They involve a high level of audience participation on the part of the children and are designed to foster a feeling of strong involvement in the event by drawing the audience in. Each show is completely portable and can be performed inside or outside as the technical requirements are minimal. Founded 1989.

Cahoots NI
109–113 Royal Avenue, Belfast BT1 1FF
tel (28) 9043 4349/4339
email info@cahootsni.com
website www.cahootsni.com
Artistic Director Paul Bosco McEneaney

A professional children's touring theatre company which concentrates on the visual potential of theatre and capitalises upon the age-old popularity of magic and illusion as an essential ingredient in the art of entertaining. It aims to provide inspiring theatrical experiences for children and to encourage appreciation of the arts in children from all sections of society. Each production is at the centre of a body of outreach work designed to maximise artistic potential, customise the individual theatre experience and extend the imaginative life of the piece beyond the actual event. Founded 2001.

Classworks Theatre
Eastern Court, 182–190 Newmarket Road, Cambridge CB5 8HE
tel (01223) 321900
email info@classworks.org.uk
website www.classworks.org.uk
Contact Gayle Macgregor, General Manager

Professional touring company which focuses on new work for and with young people. Also provides supporting workshops. Tours locally and nationally to small- and mid-scale arts venues. Founded 1983.

Cornelius & Jones
49 Carters Close, Sherington, Newport Pagnell MK16 9NW
tel/fax (01908) 612593
email admin@ corneliusjones.com
website www.corneliusjones.com
Co-directors Neil Canham and Sue Leech

A small touring theatre company which performs for children and adults in schools and theatres. The company creates its own productions and commissions scripts and music. Founded 1986.

The Hiss & Boo Company Ltd
1 Nyes Hill, Wineham Lane, Bolney, West Sussex RH17 5SD
tel (01444) 881707 *fax* (01444) 882057

email ian@hissboo.co.uk
website www.hissboo.co.uk
Managing Director Ian Liston

Not much scope for new plays, but will consider comedy thrillers/chillers and plays/musicals for children. Produces pantomimes. No unsolicited scripts – telephone first. Plays/synopses will be returned only if accompanied by an sae.

Imaginate
45A George Street, Edinburgh EH2 2HT
tel 0131-225 8050 *fax* 0131-225 6440
email info@imaginate.org.uk
Director Tony Reekie, *General Manager* Tessa Rennie

Imaginate is an arts agency committed to promoting and developing performing arts for children in Scotland. See page 372 for further information.

Kazzum Arts Project
Oxford House, Derbyshire Street, London E2 6HG
email info@kazzum.org
website www.kazzum.org
Artistic Director Daryl Beeton

Creates playful theatrical experiences in unusual places that involve the imaginations of diverse young audiences. A theatre and participative arts company which applies an innovative approach to producing theatre that allows young people to become part of a captivating experience in a safe environment. These aims are achieved through:

• outdoor productions and interactive environments for audiences aged 8 and under, and their families;
• promenade and site-specific work for audiences aged 10 and over;
• 'Pathways', a programme of arts activities for young people across Greater London's refugee and new migrant communities;
• education and outreach work in schools and community settings;
• cultural development opportunities. Founded 1989.

Konflux Theatre in Education
St Thomas's Parish Rooms, Neville Terrace, York YO31 8NF
tel/fax (01904) 611355
email info@konfluxtheatre.com
website www.konfluxtheatre.com
Artistic Director Anthony Koncsol

Tours throughout the UK with workshops and performances for children and young people. Its Creative Learning Workshops (for Early Years through to KS2) and Play in a Day project (KS1–3) involve working interactively with groups in schools, arts centres and small receiving houses, using drama to enhance personal and social development whilst at the same time enriching and extending the National Curriculum.

The Philosophy for Children project, Stone Soup, blends performance and discussion and encourages children (KS2) to question what kind of role they play within their community. Konflux has also produced work which tackles environmental issues and it works with more than 1,000 schools every year. Founded 1997.

Legend Theatre
31 Darley Road, London SW11 6SW
tel 020-8767 8886 *fax* 020-8767 8886
email admin@legendtheatre.com
website www.legendtheatre.com
Contact Bob Clayton

Tours primary schools and theatres throughout the UK with entertaining and educational productions. The emphasis is always on movement, mime, clowning, masks, puppetry. Productions are based around the education of a popular historical period relevant to KS2 and the National Curriculum. Founded 1990.

The Little Angel Theatre
14 Dagmar Passage, London N1 2DN
tel 020-7226 1787
email info@littleangeltheatre.com
website www.littleangeltheatre.com
Artistic Director Peter Glanville

The theatre is committed to working with children and families, both through schools and the local community. It is developing innovative projects to improve access to their work, offer opportunities for participation, and stimulate learning and creativity for all using puppetry. Every term it runs activities for children, families and schools, including the Saturday Puppet Club, family workshops and schools projects such as the highly successful Puppet Power. It also runs puppetry courses for teenagers and adults, as well as INSET training for teachers.

Shows last about an hour and many are toured to theatres, arts centres and festivals. The Little Angel Education Programme works with schools, youth groups and Education Authorities; it is a strategic plank in the theatre's ongoing work with children and young people.

M6 Theatre Company (Studio Theatre)
Hamer C.P. School, Albert Royds Street, Rochdale, Lancs. OL16 2SU
tel (01706) 355898 *fax* (01706) 712601
email info@m6theatre.co.uk
website www.m6theatre.co.uk
Contact Dorothy Wood

Theatre-in-education company providing high-quality theatre for children, young people and community audiences.

Magic Carpet Theatre
18 Church Street, Sutton on Hull,
East Yorks. HU7 4TS
tel (01482) 709939 *fax* (01482) 787362

email jon@magiccarpettheatre.com
website www.magiccarpettheatre.com
Director Jon Marshall

A touring company which incorporates the traditional skills of variety theatre, the circus and puppets including clown, slapstick and physical theatre to make highly entertaining productions for schools and theatres. Founded 1982.

Moby Duck
12 Reservoir Retreat, Birmingham B16 9EH
tel 0121-2420400
email guyhutchins@blueyonder.co.uk
website www.moby-duck.org
Contact Guy Hutchins

Produces stimulating, challenging and accessible work for young people and adults that celebrates the common ground between cultures. Tours throughout the UK, presenting new cross art form cross-cultural work to young children and adults in small- and middle-scale theatres, arts centres, village halls and schools. Also performs in less conventional venues, e.g. a farm equipment museum, a Crown Court and a 3-hole Georgian privy! Performances are storytelling-led and have included live Karnatic music, western jazz, Bharatanatyam dance, masks, mime, puppetry, visual arts, digital media and Eastern and Western cooking. Founded 1999.

Oily Cart
Smallwood School Annexe, Smallwood Road, London SW17 0TW
tel 020-8672 6329 *fax* 020-8672 0792
email oilies@oilycart.org.uk
website www.oilycart.org.uk
Artistic Director Tim Webb

Touring company staging at least 2 children's productions a year. Multi-sensory, highly interactive work is produced, often in specially constructed installations for 3 specific audiences: children aged 6 months–2 years, children aged 3–6 years, and young people (3–19) with profound and multiple learning disabilities or autism. Considers scripts from new writers but at present all work is generated from within the company. Founded 1981.

Playtime Theatre Company
18 Bennells Avenue, Whitstable, Kent CT5 2HP
tel (01227) 266272 *fax* (01227) 266648
website www.playtimetheatre.co.uk

Touring theatre company specialising in theatre for children, performing in schools and theatres. Takes part in European exchange drama programmes. Founded 1983.

Proteus Theatre Company
Queen Mary's College, Cliddesden Road, Basingstoke, Hants RG21 3HF
tel (01256) 354541 *fax* (01256) 356186

email info@proteustheatre.com
website www.proteustheatre.com
Artistic Director Mary Swan

Small-scale touring company particularly committed to new writing and new work, education and community collaborations. Produces 3 touring shows per year plus several community projects. Founded 1979.

Quicksilver Theatre

The New Diorama Theatre, 15–16 Triton Street, Regents Place, London NW1 3BF
tel 020-7241 2942 *fax* 020-7254 3119
email talktous@quicksilvertheatre.org
website www.quicksilvertheatre.org
Joint Artistic Director/Ceo Guy Holland, *Joint Artistic Director* Carey English

A professional touring theatre company which brings live theatre to theatres and schools all over the country. Delivers good stories, original music, kaleidoscopic design and poignant, often humorous, new writing to entertain and make children and adults think. Two to three new plays a year for 3–5 year-olds, 4–7 year-olds and children 8+ and their families. Mission: to make life-changing theatre to inspire and entertain. Founded 1977.

Red Ladder Theatre Company

3 St Peters Buildings, York Street, Leeds LS9 8AJ
tel 0113-245 5311 *fax* 0113-245 5351
email rod@redladder.co.uk
website www.redladder.co.uk
Artistic Director Rod Dixon

Theatre performances for young people (13–25) in theatre venues and youth clubs. Commissions 1–2 new plays each year. Runs the Red Grit Project, a theatre training programme for young people (18–25) in Yorkshire.

Replay Theatre Company

Old Museum Building, 7 College Square North, Belfast BT1 6AR
tel (028) 9032 2773 *fax* (028) 9032 2724
email info@replaytheatreco.org
website www.replaytheatreco.org
Artistic Director Anna Newell

Provides professional theatre that entertains, educates and stimulates children and young people. It produces educational theatre performances, activities and accompanying resource materials to primary, secondary and special schools throughout Northern Ireland and the Republic of Ireland. Founded 1988.

Sixth Sense Theatre for Young People

c/o The Wyvern Theatre, Theatre Square, Swindon SN1 1QN
tel (01793) 614864 *fax* (01793) 616715
email sstc@dircon.co.uk
website www.sixthsensetyp.co.uk

A professional theatre company prioritising work with young people. It promotes theatre and helps young people explore issues that are important to them. Each year, the company produces both issue-based and creative theatre productions and performs in schools, theatres and arts centres in Swindon and the South West region. These productions are supported by additional young people-led work, workshops, training sessions and other additional production projects.

Tangere Arts

PO Box 7330, Tansley, Matlock DE4 9BF
tel (0845) 329 8013
email admin@tangere-arts.co.uk
website www.tangere-arts.co.uk

Theatre primarily for the East Midlands area with a range of culturally diverse work for children, young people, families and communities.

Theatr Gwent Theatre

The Drama Centre, Pen-y-Pound, Abergavenny, Monmouthshire NP7 5UD
tel (01873) 853167 *fax* (01873) 853910
email gwenttie@uwclub.net
website www.gwenttheatre.com
Artistic Director Gary Meredith, *General Manager* Julia Davies

Commissions, devises and tours productions for young people to schools and communities. Offers individually designed workshops and INSET for schools, work experience for young people, an advisory service for schools, and youth theatre.

Theatr Iolo

The Old School Building, Cefn Road, Mynachdy, Cardiff CF14 3HS
tel 029-2061 3782 *fax* 029-2052 2225
email info@theatriolo.com
website www.theatriolo.com
Artistic Director Kevin Lewis

Aims to produce and programme the best of live theatre, making it widely accessible to children and young people in Cardiff and the Vale of Glamorgan, to 'stir the imagination, inspire the heart and challenge the mind'. The company works alongside teachers and subject advisers to enhance teaching and learning across the curriculum.

Theatr Spectacle Theatre

Coleg Morgannwg Rhondda, Llwynypia, Tonypandy, Rhondda Cynon Tâf CF40 2TQ
tel (01443) 430700 *fax* (01443) 439640
email info@spectacletheatre.co.uk
website www.spectacletheatre.co.uk
Artistic Director Steve Davis

Creates quality theatre for schools, communities and theatre venues throughout Wales and further afield.

Theatre Centre

Shoreditch Town Hall, 380 Old Street, London EC1V 9LT

tel 020-7729 3066 *fax* 020-7739 9741
email admin@theatre-centre.co.uk
website www.theatre-centre.co.uk
Artistic Director Natalie Wilson

New writing company producing 3 plays a year and touring nationally and internationally. All productions are for children and/or young people, staged in schools, arts centres and other venues. Recently produced work includes *Trashed* by Noël Greig, *God is a DJ* by Oladipo Agboluaje, *Romeo in the City* by Amber Lone, *Rigged* by Ashmeed Sohoye and *The Day The Waters Came* by Lisa Evans. Also manages the Brian Way Award and Adrienne Benham Award. Keen to hear from writers from ethnic minority groups. Founded 1953.

The Theatre Co Blah Blah Blah

The West Park Centre, Spen Lane, Leeds LS16 5BE
tel 0113-274 0030
email admin@blahs.co.uk
website www.blahs.co.uk
Artistic Director Anthony Haddon

Specialises in touring theatre for children and young people and residency work in schools and youth centres. Founded 1985.

Theatre Hullabaloo

Arts Centre, Vane Terrace, Darlington DL3 7AX
tel (01325) 352004 *fax* (01325) 369404
email info@theatrehullabaloo.org.uk
website www.theatrehullabaloo.org.uk
Creative Producer Miranda Thain

The North East's specialist theatre company creating and touring work for young audiences. Creates theatre experiences for children and young people which aim to contribute to their emotional, spiritual and social development. Promotes greater awareness of the value of theatre to children and young people by working with teachers and others through courses, events and publications. Tours professional theatre productions to schools and venues within Tees Valley, the North East and nationally. Organiser of the annual Take Off Festival since 1994.

Theatre Is...

The Innovation Centre, College Lane,
Hatfield AL10 9AB
tel (01707) 281100 *fax* (01707) 281038

email info@theatreis.org
website www.theatreis.org
Contact Michael Corley

Challenging and creating new models of live performance by, with and for young audiences across the East of England.

Theatre Workshop

34 Hamilton Place, Edinburgh EH3 5AX
tel 0131-225 7942 *fax* 0131-220 0112
email enquiries.tws@hotmail.co.uk
website www.theatre-workshop.com
Artistic Director Robert Rae

Cutting edge, professional, inclusive theatre company. Plays include new writing/community/children's/disabled. Scripts from new writers considered.

Travelling Light Theatre Company

Barton Hill Settlement, 41–43 Ducie Road,
Lawrence Hill, Bristol BS2 0AX
tel 0117-377 3166 *fax* 0117-377 3167
email info@travellinglighttheatre.org.uk
website www.travellinglighttheatre.org.uk
Artistic Producer Jude Merrill

A professional touring company performing at schools, theatres, community venues and festivals in the UK, Europe and beyond. It presents new work, either devised or commissioned scripts, exploring themes and issues of special interest and relevance to young people. The performance style is highly physical, visual and musical.

Tutti Frutti Productions

Shine, Harehills Road, Harehills, Leeds LS8 5DR
tel 0113-388 0027
email emma@tutti-frutti.co.uk
website www.tutti-frutti.co.uk
Artistic Director Wendy Harris

Professional theatre aimed specifically at family audiences (age 3+ and adults). Productions are adaptations of children's books or specially commissioned pieces and include original music together with different artforms, i.e. puppetry, dance, movement. Tours nationally and performs in a host of different small-scale venues, including arts centres, village halls, rural touring schemes and schools, undertaking approx. 200 performances a year. Founded 1991.

Theatre

Resources for children's writers
Setting up a website

Suna Cristall explains the procedure for setting up a website and presents the options for its design. She includes points to consider if the target audience includes children.

Having your own personal website is a fantastic promotional tool and will allow you to display your work and achievements to a global audience spanning all age ranges, genders and economic stratums. The internet is increasingly becoming the first place people look to find information and, with a staggering 18.3 million households with internet access in the UK alone (according to the National Statistics website, www.statistics.gov.uk), it is worthwhile making yourself accessible through this media.

Setting up a website can seem like a daunting task, especially if you're not very technically literate. However, there is absolutely no need to feel intimidated as there are options available to suit all budgets and levels of web-programming skills (even if you have none to speak of).

Getting started

First things first – you will need a web address, otherwise known as a domain name. It is basically the equivalent of a home or business address; people can only come and visit if they have an address to navigate to. Try to keep your domain name as simple as possible as this will make it easier for people to remember. It should also be something relevant to you, or to your work. This is particularly pertinent not only so that people can make a clear connection between you and your web address, but to avoid any potential legal issues. For example, HarryPotter.com is indubitably a memorable domain name, but it is rather likely that the author's, publisher's, and film company's legal teams will have a few things to say about you using it for yourself.

If you decide to hire a professional designer he or she can take care of the actual purchasing for you, but do note that they will charge you further for the privilege. There are a multitude of different companies you can buy a domain name from, all unfortunately with varying prices, so it is highly recommended that you shop around. It is also advisable to confirm that the company is ICANN certified. ICANN is the Internet Corporation for Assigned Names and Numbers and acts as the regulatory body for domain registrars. A list of ICANN certified domain registrars can be found on their website: www.icann.org/registrars/accredited-list.html

Planning your website

As with any form of design there are certain principles to follow which will ensure your end product is successful. Even if you choose to hire someone to create your website for you, it is worth noting the following basic guidelines for good web design as they will help you make an informed decision when it comes to finalising your layout.

• **Clear navigation.** Your visitor could be aged nine or 90, but if they cannot easily navigate their way around your website they will be equally frustrated by the experience. If someone gets lost whilst browsing your website, it is likely that you will lose them completely – people are more liable to log off than persevere as few like their patience challenged in that manner.

• **Be consistent.** This goes hand in hand with keeping your site navigation clear as it helps your visitors recognise where they are. Changing the look and structure of your website from page to page will only serve to confuse and disorientate people. It is the online equivalent of having different wallpaper and flooring in every room in your house. You want your website to flow and appear organised, with a clear design concept executed throughout.

• **Structure your text.** The average individual spends approximately 20 seconds per web page, and tends to simply 'scan' it as opposed to reading every line. With this in mind, it is highly recommended that you label your sections clearly to help your visitors find the information they require more easily. Also, make points of interest bold and eye-catching. This does *not* mean using lots of flashing images or text as those sorts of devices tend only to be effective at irritating people. It is also worth noting that most children are reluctant to scroll, so try to keep your content concise and constrained to the immediate visual area of the screen.

• **Readability.** Dark text on light backgrounds is best for the purposes of reading onscreen as it is the easiest on the eyes but, whatever your colour choice, make sure there is a high contrast between these two elements otherwise your copy simply blends into the background. Make sure to apply an appropriate font size, so that text is large enough to be legible, but not so large it looks like you are SHOUTING.

• **Fonts.** Sans-serif fonts, such as Geneva, Arial or Helvetica are the easiest to read on a computer screen. As an added bonus, these also happen to be 'web-safe' fonts. Web-safe fonts basically refer to the standard fonts that are on every computer system. They may be prettier but non-web-safe fonts are not universally installed, and using one would be a gamble as you run the risk of your visitors' computers not being able to recognise your specified font.

• **Current content.** Be wary of your site 'dating' itself. The content may be current at the time of construction, but how will it read six months later? To avoid your content being classified as *passé*, use the present or present-perfect tense as much as possible. Likewise, try to update your site regularly as this will help to generate repeat visitors.

• **Screen size.** Monitors come in all different sizes, with varying default resolutions. With this in mind it is good practice to design your site for the smaller screens – 800 (width) by 600 (height) pixels. People with larger screens will still be able to view all of the content on your site, whereas the reverse will cause unsightly bottom and side scrollbars (a rather unfortunate web design *faux-pas* that is easily avoided).

• **Page size.** Download time varies according to file size and the speed of internet connection. Faster connections are rapidly becoming the norm for business and home use, but it is still advisable to keep your web pages as small as possible so that people with slow dialup connections can still access your site at a reasonable speed. Graphics, animations and audio clips are generally the biggest culprits for bumping up file sizes, so keep your image resolutions low and your sound bytes short. If you want to include things such as high resolution images, provide a thumbnail of the image with an option of clicking to download the larger version.

• **Accessibility.** Making websites accessible to disabled users is not only good practice, but with new legislations being regularly introduced, this will eventually be *standard* practice. To ensure your website is up to scratch on this level, you will need to provide basic text equivalents for things such as images, audio/video clips, animations, etc describing what they are so that a web reader can process the information. ALT tags are the most commonly used for this purpose (these are the buttercup-yellow text boxes that pop up when you hover the cursor over an image).

Know your audience

Knowing who your website is targeted at is a key step in the process, as your design and content will alter depending on whom you wish to reach. Even though your creative work may be aimed at children you will need to make certain you do not alienate parents, teachers, or people offering potential commissions. Fortunately, what makes a successful website does not differ between age groups as much as one might think, although there are certain deviations worth noting. In a study conducted by the Neilsen Norman Group, interesting revelations were made regarding how both children (aged 6–12) and teenagers (aged 13–17) use the web and it highlighted the unique distinctions between the two groups as well as the general similarities. They discovered that the younger age group participants were able to successfully use the sites that were aimed at adults, such as Google, successfully as they are minimally designed with clear navigation. They also responded well to animation and sound effects – the fun stuff. If you would like to include these elements in your website, it is advisable you do so as add-ons and not at the expense of your navigation, as the children were uniformly flummoxed when the navigation was convoluted. Notably, the children rarely scrolled down a screen, but instead randomly moved their cursor over the page looking for clickable areas.

The teens were online more often on a regular basis, as they purported to utilise the internet for school projects, hobbies, news and information, and e-commerce as well as entertainment (which was the main reason given for use by the younger age group). They responded particularly well to cool looking graphics and clean designs.

Most importantly, both groups demanded an element of interactivity to hold their interest – sites lacking this component were quickly classified as boring and the children did not hang around. Interactivity can be achieved in an assortment of ways and it is essential to have at least one of these attributes on your website for children and teenagers:
• quizzes
• forums or message boards
• voting
• games
• contact details, such as an email address.

Designing your site

Now that you've got your domain name, understand the basic principles of good web design and have somewhat of a clue as to what children want (at least pertaining to websites), you are ready to start building your website.

As previously mentioned, there are a variety of options available to you with regard to designing and building your site. There is a solution out there to suit every level of available finances and technical savviness. They can be divided into three groups: DIY, ready-made, and professional.

• **The DIY option.** Although this option is cost effective, it requires a basic knowledge of HTML (HyperText MarkUp Language) and some time and patience on your part. HMTL is a language like any other and can be learned should you have the inclination. It is this vernacular that formats your web page and allows the browser to interpret text styles, links, images, etc. If you have never encountered it before, it can certainly look rather complicated (like sci-fi robot-speak) but rest assured it really is quite straightforward and follows a very simple logic. Should you decide to learn some HTML or already have a basic knowledge, this will most certainly be an asset when it comes to creating and maintaining your website. There are some extremely helpful software programmes on the market to assist you in building your website. Two of the most popular are Macromedia Dreamweaver and Microsoft FrontPage. These programmes are designed to be as user-friendly as possible and code parts of your site automatically for ease. They also come equipped with pre-designed web templates, so if you are feeling slightly less adventurous, you can simply add your content and images within their pre-established parameters. As an added bonus, there are plenty of books, online tutorials and forums that offer assistance should you find yourself in need.

• **The ready-made option.** Realising that there are a vast amount of individuals and businesses that desire websites, but lack the technical ability, time and patience to create their own or have insufficient resources to hire a professional designer, a few companies have recently emerged offering a ready-made option (the greatest invention of convenience since the TV dinner). These companies have already gone to all of the trouble for you and have created a complete professionally designed website. You simply choose your design and add your content through their interface, which is purposefully constructed for even the most technically challenged amongst us. They tend to charge on a monthly basis, but are truly affordable. The main drawback with this option is that you are constrained by their design templates and it is likely that other people will have chosen the same template as you, so your visitors may be struck by a case of *déjà vu*. However, the instant gratification of having a complete and professional looking website in a matter of hours more than makes up for the lack of creative freedom.

In a similar vein, you might want to consider using a blogging or social network site, such as Wordpress or Facebook. These are free to use once you register and open your blog or personal profile up to a pre-existing online community. Although these will not entirely replace having a personal website, they are a great way to instantly get yourself online.

• **Employing a professional.** It pains me to say that we're a dime a dozen, but there is no denying that there are a ridiculous number of web designers out there. A recommendation from a trusted source, as with anything, is always helpful. However, if one is not forthcoming, make a note of the name of design companies that have created sites you like. When choosing a designer, it's worth assessing them on:

• *examples of their previous work* – they may be your sister's husband's first cousin on his mother's side, but if you don't like their style of design, don't employ them; no rabbits will be pulled out of any hats just because you're 'family';

• *company history* – this will give you a better idea of their level of experience and professionalism;

• *references* – they are working for you, so do not be afraid to ask for testimonials of satisfied clients;

• *charges* – you need to clarify how much they will charge you for the initial build as well as if there are any further charges for updates, etc.

Going online

Once you have successfully built your website (or had it built for you) it is time to put it 'live'. To get your website online you will need to purchase a hosting package. Your website, for all intents and purposes, is a file and needs to be stored somewhere which will allow public access. This is where the hosting company comes in – they provide the crucial disk space on their servers which will host your website.

Again, much like with domain registrars, there are many hosting companies in operation with varying annual charges, so by all means, do your research and compare price plans. Obviously, this step is only applicable if you have designed the site yourself. Otherwise, you have duly paid for the luxury not to have to worry about these things.

As soon as you have chosen and paid for your hosting package, you will receive a confirmation email supplying you with the information you need to transfer your files over to them. The first step will be to log into the account you created when you purchased your domain name and change the name server to the one specified by your hosting company. This is a straightforward process, but do not hesitate to contact your domain registrar if you need assistance. This change tends to take approximately 48 hours to propagate. Whilst you are waiting for this to happen you can proceed with uploading your website to your hosting account. This is achieved by using a FTP (File Transfer Protocol) client or your web page editor and again, is a very simple process but do feel free to contact your hosting company if you are having trouble.

All that is left for you to do now is to promote your website – people won't know to visit if they don't know it exists. Add your web address to your business cards, as your email footer and post your web address on other websites that have relevance to yours. Also post it within blog comments, forums, message boards, and/or by requesting a link (offering a reciprocal link is polite and always appreciated). As well as increasing targeted awareness of your website, the links also serve to improve your search engine rating (i.e. how high on the search results page your website appears). It really pays to be proactive on this front as the more traffic you encourage, the more people will know about your work, which of course is the whole point of all this rigmarole.

Suna Cristall lives in London and works as a freelance web designer.

Learning to write for children

Many people have what they consider to be brilliant ideas for children's books but have no experience of writing. But lack of experience need not get in the way of bringing an idea to fruition as there is guidance available in the form of courses. Alison Sage demystifies what happens on a writing course for children and outlines the benefits to be gained.

Can you teach people to write for children?

There are quite a few who think you can't. There is an implicit idea that writing is a talent you are born with and that one day, sitting at your laptop in your kitchen (why is it always the kitchen?) your innate ability will suddenly surface like a lottery ticket, and you will write a bestseller that will pay your mortgage and take you on exotic holidays for life.

After many years working in publishing and talking to would-be writers, I have come to the conclusion that this is only a tiny fraction of the truth. Writing is like any other talent and it improves with being used. Dancers dance, musicians play and writers have to write and write and write to get better.

There is no doubt that some people have more aptitude for writing than others. But besides natural talent, a writer must have something to say.

Next, a writer needs to have the persistence and self belief to continue to write through all kinds of distractions and discouragement. And finally, if a writer wants to be published successfully, he or she needs a certain amount of luck.

The role of writing classes

First and most importantly, writing classes can give the writer a chance to explore different kinds of writing in a non-judgemental atmosphere. It is the job of the teacher to help students to experiment until they find what suits them.

Students can also meet other people in the same situation. Writing can be a very lonely pursuit. A writer's friends are usually embarrassed to give their honest opinion about a story because it is a recipe for falling out. Every writer knows the despair of writing something which at first sounds wonderful and then on re-reading sounds rubbish. Where can writers find an independent judgement? Whoever they ask must be someone they can trust to be impartial, someone who can suggest where their good ideas become woolly and perhaps even how they might go about improving things. However, these must always be *suggestions*. It is the writer who must decide how, where, and in what way to alter the manuscript.

In an ideal world, the publisher's editor would help new writers endlessly until they achieved a best-selling novel. The reality is that publishers' editors are too busy to nurture every single would-be talent. Therefore, it is up to the writer either to go it alone – which many do – or to find someone else to act as a sounding board. This is where writing classes can help.

Who benefits most from writing classes?

It is impossible to guess at the beginning of a course how far students will develop their talent or even who will actually get published. Obviously, different teachers suit different people, but I have found an astonishing range amongst my students. That is what makes it so exciting and rewarding – and so unpredictable. The only student who is unlikely to be happy is the one who says: 'Teach me to write a bestseller.' This is frankly impossible and anyone who believes that writing is an exact science is bound to be disappointed.

Interestingly enough, the one thing that can indicate how far a student will get – apart from their persistence, of course – is how flexible they are. Often, people who are highly educated are actually at a disadvantage. They believe they have been taught how to write correctly – and that there is a 'right' and a 'wrong' way to do it. Nothing could be further from the truth, particularly when writing for children. Therefore, I have seen an Oxford graduate watch enviously as another student, still at school, sends the whole class into fits of laughter with a perfect story. I have had students who were models, refugees, counsellors, puppeteers, housewives, diplomats, postmen, soldiers, office managers, nurses, with children, without children or simply out of work. One of my best students left school aged 15. He is now editing a magazine and I still wonder if he will ever write his children's novel.... Another is now a published author/illustrator, through his own talent and a great deal of effort. Yet another is looking after her children – and one day perhaps the quiet brilliance of her writing will find a publisher.

A typical course outline

Every course is different because every student is asked what they hope to achieve and this obviously affects what we do. However, certain things are always included in some form.

It may sound self evident, but central to a writing course is getting students to write. Students develop through putting new ideas into practice. Therefore, every class includes about 15 minutes' writing time and students read out and talk about what they have written. Most students are nervous at first, because they feel they are unprepared. But this rarely lasts because writing on the spot seems to bring the group closer together. It also relaxes everyone, as no one can be expected to write a bestseller in 15 minutes and at this point, students invariably have brilliant ideas and express them unbelievably well. If anyone gets stuck, they simply explain that the topic hasn't worked for them. Different students shine at different topics and this helps to steer them towards what they ultimately want to write.

Finding a story

The first place to look for a story is in your own experience. All students are asked to write something about their first memories of their baby brothers or sisters because when students genuinely remember their own childhood, their language becomes simpler, their writing more powerful and direct. They write in a way they never would if they were consciously trying to 'write for children'. This is a very important step in trying to discover what is your own voice. Writers need to know not only what they want to say, but also how they are going to put it over.

The class then usually discusses what kinds of story are appropriate for different ages. Perhaps one of the most common mistakes made by new children's writers is that they write about very young topics in a very sophisticated fashion. If you are aiming to write a picture book for a three year-old, you need to understand a little of what a three year-old can cope with. It is no use writing a story that is 10,000 words long.

However, a nine year-old is not going to be interested in stories designed for a three year-old – even if technically they are suitable. In fact, a good rule of thumb is that children are interested in most of the things that adults are – except they are not used to dealing with concepts. A child may love a book about a character who is alone, or brave, or funny.

They will not be so interested in loneliness, heroism or humour in the *abstract*. Children are also not very comfortable with irony until they are about nine or ten years old, tending to take the printed word at its face value. However, when they *do* discover it, they love it.

The beginning

The next thing to stress is the importance of the beginning. Many students think that page one is where a writer finds his feet and that the story proper starts about page six. This is not true. The first paragraph of a book is crucial. Children invest a lot of energy in reading a book and they want to be convinced pretty quickly that this effort is going to be worthwhile. A dull first page means that the book will be put down, never to be opened again. Even more to the point, perhaps, a busy editor reading an unsolicited manuscript will also lose interest if the beginning of the story is dull or confusing and they will make this the excuse they need to return it immediately. The beginning must draw the reader in. If a story is the solving of a problem, then the beginning must make that problem sound exciting and tantalising.

At this point, it is usually a good idea for the class to discuss strategies for keeping going with a story. Finishing a story gives a student a great boost and in itself, is a huge learning curve. Different strategies are helpful for different people. Some students need a writing routine – a special chair or table or cup of coffee. For others this is either no use or impossible to maintain. Some find writing notes at the end of each writing session is helpful, so that they can more easily get into the flow of ideas where they broke off. And most people find a notebook helpful, where they can record interesting ideas and experiences to be used as the raw material for future stories. If you are able to go into a school and help with reading, this can be a great eye opener as you will see first hand which stories children struggle over and which really work.

A vital ingredient

Another vital topic usually covered at this stage of the course is tension. Tension is what makes you want to continue reading and without tension, a story is as dull as a meal without salt. Just as a joke falls flat if the timing is wrong, so a fascinating story can become boringly muddled if the author does not build to a climax. It is about choosing selective details and using the reader's own imagination to create suspense. A description of the monster's claw grasping from behind the door is far more terrifying than a complete run-down of the whole creature.

If you think of your own favourite childhood story, it is often not the end that sticks in your mind. It is the bit just before the climax. That is when the tension and suspense should be strongest. At the end of the story, you can ask a question or add a twist, to give the impression that your characters will continue even after the book has been shut.

Talk about getting published

Finally, most students are interested in the mechanics of getting published, and this is a minefield for would-be authors. It is difficult to get your work singled out from a pile of unsolicited manuscripts and while (eventually) good writers are usually discovered, it can be a long and tortuous process.

There are things you can do to improve your chances and while they are mostly common sense, this is probably an area where a good writing class can help. Look in your local bookshop for the publishers which produce the kind of books you admire. There is an outside chance that if you like them, they might like you. Far too many good manuscripts are sent to the wrong places and if a publisher produces medical books, he or she is not likely to be interested in a children's manuscript, even if it is *Harry Potter*.

Sharing an interest

Perhaps the most important thing is to enjoy writing and to meet other people who are also interested. That way, students can keep each other going through the rejections and at the very least, improve at something they want to do. There are a great many courses which cater for all different kinds of interests, attitudes and expectations. The best place to look is probably at the local adult education institute. If there is no course specifically listed for writing for children, it is worth ringing up and asking if they would like to start one. You could also put up a notice in your local library for anyone else who might be interested and as soon as you are a group, the authority will take notice of you. You could even start your own independent writing group!

There are also several residential courses (such as the Arvon Foundation courses), and they are a very enjoyable and relaxing way to take your ambitions further. Look on the internet, as these courses constantly change and new ones are added every year. Several universities and colleges also run long and short courses in children's writing and you can achieve a diploma in Writing for Children, although this would take you at least a year.

So can writing be taught?

The debate will certainly continue, as people point out that teachers on courses rarely become as famous as some of their students. However, there *are* things which are helpful to discover when you are starting out as a children's writer. And perhaps the encouragement of the group will make sure that you continue writing until instead of your returned manuscript, it is the publisher's contract that drops through your letterbox!

Alison Sage is an experienced commissioning editor of children's books and has worked for a variety of publishers including Oxford University Press, HarperCollins and Random House. Alison is also a writer and anthologist and her *Treasury of Children's Literature* won the Children's Book of the Year Award in 1995. She has run many courses on creative writing for children for Kensington & Chelsea and Hammersmith adult education institutes.

See also...
- *Children's writing courses and conferences,* page 346
- *Online resources about children's books,* page 348

Indexing children's books

Valerie A. Elliston is a Fellow of the Society of Indexers.

What is an index?

An index is 'a systematic arrangement of entries designed to enable users to locate information in a document' (British Standard BS ISO 999: 1996). Unlike the general contents page, it is a key to far more specific detail. There are two basic categories of reader: those who have not read the book and those who have. A good index will help the former to decide whether the book suits his or her needs. It will help the latter to revisit any part of it without having to riffle through all the pages. These statements apply equally to publications for children as well as for adults; the benefits can be enjoyed by both, especially if the skill of using an index is learned in the early years.

Further information

Society of Indexers
Woodbourn Business Centre, 10 Jessell Street, Sheffield S9 3HY
tel 0114-244 9561, 0845 872 6807
fax 0114-244 9563
email admin@indexers.org.uk
website www.indexers.org.uk
Administrator Wendy Burrow
Membership £95.50 p.a. UK/Europe, £120 outside Europe; corporate: fewer than 50 employees £191, more than 50 employees £287

Visit the website or contact the Administrator for further information. Publishers and authors seeking to commission an indexer should consult *Indexers Available* on the website.

Useful websites
www.nc.uk.net/nc/contents
www.standards.dfes.gov.uk/primary/publications

Why index children's books?

The vital importance of indexing information books for children has been highlighted over many years, at least since the mid-1930s. This was confirmed in a survey sponsored by the British Library Research and Innovation Centre (Williams and Bakewell 1997). All 16 publishers participating in this investigation rated this importance very highly. Yet, fewer than one-third said that they always included an index in publications for children, with reasons for exclusion given chiefly as restrictions on budget, time and space. Sometimes the contents page is considered sufficient, even though this lacks essential details.

Advantages of indexes

Firstly, the National Curriculum (2000) requires that children should be taught sound information retrieval practice, using organisational features and systems to locate texts. Secondly, the Primary National Strategy includes in its non-fiction objectives: understanding the purpose of contents pages and indexes; finding information by page numbers and initial letters of words. Later, the aim includes finding parts of text that give particular information. Children should also use dictionaries to find words by using initial letters, and the teacher is advised to demonstrate scanning the index for information, asking the children to familiarise themselves with the contents pages, indexes and glossaries of the information books. Thirdly, using an index is one of the earliest tools of independent research as well as helping to promote analytical skills. Despite increasing use of the internet, books will be with us for a long time yet, and children are being encouraged more and more to read them, not only for enjoyment but in preparation for future studies. Finally, skill in using indexes can help when searching for information on the internet.

Disadvantages of a book that lacks an index

The Williams and Bakewell survey found a number of negative effects, chiefly that children lose patience and interest if they have to spend time looking through a whole book for specific information. Younger ones often find scanning difficult, and can therefore fail to develop independent searching methods, remaining reliant on the teacher or librarian. The survey also found that primary school children viewed the index as a highly important feature and assumed that every non-fiction book would have one. An 11 year-old asked how they were supposed to find anything in a book without an index. Workshops conducted by an indexer in a secondary school confirmed children's intelligent interest in the use of indexes. They were quick to grasp the importance of choosing relevant terms and of keeping the number of page references to a minimum. In fact, by the end of each session, the participants were able to criticise a selection of books from the school library, rejecting those without an index and rating the rest according to the quality of the index while taking into account the overall layout and appropriateness of the entries. Another indexer worked with groups of 10–11 year-olds who examined a selection of books and decided which were the key topics on each page before checking in the index. They gave points for inclusion and accuracy, becoming ever more discriminating as they progressed.

Quality of the indexes

Indexes for children's books should be just as high quality as for adults' books, perhaps even more so as children need to be taught with the best examples against which future use can be measured. A clear, accurate and well-presented index can encourage their use, just as a disappointing one can reduce their interest. It follows, therefore, that the index should be carefully planned, not tacked on as an afterthought or made by a computer without any consideration for the particular needs of the young user.

• **Terminology** should be appropriate for the age group, using words that children would be expected to know. Most will be taken from the text, but sometimes thought has to be given to the choice between additional entries or cross-referencing which can be a problem for younger users. For example, the text might mention 'currency' but it would be helpful to also include 'money' in the index or to cross-reference it with '*see also* money', according to the age group.

• **Subheadings** should be avoided if possible as they can confuse younger children. However, they might be necessary to avoid using too many locators (i.e. page or paragraph numbers).

• **Indexing names** needs careful consideration as there are many options. Should rulers be indexed individually or be listed as subheadings under the main entries 'kings' and 'queens'? Should titles or surnames be inverted as in indexes to adult books? The most suitable form of the name should be chosen for the particular index (e.g. 'Geldof, Bob' as opposed to 'Geldof, Sir Robert'). Correct spelling is essential, of course.

• **Consistency** is also important: should singular or plural terms be used for countable nouns? The British Standard already quoted recommends the use of the plural form for 'countables' and singular for 'non-countables'. For example, the countables 'chairs', 'cars' not 'chair' and 'car'. The plural is unlikely to arise for non-countable nouns, e.g. 'furniture', 'traffic', 'coffee'. The British Standard recommends lower case initial letters except for proper nouns.

• **Omission** of key topics is a major fault as, if children cannot find the item in the index, they will often assume it is not dealt with in the text and will give up. The index needs to be attractive and reliable, to appeal to the eye yet remain an invaluable tool.

Presentation of indexes

Presentation is particularly important to children.

• **Length** is determined by length of text and space available but, ideally, the index should adequately reflect the book.

• If the **font size** is small in proportion to the text, this can make the index seem relatively unimportant and sometimes more difficult to read, another reason for giving up.

• **Alphabetical order** can be used in two ways: word by word or letter by letter, but the chosen style must be used consistently. Many children's books print the entire alphabet on the first or each index page to help them locate the initial letters. Space between each section beginning with the same letter can be helpful, especially if the section is headed with the appropriate large upper case letter.

• **Illustrations** should be indexed but the difference between references to text and references to illustrations needs to be distinguished, perhaps by use of bold or italic type for the latter. If illustrations are also used purely for decoration, confusion should be avoided; the index pages should be as clear as possible. Another source of confusion could be a combined index and glossary; keeping them separate emphasises the different functions of each.

• **Locators (page or paragraph numbers)** can be shown with each page listed individually (4, 5, 6, 7, 8, 10, 11, 12, i.e. a separate reference to the topic on each page) or in ranges indicated by hyphens or en-rules (4–8, 10–12, i.e. a continuous reference over more than one page). This practice can be explained to children early on in their study of indexes so that they become familiar with it as soon as possible.

• **Passing mention** of a topic should be ignored as it is frustrating for children who find it is mentioned only in connection with something entirely different. Again, here is another reason for children giving up using an index. A further source of frustration is a long string of page numbers; children in the index workshop mentioned above were quick to notice them, announcing that they would certainly give up checking each one. Here then, is a sound reason for making more main entries or using subheadings.

• **Cross-references.** Using '*see*' and '*see also*' is often a problem, especially to younger children for whom additional entries might be more straightforward. The Williams and Bakewell survey found that the majority of respondents were in favour of keeping these traditional terms so that children could become accustomed to them in preparation for using adult books. Others suggested using double or additional entries or introducing different phrases such as 'try the word . . .' or 'also look up . . .' but the latter solution means the children will still have to learn the traditional phrases later on.

In view of all the foregoing, it might not be surprising that one of the 21 recommendations in the Williams and Bakewell report on indexes to children's information books is that such indexes should be compiled by a professional indexer who should have some knowledge of the subject matter. These recommendations appear in the Society of Indexers 'Occasional Paper No 5' which is derived largely from that investigation.

Valerie A. Elliston is a Fellow of the Society of Indexers, and a former adult education lecturer in English Language and Literature.

Further reading

Bakewell, K.G.B. and Williams, Paula L. with contributions from Elizabeth Wallis MBE and Valerie A. Elliston, *Indexing Children's Books*, 'Occasional Paper on Indexing No 5', Society of Indexers, 2000

British Standards Institution, *Information and Documentation: Guidelines for the content, organization and presentation of indexes*, BS ISO 999: 1996, 1997

Department for Educational Standards, *Key Stages 1 & 2 of the National Curriculum*, DfES, 2000

Williams P.L. and Bakewell K.G.B., *Indexes to Children's Information Books: A study of the provision and quality of book indexes for children at National Curriculum Key Stage 2. Final Report on Project RIC/G/330 (British Library Research and Innovation Report 129)*, 1997

Children's writing courses and conferences

Anyone wishing to participate in a writing course should first satisfy themselves as to its content and quality. For day and evening courses consult your local Adult Education Centre.

The Arvon Foundation

Lumb Bank, The Ted Hughes Arvon Centre,
Heptonstall, Hebden Bridge,
West Yorkshire HX7 6DF
tel (01422) 843714 *fax* (01422) 843714
email lumbbank@arvonfoundation.org
website www.arvonfoundation.org
Contact Ilona Jones
Moniack Mhor, Teavarran, Kiltarlity, Beauly,
Inverness-shire IV4 7HT
tel (01463) 741675 *fax* (01463) 741733
email moniackmhor@arvonfoundation.org
Contact Lyndy Batty
The Arvon Foundation, Totleigh Barton, Sheepwash,
Beaworthy, Devon EX21 5NS
tel (01409) 231338 *fax* (01409) 231144
email totleighbarton@arvonfoundation.org
Contact Julia Wheadon
The Hurst – The John Osborne Arvon Centre
Clunton, Craven Arms, Shrops. SY7 0JA
tel (01588) 640658 *fax* (01588) 640509
email thehurst@arvonfoundation.org
Contact Dan Pavitt

The Federation of Children's Book Groups Conference

Details Martin and Sinead Kromer,
2 Bridge Wood View, Horsforth, Leeds LS18 5PE
email info@fcbg.org.uk
website www.fcbg.org.uk
Takes place 3 days in April

Held annually, guest speakers include well-known children's authors as well as experts and publishers in the field of children's books. Publishers also exhibit their newest books and resources.

IBBY Congress

Nonnenweg 12, Postfach, CH-4003-Basel,
Switzerland
tel (4161) 272 2917 *fax* (4161) 272 2757
email liz.page@ibby.org, ibby@ibby.org
British Section 10 Hall's Drive, Gressenhall, East
Dereham, Norfolk NR20 4EJ
tel (01362) 860886
email annlazim@googlemail.com
website www.ibby.org

A biennial international congress for IBBY (International Board on Books for Young People) members and other people involved in children's books and reading development. Every other year a different National Section of IBBY hosts the congress and several hundred people from all over the world attend the professional programme.

Forthcoming congresses: 2012 Congress to be held on 21–24 August in London, UK on the theme 'Translations and Migrations'; 2014 Congress to be held 15–21 September in Mexico City, on the theme 'Reading as a Social Inclusion Tool: in the classroom, the library, and other social spaces'. See also page 372.

NCRCL British IBBY Conference

Department of English and Creative Writing,
Roehampton University, Digby Stuart College,
London SW15 5PU
tel 020-8392 3008 *fax* 020-8392 3819
email l.atkins@roehampton.ac.uk
website www.ncrcl.ac.uk

Conference held annually in November on a specific theme.

Oxford University Day and Weekend Schools

Department for Continuing Education,
Oxford University, Rewley House,
1 Wellington Square, Oxford OX1 2JA
tel (01865) 270368
email ppdayweek@conted.ox.ac.uk
website www.conted.ox.ac.uk
Contact Day School Administrator

Effective Writing: a series of 3-day accredited courses for creative writing. Topics vary from year to year. Courses always held on Fridays. See website for futher courses on creative writing.

Pitstop Refuelling Writers' Weekend Workshops – see The Winchester Writers' Conference Festival and Bookfair, Centre for Research and Knowledge Exchange

Swanwick, The Writers' Summer School

Hayes Conference Centre, Swanwick,
Derbyshire DE55 1AU
tel (01292) 442786
email secretary@swanwickwritersschool.co.uk
website www.swanwickwritersschool.co.uk
Takes place 13–19 August 2011

Resources for children's writers

Six-day programme of events for writers of all ages and genres featuring courses, talks and workshops. Attracts top speakers such as Iain Banks, Kate Mosse, Simon Brett, Katie Fforde and other best-selling authors, playwrights, journalists and comedy writers plus the literary agents and publishers who represent them. Full-board accommodation available onsite; day tickets also available. Established 1947.

Tŷ Newydd

Tŷ Newydd, National Writers' Centre for Wales, Llanystumdwy, Cricieth, Gwynedd LL52 0LW
tel (01766) 522811 *fax* (01766) 523095
email post@tynewydd.org
website www.tynewydd.org

Week and weekend courses on all aspects of creative writing. Full programme available.

The Winchester Writers' Conference Festival and Bookfair, Centre for Research and Knowledge Exchange

University of Winchester, Winchester, Hants SO22 4NR
tel (01962) 827238
email barbara.large@winchester.ac.uk
website www.writersconference.co.uk
Conference Director Barbara Large MBE, FRSA, HFUW,
Honorary Patrons Jacqueline Wilson OBE, Maureen Lipman, Colin Dexter OBE, Baroness James OBE
Takes place University of Winchester, July

This Festival of Writing, celebrating its 32nd year in 2012, attracts 65 internationally renowned authors, poets, playwrights, agents and commissioning editors who give 12 mini-courses, 22 workshops, 60 talks, seminars and 500 one-to-one appointments to help writers harness their creativity and develop their writing, editing and marketing skills. Seventeen writing competitions, including Writing for Children, are adjudicated and 70 prizes are awarded at the Writers' Awards Reception. All first place winners are published annually in *The Best of* series.

The Bookfair offers delegates a wide choice of exhibits including authors' and internet services, publishers, booksellers, printers and trade associations.

Pitstop Refuelling Writers' Weekend Workshops are planned for 28–30 October 2011, including Writing Marketable Children's Fiction and Non-fiction; Editing and Marketing your Novel; and How to Self-Publish Your Book day workshops on 12 September and 18 November 2011 at a major book production company, CPI Antony Rowe, Chippenham.

A retreat in Mallorca, the Great Fiction Workshop, is planned for 10–15 October 2011 (www.centromallorca.com) to cover creating, writing, editing and marketing fiction.

Writers Advice Centre for Children's Books – see page 381

The Writers' Workshop

7 Market Street, Charlbury, Oxon OX7 3PH
tel 0845 459 9560
email info@writersworkshop.co.uk
website www.writersworkshop.co.uk
Contacts Harry Bingham, Laura Wilkins, Nikki Holt

Offers a range of courses, including one-day workshops, online writing courses and a unique Comprehensive Writing Course. Topics covered range from How to Write a Novel for beginners, through to Screenwriting and Self-editing your Novel. See website for full details.

YLG Conference

Bromley Central Library, High Street, Bromley BR1 1EX
tel 020-8461 7193 *fax* 020-8313 9975
email ian.dodds@bromley.gov.uk
website www.cilip.org.uk/specialistinterestgroups
Secretary Ian Dodds
Takes place September

This annual conference run by the Youth Libraries Group (YLG) of CILIP is a forum for discussion and debate on current issues for everyone working with and for children in libraries. It also provides an opportunity for experts, authors, illustrators, publishers and all those involved in the children's book trade to meet informally.

POSTGRADUATE COURSES

Bath Spa University

School of Humanities and Cultural Industries, Bath Spa University, Newton Park, Newton St Loe, Bath BA2 9BN
tel (01225) 875875 *fax* (01225) 875503
email s.may@bathspa.ac.uk
website www.bathspa.ac.uk

MA in Writing for Young People, taught by a team of published children's writers. Informal enquires to Julia Green, course leader (j.a.green@bathspa.ac.uk). Also MA in Creative Writing and PhD in Creative Writing.

University of Winchester

Winchester SO22 4NR
tel (01962) 827234 *fax* (01962) 827406
email course.enquiries@winchester.ac.uk
website www.winchester.ac.uk
Contact Course Enquiries & Admissions

MA Writing for Children and MA Creative and Critical Writing.

Online resources about children's books

This is a representation of some of the many websites relating to children's books and reading. Individual author websites can be accessed via the ACHUKA or Contemporary Writers websites. See *Societies, associations and organisations* on page 364 for other resources.

About Children's Books
www.childrensbooks.about.com

Part of About.com, this site holds international information on children's books plus a newsletter.

ACHUKA Children's Books UK
www.achuka.co.uk

Up-to-date and comprehensive online guide to children's books and what's new in children's publishing. With author interviews, children's book news across the globe plus links to many other sites.

Armadillo
email armadilloeditor@googlemail.com
website http://sites.google.com/site/armadillomagazine/
Editor Louise Ellis-Barrett

Magazine about children's books, including reviews, interviews, features and profiles, now available only online. New issues are posted at the end of March, June, September and December. New reviewers and writers are always welcome but there is no payment; reviewers keep the books. The editor instructs reviewers to obtain specific titles direct from publishers. Founded in 1999 by author Mary Hoffman as a review publication for children's books.

Amazon
www.amazon.co.uk, www.amazon.com

UK and US online bookstore with millions of books available on their websites at discounted prices, plus a personal notification service of new releases, reader reviews, bestsellers and book information.

BBC Education
www.bbc.co.uk/schools

Information about UK schools' curriculum. Essential for those wishing to write for educational publishers but also for keeping abreast of curricular topics.

The Best Kids Book Site
www.thebestkidsbooksite.com

US site 'where children's books, crafts and collectibles intersect with your interests.' Useful links to Children's Book Awards, children's series fiction and author websites. Also gives access to the Book Wizard, an information tool to help track down children's books.

Quentin Blake
www.quentinblake.com

The official Quentin Blake website. It includes downloads for children and suggestions for teachers on using books in the classroom.

BookHive
www.cmlibrary.org/bookhive

US guide to children's books for children, parents, teachers or anyone interested in reading about children's books. Includes book reviews.

Booktrust
www.booktrustchildrensbooks.org.uk

Dedicated children's division of Booktrust and an essential site for professionals working with young readers. Information on events, prizes, books, authors, etc.

Canadian Children's Book Centre
www.bookcentre.ca

The site of the Canadian Children's Book Centre includes profiles of authors, illustrators, information on recent books, a calendar of upcoming Canadian events, information on publications and tips from Canadian children's authors.

Children's BBC
www.bbc.co.uk/cbbc

Website of the CBBC channel with games, activities and news for children.

The Children's Book Council
www.cbcbooks.org

The Children's Book Council in the USA is dedicated to encouraging literacy and the enjoyment of children's books. The website includes reviews of children's books published in the USA, forthcoming publications, author profiles and features 'sneek peeks at publishers' newest and hottest titles.' A good site for checking out the US marketplace.

Children's Books Online: the Rosetta Project
www.childrensbooksonline.org

An online library of antique children's books.

Children's Laureate
www.childrenslaureate.org.uk

Official website of the Children's Laureate with resources and activities for children.

Children's Literature
www.childrenslit.com

US website of the Children's Literature Comprehensive Database (CLCD), an ever-growing online database with over 400,000 reviews of children's books. Plus a blog giving news about the world of children's literature.

Classic Children's Stories
www.childhoodreading.com

Many classic stories that have carried on through generations, including illustrations.

Contemporary Writers
www.contemporarywriters.com

Searchable database containing up-to-date profiles of some of the UK and Commonwealth's most important living writers – biographies, bibliographies, critical reviews, prizes and photographs.

Cool Reads
www.cool-reads.co.uk

Find out what children think are cool reads! A website set up by teenagers with reviews, genres, ideas and much more.

Roald Dahl Club
www.roalddahlclub.com

Everything you ever wanted to know about Dahl's books with a section for teachers, children's activities plus the online Roald Dahl Club magazine *The Gobblefunk Gazette*.

The Guardian
www.guardian.co.uk/education

The *Guardian's* education pages online.

Guy's Read
www.guysread.org

US web-based literacy programme to help boys find material they like to read.

The Horn Book
www.hbook.com

US website hosting *The Horn Book Guide Online*, a comprehensive, fully searchable database of over 80,000 book titles for children and young adults, and a monthly e-newsletter for parents, *Notes from the Horn Book*. Plus much more.

ipl2 For Kids
www.ipl.org/div/kidspace

Children's reference zone of the Internet Public Library (IPL), a public service organisation and learning/teaching environment at the University of Michigan School of Information, USA.

ipl2 For Teens
www.ipl.org/div/teen

Teenagers' reference zone of the Internet Public Library (IPL).

Kids' Bookline
www.cllc.org.uk/gwasanaethau-services/plant-children

Website of the Children's Books Department of the Welsh Books Council. It offers a range of activities including book competitions, a book club, awards and prizes as well as services to schools.

Kids' Reads
www.kidsreads.com

Excellent US website with information, reviews, author links and features on children's books. Part of The Book Report Network.

Mrs Mad's Book-a-Rama
www.mrsmad.com

Children's book reviews from an independent reviewer – great fun and informative.

National Curriculum Online
http://curriculum.qcda.gov.uk

The National Curriculum website contains the statutory programmes of study and attainment targets for Key Stages 1–4.

National Literacy Trust
www.literacytrust.org.uk

National Young Readers' Programme
www.literacytrust.org.uk/nyrp

Details of the NLT's initiative to motivate disadvantaged children and young people to read for pleasure plus lots of news and information about children's books.

On-Lion for Kids!
http://kids.nypl.org

New York Public Library children's book site which includes 100 Picture Books Everyone Should Know, 100 Favourite Children's Books and annual lists of 100 Titles for Reading and Sharing.

Picturing Books
www.picturingbooks.com

A website dedicated to picture books. Includes a database of picture book authors and illustrators, explanations of how a picture book is made and a link to the *New York Times* list of best-selling picture books.

Reading Matters
www.readingmatters.co.uk

Website about books and ideas for children and teenagers, written for intelligent young readers who want to choose their own books. It has 328 detailed children's book reviews and more are being added all the time.

ReadingZone.com
www.readingzone.com

Dedicated to helping young people, parents and adults and teachers to find out about children's books. Each area on the site provides information about new and classic titles with expert advice to help you find the best children's books available.

Scottish Book Trust
www.scottishbooktrust.com

Information on books for children of all ages in Scotland plus a national programme of events with children's writers: author tours, festivals, writing competitions and exciting activities.

Stories from the Web
www.storiesfromtheweb.org

A development between Leeds, Bristol and Birmingham Library Services and the UK office for Library and Information Networking to provide information on library clubs, stories, and a chance to email authors.

The Story Museum
website www.storymuseum.org.uk/1001stories

1001 inspirational stories from around the world to watch, hear, read and tell.

Teen Reads
www.teenreads.com

Excellent US website with information, reviews, author links and features on teenage books. Part of The Book Report Network.

UK Children's Books
www.ukchildrensbooks.co.uk

Directory of authors, illustrators and publishers involved in children's books and reading promotion.

The Word Pool
www.wordpool.co.uk

Independent website which profiles authors of children's books and gives information and advice for aspiring writers. Access to the free monthly newsletter.

World of Reading
www.worldreading.org

Website created by Ann Arbor District Library in USA devoted to book reviews written by and for children around the world.

Write4Kids
www.write4kids.com

US site with articles and information about the art of writing children's books. Also *Children's Book Insider* newsletter.

Books about children's books

There are many books written about children's books. Some offer practical advice on selecting books. Others provide invaluable research material for those pursuing degrees and diplomas in children's literature. Here is a small selection.

Best Book Guide for Children and Young Adults
Published by Booktrust
Paperback pub. annually
website www.booktrustchildrensbooks.org.uk

Booktrust's independent annual 'pick of the best' in children's paperback fiction published in the previous calendar year. It is designed to help parents, teachers, librarians, booksellers and anyone interested in children's reading to select books for children, from babies to teenagers. Printed in full colour, each book featured has a short review, colour coding to indicate reading age and interest level, and bibliographic information.

The Book about Books
by Chris Powling
Published by A&C Black
ISBN 9780713654790
Paperback 2001

Using interviews with authors and illustrators, this book asks: what makes a classic? How do you get a book published? How do writers come up with their ideas? A light-hearted and informative book for children, perfect as a resource for Children's Book Week.

The Cambridge Guide to Children's Books in English
Edited by Victor Watson
Published by Cambridge University Press
ISBN 9780521550642
Hardback 2001

Reference work providing a critical and appreciative overview of children's books written in English across the world. It includes the history of children's books from pre-Norman times to the present, taking on board current developments in publishing practices and in children's own reading. Entries on TV, comics, annuals and the growing range of media texts are included.

The Oxford Companion to Children's Literature
Edited by Humphrey Carpenter and Mari Prichard
Published by Oxford University Press
ISBN 9780198602286
Paperback 1999

An indispensable reference book for anyone interested in children's books. Over 900 biographical entries deal with authors, illustrators, printers, publishers, educationalists and others who have influenced the development of children's literature. Genres covered include myths and legends, fairy tales, adventure stories, school stories, fantasy, science fiction, crime and romance. This book is of particular interest to librarians, teachers, students, parents and collectors.

The Reading Bug – and how you can help your child to catch it
by Paul Jennings
Published by Penguin Books
ISBN 9780141318400
Paperback 2004

Paul Jennings is a well-known children's author. This book explains, in his unique humorous style, how readers can open up the world through a love of books. He cuts through the jargon and the controversies to reveal the simple truths, which should enable adults to infect children with the reading bug.

The Rough Guide to Books for Teenagers
Edited by Nicholas Tucker and Julia Eccleshare
Published by Rough Guides
ISBN 9781843531388
Paperback 2003, repr. 2005

A resource for teenagers who love reading, this *Guide* is also ideal for adults looking to recommend and buy books for teenagers. More than 200 books are reviewed – mainly fiction – ranging from classics such as *Wuthering Heights* to more controversial and best-selling titles such as Melvin Burgess's *Junk* and Judy Blume's *Forever*. Graphic novels and some narrative non-fiction are also included.

Sticks and Stones: The Troublesome Success of Children's Literature from Slovenly Peter to Harry Potter
by Jack Zipes
Published by Routledge
ISBN 9780415938808
Paperback 2002

Jack Zipes – translator of the Grimm tales, teacher, storyteller, and scholar – questions whether children ever really had a literature of their own. He sees children's literature in many ways as being the 'grown-ups' version' – a story about childhood that adults tell kids. He discusses children's literature from the 19th century moralism of Slovenly Peter (whose fingers get cut off) to the wildly successful *Harry Potter* books. Children's literature is a booming market but its success, this author says, is disguising its limitations. *Sticks and Stones* is a forthright and engaging book by someone who clearly cares deeply about what and how children read.

The Ultimate Book Guide

Edited by Daniel Hahn, Leonie Flynn and Susan Reuben
Published by A&C Black
ISBN 9781408104385
Paperback 2009

Over 600 entries covering the best books for children aged 8–12, from classics to newly released titles. Funny, friendly and frank recommendations written for children by their favourite and best-known authors including Anthony Horowitz, Jacqueline Wilson, Celia Rees, Darren Shan, David Almond and Dick King-Smith. Plus features on the most popular genres.

The Ultimate First Book Guide

by Leonie Flynn and Daniel Hahn
Published by A&C Black
Paperback 2008
ISBN 9780713673319

Comprehensive reference to help children aged 0–7 with their first steps into the world of books. Covers board books and novelty books, through to classic and contemporary picture books, chapter books and more challenging reads. It includes recommendations and features from top authors and experts in the field of children's books, including former Children's Laureate Michael Rosen, Tony Bradman, Malachy Doyle and Wendy Cooling. There are also special features on a variety of topics and themed lists, and a selection of cross-references to other titles children may enjoy.

The Ultimate Teen Book Guide

Edited by Daniel Hahn and Leonie Flynn
Published by A&C Black
Paperback 2010 (2nd edn)
ISBN 9781408104378

Listings of over 700 books that might interest teenage readers, recommended and reviewed by authors such as Melvin Burgess, Anthony Horowitz, Meg Cabot, Eoin Colfer and Philip Pullman. Reviews cover the classics to cult fiction, and graphic novels to bestsellers, and each is cross-referenced to other titles as suggestions of what to read next. The book also contains essays on areas of teenage writing including *Race in Young Adult Fiction* by Bali Rai and *Off the Rails* by Kevin Brooks. There are also the results of a national teen readers' poll, plus reviews from teen readers.

Societies, prizes and festivals

The Society of Authors

The Society of Authors is an independent trade union, representing writers' interests in all aspects of the writing profession, particularly publishing, but also broadcasting, television and film, theatre and translation.

Founded over 100 years ago, the Society now has more than 8,500 members. It has a professional staff, responsible to a Management Committee of 12 authors, and a Council (an advisory body meeting twice a year) consisting of 60 eminent writers.

Specialist groups

There are specialist groups within the Society to serve particular needs: the Broadcasting Group, the Children's Writers and Illustrators Group (see below), the Educational Writers Group and the Translators Association. There are also groups representing Scotland and the North of England.

The Children's Writers and Illustrators Group

The Children's Writers and Illustrators Group (CWIG) was formed in 1963. Besides furthering the interests of writers and artists and defending them whenever they are threatened, the Group seeks to bring members together professionally and socially, and in general to raise the status of children's books.

The Group has its own Executive Committee with representation on the Management Committee of the Society of Authors. Meetings and socials are held on a regular basis. Speakers have so far included publishers, librarians, booksellers and reviewers, and many distinguished writers and illustrators for children.

The annual subscription to the Society of Authors includes membership of all its groups. Membership of the CWIG is open to writers and illustrators who have had at least one

Membership

The Society of Authors
84 Drayton Gardens, London SW10 9SB
tel 020-7373 6642
email info@societyofauthors.org
website www.societyofauthors.org
General Secretary Nicola Solomon

Membership is open to authors who have had a full-length work published, broadcast or performed commercially in the UK and to those who have had a full-length work accepted for publication, but not yet published; and those who have had occasional items broadcast or performed, or translations, articles, illustrations or short stories published. The owner or administrator of a deceased author's copyrights can become a member on behalf of the author's estate. Writers who have been offered a contract seeking a contribution towards publication costs may apply for associate membership and have the contract vetted.

The annual subscription (which is tax deductible) is £90 (£85 by direct debit after the first year). There is a special rate for partners living at the same address. Authors under 35 not yet earning a significant income from writing, may pay a lower subscription of £64. Authors over 65 may pay at the reduced rate after their first year of membership.

Contact the Society for a membership booklet or visit the website for an application form.

book published by a reputable British publisher, five short stories or more than 20 minutes of material broadcast on national radio or television. Election is at the discretion of the Committee.

What the Society does for members

Through its permanent staff (including a solicitor), the Society is able to give its members a comprehensive personal and professional service covering the business aspects of authorship, including:

'It does no harm to repeat, as often as you can, "Without me the literary industry would not exist: the publishers, the agents, the sub-agents, the accountants, the libel lawyers, the departments of literature, the professors, the theses, the books of criticism, the reviewers, the book pages – all this vast and proliferating edifice is because of this small, patronised, put-down and underpaid person."' – *Doris Lessing*

• providing information about agents, publishers, and others concerned with the book trade, journalism, broadcasting and the performing arts;
• advising on negotiations, including the individual vetting of contracts, clause by clause, and assessing their terms both financial and otherwise;
• helping with members' queries, major or minor, over any aspect of the business of writing;
• taking up complaints on behalf of members on any issue concerned with the business of authorship;
• pursuing legal actions for breach of contract, copyright infringement, and the non-payment of royalties and fees, when the risk and cost preclude individual action by a member and issues of general concern to the profession are at stake;
• holding conferences, seminars, meetings and social occasions;
• producing a comprehensive range of publications, free of charge to members, including the Society's quarterly journal, *The Author*. *Quick Guides* cover many aspects of the profession such as: copyright, publishing contracts, libel, income tax, VAT, authors' agents, permissions, indexing and self-publishing. The Society also publishes occasional papers on subjects such as film agreements and packaged books.

The Society frequently secures improved conditions and better returns for members. It is common for members to report that, through the help and facilities offered, they have saved more, and sometimes substantially more, than their annual subscriptions (which are an allowable expense against income tax).

Further membership benefits

Members have access to:
• books, hotels and other products and services at special rates;
• free membership of the Authors' Licensing and Collecting Society (ALCS);
• a group Medical Insurance Scheme with BUPA;
• the Contingency Fund (which provides financial relief for authors or their dependents in sudden financial difficulties);
• the Pension Fund (which offers discretionary pensions to a number of members);
• membership of the Royal Over-Seas League at a discount.

What the Society does for authors

The Society lobbies Members of Parliament, Ministers and Government Departments on all issues of concern to writers, litigates in matters of importance to authors and campaigns for better terms for writers.

The Society is recognised by the BBC for the purpose of negotiating rates for writers' contributions to radio drama, as well as for the broadcasting of published material. It was instrumental in setting up the ALCS (see page 276), which collects and distributes fees from reprography and other methods whereby copyright material is exploited without direct payment to the originators.

The Society keeps in close touch with the Association of Authors' Agents, the Booksellers Association and Publishers Association, the British Council, the Department for Culture, Media and Sport, the National Union of Journalists and the Writers' Guild of Great Britain. It is a member of the European Writers Council and the British Copyright Council.

Awards

The Society of Authors administers:

• the Authors' Foundation and Kathleen Blundell Trust, which give grants to assist authors working on their next book;

• the Francis Head Bequest for assisting authors who, through physical mishap, are temporarily unable to maintain themselves or their families;

• Travelling Scholarships which give honorary awards;

• three prizes for novels: the Betty Trask Awards, the Encore Award and the McKitterick Prize;

• the Somerset Maugham Awards for a full-length published work;

• two poetry awards: the Eric Gregory Awards and the Cholmondeley Awards;

• the Tom-Gallon Award for short story writers;

• two radio drama prizes: the Richard Imison Award for a writer new to radio drama and the Peter Tinniswood Award;

• awards for translations from Arabic, Dutch/Flemish, French, German, Greek, Italian, Portuguese, Spanish and Swedish into English;

• educational book awards.

Societies, prizes and festivals

Society of Children's Book Writers & Illustrators

The Society of Children's Book Writers & Illustrators (SCBWI) is the only international professional organisation dedicated to serving people who share a vital interest in children's literature, magazines, film, television and/or multimedia.

Whether you're a professional children's writer or illustrator, or a newcomer to the field, the SCBWI has plenty to offer you, from local to national to international events, from advice on getting your first deal to help in navigating your career as a writer or illustrator. Established in 1971, SCBWI now has over 22,000 members in 70 regional chapters worldwide. Membership benefits include professional development and networking opportunities, marketing information, events, publications, online profiles, grants and awards.

What does SCBWI British Isles do?

SCBWI British Isles is a dynamic and friendly chapter of 500 members, which aims to support aspiring and published writers and illustrators and provide opportunities for them to network, hone their craft and develop their careers. Events include an annual two-day conference, writing retreats, an annual Agents' Party, the Professional series (six talks a year in London aimed at professional development on a variety of topics), the Illustrators' series (Saturday workshops with a hands-on craft element), sketch and scrawl crawls, masterclasses and PULSE events (SCBWI Pulse is a new initiative providing workshops, lectures and professional development for published children's book writers and illustrators). A network of regional coordinators run local critique groups and organise workshops and speaker and social events across the country.

What SCBWI does for its members

• SCBWI is a professional guild. It speaks as a consolidated global voice for professional children's writers and illustrators. In recent years, the SCBWI has successfully lobbied for such issues as new copyright legislation, equitable treatment of authors and artists, and fair contract terms;

• It keeps members up to date with industry developments through the SCBWI PULSE series of events, with opportunities to learn more about the 'business' of writing and illustrating, and network with librarians and booksellers at exclusive events;

• It offers members invaluable exposure to editors, art directors and agents through one-to-one manuscript or portfolio reviews at the annual conference and retreat, the members-only Agents' Party, and the Slush Pile Challenge and biennial SCBWI Undiscovered Voices (www.undiscoveredvoices.com) competitions;

• It supports professional development for members to hone their craft through the Masterclass series, conference workshops and highly successful critique groups;

• It gives members increased visibility online with a free profile on the main SCBWI and the social networking NING websites, both of which are often a point of call for agents and editors;

• It provides support and a network of like-minded people, helping to answer members' queries through a variety of online resources, including an email forum and social networking site;

• It facilitates networking opportunities with professionals worldwide;

• Publications include the *Bulletin*, the SCBWI international magazine, *Words & Pictures* newsletter blog and resources including the annual publications and market guide.

Further information

Society of Children's Book Writers & Illustrators (SCBWI)
website www.scbwi.org, www.britishscbwi.org
Regional Advisor (Chair) Natascha Biebow
email ra@britishscbwi.org
Membership Coordinator Sue Hyams
email membership@britishscbwi.org
Membership £50 p.a.

The SCBWI administers a number of awards and grants:

• The **Golden and Crystal Kite Awards** for the most outstanding books published by SCBWI members each year, voted for by SCBWI peers;

• The **Sid Fleischman Humour Award** is presented to authors whose work exemplifies the excellence of writing in the genre of humour;

• Magazine Merit Awards are presented for outstanding original magazine work for young people published during that year;

• The **Sue Alexander Most Promising New Work Award** is presented to the best manuscript submitted for individual critique at the LA Conference;

• The **Portfolio Award** is presented to the best art portfolio on view at the Juried Portfolio Display at the LA conference;

• Student Illustrator Scholarship – four conference scholarships for full-time graduate and undergraduate students of children's book illustration;

• Work-in-progress Grants – several grants are available each year.

Societies, prizes and festivals

Booktrust

Booktrust is the largest literature organisation in the UK.

Booktrust is an independent charity dedicated to encouraging people of all ages and cultures to engage with books. It is supported by Arts Council England and the Department for Education, and has a broad range of activities aimed at promoting books and reading.

Booktrust administers a number of literary prizes, including the Orange Prize for Fiction and the BBC National Short Story Award for adults, and the Roald Dahl Funny Prize for children, as well as promoting books and reading for all ages through various campaigns.

Further information

Booktrust
Book House, 45 East Hill, London SW18 2QZ
tel 020-8516 2977 *fax* 020-8516 2978
email query@booktrust.org.uk
website www.booktrustchildrensbooks.org.uk,
www.booktrust.org.uk, www.bookstart.org.uk,
www.booktime.org.uk, www.bookedup.org.uk,
www.childrenslaureate.org.uk

Booktrust and children

• The Booktrust children's books website (www.booktrustchildrensbooks.org.uk) has a searchable database of more than 2,000 book reviews, resources for teachers, an illustrators' gallery featuring the best artists currently working in children's books, interviews with authors and illustrators and news about children's book prizes and events happening throughout the UK.

• Booktrust coordinates four national bookgifting programmes. Bookstart gives free advice and books to parents/carers attending their baby's health checks (see *Books for babies*, page 105). Booktime promotes reading for pleasure by giving a book pack to children across the UK shortly after they start school. Booked Up encourages children to read for pleasure by providing each Year 7 child with a free book from a selection. The Letterbox Club provides a parcel of books and other materials for looked after children aged 7–11, every month for six months.

• The best books of the year are chosen for inclusion in Booktrust's annual *Best Book Guide*, which is available as a free download from the website.

• Booktrust runs the Roald Dahl Funny Prize (see page 385), which aims to celebrate, publicise and honour the funniest books of the year. This is part of a wider campaign to promote and draw attention to humour in children's literature.

• With Bookstart, Booktrust hopes to promote and make the exciting range of books being published today for babies, toddlers and preschool children accessible to as wide an audience as possible.

• Booktrust runs the Everybody Writes programme, which aims to ensure that, during their life at school, every child encounters opportunities to work with professional writers who inspire them creatively.

• Booktrust administers the Children's Laureate (Julia Donaldson 2011–13); see page 384.

• Booktrust administers Children's Book Week (see page 393).

• Booktrust administers the Blue Peter Children's Book Awards (see page 383).

Seven Stories, the Centre for Children's Books

At Seven Stories the rich heritage of British children's books is collected, explored and celebrated.

sevenstories
the centre for children's books

Once upon a time an idea was born on the banks of the Tyne to create a national home for children's literature – a place where the original work of authors and illustrators could be collected, treasured and celebrated. After ten years of pioneering work by founding directors Elizabeth Hammill and Mary Briggs, that dream became a reality. In August 2005 Seven Stories, the Centre for Children's Books, opened in an award-winning converted seven storey Victorian granary in the Ouseburn Valley, a stone's throw from Newcastle's vibrant quayside.

The collection

At the heart of Seven Stories is a unique and growing collection of manuscripts, artwork and other pre-publication materials. These treasures record the creative process involved in making a children's book and provide illuminating insights into the working lives of modern authors and illustrators. The collection focuses on work created in modern Britain. It already contains thousands of items by authors such as Peter Dickinson, Berlie Doherty, Jan Mark, Philip Pullman, Michael Rosen, Robert Westall and Ursula Moray Williams; illustrators like Edward Ardizzone, Faith Jaques, Harold Jones, Anthony Maitland, Pat Hutchins, Helen Cooper, Jan Ormerod and Jane Ray; and editors and other practitioners such as Kaye Webb. Many more bodies of work are pledged. A catalogue of the collection is available via the Seven Stories website.

Exhibitions

A celebration of creativity underpins the Seven Stories project: its collection documents the creative act, and its exhibitions and programmes interpret this original material in unconventional but meaningful ways. The aim is to cultivate an appreciation of books and their making, and inspire creativity in its audience.

Seven Stories, known during its development as the Centre for the Children's Book, has been mounting exhibitions since 1998 – first in borrowed venues and now in its own home. Here it provides the only exhibition space in the UK wholly dedicated to showcasing the incomparable legacy of British writing and illustrating for children. Its current exhibitions are *There's Nuffin Like a Puffin!* and *Through the Magic Mirror, the World of Anthony Browne*. Seven Stories has been fulfilling its national remit by touring exhibitions since 2003. These include *What's in the Book?*, the 17 million books of Jane and Allan Ahlberg, *Miffy*, and *Snozzcumbers and Frobscottle*.

Throughout its seven storeys – from the Creation Station to the bookshop and café to the Artist's Attic, visitors of all ages are invited to engage in a unique, interactive exploration

Societies, prizes and festivals

of creativity, literature and art. In this ever changing literary playground and landscape for the imagination, they can become writers, artists, explorers, designers, storytellers, readers or collectors, in the company of storytellers, authors, illustrators and Seven Stories' own facilitators and education team.

Seven Stories aims to place children, young people and their books at the heart of the UK's national literary culture. An independent educational charity, it is committed to access for all and has initiated several innovative participation projects. The centre has developed close links with the Newcastle and regional community, and is currently working with the Children's Literature Unit in the Department of English Literature, Language and Linguistics at Newcastle University to develop the Seven Stories collection and maximise its potential for research and display.

In Seven Stories, Britain has found a long needed home dedicated to the celebration of children's literature and was the 2010 winner of the Eleanor Farjeon Award. Supported by Arts Council England and Newcastle City Council.

Further information

Seven Stories, the Centre for Children's Books
30 Lime Street, Ouseburn Valley,
Newcastle upon Tyne NE1 2PQ
tel (0845) 271 0777 *fax* 0191-261 1931
email info@sevenstories.org.uk
website www.sevenstories.org.uk
Registered Charity No 1056812.
Public opening hours Mon–Sat 10am–5pm,
Sun 10am–4pm
Admission charges Adult (17 and over) £6.50;
child/concession £5.50; family £19. Annual passes available

The Children's Book Circle

Rachel Boden of the Children's Book Circle introduces the organisation.

Are you passionate about children's books? The Children's Book Circle (CBC) provides an exciting forum in which you can develop your interest, build your contacts and enrich your engagement with the children's book world. The CBC's membership consists of publishers, librarians, authors, illustrators, agents, teachers, booksellers and anyone with an active interest in the field. If you're an aspiring author or illustrator, you'll already know how important it is to become as knowledgeable as possible about the current marketplace for children's books. The CBC is the ideal place to broaden your knowledge. It's not the place to try for a publishing contract, but it will give you the forum to take part in discussions with people from the industry in an informal and enjoyable context.

> ### Further information
>
> **The Children's Book Circle**
> *email* childrensbookcircle@googlemail.com
> *website* www.childrensbookcircle.org.uk
> *Membership* £20 p.a.

The CBC meets regularly at venues in London. At our speaker meetings, invited guest speakers debate key issues relating to the world of children's books. Recent events have included a discussion on how to get boys reading, a debate on what the future of children's publishing will look like, and a Q&A session on how to make your mark in children's books.

Members also have the opportunity to attend the annual Eleanor Farjeon award ceremony and reception, and the Patrick Hardy Lecture. The Eleanor Farjeon Award recognises an outstanding contribution to the world of children's books, either by an individual or an organisation, and is voted for by CBC members. Recent winners include Malorie Blackman, Chris Brown, Jane Nissen and Wendy Cooling. The Patrick Hardy lecture is delivered each year by a distinguished speaker on a relevant topic of their choice. Past speakers have included Michael Rosen, Jeremy Strong, Meg Rosoff, Verna Wilkins (founder of Tamarind Books) and Anthony Horowitz.

Another highlight of the CBC calendar is the summer quiz, which offers members a chance to show off their children's book knowledge.

Societies, prizes and festivals

Federation of Children's Book Groups

The aim of the Federation of Children's Book Groups is to bring children and books together and have fun. Sinead Kromer of the FCBG introduces the organisation.

The Federation of Children's Book Groups (now a registered charity) was formed in 1968 by Anne Wood to co-ordinate the work of the many different children's book groups that were coming together across the country. Over the next eight years the organisation expanded and a system of regionalisation was introduced to link groups together in each part of the country.

In 1976 National Tell-A-Story-Week was introduced and became an immediate success. This has now grown into National Share-A-Story-Month and takes place each May. It enables groups to focus on the power of story and to hold events which celebrate this. Each year the National Launch is held in a different part of the country.

In 1977, the first Federation anthology was published, and since then there have been nine more titles. Plans are under way to consider a new anthology. We also regularly produce new booklists on a variety of topics, which are available free of charge to anyone interested.

In 1981 the Federation inaugurated one of its most successful ventures – the Children's Book Award, a prize given for the best book of the year judged entirely by children. The first winner was *Mr Magnolia* by Quentin Blake and the present holder is Suzanne Collins for H*unger Games*. The Award for 2011 was presented at the Botanical Gardens in Birmingham in June. Children from all over the country came together to celebrate all that is best in children's books. For the past ten years the Award has been supported by Red House and their financial commitment has enabled the Award to go from strength to strength, providing opportunities for children all over the country, who are not members of the Federation, to become involved in the final round of judging.

In 2010 the Federation began National Non-Fiction Day to celebrate the quality and variety of information books available for children. It will take place on the first Thursday of each November.

Each year the Federation invites a Group to organise the Annual Conference. This ensures that the Conference moves around the country and that its organisation involves many different members. Venues have included Edinburgh, Bradford, Plymouth, Stratford-upon-Avon, Brighton and Cirencester. The 2011 conference was held at Worth School, south of London. Over 200 delegates attended during the weekend and listened to speakers as diverse as David Almond, Steve Cole and Julia Hearn.

Further information

Federation of Children's Book Groups
tel 0113-2588910
email info@fcbg.org.uk
website www.fcbg.org.uk
Registered Charity No 268289

The Children's Book Groups

So where are the book groups and who are its members? Federation Groups exist in many parts of England, Scotland and Wales; from Plymouth to Dundee; from Grantham to St

David's and from Harrogate to Lewes. Membership of a book group is made up of parents, carers, teachers, librarians and, in some cases, children's authors and illustrators. The passion of Federation members for bringing books and children together is the reason that the organisation has continued and developed over the past 40 years.

Each of the member groups is self supporting in terms of money and organisation, but has the advantage of a parent body to support and encourage its activities. These are as varied and diverse as the book groups themselves, serving their own community's needs. They might include author visits, children's events and celebrations. But above all the Federation is an organisation that is passionate about children's books, bringing together ordinary book-loving families, empowering parents, grandparents, carers and their children to become enthusiastic and excited about all kinds of good books. Local book groups encourage everyone to talk about books and reading, and thus enthusiasm for good children's literature is passed on at all levels.

Membership of the Federation is also available to those who live too far away to join a local book group. Individuals can join, as can organisations involved with children and reading.

Societies, prizes and festivals

Societies, associations and organisations

The societies and associations listed here include appreciation societies devoted to specific authors (see also online resources on page 348), professional bodies and national institutions. Some also offer prizes and awards (see page 382).

Academi – see Literature Wales

AccessArt
6 West Street, Comberton, Cambridge CB23 7DS
tel (01223) 262134
email info@accessart.org.uk
website www.accessart.org.uk

A fun, creative and dynamic learning tool for pupils across all the key stages, and for home-users of all ages. AccessArt gives users access to arts educational activities that would otherwise reach only a small audience. The website allows access to:

• a series of visually exciting and innovative 'online workshops' which condense and articulate artist-led teaching which has taken place in schools, museums and galleries; and
• teachers notes and learners' printouts. Each online workshop is accompanied by explanatory notes for the educators and printable resource material which can be used directly by the learner.

Action for Children's Arts
PO Box 2620, Purley CR8 3WA
email admin@childrensarts.org.uk
website www.childrensarts.org.uk
Membership £30 p.a. individuals; see website for organisation rates

A membership charity organisation that values children, childhood and the arts. It embraces the UN Convention on the Rights of the Child:

• by campaigning for the right of all children in the UK to experience high-quality arts experiences as an integral part of their childhood;
• by connecting people within and across the cultural and education sectors, across art-forms and across the regions and nations of the UK;
• by celebrating achievement, dedication and best practice in artistic activity for and with children. The J.M. Barrie Award is given annually to a children's arts practitioner or organisation whose work, in the view of ACA, will stand the test of time. Winners: Dick King-Smith (2005), Judith Kerr (2006), Oliver Postgate and Peter Firmin (2007), Quentin Blake (2008), Roger McGough (2009), Shirley Hughes (2010). Founded 1998.

Louisa May Alcott Memorial Association
Orchard House, 399 Lexington Road, PO Box 343, Concord, MA 01742–0343, USA
tel 978-369-4118 *fax* 978-369-1367
email info@louisamayalcott.org
website www.louisamayalcott.org

A private, not-for-profit association that provides the financial and human resources required to conduct public tours, special programmes, exhibits and the curatorial work which continue the tradition of the Alcotts, a unique 19th century family. Founded 1911.

American Society of Composers, Authors and Publishers
One Lincoln Plaza, New York, NY 10023, USA
tel 212-621-6000 *fax* 212-621-8453
London contact: 8 Cork Street, London W1S 3LT
website www.ascap.com
President & Chairman Paul Williams

Amgueddfa Cymru – National Museum Wales
Cathays Park, Cardiff CF10 3NP
tel 029-2039 7951 *fax* 029-2057 3321
website www.museumwales.ac.uk

Arab Children's Book Publisher's Forum
website www.acbpub.org

Aims to improve the level and quality of children's book publishing and reinforce the mission of Arab children's book publishers.

Arts Council England
14 Great Peter Street, London SW1P 3NQ
tel (0845) 300 6200 *fax* (0161) 934 4426
email enquiries@artscouncil.org.uk
website www.artscouncil.org.uk
Chief Executive Alan Davey

The national development agency for the arts in England, distributing public money from Government and the National Lottery. Arts Council England's main funding programme is Grants for the Arts, which is open to individuals, arts organisations, national touring companies and other people who use the arts in their work.

Arts Council England has one national and 9 regional offices. It has a single contact telephone and email address for general enquiries (see above). Founded 1946.

East
Eden House, 48–49 Bateman Street, Cambridge CB2 1LR

tel (0845) 300 6200 *textphone* (01223) 306893
fax (0870) 242 1271

East Midlands
St Nicholas Court, 25–27 Castle Gate, Nottingham
NG1 7AR
tel (0845) 300 6200 *fax* 0115-950 2467

London
14 Great Peter Street, London SW1P 3NQ
tel (0845) 300 6200 *textphone* 020-7973 6564
fax 020-7608 4100

North East
Central Square, Forth Street, Newcastle upon Tyne
NE1 3PJ
tel (0845) 300 6200 *textphone* 0191-255 8585
fax 0191-230 1020

North West
The Hive, 49 Lever Street, Manchester M1 1FN
tel (0845) 300 6200 *textphone* 020-7973 6564
fax (0161) 934 4426

South East
Sovereign House, Church Street, Brighton BN1 1RA
tel (0845) 300 6200 *textphone* (01273) 710659
fax (0870) 2421257

South West
Senate Court, Southernhay Gardens, Exeter EX1 1UG
tel (0845) 300 6200 *textphone* (01392) 433503
fax (01392) 98546

West Midlands
82 Granville Street, Birmingham B1 2LH
tel (0845) 300 6200 *textphone* 0121-643 2815
fax 0121-643 7239

Yorkshire
21 Bond Street, Dewsbury, West Yorkshire
WF13 1AX
tel (0845) 300 6200 *textphone* (01924) 438585
fax (01924) 38585

Arts Council/An Chomhairle Ealaíon

70 Merrion Square, Dublin 2, Republic of Ireland
tel (01) 618 0200 *fax* (01) 6761302
email stephanie.ocallaghan@artscouncil.ie
website www.artscouncil.ie
Arts Programme Director John O'Kane

The national development agency for the arts in
Ireland. Founded 1951.

Arts Council of Northern Ireland

77 Malone Road, Belfast BT9 6AQ
tel 028-9038 5200 *fax* 028-90661715
email info@artscouncil-ni.org
website www.artscouncil-ni.org
Chief Executive Roisín McDonough, *Literature Officer*
Damian Smyth, *Visual Arts Officer* Suzanne Lyle

Promotes and encourages the arts throughout
Northern Ireland. Artists in drama, dance, music and

jazz, literature, the visual arts, traditional arts and
community arts can apply for support for specific
schemes and projects. The value of the grant will be
set according to the aims of the application.
Applicants must have contributed regularly to the
artistic activities of the community, and been resident
for at least one year in Northern Ireland.

Arts Council of Wales

Bute Place, Cardiff CF10 5AL
tel 0845-873 4900 *fax* 029-2044 1400
email info@artswales.org.uk
website www.artswales.org.uk
Chairman Prof. Dai Smith, *Arts Director* David
Alston, *Head of Communications* Betsan Moses, *Wales
Arts International Director* Eluned Haf

National organisation with specific responsibility for
the funding and development of the arts in Wales.
Arts Council of Wales receives funding from the
National Assembly for Wales and also distributes
National Lottery funds for the arts in Wales. From
these resources, Arts Council of Wales makes grants
to support arts activities and facilities. Some of the
funds are allocated in the form of annual revenue
grants to full-time arts organisations such as
Literature Wales. It also operates schemes which
provide financial and other forms of support for
individual artists or projects. Arts Council of Wales
undertakes this work in both the English and Welsh
languages. Wales Arts International is the unique
partnership between the Arts Council of Wales and
British Council Wales, which works to promote
knowledge about contemporary arts and culture from
Wales and encourages international exchange and
collaboration.

North Wales Regional Office
36 Princes Drive, Colwyn Bay LL29 8LA
tel (01492) 533440 *minicom* (01492) 532288
fax (01492) 533677

Mid and West Wales Regional Office
6 Gardd Llydaw, Jackson Lane, Carmarthen
SA31 1QD
tel (01267) 234248 *minicom* (01267) 223496
fax (01267) 233084

South Wales Office
Bute Place, Cardiff CF10 5AL
tel 0845-873 4900 *fax* 029-2044 1400

Association for Library Service to Children

American Library Association, 50 East Huron,
Chicago, IL 60611–2795, USA
tel 800-545-2433 ext. 2163 *fax* 312-280-5271
email alsc@ala.org
website www.ala.org/alsc

Develops and supports the profession of children's
librarianship by enabling and encouraging its

Societies, prizes and festivals

practitioners to provide the best library service to US children.

Association for Scottish Literary Studies (ASLS)

c/o Dept of Scottish Literature, 7 University Gardens, University of Glasgow G12 8QH
tel 0141-330 5309
email office@asls.org.uk
website www.asls.org.uk
Hon. President Ian Brown, *Hon. Secretary* Lorna Borrowman Smith, *Publishing Manager* Duncan Jones
Membership £45 p.a. individuals, £10 UK students, £75 corporate

Promotes the study, teaching and writing of Scottish literature and furthers the study of the languages of Scotland. Publishes annually an edited text of Scottish literature, an anthology of new Scottish writing, a series of academic journals and a newsletter (2 p.a.). Also publishes *Scotnotes* (comprehensive study guides to major Scottish writers), literary texts and commentary CDs designed to assist the classroom teacher, and a series of occasional papers. Organises 3 conferences a year. Founded 1970.

Association of American Publishers Inc.

71 Fifth Avenue, New York, NY 10003, USA
tel 212-255-0200 *fax* 212-255-7007
email jplatt@publishers.org
website www.publishers.org
President & Ceo Tom Allen

Founded 1970.

The Association of Authors' Agents

10 Iron Bridge House, Bridge Approach, London NW1 8BD
tel 020-7722 7674
website www.agentsassoc.co.uk
President Anthony Goff, *Secretary* Olivia Guest

Maintains a code of professional practice to which all members commit themselves; holds regular meetings to discuss matters of common professional interest; provides a vehicle for representing the view of authors' agents in discussion of matters of common interest with other professional bodies. Founded 1974.

Association of Authors' Representatives Inc.

676ᴀ, Suite 312 9th Avenue, New York, NY 10036, USA
tel 212-840-5770
email administrator@aaronline.org
website www.aaronline.org

Founded 1991.

Association of Booksellers for Children

ABC National Office, 6538 Collin Avenue, Suite 168, Miami Beach, FL 33141

tel 617-390-7759 *fax* 617-344-0540
Executive Director Kristen McLean

A national membership association that offers a support network for professional independent children's booksellers who share the goal of encouraging quality and service within the children's book industry.

Association of Canadian Publishers

174 Spadina Avenue, Suite 306, Toronto, Ontario M5T 2C2, Canada
tel 416-487-6116 *fax* 416-487-8815
email admin@canbook.org
website www.publishers.ca
Executive Director Carolyn Wood

Founded 1976; formerly Independent Publishers Association, 1971.

The Association of Illustrators

2nd Floor, Back Building, 150 Curtain Road, London EC2A 3AT
tel 020-7613 4328 *fax* 020-7613 4417
email info@theaoi.com
website www.theaoi.com
Contact Membership Coordinator

Exists to support illustrators, promote illustration and encourage professional standards in the industry. Publishes *Varoom* magazine (3 p.a.); presents an annual programme of events; annual competition, exhibition and tour of Images – the Best of British Contemporary Illustration (call for entries: July/August). Founded 1973.

Australia Council

PO Box 788, Strawberry Hills, NSW 2012, Australia
located at 372 Elizabeth Street, Surry Hills, NSW 2010, Australia
tel (02) 9215 9000 *fax* (02) 9215 9111
email mail@australiacouncil.gov.au
website www.australiacouncil.gov.au
Ceo Kathy Keele

Provides a broad range of support for the arts in Australia, embracing music, theatre, literature, visual arts, crafts, Aboriginal arts, community and new media arts. It has 7 Boards: Literature, Visual Arts, Music, Theatre, Dance, Major Performing Arts, as well as the Aboriginal and Torres Strait Islander Arts Board.

The Literature Board's chief objective is to support the writing of all forms of creative literature – novels, short stories, poetry, plays and literary non-fiction. It also assists with the publication of literary magazines, has a book publishing subsidies programme, and initiates and supports projects of many kinds designed to promote Australian literature both within Australia and abroad.

Australian Copyright Council

PO Box 1986, Strawberry Hills, NSW 2012, Australia
tel (02) 8815 9777 *fax* (02) 8815 9799

email info@copyright.org.au
website www.copyright.org.au

An independent non-profit organisation which aims to assist creators and other copyright owners to exercise their rights effectively; raise awareness in the community generally about the importance of copyright; research and identify areas of copyright law which are inadequate or unfair; seek changes to law and practice to enhance the effectiveness and fairness of copyright; foster cooperation amongst bodies representing creators and owners of copyright.

The Council comprises 23 organisations or associations of owners and creators of copyright material, including the Australian Society of Authors, the Australian Writers Guild and the Australian Book Publishers Association. Founded 1968.

Australian Publishers Association (APA)

60–89 Jones Street, Ultimo, NSW 2007, Australia
tel (02) 9281 9788 *fax* (02) 9281 1073
email apa@publishers.asn.au
website www.publishers.asn.au
Ceo Maree McCaskill

Australian Writers' Guild (AWG)

5 Blackfriars Street, Chippendale, NSW 2008
tel (02) 9319 0339 *fax* (02) 9319 0141
email admin@awg.com.au
website www.awg.com.au
Executive Director Jacqueline Woodman

The professional association for all performance writers, i.e. writers for film, TV, radio, theatre, video and new media. The AWG is recognised throughout the industry in Australia as being the voice of performance writers. Established 1962.

Authors' Licensing and Collecting Society Ltd – see page 276

Barnardo's Image Archive

Tanners Lane, Barkingside, Ilford, Essex IG6 1QG
tel 020-8498 7345 *fax* 020-8550 0429
email stephen.pover@barnados.org.uk
website www.barnardos.org.uk

Extensive collection of b&w and colour images dating from 1874 to the present day covering social history with the emphasis on children and child care. Also 300 films dating from 1905. Founded 1872.

Enid Blyton Society

93 Milford Hill, Salisbury, Wilts. SP1 2QL
tel (01722) 331937
email tony@enidblytonsociety.co.uk
website www.enidblytonsociety.co.uk
Contact Anita Bensoussane

To provide a focal point for collectors and enthusiasts of Enid Blyton through its magazine *The Enid Blyton*

Society Journal (3 p.a.) and the annual Society Day which attracts in excess of a hundred members each year. Founded 1995.

The Booksellers Association of the United Kingdom & Ireland Ltd

272 Vauxhall Bridge Road, London SW1V 1BA
tel 020-7802 0802 *fax* 020-7802 0803
email mail@booksellers.org.uk
website www.booksellers.org.uk
Chief Executive T.E. Godfray

Founded 1895.

Booktrust – see page 358

The British Council

London office 10 Spring Gardens, London SW1A 2BN
tel 020-389 4385 *fax* 020-7839 6347
email general.enquiries@britishcouncil.org
Headquarters Bridgewater House, 58 Whitworth Street, Manchester M1 6BB
tel 0161-957 7000
website www.britishcouncil.org,
www.britishcouncil.org/arts,
www.contemporarywriters.com,
www.encompassculture.com
Chair The Rt Hon. Lord Kinnock, *Chief Executive* Martin Davidson, *Director of Arts* Graham Sheffield

The British Council connects people worldwide with learning opportunities and creative ideas from the UK, and builds lasting relationships between the UK and other countries. It has 6,000 staff in offices, teaching centres, libraries, and information and resource centres in the UK and 110 countries and territories worldwide.

Working in close collaboration with book trade associations, British Council offices participate in major international book fairs.

The British Council is an authority on teaching English as a second or foreign language. It also gives advice and information on curriculum, methodology, materials and testing.

The British Council promotes British literature overseas through writers' tours, academic visits, workshops, conferences, seminars and exhibitions. It publishes *New Writing*, an annual anthology of unpublished short stories, poems and extracts from works in progress and essays; and a series of literary bibliographies, including *Tbooks: UK Teenage Literature*, *Crime Literature* and *Reading in the City*. Through its Literature Department, the British Council provides an overview of UK literature and a range of online resources (see above). This includes a literary portal, information about UK and Commonwealth authors, translation workshops and a worldwide online book club and reading group for adults, teenagers and children with over 10,000 books plus reading group advice.

The Visual Arts Department, part of the British Council's Arts Group, develops and enlarges overseas knowledge and appreciation of British achievement in the fields of painting, sculpture, printmaking, design, photography, the crafts and architecture, working closely with the British Council's overseas offices and with professional colleagues in the UK and abroad.

Further information about the work of the British Council is available from Arts Press at the above address, or from British Council offices overseas by emailing arts@britishcouncil.org.

British Museum

Great Russell Street, London WC1B 3DG
tel 020-7323 8000/8299
email information@thebritishmuseum.ac.uk
website www.thebritishmuseum.org

Young Explorers

website www.britishmuseum.org/explore/young_explorers1.aspx

An online opportunity for children to discover world cultures using games and activities.

Randolph Caldecott Society

Secretary Kenn Oultram, Blue Grass Cottage, Clatterwick Lane, Little Leigh, Northwich, Cheshire CW8 4RJ
tel (01606) 891303 (office), 781731 (evening)
website www.randolphcaldecott.org.uk
Membership £12.50 p.a. individual, £17.50 p.a. families/corporate

Aims to encourage an interest in the life and works of Randolph Caldecott (1846–86), the Victorian artist, illustrator and sculptor. Caldecott produced 16 picture books, each based on the words of a nursery rhyme or well-known nonsense verse. Meetings held in Chester. Liaises with the American Caldecott Society. Founded 1983.

Canadian Authors Association

PO Box 851, Stn Main Orillia, Ontario L3V 6KS, Canada
tel 705-653-0323, 866-216-6222 (toll free)
email admin@canauthors.org
website www.canauthors.org
President Anthony Dalton, *Executive Director* Anita Purcell

The Canadian Children's Book Centre (CCBC)

Suite 101, 40 Orchard View Blvd, Toronto, Ontario M4R 1B9, Canada
tel 416-975-0010 *fax* 416-975-8970
email info@bookcentre.ca
website www.bookcentre.ca

A national, not-for-profit organisation dedicated to encouraging, promoting and supporting the reading, writing and illustrating of Canadian books for young readers. CCBC programmes and publications offer a wide range of resources to anyone who is interested

in quality reading for children and teens. Founded 1976.

Canadian Publishers' Council

250 Merton Street, Suite 203, Toronto, Ontario M4S 1B1, Canada
tel 416-322-7011 *fax* 416-322-6999
website www.pubcouncil.ca
Executive Director Jacqueline Hushion

CANSCAIP (Canadian Society of Children's Authors, Illustrators & Performers)

40 Orchard View Boulevard, Suite 104, Toronto, Ontario M4R 1B9, Canada
tel 416-515-1559
email office@canscaip.org
website www.canscaip.org
Administrative Director Lena Coakley
Membership $85 p.a. Full member (published authors and illustrators), $45 Friend

A non-profit support network for children's artists. Promotes children's literature and performances through Canada and internationally. Founded 1977.

Careers Writers' Association

Membership Secretary Ann Goodman, 16 Caewal Road, Llandaff, Cardiff CF5 2BT
tel 029-2056 3444 *fax* 029-2065 8190
email gm.sharp@virgin.net
website www.careerswriting.co.uk
Membership £40 p.a.

Society for established writers on the interrelated topics of education, training and careers. Holds occasional meetings on subjects of interest to members, and circulates details of members to information providers. Founded 1979.

The Lewis Carroll Society

Secretary Bob Cole, 50 Lauderdale Mansions, Lauderdale Road, London W9 1NE
email markrichards@aznet.co.uk
website www.lewiscarrollsociety.org.uk
Membership £20 p.a. UK, £23 Europe, £26 elsewhere; special rates for institutions

Aims to promote interest in the life and works of Lewis Carroll (Revd Charles Lutwidge Dodgson) (1832–98) and to encourage research. Activities include regular meetings, exhibitions, and a publishing programme that includes the first annotated, unexpurgated edition of his diaries in 9 volumes, the Society's journal *The Carrollian* (2 p.a.), a newsletter, *Bandersnatch* (quarterly) and the *Lewis Carroll Review* (occasional). Founded 1969.

Lewis Carroll Society (Daresbury)

Secretary Kenn Oultram, Blue Grass Cottage, Clatterwick Lane, Little Leigh, Northwich, Cheshire CW8 4RJ

tel (01606) 891303 (office), 781731 (evening)
Membership £7 p.a., £10 families/corporate

Aims to encourage an interest in the life and works of Lewis Carroll (1832–98), author of *Alice's Adventures*. Meetings take place at Carroll's birth village (Daresbury, Cheshire). Founded 1970.

Lewis Carroll Society of North America (LCSNA)

11935 Beltsville Drive, Beltsville, MD 20705, USA
email wrabbit@idiom.com
website www.lewiscarroll.org
President Mark Burstein
Membership $35 p.a. USA; $50 elsewhere

An organisation of Carroll admirers of all ages and interests and a centre for Carroll studies. It is dedicated to furthering Carroll studies, increasing accessibility of research material, and maintaining public awareness of Carroll's contributions to society. The Society has a worldwide membership and meets twice a year. The Society maintains an active publication programme and members receive copies of the Society's magazine *Knight Letter*. An interest in Lewis Carroll, a simple love for Alice (or the Snark for that matter) qualifies for membership. Founded in 1974.

The Center for Children's Books (CCB)

Graduate School of Library and Information Science, University of Illinois at Urbana–Champaign, 501 East Daniel Street, Champaign, IL 61820, USA
tel 217-244-9331 *fax* 217-333-5603
email ccb@uiuc.edu
website http://ccb.lis.illinois.edu

CCB houses a non-circulating collection of more than 16,000 recent and historically significant trade books for children, plus review copies of nearly all trade books published in the USA in the current year. There are over 1,000 professional and reference books on the history and criticism of literature for youth, literature-based library and classroom programming, and storytelling. Although the collection is non-circulating, it is available for examination by scholars, teachers, librarians, students, and other educators.

Centre for Literacy in Primary Education (CLPE)

Webber Street, London SE1 8QW
tel 020-7401 3382/3 *fax* 020-7928 4624
email info@clpe.co.uk
website www.clpe.co.uk

A centre for children's language, literacy, literature and educational assessment which provides in-service training for teachers and courses for parents and contains a reference library of children's books plus teachers' resources. CLPE also publishes booklists and teaching resources relating to literacy in the primary classroom.

The Children's Book Circle – see page 361

The Children's Book Circle – see page 361

The Children's Book Council (CBC)

54 West 39th Street, 14th Floor, New York, NY 10018, USA
tel 212-966-1990 *fax* 212-966-2073
email info@cbcbooks.org
website www.cbcbooks.org

The non-profit trade association of publishers and packagers of trade books and related materials for children and young adults. The goals of the CBC are to make the reading and enjoyment of children's books an essential part of the USA's educational and social goals; to enhance public perception of the importance of reading by disseminating information about books and related materials for young people and information about children's book publishing; and to create materials to support literacy and reading encouragement programmes and to encourage the annual observance of National Children's Book Week.

Children's Book Council of Australia

PO Box 3203, Norwood, SA 5067, Australia
tel (08) 8332 2845 *fax* (08) 8333 0394
website www.cbca.org.au

Aims to foster children's enjoyment of books through managing the Children's Book of the Year Awards; providing information on and encouragement to authors and illustrators; organising exhibitions and activities during Children's Book Week; supporting children's library services; and promoting high standards in book reviewing.

The Children's Book Guild of Washington DC

email theguild@childrensbookguild.org
website www.childrensbookguild.org
President Patty Steelman

A regional association of writers, artists, librarians and other specialists dedicated to the field of children's literature. Its aims are to uphold and stimulate high standards of writing and illustrating for children; to increase knowledge and use of better books for children in the community; and to cooperate with other groups having similar purposes. Founded 1945.

Children's Books Ireland

17 North Great Georges Street, Dublin 1, Republic of Ireland
tel (01) 872 7475 *fax* (01) 872 7476
email info@childrensbooksireland.com
website www.childrensbooksireland.ie
Director Mags Walsh, *Administrator* Jenny Murray
Membership €30/£20 p.a. individual, €50/£35 p.a. institutions, €45/£30/$55 p.a. overseas individual, €60/£40/$70 p.a. overseas institutions, €20/£15 p.a. student

Dedicated to ensuring that books are at the centre of young people's lives, through advocacy, resource and innovative programming and outreach. Founded 1996.

Children's Literature Association (ChLA)

PO Box 138, Battle Creek, MI 49016–0138, USA
tel 269-965-8180 *fax* 269-965-3568
email info@childlitassn.org
website www.childlitassn.org
Membership Open to both individuals and institutions. Individual membership $75 (USA), $105 (non-US/Canada). Discounts available for concessions. Institutional membership $155 (USA), $185 (non-USA/Canada)

An organisation encouraging high standards of criticism, scholarship, research and teaching in children's literature. Individual members are entitled to the *ChLA Quarterly* and the annual volume of *Children's Literature*.

Children's Literature Centre (CLC)

Martynas Mazvydas National Library of Lithuania, Gedimino pr. 51, LT–01504, Vilnius, Lithuania
tel (370) 5 2398560 *fax* (370) 5 2496129
email vaikai@lnb.lt
website www.lnb.lt

Accumulates, processes, and stores children's literature, both original and in translation, as well as works on history, theory and literary criticism, informative and reference publications from various countries related to children's literature. Its aim is to acquire, as fully as possible, earlier Lithuanian and translated children's books and books published by Lithuanian exiles.
   CLC organises children's reading research, analyses book popularity, design, illustrations, quality of translations. It arranges international children's book exhibitions, seminars and conferences on children's book and reading. Presentation of new books, meetings with authors, publishers and designers are regularly carried out. CLC is the coordination and monitoring centre of children's libraries in Lithuania. Founded 1994.

Children's Writers and Illustrators Group – see The Society of Authors, page 353

Comhairle nan Leabhraichean/The Gaelic Books Council

32 Mansfield Street, Glasgow G11 5QP
tel 0141-337 6211 *fax* 0141-353 0515
email brath@gaelicbooks.net
website www.gaelicbooks.org
Chair Donald-Iain Brown

Stimulates Scottish Gaelic publishing by awarding publication grants for new books, commissioning authors and providing editorial services and general assistance to writers and readers. Has its own bookshop of all Gaelic and Gaelic-related books in print and runs a book club. All the stock is listed on the website and a paper catalogue is also available. Founded 1968.

Creative Scotland

12 Manor Place, Edinburgh EH3 7DD
tel 0330 333 2000
email enquiries@creativescotland.com
website www.creativescotland.com

The lead body for Scotland's arts, screen and creative industries. Helps Scotland's creativity shine at home and abroad. Creative Scotland, established on 1 July 2010, took over the functions and resources of Scottish Screen and the Scottish Arts Council but also has a wider set of responsibilities for developing the sector.

Cwlwm Cyhoeddwyr Cymru

c/o Elena Gruffudd, Aran Fair, Broom Road, Aberystwyth, Ceredigion SY23 1NA
tel (01970) 625659
email geiriau@googlemail.com
website www.cwlwmcyhoeddwyr.com (Welsh language only)

Represents and promotes Welsh-language publishers. Founded 2002.

Cyngor Llyfrau Cymru – see Welsh Books Council/Cyngor Llyfrau Cymru

Roald Dahl Foundation

81A High Street, Great Missenden, Bucks. HP16 0AL
tel (01494) 890465
email enquiries@roalddahlfoundation.org
website www.roalddahl.com,
www.roalddahlfoundation.org

A UK-based registered charity offering a programme of grant-giving to charities, hospitals and individuals in the UK. It supports many varied projects, in the same way Roald Dahl did when he was alive, offering practical assistance to children and families in 3 areas: neurology, haematology and literacy.
   The websites are illustrated with the artworks of Quentin Blake, Roald Dahl's principal illustrator and include full information about the author, his life and his works. The Roald Dahl website includes a free online club for children and the online magazine *Dahl-y Telegraph*.

The Roald Dahl Museum and Story Centre

81–83 High Street, Great Missenden, Bucks. HP16 0AL
tel (01494) 892192
website www.roalddahlmuseum.org
Housing Roald Dahl's unique archive, the Roald Dahl Museum and Story Centre has two biographical galleries and a hands-on Story Centre that inspires visitors to write creatively.

Walter de la Mare Society
PO Box 25351, London NW5 1ZT
tel 020-8886 1771
Membership £15 p.a.

To promote the study and deepen the appreciation of the works of Walter de la Mare (1873–1956) through a magazine, talks, discussions and other activities. Founded 1997.

Discover
383–387 High Street, Stratford, London E15 4QZ
tel 020-8536 5555 *fax* (020) 8522 1003
email team@discover.org.uk
website www.discover.org.uk

Discover Children's Story Centre is the UK's first hands-on creative literacy centre for children aged 0–11 years and their families, carers and teachers. Its mission is to spark children and adults' imagination, curiosity and creativity in a magical and stimulating environment. It offers a variety of programmes including schools workshops, family art activities, a literature programme led by children's writers and illustrators, community and education projects, artist residencies in schools and training for professionals that work with children and families. Artists are commissioned to create multisensory installations and exhibitions. Registered charity.

The Arthur Conan Doyle Society
Organisers Christopher and Barbara Roden,
PO Box 1360, Ashcroft, BC V0K 1A0, Canada
tel 250-453-2045 *fax* 250-453-2075
email sirhenry@telus.net
website www.ash-tree.bc.ca/acdsocy.html

Promotes the study of the life and works of Sir Arthur Conan Doyle (1859–1930). Publishes *ACD* journal (bi-annual) and occasional reprints of Conan Doyle material. Occasional conventions. Founded 1989.

Educational Publishers Council
The Publishers Association, 29ʙ Montague Street, London WC1B 5BW
tel 020-7691 9191 *fax* 020-7691 9199
email mail@publishers.org.uk
website www.publishers.org.uk

Provides a forum for publishers of printed and electronic learning resources for the school and college markets. It runs a series of events and meetings for its members and provides an information service. It also promotes the industry through the media.

Educational Writers Group – see The
Society of Authors, page 353

English Association
University of Leicester, University Road, Leicester LE1 7RH

tel 0116-229 7622 *fax* 0116-229 7623
email engassoc@leicester.ac.uk
website www.le.ac.uk/engassoc
Chair Adrian Barlow, *Chief Executive* Helen Lucas

Aims to further knowledge, understanding and enjoyment of English literature and the English language, by working towards a fuller recognition of English as an essential element in education and in the community at large; by encouraging the study of English literature and language by means of conferences, lectures and publications; and by fostering the discussion of methods of teaching English of all kinds.

Federation of Children's Book Groups – see page 362

Federation of European Publishers
Rue Montoyer 31 Bte 8, B–1000 Brussels, Belgium
tel (0032 2) 770 11 10 *fax* (0032 2) 771 20 71
email info@fep-fee.eu
website www.fep-fee.be
President Fergal Tobin, *Director* Anne Bergman-Tahon

Represents the interests of European publishers on EU affairs; informs members on the development of EU policies which could affect the publishing industry. Founded 1967.

The Federation of Indian Publishers
18/1C Institutional Area,
Aruna Asaf Ali Marg (near JNU), New Delhi 110067, India
tel 26852263, 26964847 *fax* 26864054
email fip1@sify.com
website www.fipindia.org
President Shri Anand Bhushan

Federation of Spanish Publishers' Association
(Federación de Gremios de Editores de España)
Cea Bermúdez, 44–2 Dcha. 28003 Madrid, Spain
tel (91) 534 51 95 *fax* (91) 535 26 25
email fgee@fge.es
website www.federacioneditores.org
President Sr D. Antoni Comas

French Publishers' Association
(Syndicat National de l'Edition)
115 Blvd St Germain, 75006 Paris, France
tel (1) 44 41 40 50 *fax* (1) 44 41 40 77
website www.sne.fr

The Gaelic Books Council – see Comhairle
nan Leabhraichean/The Gaelic Books Council

The Greeting Card Association
United House, North Road, London N7 9DP
tel 020-7619 0396

website www.greetingcards4kids.org
Chief Executive Sharon Little

The trade association for greeting card publishers. See website for information, including teachers' resources, lesson plans and card-making projects for children of all ages. Official magazine: *Progressive Greetings Worldwide.*

Guernsey Arts Council
St James's Street, St James's Concert Hall,
St Peter Port, Guernsey GY1 2NZ
tel (01481) 721902
Chairman Michael Rivett-Carnac

Hayward Gallery
Southbank Centre, Belvedere Road, London SE1 8XX
tel 020-7921 0813 *fax* 0871-663 2596
email customer@southbankcentre.co.uk
website www.southbankcentre.co.uk/visualarts

Imaginate
45A George Street, Edinburgh EH2 2HT
tel 0131-225 8050 *fax* 0131-225 6440
email info@imaginate.org.uk
website www.imaginate.org.uk
Director Tony Reekie, *General Manager* Tessa Rennie

An arts organisation that promotes and develops the performing arts for children and young people in Scotland. Its aim is that children and young people aged up to 18 have regular access to a diverse range of high-quality performing arts activity, from home and abroad, that will entertain, enrich, teach and inspire them. Its mission is to act as an advocate for the provision of high-quality performing arts for children across Scotland. Imaginate produces an annual programme of events and initiatives.

Imaginate produces the Bank of Scotland Imaginate Festival (see page 392). It also produces WYSIWYG (What You See Is What You Get), Scotland's showcase and conference of performing arts for children and young people that takes place every 2 years. In the intervening years, a laboratory event is held with presentations from leading thinkers in the industry, workshops and work in progress.

Other areas of Imaginate's work include: development opportunities for artists and producers, professional development for teachers and other educators, and strategic development, i.e. research, advocacy and initiatives to increase access and participation and enhance the experience for children and young people.

Imperial War Museum
Lambeth Road, London SE1 6HZ
tel 020-7416 5000
website www.iwm.org.uk

Independent Publishers Guild
PO Box 12, Llain, Whitland SA34 0WU
tel (01437) 563335 *fax* (01437) 562071

website www.ipg.uk.com
Membership Open to new and established publishers and book packagers

Provides an information and contact network for independent publishers. Also voices concerns of member companies within the book trade. Founded 1962.

Independent Theatre Council (ITC)
12 The Leather Market, Weston Street,
London SE1 3ER
tel 020-7403 1727 *fax* 020-7403 1745
email admin@itc-arts.org
website www.itc-arts.org
Membership Varies

Represents a wide range of performing arts organisations, venues and individuals in the fields of drama, dance, opera, music theatre, puppetry, mixed media, mime, physical theatre and circus. These organisations predominantly work on the middle and small scale around the UK. It has around 700 members across the performing arts who are united by their commitment to producing innovative, contemporary work (24% of the membership work specifically in the educational field reaching over 2 million children and young people). Founded 1974.

International Board on Books for Young People (IBBY)
Nonnenweg 12, Postfach, CH–4003–Basel,
Switzerland
tel (4161) 272 2917 *fax* (4161) 272 2757
email ibby@ibby.org, liz.page@ibby.org
British Section 10 Hall's Drive, Gressenhall, East Dereham, Norfolk NR20 4EJ
tel (01362) 860886
email annlazim@googlemail.com
website www.ibby.org

A non-profit organisation which represents an international network of people from all over the world who are committed to bringing books and children together. Its aims are:

• to promote international understanding through children's books;
• to give children everywhere the opportunity to have access to books with high literary and artistic standards;
• to encourage the publication and distribution of quality children's books, especially in developing countries;
• to provide support and training for those involved with children and children's literature;
• to stimulate research and scholarly works in the field of children's literature.

IBBY is composed of more than 70 National Sections all over the world and represents countries with well-developed book publishing and literacy programmes, and other countries with only a few dedicated professionals who are doing pioneer work in children's book publishing and promotion. Founded in Zurich, Switzerland in 1953.

International Publishers Association

3 avenue de Miremont, CH–1206 Geneva, Switzerland
tel (022) 704 18 20 *fax* (022) 704 18 21
email secretariat@internationalpublishers.org
website www.internationalpublishers.org
President Youngsuk (Y.S.) Chi, *Secretary-General* Mr Jens Bammel

Founded 1896.

The Irish Book Publishers' Association – see Publishing Ireland – Foilsiú Éireann

Irish Writers' Centre

19 Parnell Square, Dublin 1, Republic of Ireland
tel (01) 8721302 *fax* (01) 8726282
email info@writerscentre.ie
website www.writerscentre.ie
Chairperson Jack Harte

National organisation for the promotion of writers, writing and literature in Ireland. Provides a wide range of services and facilities to individual writers. Runs an extensive programme of events at its headquarters, including readings and book launches, seminars and discussions. Offers an education programme of workshops and masterclasses in writing and provides a venue for visiting international writers. See website for further details. Founded 1987.

The Kipling Society

Hon. Secretary Jane Keskar, 6 Clifton Road, London W9 1SS
tel 020-7286 0194
email jmkeskar@btinternet.com
website www.kipling.org.uk
Membership £24 p.a. (£22 p.a. standing orders; £12 under age 23)

Aims to honour and extend the influence of Rudyard Kipling (1865–1936), to assist in the study of his writings, to hold discussion meetings, to publish a quarterly journal, and to maintain a Kipling Library in London and a Kipling Room in The Grange, Rottingdean, near Brighton.

C.S. Lewis Society (Oxford)

Pusey House, St Giles, Oxford OX1 3LZ
email oulewis@herald.ox.ac.uk
website http://lewisinoxford.googlepages.com

Meets 8.15pm, Tuesday term-time at Pusey House, to promote knowledge of C.S. Lewis (1898–1963) and the writers who influenced him, including J.R.R. Tolkien, Charles Williams, Dorothy L. Sayers, G.K. Chesterton and George MacDonald. Open to non-University members.

The C.S. Lewis Society (New York)

Secretary Clare Sarrocco, 84–23, 77th Avenue, Glendle, NY 11385–7706, USA
email subscribe@nycslsociety.com
website www.nycslsociety.com

The oldest society for the appreciation and discussion of C.S. Lewis (1898–1963). Founded 1969.

Literature Wales

(formerly Adacemi)
Main Office 3rd Floor, Mount Stuart House, Mount Stuart Square, Cardiff CF10 5FQ
tel 029-2047 2266 *fax* 029-2049 2930
email post@literaturewales.org
and Academi Glyn Jones Centre, Wales Millennium Centre, Cardiff Bay, Cardiff CF10 5AL
tel 029-2047 2266 *fax* 029-2047 0691
email post@literaturewales.org
North West Wales Office Tŷ Newydd, Llanystumdwy, Cricieth, Gwynedd LL52 0LW
tel (01766) 522817 *fax* (01766) 523095
email tynewydd@literaturewales.org
South West Wales Office Dylan Thomas Centre, Somerset Place, Swansea SA1 1RR
tel (01792) 463980 *fax* (01792) 463993
website www.literaturewales.org
Chief Executive Peter Finch

The national organisation responsible for developing and promoting literature. It is made up of Yr Academi Gymreig (Welsh Academy), the Society for Writers of Wales, and Tŷ Newydd Writers' Centre. Its activities include Wales Book of the Year, the National Poet of Wales, Writers on Tour funding scheme, writing courses at Tŷ Newydd, Translators' House Wales, funding and advice for writers, the BayLit and Tŷ Newydd festivals, Young People's Writing Squads and fieldworkers in the south Wales valleys and north Wales.

Literature Wales represents the interests of Welsh writers in all genres and languages, both inside Wales and internationally. It offers advice, support, bursaries, mentoring and opportunities to meet other writers. It works with the support of the Arts Council of Wales and the Welsh Assembly Government. It is one of the resident organisations of the Wales Millennium Centre, where it runs the Glyn Jones Centre.

Little Theatre Guild of Great Britain

Guild Secretary Caroline Chapman, Satley House, Satley, near Bishop Auckland, Co. Durham DL13 4HU
tel (01388) 730042
website www.littletheatreguild.org

Aims to promote closer cooperation amongst the little theatres constituting its membership; to act as coordinating and representative body on behalf of the little theatres; to maintain and advance the highest standards in the art of theatre; and to assist in encouraging the establishment of other little theatres.

Magazines Canada (Canadian Magazine Publishers Association)
425 Adelaide Street West, Suite 700, Toronto, Ontario M5V 3C1, Canada
tel 416-504-0274 *fax* 416-504-0437
email friends@magazinescanada.ca
website www.magazinescanada.ca
Chief Executive Mark Jamison

L.M. Montgomery Heritage Society
L.M. Montgomery Institute,
University of Prince Edward Island,
550 University Avenue, Charlottetown,
Prince Edward Island, Canada C1A 4P3
tel 902-628-4346 *fax* 902-628-4305
email lmmi@upei.ca
website www.lmmontgomery.ca

Dedicated to protecting L.M. Montgomery's (1874–1942) Prince Edward Island literary and historic legacy for the benefit, education and enjoyment of the public. The Society is a non-profit organisation made up of representatives from Island heritage sites and groups with a mutual interest in preserving and promoting Montgomery's Island home. The Society holds events honouring the life and times of Montgomery, including an annual birthday celebration held each November and the L.M. Montgomery Festival held each August. L.M. Montgomery is the author of *Anne of Green Gables* and *Emily of New Moon*. Founded 1994.

Museum of London
150 London Wall, London EC2Y 5HN
tel (0870) 444 3851 *fax* (0870) 444 3853
email info@museumoflondon.org.uk
website www.museumoflondon.org.uk

The Mythopoeic Society
Corresponding Secretary Edith Crowe,
The Mythopoeic Society, PO Box 6707, Altadena, CA 91003-6707, USA
email correspondence@mythsoc.org
website www.mythsoc.org
Membership with *Mythprint* $20 p.a. (USA), $36 p.a. (rest of world)

A non-profit international literary and educational organisation for the study, discussion, and enjoyment of fantastic and mythic literature, especially the works of Tolkien, C.S. Lewis, and Charles Williams. The word 'mythopoeic' (myth-oh-PAY-ik or myth-oh-PEE-ic), meaning 'mythmaking' or 'productive of myth', aptly describes much of the fictional work of the 3 authors who were also prominent members of an informal Oxford literary circle (1930s–1950s) known as the Inklings. Membership is open to all scholars, writers, and readers of these literatures. The Society sponsors 3 periodicals: *Mythprint* (a monthly bulletin of book reviews, articles and events), *Mythlore* (scholarly articles on mythic and fantastic

literature), and *Mythic Circle* (a literary annual of original poetry and short stories). Each summer the Society holds an annual conference. Founded 1967.

National Art Library
Victoria & Albert Museum, South Kensington, London SW7 2RL
tel 020-7942 2400
email nal.enquiries@vam.ac.uk
website www.vam.ac.uk/nal

A major reference library and the Victoria & Albert Museum's curatorial department for the art, craft and design of the book. All are welcome to use the facilities.

National Association for the Teaching of English (NATE)
50 Broadfield Road, Sheffield S8 0XJ
tel 0114-255 5419 *fax* 0114-255 5296
email info@nate.org.uk
website www.nate.org.uk

The professional association for all those working in English education in the UK. NATE provides information about current developments, publications and resource materials. It also conducts research, in-service training and holds annual and regional conferences. Annual membership gives members termly copies of *NATE Classroom* (the Association's magazine which includes practical teaching strategies and resources for both Primary and Secondary teachers); *English in Education* (the Association's academic journal); *English Drama Media* magazine (the Association's professional journal with curriculum and pedagogy updates); and *NATE News* (a newsletter on Association matters). Membership also gives discounts on publications, courses and conferences. See website for details of how to join.

National Association of Writers' Groups
Secretary Aine Chadwick, PO Box 9891, Market Harborough LE16 0FU
tel (01262) 609228
email secretary@nawg.co.uk
website www.nawg.co.uk
Membership £35 p.a. plus £5 registration per group; £16 Associate individuals

Aims 'to advance the education of the general public throughout the UK, including the Channel Islands, by promoting the study and art of writing in all its aspects'. Publishes *Link* bimonthly magazine. Annual Festival of Writing held in Durham in September. Annual Creative Writing Competition. Founded 1995.

National Association of Writers in Education (NAWE)
PO Box 1, Sheriff Hutton, York YO60 7YU
tel (01653) 618429

email paul@nawe.co.uk
website www.nawe.co.uk
Director Paul Munden

Represents and supports writers, teachers and all those involved in the development of creative writing in education. Useful resource of writers who work in schools and communities is held on the website.

National Centre for Language and Literacy (NCLL)

University of Reading, Bulmershe Court, Reading RG6 1HY
tel 0118-378 8820
email ncll@reading.ac.uk
website www.ncll.org.uk

An independent organisation concerned with all aspects of language and literacy learning. The Centre supports teachers through its unique collection of resources and ongoing research.

National Centre for Research in Children's Literature (NCRCL)

Department of English and Creative Writing, Digby Stuart College, Roehampton University, Roehampton Lane, London SW15 5PH
tel 020-8392 3008 *fax* 020-8392 3819
email g.lathey@roehampton.ac.uk, l.sainsbury@roehampton.ac.uk
website www.ncrcl.ac.uk

Facilitates and supports research exchange in the field of children's literature. The NCRCL is based in Roehampton University, which houses a Children's Literature Collection and a number of Archives (including the Richmal Crompton archive) and Special Collections in the library. The website provides information on resources, activities and children's literature-related events and links to websites.

National Galleries of Scotland

National Gallery Complex, The Mound, Edinburgh EH2 2EL
tel 0131-624 6200, 0131-624 6332 (press office)
fax 0131-343 3250 (press office)
email pressinfo@nationalgalleries.org
Scottish National Portrait Gallery, 1 Queen Street, Edinburgh EH2 1JD
Scottish National Gallery of Modern Art, Belford Road, Edinburgh EH4 3DR
The Dean Gallery, Belford Road, Edinburgh EH4 3DS
website www.nationalgalleries.org

National Gallery

Information Department, Trafalgar Square, London WC2N 5DN
tel 020-7747 2885 *fax* 020-7747 2423
email information@ng-london.org.uk
website www.nationalgallery.org.uk

National Literacy Association

87 Grange Road, Ramsgate, Kent CT11 9QB
tel/fax (01843) 239952
email wendy@nla.org.uk
website www.nla.org.uk

Campaigns to raise awareness of the needs of underachievers and aims to ensure that school leavers will have adequate literacy for their needs in daily life. Produces publications and other resources including *The Guide to Literacy Resources*, which is distributed free to schools, parent groups, libraries and others.

National Literacy Trust – see page 397

National Museum Wales – see Amgueddfa Cymru – National Museum Wales

National Museums Liverpool

127 Dale Street, Liverpool L2 2JH
tel 0151-207 0001 *fax* 0151-478 4790
website www.liverpoolmuseums.org.uk

Venues: World Museum, Walker Art Gallery, National Conservation Centre, Merseyside Maritime Museum, International Slavery Museum, Lady Lever Art Gallery, Sudley House, Museum of Liverpool (opened summer 2011).

National Museums Scotland

Chambers Street, Edinburgh EH1 1JF
tel 0300 123 6789
website www.nms.ac.uk

National Portrait Gallery

St Martin's Place, London WC2H 0HE
tel 020-7306 0055
email personnel@npg.org.uk
website www.npg.org.uk

National Society for Education in Art and Design

3 Mason's Wharf, Potley Lane, Corsham, Wilts. SN13 9FY
tel (01225) 810134 *fax* (01225) 812730
website www.nsead.org
General Secretary Dr John Steers NDD, ATC, PhD

The leading national authority concerned with art, craft and design across all phases of education in the UK. Offers the benefits of membership of a professional association, a learned society and a trade union. Has representatives on National and Regional Committees concerned with Art and Design Education. Publishes *International Journal of Art and Design Education* (3 p.a.; Blackwells) and *AD* magazine for schools. Founded 1888.

Natural History Museum

Cromwell Road, London SW7 5BD
tel 020-7942 5000
website www.nhm.ac.uk

The Edith Nesbit Society

21 Churchfields, West Malling, Kent ME19 6RJ
email mccarthy804@aol.com
website www.edithnesbit.co.uk
Membership £7 p.a., £14 organisations/overseas

Aims to promote an interest in the life and works of Edith Nesbit (1858–1924) by means of talks, a regular newsletter and and other publications, and visits to relevant places. Founded 1996.

New Writing North

PO Box 1277, Newcastle upon Tyne NE99 5BP
tel 0191-233 3850 *fax* 0191-447 7686
email office@newwritingnorth.com
website www.newwritingnorth.com
Director Claire Malcolm

The literature development agency for the North East. Offers advice and support to writers of poetry, prose and plays. See website for details. Founded 1996.

Newcastle University Library

Robinson Library, Newcastle University,
Newcastle upon Tyne NE2 4HQ
tel 0191-222 7662
email lib-readersservices@ncl.ac.uk
website www.ncl.ac.uk/library

Historical children's books and other material relevant to the history of childhood and education. Over 100 collections of material ranging from rare books and archives to woodblocks and illustrations, from the mid 15th–21st century.

The Special Collections

tel 0191-222 5146
email lib-specenq@ncl.ac.uk
website www.ncl.ac.uk/library/specialcollections
Contains many historical children's books as well as a wealth of other material relevant to the history of childhood and education, especially 18th and 19th century chapbooks (cheap, popular pamphlets sold by itinerant traders, and often used by children). Most of these are to be found in the internationally important Robert White Collection. Special collections of children's books – the Chorley Collection of over 200 books published in the 19th and early 20th centuries; the Meade Collection of 184 books written by the children's author L.T. Meade (1854–1914); the Joan Butler Collection of about 5,000 children's books published up to the mid-20th century (uncatalogued). Other collections include the Wallis Collection which contains material designed for the instruction of children; the Crawhall Collection which includes items such as the children's ABC books illustrated with woodcuts by Joseph Crawhall; the Bradshaw-Bewick Collection which contains several books designed for children and illustrated with woodcuts by Thomas Bewick. It also holds collections built up by schools from North-East England since the 16th century.

Special Collections at the Robinson Library is working in conjunction with Seven Stories to collect and preserve neglected collections of historical children's books.

The Booktrust Collection

tel 0191-222 7656
website www.ncl.ac.uk/library/specialcollections/
collections/subject/childrens/booktrust.php
Contact Lucy Keating

Since the 1970s, most UK publishers have sent copies of every children's book they publish to Booktrust (see page 358), so that these books may be inspected and researched by the public. The Booktrust Collection is now housed in the Robinson library. Recent additions are catalogued. The collection currently contains approx. 60,000 items, including examples of toy and board books, picture books, young fiction and non-fiction. This number grows substantially each year. The collection provides an overview of British children's book publishing of the recent period and therefore of illustration, pedagogy, printing, images of childhood, design, typography, and so on, i.e. all the many areas included in the making of books for children. This is as complete a collection of recent and contemporary British children's books as exists anywhere. Open access is available to all users, except to the novelty books, which are only available for reference on request.

The Seven Stories Archive

Since 1997, Seven Stories (see page 359) has been forming a collection of manuscripts and artwork by British writers and illustrators for children, from 1945 to the present day. Some of this archive is housed in the library.

Office for Standards in Education (OFSTED)

Royal Exchange Buildings, St Ann's Square,
Manchester M2 7LA
tel 0300-123 1231
email enquiries@ofsted.gov.uk
website www.ofsted.gov.uk

A non-ministerial government department established under the Education (Schools Act) 1992. Since April 2001 OFSTED has been responsible for inspecting all educational provision for 16–19 year-olds to establish and monitor an independent inspection system for maintained schools in England. Its inspection role also includes the inspection of local educational authorities, teacher training institutions and youth work.

The Office of Communications (Ofcom)

Riverside House, 2A Southwark Bridge Road,
London SE1 9HA
tel 020-7981 3000 *fax* 020-7981 3333
email contact@ofcom.org.uk
website www.ofcom.org.uk

The independent regulator and competition authority for the UK communications industries, with responsibilities across TV, radio, telecommunications and wireless communications services. Established 2003.

The Poetry Book Society – see page 191

The Poetry Library – see page 193

The Poetry Society – see page 192

Poetry Society Education – see page 198

Positive Images
Millennium House, 207 Coatsworth Road, Bensham, Gateshead NE8 1SR
website www.positiveimages.org.uk

A registered charity dedicated to training anyone working with children in the identification and elimination of racist images, language and sterotypes in children's books, resources and play materials.

The Beatrix Potter Society
c/o The Lodge, Salisbury Avenue, Harpenden, Herts. AL5 2PS
tel (01582) 769755
email beatrixpottersociety@tiscali.co.uk
website www.beatrixpottersociety.org.uk
Membership £25 p.a. UK (£31 overseas), £30/£36 commercial/institutional

Promotes the study and appreciation of the life and works of Beatrix Potter (1866–1943) as author, artist, diarist, farmer and conservationist. Regular lecture meetings, conferences and events in the UK and USA. Quarterly newsletter. Small publishing programme. Founded 1980.

The Publishers Association
29B Montague Street, London WC1B 5BW
tel 020-7691 9191 *fax* 020-7691 9199
email mail@publishers.org.uk
website www.publishers.org.uk
Ceo Richard Mollet, *President* Rod Bristow, *Director of International and Trade Services* Emma House, *Director of Educational, Academic & Professional Publishing* Graham Taylor, *Operations Director* Mark Wharton

Founded 1896.

Publishers Association of New Zealand (PANZ)
PO Box 102006, North Shore 0745, Auckland, New Zealand
tel (09) 477-5589 *fax* (09) 477-5570
email admin@publishers.org.nz
website www.publishers.org.nz
Association Director Anne de Lautour

Publishing Ireland – Foilsiú Éireann
Guinness Enterprise Centre, Taylor's Lane, Dublin 8, Republic or Ireland

tel (1) 415 1210
email info@publishingireland.com
website www.publishingireland.com
President Jean Harrington

Publishing Scotland
(formerly Scottish Publishers Association)
Scottish Book Centre, 137 Dundee Street, Edinburgh EH11 1BG
tel 0131-228 6866 *fax* 0131-228 3220
email enquiries@publishingscotland.org
website www.publishingscotland.org
Chair Caroline Gorham, *Chief Executive* Marion Sinclair

Founded 1973.

The Arthur Ransome Society Ltd (TARS)
Abbott Hall Museum, Kendal, Cumbria LA9 5AL
website www.arthur-ransome.org
President Gabriel Woolf

To celebrate the life, promote the works, and diffuse the ideas of Arthur Ransome (1884–1967), author of the world-famous *Swallows and Amazons* series of books for children. The Society seeks in particular to encourage children and others to engage, with due regard to safety, in adventurous pursuits; educate the public generally about Ransome and his work; sponsor research in relevant areas; be a communications link for those interested in any aspect of Arthur Ransome's life and works. Founded 1990.

Readathon
The Parsonage, St Mary's, Chalford, Stroud GL6 8QB
tel (0870) 240 1124
email reading@readathon.org
website www.readathon.org

Readathon was set up to encourage children to read more books. Children undertake to read books, or do other literacy-based activities, in return for pledges of money, for charity, from family and friends. Thousands of schools have contributed to this success, and have made the Readathon campaign Britain's largest sponsored literary event. On joining, a free pack containing everything needed to run a successful Readathon is supplied.

Since it began Readathon has raised well over £20 million, helping two charities, the Roald Dahl Foundation and CLIC Sargent. Fundraising costs are kept to a minimum because Readathon receives support from booksellers, children's publishers, and many organisations concerned with books and reading. Part of the RFG charity. Founded 1984.

RNIB National Library Service
Far Cromwell Road, Bredbury, Stockport SK6 2SG
tel 0303-123 9999 *fax* 0161-355 2098
email library@rnib.org.uk
website www.rnib.org.uk/library

Societies, prizes and festivals

The largest specialist library for readers with sight loss in the UK. It offers a comprehensive range of books and accessible information for children and adults in a range of formats including braille, Moon, large print and unabridged audio. It also provides free access to online reference material, braille sheet music, themed book lists and a quarterly reader magazine.

The Malcolm Saville Society
6 Redcliffe Street, London SW10 9DS
email mystery@witchend.com
website www.witchend.com
Membership £10 p.a. (£12.50 Europe, £16 elsewhere)

Aims to remember and promote interest in the work of Malcolm Saville (1901–82), children's author. Regular social activities, library, contact directory and magazine (4 p.a.). Founded 1994.

Scattered Authors Society
Secretary Damian Harvey, 15 Wyreside Drive, Hambleton, Poulton-le-Fylde, Lancs. FY6 9DP
email author@damianharvey.co.uk
website www.scatteredauthors.org

Aims to provide a forum for informal discussion, contact and support for professional writers in children's fiction. Founded 1998.

School Library Association
Unit 2, Lotmead Business Village, Lotmead Farm, Wanborough, Swindon SN4 0UY
tel (01793) 791787 *fax* (01793) 791786
email info@sla.org.uk
website www.sla.org.uk

Promotes the development of school libraries and information literacy as central to the curriculum. It publishes booklists and guidelines for library and resource centres, a quarterly journal and provides training and an information service.

Science Museum
Exhibition Road, London SW7 2DD
tel (0870) 870 4868
email sciencemuseum@sciencemuseum.org.uk
website www.sciencemuseum.org.uk

Scottish Arts Council – see Creative Scotland

Scottish Book Trust (SBT)
Sandeman House, 55 High Street, Edinburgh EH1 1SR
tel 0131-524 0160 *fax* 0131-524 0161
email info@scottishbooktrust.com
website www.scottishbooktrust.com

With a responsibility towards Scottish writing, SBT exists to inspire readers and writers, and through the promotion of reading, to reach and create a wider reading public. Programmes include: management of Live Literature funding, a national initiative enabling Scottish citizens to engage with authors, playwrights, poets, storytellers and illustrators; Writer Development, offering mentoring and professional development for emerging and established writers; an ambitious children's programme including national tours, a children's festival and the Royal Mail Scottish Children's Book Awards; and readership development programmes. An information service for readers, writers and occasional exhibitions and publications all contribute to SBT's mission to bring readers and writers together.

The Scottish Storytelling Forum
The Scottish Storytelling Centre, 43–45 High Street, Edinburgh EH1 1SR
tel 0131-556 9579 *fax* 0131-557 5224
email reception@scottishstorytellingcentre.com
website www.scottishstorytellingcentre.co.uk

Scotland's national charity for oral storytelling, established to encourage and support the telling and sharing of stories across all ages and all sectors of society, in particular those who, for reasons of poverty or disability, were excluded from artistic experiences. The Scottish Storytelling Centre is the Forum's resource and training centre. The Storytelling Network has over 100 professional storytellers across Scotland. Founded 1992.

Seven Stories – the Centre for Children's Books – see page 359

Society for Editors and Proofreaders (SfEP)
Office Erico House, 93–99 Upper Richmond Road, London SW15 2TG
tel 020-8785 5617
email admin@sfep.org.uk
website www.sfep.org.uk

Works to promote high editorial standards and achieve recognition of its members' professional status, through local and national meetings, an annual conference, email discussion groups, a regular magazine and a programme of reasonably priced workshops/training sessions. These sessions help newcomers to acquire basic skills, enable experienced editors to update their skills or broaden their competence, and also cover aspects of professional practice or business for the self-employed. An online Directory of editorial services is available. The Society supports moves towards recognised standards of training and accreditation for editors and proofreaders and has developed its own Accreditation in Proofreading qualification. It has close links with the Publishing Training Centre and the Society of Indexers, is represented on the BSI Technical Committee dealing with copy preparation and proof correction (BS 5261), and works to foster good relations with all relevant bodies and organisations in the UK and worldwide. Founded 1988.

Societies, prizes and festivals

Society for Storytelling (SfS)
The Morgan Library, Aston Street, Wem,
Shropshire SY4 5AU
tel (07534) 578386
email admin@sfs.org.uk
website www.sfs.org.uk

Provides information on oral storytelling, events, storytellers and traditional stories. SfS volunteers have specialist knowledge of storytelling in education, health, therapy and business settings. To increase public awareness of the art it promotes National Storytelling Week, which takes place in the first week of February. The SfS provides a network for anyone interested in the art of oral storytelling whether they are full-time storytellers, use storytelling in their work, tell for the love or it or just want to listen. It holds an annual conference each Spring and produces a quarterly newsletter, a *Directory of Storytellers* and a variety of books and fact sheets. Founded 1993.

Society of Artists Agents
website www.saahub.com

Formed to promote professionalism in the illustration industry and to forge closer links between clients and artists through an agreed set of guidelines. The Society believes in an ethical approach through proper terms and conditions, thereby protecting the interests of the artists and clients. Founded 1992.

The Society of Authors – see page 353

Society of Children's Book Writers and Illustrators (SCBWI) – see page 356

Society of Editors
Director Bob Satchwell, University Centre,
Granta Place, Mill Lane, Cambridge CB2 1RU
tel (01223) 304080 *fax* (01223) 304090
email info@societyofeditors.org
website www.societyofeditors.org
Membership £230 p.a.

Formed from the merger of the Guild of Editors and the Association of British Editors, the Society has more than 400 members in national, regional and local newspapers, magazines, broadcasting, new media, journalism education and media law, campaigning for media freedom. Founded 1999.

Society of Young Publishers
Contact The Secretary,
c/o The Publishers Association,
29B Montague Street, London WC1B 5BW
email sypchair@thesyp.org.uk
website www.thesyp.org.uk
Membership Open to anyone employed in publishing or hoping to be soon; £30 p.a. standard, £24 student/unwaged

Organises monthly speaker meetings at which senior figures talk on topics of key importance to the industry today, and social and other events. Runs a job database advertising the latest vacancies and internships. Meetings are held in Central London, usually on the last Wednesday of the month at 6.30pm. Also a branch in Oxford. Founded 1949.

Speaking of Books
46B Vanbrugh Park, London SE3 7JQ
tel/fax 020-8858 6616
email jan@speakingofbooks.co.uk
website www.speakingofbooks.co.uk

Arranges school visits by writers, illustrators and storytellers. Also in-service training days relating to literacy.

The Robert Louis Stevenson Club
Secretary John W.S. Macfie, 17 Heriot Row,
Edinburgh EH3 6HP
tel/fax 0131-556 1896
email mail@stevenson-house.co.uk
Membership £20 p.a., £150 10 years

Aims to foster interest in Robert Louis Stevenson's life (1850–94) and works through various events and its newsletter. Founded 1920.

The Story Museum
Rochester House, 42 Pembroke Street,
Oxford OX1 1BP
tel (01865) 790050
email office@storymuseum.org.uk
website www.storymuseum.org.uk

Exists to celebrate children's stories and to share 1001 enjoyable ways for young people to learn through stories as they grow. It takes story performances, exhibitions, activities and ideas to schools and communities. The museum plans to open a magical new centre of children's literature and storytelling in the heart of Oxford in 2014.

The Swedish Institute for Children's Books (Svenska barnboksinstitutet)
Odengatan 61, SE–113 22 Stockholm, Sweden
tel (0)8-54 54 20 50 *fax* (0)8-54 54 20 54
email info@sbi.kb.se
website www.sbi.kb.se

A special library open to the public and an information centre for children's and young people's literature. The aim is to promote this kind of literature in Sweden as well as Swedish children's and young people's literature abroad. Founded 1967.

Teenage Magazine Arbitration Panel (TMAP)
28 Kingsway, London WC2B 6JR
tel 020-7400 7520 *fax* 020-7404 4167
email james.evans@ppa.co.uk
website www.tmap.org.uk

The magazine industry's self-regulatory body which ensures that the sexual content of teenage magazines is presented in a responsible and appropriate manner.

The Tolkien Society

Membership Secretary Marion Kershaw,
655 Rochdale Road, Walsden, Todmorden,
Lancashire OL14 6SX
email membership@tolkiensociety.org
website www.tolkiensociety.org
Membership £21 p.a. (Full), £10.50 p.a. (Associate),
£2 p.a. (Entings)

United Kingdom Literacy Association (UKLA)

University of Leicester, Leicester LE1 7RH
tel (0116) 223 1664 *fax* (0116) 223 1665
email admin@ukla.org
website www.ukla.org

UKLA is a registered charity, which has as its sole object the advancement of education in literacy. It is committed to promoting good practice nationally and internationally in literacy and language teaching and research. Its activities include:

• a conference programme of international, national and local conferences reflecting language and literacy interests;
• an active publications committee. Members are kept up to date via UKLA journals and website. Members receive a copy of the newsletter, *UKLA News* (3 p.a.), and the journal *Literacy* (see page 294). For an additional subscription, members can receive the *Journal of Research in Reading*. Both of the UKLA journals are refereed and include research reports, both qualitative and quantitative research, and critiques of current policy and practice as well as discussions and debates about current issues. UKLA also produces a range of books, written mainly with teachers and students in mind. In addition UKLA offers *English 4–11* published jointly with the English Association;
• regular responses to national consultations, including those organised through the DfES or QCA. Consequently, the UKLA often seeks information and responses from its members, as well as establishing a UKLA response to particular issues;
• promoting and disseminating research. UKLA provides support and small grants for literacy research;
• networking – UKLA helps its members to network both in the UK and through its worldwide contacts. UKLA's affiliation to the International Reading Association enables it to keep members in touch with events and ideas in other parts of the world. UKLA is also involved in specific international projects such as Project Connect, for which it provides some support for literacy education in Uganda.
    Founded in 1963 as the United Kingdom Reading Association; renamed in 2003.

V&A Museum of Childhood

Cambridge Heath Road, London E2 9PA
tel 020-8983 5200 *fax* 020-8983 5225

website www.museumofchildhood.org.uk

Holds one of the largest and oldest collections of toys and childhood artefacts in the world. As well as its permanent displays, the museum has temporary exhibitions, workshops and activities for all.

Victoria and Albert Museum

South Kensington, London SW7 2RL
tel 020-7942 2000
email vanda@vam.ac.uk
website www.vam.ac.uk

Voice of the Listener & Viewer Ltd (VLV)

PO Box 401, Gravesend, Kent DA12 9FY
tel (01474) 338711/338716 *fax* (01474) 325440
email info@vlv.org.uk
website www.vlv.org.uk
Administrative Secretary Sue Washbrook

Represents the citizen and consumer interests in broadcasting: it is an independent, non-profit-making society working to ensure independence, quality and diversity in broadcasting. VLV does not handle complaints. Founded 1984.

Volunteer Reading Help (VRH)

VRH Central Office, Charity House,
14–15 Perseverance Works, 38 Kingsland Road,
London E2 8DD
tel 020-7729 4087 *fax* 020-7729 7643
email info@vrh.org.uk
website www.vrh.org.uk

A national charity that exists to inspire disadvantaged children with poor literacy and communication skills to become confident and literate for life. VRH recruits and trains volunteers to work one-on-one with at least three children, aged 6–11, in two hour-and-a-half sessions every week.

Welsh Animation Group (WAG)

Details Georgia Anderegg, WAG Treasurer,
13 Bangor Street, Cardiff CF24 3LQ
tel 029-2048 1420
email enquiries@siriol.co.uk
website http://wag.sequence.co.uk
Chair Robin Lyons
Membership £25 p.a. waged, £15 unemployed, £5 student, £200 studio/corporate

Aims to bring together everybody working in animation in Wales, 'to build on the creative and economic successes of animation in Wales... to promote Welsh animation both nationally and throughout the world... to lobby for economic growth and the creation of jobs in the industry, and nurture the creative talent that has already brought Welsh animation international acclaim.' Holds regular meetings where animators can show their work, network, and voice their opinions. Helps to organise the Animation Day at the International Film Festival of Wales. Founded 1999.

Welsh Books Council/Cyngor Llyfrau Cymru

Castell Brychan, Aberystwyth, Ceredigion SY23 2JB
tel (01970) 624151 *fax* (01970) 625385
email castellbrychan@cllc.org.uk
website www.cllc.org.uk, www.gwales.com
Director Elwyn Jones

A national body funded directly by the Welsh Assembly Government which provides a focus for the publishing industry in Wales. Awards grants for publishing in Welsh and English. Provides services to the trade in the fields of editing, design, marketing and distribution. The Council is a key enabling institution in the world of books and provides services and information in this field to all who are associated with it. Founded 1961.

The Henry Williamson Society

General Secretary Sue Cumming, 7 Monmouth Road, Dorchester, Dorset DT1 2DE
tel (01305) 264092
email zseagull@aol.com
Membership Secretary Margaret Murphy, 16 Doran Drive, Redhill, Surrey RH1 6AX
tel (01737) 763228
email mm@misterman.freeserve.co.uk
website www.henrywilliamson.co.uk
Chairman Tony Boakes
Membership £15 p.a.

Aims to encourage a wider readership and greater understanding of the literary heritage left by Henry Williamson (1895–1977). Two meetings annually; also weekend activities. Publishes an annual journal. Founded 1980.

Writers Advice Centre for Children's Books

16 Smith's Yard, London SW18 4HR
tel 07979 905353
email info@writersadvice.co.uk
website www.writersadvice.co.uk
Managing Editor Louise Jordan

Dedicated to helping new and published children's writers by offering both editorial advice and tips on how to get published. The Centre also runs an online children's writing correspondence course plus a mentoring scheme for both ideas and manuscripts. Founded 1994.

The Writers' Guild of Great Britain

40 Rosebery Avenue, London EC1R 4RX
tel 020-7833 0777
email admin@writersguild.org.uk
website www.writersguild.org.uk
General Secretary Bernie Corbett
Full, Candidate and Student membership available

A trade union for professional and aspiring writers in TV, radio, film, theatre, books and videogames. 2,000 members, affiliated to the Trades Union Congress. The Guild negotiates collective minimum terms agreements with the main broadcasters and trade bodies for producers and subsidised theatre – these cover fees, advances, royalties, residuals, pension contributions, rights, credits and other matters. Guild members have access to free contract vetting, legal advice and representation in work-related disputes, and the Writers' Guild Welfare Fund gives emergency assistance to members in financial trouble. Also offered are professional, cultural and social activities to help provide writers with a sense of community, making writing a less isolated occupation. Members receive *UK Writer*, a quarterly magazine, plus a weekly email bulletin containing news and work opportunities. The Writers' Guild Awards, presented every November, recognise the best writing across all arts and entertainment media. The Writers' Guild Books Co-operative helps authors to self-publish and market their works.

Young at Art

15 Church Street, Belfast BT1 1PG
tel (028) 9023 0660
website www.youngatart.co.uk

Coordinates the annual Belfast Children's Festival as well as a wide variety of projects that encourage children and young people under 18 to enjoy the arts, develop awareness of its impact on their lives, and have a say in what their arts provision should be. These include workshop programmes, commissions, regional touring, seminars, training, research, publications and online resources.

Youth Libraries Group (YLG)

c/o Hampshire School Library Service, 5&6 Moorside Place, Moorside Road, Winchester SO23 7ZF
tel (01962) 826663
email hannah.plom@hants.gov.uk
website www.cilip.org.uk/specialinterestgroups/bysubject/youth
Secretary Hannah Plom

The YLG is open to all members of the Chartered Institute for Library and Information Professionals (CILIP) who are interested in children's work. At a national level its aims are:

• to influence the provision of library services for children and the provision of quality literature;
• to inspire and support all librarians working with children and young people; and
• to liaise with other national professional organisations in pursuit of such aims.

At a local level, the YLG organises regular training courses, supports professional development and provides opportunities to meet colleagues. It holds an annual conference and judges the CILIP Carnegie and Kate Greenaway Awards (see page 384). It also produces the journal *Youth Library Review*.

Children's book and illustration prizes and awards

This list provides details of prizes, competitions and awards for children's writers and artists. See page 391 for a *Calendar of awards.*

The Hans Christian Andersen Awards
Details International Board on Books for Young People, Nonnenweg 12, Postfach, CH–4003 Basel, Switzerland
tel (61) 272 29 17 *fax* (61) 272 27 57
email ibby@ibby.org, liz.page@ibby.org
website www.ibby.org

The Medals are awarded every 2 years to a living author and an illustrator who by the outstanding value of their work are judged to have made a lasting contribution to literature for children and young people. 2010 winners: David Almond from the UK (author) and Jutta Bauer from Germany (illustrator).

Angus Book Award
Details Moyra Hood,
Educational Support Officer Literacy,
Educational Resources Service, Angus Council,
Leisure Services, Bruce House, Wellgate,
Arbroath DD11 3TL
tel (01241) 435045
email hoodm@angus.gov.uk
website www.angus.gov.uk/bookaward

An annual award originally set up as an Angus Council initiative to encourage pupils to read and enjoy quality teenage fiction. It is based on pupils not only voting for the winner but actively participating in all aspects of the award from selection of the shortlist to the award ceremony. The award involves 3rd-year pupils from all 8 secondary schools in Angus in reading 5 shortlisted titles. The shortlist is selected by teachers, librarians and pupils from books appropriate for the 14–15 year-old age group, written by authors living in the UK and published in paperback between July and June of the preceding year. Titles are chosen that reflect the range of themes which interest teenagers whilst challenging and interesting both committed and less enthusiastic readers. As part of the shortlisting process authors agree to visit schools and attend the Award ceremony, which takes place in May. The winner receives a miniature replica of the Aberlemno Serpent stone and £500. 2011 winner: *When I Was Joe* by Keren David (Frances Lincoln Children's Books). Launched 1996.

Arts Council England, London
Details Literature Administrator,
Arts Council England, London, 2 Pear Tree Court,
London EC1R 0DS
tel (0845) 300 6200 *fax* 020-7973 6590
website www.artscouncil.org.uk/regions/london/
Contact Gemma Seltzer

Arts Council England, London, is the regional office for the Capital, covering 33 boroughs and the City of London. Grants are available through the 'Grants for the arts' scheme throughout the year to support a variety of literature projects, concentrating particularly on:

• original works of poetry and literary fiction and professional development for individual writers, including writers of children's books;
• touring and live literature;
• small independent literary publishers; and
• literary translation into English.

Contact the Literature Unit for more information, or see website for an application form.

Arts Council YouWriteOn.com Book Awards
tel (07948) 392634
email edward@youwriteon.com
website www.youwriteon.com

Arts Council-funded publishing awards for new fiction writers. Random House provides free professional critiques for the highest rated new writers' opening chapters and short stories on YouWriteOn.com each month. The highest rated writers of the year are then published, 3 in each of the adult and children's categories, through YouWriteOn's free paperback publishing service for writers. The novel publishing awards total £1,000. Writers can enter at any time throughout the year by joining the website. Closing date: 31 December each year. 2010 winner: *The Scarlet Heart* by Justine Windsor. Founded 2005.

Association for Library Service to Children Awards
American Library Association, 50 East Huron Street, Chicago, IL 60611, USA
tel 800-545-2433 ext. 2163 *fax* 312-944-7671
email alsc@ala.org
website www.ala.org

The following awards are administered by ALSC:

• The Caldecott Medal (named in honour of the 19th century English illustrator Randolph Caldecott) is

awarded annually to the artist of the most distinguished US picture book for children.
• The Newbery Medal (named after the 18th century British bookseller John Newbery) is awarded annually to the author of the most distinguished contribution to US literature for children.
• The Theodor Seuss Geisel Award (named after the world-renowned children's author a.k.a. Dr Seuss) is given annually to the author(s) and illustrator(s) of the most distinguished contribution to the body of children's literature known as beginning reader books published in the USA during the preceding year.
• The Robert F. Sibert Informational Book Award is given annually to the author of the most distinguished informational book published in English during the preceding year.
• The Wilder Medal, a bronze medal, honours an author or illustrator whose books, published in the USA, have made, over a period of years, a substantial and lasting contribution to literature for children.

Bardd Plant Cymru (Welsh-Language Children's Poet Laureate)

Welsh Books Council, Castell Brychan, Aberystwyth, Ceredigion SY23 2JB
tel (01970) 624151 *fax* (01970) 625385
email castellbrychan@wbc.org.uk
website www.cllc.org.uk

The main aim is to raise the profile of poetry amongst children and to encourage them to compose and enjoy poetry. During his/her term of office the bard will visit schools as well as helping children to create poetry through electronic workshops.

The scheme's partner organisations are: S4C, the Welsh Books Council, Urdd Gobaith Cymru, Literature Wales and the Welsh Language Board.

Best New Illustrators Award

Booktrust, Book House, 45 East Hill,
London SW18 2QZ
020-8516 2977
email education@booktrust.org.uk

This award celebrates the best rising talent in the field of children's illustration today. First awarded in 2008, and then again in 2011, the prize is given to 10 emerging illustrators whose work demonstrates remarkable creative flair, artistic skill and boundless imagination. 2011 winners: Joe Berger, Claudia Boldt, Katie Cleminson, Chris Haughton, Alice Melvin, Sara Ogilvie, Levi Pinfold, Salvatore Rubbino, Viviane Schwarz and Kevin Waldron.

The Bisto Book of the Year Awards – see

The CBI Bisto Book of the Year Awards

Blue Peter Book Awards

Booktrust, Book House, 45 East Hill,
London SW18 2QZ
tel 020-8516 2972

email prizes@booktrust.org.uk
website www.booktrust.org.uk

Awarded annually, winners are shortlisted by a panel of expert adult judges, then a group of young *Blue Peter* viewers judge the 3 categories, which are: Favourite Story, The Best Book with Facts and The Most Fun Story with Pictures. There is a winner in each category and an overall winner, which wins the accolade Blue Peter Book of the Year. Winning books are announced on *Blue Peter* in March.

2011 Overall Winner and Favourite Story: *Dead Man's Cove* by Lauren St John (Orion Children's Books); The Best Book with Facts: *Do Igloos Have Loos?* by Mitchell Symons (Doubleday); *The Most Fun Story with Pictures: Lunatics and Luck* by Marcus Sedgwick, illustrated by Pete Williamson (Orion Children's Books). Established 2000.

BolognaRagazzi Award

Piazza Costituzione 6, 40128 Bologna, Italy
tel (051) 282242/282361 *fax* (051) 6374011
email bookfair@bolognafiere.it
website www.bolognachildrensbookfair.com
Takes place March

Winners of the BolognaRagazzi Award are displayed at the Bologna Children's Book Fair. Prizes are given to encourage excellence in children's publishing in the categories of fiction, non-fiction, 'new horizons' (books from emerging countries) and Opera Prima (works by authors or illustrators being published for the first time). The books are judged on the basis of their creativity, educational value and artistic design.

Booktrust Early Years Awards

(formerly the Sainsbury's Baby Book Award)
Booktrust, Book House, 45 East Hill,
London SW18 2QZ
tel 020-8516 2972
email prizes@booktrust.org.uk
website www.booktrust.org.uk
Contact Claire Shanahan

The winners of each of 3 categories, The Best Book for Babies under one year old, The Best Picture Book for children up to 5 years old, and Best Emerging Illustrator, each receive a cheque for £2,000 and a crystal award. The winner of the Best Emerging Illustrator also receives a specially commissioned piece of artwork from a well-known children's illustrator. Closing date: Suspended for 2011. Established 1999.

2010 winners: The Best Book for Babies under one year old – *I love my Mummy* by Giles Andreae, illustrated by Emma Dodd (Orchard); The Best Picture Book for children up to 5 years old – *One Smart Fish* by Chris Wormell (Jonathan Cape); Best Emerging Illustrator – *The Django* by Levi Pinfold (Templar).

The Booktrust Teenage Prize

Booktrust, Book House, 45 East Hill,
London SW18 2QZ

tel 020-8516 2972
email prizes@booktrust.org.uk
website www.booktrust.org.uk
Contact Claire Shanahan

The first annual national book prize to recognise and celebrate the best in young adult fiction. The author of the best book for teenagers receives £2,500 and is chosen from a shortlist of 6–8. The prize is open to works of fiction and non-fiction (including short story collections, graphic novels, poetry and reference books), aimed at teenagers aged 13–16 and written in English by a citizen of the UK, or an author resident in the UK. The work must be published between 1 July and the following 30 June by a UK publisher. Closing date: Suspended for 2011. Established 2003.

2010 winner: Gregory Hughes for *Unhooking the Moon* (Quercus).

The Branford Boase Award

Library and Information HQ, 5–6 Moorside Place, Moorside Road, Winchester SO23 7FZ
tel (01962) 826658
email anne.marley@tiscali.co.uk
website www.branfordboaseaward.org.uk

An annual award of £1,000 is made to a first-time writer of a full-length children's novel (age 7+) published in the preceding year; the editor is also recognised. Its aim is to encourage new writers for children and to recognise the role of perceptive editors in developing new talent. The Award was set up in memory of the outstanding children's writer Henrietta Branford and the gifted editor and publisher Wendy Boase who both died in 1999. Closing date for nominations: end of December. 2010 winner: *Stolen* by Lucy Christopher (Chicken House). 2011 shortlist: *I Am the Blade* by J.P. Buxton (Hachette), *When I Was Joe* by Keren David (Frances Lincoln), *Tall Story* by Candy Gourlay (David Fickling), *Unhooking the Moon* by Gregory Hughes (Quercus), *Out of Shadows* by Jason Wallace (Andersen Press), *The Crowfield Curse* by Pat Walsh (Chicken House). Founded 2000.

British Book Awards – see Galaxy National Book Awards

Carnegie Medal – see The CILIP Carnegie and Kate Greenaway Awards

The CBI Bisto Book of the Year Awards

Details The Administrator, Children's Books Ireland, 17 North Great Georges Street, Dublin 1, Republic of Ireland
tel (01) 8727475 *fax* (01) 8727476
email info@childrensbooksireland.ie
website www.childrensbooksireland.ie

Awards made annually to authors and illustrators born or resident in Ireland, open to books written in Irish or English. Closing date: December for work

published between 1 January and 31 December. Winners announced in May. Sponsored by Bisto (Premier Foods). Founded 1990.

The CBI Bisto Book of the Year Award

An award of €10,000 is presented to the overall winner (text and/or illustration). 2010 award winner: *A Bit Lost* by Chris Haughton (Walker).

The CBI Bisto Honour Awards

An award of €2,000 each is given for fiction and illustration.

The CBI Bisto Eilís Dillon Award

An award of €3,000 is presented to an author for a first children's book.

Cheltenham Illustration Awards

The CIA, University of Gloucestershire, Pittville Studios, Cheltenham, Glos. GL52 3JG
tel (01242) 714953
email cheltillustrationawards@glos.ac.uk
website www.cheltenham-illustration-awards.com

Awards for student and new illustrators. The winning entries together with a selection of runners up will have their work exhibited and also published as a full colour annual. The Emerging Talent First Prize is £1,500 and the runner up will receive £750, and both will have their work showcased. Artwork must be supplied as jpegs on CD-Rom; up to 5 entries per person. Entry fee: £10 per entry. See website for details.

The Children's Laureate

Booktrust, Book House, 45 East Hill, London SW18 2QZ
tel 020-8516 2977
email childrenslaureate@booktrust.org.uk
website www.childrenslaureate.org.uk
Contact Katherine Woodfine

The role of Children's Laureate, which has a bursary of £15,000, is awarded once every 2 years to honour a writer or illustrator of children's books to celebrate outstanding achievement. It highlights the importance of exceptional children's book creators in developing the readers of tomorrow. Children's Laureates: Julia Donaldson (2011–13), Anthony Browne (2009–11), Michael Rosen (2007–9), Jacqueline Wilson (2005–7), Michael Morpurgo (2003–5), Anne Fine (2001–3), Quentin Blake (1999–2001). Founded 1998.

The CILIP Carnegie and Kate Greenaway Awards

CILIP, 7 Ridgmount Street, London WC1E 7AE
tel 020-7255 0650 *fax* 020-7255 0651
email ckg@cilip.org.uk
website www.carnegiegreenaway.org.uk

Recommendations for the following 2 awards are invited from members of CILIP (the Chartered

Institute of Library and Information Professionals), who are asked to submit a preliminary list of not more than 2 titles for each award, accompanied by a 50-word appraisal justifying the recommendation of each book. The awards are selected by the Youth Libraries Group of CILIP.

Carnegie Medal

Awarded annually for an outstanding book for children (fiction or non-fiction) written in English and first published in the UK during the preceding year or co-published elsewhere within a 3-month time lapse.

2011 winner: *Monsters of Men* by Patrick Ness (Walker).

Kate Greenaway Medal

Awarded annually for an outstanding illustrated book for children first published in the UK during the preceding year or co-published elsewhere within a 3-month time lapse. Books intended for older as well as younger children are included, and reproduction will be taken into account. The Colin Mears Award (£5,000) is awarded annually to the winner of the Kate Greenaway Medal.

2011 winner: *Farther* by Grahame Baker-Smith (Templar).

The CLPE Poetry Award

Details CLPE, Webber Street, London SE1 8QW
tel 020-7401 3382/3 *fax* 020-7928 4624
email ann@clpe.co.uk
website www.clpe.co.uk

An award that aims to honour excellence in children's poetry. Organised by the Centre for Literacy in Primary Education, it is presented annually in June/July for a book of poetry published in the preceding year. The book can be a single-poet collection or an anthology. Submissions deadline: end of February. 2010 winner: *New and Collected Poems for Children* by Carol Ann Duffy (Faber & Faber).

Costa Book Awards

(formerly the Whitbread Book Awards)
Details The Booksellers Association, Minster House, 272 Vauxhall Bridge Road, London SW1V 1BA
tel 020-7802 0802 *fax* 020-7802 0803
email info@costabookawards.com
website www.costabookawards.co.uk
Contact Naomi Gane

The awards celebrate and promote the most enjoyable contemporary British writing. Judged in 2 stages and offering a total of £50,000 prize money, there are 5 categories: Novel, First Novel, Biography, Poetry and Children's. They are judged by a panel of 3 judges and the winner in each category receives £5,000. Nine final judges then choose the Costa Book of the Year from the 5 category winners. The overall winner receives £25,000. Writers must be resident in Great Britain or Ireland for 3 or more years.

Submissions must be received from publishers. Closing date: end of June.

2010 Costa Children's Book Award winner: *Out of the Shadows* by Jason Wallace (Anderson).

Creative Scotland

(formerly Scottish Arts Council)
tel 0330 333 2000
email enquiries@creativescotland.com
website www.creativescotland.com

A limited number of writers' bursaries of up to £15,000 each are offered to enable professional writers based in Scotland, including writers for children, to devote more time to writing. Priority is given to writers of fiction and verse and playwrights, but writers of literary non-fiction are also considered. Applications may be discussed with Gavin Wallace. See also Royal Mail Awards for Scottish Children's Books (page 388).

The Roald Dahl Funny Prize

Book House, 45 East Hill, London SW18 2QZ
tel 020-8516 2972
email prizes@booktrust.org.uk
website www.roalddahlprize.org
Contact Claire Shanahan

Founded by Michael Rosen, Children's Laureate 2007–9, this prize is unique in its aim to honour the funniest children's books of the year. This is part of the wider objective of promoting and drawing attention to humour in children's literature. The winners of the 2 categories, the Funniest Book for Children Aged 6 and Under and the Funniest Book for Children Aged 7–14, are awarded £2,500 each, as well as both receiving a bottle of wine from the Dahl family's wine cellar. Fiction, non-fiction and poetry are welcomed in each category. Closing date: late June.

2010 winners: Funniest Book for Children Aged 6 and Under: Louise Yates for *Dog Loves Books* (Jonathan Cape); Funniest Book for Children Aged 7–14: Louise Rennison for *Withering Tights* (HarperCollins Children's Books). Established 2008.

Etisalat Prize for Arabic Children's Literature

website www.acbpub.org

The prize of one million dirhams (about £79,000) is open only to children's books written in Arabic. Translated titles are not eligible. Organised by the The Arab Children's Book Publishers Forum.

The Eleanor Farjeon Award

website www.childrensbookcircle.org.uk

An annual award may be given to an individual or an organisation. Librarians, authors, publishers, teachers, reviewers and others who have given exceptional service to the children's book industry are eligible for nomination. It was instituted in 1965 by the

Children's Book Circle (page 361) for distinguished services to children's books and named after the much-loved children's writer Eleanor Farjeon. 2010 winner: Seven Stories, the Centre for Children's Books (see page 359).

Foyle Young Poets of the Year Award – see page 199

Galaxy National Book Awards

Details Merric Davidson, PO Box 60, Cranbrook, Kent TN17 2ZR
tel (01580) 212041
email merric@agile-ideas.com
website www.galaxynationalbookawards.com

Award categories include: Children's Book of the Year. 2010 winner: Julia Donaldson and Axel Scheffler for *Zog*. Founded 1989.

Grampian Children's Book Award

tel (01651) 871213
email marion.wands@aberdeenshire.co.uk
website www.aberdeenshire.gov.uk/libraries/young_people

This award is for best fiction book, judged solely by pupils in participating secondary schools in Aberdeen City, Aberdeenshire and Moray and children in Aberdeen Central Children's Library. The award is given to a children's book published in paperback between July and June of the previous year. 2011 joint winners: *The Enemy* by Charlie Higson (Puffin) and *Grass* by Catherine MacPhail (Bloomsbury).

Kate Greenaway Medal – see The CILIP Carnegie and Kate Greenaway Awards

The Guardian Children's Fiction Prize

tel 020-3353 2000
email books@guardian.co.uk

The *Guardian's* annual prize of £1,500 is for a work of children's fiction for children over 8 (no picture books) published by a British or Commonwealth writer. The winning book is chosen by the Children's Book Editor together with a team of 3–4 authors of children's books. 2010 winner: *Ghost Hunter* by Michelle Paver (Orion).

Kelpies Prize

New Scottish Writing for Children, Floris Books, 15 Harrison Gardens, Edinburgh EH11 1SH
tel 0131-337 2372 *fax* 0131-347 9919
email floris@florisbooks.co.uk
website www.florisbooks.co.uk/kelpiesprize

A prize open to writers of fiction suitable for both boys and girls aged 8–12. Stories must be set wholly, or mainly, in Scotland and must not have been previously commercially published. MSS must be 40,000–70,000 words in length. The winner receives £2,000 and their book will be published in the *Kelpies*

range of Scottish fiction by Floris Books. Closing date: end February. Winner announced in August. 2010 winner: *Red Fever* by Caroline Clough (Floris Books). See website for full details.

Lancashire County Library Children's Book of the Year Award

Details LCC, Library & Information Service, East Cliff, PO Box 162, Preston PR1 3EA
tel (01772) 534008 *fax* (01772) 534880
email library@lcl.lancscc.gov.uk
website www.lancashire.gov.uk/libraries/services/children
Contact Jake Hope

A prize of £1,000 and an engraved decanter is awarded to the best work of fiction for 12–14 year-olds, written by a UK author and first published between 1 September and 31 August of the previous year. The winner is announced in June. 2010 winner: *When I Was Joe* by Keren David (Frances Lincoln).

The Frances Lincoln Diverse Voices Children's Book Award

Seven Stories, 30 Lime Street, Newcastle upon Tyne NE1 2PQ
tel (0845) 2710777
email diversevoices@sevenstories.org.uk
website www.sevenstories.org.uk
Contact Helena McConnell

A prize of £1,500 plus the option for Frances Lincoln Children's Books to publish the winning novel is awarded to the best MS for 8–12 year-olds that celebrates diversity in the widest possible sense. Closing date: 25 February 2012. 2011 winner: *Om Shanti, Babe* by Helen Limon (Frances Lincoln). Created in memory of Frances Lincoln and supported by Frances Lincoln Ltd and Arts & Business. Founded 2009.

The Astrid Lindgren Memorial Award

Swedish Arts Council, PO Box 27215, SE–102 53 Stockholm, Sweden
tel (08) 519 264 00 *fax* (08) 519 264 99
email literatureaward@alma.se
website www.alma.se

An award to honour the memory of Astrid Lindgren, Sweden's favourite author, and to promote children's and youth literature around the world. The award is 5 million Swedish kronas, the world's largest for children's and youth literature, and the second-largest literature prize in the world. It is awarded annually to one or more recipients, regardless of language or nationality.

Authors, illustrators, storytellers and promoters of reading are eligible. The award is for life-long work or artistry rather than for individual pieces. The prize can only be awarded to living people. The body of work must uphold the highest artistic quality and evoke the deeply humanistic spirit of Astrid Lindgren.

The winner is selected by a jury based on nominations for outstanding achievement from selected nominating bodies around the world. The jury has the right to suggest nominees of their own. Neither individuals nor organisations may nominate themselves. 2011 winner: Shaun Tan. The Astrid Lindgren Memorial Award is administered by the Swedish Arts Council. Founded 2002.

The Macmillan Prize for Children's Picture Book Illustration

Applications Macmillan Children's Books, 20 New Wharf Road, London N1 9RR
tel 020-7014 6124
email children@macmillan.co.uk

Four prizes are awarded annually for unpublished children's book illustrations by art students in higher education establishments in the UK. Prizes: £1,000 (1st), £500 (2nd) and £250 (3rd) and the Lara Jones award for the entry that shows most promise as an illustrator of books for preschool (£500). 2011 winner: Gemma Merino for *The Crocodile Who Didn't Like Water*.

Marsh Award for Children's Literature in Translation

Administered by The English-Speaking Union, Dartmouth House, 37 Charles Street, London W1J 5ED
tel 020-7529 1550
email education@esu.org
website www.esu.org
Contact Kate McCulloch

This biennial award of £2,000 is given to the translator of a book for children (aged 4–16) from a foreign language into English and published in the UK by a British publisher. Electronic books, and encyclopedias and other reference books, are not eligible. Next award: January 2013. Founded 1996.

The Mythopoeic Fantasy Award for Children's Literature

David Oberhelman, Award Administrator, The Mythopoeic Society, 3700 West 19th Street, Suite K3, Stillwater, OK 74074–1678, USA
website www.mythsoc.org

This award honours books for younger readers (from young adults to picture books for beginning readers), in the tradition of *The Hobbit* or *The Chronicles of Narnia*. 2010 winner: *Where the Mountain Meets the Moon* by Grace Lin (Little, Brown Young Readers). 2011 shortlist: *Incarceron and Sapphique* by Catherine Fisher (Dial), *I Shall Wear Midnight* by Terry Pratchett (HarperCollins), *The Grimm Legacy* by Polly Shulman (Putnam Juvenile), *Toads and Diamonds* by Heather Tomlinson (Henry Holt), *The Queen's Thief* series, consisting of *The Thief*, *The Queen of Attolia*, *The King of Attolia* and *A Conspiracy*

of Kings by Megan Whalen Turner (Greenwillow Books).

nasen Awards – Celebrating Inclusive Practice

Nasen House, 4–5 Amber Business Village, Amber Close, Amington, Tamworth B77 4RP
tel (01827) 311500
email janec@nasen.org.uk
website www.nasen.org.uk
Contact Jane Cobby

These awards were created to recognise the authors and publishers of high-quality books and resources that inspire both children with special educational needs and their teachers. A prize of £500 will be presented to the winning authors of each of 9 categories: the Inclusive Children's Book Award; the Special Educational Needs Academic Book Award; the Book to Support Teaching and Learning Award; Pupil Book and Educational Practitioner's Book; the Inclusive Resource for Primary Classrooms Award; and the Inclusive Resource for Secondary Classrooms Award; ICT Accessibility (Software) Resource, ICT Accessibility (Hardware) Resource.

Publishers will have winning entries featured in *Special* magazine. All entries must have been published in the UK. See website for details. 2010 Inclusive Children's Book Award winner: *The Pasta Detectives* by Andrea Steinhöfel (Chicken House).

New Zealand Post Book Awards for Children and Young Adults

Details c/o Booksellers New Zealand, PO Box 25033, Panama Street, Wellington 6146, New Zealand
tel (04) 472 1908 *fax* (04) 472 1912
email info@booksellers.co.nz
website www.bookseller.co.uk/awards

Annual awards to celebrate excellence in, and provide recognition for, the best books for children and young adults published annually in New Zealand. Awards are presented in 4 categories: non-fiction, picture book, junior fiction and young adult fiction. The winner of each category wins $7,500. One category winner is chosen as the *New Zealand Post Book of the Year* and receives an additional $7,500. Eligible authors' and illustrators' books must have been published in New Zealand in the calendar year preceding the awards year. Closing date: December. Founded 1990.

North East Book Award

Details Eileen Armstrong, Cramlington Learning Village, Cramlington, Northumberland NE23 6BN
tel (01670) 712311 *fax* (01670) 730598
email earmstrong@cramlingtonlv.co.uk
website http://northeastbookaward.wordpress.com

Awarded to a book written by a UK resident author and first published in paperback the previous year.

The shortlist is selected by school librarians, teachers and the previous year's student judges. The final winner is decided entirely by the student judges (Year 7/8). Winner announced in April. 2011 shortlist: *Wishful Thinking* by Ali Sparkes (OUP), *Flood and Fang* by Marcus Sedgwick (Orion Children's), *Castle of Shadows* by Ellen Renner (Orchard), *Young Sherlock Holmes: Death Cloud* by Andrew Lane (Macmillan Children's), *Flyaway* by Lucy Christopher (Chicken House).

North East Teenage Book Award

Details Eileen Armstrong,
Cramlington Learning Village, Cramlington,
Northumberland NE23 6BN
tel (01670) 712311 *fax* (01670) 730598
email earmstrong@cramlingtonlv.co.uk
website http://northeastteenagebookaward.wordpress.com

Awarded to a book written by a UK resident author and first published in paperback during the previous year. The shortlist is selected by school librarians, teachers and the previous year's student judges. The final winner is decided entirely by the teenage student judges (Year 9+). Winner announced in January. 2010 winner: *When I Was Joe* by Keren David (Frances Lincoln).

Nottingham Children's Book Awards

Nottingham City Libraries and Information Service,
Sneinton Library, Sneinton Boulevard,
Nottingham NG2 4FD
tel 0115-915 1173
website www.nottinghamchildrensbookaward.co.uk
Contact Elaine Dykes, Deborah Sheppard

Nottingham children aged 3–5 years choose their favourite picture book of the year. A shortlist of titles is chosen in November with the help of local nurseries and voting takes place in Under 5 settings and libraries in Spring. Winners are announced and authors/illustrators invited to meet children and receive their award in June. Launched 1999.

Phoenix Award

Children's Literature Association, PO Box 138,
Battle Creek, MI 49016–0138, USA
tel 269-965-8180 *fax* 269-965-3568
website www.childlitassn.org

This Award is presented by the Children's Literature Association (ChLA) for the most outstanding book for children originally published in the English language 20 years earlier which did not receive a major award at the time of publication. It is intended to recognise books of high literary merit. 2011 winner: *The Mozart Season* by Virginia Euwer Wolff (Henry Holt). Founded 1985.

The Red House Children's Book Award

Details Sinead Kromer, 2 Bridge Wood View,
Horsforth, Leeds, West Yorkshire LS18 5PE

tel 0113-258 8910
email info@fcbg.org.uk
website www.redhousechildrensbookaward.co.uk

This award is given annually to authors of works of fiction for children published in the UK. Children participate in the judging of the award. 'Pick of the Year' book list is published in conjunction with the award. Founded in 1980 by the Federation of Children's Book Groups.

Royal Mail Awards for Scottish Children's Books

Scottish Book Trust, Sandeman House,
Trunk's Close, 55 High Street, Edinburgh EH1 1SR
tel 0131-524 0160 *fax* 0131-524 0161
email anna.gibbons@scottishbooktrust.com
website www.scottishbooktrust.com/royalmailawards
Contact Anna Gibbons, Children's Programme Manager

Awards totalling £12,000 are given to new and established authors of published books in recognition of high standards of writing for children in 3 age group categories: Bookbug Readers (0–7 years), Younger Readers (8–11 years) and Older Readers (12–16 years). A shortlist is drawn up by a panel of children's book experts and then a winner in each category is decided by children and young people by voting for their favourites in book groups in schools and libraries across Scotland. An award of £3,000 is made for the winner in each category and £500 for runners-up. Books published in the preceding calendar year are eligible. Authors should be resident in Scotland. Guidelines available on request. Closing date: 31 March. Award presented: February. Administered by Scottish Book Trust, in partnership with Creative Scotland.

RSPCA Young Photographer Awards (YPA)

Details Publications Department, RSPCA,
Wilberforce Way, Southwater, Horsham,
West Sussex RH13 9RS
tel (0300) 123 0455 *fax* (0303) 123 0455
email publications@rspca.org.uk
website www.rspca.org.uk/ypa

Annual awards are made for animal photographs taken by young people in categories: under 12; 12–18 year-olds; Portfolio (5 pictures); Pets Personalities. Prizes: overall winner (photography break, £1,000-worth of Olympus vouchers), age group winners (cameras, photoshoots). Four runners-up in each age group receive a camera. Closing date for entries: September. Founded 1990.

Sainsbury's Baby Book Award – see Booktrust Early Years Awards

Sheffield Children's Book Award

Details Book Award Co-ordinator,
Schools Library Service, Sheffield

tel 0114-250 6844
email jennifer.wilson@sheffield.gov.uk
website www.sheffield.gov.uk

Presented annually in November to the book chosen as the most enjoyable by the children of Sheffield. There are 3 category winners and one overall winner. 2010 winners – Picture Book and Overall Winner: *Morris the Mankiest Monster* by Giles Andreae and Sarah McIntyre; Longer Novel: *Gone* by Michael Grant; Shorter Novel: *Boom!* by Mark Haddon.

WHSmith Children's Book of the Year – see Galaxy National Book Awards

The Times/Chicken House Children's Fiction Competition

Details Chicken House, 2 Palmer Street, Frome, Somerset BA11 IDS
tel (01373) 454488
email claire@doublecluck.com
website www.doublecluck.com
Contact Claire Skuse

This annual competition is open to first-time writers of a full-length children's novel (age 9–16). Entrants must be over 18 and novels must not exceed 80,000 words in length. The winner will be announced in *The Times* and receives a worldwide publishing contract with Chicken House with a royalty advance of £10,000. The winner is selected by a panel of judges which includes children's authors, journalists, publishers, librarians and others involved in children's literature. Submissions are invited between August and the end of October, with a shortlist announced the following February and the winner chosen at Easter. See website for further details. 2011 winner: *Plumpscuttle's Peculiars* by Kieran Larwood. Previous winners: *Reavers' Ransom* by Emily Diamand (2008), *Threads* by Sophia Bennett (2009), *Muncle Trogg* by Janet Foxley (2010).

Tir na n-Og Awards

Details Welsh Books Council, Castell Brychan, Aberystwyth, Ceredigion SY23 2JB
tel (01970) 624151 *fax* (01970) 625385
email delyth.humphreys@cllc.org.uk
website www.cllc.org.uk

Established with the intention of raising the standard of children's and young people's books published during the year, and to encourage the buying and reading of good books. Three awards are presented annually:

• The best English language book of the year with an authentic Welsh background. Fiction and factual books originally in English are eligible; translations from Welsh or any other language are not eligible. Prize: £1,000.
• Welsh language books aimed at the primary sector. Prize: £1,000.

• Welsh language books aimed at the secondary sector. Prize: £1,000.

Sponsored by the Chartered Institute of Library and Information Professional and the Welsh Books Council. Founded 1976.

2011 winners – English language book: *Three Little Sheep* by Rob Lewis (Pont Books/Gomer Press); Welsh language book – Primary Sector: *Dirgelwch y Bont* by Hywel Griffiths (Gwasg Gomer); Welsh language book – Secondary Sector: *Stwff Guto S. Tomos* by Lleucu Roberts (Y Lolfa).

Christopher Tower Poetry Prize – see page 199

UKLA Children's Book Awards

Details Lynda Graham
tel (0116) 223 1664
email lynda_j_graham@hotmail.com
Submissions Administrator, United Kingdom Literacy Association, University of Leicester LE1 7RH
website www.ukla.org

The award is presented for excellence in the field of literacy. Literacy is interpreted here as being about 'the expression of meaning and ideas through challenging use of language, imaginative expression, illustration and other graphics'. The awards are given for content, expression and to honour writers whose use of language has a powerful impact on the reader. The shortlist is decided by teachers based on which books engage young readers. The shortlist is announced in the Spring and the prize awarded at the UKLA International Conference in July.

The V&A Illustration Awards

Enquiries The Word & Image Dept, Victoria & Albert Museum, London SW7 2RL
tel/fax 020-7942 2385
email villa@vam.ac.uk
website www.vam.ac.uk/illustrationawards
Contact Martin Flynn

These annual awards are given to practising book and magazine illustrators, for work first published in the UK during the 12 months preceding the closing date of the awards. Cash prizes will be awarded for best book cover, illustrated book and newspaper, magazine and comic illustration. Also student illustrator of the year category. Closing date: December.

Waterstone's Children's Book Prize

Waterstone's, Capital Court, Capital Interchange Way, Brentford, Middlesex TW8 0EX
tel 020-8742 3800 *fax* 020-8742 0215
email sarah.clarke@waterstones.com
website www.waterstones.com
Contact Sarah Clarke, Children's Buying Manager

An annual award of £5,000 plus a major promotion in Waterstone's which aims to support new children's authors and introduce them to a wide audience. Books submitted should be fiction for children aged 7–14 with a focus on text rather than illustration. Open to new authors of any nationality with not more than 2 previously published fiction titles (for adults or children). Publishers must declare any titles written under another name, including series fiction. All submitted titles must be newly available in paperback for a period of shortlist promotion in January/February but can have been available previously in hardback. Titles can be the first part of a series or trilogy but must stand alone as a novel. See website for submission deadline. 2011 winner: *Artichoke Hearts* by Sita Brahmachari (Macmillan's Children's). Founded 2005.

Whitbread Book Awards – see Costa Book Awards

Winchester Writers' Conference Competitions

Contact Barbara Large, Faculty of Arts, University of Winchester, Winchester, Hants SO22 4NR
tel (01962) 827238
email barbara.large@winchester.ac.uk
website www.writersconference.co.uk
Honorary Patrons Jacqueline Wilson OBE, Maureen Lipman, Baroness James OBE, Colin Dexter OBE

Seventeen writing competitions are attached to this major international Festival of Writing, which takes place at the end of June/early July (see page 347). Each entry is adjudicated and 70 sponsored prizes are presented at the Writers' Awards Dinner. In addition to two Writing for Children Competitions sponsored by Little Tiger Press and Greenhouse Literary Consultancy, other categories include the First Three Pages of the Novel, Short Stories, Shorter Short Stories, A Page of Prose, Lifewriting, Slim Volume, Small Edition, Poetry, Retirement, Writing Can be Murder, Local History, Young Writers' Poetry Competition and Sustainability of our Climate. Deadline for entries: June.

Write A Story for Children Competition

Entry forms The Academy of Children's Writers, PO Box 95, Huntingdon, Cambs. PE28 5RL
tel (01487) 832752
website www.childrens-writers.co.uk

Three prizes (1st £2,000, 2nd £300, 3rd £200) are awarded annually for a short story for children, maximum 1,500 words, by an unpublished writer of children's fiction. Send sae for details or see website. Founded 1984.

Young Writers' Programme

Details Young Writers' Programme, Royal Court Young Writers' Programme, Sloane Square, London SW1W 8AS
tel 020-7565 5050 *fax* 020-7565 5001
email info@royalcourttheatre.com
website www.royalcourttheatre.com

Competition open to 18–25 year olds. See website for further information for how to submit plays and the progression for the winners.

YoungMinds Book Award

48–50 St John Street, London EC1M 4DG
email hannah.smith@youngminds.org.uk
website www.youngminds.org.uk
Contact Hannah Smith

This annual book award of £2,000 seeks to raise awareness and create understanding of mental health needs of children and young people. Eligible books must have been published between 1 June and 31 May and may be works of fiction or biography for young people aged 12+ which helps them to cope with the stresses and challenges of growing up. Founded 2003.

YouWriteOn.com – see Arts Council YouWriteOn.com Book Awards

Calendar of awards

Announcements of awards are subject to change. See page 382 for listings.

January
• The Marsh Award for Children's Literature in Translation (biennial, 2013)
• Costa Book Awards
• North East Teenage Book Award

February
• Royal Mail Awards for Scottish Children's Books

March
• Hans Christian Andersen Awards (biennial, 2012)
• Blue Peter Children's Book Awards
• BolognaRagazzi Award

April
• The Frances Lincoln Diverse Voices Children's Book Award
• North East Book Award

May
• Angus Book Award
• The CBI Bisto Book of the Year Awards
• Grampian Children's Book Award
• The Macmillan Prize for Children's Picture Book Illustration
• nasen Awards – Celebrating Inclusive Practice
• Red House Children's Book Award

June
• Carnegie Medal
• Kate Greenaway Medal
• Lancashire County Library Children's Book of the Year Award
• Nottingham Children's Book Awards
• Tir na n-Og Awards
• The V&A Illustration Awards

July
• The Branford Boase Award
• UKLA Children's Book Awards

August
• Kelpies Prize

September
• Booktrust Early Years Awards (suspended for 2011)
• The CLPE Poetry Award
• The Guardian Children's Fiction Prize

October
• The Booktrust Teenage Prize (suspended for 2011)

November
• The Roald Dahl Funny Prize
• The Eleanor Farjeon Award
• Sheffield Children's Book Award

Societies, prizes and festivals

Children's literature festivals and trade fairs

Some of the literature festivals in this section are specifically related to children's books and others are general arts festivals which include literature events for children.

Aspects Irish Literature Festival

Town Hall, The Castle, Bangor, Co. Down BT20 4BT
tel (028) 91 278032, 91 271200 (box office)
fax (028) 91 271370
website www.northdown.gov.uk
Contact Gail Prentice, Arts Officer/Festival Director
Takes place 20–25 September 2011

An annual celebration of contemporary Irish writing with novelists, poets and playwrights. Includes writers' visits to schools and Young Aspects Showcase, where young people are given opportunity to publicly read their own work.

Bank of Scotland Imaginate Festival

45A George Street, Edinburgh EH2 2HT
tel 0131-225 8050 *fax* 0131-225 6440
email info@imaginate.org.uk
website www.imaginate.org.uk
Takes place 7–14 May 2012

As the largest performing arts festival for children and young people in the UK, this annual festival provides the opportunity for school children and their teachers, families and industry professionals to see the best children's theatre the world has to offer. Produced by Imaginate (page 372), the festival's aim is that children and young people aged up to 18 have regular access to a diverse range of high-quality performing arts activity, from home and abroad, that will entertain, enrich, teach and inspire them. Each year the festival presents around 16 national and international productions attracting an audience of over 15,000, and tours to both rural and urban areas throughout Scotland. Founded 1990.

Bath Festival of Children's Literature

PO Box 4123, Bath BA1 0FR
email info@bathkidslitfest.co.uk
website www.bathkidslitfest.co.uk
Festival Directors John McLay, Gill McLay
Takes place 23 September–2 October 2011

A 10-day celebration of children's books and reading. Authors and illustrators taking part include Francesca Simon, Charlie Higson, Julia Donaldson, Lauren Child, Judith Kerr, Patrick Ness, Andy Stanton. In addition to big name authors, there will be events for the youngest readers and readers-to-be. Sponsored by *The Daily Telegraph* and Waterstone's Booksellers.

Bath Literature Festival

Bath Festivals, Abbey Chambers, Kingston Buildings, Bath BA1 1NT

tel (01225) 462231 *fax* (01225) 445551
Box Office *tel* (01225) 463362
email info@bathfestivals.org.uk
website www.bathlitfest.org.uk
Artistic Director James Runcie
Takes place 25 February–6 March 2012

An annual 9-day festival with leading guest writers. Includes readings, debates, discussions and workshops, and events for children and young people. Programme available in December.

Beyond the Border: The Wales International Storytelling Festival

St Donats Arts Centre, St Donats Castle,
Nr Llantwit Major, Vale of Glamorgan CF61 1WF
tel (01446) 799095 (marketing), 799100 (box office)
fax (01446) 799101
email enquiries@stdonats.com,
davidambrose@beyondtheborder.com
website www.beyondtheborder.com
Programme Director David Ambrose
Takes place July

A biennial international festival celebrating oral tradition and bringing together storytellers, poets and musicians from around the world. This is the largest event of its type in the UK. On the last day there is a competition for young storytellers aged 10–20 to be BTB Young Storyteller of the Year.

Bologna Children's Book Fair

Piazza Costituzione 6, 40128 Bologna, Italy
tel (051) 282242/282361 *fax* (051) 6374011
email bookfair@bolognafiere.it
website www.bolognachildrensbookfair.com
Takes place March

Held annually, the Bologna Children's Book Fair is the leading children's publishing event. Publishers, authors and illustrators, literary agents, licensors and licensees, and many other members of the children's publishing community meet in Bologna to buy and sell copyrights, establish new contacts and strengthen their professional relationships, discover new illustrators, develop new business opportunities, learn about the latest trends and developments and explore children's educational materials, including new media products. Approximately 4,000 professionals active in children's publishing attend from 70 countries. Entry is restricted to those in the publishing trade.

Selected by a jury, the Bologna Illustrators Exhibition showcases fiction and non-fiction children's book illustrators, both new and established, from all over the world. Many illustrators also visit the Fair to show their latest portfolios to publishers.

Winners of the BolognaRagazzi Award are displayed. Prizes are given to encourage excellence in children's publishing in the categories of fiction, non-fiction, 'new horizons' (books from emerging countries) and Opera Prima (works by authors or illustrators being published for the first time), and books are judged on the basis of their creativity, educational value and artistic design. The Hans Christian Andersen Award and the Astrid Lindgren Memorial Award are announced at the Fair.

The Times Cheltenham Literature Festival

109–111 Bath Road, Cheltenham, Glos. GL53 7LS
tel (01242) 774400
email nicola.tuxworth@cheltenhamfestivals.com
website www.cheltenhamfestivals.com
Book It! Director Jane Churchill
Takes place 7–16 October 2011

This annual festival is the largest of its kind in Europe. Events include talks and lectures, poetry readings, novelists in conversation, exhibitions, discussions, workshops and a large bookshop. *Book It!* is a festival for children within the main festival with an extensive programme of events. Brochures are available in August.

Chester Literature Festival

Chester Railway Station, 1st Floor,
West Wing Offices, Chester CH1 3NT
tel (01244) 405605
email info@chesterfestivals.org
website www.chesterfestivals.co.uk
Programme Manager Katherine Seddon
Takes place 17–30 October 2011

An annual festival with events featuring international, national and local writers and poets, as well as a literary lunch and festival dinner. There is a poetry competition for school children, events for children and workshops for adults. A Cheshire Prize for Literature is awarded each year; only residents of Cheshire are eligible.

Children's Book Festival

Festival Office, Childrens Books Ireland,
17 North Great Georges Street, Dublin 1,
Republic of Ireland
tel (1) 872 7475 *fax* (1) 872 7476
email info@childrensbooksireland.ie
website www.childrensbooksireland.ie
Takes place Throughout October

Annual nationwide celebration of reading and books in Ireland for young people.

Children's Book Week

Booktrust, Book House, 45 East Hill,
London SW18 2QZ

tel 020-8516 2977
email education@booktrust.org.uk
website www.childrensbookweek.org.uk
Contact Katherine Woodfine
Takes place First full week of October

An annual celebration of reading for pleasure for children of primary school age. Free teachers' packs are sent to schools, libraries and teacher training institutions in England, and during the week, schools, libraries, and other venues hold a range of events and activities.

Edinburgh International Book Festival

5A Charlotte Square, Edinburgh EH2 4DR
tel 0131-718 5666 *fax* 0131-226 5335
email admin@edbookfest.co.uk
website www.edbookfest.co.uk
Director Nick Barley
Takes place August

Now established as Europe's largest book event for the public. In addition to a unique independent bookselling operation, more than 800 writers contribute to the programme of events. Programme details available in June.

Essex Poetry Festival

2 The Drive, Hullbridge, Essex SS5 6LN
tel (01702) 230596
email derek@essex-poetry-festival.co.uk
website www.essex-poetry-festival.co.uk
Contact Derek Adams
Takes place October

A poetry festival across Essex. Also includes the Young Essex Poet of the Year Competition.

The Festival of Writing

The Writers' Workshop, 7 Market Street, Charlbury,
Oxon OX7 3PH
tel 0845 459 9560
email info@writersworkshop.co.uk
website www.festivalofwriting.com
Director Harry Bingham
Takes place late March/early April

A festival for new writers providing the opportunity to meet literary agents, publishers, professional authors and book doctors. Keynote speakers from across the industry. Also workshops, competitions, networking events, Q&A panels and the chance to pitch work directly to literary agents.

Folkestone Book Festival

Creative Foundation Offices, The Block,
65–69 Tontine Street, Folkestone, Kent CT20 1JR
tel (01303) 245799
email info@creativefoundation.org.uk (FAO
Folkestone Book Festival)
website www.folkestonebookfest.com
Takes place November

An annual festival with over 40 events, including a Children's Day.

Hay Festival – see The Telegraph Hay Festival

Ilkley Literature Festival
The Manor House, 2 Castle Hill, Ilkley LS29 9DT
tel (01943) 601210 *fax* (01943) 817079
email admin@ilkleyliteraturefestival.org.uk
website www.ilkleyliteraturefestival.org.uk
Festival Director Rachel Feldberg
Takes place First 2 weeks in October

The north of England's most prestigious literature
festival with over 180 events, from author's
discussions to workshops, readings, literary walks,
children's events and a festival fringe.

Imagine: Writers and Writing for Children
Purcell Room, South Bank Centre, London SE1 8XX
tel 020-7921 0906 (administration), 020-7921 0971
(programme), (0870) 160 2520 (box office)
fax 020-7928 2049
email literature&talks@southbankcentre.co.uk
website www.southbankcentre.co.uk/festivals-series/
imagine
Takes place February

An annual festival celebrating writing for children.
Three days featuring a selection of poets, storytellers
and illustrators.

Jewish Book Week
Jewish Book Council, ORT House, 126 Albert Street,
London NW1 7NE
tel 020-7446 8771 *fax* 020-7446 8777
email info@jewishbookweek.com
website www.jewishbookweek.com
Administrator Pam Lewis
Takes place Feb/March

A festival of Jewish writing, with contributors from
around the world and sessions in London and
nationwide. Includes events for children and
teenagers.

Lincoln Book Festival
Freeschool Lane, Lincoln, Lincs. LN2 1EY
tel (01522) 545458 *fax* (01522) 842718
email sara.bullimore@lincoln.gov.uk,
info@lincolnbookfestival.co.uk
website www.lincolnbookfestival.co.uk
Contact Sara Bullimore (Arts & Cultural Sector
Officer)
Takes place May

A festival that celebrates books but also includes
other art forms that books initiate and inspire –
comedy, film, performance, conversation. It aims to
celebrate local, national and international writers and
artists, historical and contemporary works of art as
well as offering the public a chance to see both
emerging and well-known writers and artists.
Includes a programme of children's events.

London Literature Festival
Southbank Centre, Belvedere Road, London SE1 8XX
tel 020-7960 4200
email customer@southbankcentre.co.uk
website www.southbankcentre.co.uk,
www.londonlitfest.com
Takes place July

A 2-week festival featuring international and prize-
winning authors, historians, poets, performers and
artists, children's events, specially commissioned
work, debate and discussion, interactive and
improvised writing and performance. Established
2007.

Lowdham Book Festival
c/o The Bookcase, 50 Main Street,
Lowdham NG14 7BE
tel 0115-966 4143
email info@fiveleaves.co.uk
website www.lowdhambookfestival.co.uk
Contact Jane Streeter, Ross Bradshaw
Takes place June

An annual 10-day festival of literature events for
adults and children, with a daily programme of high-
profile national and local writers. The last day always
features dozens of free events and a large book fair.

Manchester Children's Book Festival
The Manchester Writing School, Dept of English,
Manchester Metropolitan University (MMU),
All Saints Building, All Saints, Manchester M15 6BH
tel 0161-247 1787
email mcbf@mmu.ac.uk
website www.manchesterchildrensbookfestival.co.uk
Festival Directors Carol Ann Duffy, James Draper,
Kaye Tew
Takes place July

A new festival featuring some of today's favourite
children's writers and artists for children (aged 0–15)
and anyone who loves children's books.

Northern Children's Book Festival
Newcastle City Library, Charles Avison Building,
33 Newbridge Street, Newcastle upon Tyne NE1 8AX
website www.ncbf.org.uk
Chairperson Janice Hall
Takes place November

An annual festival to bring authors, illustrators, poets
and performers to children in schools, libraries and
community centres across the North East of England.
About 36 authors visit the North East over the
2-week period for 2–8 days, organised by the 12 local
authorities. The climax of the festival is a huge public
event in a different part of the North East each year
when over 4,000 children and their families visit to
take part in author seminars, drama workshops, and
to enjoy a variety of book-related activities.

Off the Shelf Literature Festival
Central Library, Surrey Street, Sheffield S1 1XZ
tel 0114-273 4716

email offtheshelf@sheffield.gov.uk
website www.offtheshelf.org.uk
Contact Maria de Souza, Su Walker, Lesley Webster
Takes place October

The festival comprises a wide range of events for adults and children, including author visits, writing workshops, storytelling, competitions and exhibitions. Programme available in September.

Oundle Festival of Literature
2 New Road, Oundle, Peterborough,
Northants PE8 4LA
tel (01832) 273050
email enquiries@oundlelitfest.org.uk
website www.oundlelitfest.org.uk
Contact Liz Dillarstone (Publicity)
Takes place March (festival fortnight) plus all-year-round programme

Featuring a full programme of author events, poetry, philosophy, politics, storytelling, biography, illustrators and novelists for young and old. Includes events for children.

The Sunday Times Oxford Literary Festival
Christ Church, Oxford OX1 1DP
tel (01865) 276152
email info@oxfordliteraryfestival.co.uk
website www.oxfordliteraryfestival.com
Festival Chief Executive Sally Dunsmore
Takes place March/April

An annual 6-day festival for both adults and children. Presents topical debates, fiction and non-fiction discussion panels, and adult and children's authors who have recently published books. Topics range from contemporary fiction to discussions on politics, history, science, gardening, food, poetry, philosophy, art and crime fiction. An additional 2 days of events for schools.

Oxford Literary Festival – see The Sunday Times Oxford Literary Festival

Readathon
The Parsonage, St Mary's Chalford, Stroud GL6 8QB
tel (0870) 240 1124
website www.readathon.org

Run in schools throughout the year, especially for Children's Book Week and World Book Day. Children undertake to read books for pledges of money. All the money raised is donated to children's charities. Readathon is part of the Read for Good charity. See page 377.

Redbridge Book and Media Festival
London Borough of Redbridge, Arts & Events Team,
3rd Floor, Central Library, Clements Road,
Ilford IG1 1EA
tel 020-8708 2855

website www.redbridge.gov.uk
Contact Arts & Events Team
Takes place April and May

Features author talks, performances, panel debates, Urdu poetry events, an exhibition, workshops, children's activities and events, and a schools outreach programme.

Richmond upon Thames Literature Festival, Arts Service
Orleans House Gallery, Riverside,
Twickenham TW1 3DJ
tel 020-8831 6000 fax 020-8744 0501
email artsinfo@richmond.gov.uk
website www.richmondliterature.com
Takes place November

An annual literature festival covering a broad range of subjects. Leading contemporary authors hold discussions, talks, debates and readings. There are also exhibitions and storytelling sessions for children and adults.

Royal Court Young Writers' Festival
The Royal Court Theatre, Sloane Square,
London SW1W 8AS
tel 020-7565 5050
email studio@royalcourttheatre.com
website www.royalcourttheatre.com
Contact Nina Lyndon, Administrator
Takes place January–March 2012 (biennial)

A national festival which anyone aged 18–25 can enter. Promising plays which arise from the workshops are then developed and performed at the Royal Court's Theatre Upstairs.

Scottish International Storytelling Festival
43–45 High Street, Edinburgh EH1 1SR
tel 0131-556 9579 fax 0131-557 5224
email reception@scottishstorytellingcentre.com
website www.scottishstorytellingcentre.co.uk
Festival Director Donald Smith
Takes place 21–30 October 2011

A celebration of Scottish storytelling set in its international context, complemented by music, ballad and song. The main theme of the 2011 Festival will be 'Island Odyssey — Scotland and Old Europe'. Takes place at the Scottish Storytelling Centre and partner venues across Edinburgh and the Lothians.

StAnza: Scotland's International Poetry Festival
tel (01334) 475000 (box office), (01334) 474610 (programmes)
email info@stanzapoetry.org
website www.stanzapoetry.org
Festival Director Eleanor Livingstone
Takes place March

The festival engages with all forms of poetry: read and spoken verse, poetry in exhibition, performance poetry, cross-media collaboration, schools work, book launches and poetry workshops, with numerous UK and international guests and weekend children's events.

Stratford-upon-Avon Poetry Festival

Shakespeare Centre, Henley Street,
Stratford-upon-Avon CV37 6QW
tel (01789) 204016 *fax* (01789) 296083
email info@shakespeare.org.uk
website www.shakespeare.org.uk
Takes place June/July

An annual festival to celebrate poetry past and present with special reference to the works of Shakespeare. Events include: evenings of children's verse, a Poetry Mass and a local poets' evening. Full details available on the website from March. Sponsored by The Shakespeare Birthplace Trust.

The Telegraph Hay Festival

Festival Office, The Drill Hall, 25 Lion Street,
Hay-on-Wye HR3 5AD
tel (01497) 822620 (admin)
email sophie@hayfestival.com
website www.hayfestival.com
Takes place May/June

This annual festival aims to celebrate the best in writing and performance from around the world, to commission new work, and to promote and encourage writers of excellence and potential. More than 500 events over 10 days, with leading guest writers. Programme published April.

Wigtown Book Festival

County Buildings, Wigtown,
Dumfries & Galloway DG8 9JH
tel (01988) 402036
email mail@wigtownbookfestival.com
website www.wigtownbookfestival.com
Festival Director Adrian Turpin
Takes place 23 September–2 October 2011

An annual celebration of literature and the arts in Scotland's National Book Town. Over 150 events including author events, theatre, music, film and a full children's programme.

Winchester Writers' Conference, Bookfair and Weeklong Workshops – see page 346

Word – University of Aberdeen Writers Festival

University of Aberdeen, Office of External Affairs,
University of Aberdeen, King's College,
Aberdeen AB24 3FX

tel (01224) 273874 *fax* (01224) 272086
email word@abdn.ac.uk
website www.abdn.ac.uk/word
Artistic Director Alan Spence
Takes place May

Over 70 of the world's finest writers and artists take part in a packed weekend of readings, music, art exhibitions and film screenings. The festival hosts some of the UK's best-loved children's writers and some of the richest talents in Gaelic literature.

World Book Day

c/o The Booksellers Association,
272 Vauxhall Bridge Road, London SW1V 1BA
tel (01634) 729810
email wbd@education.co.uk
website www.worldbookday.com
Takes place March

An annual celebration of books and reading aimed at promoting their value and creating the readers of the future. Every schoolchild in full-time education receives a £1 book token. Events take place all over the UK in schools, bookshops, libraries and arts centres. World Book Day was designated by UNESCO as a worldwide celebration of books and reading, and is marked in over 30 countries. It is a partnership of publishers, booksellers and interested parties who work together to promote books and reading for the personal enrichment and enjoyment of all.

See also Readathon (page 377).

Young Readers Birmingham

Children's Office, Central Library,
Chamberlain Square, Birmingham B3 3HQ
tel 0121-303 3368 *fax* 0121-464 1004
email patsy.heap@birmingham.gov.uk
website www.birmingham.gov.uk/youngreaders
Contact Patsy Heap
Takes place May–June

An annual festival targeted at children, young people and families. It aims to promote the enjoyment of reading; to provide imaginative access to books, writers, performers and storytellers; to encourage families to use libraries and to share reading for pleasure; to provide a focus for the celebration of books and reading for children and young people and help raise the media profile of children's books and writing. Approximately 150 events take place.

National Literacy Trust
– better literacy for all

The National Literacy Trust is an independent charity that transforms lives through literacy.

The National Literacy Trust (NLT) wants you to help it campaign for better literacy for all. The organisation believes that literacy transforms lives, and that with better literacy, everyone can succeed in life. For the NLT, 'better literacy', means the combination of reading, writing, speaking and

Further information

National Literacy Trust
68 South Lambeth Road, London SW8 1RL
tel 020-7587 1842
email contact@literacytrust.org.uk
website www.literacytrust.org.uk

listening skills necessary for a fair chance in life, and the belief that society will only be fair when everyone can communicate as well as they need. The NLT believes that with better literacy skills a greater number of people will have the opportunity to improve their skills and transform their lives, and to contribute more to society.

Even today, one in six people in the UK do not have the reading and literacy skills they need to fulfil their potential. The NLT campaigns to improve public understanding of the vital importance and impact of literacy. It believes that everyone is entitled to Reading Rights, the benefits enjoyed by everyone with good literacy skills. Research shows that with good literacy skills, people are happier, healthier, more successful and more likely to contribute to society. The NLT's Reading Rights are:
• The right to learn, to understand and to empathise
• The right to communicate and to be understood
• The right to work, and to be independent
• The right to comprehend and secure our rights as a citizen
• The right to support and encourage our families
• The right to be happy, healthy and secure
• The right to participate, and contribute to society.

Societies, prizes and festivals

Finance for writers and artists

FAQs for writers

Peter Vaines, a chartered accountant and barrister, addresses some frequently asked questions.

What can a working writer claim against tax?

A working writer is carrying on a business and can therefore claim all the expenses which are incurred wholly and exclusively for the purposes of that business. A list showing most of the usual expenses can be found in the article on *Income tax*, starting on page 401 of this *Yearbook*, but there will be other expenses that can be allowed in special circumstances.

Strictly, only expenses which are incurred for the sole purpose of the business can be claimed; there must be no 'duality of purpose' so an item of expenditure cannot be divided into private and business parts. However, HM Revenue & Customs are now able to allow all reasonable expenses (including apportioned sums) where the amounts can be commercially justified.

Allowances can also be claimed for the cost of business assets such as a motor car, personal computers, fax, copying machines and all other equipment (including books) which may be used by the writer. An allowance of 100% of the cost can now be claimed for most assets except cars, for which a lower allowance can be claimed. See the article on *Income tax* (page 401) for further details of the deductions available in respect of capital expenditure.

Can I request interest on fees owed to me beyond 30 days of my invoice?

Yes. A writer is like any other person carrying on a business and is entitled to charge interest at a rate of 8% over bank base rate on any debt outstanding for more than 30 days – although the period of credit can be varied by agreement between the parties. It is not compulsory to claim the interest; it is up to you to decide whether to enforce the right.

What can I do about bad debts?

A writer is in exactly the same position as anybody else carrying on a business over the payment of his or her invoices. It is generally not commercially sensible to insist on payment in advance but where the work involved is substantial (e.g. a book), it is usual to receive one third of the fee on signature, one third of the fee on delivery of the manuscript and the remaining one third on publication. On other assignments, perhaps not as substantial as a book, it could be worthwhile seeking 50% of the fee on signature and the other 50% on delivery. This would provide a degree of protection in case of cancellation of the assignment because of changes of policy or personnel at the publisher.

What financial disputes can I take to the Small Claims Court?

If somebody owes you money you can take them to the Small Claims Section of your local County Court, which deals with financial disputes up to £5,000. The procedure is much less formal than normal court proceedings and involves little expense. It is not necessary to have a solicitor. You fill in a number of forms, turn up on the day and explain the background to why you are owed the money (see www.courtservice.gov.uk).

If I receive an advance, can I divide it between two tax years?

Yes. There is a system known as 'averaging'. This enables writers (and others engaged in the creation of literary, dramatic works or designs) to average the profits of two or more consecutive years if the profits for one year are less than 75% of the profits for the highest year. This relief can apply even if the work takes less than 12 months to create and it allows the writer to avoid the higher rates of tax which might arise if the income in respect of a number of years' work were all to be concentrated in a single year.

How do I make sure I am taxed as a self-employed person so that tax and National Insurance contributions are not deducted at source?

To be taxed as a self-employed person you have to make sure that the contract for the writing cannot be regarded as a contract of employment. This is unlikely to be the case with a professional author. The subject is highly complex but one of the most important features is that the publisher must not be in a position to direct or control the author's work. Where any doubt exists, the author might find the publisher deducting tax and National Insurance contributions as a precaution and that would clearly be highly disadvantageous. The author would be well advised to discuss the position with the publisher before the contract is signed to agree that he or she should be treated as self-employed and that no tax or National Insurance contributions will be deducted from any payments. If such agreement cannot be reached, professional advice should immediately be sought so that the detailed technical position can be explained to the publisher.

Is it a good idea to operate through a limited company?

It can be a good idea for a self-employed writer to operate through a company but generally only where the income is quite large. The costs of operating a company can outweigh any benefit if the writer is paying tax only at the basic rate. Where the writer is paying tax at the higher rate of 40% (or 50%), being able to retain some of the income in a company at a tax rate of only 20% is obviously attractive. However, this will be entirely ineffective if the writer's contract with the publisher would otherwise be an employment. The whole subject of operating through a company is complex and professional advice is essential.

When does it become necessary to register for VAT?

Where the writer's self-employed income (from all sources, not only writing) exceeds £73,000 in the previous 12 months or is expected to do so in the next 30 days, he or she must register for VAT and add VAT to all his/her fees. The publisher will pay the VAT to the writer, who must pay the VAT over to the Customs and Excise each quarter. Any VAT the writer has paid on business expenses and on the purchase of business assets can be deducted. It is possible for some authors to take advantage of the simplified system for VAT payments which applies to small businesses. This involves a flat rate payment of VAT without any need to keep records of VAT on expenses.

If I make a loss from my writing can I get any tax back?

Where a writer makes a loss, HM Revenue & Customs may suggest that the writing is only a hobby and not a professional activity thereby denying any relief or tax deduction for the loss. However, providing the writing is carried out on a sensible commercial basis with an expectation of profits, any resulting loss can be offset against any other income the writer may have for the same or the previous year.

Income tax

Despite attempts by successive Governments to simplify our taxation system, the subject has become increasingly complicated. Peter Vaines, a chartered accountant and barrister, gives a broad outline of taxation from the point of view of writers and other creative professionals. The proposals in the March 2011 Budget are broadly reflected in this article.

How income is taxed

Generally

Authors are usually treated for tax purposes as carrying on a profession and are taxed in a similar fashion to other self-employed professionals. This article is directed to self-employed persons only, because if a writer is employed he or she will be subject to the much less advantageous rules which apply to employment income.

Attempts are often made by employed persons to shake off the status of 'employee' and to attain 'freelance' status so as to qualify for the tax advantages, such attempts meeting with varying degrees of success. The problems involved in making this transition are considerable and space does not permit a detailed explanation to be made here – individual advice is necessary if difficulties are to be avoided.

Particular attention has been paid by HM Revenue & Customs to journalists and to those engaged in the entertainment industry with a view to reclassifying them as employees so that PAYE is deducted from their earnings. This blanket treatment has been extended to other areas and, although it is obviously open to challenge by individual taxpayers, it is always difficult to persuade HM Revenue & Customs to change its views.

There is no reason why employed people cannot carry on a freelance business in their spare time. Indeed, aspiring authors, painters, musicians, etc, often derive so little income from their craft that the financial security of an employment, perhaps in a different sphere of activity, is necessary. The existence of the employment is irrelevant to the taxation of the freelance earnings although it is most important not to confuse the income or expenditure of the employment with the income or expenditure of the self-employed activity. HM Revenue & Customs is aware of the advantages which can be derived by an individual having 'freelance' income from an organisation of which he or she is also an employee, and where such circumstances are contrived, it can be extremely difficult to convince an Inspector of Taxes that a genuine freelance activity is being carried on. Where the individual operates through a company or partnership providing services personally to a particular client, and would be regarded as an employee if the services were supplied directly by the individual, additional problems arise from the notorious IR35 legislation and professional advice is essential.

For those starting in business or commencing work on a freelance basis HM Revenue & Customs produces a very useful booklet, *Thinking of Working for Yourself?* (SE1), which is available from any tax office.

Income

For income to be taxable it need not be substantial, nor even the author's only source of income; earnings from casual writing are also taxable but this can be an advantage, because occasional writers do not often make a profit from their writing. The expenses incurred in connection with writing may well exceed any income receivable and the resultant loss may then be used to reclaim tax paid on other income. There may be deducted from the income certain allowable expenses and capital allowances which are set out in more detail below. The possibility of a loss being used as a basis for a tax repayment is fully appreciated by HM Revenue & Customs, which sometimes attempts to treat casual writing as a hobby so that any losses incurred cannot be used to reclaim tax; of course by the same token any income receivable would not be chargeable to tax. This treatment may sound attractive but it should be resisted vigorously because HM Revenue & Customs does not hesitate to change its mind when profits begin to arise. In the case of exceptional or non-recurring writing, such as the autobiography of a sports personality or the memoirs of a politician, it could be better to be treated as pursuing a hobby and not as a professional author. Sales of copyright cannot be charged to income tax unless the recipient is a professional author. However, the proceeds of sale of copyright may be charged to capital gains tax, even by an individual who is not a professional author.

Royalties

Where the recipient is a professional author, a series of cases has laid down a clear principle that sales of copyright are taxable as income and not as capital receipts. Similarly, lump sums on account of, or in advance of royalties are also taxable as income in the year of receipt, subject to a claim for averaging relief (see below).

Arts Council awards

Arts Council category A awards
- Direct or indirect musical, design or choreographic commissions and direct or indirect commission of sculpture and paintings for public sites.
- The Royalty Supplement Guarantee Scheme.
- The contract writers' scheme.
- Jazz bursaries.
- Translators' grants.
- Photographic awards and bursaries.
- Film and video awards and bursaries.
- Performance Art Awards.
- Art Publishing Grants.
- Grants to assist with a specific project or projects (such as the writing of a book) or to meet specific professional expenses such as a contribution towards copying expenses made to a composer or to an artist's studio expenses.

Arts Council category B awards
- Bursaries to trainee directors.
- Bursaries for associate directors.
- Bursaries to people attending full-time courses in arts administration (the practical training course).
- In-service bursaries to theatre designers and bursaries to trainees on the theatre designers' scheme.
- In-service bursaries for administrators.
- Bursaries for actors and actresses.
- Bursaries for technicians and stage managers.
- Bursaries made to students attending the City University Arts Administration courses.
- Awards, known as the Buying Time Awards, made not to assist with a specific project or professional expenses but to maintain the recipient to enable him or her to take time off to develop his personal talents. These at present include the awards and bursaries known as the Theatre Writing Bursaries, awards and bursaries to composers, awards and bursaries to painters, sculptures and print makers, literature awards and bursaries.

Copyright royalties are generally paid without deduction of income tax. However, if royalties are paid to a person who normally lives abroad, tax must be deducted by the payer or his agent at the time the payment is made unless arrangements are made with HM Revenue & Customs for payments to be made gross under the terms of a Double Taxation Agreement with the other country.

Arts Council grants

Persons in receipt of grants from the Arts Council or similar bodies will be concerned whether or not such grants are liable to income tax. HM Revenue & Customs has issued a Statement of Practice after detailed discussions with the Arts Council regarding the tax treatment of the awards. Grants and other receipts of a similar nature have now been divided into two categories (see box) – those which are to be treated by HM Revenue & Customs as chargeable to tax and those which are not. Category A awards are considered to be taxable; awards made under category B are not chargeable to tax.

This Statement of Practice has no legal force and is used merely to ease the administration of the tax system. It is open to anyone in receipt of a grant or award to disregard the agreed statement and challenge HM Revenue & Customs view on the merits of their particular case. However, it must be recognised that HM Revenue & Customs does not issue such statements lightly and any challenge to their view would almost certainly involve a lengthy and expensive action through the Courts.

The tax position of persons in receipt of literary prizes will generally follow a decision by the Special Commissioners in connection with the Costa Book Awards (previously called the Whitbread Book Awards). In that case it was decided that the prize was not part of the author's professional income and accordingly not chargeable to tax. The precise details are not available because decisions of the Special Commissioners were not, at that time, reported unless an appeal was made to the High Court; HM Revenue & Customs chose not to appeal against this decision. Details of the many literary awards that are given each year start on Children's book and illustration prizes and awards, and this decision is of considerable significance to the winners of each of these prizes. It would be unwise to assume that all such awards will be free of tax as the precise facts which were present in the case of the Whitbread awards may not be repeated in another case; however it is clear that an author winning a prize has some very powerful arguments in his or her favour, should HM Revenue & Customs seek to charge tax on the award.

Allowable expenses

To qualify as an allowable business expense, expenditure has to be laid out wholly and exclusively for business purposes. Strictly there must be no 'duality of purpose', which means that expenditure cannot be apportioned to reflect the private and business usage, e.g. food, clothing, telephone, travelling expenses, etc. However, HM Revenue & Customs are now able to allow all reasonable expenses (including apportioned sums) where the amounts can be commercially justified.

It should be noted carefully that the expenditure does not have to be 'necessary', it merely has to be incurred 'wholly and exclusively' for business purposes. Naturally, however, expenditure of an outrageous and wholly unnecessary character might well give rise to a presumption that it was not really for business purposes. As with all things, some expenses are unquestionably allowable and some expenses are equally unquestionably not allowable – it is the grey area in between which gives rise to all the difficulties and the outcome invariably depends on negotiation with HM Revenue & Customs.

Great care should be taken when claiming a deduction for items where there may be a 'duality of purpose' and negotiations should be conducted with more than usual care and courtesy – if provoked the Inspector of Taxes may well choose to allow nothing. An appeal is always possible although unlikely to succeed as a string of cases in the Courts has clearly demonstrated. An example is the case of *Caillebotte* v. *Quinn* where the taxpayer (who normally had lunch at home) sought to claim the excess cost of meals incurred because he was working a long way from his home. The taxpayer's arguments failed because he did not eat only in order to work, one of the reasons for his eating was in order to sustain his life; a duality of purpose therefore existed and no tax relief was due.

Other cases have shown that expenditure on clothing can also be disallowed if it is the kind of clothing which is in everyday use, because clothing is worn not only to assist the pursuit of one's profession but also to accord with public decency. This duality of purpose may be sufficient to deny relief – even where the particular type of clothing is of a kind not otherwise worn by the taxpayer. In the case of *Mallalieu* v. *Drummond* a barrister failed to obtain a tax deduction for items of sombre clothing that she purchased specifically for wearing in Court. The House of Lords decided that a duality of purpose existed because clothing represented part of her needs as a human being.

Allowances

Despite the above, Inspectors of Taxes are not usually inflexible and the following list of expenses are among those generally allowed.

(a) Cost of all materials used up in the course of preparation of the work.

(b) Cost of typewriting and secretarial assistance, etc; if this or other help is obtained from one's spouse then it is entirely proper for a deduction to be claimed for the amounts paid for the work. The amounts claimed must actually be paid to the spouse and should be at the market rate although some uplift can be made for unsocial hours, etc. Payments to a wife (or husband) are of course taxable in her (or his) hands and should therefore be most carefully considered. The wife's earnings may also be liable for National Insurance contributions and it is important to take care because otherwise you may find that these contributions outweigh the tax savings. The impact of the National Minimum Wage should also be considered.

(c) All expenditure on normal business items such as postage, stationery, telephone, email, fax and answering machines, agent's fees, accountancy charges, photography, subscriptions, periodicals, magazines, etc, may be claimed. The cost of daily papers should not be overlooked if these form part of research material. Visits to theatres, cinemas, etc, for research purposes may also be permissible (but not the cost relating to guests). Unfortunately, expenditure on all types of business entertaining is specifically denied tax relief.

(d) If work is conducted at home, a deduction for 'use of home' is usually allowed providing the amount claimed is reasonable. If the claim is based on an appropriate proportion of the total costs of rent, light and heat, cleaning and maintenance, insurance, etc (but not the Council Tax), care should be taken to ensure that no single room is used 'exclusively' for business purposes, because this may result in the Capital Gains Tax exemption on the house as the only or main residence being partially forfeited. However, it would be a strange household where one room was in fact used exclusively for business purposes and for no other purpose whatsoever (e.g. storing personal bank statements and other private papers); the usual formula is to claim a deduction on the basis that most or all of the rooms in the house are used at one time or another for business purposes, thereby avoiding any suggestion that any part was used exclusively for business purposes.

(e) The appropriate business proportion of motor running expenses may also be claimed although what is the appropriate proportion will naturally depend on the particular circumstances of each case; it should be appreciated that the well-known scale of benefits, whereby employees are taxed according to the size of the car's CO_2 emissions, do not apply to self-employed persons.

(f) It has been long established that the cost of travelling from home to work (whether employed or self-employed) is not an allowable expense. However, if home is one's place of work then no expenditure under this heading is likely to be incurred and difficulties are unlikely to arise.

(g) Travelling and hotel expenses incurred for business purposes will normally be allowed but if any part could be construed as disguised holiday or pleasure expenditure, considerable thought would need to be given to the commercial reasons for the journey in order to justify the claim. The principle of 'duality of purpose' will always be a difficult hurdle in this connection – although not insurmountable.

(h) If a separate business bank account is maintained, any overdraft interest thereon will be an allowable expense. This is the only circumstance in which overdraft interest is allowed for tax purposes and care should be taken to avoid overdrafts in all other circumstances.

(i) Where capital allowances (see below) are claimed for a personal computer, fax, modem, television, video, CD or tape player, etc, used for business purposes the costs of maintenance and repair of the equipment may also be claimed.

Clearly many other allowable items may be claimed in addition to those listed. Wherever there is any reasonable business motive for some expenditure it should be claimed as a deduction although it is necessary to preserve all records relating to the expense. It is sensible to avoid an excess of imagination as this would naturally cause the Inspector of Taxes to doubt the genuineness of other expenses claimed.

The question is often raised whether the whole amount of an expense may be deducted or whether the VAT content must be excluded. Where VAT is reclaimed from the Customs and Excise by someone who is registered for VAT, the VAT element of the expense cannot be treated as an allowable deduction. Where the VAT is not reclaimed, the whole expense (inclusive of VAT) is allowable for income tax purposes.

Capital allowances

Allowances

Where expenditure of a capital nature is incurred, it cannot be deducted from income as an expense – a separate and sometimes more valuable capital allowance being available instead. Capital allowances are given for many different types of expenditure, but authors and similar professional people are likely to claim only for 'plant and machinery'; this is a very wide expression which may include motor cars, personal computers, fax and photocopying machines, modems, televisions, CD, video and cassette players used for business purposes. Plant and machinery generally qualifies for an allowance of 100% (reduced to 20% for expenditure over £25,000). Where the useful life of an asset is expected to be short, it is possible to claim special treatment as a 'short life asset' enabling the allowances to be accelerated.

The reason these allowances can be more valuable than allowable expenses is that they may be wholly or partly disclaimed in any year that full benefit cannot be obtained – ordinary business expenses cannot be similarly disclaimed. Where, for example, the income of an author does not exceed his personal allowances, he would not be liable to tax and a claim for capital allowances would be wasted. If the capital allowances were to be disclaimed their benefit would be carried forward for use in subsequent years. This would also be advantageous where the income is likely to be taxable at the higher rate of 40% (or even the new 50% rate) in a subsequent year. Careful planning with claims for capital allowances is therefore essential if maximum benefit is to be obtained.

As an alternative to capital allowances, claims can be made on the 'renewals' basis whereby all renewals are treated as allowable deductions in the year; no allowance is obtained for the initial purchase, but the cost of replacement (excluding any improvement element) is allowed in full. This basis is no longer widely used, as it is considerably less advantageous than claiming capital allowances as described above.

Leasing is a popular method of acquiring fixed assets, and where cash is not available to enable an outright purchase to be made, assets may be leased over a period of time. Whilst leasing may have financial benefits in certain circumstances, in normal cases there is likely to be no tax advantage in leasing an asset where the alternative of outright purchase is available.

Books

The question of whether the cost of books is eligible for tax relief has long been a source of difficulty. The annual cost of replacing books used for the purposes of one's professional activities (e.g. the cost of a new *Children's Writers' & Artists' Yearbook* each year) has always been an allowable expense; the difficulty arose because the initial cost of reference books, etc (e.g. when commencing one's profession) was treated as capital expenditure but no allowances were due as the books were not considered to be 'plant'. However, the matter was clarified by the case of *Munby* v. *Furlong* in which the Court of Appeal decided that the initial cost of law books purchased by a barrister was expenditure on 'plant' and eligible for capital allowances. This is clearly a most important decision, particularly relevant to any person who uses expensive books in the course of exercising his or her profession.

Pension contributions

Where a self-employed person makes contributions to a pension scheme, those contributions are usually deductible.

These arrangements are generally advantageous in providing for a pension as contributions are usually paid when the income is high (and the tax relief is also high) and the pension (taxed as earned income when received) usually arises when the income is low and little tax is payable. There is also the opportunity to take part of the pension entitlement as a tax-free lump sum. It is necessary to take into account the possibility that the tax advantages could go into reverse. When the pension is paid it could, if rates rise again, be taxed at a higher rate than the rate of tax relief at the moment. From 6 April 2006 a whole new regime for pensions was introduced to create a much simpler system. Each individual has a lifetime allowance of £1.8 million and when benefits crystallise, which will generally be when a pension begins to be paid, this is measured against the individual's lifetime allowance; any excess will be taxed at 25%, or at 55% if the excess is taken as a lump sum.

Each individual also has an annual allowance for contributions to the pension fund which is set at £50,000 for 2011/12 but may change in later years. If the annual increase in an individual's rights under all registered schemes of which he is a member exceeds the annual allowance, the excess is chargeable to tax.

For many writers and artists this means that they can contribute a large part of their earnings to a pension scheme (if they can afford to do so) without any of the previous complications. It is still necessary to be careful where there is other income giving rise to a pension because the whole of the pension entitlement has to be taken into account.

Flexible retirement is possible allowing members of occupational pension schemes to continue working while also drawing retirement benefits. As part of this reform, however, the normal minimum pension age was raised from 50 to 55 on 6 April 2010.

Class 4 National Insurance contributions

Allied to pensions is the payment of Class 4 National Insurance contributions, although no pension or other benefit is obtained by the contributions; the Class 4 contributions are designed solely to extract additional amounts from self-employed persons and are payable in addition to the normal Class 2 (self-employed) contributions. The rates are changed each year and for 2011/12 self-employed persons will be obliged to contribute 9% of their profits between the range £7,225–£42,475 per annum plus 2% on earnings above £42,475. This amount is collected in conjunction with the annual income tax liability.

Averaging relief
Relief for copyright payments

For many years special provisions enabled authors and similar persons engaged on a literary, dramatic, musical or artistic work for a period of more than 12 months, to spread certain amounts received over two or three years depending on the time spent in preparing the work.

Since 2001 there has been a simpler system of averaging. Under these rules, professional authors and artists engaged in the creation of literary, dramatic works or designs may claim to average the profits of two or more consecutive years if the profits for one year are less than 75% of the profits for the highest year. This new relief can apply even if the work took less than 12 months to create and is available to people who create works in partnership with others.

The purpose of the relief is to enable the creative artist to utilise his allowances fully and to avoid the higher rates of tax which might apply if all the income were to arise in a single year.

Collection of tax
Self-assessment

In 1997, the system of sending in a tax return showing all your income and HM Revenue & Customs raising an assessment to collect the tax was abolished. So was the idea that you pay tax on your profits for the preceding year. Now, when you send in your tax return you have to work out your own tax liability and send a cheque; this is called 'self-assessment'. If you get it wrong, or if you are late with your tax return or the payment of tax, interest and penalties will be charged.

Under this system, HM Revenue & Customs rarely issue assessments; they are no longer necessary because the idea is that you assess yourself. A colour-coded tax return was created, designed to help individuals meet their tax obligations. This is a daunting task but the term 'self-assessment' is not intended to imply that individuals have to do it themselves; they can (and often will) engage professional help. The term is only intended to convey that it is the taxpayer, and not HM Revenue & Customs, who is responsible for getting the tax liability right and for it to be paid on time.

The deadline for sending in the tax return is 31 October following the end of the tax year. This is the deadline for paper tax returns. You can file online, in which case you have until 31 January following the end of the tax year. If for some reason you are unwilling or unable to calculate the tax payable, you can ask HM Revenue & Customs to do it for you on your paper tax return.

Income tax on self-employed earnings remains payable in two instalments on 31 January and 31 July each year. Because the accurate figures may not necessarily be known, these payments in January and July will therefore be only payments on account based on the previous year's liability. The final balancing figure will be paid the following 31 January together with the first instalment of the liability for the following year.

When HM Revenue & Customs receives the self-assessment tax return, it is checked to see if there is anything obviously wrong; if there is, a letter will be sent to you immediately. Otherwise, HM Revenue & Customs has 12 months from the filing date in which to make further enquiries; if it doesn't, it will have no further opportunity to do so and your tax liabilities are final – unless there is something seriously wrong such as the omission of income or capital gains. In that event, HM Revenue & Customs will raise an assessment later to collect any extra tax together with appropriate penalties. It is essential for the operation of the new system that all records relevant to your tax returns are retained for at least 12 months in case they are needed by HM Revenue & Customs. For the self-employed, the record-keeping requirement is much more onerous because the records need to be kept for nearly six years. One important change in the rules is that if you claim a tax deduction for an expense, it will be necessary to have a receipt or other document proving that the expenditure has been made. Because the existence of the underlying records is so important to the operation of self-assessment, HM Revenue & Customs will treat them very seriously and there is a penalty of £3,000 for any failure to keep adequate records.

Interest

Interest is chargeable on overdue tax at a variable rate, which at the time of writing is 3% per annum. It does not rank for any tax relief, which can make HM Revenue & Customs an expensive source of credit.

However, HM Revenue & Customs can also be obliged to pay interest (known as repayment supplement) tax-free where repayments are delayed. The rules relating to re-payment supplement are less beneficial and even more complicated than the rules for interest payable but they do exist and can be very welcome if a large repayment has been delayed for a long time. Unfortunately, the rate of repayment supplement is only 0.5% and is always less than the rate charged by HMRC on overdue tax.

Value added tax

The activities of writers, painters, composers, etc are all 'taxable supplies' within the scope of VAT and chargeable at the standard rate. (Zero rating which applies to publishers, booksellers, etc on the supply of books does not extend to the work performed by writers.) Accordingly, authors are obliged to register for VAT if their income for the past 12 months exceeds £73,000 or if their income for the coming month will exceed that figure.

Delay in registering can be a most serious matter because if registration is not effected at the proper time, the Customs and Excise can (and invariably do) claim VAT from all the income received since the date on which registration should have been made. As no VAT would have been included in the amounts received during this period the amount claimed by the Customs and Excise must inevitably come straight from the pocket of the author.

The author may be entitled to seek reimbursement of the VAT from those whom he or she ought to have charged VAT but this is obviously a matter of some difficulty and may indeed damage his commercial relationships. Apart from these disadvantages there is also a penalty for late registration. The rules are extremely harsh and are imposed automatically even in cases of innocent error. It is therefore extremely important to monitor the income very carefully because if in any period of 12 months the income exceeds the £73,000 limit, the Customs and Excise must be notified within 30 days of the end of the period. Failure to do so will give rise to an automatic penalty. It should be emphasised that this is a penalty for failing to submit a form and has nothing to do with any real or potential loss of tax. Furthermore, whether the failure was innocent or deliberate will not matter. Only the existence of a 'reasonable excuse' will be a defence to the penalty. However, a reasonable excuse does not include ignorance, error, a lack of funds or reliance on any third party.

However, it is possible to regard VAT registration as a privilege and not a penalty, because only VAT registered persons can reclaim VAT paid on their expenses such as stationery, telephone, professional fees, etc, and even computers and other plant and machinery (excluding cars). However, many find that the administrative inconvenience – the cost of maintaining the necessary records and completing the necessary forms – more than outweighs the benefits to be gained from registration and prefer to stay outside the scope of VAT for as long as possible.

Overseas matters

The general observation may be made that self-employed persons resident and domiciled in the UK are not well treated with regard to their overseas work, being taxable on their worldwide income. It is important to emphasise that if fees are earned abroad, no tax saving can be achieved merely by keeping the money outside the country. Although exchange control regulations no longer exist to require repatriation of foreign earnings, such income remains taxable in the UK and must be disclosed to HM Revenue & Customs; the same applies to interest or other income arising on any investment of these earnings overseas. Accordingly, whenever foreign earnings are likely to become substantial, prompt and effective action is required to limit the impact of UK and foreign taxation. In the case of non-resident authors it is important that arrangements concerning writing for publication in the UK, e.g. in newspapers, are undertaken with great care. A case concerning the wife of one of the great train robbers who provided detailed information for a series of articles in a Sunday newspaper is most instructive. Although she was acknowledged to be resident in Canada for all the relevant years, the income from the articles was treated as arising in this country and fully chargeable to UK tax.

The UK has double taxation agreements with many other countries and these agreements are designed to ensure that income arising in a foreign country is taxed either in

Finance for writers and artists

that country or in the UK. Where a withholding tax is deducted from payments received from another country (or where tax is paid in full in the absence of a double taxation agreement), the amount of foreign tax paid can usually be set off against the related UK tax liability. Many successful authors can be found living in Eire because of the complete exemption from tax which attaches to works of cultural or artistic merit by persons who are resident there. However, such a step should only be contemplated having careful regard to all the other domestic and commercial considerations and specialist advice is essential if the exemption is to be obtained and kept; a careless breach of the conditions could cause the exemption to be withdrawn with catastrophic consequences.

Further information concerning the precise conditions to be satisfied for exemption from tax in Eire can be obtained from the Revenue Commissioners in Dublin or from their website (www.revenue.ie).

Companies

When an author becomes successful the prospect of paying tax at the higher rate may drive them to take hasty action such as the formation of companies, etc, which may not always be to their advantage. Indeed some authors seeing the exodus into tax exile of their more successful colleagues even form companies in low tax areas in the naive expectation of saving large amounts of tax. HM Revenue & Customs is fully aware of these possibilities and have extensive powers to charge tax and combat avoidance. Accordingly, such action is just as likely to increase tax liabilities and generate other costs and should never be contemplated without expert advice; some very expensive mistakes are often made in this area which are not always able to be remedied.

To conduct one's business through the medium of a company can be a most effective method of mitigating tax liabilities, and providing it is done at the right time and under the right circumstances very substantial advantages can be derived. However, if done without due care and attention the intended advantages will simply evaporate. At the very least it is essential to ensure that the company's business is genuine and conducted properly with regard to the realities of the situation. If the author continues his or her activities unchanged, simply paying all the receipts from his work into a company's bank account, he cannot expect to persuade HM Revenue & Customs that it is the company and not himself who is entitled to, and should be assessed to tax on, that income.

It must be strongly emphasised that many pitfalls exist which can easily eliminate all the tax benefits expected to arise by the formation of the company. For example, company directors are employees of the company and will be liable to pay much higher National Insurance contributions; the company must also pay the employer's proportion of the contribution and a total liability of nearly 24% of gross salary may arise. This compares most unfavourably with the position of a self-employed person. Moreover, on the commencement of the company's business the individual's profession will cease and the possibility of revisions being made by HM Revenue & Customs to earlier tax liabilities means that the timing of a change has to be considered very carefully.

The tax return

No mention has been made above of personal reliefs and allowances; this is because these allowances and the rates of tax are subject to constant change and are always set out in detail in the explanatory notes which accompany the Tax Return. The annual Tax Return is an important document and should be completed promptly with extreme care, particularly since the introduction of self-assessment. If filling in the Return is a source of difficulty or anxiety, comfort may be found in the Consumer Association's publication *Money Which? – Tax Saving Guide*, which is published in March of each year and includes much which is likely to be of interest and assistance.

Peter Vaines FCA, CTA, barrister, is a partner in the international law firm of Squire Sanders Hammonds and writes and speaks widely on tax matters. He is on the Editorial Boards of *Taxation* and *Personal Tax Planning Review*, tax columnist of the *New Law Journal* and author of a number of books on taxation.

Social security contributions

In general, every individual who works in Great Britain either as an employee or as a self-employed person is liable to pay social security contributions. The law governing this subject is complex and Peter Arrowsmith FCA gives here a summary of the position. This article should be regarded as a general guide only.

All contributions are payable in respect of years ending on 5 April. See box (below) for the classes of contributions.

Employed or self-employed?

The question as to whether a person is employed under a contract *of* service and is thereby an employee liable to Class 1 contributions, or performs services (either solely or in partnership) under a contract *for* service and is thereby self-employed liable to Class 2 and Class 4 contributions, often has to be decided in practice. One of the best guides can be found in the case of *Market Investigations Ltd* v. *Minister of Social Security* (1969 2 WLR 1) when Cooke J. remarked:

'...the fundamental test to be applied is this: "Is the person who has engaged himself to perform these services performing them as a person in business on his own account?" If the answer to that question is 'yes', then the contract is a contract for services. If the answer is 'no', then the contract is a contract of service. No exhaustive list has been compiled and perhaps no exhaustive list can be compiled of the considerations which are relevant in determining that question, nor can strict rules be laid down as to the relative weight which the various considerations should carry in particular cases. The most that can be said is that control will no doubt always have to be considered, although it can no longer be regarded as the sole determining factor; and that factors which may be of importance are such matters as:

• whether the man performing the services provides his own equipment,
• whether he hires his own helpers,
• what degree of financial risk he takes,
• what degree of responsibility for investment and management he has, and
• whether and how far he has an opportunity of profiting from sound management in the performance of his task.'

The above case has often been considered subsequently – notably in November 1993 by the Court of Appeal in the case of *Hall* v. *Lorimer*. In this case a vision mixer with around 20 clients and undertaking around 120–150 separate engagements per annum was held to be self-employed. This follows the, perhaps surprising, contention of the former Inland Revenue that the taxpayer was an employee.

> ### Classes of contributions
>
> **Class 1** These are payable by employees (primary contributions) and their employers (secondary contributions) and are based on earnings.
>
> **Class 1A** Payable only by employers in respect of all taxable benefits in kind.
>
> **Class 1B** Payable only by employers in respect of PAYE Settlement Agreements entered into by them.
>
> **Class 2** These are weekly flat rate contributions, payable by the self-employed.
>
> **Class 3** These are weekly flat rate contributions, payable on a voluntary basis in order to provide, or make up entitlement to, certain social security benefits.
>
> **Class 4** These are payable by the self-employed in respect of their trading or professional income and are based on earnings.

Exceptions

There are certain exceptions to the above rules, those most relevant to artists and writers being:

• The employment of a wife by her husband, or vice versa, is disregarded for social security purposes unless it is for the purposes of a trade or profession (e.g. the employment of his wife by an author would not be disregarded and would result in a liability for contributions if her salary reached the minimum levels). The same provisions also apply to civil partners from 5 December 2005.

• The employment of certain relatives in a private dwelling house in which both employee and employer reside is disregarded for social security purposes provided the employment is not for the purposes of a trade or business carried on at those premises by the employer. This would cover the employment of a relative (as defined) as a housekeeper in a private residence.

In general, lecturers, teachers and instructors engaged by an educational establishment to teach on at least four days in three consecutive months are regarded as employees for social security purposes, although this rule does not apply to fees received by persons giving public lectures.

Freelance film workers

There is a list of grades in the film industry in respect of which PAYE need not be deducted and who are regarded as self-employed for tax purposes.

Further information can be obtained from the guidance notes on the application of PAYE to casual and freelance staff in the film industry, a revised edition of which was issued by HMRC in April 2011. In view of the HMRC announcement that the same status will apply for PAYE and National Insurance contributions purposes, no liability for employee's and employer's contributions should arise in the case of any of the grades mentioned above.

However, in the film and television industry this general rule was not always followed in practice. In December 1992, after a long review, the DSS agreed that individuals working behind the camera and who have jobs on the Inland Revenue Schedule D list are self-employed for social security purposes.

There are special rules for, *inter alia*, personnel appearing before the camera, short engagements, payments to limited companies and payments to overseas personalities.

Artistes, performers/non-performers

The status of artistes and performers for tax purposes will depend on the individual circumstances but for social security purposes new regulations which took effect on 17 July 1998 require most entertainers, including actors, musicians or similar performers to be treated as employees, whether or not this status applies under general and/or tax law. It also applies whether or not the individual is supplied through an agency. The above position has been confirmed and strengthened in most cases by the First-tier Tribunal case *ITV Services Ltd* v. *HMRC* TC 836. However, ITV may well appeal the decision.

Personal service companies

From 6 April 2000, those who have control of their own 'one-man service companies' are subject to special rules. If the work that the owner of the company does for the company's customers would – but for the one-man company – be considered as an employment of that individual (i.e. rather than self-employment), a deemed salary may arise. If it does, then some or all of the income of the company will be treated as salary liable to PAYE and National Insurance contributions. This will be the case whether or not such salary is actually paid by the company. The same situation may arise where the worker owns as little as 5% of a company's share capital.

The calculations required by HM Revenue & Customs are complicated and have to be done very quickly at the end of each tax year (even if the company's year-end does not coincide). It is essential that affected businesses seek detailed professional advice about these rules which may also, in certain circumstances, apply to partnerships.

In order to escape the application of these rules, a number of workers have arranged their engagements through 'managed service companies', etc where the promoter is heavily involved in all the company management to the exclusion of the workers themselves. Such companies are now subjected to similar, but different, rules from 6 April 2007 for tax and 6 August 2007 for NIC.

Pension age

The current pensionable age for men is 65. In the case of women the previous age of 60 no longer applies as from 6 April 2010 to 5 April 2020 the female pensionable age is now rising to 66. This means that National Insurance contributions (NICs) will be payable by women up to the extended pension age. In 2011 and 2012 women will reach state pension age on the following dates dependent on date of birth:

Date of birth	Pension age
6 August 1950 to 5 September 1950	6 January 2011
6 September 1950 to 5 October 1950	6 March 2011
6 October 1950 to 5 November 1950	6 May 2011
6 November 1950 to 5 December 1950	6 July 2011
6 December 1950 to 5 January 1951	6 September 2011
6 January 1951 to 5 February 1951	6 November 2011
6 February 1951 to 5 March 1951	6 January 2012
6 March 1951 to 5 April 1951	6 March 2012
6 April 1951 to 5 May 1951	6 May 2012
6 May 1951 to 5 June 1951	6 July 2012
6 June 1951 to 5 July 1951	6 September 2012
6 July 1951 to 5 August 1951	6 November 2012

From late 2018 the pensionable age for both men and women will rise to 66 (by March 2020), and will rise further to 67 over the two-year period from 2034–6 and then similarly to 68 from 2044–6. The increases to 67 and 68 are under review by the coalition government and may yet be accelerated.

Class 1 contributions

As mentioned above, these are related to earnings, the amount payable depending upon whether the employer has applied for his employees to be 'contracted-out' of the State earnings-related pension scheme; such application can be made where the employer's own pension scheme provides a requisite level of benefits for his or her employees and their dependants (salary related, COSR) or, in the case of a money purchase scheme (COMPS) certain minimum safeguards are covered. Contracting-out through a COMPS arrangement will not attract any reduction in Class 1 contributions with effect from 6 April 2012.

Employers with employees contributing to 'stakeholder pension plans' continue to pay the full not contracted-out rate. Such employees have their contracting out arrangements handled separately by government authorities.

Contributions are payable by employees and employers on earnings that exceed the earnings threshold. Contributions are normally collected via the PAYE tax deduction machinery, and there are penalties for late submission of returns and for errors therein. From 19 April 1993, interest is charged automatically on PAYE and social security contributions paid late.

Employees liable to pay

Contributions are payable by any employee who is aged 16 years and over (even though they may still be at school) and who is paid an amount equal to, or exceeding, the earnings threshold. Nationality is irrelevant for contribution purposes and, subject to special rules covering employees not normally resident in Great Britain, Northern Ireland or the Isle of Man, or resident in EEA countries or those with which there are reciprocal agreements, contributions must be paid whether the employee concerned is a British subject or not provided he is gainfully employed in Great Britain.

Employees exempt from liability to pay

Persons over pensionable age are exempt from liability to pay primary contributions, even if they have not retired. However, the fact that an employee may be exempt from liability does not relieve an employer from liability to pay secondary contributions in respect of that employee.

Employees' (primary) contributions

From 6 April 2011, the rate of employees' contributions on earnings from the employee earnings threshold to the upper earnings limit is 12% (for contracted-out employment 10.4% up to the upper accrual point, then 12% to the upper earnings limit). Certain married women who made appropriate elections before 12 May 1977 may be entitled to pay a reduced rate of 5.85%. However, they will have no entitlement to benefits in respect of these contributions. It should be noted that from 6 April 2011 the employee and employer earnings thresholds are no longer the same.

From April 2003, earnings above the upper earnings limit attract an employee contribution liability at the additional rate. Previously, this was 1% but from 6 April 2011 is 2%.

Employers' (secondary) contributions

All employers are liable to pay contributions on the gross earnings of employees. As mentioned above, an employer's liability is not reduced as a result of employees being exempted from contributions, or being liable to pay only the reduced rate (5.85%) of contributions.

For earnings paid on or after 6 April 2011 employers are liable at a rate of 13.8% on earnings paid above the employer earnings threshold (without any upper earnings limit), 10.1% where the employment is contracted out (salary related) or 12.4% contracted out (money purchase). In addition, special rebates apply in respect of earnings falling between the lower earnings limit and the earnings threshold. This provides, effectively, a negative rate of contribution in that small band of earnings. It should be noted that the contracted-out rates of 10.1% and 12.4% now apply only up to the upper accrual point. Thereafter, the not contracted-out rate of 13.8% is applicable. Prior to 6 April 2009 the contracted-out rates applied up to the upper earnings limit.

Finance for writers and artists

The employer is responsible for the payment of both employees' and employer's contributions, but is entitled to deduct the employees' contributions from the earnings on which they are calculated. Effectively, therefore, the employee suffers a deduction in respect of his or her social security contributions in arriving at his weekly or monthly wage or salary. Special rules apply to company directors and persons employed through agencies.

Items included in, or excluded from, earnings

Contributions are calculated on the basis of a person's gross earnings from their employment. This will normally be the figure shown on the deduction working sheet, except where the employee pays superannuation contributions and, from 6 April 1987, charitable gifts under payroll giving – these must be added back for the purposes of calculating Class 1 liability.

Earnings include salary, wages, overtime pay, commissions, bonuses, holiday pay, payments made while the employee is sick or absent from work, payments to cover travel between home and office, and payments under the statutory sick pay, statutory maternity pay, statutory paternity pay and statutory adoption pay schemes.

However, certain payments, some of which may be regarded as taxable income for income tax purposes, are ignored for Class 1 purposes. These include:
• certain gratuities paid other than by the employer;
• redundancy payments and some payments in lieu of notice;
• certain payments in kind;
• reimbursement of specific expenses incurred in the carrying out of the employment;
• benefits given on an individual basis for personal reasons (e.g. wedding and birthday presents);
• compensation for loss of office.

Booklet CWG 2 (2011 edition) gives a list of items to include in or exclude from earnings for Class 1 contribution purposes. Some such items may, however, be liable to Class 1A (employer only) contributions.

Miscellaneous rules

There are detailed rules covering a person with two or more employments; where a person receives a bonus or commission in addition to a regular wage or salary; and where a person is in receipt of holiday pay. From 6 April 1991 employers' social security contributions

Rates of Class 1 contributions and earnings limits from 6 April 2011

Earnings per week	Rates payable on earnings in each band			
	Not contracted out		Contracted out	
	Employee	Employer	Employee	Employer
£	%	%	%	%
Below 102.00	–	–	–	–
102.00–135.99	–	–	– (*)	– (*)
136.00–138.99	–	13.8	– (*)	10.1 or 12.4
139.00–769.99	12	13.8	10.4	10.1 or 12.4
770.00–817.00	12	13.8	12	13.8
Over 817.00	2	13.8	2	13.8

* Special rebates deductible in respect of this band of earnings.

arise under Class 1A in respect of the private use of a company car, and of fuel provided for private use therein. From 6 April 2000, this charge was extended to cover most taxable benefits in kind. The rate is now 13.8%. From 6 April 1999, Class 1B contributions are payable by employers using PAYE Settlement Agreements in respect of small and/or ir-regular expense payments and benefits, etc. This rate is also currently 13.8%.

Upper accrual point

From 6 April 2009 there was introduced a new upper accrual point (UAP) from which entitlement to benefit (principally earnings-related state pension) ceases, even though main rate Class 1 contributions continue to be due. This impacts on contracted-out employees in particular. The UAP is fixed at a constant cash amount of £770 per week and will eliminate any earnings-related element of the state pension by around 2031.

Class 2 contributions

Class 2 contributions are payable at the weekly rate of £2.50 as from 6 April 2011. Exemp-tions from Class 2 liability are:
• A person over pensionable age.
• A person who has not attained the age of 16.
• A married woman or, in certain cases, a widow either of whom elected prior to 12 May 1977 not to pay Class 2 contributions.
• Persons with small earnings (see below).
• Persons not ordinarily self-employed (see below).

Small earnings

Application for a certificate of exception from Class 2 contributions may be made by any person who can show that his or her net self-employed earnings per his profit and loss account (as opposed to taxable profits):
• for the year of application are expected to be less than a specified limit (£5,315 in the 2011/12 tax year); or
• for the year preceding the application were less than the limit specified for that year (£5,075 for 2010/11) and there has been no material change of circumstances.

Certificates of exception must be renewed in accordance with the instructions stated thereon. At HM Revenue & Customs' discretion the certificate may commence up to 13 weeks before the date on which the application is made. Despite a certificate of exception being in force, a person who is self-employed is still entitled to pay Class 2 contributions if they wish, in order to maintain entitlement to social security benefits.

Persons not ordinarily self-employed

Part-time self-employed activities (including as a writer or artist) are disregarded for con-tribution purposes if the person concerned is not ordinarily employed in such activities and has a full-time job as an employee. There is no definition of 'ordinarily employed' for this purpose. Persons qualifying for this relief do not require certificates of exception but may be well advised to apply for one nonetheless.

Method of payment

Class 2 contributions may be paid by monthly or six-monthly direct debit in arrears or, alternatively, by cheque, bank giro, etc following receipt of a six-monthly (in arrears) bill.

Overpaid contributions

If, following the payment of Class 2 contributions, it is found that the earnings are below the exception limit (e.g. the relevant accounts are prepared late), the Class 2 contributions

Finance for writers and artists

that have been overpaid can be reclaimed, provided a claim is made between 6 April and 31 January immediately following the end of the tax year. Such a refund may, however, prejudice entitlement to contributory benefits.

Class 3 contributions

Class 3 contributions are payable voluntarily, at the weekly rate of £12.60 per week from 6 April 2011, by persons aged 16 or over with a view to enabling them to qualify for a limited range of benefits if their contribution record is not otherwise sufficient. In general, Class 3 contributions can be paid by employees, the self-employed and the non employed.

Broadly speaking, no more than 52 Class 3 contributions are payable for any one tax year, and contributions cannot be paid in respect of tax years after the one in which the individual concerned reaches state pension age. Class 3 contributions may be paid in the same manner as Class 2 (see above) or by annual cheque in arrears.

Class 4 contributions

In addition to Class 2 contributions, self-employed persons are liable to pay Class 4 contributions. These are calculated at the rate of 9% on the amount of profits or gains chargeable to income tax which exceed £7,225 per annum but which do not exceed £42,475 per annum for 2011/12. Profits above the upper limit of £42,475 attract a Class 4 charge at the rate of 2%. The income tax profit on which Class 4 contributions are calculated is after deducting capital allowances and losses, but before deducting personal tax allowances or retirement annuity or personal pension or stakeholder pension plan premiums.

Class 4 contributions produce no additional benefits, but were introduced to ensure that self-employed persons as a whole pay a fair share of the cost of pensions and other social security benefits, yet without those who make only small profits having to pay excessively high flat rate contributions.

Payment of contributions

In general, Class 4 contributions are now self-assessed and paid to HM Revenue & Customs together with the income tax as a result of the self-assessment income tax return, and accordingly the contributions are due and payable at the same time as the income tax liability on the relevant profits. Under self-assessment, interim payments of Class 4 contributions are payable at the same time as interim payments of tax.

Further information

Further information can be obtained from the many booklets published by HM Revenue & Customs, available from local Enquiry Centres and on their website (www.hmrc.gov.uk).

National Insurance Contributions Office, International Caseworker
Newcastle upon Tyne NE98 1ZZ
tel (08459) 154811 (local call rates apply)
Address for enquiries for individuals resident abroad.

Class 4 exemptions

The following persons are exempt from Class 4 contributions:
• Persons over state pension age at the commencement of the year of assessment (i.e. on 6 April).
• An individual not resident in the UK for income tax purposes in the year of assessment.
• Persons whose earnings are not 'immediately derived' from carrying on a trade, profession or vocation (e.g. sleeping partners).

• A child under 16 on 6 April of the year of assessment.
• Persons not ordinarily self-employed.

Married persons and partnerships

Under independent taxation of husband and wife from 1990/1 onwards, each spouse is responsible for his or her own Class 4 liability.

In partnerships, each partner's liability is calculated separately. If a partner also carries on another trade or profession, the profits of all such businesses are aggregated for the purposes of calculating their Class 4 liability.

When an assessment has become final and conclusive for the purposes of income tax, it is also final and conclusive for the purposes of calculating Class 4 liability.

Maximum contributions

There is a form of limit to the total liability for social security contributions payable by a person who is employed in more than one employment, or is also self-employed or a partner.

Where only not contracted-out Class 1 contributions, or not contracted-out Class 1 and Class 2 contributions, are payable, the maximum contribution payable at the main rates (12%, 10.4% or 5.85% as the case may be) is limited to 53 primary Class 1 contributions at the maximum weekly not contracted-out standard rate. For 2011/12 this 'maximum' will thus be £4,312.08 (amounts paid at only 2% are to be excluded in making this comparison).

However, where contracted-out Class 1 contributions are payable, the maximum primary Class 1 contributions payable for 2011/12 where all employments are contracted out are £3,745.61 (again excluding amounts paid at only 2%).

Where Class 4 contributions are payable in addition to Class 1 and/or Class 2 contributions, the Class 4 contributions payable at the full 9% rate are restricted for 2011/12 so that they shall not exceed the excess of £3,305.00 (i.e. 53 Class 2 contributions plus maximum Class 4 contributions) over the aggregate of the Class 1 and Class 2 contributions paid at the full (i.e. other than 2%) rates.

Transfer of government departmental functions

The administrative functions of the former Contributions Agency transferred to the Inland Revenue from 1 April 1999. Responsibility for National Insurance contribution policy matters was also transferred from DSS Ministers to the Inland Revenue and Treasury Ministers on the same date. The DSS is now known as the Department for Work and Pensions (DWP). From 18 April 2005, the functions of the former Inland Revenue and former HM Customs and Excise were merged to become HM Revenue & Customs.

Merger with income tax

It was announced in the 2011 Budget that consultation will take place on a possible merger of income tax and social security contributions. Even if this proceeds, it will take many years to come to fruition.

Peter Arrowsmith FCA is a sole practitioner specialising in National Insurance matters. He is a member and former chairman of the Employment Taxes and National Insurance Committee of the Institute of Chartered Accountants in England and Wales.

Finance for writers and artists

Index

Abbey Home Media Group Ltd   5, 61
Abingdon Press   39
Harry N. Abrams Inc.   39
abridgedments   307
Absey and Co. Inc.   39
Academi   364
AccessArt   364
accounts, publishers'   260
ACER Press   28
acquisitions   206
action books   116
Action for Children's Arts   364
Action Publishing, LLC   39
activity books   103
Adams Literary   222
Adams, Richard   117
adaptations of works   312, 322
advances (against royalties)   182, 210,
    257–258, 400, 402
Adventure Box   284
advertising in schools   169
Advocate   252
age groups   137
age ranging   115
Agency (London) Ltd, The   212
agents
  illustrators'   202, 243
  literary   2, 81, 90, 178, 201, 208, 258, 297,
    301
  television and film   297
agreements (contracts) see publishing
    agreements
Aiken, Joan   110
Aitken Alexander Associates Ltd   212
Aladdin Books Ltd   63
Aladdin Paperbacks   39
Alanna Books   5
Albion Press Ltd, The   63
Louisa May Alcott Memorial Association   364
All About Animals   284
All About Kids Publishing   39
Philip Allan   5
Allen & Unwin Pty Ltd   28
Allen, John   317
Alliance of Literary Societies (ALS)   193
Allied Artists/Artistic License   252

Alligator Books Ltd   5
Altair-Australia Literary Agency   220
Alyson Publications, Inc.   39
American Girl Publishing, Inc.   40
American Society of Composers, Authors and
    Publishers   364
Americanisation   178
Amgueddfa Cymru – National Museum
    Wales   5, 364
Amistad   40
Amistad Press   40
Grupo Anaya   38
Hans Christian Andersen Awards, The   382
Andersen Press Ltd   5
Darley Anderson Children's Book Agency
    Ltd   212
Julie Andrews Collection, The   40
Angus Book Award   170, 382
Animal Action   284
animal and nature stories   117
Animals and You   284
animation   84, 298, 310, 335
Anness Publishing   5
Annick Press Ltd   30
Anova Children's Books   5
anthologies, poetry   185–186
Anvil Books/Children's Press, The   5
Apples & Snakes   196
Apples & Snakes Performance Poetry   195,
    196
Aquila   284
Arab Children's Book Publisher's Forum   364
Arad Goch   328
Arcturus Publishing Ltd   6
Ardagh, Philip   208
Arena   252
Edizoni Arka srl   34
Armadillo   293
Armitage, Ronda and David   318
Arrowsmith, Peter   412
Art Agency, The   252
Art Attack   284
artistic directors   319
artistic freedom   87
Arts Council England   191, 193, 364
  grants   403

Arts Council England, London 382
Arts Council/An Chomhairle Ealaíon 365
Arts Council of Northern Ireland 365
Arts Council of Wales 193, 365
Arts Council YouWriteOn.com Book
    Awards 382
Artworks, The 252
Arvon Foundation, The 196, 341, 346
    International Poetry Competition 196
Askews 71
Aspects Irish Literature Festival 392
Association for Library Service to
    Children 365
Association for Library Service to Children
    Awards 382
Association for Scottish Literary Studies
    (ASLS) 366
Association of American Publishers Inc. 366
Association of Authors' Agents, The 366
Association of Authors' Representatives
    Inc. 366
Association of Booksellers for Children 366
Association of Canadian Publishers 366
Association of Illustrators 267, 366
Astonishing Spider-Man 284
Atheneum Books for Young Readers 40
Atlantic Europe Publishing Co. Ltd 6
Atom 6
audience participation 320
audiobooks 305
AudioGO Ltd 6
Aurora Metro 6
Austin Clarke Library 192
Australia Council 366
Australian Copyright Council 366
Australian Literary Management 220
Australian Publishers Association (APA) 367
Australian Writers' Guild (AWG) 367
Author, The 354
Author Literary Agents 212
authors
    and marketing 168
    as brands 182
    tracing 277
Authors' Licensing and Collecting Society
    (ALCS) 270, 274, 276, 354, 367
authorship 266
Autumn Publishing 6
Avengers Unconquered 284
Avisson Press, Inc. 40
Avon Books 40
Award Publications Ltd 6

b small publishing limited 6
baby books 97, 105, 181

Baby TV 314
Badger Books 71
Badger Publishing 6
BAFTA Children's Writer Awards 298
Baggins Book Bazaar 194
Baker Books 69
Bank of Scotland Imaginate Festival 392
Bantam Books 40
Bantam Press (children's) 6
Barbie 284
barcodes 263
Bardd Plant Cymru (Welsh-Language
    Children's Poet Laureate) 383
Barefoot Books Ltd 6, 40, 61
Barnardo's Image Archive 367
Barrington Stoke 7, 61
Barron's Educational Series Inc. 40
David Bateman Ltd 35
bath books 105
Bath Festival of Children's Literature 392
Bath Literature Festival 392
Bath Spa University 347
Batman: Legends 285
Nicola Baxter Ltd 63
BBC, and Society of Authors 355
BBC Audiobooks Ltd 7
BBC Children's Books 7
BBC Children's Radio 316
BBC Cover to Cover 61
BBC radio 303
BBC School Radio 316
BBC writersroom 314
Glenys Bean Writer's Agent 221
Beano, The 285
Beehive Illustration 252
beginner readers 124, 181
Belair 7
Belgrade Theatre, Coventry 317
Bell Lomax Moreton Agency, The 212
Ben 10 Magazine 285
Bender Richardson White 63
Best New Illustrators Award 383
Beyond the Border:Wales International
    Storytelling Festival, The 392
BFC Books for Children 69
Bibliophile 69
Bick Publishing House 40
Big Idea Entertainment 40
Big Read 105
Bisto Book of the Year Awards, The 383
A&C Black 7
Blackman, Malorie 118, 148, 304
Blackwater Press 7
Blackwell Rare Books 73

Blake, Quentin   229, 255
Blanch, David   362
Blast Off!   285
Blast-Off Books   71
Bliss   285
Blogger.com   336
blogging   205, 336
Blooming Tree Press   41
Bloomsbury Publishing Plc   7, 61
Bloomsbury Publishing PTY Limited   28
Bloomsbury Publishing USA   41
Blue Balloon   35
Blue Peter Book Awards   383
Blue Sky Press   41
Blume, Judy   117
blurb   260
Enid Blyton Society   367
board books   97, 105
Boardwalk Books   30
Bob the Builder   285
Bodley Head Children's Books   8
Bologna Children's Book Fair   203, 392
BolognaRagazzi Award   383
book clubs   171
Book Guild Ltd, The   63
Book House, The   71
Book Industry Communication website   263
Book Marketing Ltd   101, 181
Book People Ltd, The   69
Book Street Ltd   63
Bookmark Children's Books   73
Bookmart Ltd   63
Books for Keeps   1, 169, 293
books, purchased, tax relief on   406
Bookseller, The   171, 178, 293
Booksellers Association of the United Kingdom
    & Ireland Ltd, The   367
Bookspread Ltd   71
Bookstart   103
BookStop Literary Agency   222
Booktrust   358, 367
Booktrust Early Years Awards   383
Booktrust Teenage Prize, The   383
Bookwork Ltd   63
Bookworm Ltd   71
Boomerang   314
Booster Cushion Theatre   328
Boxer Books Ltd   8
Boyds Mills Press   41
Braille at Bedtime   285
Brainwaves Ltd   64
Branford Boase Award, The   384
Branford, Henrietta   117
Brathwaite, Val   237

Breslin, Theresa   117
brief, writing to a   310
Briggs, Raymond   227, 229
Briggs, Stephen   322
Bright Agency, The   252
Bright Art Licensing   252
Bright Red Publishing   8
Brilliant Publications   8
British Book Awards   171, 384
British Council, The   194, 367
British Haiku Society, The   191
British Museum   368
British Museum Company Ltd   8
Andrew Brodie   8
Bromley, Adam   299
Brook Green Bookshop   71
Brown, Anthony   75
Jenny Brown Associates   212, 252
Brown Bear Books Ltd   64
John Brown Group – Children's Division   64
Andrea Brown Literary Agency   222
Brown Wells & Jacobs Ltd   64
Pema Browne Ltd   222
Browne & Miller Literary Associates   222
Browns Books For Students   71
Felicity Bryan Associates   213
Bryson Agency Australia Pty Ltd   220
budgets   323
buggy buddies   106
Burgess, Melvin   117
Buster Books   8
Mary Butts Books   74
buy-out clause   163
Byre Theatre of St Andrews, The   326

Cahoots NI   329
Randolph Caldecott Society   368
Calkins Creek Books   41
Cambridge Publishing Management Ltd   64
Cambridge University Press   8, 37
Camden Poetry Group   196
Campaign for the Book   103
Campbell Books   9
Canadian Authors Association   368
Canadian Children's Book Centre (CCBC),
    The   368
Canadian Publishers' Council   368
Candlewick Press   41
Cannon Poets   196
CANSCAIP (Canadian Society of Children's
    Authors, Illustrators & Performers)   368
Jonathan Cape Children's Books   9

capital allowances   405
Careers Writers' Association   368
Carl Hanser Verlag   34
Carlsen Verlag   34
Carlton Poets   195
Carlton Publishing Group   9
Carnegie Medal   384
Carolrhoda Books   41
Carousel   1, 169, 293
Lewis Carroll Society (Daresbury)   368
Lewis Carroll Society, The   368
Lewis Carroll Society of North America
     (LCSNA)   369
Cars Magazine   285
Cartoon Network   315
cartoon novels   92
cartoons, cartoonists   227
Cartwheel Books   41
Maria Carvainis Agency Inc.   222
Cassidy, Anne   143
Celia Catchpole   213, 252
categorising children's books   181
Caterpillar Books   9
Catnip Publishing Ltd   9
CB1 Poetry   195
CBBC   314
CBeebies   304, 314
CBeebies Animals   285
CBeebies Art   285
CBeebies Weekly Magazine   285
CBI Bisto Book of the Year Awards, The   384
Cengage Learning Australia   28
Cengage Learning New Zealand   35
Center for Children's Books (CCB), The   369
Centerprise Literature Development
     Project   196
Centre for Children's Books   359
Centre for Literacy in Primary Education
     (CLPE)   369
CGP   9
Chameleon Books   71
Channel 4   315
Channel 5   315
Paul Chapman Publishing   9
Chapter One Bookshop   71
Charlesbridge Publishing   41
Charlie and Lola   286
Cheltenham Illustration Awards   384
Times Cheltenham Literature Festival,
     The   393
Cherokee Literary Agency   221
Cherrytree Books   9
Chester Literature Festival   393
Chicago Review Press   42

Chichester Festival Theatre   327
Chicken House, The   9
Child Education PLUS   293
Child, Lauren   84, 229
Children's Book Circle   361, 369
Children's Book Council (CBC), The   369
Children's Book Council of Australia   369
Children's Book Festival   393
Children's Book Guild of Washington DC,
     The   369
Children's Book Week   393
Children's Books Ireland   369
Children's Bookshop, The   71
Children's Bookshop – Hay on Wye   71
Children's Bookshop (Huddersfield)   72
Children's Bookshop (Muswell Hill)   72
Children's Hour   303
Children's Laureate   75, 229, 384
Children's Literature Association (ChLA)   370
Children's Literature Centre (CLC)   370
Children's Poetry Bookshelf   69
Children's Writers and Illustrators Group   370
Childrens@Blackwells   71
Child's Play (International) Ltd   9
Chivers Children's Audiobooks   61
Christian Education   9
Chronicle Books   42
Chrysalis Children's Books   9
Chudney Agency, The   222
CILIP Carnegie and Kate Greenaway Awards,
     The   384
CITV   315
City Lit   197
City University Creative Writing and Poetry
     Courses   197
Claire Publications   9
Clarion Books   42
Classical Comics   10
classics   94, 312
classrooms, plays in   317, 323
Classworks Theatre   329
Clear Light Books   42
Clever Books Pty Ltd   37
cliffhangers   148
Clitheroe Books Open Floor Readings   195
Cló Iar-Chonnachta Teo.   61
cloth books   106
CLPE Poetry Award, The   385
Clwyd Theatr Cymru Theatre for Young
     People   327
CMX   42
co-authorship   266
co-editions   178, 259
co-productions   298

Coffee House Poetry 195
Melanie Colbert 220
Colfer, Eoin 82, 118–119, 304
Collins Education 10
Colourpoint Books 10
comedy writing
for children's television 298–299
scripted 300
Comhairle nan Leabhraichean/Gaelic Books
Council, The 370
Commando 286
commissioning of scripts 301
Commonword 191
company, operating as 400, 410
compilers 266
Contact Theatre Company 327
Continuum International Publishing Group
Ltd, The 10
contracts *see* publishing agreements
Conville & Walsh Ltd 213
David C. Cook 42
Cooke Agency, The 220
Cooling, Wendy 105
Cooper Square Publishing 42
Doe Coover Agency, The 222
copy-editing 95, 166
copying 277
copyright 259, 266, 271
assignment of 271
duration of 271
infringement of 272
and libel 274
photographs 272
royalties 403
use of symbol 272
Copyright, Designs and Patents Act
(1988) 271
Copyright Licensing Agency (CLA) 274, 276
Copyrights Group Ltd, The 253
core fiction 181
Corgi Children's Books 10
Cormier, Robert 116
Corneliu M. Popescu Prize for European
Poetry in Translation 192
Cornelius & Jones 329
Corner to Learn 10
Costa Book Awards 385
Costa Children's Book Award 130
Joanna Cotler Books 42
covering letter 206
covers and jackets 166, 169–170, 179, 260
covert art 238
Cowley Robinson Publishing Ltd 64
cp publishing 10

Creations for Children International 64
Creative Arts East 191
Creative Authors Ltd 213
Creative Plus Publishing Ltd 64
Creative Rights Agency, The 213
Creative Scotland 370, 385
Creech, Sharon 118
Cricket Books 42
crime fiction 118, 143
Cristall, Suna 333
Cross, Gillian 116
crossover books 91, 137, 150, 172, 181
Crown Books 43
Crown House Publishing Ltd 10
Editorial Cruilla 38
CSA Word 61
Cunningham, Barry 90
Curtis Brown Group Ltd 213
Curtis Brown Ltd 223
cutting 324
Cwlwm Cyhoeddwyr Cymru 370
Cyngor Llyfrau Cymru 370

Roald Dahl Foundation 370
Roald Dahl Funny Prize, The 385
Dahl, Roald 304, 320
Dandy Xtreme, The 286
Darby Creek Publishing 43
Jenny Darling & Associates 220
Dawn Publications 43
Liza Dawson Associates 223
DC Comics 43
De Agostini Editore 34
Walter de la Mare Society 371
Dead Good Poets Society 195
Dean 10
debts 399
Delacorte Press Books for Young Readers 43
Department for Work and Pensions
(DWP) 419
design 166, 170, 227, 273
Design and Artists Copyright Society
(DACS) 274
Design Eye Ltd 64
design templates 336
designers 333
Destino Infantil & Juvenil 38
Deutscher Taschenbuch Verlag (dtv
junior) 34
Dial Books for Young Readers 43
dialogue 322
digitisation 277
Sandra Dijkstra Literary Agency 223

direct marketing   171
disabled website users   335
Discover   371
Discovery Box   286
Disney & Me   286
Disney Books for Young Readers   43
Disney Channel UK   315
Disney Girl   286
Disney Tinker Bell   286
Disney's Princess   286
DNA Press   43
Doctor Who Adventures   286
Doctor Who Magazine   286
Dog-Eared Publications   43
Tom Doherty Associates, LLC   43
domain name   333
Donaldson, Julia   102
Dora the Explorer   287
Dorling Kindersley   10
double taxation agreements   403, 409
Doubleday Books for Young Readers   44
Doubleday Children's Books   10
Dover Publications Inc.   44
Arthur Conan Doyle Society, The   371
Dragon Books   44
Dragonfly Books   44
dramatisations   322
Dref Wen   10, 61
Dundurn Press   30
Dunham Literary, Inc.   223
Dutton Children's Books   44
Dwyer & O'Grady Inc.   223
Dystel & Goderich Literary Management   223

early learning books   103
Early Years Awards   105
ebooks   101
L'Ecole des Loisirs   33
EDCON Publishing Group   44
Eddison Pearson Ltd   213
Edinburgh Bookshop, The   72
Edinburgh International Book Festival   393
editing   95, 166
editors   86, 164, 172, 266
Edizioni El/Einaudi Ragazzi/Emme
      Edizioni   34
Educat Publishers Pty Ltd   37
Educational Company of Ireland, The   11, 61
Educational Design Services LLC   223
Educational Explorers (Publishers)   11
educational publishing   157
Educational Recording Agency (ERA)   277

Educational Writers Group   371
Edupress   44
Eerdmans Publishing Company   44
Egg, The   327
Egmont UK Ltd   11
Egmont USA   44
Ethan Ellenberg Literary Agency, The   223
Elliston, Valerie A.   342
Elm Grove Books Ltd   64
Paul Embleton   74
Enchanted Wood   72
Encyclopaedia Britannica Inc.   44
English Association   371
English, John   317
Enslow Publishers, Inc.   44
Eos   44
Epsom Writers' Workshop   197
Essential X-Men   287
Essex Poetry Festival   393
Etisalat Prize for Arabic Children's
      Literature   385
Evan-Moor Educational Publishers   44
Evans Publishing Group   11
Everyman Theatre   327
expenses, claimed against tax   399, 403
Express Excess   195

Faber and Faber Ltd   11
fairy stories   119
CJ Fallon   11
family stories   117
fantasy   115, 117, 170, 182
Eleanor Farjeon Award, The   385
Farrago Poetry   195
Farrar, Straus and Giroux, LLC   45
Featherstone Education   12
Federation of Children's Book Groups
      Conference, The   346, 362, 371
Federation of European Publishers   371
Federation of Indian Publishers, The   371
Federation of Spanish Publishers'
      Association   371
fees   272
Festival of Writing, The   393
David Fickling Books   12, 45
Fickling, David   78, 93
Fidra Books   12
Fifi and the Flowertots   287
films   84
finance   399
Fine, Anne   109
Firebird   45
Fireman Sam Magazine   287

First and Best in Education   12
FirstNews   287
Fitzhenry & Whiteside Ltd   30
Flame Tree Publishing   12
Flammarion   33
Flannery Literary   224
Floris Books   12
Flux Books/Llewellyn Worldwide   45
Folens Publishers   12   12
Folkestone Book Festival   393
fonts   334
Foreman, Michael   318
Foster, John   185
Walter Foster Publishing Inc.   45
Foyle Young Poets of the Year Award   192,
    199, 386
Fraser Ross Associates   213
Free Spirit Publishing   45
freelance (self-employed) status   401
French, Jackie   304
French Publishers' Association   371
French, Samuel   320
French's Theatre Bookshop   321
Front Street   45
FTP (File Transfer Protocol)   337
Fulcrum Resources   45
David Fulton   12
Fun Kids   316
Fun to Learn Bag-o-Fun   287
Fun to Learn Discovery   287
Fun to Learn Favourites   287
Fun to Learn Friends   287
Fun to Learn Peppa Pig   287
Futurama (UK)   288

Gaelic Books Council, The   371
gag writing   301
Galaxy National Book Awards   386
Galaxy Children's Large Print   12
Gale Cengage Learning   46
Gallimard Jeunesse   33
Galore Park Publishing Ltd   12
Gardner Education Ltd   13
Garnett, Michelle   281
Gavin, Jamila   118
Gecko Press   36
genres   85, 88, 98, 115
Laura Geringer Books   46
ghost stories   115
ghostwriting   161, 163
Gill, Richard   319
Ginn   13
Girl Talk   288

Girl Talk Extra   288
Giunti Editore SpA   35
GL Assessment   13
Mary Glasgow Magazines   293
Gliori, Debi   244
Glowworm Books & Gifts Ltd   72
Glyndebourne Children's Theatre   317
Go Girl Magazine   288
Gold Smarties Book Prize   170
Barry Goldblatt Literary LLC   224
Golden and Crystal Kite Awards, The   357
Golden Books for Young Readers   46
Golden Treasury (Southfields)   72
Golvan Arts Management   220
Gomer Press   13
Goodie Bag Mag   288
Google   335
Gorey, Edward   235
Graham, Kenneth   94
W.F. Graham   13
Graham-Cameron Publishing &
    Illustration   65, 253
Grampian Children's Book Award   386
Granada Learning   13
Graphia   46
graphic novels   119, 227
graphic story treatments   92
Gravett, Emily   234
Gray, Keith   116
Ashley Grayson Literary Agency   224
Annette Green Authors' Agency   213
Green, Jim   157
Kate Greenaway Medal   386
Greene & Heaton Ltd   214
Greenhaven Press   46
Greenhouse Literary Agency, The   214, 224
Greenwillow Books   46
Greeting Card Association, The   371
greetings cards   1
Grey, Alison Allen   118
Grosset & Dunlap   46
Gryphon House, Inc.   46
Guardian Children's Fiction Prize, The   386
Guernsey Arts Council   372
Guiding Magazine   288
Gullane Children's Books   13
Marianne Gunn O'Connor Literary
    Agency   214

Hachai Publishing   46
Hachette Australia Pty Ltd   28
Hachette Book Group USA   46
Hachette Children's   61

Hachette Children's Books 13
Hachette Livre/Gautier-Languereau 33
Hachette UK 13
Haldane Mason Ltd 14
Halse Anderson, Laurie 117
Hammer and Tongue 195
Handprint Books 46
Harcourt School Publishers 46
Harcourt Trade Publishers 47
HarperCollins Audio Books 61
HarperCollins Publishers 14, 47
HarperCollins Publishers (Australia) Pty Ltd
    Group 28
HarperCollins Publishers Ltd 30
HarperCollins Publishers (New Zealand)
    Ltd 36
Harry Potter 116, 129, 146
Hart McLeod Ltd 65
Antony Harwood Ltd 214
Hawcock Books 65
John Hawkins & Associates Inc. 224
Hawthorn Press 14
Hay Festival 394
Hayward Gallery 372
Headliners 288
Health Press NA Inc. 48
A.M. Heath & Co. Ltd 214
Heath Educational Books 72
Heinemann 14
Heinemann Publishers (South Africa) 37
High School Musical 288
David Higham Associates Ltd 214, 253
Hippo 14
Hiss & Boo Company Ltd, The 329
historical novels 118, 135
History Compass LLC 48
HL Studios Ltd 65
Hodder Children's Books 14
Hodder Education Group 14
Hodder Gibson 14
Hodder Headline Ltd 15
Ian Hodgkins & Co Ltd 74
John Hodgson Agency 253
Hogs Back Books Ltd 15
Hole, John 317
Holiday House Inc. 48
Holland, Guy 319
Henry Holt and Company LLC 48
Hooker, Yvonne 164
Hopscotch Educational Publishing Ltd 15
Horn, Caroline 101, 181
Horowitz, Anthony 116, 118–119, 132, 148,
    304
horror stories 115, 132

hosting company 337
Hothouse Fiction Ltd 65
Houghton Mifflin Harcourt 48
House of Illustration 255
HTML (HyperText MarkUp Language) 336
Human & Rousseau 37
humour 118, 126, 133, 180
Hunter House Publishers 49
Hurrell, Emma 314
Hutchinson Children's Books 15
Hyperion Books for Children 49

IBBY Congress 346
Ideals Publications LLC 49
Igloo Books Ltd 15
Ilkley Literature Festival 394
Illumination Arts Publishing 49
Illustration Cupboard, The 253
illustrations, illustrators 2, 84, 97, 107, 166,
    227, 240, 244, 248, 266
Imaginate 329, 372
Imagine: Writers and Writing for
    Children 394
Impact Publishers Inc. 49
Imperial War Museum 15, 372
Impress Books Ltd 15
In the Night Garden 288
Incentive Publications Inc. 49
income tax 399, 401
  interest on overdue 408
  self-assessment 407
  tax return 407
Independent Publishers Guild 372
Independent Theatre Council (ITC) 372
Indepenpress Publishing Ltd 15
indexing children's books 342
Inis – Children's Books Ireland Magazine,
    The 293
innovativeKids 50
interactive books 238
interactivity 335
International Board on Books for Young
    People (IBBY) 372
International Federation of Reproduction
    Rights Organisations (IFRRO) 275
International Publishers Association 373
International Schools Book Club (ISBC) 69
Internet 321, 333
  and copyright 272
  marketing to 170
  poetry groups on 198
Internet Corporation for Assigned Names and
    Numbers (ICANN) 333

intertexts 87
interviews, copyright in 272
iPad 102
iPhone 102
Ireland, Vicky 319
Irish Book Publishers' Association, The 373
Irish Writers' Centre 373
ISBNs 265, 267
  FAQs about 262
ISSNs 263

jackets, book 166, 169–170, 179, 260
Jacklin Enterprises (Pty) Ltd 37
Jackson, Peter 147
James W. Hackett International Haiku
  Award 191
JCA Literary Agency Inc. 224
Jeannetta Cochrane Theatre 321
Jeffers, Oliver 229, 248
Jenner, Caryl 317
Jewish Book Week 394
John Kinsella's 198
Johnson & Alcock Ltd 215
Johnson, Catherine 118
Jolly Learning Ltd 15
Jones, Janey Louise 173
Jubileebooks.co.uk 72
Junior 294
Junior Puzzles 288
Just Us Books, Inc. 50

Kaeden Books 50
Kaléidoscope 34
Kar-Ben Publishing 50
Kazzum Arts Project 329
Miles Kelly Packaging 65
Miles Kelly Publishing 15
Kelpies Prize 15, 386
Kenny, Mike 321
Kent & Sussex Poetry Society 197
Key Porter Books Ltd 30
KidHave Press 50
Kids Alive! (Young Soldier), The 289
Kids Can Press Ltd 31
kill fees 272
Kindle 102
King, Clive 304
King Smith, Dick 117
King-Smith, Dick 318
Kingfisher 15, 50
King's England Press, The 15
Kingscourt/McGraw-Hill 16

Jessica Kingsley Publishers 16
Kipling Society, The 373
Robert J. Kirkpatrick 74
KISS 289
Kloet, Chris 97
Klutz 50
Alfred A. Knopf Books for Young Readers 50
Knopf Trade 50
Konflux Theatre in Education 329
Barbara S. Kouts, Literary Agent 224
kt literary 224
Kube Publishing Ltd 16

Ladybird 16
Ladybird Books 61
Wendy Lamb Books 50
Lancashire County Library Children's Book of
  the Year Award 386
Lancaster University 197
language and style 137
Lassiter, Rhiannon 118
Laureate, Children's 75, 229, 384
Laurel-Leaf Books 50
LAW (Lucas Alexander Whitley Ltd) 215, 253
LB Kids 50
Leckie & Leckie 16
Lee & Low Books, Inc. 50
Leeds Children's Theatre 327
Legat, Michael 271
Legend Theatre 330
Leighton Buzzard Children's Theatre 327
Lemniscaat BV 35
Lerner Publishing Group 50
Letterbox Library 69
Arthur A. Levine Books 51
C.S. Lewis Society (New York), The 373
David Lewis Agency 253
libraries 103, 169
  talks at 79
Library Theatre Company 327
Libros del Zorro Rojo 38
Editorial Libsa 38
licence to copy 274
licensing 257
lift-the-flap books 106
Lincoln Book Festival 394
Frances Lincoln Diverse Voices Children's
  Book Award, The 386
Frances Lincoln Ltd 16
Astrid Lindgren Memorial Award, The 386
Madeleine Lindley Ltd 72
Lindsay Literary Agency 215
Lion and the Unicorn, The 294

Lion and Unicorn Bookshop, The 72
Lion Hudson plc 16
Literacy 294
Literature Wales 191, 373
Little Angel Theatre, The 330
Little, Brown & Company 51
Little, Brown Book Group 16
Little Hare Books 28
Christopher Little Literary Agency 215
Little People Books 65
Little Theatre Guild of Great Britain 373
Little Tiger Press 16
Llewellyn Worldwide 51
London Independent Books 215
London Literature Festival 394
Longman 16
Lowdham Book Festival 394
Lucas, David 229
Lucent Books 51
Jennifer Luithlen Agency 215
Luna Rising 51

M6 Theatre Company (Studio Theatre) 330
Gina Maccoby Literary Agency 224
Margaret K. McElderry Books 51
McGraw-Hill Book Company New Zealand
    Ltd 36
McGraw-Hill Education 29
McGraw-Hill Professional 51
McGraw-Hill Ryerson Ltd 31
McIntosh & Otis Inc. 224
Frances McKay Illustration 253
Macmillan Digital Audio 62
Macmillan Education Australia Pty Ltd 29
Macmillan Prize for Children's Picture Book
    Illustration, The 387
Macmillan Publishers Ltd 16
Eunice McMullen Ltd 215
Macromedia Dreamweaver 336
Madison Press Books 31
Magazine Merit Awards 357
Magazines Canada (Canadian Magazine
    Publishers Association) 374
Magi Publications 17
Magic Carpet Theatre 330
Magorian, Michelle 117
Mallinson Rendel Publishers Ltd 36
Manchester Children's Book Festival 394
manga novels 119
Andrew Mann Ltd 216
Sarah Manson Literary Agent 216
Mantra Lingua TalkingPEN Ltd 17
manuscripts (MSS) 3, 84, 97, 206, 208, 240

Marchpane Children's Books 74
Marjacq Scripts 216
marketing 97, 166, 168
    to US 177
Barbara Markowitz Literary Agency 224
Marsh Award for Children's Literature in
    Translation 387
Marshall Cavendish Benchmark 51
Marshall Cavendish Children's Books 51
Marshall Cavendish 17
Marshall Editions Ltd 65
Marvel Heroes 289
Maskew Miller Longman (Pty) Ltd 37
Match of the Day 289
Max, The 289
Kevin Mayhew Ltd 17
MBA Literary Agents Ltd 216
McCaughrean, Geraldine 120, 304
McCombie, Karen 152
McKenzie, Sophie 146
Meadowside Children's Books 18
Mercier Press, The 18
Mews Books 225
Meyer, Stephenie 103
Microsoft FrontPage 336
Midlands Arts Centre 317
Mighty World of Marvel 289
Miles Stott Children's Literary Agency 216
Milet Publishing, LLC 52
Milkweed Editions 52
Millbrook Press 52
Milnes-Smith, Philippa 201
MINX 52
Missy 289
Mitchell, Adrian 321
Mitchell Lane Publishers, Inc. 52
Mizz 289
MM House Publishing 36
Moby Duck 330
Arnoldo Mondadori Editore S.p.A
    (Mondadori) 35
Mondo Publishing 52
Monkey Feet Illustration Agency, The 253
Monkey Puzzle Media Ltd 65
L.M. Montgomery Heritage Society 374
Morden Tower 195
Morgan Reynolds Publishing 52
Morpurgo, Michael 117
William Morris Agency Inc. 225
MSS see manuscripts
Muchamore, Robert 116
Erin Murphy Literary Agency 225
Muse Literary Management 225
Museum of London 374

mystery and adventure stories   116
Mythopoeic Fantasy Award for Children's
    Literature, The   387
Mythopoeic Society, The   374

Napoleon & Company   31
narrative verse   118, 322
nasen Awards – Celebrating Inclusive
    Practice   387
Nasou Via Afrika   37
NATE Classroom (National Association for the
    Teaching of English)   294
National Art Library   374
National Association for the Teaching of
    English (NATE)   18, 374
National Association of Writers' Groups
    (NAWG)   193, 374
National Association of Writers in Education
    (NAWE)   198, 374
National Centre for Language and Literacy
    (NCLL)   375
National Centre for Research in Children's
    Literature (NCRCL)   375
National Curriculum, The   110, 121, 157, 342
National Galleries of Scotland   375
National Gallery   375
National Insurance Contributions   400, 404,
    407, 410, 414
  exemptions   418
  maximum   419
National Literacy Association   375
National Literacy Strategy   186
National Literacy Trust (NLT)   357, 397
National Museum Wales   375
National Museums Liverpool   375
National Museums Scotland   375
National Poetry Competition   192, 196
National Poetry Day   192
National Portrait Gallery   375
National Share-A-Story-Month   362
National Society for Education in Art and
    Design   375
National Theatre   318
National Theatre Bookshop   321
National Union of Journalists   271
Natural History Museum   375
Naxos AudioBooks   62
NB Illustration   254
NB Publishers (Pty) Ltd   38
NCRCL British IBBY Conference   346
Neate Publishing   18
Neilsen Norman Group   335
Nelson Education   31

Thomas Nelson Publisher   52
Nelson Thornes Ltd   18
Edith Nesbit Society, The   376
Ness, Patrick   103, 145
Net Book Agreement (NBA)   96, 171
New Africa Books (Pty) Ltd   38
New Frontier Publishing   29
New Writing North   376
New Zealand Council for Educational
    Research   36
New Zealand Post Book Awards for Children
    and Young Adults   387
Newcastle University Library   376
Newspaper, The   289
Nicholson, William   129
Nickel Books   72
Nickleodeon UK   315
Jane Nissen Books   18
No.1 Manchester Literary Agency, The   216
Nobuyuki Yuasa Annual International Award
    for Haibun   191
Norfolk Children's Book Centre   72
North East Book Award   387
North East Teenage Book Award   388
North–South Books   52
Northern and Southern Arts Councils of
    Ireland   192
Northern Children's Book Festival   394
Northern Poetry Library, The   193
NorthWord Books for Young Readers   52
Norwich Puppet Theatre   327
Nosy Crow   18
Nottingham Children's Book Awards   388
Nottingham Playhouse   328
novelty books   238
Nursery Education Plus   294
nursery rhyme books   106
Nursery World   294

Oberon Books   18
Oberon Press   31
O'Brien Press Ltd, The   18
Off the Shelf Literature Festival   394
Office for Standards in Education
    (OFSTED)   376
Office of Communications (Ofcom), The   376
Oily Cart   319, 330
Oliver Press, Inc., The   52
Orca Book Publishers   31
Orchard Books   19, 52
Organisation, The   254
originality of work   133
Orion Publishing Group Ltd, The   19, 62

Orpheus Books Ltd   66
Oundle Festival of Literature   395
Oundle School Bookshop   72
Overlook Press, The   52
overseas, earnings from   409
Richard C. Owen Publishers, Inc.   53
Oxford Literary Festival   395
Sunday Times Oxford Literary Festival,
    The   395
Oxford University Day and Weekend
    Schools   346
Oxford University Press   19, 53
Oxford University Press Southern Africa   38

Pacific View Press   53
page size   334
Palace Theatre, Watford   317
Pan Macmillan Australia Pty Ltd   29
pantomimes   317, 320
Parragon Books Ltd   19
Parragon Publishing   53
Patten, Brian   189
Pamela Paul Agency   221
Paver, Michelle   117, 135
Pavilion Children's Books   19
Payne-Gallway   19
PCET Publishing   19
Peachtree Publishers   53
Pearson Canada   32
Pearson Education   53
Pearson Education Australia   29
Pearson Education New Zealand Ltd   36
Pearson Scott Foresman   53
Pearson UK   20
Pelican Publishing Company   53
Penguin Audiobooks   62
Penguin Group (Australia)   29
Penguin Group (Canada)   32
Penguin Group (NZ)   36
Penguin Group (UK)   20
Penguin Group (USA), Inc.   54
Penguin Longman   20
pensions   406
permission to quote   271
Peters Bookselling Services   72
Phaidon Press Ltd   20
Philomel   55
Phoenix Award   388
Phoenix Yard Books   20
photographs, copyright in   272
Alison Picard, Literary Agent   225
Piccadilly Press   20
Picthall & Gunzi Ltd   21, 66

picture books   76, 86, 97, 102, 107, 109, 120,
    181, 234, 237, 240, 244, 248, 257
Pinwheel   66
Pinwheel Children's Books   21
Pipers' Ash Ltd   21
Pippin Properties Inc.   225
Pippin Publishing Corporation   32
Pitstop Refuelling Writers' Weekend
    Workshops   346
Play & Learn Thomas & Friends   289
playground marketing   170
Playne Books Ltd   66
plays   312, 317, 319, 323
Playtime Theatre Company   330
playwrights   321
plots   84, 109
Plum Pudding Illustration   254
Plurabelle Books   74
Poems in the Waiting Room (PitWR)   194
poetry   111, 115, 118, 185,
Poetry Book Society, The   191, 377
Poetry Bookshop, The   194
Poetry Business, The   191
Poetry Café   196
Poetry Can, The   192
poetry, children's   189
Poetry Ireland   192
Poetry Kit   194, 198
Poetry Landmarks of Britain   192
Poetry Library, The   193, 196, 198, 377
Poetry on Loan   192
Poetry Prescription   192
Poetry School, The   197
Poetry Society, The   192, 377
Poetry Society Education   198, 377
Poetry Society of America   194
Poetry Trust, The   194, 198
Poetry-next-the-Sea   195
Poets Anonymous   197
Poet's House/Teach na hÉigse, The   197
Sylvie Poggio Artists Agency   254
Point   21
Polka Theatre   318, 326
Pollinger Limited   216
Pont Books   21
PONY Magazine   290
Poolbeg Press Ltd   21
POP   316
pop-up books   202, 238
Poppy   55
portfolio   2, 237, 239
Portfolio Award, The   357
Portland Press Ltd   21
Positive Images   377

postcards 238
Postman Pat 290
Potter, Beatrix 174
Beatrix Potter Society, The 377
Tony Potter Publishing Ltd 66
Pottermore.com 102
Practical Parenting 295
Pratchett, Terry 304, 322
preschool books 238
Mathew Price Ltd 55
Price Stern Sloan 55
Priddy Books 21
Prim-Ed Publishing 21
Prim-Ed Publishing Pty Ltd 29
prizes and awards, tax position 403
production, author and 260
promotional material 238
proofreading 166, 260
Proteus Theatre Company 330
Public Lending Right Act 1979 264
Public Lending Right (PLR) 103, 163, 264,
    276
  books eligible for 267
  reciprocal arrangements 270
  sampling arrangements 267
publicity 169
publishers 321
  agreements (contracts) 2, 209, 257, 260
  approaching 97, 210, 240, 249
  educational 157
  and ISBNs 263
  US 178
Publishers Association, The 377
Publishers Association of New Zealand
    (PANZ) 377
Publishers Licensing Society (PLS) 274, 276
Publishers Weekly 178, 295
publishing agreements (contracts) 2, 209,
    257, 260
Publishing Ireland – Foilsiú Éireann 377
Publishing Scotland 377
Puffin Audiobooks 62
Puffin Book Club 69
Puffin Books 21, 29, 55
Pullman, Philip 118
Simon Pulse Paperback Books 55
Pure 290
Puzzle House, The 66
Puzzler Quiz Kids 290

QED Publishing 21
Quarto Group, Inc., The 21, 66
Queen's Theatre, Hornchurch 328

University of Queensland Press 29
Quentaris Chronicles, The 29
Quest 22
Quicksilver 319
Quicksilver Theatre 331

racism 115
Radio Telefis Eireann (RTE) 316
Ragged Bears Publishing Ltd 22
Rai, Bali 117
Raincoast Books 32
Raintree 22
Random House Audio Books 62
Random House Australia Pty Ltd 29
Random House Children's Books 78
Random House Group Ltd, The 22
Random House Inc. 55
Random House Mondadori 38
Random House New Zealand Ltd 36
Random House of Canada Ltd 32
Ransom Publishing Ltd 22
Arthur Ransome Society Ltd (TARS),
    The 377
Ravensburger Buchverlag 34
Rayo 56
Razorbill 56
RDC Agencia Literaria SL 221
readability 334
Readathon 377, 395
Reader's Digest Children's Publishing Ltd 23
reading aloud, books for 109
Reading Rights 397
real life/contemporary stories 117
reciprocal arrangements, PLR 270
Red Bird Publishing 23
Red Deer Press 32
Red Fox Children's Books 23
Red House 69
Red House Children's Book Award, The 388
Red Kite Books 23
Red Ladder Theatre Company 331
Redbridge Book and Media Festival 395
Redhammer Management Ltd 217
Redmond, Di 161, 310
Reeve, Philip 118
reference books 115
Remedial Literacy books 122
Rennison, Louise 112, 118
Replay Theatre Company 331
Report 295
Rhyme & Reason 72
Richards Literary Agency 221
Richmond upon Thames Literature Festival,
    Arts Service 395

Rigby   23
Right Start   295
rights   209, 257, 319
  assignment of   260
  authors'   277
  electronic   260, 272
  foreign   178, 209, 258
  moral   259, 271
  reversion of   260
  serial   271
  subsidiary   205, 259
Peter Riley   194
Riordan, Rick   119
Ripping Yarns Bookshop   74
Rising Moon   56
Rising Stars   23
Roar Publishing   23
Roaring Brook Press   56
Rockpool Children's Books Ltd   23
Rogers, Coleridge & White Ltd   217
romance and love stories   117
Ronsdale Press   32
Rosen, Michael   87, 231
Rose's Books   74
Rosoff, Meg   139
Ross, Tony   229, 240
Roving Books Ltd (Roving Bookshop),
  The   73
Rowling, J.K.   81, 102, 118, 130
Elizabeth Roy Literary Agency   217, 254
Royal Court Young Writers' Festival   395
Royal Mail Awards for Scottish Children's
  Books   388
RNIB National Library Service   377
Royal Shakespeare Company   318, 328
royalties   179, 258
RSPCA Young Photographer Awards
  (YPA)   388
RSVP Publishing Company   36
Rubinstein Publishing   35
Running Press Book Publishers   57
Uli Rushby-Smith Literary Agency   217
Ruskin, Sheila   320
Russell, Gillie   149

S4C   316
Sacher, Louis   117
Sage, Alison   338
SAGE Publications Ltd   23
Sainsbury's Baby Book Award   388
Adriano Salani Editore S.p.A.   35
Salariya Book Company Ltd   23
sampling arrangements, PLR   267

Rosemary Sandberg Ltd   217
Sandcastle Books   33
Lennart Sane Agency AB   221
Editions Sarbacane   34
Sasakawa Prize   191
Malcolm Saville Society, The   378
Scattered Authors Society   2, 378
scenery   323
Schofield & Sims Ltd   23
Scholastic Australia Pty Ltd   30
Scholastic Book Clubs and Fairs   69
Scholastic Book Fairs   70
Scholastic Canada Ltd   33
Scholastic Education   57
Scholastic Inc.   57
Scholastic Ltd   23
Scholastic New Zealand Ltd   36
School Librarian, The   171, 295
School Library Association   378
school stories   117
schools
  drama in   318
  marketing to   98, 157, 202
  talks to   79
  in US   179
Susan Schulman, A Literary Agency   225
Schwartz & Wade Books   58
science fiction   118
Science Museum   378
Scooby-Doo   290
Scottish Arts Council   378
Scottish Book Trust (SBT)   378
Scottish International Storytelling
  Festival   395
Scottish Poetry Library, The   194
Scottish Storytelling Forum, The   378
SCP Publishers Ltd   24
screenplays   322
scripts   324
Scripture Union   24
Scrivener, Richard   177
Seamus Heaney Centre for Poetry, The   192
search engine ratings   337
self-employed status   400, 412
self-publishing   173, 175
SEMERC   24
SEN Press Ltd   24
series fiction   145, 152–153, 182, 312
Seven Stories – the Centre for Children's
  Books   73, 359, 378
Shan, Darren   116
Shape Game   75
Sharpe, Tom   322
Sharratt, Nick   79

Sheffield Children's Book Award 388
Caroline Sheldon Literary Agency Ltd 217, 254
Sherman Cymru 328
Short Books Ltd 24
short stories 118
Shortlands Poetry Circle 197
Shout 290
Showtime Magazine 290
Shuter and Shooter Publishers (Pty) Ltd 38
Sid Fleischman Humour Award, The 357
Silver Moon Press 58
Dorie Simmonds Agency 217
Simon & Schuster Children's Publishing Division 58
Simon & Schuster UK Ltd 24
Simon, Francesca 155
Simpsons Comics 290
Simpsons Comics Presents 290
Sixth Sense Theatre for Young People 331
Sjaloom & Wildeboer, Uitgevers 35
sketch writing 301
Sleeping Bear Press 59
slush pile 208
Small Claims 399
Small World Design 66
Smart Learning 24
SmartPass Ltd 62
WHSmith Children's Book of the Year 389
social networking 205
social problems 320
social security contributions 412
Society for Editors and Proofreaders (SfEP) 378
Society for Storytelling (SfS) 379
Society of Artists Agents 379
Society of Authors 209, 257, 271, 353, 379
Children's Writers and Illustrators Group (CWIG) 353
Society of Children's Book Writers and Illustrators (SCBWI), The 356, 379
Society of Editors 379
Society of Young Publishers 379
Soho Theatre 326
Le Sorbier 34
Henry Sotheran Ltd 74
sound effects 335
South Norwood Writers' Workshop 197
Sparkle World 290
Speak 59
Speaking of Books 379
special effects 324
Specs Art 254
Spectacular Spider-Man 290

SpongeBob SquarePants 291
sports stories 117
Spread the Word 197
spy thrillers 116
Stacey International 25
stage plays 312, 317, 319, 323
standalone novels 145, 153
Standen Literary Agency, The 217
Stanley, Alison 1, 124
StAnza: Scotland's International Poetry Festival 195, 395
Star Trek Magazine 291
Star Wars Clone Wars Comic 291
StarScape 59
Start-Ups 30
Abner Stein 218
Sterling Publishing Co., Inc. 59
Gareth Stevens Publishing 59
Robert Louis Stevenson Club, The 379
Stevenson, Robert Louis 88
Stimola Literary Studio, Inc. 225
Story Museum, The 379
Storybox 291
Storysack Ltd 25
Stratford-upon-Avon Poetry Festival 396
Strident Publishing Ltd 25
Stripes 25
Strong, Jeremy 118, 126
Student Illustrator Scholarship 357
style 234
submission guidelines 206
submissions 2, 206
subplots 320, 324
subsidiary rights 205, 259
Sarah Such Literary Agency 218
suddenlies 319
Sue Alexander Most Promising New Work Award, The 357
supermarkets, as booksellers 171
Surrey Poetry Circle 197
survival stories 116
Survivors Poetry 192
Swan Theatre, Worcester 317
Swanwick, Writers' Summer School, The 346
Carolyn Swayze Literary Agency Ltd 221
Swedish Institute for Children's Books (Svenska barnboksinstitutet), The 379
Sweetens of Bolton 194
Swindells, Robert 117
symbols 89
synopsis 99, 320

talent, spotting 90
Tales On Moon Lane 73

Tamarind Books   25
Tangere Arts   331
Tangerine Designs Ltd   66
Tango Books Ltd   25, 67
target readership   206
Tarquin Publications   25
Tax
  double agreements   403, 409
  expenses, claimed against   399, 403
  income   399, 401, 407, 408
  prizes and awards   403
  relief on books purchased   406
  return   410
  Value Added   400, 408
Taylor and Francis Group   25
tBkmag   291
teenage fiction   99, 113, 122, 139, 143, 149,
  180–181
Teenage Magazine Arbitration Panel
  (TMAP)   379
teenage
  books for   99, 113, 122, 139, 143, 149,
    180–181
  magazines   281
  protagonists   147
  thrillers, for   119, 142, 146–147, 151
Katherine Tegen Books   59
Telegraph Hay Festival, The   396
Teller, Neville   303
Templar Company Ltd, The   25, 67
territory (granted to publisher)   257
TES, The   295
TES Cymru, The   295
TESS, The   296
Theatr Gwent Theatre   331
Theatr Iolo   331
Theatr Spectacle Theatre   331
theatre, amateur   322
Theatre Centre   317, 331
Theatre Co Blah Blah Blah, The   332
Theatre Hullabaloo   332
Theatre Is…   332
Theatre Workshop   332
Theatre-Rites   326
theatrical techniques   319
Thomas & Friends   291
Vicki Thomas Associates   254
D.C. Thomson & Co. Ltd – Publications   25
thrillers   115
  for teenagers   119, 142, 146–147, 151
Thwaites, Stephanie   205
TickTock Books Ltd   25
Tide Mill Press   25
TIE Company   317

Times Educational Supplement, The   296
Times Educational Supplement Scotland,
  The   296
Times/Chicken House Children's Fiction
  Competition, The   389
Tiptoe Books   67
Tir na n-Og Awards   389
Titan Books   25
toddlers, books for   97, 106
TOKYOPOP   59
Tolkien Society, The   380
Tom and Jerry   291
Tongues and Grooves   196
Top of the Pops   291
Top That! Publishing plc   26
Tor Books   59
Total Fiction Services   221
Toucan Books Ltd   67
touring companies   318
Christopher Tower Poetry Prize   199, 389
Tower Poetry Society   193
Towngate Theatre, Basildon   319
Toxic Magazine   291
Toybox   292
Transatlantic Literary Agency   221
translators   266
Transworld   78
Travelling Book Company   70
Travelling Light Theatre Company   332
Emma Treehouse Ltd   67
S©ott Treimel NY   225
Trentham Books Ltd   26
Tricycle Press   59
Trotman   26
T.S. Eliot Prize   191
Tucker Slingsby Ltd   67
Tundra Books Inc.   33
Turnbull, Ann   117
Tutti Frutti Productions   332
Twenty-first Century Books   60
Twist in the Tale   73
Twitter   206
2000 AD   292
Two-Can   60
Tŷ Newydd   197, 347
typography   227

UKLA Children's Book Awards   389
Umansky, Kaye   304
Umbrella Books   67
Under 5   296
under-fives, drama for   318
Unicorn   317

Unicorn Theatre   326
unique selling point (USP)   3
United Agents   218, 254
United Kingdom Literacy Association
    (UKLA)   380
unsolicited manuscripts   84, 97, 208, 240
Usborne Publishing Ltd   26   62

Vaines, Peter   399, 401
Van Goor   35
V&A Illustration Awards, The   389
V&A Museum of Childhood   380
VAT (value added tax)   400, 408
Vibe   292
Vicens Vives SA   39
Ralph M. Vicinanza Ltd   226
Ed Victor Ltd   218
Victoria and Albert Museum   380
Victoria Park Books   73
Viking Children's Books   60
Voice, The   292
Voice of the Listener & Viewer Ltd
    (VLV)   380
Volunteer Reading Help (VRH)   380
VSP Books   60

Wade, Rachel, and Baker, Miranda   361
Walker & Co.   60
Walker Books Ltd   26, 62
Walsh, Caroline   257
war stories   117
Ward Lock Educational Co. Ltd   26
Warne   26
Waterstone's Children's Book Prize   389
Watson, Little Ltd   218
AP Watt Ltd   218
Franklin Watts   26
Watts Publishing Group Ltd, The   26
Waverley Books Ltd   26
Way, Brian   317
Way, Charles   321
Waybuloo   292
Wayland   27
web design   335
web page editor   337
Webb, Tim   319
websites   205
    setting up   333
Weigl Publishers Inc.   60
Weldon Owen Education   37
Well Wisher Children's Bookshop, The   73
Welsh Animation Group (WAG)   380

Welsh Books Council/Cyngor Llyfrau
    Cymru   381
David West Children's Books   67
Whirligig   319
Whirligig Theatre   326
Whispering Buffalo Literary Agency Ltd   218
Whitbread Book Awards   390
Whitbread Literary Award   403
Eve White   219
Whitecap Books Ltd   33
Albert Whitman & Company   60
Wigtown Book Festival   396
Willesden Bookshop   73
Henry Williamson Society, The   381
Wilson, Jacqueline   78, 117
Wimbledon and Merton Poetry Group   197
University of Winchester   347
Winchester Writers' Conference
    Competitions   390, 396
Winchester Writers' Conference Festival and
    Bookfair, The   347
Windmill Books Ltd   68
WingedChariot Press   27
Paula Wiseman   60
Wizard Books Ltd   27
WizzBook Ltd   27
Wolverine and Deadpool   292
Women's Press   33
Wood, Annie   319
Wood, David   317
Word – University of Aberdeen Writers
    Festival   396
Word Hoard, The   193
wordless books   105
Wordsong   60
Wordsworth Editions Ltd   27
Work-in-progress Grants   357
Working Partners Ltd   68
Workman Publishing Company   60
World Book Day   105, 169, 396
World Book, Inc.   60
Write A Story for Children Competition   390
Writers Advice Centre for Children's
    Books   347, 381
Writers' Guild of Great Britain   257, 271, 381
Writers House LLC   226
Writers' Workshop, The   347
writing classes/courses   204, 338
Wyndham, John   118

Y Lolfa Cyf.   27
Yearling Books   60
Susan Yearwood Literary Agency   219

Index

Yen Press   60
YLG Conference   347
York Notes   27
young adult fiction   115, 117, 122
Young at Art   381
Young Browsers Bookshop   73
Young Europeans Bookstore   73
Young Picador   27
Young Readers Birmingham   396
Young Scot   292
Young Vic Theatre Company   326
Young Writer Magazine   292
Young Writers' Programme   390

younger readers, books for   85, 98, 121, 181, 202
YoungMinds Book Award   390
youth groups   318
Youth Libraries Group (YLG)   381
youth theatre   318
YouWriteOn.com   390

Zero to Ten Ltd   27
ZigZag Education   27
Zirkoon Uitgevers / Baekens Books   35
ZooBooKoo International Ltd   27
Zuza Books   68